The Canadian Writer's Handbook

THIRD EDITION

For Ann and Betty.

Canadian Cataloguing in Publication Data

Messenger, William E., 1931– .
       The Canadian writer's handbook, third edition.

Includes index.
ISBN 0-13-287574-8

1. English language–Composition and exercises.
2. English language–Grammar.
I. de Bruyn, Jan, 1918– . II. Title.

PE1408.M47 1995   808'.042   C94-931935-X

Prentice-Hall, Inc., Englewood Cliffs, New Jersey
Prentice-Hall International (UK) Limited, London
Prentice-Hall of Australia, Pty. Limited, Sydney
Prentice-Hall Hispanoamericana, S.A., Mexico City
Prentice-Hall of India Private Limited, New Delhi
Prentice-Hall of Japan, Inc., Tokyo
Simon & Schuster Asia Private Limited, Singapore
Editora Prentice-Hall do Brasil, Ltda., Rio de Janeiro

ISBN 0-13-287574-8

Acquisitions Editor: Marjorie Munroe
Developmental Editor: Linda Gorman
Production Editor: Kelly Dickson
Copy Editor: Mary de Souza
Production Coordinator: Deborah Starks
Cover and Interior Design: Alex Li
Page Layout: Jaytype Inc./Debbie Fleming

1 2 3 4 5 RRD 99 98 97 96 95

Printed and bound in the USA.

Every reasonable effort has been made to obtain permissions for all articles and data used in this edition. If errors or omissions have occurred, they will be corrected in future editions provided written notification has been received by the publisher.

 This book is printed on recycled paper.

The
Canadian
Writer's
Handbook

THIRD EDITION

William E. Messenger
University of British Columbia

Jan de Bruyn
University of British Columbia

Editorial Consultant
Judy Brown
University of British Columbia

Prentice Hall Canada Inc.
Scarborough, Ontario

CONTENTS

PART TWO
MECHANICS   223

PREFACE
How to Use This Book

The third edition of *The Canadian Writer's Handbook*, like its predecessors, is intended to help you improve your use of English, especially to help you write correctly and effectively. If you use it conscientiously and carefully, this book will be a trustworthy and helpful authority and guide as you work to improve your writing. It covers all you should need to know about the conventions of grammar and syntax, punctuation, mechanics, spelling, and usage—including not just the conventions and principles themselves, but background and other facts intended to enable you to understand the reasons for them. It also provides substantial sections on such rhetorical matters as clarity and emphasis, effective sentences and paragraphs, argument, and the entire writing process, including planning and organization. All parts of the book have been improved, some in relatively small ways, others in larger ways. The chapter on writing a research paper has been thoroughly revised and updated, and this new edition also offers many new and improved exercises, some designed particularly for those whose first language is not English. Though it remains a handbook—basically a reference book—it is also a text that can be taught and, above all, a text that can be studied.

Overview

First, begin to familiarize yourself with the book. See what it has to offer: useful advice won't help you if you never discover that it's there. Browse through the table of contents and the index. Look up some sections that arouse your interest or curiosity. Flip through the pages, pausing now and then for a closer look. Note the running heads and symbols at the tops and bottoms of pages; note also the list of sections inside the front cover, the list of correction symbols inside the back cover, and the list of exercises following the index: they can help you find things in a hurry.

Organization

Notice how the material is arranged. Begin to think about how you can best approach it all. Some will want to begin at the beginning and proceed carefully through the book; many points in later chapters won't be clear to you unless you understand the material in the early chapters. But if you already understand basic grammar—the functions of the parts of speech and the principles governing English sentences—you may need only a quick review of the first three chapters. Test yourself by trying some of the exercises in each section.

Treating Specific Problems

Concentrate on any specific weaknesses you may have. Do the relevant exercises and have someone check them. An instructor may assign certain sections and exercises for you to work on. Or an instructor may assign certain sections and exercises to a whole class for study and discussion.

Checking Your Work Before Submitting It

When you finish a piece of writing, go through the Omnibus Checklist in Chapter XII. If you find you're not sure about something, follow the cross-references to the sections that will give you the help you need.

Correcting and Revising Returned Work

When you get a piece of writing back with marks and comments, first look it over alongside Chapter XI, "The Correction Symbols Explained." The information there may be enough to enable you to make the appropriate changes. But if you need more than a reminder about a specific error or weakness—if you don't understand the fundamental principles it violates—follow the cross-references and study the sections that discuss and illustrate those principles in greater detail. You should then be able to correct and revise with understanding and confidence.

An important feature of this book is that it discusses and illustrates various kinds of weaknesses and errors in several places: in the main discussions and in the exercises that accompany them, in the review exercises at the ends of major chapters and sections, in the sample essays in Chapter X, and in Chapter XI. If one or another of these isn't enough to clarify a point, remember that you may not yet have exhausted the available resources: try the index to see if it will lead you to still other relevant places.

Numbering and Cross-Referencing

The book's sections and subsections are numbered consecutively throughout, without regard to chapters (see the list inside the front cover). Cross-references are to section and subsection numbers, or occasionally to chapters. In the index, references are to page numbers. Exercises are numbered according to their sections or subsections; some sections do not include exercises.

Important Terms

The first time or two an important term occurs, it is in **boldface**. Pay attention to these terms, for they make up the basic vocabulary necessary for the intelligent discussion of grammar, syntax, and style.

Acknowledgments

A thoroughly revised essay may bear little resemblance to its preliminary notes, or perhaps even to its early drafts; but the original matter—thoughts, feelings, even words and phrases—however transmogrified, still gives life and substance to the final product. So too with the third edition of *The Canadian Writer's Handbook*. The contributions of colleagues and of generations of students, of friends, fellow writers, and editors, continue to sustain this new version. Our gratitude to all of them also continues.

PART 1

SENTENCE GRAMMAR AND PUNCTUATION

INTRODUCTION:
The Conventions of Language

Words are the building blocks that people use to put together language structures that enable them to communicate. Combinations of words produce sentences; combinations of sentences produce paragraphs; combinations of paragraphs can form stories, detailed expositions, descriptions, arguments.

When people write they represent speech sounds with symbols called letters which combine to form the units called words. Those who share a familiarity with a particular language are able to communicate because each person knows the meaning of the sounds. If you said "Look" when you meant "Listen," you would fail to communicate. The success of the process depends upon the **conventions**, the shared acceptance of what particular words mean.

Putting words together to make sentences is similarly subject to conventions. We use particular word orders and other standard ways of showing how words are related to each other; and since writing represents speech, we use certain visual devices to help clarify meaning and make communication easier. The conventions governing the arrangement of words and the relations between them constitute the **grammar** of a language. The techniques that help us "hear" writing as something like speaking constitute the conventions of **punctuation**.

These first four chapters describe and illustrate these conventions and ways of avoiding common errors in their use. Although on occasion we use terms like *rules* and *right* and *wrong* and *correct*, try to think of yourself as studying not the "rules" of grammar and punctuation but their *conventions*; and don't think in terms of what is "right" or "correct" but of what is *conventional*—that is, mutually agreed upon, and therefore understandable, and therefore effective.

Grammar

The term *grammar* here is virtually equivalent to the term *syntax*, which refers to the relations among words and the order of words in individual sentences. The first four chapters are about sentences, the primary units of communication: how they work, what goes into them, what their varieties are, how their parts are arranged, and how they are punctuated. You may be able to write fairly well without knowing much about these grammatical principles. But if you have any difficulties writing correct and effective sentences, you'll find it much easier to overcome them if you know how sentences work. And you'll find an understanding of sentence grammar especially helpful in improving both the correctness and the effectiveness of your punctuation.

Don't be intimidated or otherwise made uncomfortable by the thought that you're studying "grammar." For one thing, although you may sometimes find yourself enjoying it for its own sake, you're studying it primarily as a means to an end. Besides, if you can read these sentences and understand what we're saying, you already know a great deal of grammar; chances are you absorbed it, unconsciously, early in life. Now you need only raise some of that understanding into consciousness so that you can use it—when you need it—to help you stick to the conventions and make your writing more effective. You may often be able to trust your unconscious grasp of the way English words and sentences work; but if you find yourself having trouble, especially if English isn't your first language, you may have to consult the principles more often and apply them more consciously.

We use the vocabulary of traditional grammar both because it has for many the virtue of simplicity and familiarity and because it is usually the vocabulary used to study another language. It is also the vocabulary used by dictionaries and other reference books in their definitions and discussions of usage.

Learning these terms shouldn't be difficult. Many people learn the basic details presented in this and other such books in a matter of only a few days; much of it is after all entirely mechanical. If you find the going rough, you may be making it unnecessarily hard for yourself; if you fight the material, it may well fight back. But if you approach it with interest and a desire to learn, you'll find that it will cooperate and that the quality of your writing will improve as you increase your mastery of the conventions. Further, you will not only be learning to follow "rules" in order to produce "correct" sentences but also learning how to choose one form or usage or order rather than another. Good writing is often a result of being able to make intelligent choices from the alternatives available to you.

CHAPTER 1

SENTENCES:
Their Elements and Basic Patterns

This chapter introduces the basic elements and patterns of English sentences and defines and classifies different kinds of sentences. Awareness of these patterns and an ability to recognize phrases and clauses are essential to an understanding of sentence grammar.

1 The Conventions of Sentences

All sentences have a purpose, namely to communicate ideas or feelings. And there are **conventional** ways to convey these ideas or feelings. For example, if someone tells you,

> I didn't finish my homework last night.

you know that the sentence is stating a fact, or a supposed fact. If the same person then says,

> Did you get your history essay written?

you know that you are being asked a question and that you are expected to give an answer. If your friend then says,

> Leave me alone for a while.

you know you are being told to do something, being given a mild command. And when your fellow-student says,

> What a tough assignment!

you know you are hearing an emphatic expression of strong feeling.

We all know how to take these different kinds of utterances because we all understand and accept the *conventions* of the way sentences communicate. Sentences are classified according to the kind of purpose each has. Sentences that *make statements* are called **declarative**:

> Canada is a large country.
> The police officer asked me a question.
> There will be a quiz on this material Wednesday.

Sentences that *ask questions* are **interrogative**; in speech, they often (but not always) end with a rise in pitch; in writing, they end with a **question mark**:

> Was John A. Macdonald an effective leader?
> Are you going to the concert?
> When? What for?

Sentences that *give commands* or *make requests*, that expect action or compliance, are **imperative**:

> Please close the door.
> Be sure to get to class on time tomorrow.
> Proofread carefully.

Sentences that *exclaim*, that express strong feeling with particular vigour or emphasis, are called **exclamatory**; they customarily end with an **exclamation point**:

> That was quite a day!
> Not if I can help it!
> Wow!

Like many other traditional categories, however, these aren't always so simple or obvious. For example, a sentence may include both *interrogative* and *declarative* elements:

> "Have you been drinking?" the police officer asked.

or both *imperative* and *declarative* elements:

> Be sure to get to class on time tomorrow: there's going to be a quiz.

or be both *imperative* and *exclamatory*:

> Stop that!

And many *imperative* sentences, especially those that make requests, are at least implicitly *interrogative* even though they don't end with a question mark:

> Please close the door. (Will you please close the door?)

Sometimes the same basic sense can be expressed in all four ways:

> I need your help.
> Will you help me?
> Help me with this.
> Help!

Nevertheless, you're seldom in doubt about the purpose of sentences you hear or read, and you're seldom if ever in doubt about the purpose or purposes of any particular sentence you speak or write. Your unconscious awareness of the *conventions* guides you: you know instinctively how to frame a sentence in order to make it do what you want.

But a more conscious grasp of sentences and the way they work will help you frame them even more effectively. It will help you when you're in doubt. And it will help you not only to avoid weaknesses and errors but also to revise and correct them when they do occur.

Since most sentences are *declarative*, their patterns are the ones you need to understand first. Most of the rest of this chapter, then, deals with the basic elements and patterns of declarative sentences.

1a Subject and Predicate, Noun and Verb

A standard declarative sentence consists of two parts: a **subject** and a **predicate**. The subject is what acts or is talked about; the predicate is what the subject does or what is said about it. For example:

subject	predicate
Grass	grows.
Cats	purr.
I	paint.

The essential element of the subject part of a sentence is a **noun** (*Grass, Cats*) or a **pronoun** (*I*) (see #2 and #3); the essential element of the predicate part of a sentence is a **verb** (*grows, purr, paint*) (see #6).

Exercise 1a

Compose ten two-word sentences similar to those above. Each must have a single-word noun or a pronoun as subject and a single-word verb as predicate.

1b Articles and Other Modifiers

Few sentences, however, consist of only a one-word subject and a one-word predicate. Frequently, for example, nouns are preceded by **articles** (*a, an, the*) (see #8c):

subject	predicate
The grass	grew.

And both subject and predicate often include **modifiers**, words that change or limit the meaning of nouns and verbs. Nouns are modified by **adjectives** (see #8):

subject	predicate
The *green* grass	grew.
An *angry* cat	will scratch.

Verbs are modified by **adverbs** (see #9):

subject	predicate
The green grass	grew *profusely.*
They	purr *contentedly.*

Exercise 1b

Rewrite five of the sentences you wrote for Exercise 1a, adding articles and single-word adjectives and adverbs to them as you think appropriate.

1c-k   Basic Sentence Patterns

Such single-word modifiers as those above, however, account for only part of the richness of many sentences, with their arrays of modifying phrases and clauses (see for example the sentences discussed in #15). Yet complicated as they may often seem, almost all English sentences use only a few basic patterns, or combinations of them. If you can recognize and understand these few simple patterns, you are well on your way to being able to analyze any sentence you read—or write.

1c   Sentence Pattern 1

This is the pattern you've already looked at and imitated. The subject, consisting of a noun (with its modifiers) or a pronoun, is followed by the predicate, consisting of a verb (with its modifiers):

subject	predicate
The Siamese cat	scratched fiercely.
Birds	fly.
These large, ungainly birds	can fly surprisingly fast.
They	soar majestically.

Exercise 1c

Return to the sentences you wrote for Exercises 1a and 1b, or compose new ones, this time adding a few more modifiers to some of the nouns and verbs.

1d Sentence Pattern 2A

In this pattern you expand the basic sentence core by adding a **direct object** to the predicate. A direct object, like a subject, must be either a noun or a pronoun, and the verb must be **transitive** (see #6a):

subject	predicate	
noun or pronoun	transitive verb	direct object
I	paint	pictures.
Lynn	threw	the ball.
Sandra	hates	television.
It	always annoys	her.
Pierre	was picking	flowers.
Farmers	grow	nutritious vegetables.
Nervous cats	scratch	careless children.

In this pattern the subject acts, the verb indicates the action, and the direct object is what the action produces (*pictures*) or is directed toward (*television, children*). Note that direct objects can, like subject-nouns, be modified by adjectives (*nutritious, careless*).

Exercise 1d

Compose five sentences following Pattern 2A, some with modifiers and some without.

1e Sentence Pattern 2B

This pattern reverses the order of the main elements of Pattern 2A. That is, the former direct object becomes the subject and the former subject moves to the end after the **preposition** *by* (see #11). The verb stays in the middle, but changes to the **passive voice**—a form of the verb *be* followed by a **past participle** (see #10d). Usually you will want to avoid the passive voice; it is often weak and wordy compared to the active voice. But occasionally it is preferable. For example a detective might say, using Pattern 2A,

Poison killed him. (active voice)

But in the circumstances it would be more natural to say

He was killed by poison. (passive voice)

Similarly, you can write some of the sentences under Pattern 2A according to Pattern 2B:

subject	predicate	
noun or pronoun	verb	prepositional phrase
Pictures	are painted	by me.
Television	is hated	by Sandra.
Flowers	are picked	by Pierre.
Nutritious vegetables	are grown	by farmers.
It	was thrown	by Lynn.

But you can see that such alternative sentences would be preferable only in unusual circumstances, for example if you wanted special emphasis on *Flowers* or *It* (i.e., *The ball*) or *Lynn*. Note that in this pattern the *by*-phrase is often omitted as unnecessary or unknown:

He	has been poisoned	(by someone).

See also #6 o-p and #18f.

Exercise 1e

Convert each sentence you wrote for Exercise 1d into Pattern 2B. How many now seem to be sentences you could use in normal discourse? Try to include them in contexts where they would be preferable to the versions you wrote for Pattern 2A. Then compose a few new sentences using Pattern 2B, ones that you like the sound of in the passive voice.

1f   **Sentence Pattern 3**

A sentence with a direct object sometimes also includes an **indirect object**, a noun or pronoun identifying *to* or *for* whom or what the action of the verb is carried out. The indirect object comes before the direct object:

subject	predicate		
noun	transitive verb	indirect object	direct object
Lynn	threw	me	the ball.
She	gave	the laundry bag	a swift kick.
He	bought	his daughter	a bicycle.

Note that you can usually vary this pattern, and still say essentially the same thing, by changing the indirect object to a prepositional phrase that comes after the direct object:

subject	predicate		
noun	transitive verb	direct object	prepositional phrase
Lynn	threw	the ball	to me.
He	bought	a bicycle	for his daughter.

Compose five sentences in Pattern 3. Then rewrite two of them so that you use a prepositional phrase, with *to* or *for*, instead of an indirect object.

1g   Sentence Pattern 4A

Some verbs—called **linking verbs** (see #6a)—require something other than an object to complete the idea, something called a **complement**. And since it is linked to the subject, it is sometimes called a **subjective complement**. The principal linking verb is *be* in its various forms (see #6f). In Pattern 4A, the verb links the subject with an adjectival modifier in the predicate part of the sentence; the modifier is therefore called a **predicate adjective**:

subject	predicate	
noun or pronoun	linking verb	subjective complement (predicate adjective)
Sharon	is	rich.
He	isn't	tired.
Computers	are becoming	indispensable.
Anchovies	taste	salty.

Compose three sentences following Pattern 4A.

1h   Sentence Pattern 4B

In this pattern a verb links the subject with a noun or pronoun as subjective complement, called a **predicate noun**:

subject	predicate	
noun or pronoun	linking verb	subjective complement (predicate noun)
Anna	is	a lawyer.
This	is	it.
Margaret Atwood	is	a well-known writer.
Computers	are	useful tools.
Raw vegetables	make	good snacks.

Compose three sentences following Pattern 4B.

1i   Sentence Pattern 5A

Such verbs as *appoint, believe, call, consider, declare, designate, elect, find, judge, make, name, nominate, select,* and *think* are sometimes followed by a direct object and an **objective complement**—a complement describing the object rather than the subject. In Pattern 5A, as in Pattern 4A, the complement is an *adjective*:

subject	predicate		
noun or pronoun	*transitive verb*	*direct object*	*objective complement (adjective)*
The members	considered	Walter	incompetent.
The jury	found	her	guilty as charged.
They	made	themselves	comfortable.

Exercise 1i

Compose three sentences following Pattern 5A.

1j   Sentence Pattern 5B

In this variation, the objective complement completes the meaning of the direct object with a *noun*:

subject	predicate		
noun or pronoun	*transitive verb*	*direct object*	*objective complement (noun)*
They	elected	Herbert	treasurer.
I	call	that idea	a winner.
Sandra	considers	television	a waste of time.

Exercise 1j

Compose three sentences following Pattern 5B.

1k   Sentence Pattern 6

This final pattern is another, like Pattern 2B, that you should use sparingly: the **expletive** pattern. In such sentences the word *There* or *It* appears at the beginning, in the place usually occupied by the subject; then comes a linking verb, usually a form of the verb *be*; and then comes the subject. The words *There* and *It* enable you to make certain kinds of statements in a more natural way or with a different emphasis than you could otherwise. For example, instead of having to say

subject	*predicate*
That life begins at forty	may be true.
No solutions	existed.
No plumbing	was in the cabin.

you can, using Pattern 6, say

expletive	*linking verb*	*complement*	*subject*
It	may be	true	that life begins at forty.
There	were		no solutions.
There	was		no plumbing in the cabin.

Here are some further examples of Pattern 6:

There were fifteen people at the meeting.
It was difficult to believe him.
It is not easy to succeed in that profession.
There wasn't a cloud in the sky.
It's delightful the way she can imitate her brother.

See also #7e, #18f, and #59a.

Exercise 1k(1)

Try converting the five examples just above into a different pattern (for example, *Fifteen people were at the meeting*). In what kinds of contexts might the alternative—and more direct—versions be preferable?

Exercise 1k(2)

Convert the following sentences into Pattern 6:
1. Ten books are on the table.
2 No way around the obstacle exists.
3. To look directly at a solar eclipse is dangerous.
4. A magnificent celebration occurred.
5. People were everywhere!
6. Waiter, a fly is in my soup.

Do some seem better in the expletive form? Why? How might context determine one's choice?

Exercise 1c-k | Identifying sentence elements and patterns

Identify the pattern of each of the following sentences. Label each subject-noun or -pronoun *S* and each predicate-verb *V*. Then label each direct object *DO*, each indirect object *IO*, each subjective complement *SC*, and each objective complement *OC*. If you wish, also label any articles and other modifiers.

1. Food nourishes.
2. Bruce finds gardening relaxing.
3. The Schmidts are excellent cooks.
4. I love spaghetti.
5 .There are nine major planets in our solar system.
6. Poor Stephen was hit by a bus.
7. Jacques brought me luck.
8. Good music can affect one's emotions.
9. The committee elected Maya secretary.
10. Most people are generous.

1-l   Other Elements: Structure Words

Most declarative sentences use one or more of the above patterns. And the elements in those patterns—subjects, verbs, modifiers, objects, and complements—make up the substance of all sentences. Most sentences, however, also include words like *and, but, for, of, under, with*. Though such words have little meaning by themselves, they are important because they connect the other elements in various ways that establish meaningful relations between them. Such words are sometimes called **structure words** or **function words**; most of them belong to two other classes of words, or "parts of speech," **conjunctions** (see #12) and **prepositions** (see #11). All of these elements are discussed and illustrated at greater length in Chapter II and Chapter III.

1m-r   Clauses and Phrases

But before you go on to Chapter II, you need to understand the difference between **clauses** and **phrases** and how they work in sentences. Clauses and phrases are groups of words that function as grammatical units or elements *within* sentences but that—except for **independent clauses**—cannot stand alone *as* sentences.

1m   Independent (Main) Clauses

A **clause** is a group of words that contains both a *subject* and a *predicate*. If it is an **independent clause**, it can, as the term indicates, stand by itself as a sentence. Each of the sample sentences in the preceding sections is an independent clause, since each contains the minimum requirement: a noun or pronoun as subject and a verb functioning in the predicate; each is a **simple sentence** (see #1z.1).

But an independent clause can also function as only part of a sentence. For example, if you start with two separate independent clauses—that is, two simple sentences:

Tuition fees went up.
Students complained.

you can combine them to form a **compound sentence** (see #1z.2):

Tuition fees went up; students complained.
Tuition fees went up, and students complained.
Tuition fees went up; therefore students complained.

Each of the two halves of these sentences is an independent clause; each could stand alone as a sentence.

1n Subordinate (Dependent) Clauses

A **subordinate clause**, unlike an independent clause, usually cannot stand by itself. Even though, as a clause, it contains a subject and a predicate, it is by definition *subordinate, dependent* on another clause—an *independent* one—for its meaning. It therefore must be treated as only part of a sentence, as in the following examples (the subordinate clauses are in italics); these are called **complex sentences** (see #1z.3):

When tuition fees went up, students complained.
Students complained *because tuition fees went up*.
Students complained *that tuition fees had gone up two years in a row*.
Tuition fees went up, *which angered many students*.

Note that subordinate clauses often begin with such words as *when, because, that*, and *which*, called **subordinators**, which often clearly signal the presence of a subordinate clause as opposed to an independent clause (see #12c).

(Of course subordinate clauses can be used separately, for example in dialogue or as answers to questions, where the context is clear: Why did students complain? *Because tuition fees went up.* Except in such special circumstances, however, a subordinate clause should not be allowed to stand by itself as if it were a sentence. See #1x and #1y.)

1o Functions of Subordinate Clauses

Like a phrase (see below), a subordinate clause functions as a grammatical unit in its sentence. That is, subordinate clauses can occupy several of the slots in the sentence patterns illustrated above. For example, a **noun clause** can serve as the subject of a sentence:

That hummingbirds can fly is astonishing. (Pattern 4A)

as a direct object:

Jill knows *what she is doing*. (Pattern 2A)

or as a predicate noun:

The problem was *what they would tell the inspector*. (Pattern 4B)

Adjectival clauses (also called **relative clauses**; see #3d) modify nouns or pronouns, such as a direct object:

The principal congratulated the student *who had won the prize*. (Pattern 2A)

or a subject:

The horse *that she had bet on* won easily. (Pattern 1)

Adverbial clauses usually modify main verbs:

He wept *because he was deeply moved*. (Pattern 1)

1p   Phrases

A **phrase** is a group of words lacking a subject and predicate but functioning as a grammatical unit in a sentence. For example, a **verb phrase** (see #6g) acts as the verb in this Pattern 1 sentence:

Most of our guests *will be leaving* in the morning.

A **prepositional phrase** (see #11) can be an adjectival modifier:

Most *of our guests* will be leaving in the morning.

or an adverbial modifier:

Most of our guests will be leaving *in the morning*.

The words *Most of our guests* constitute a **noun phrase** functioning as the subject of the sentence. Any noun or pronoun along with its modifiers—so long as the group doesn't contain a subject-predicate combination—can be thought of as a noun phrase. Similarly, a **gerund phrase** (see #10f) can function as a subject:

Losing weight can be difficult. (Pattern 4A)

or as a direct object:

They tried *losing weight*. (Pattern 2A)

A **participial phrase**—always adjectival (see #10d)—can modify a subject:

Obeying his catcher's signal, Enrique threw the batter a low curve. (Pattern 3) or a direct object:

> The car hit the man *standing on the corner*. (Pattern 2A)

An **infinitive phrase** (see #10a) can function as a direct object (noun):

> They tried *to lose weight*. (Pattern 2A)

or as a subject (noun):

> It is difficult *to lose weight*. (Pattern 6)

but it can also function as an adjective, for example one modifying the subject:

> His failure *to lose weight* was predictable. (Pattern 4A)

or as an adverb, for example one modifying the verb:

> He arranged the furniture *to suit his own taste*. (Pattern 2A)

Adverbs, whether single words or phrases, can also act as **sentence modifiers**, modifying not the verb or any other word alone but rather all the rest of the sentence (see #9a and #9d.4):

> Luckily,
> In fact,　　　　the damage from the earthquake was limited.
> To be sure,

Exercise 1m-p　Recognizing phrases and clauses

Indicate whether each of the following groups of words is an independent clause, a subordinate clause, or a phrase. Label the subject (s) and verb (v) of each clause.

1. not only Lily but Jean as well
2. never had he seen such a storm
3. for the first time in her life she was happy
4. since no one was looking
5. around the corner from our house
6. but the minister was not in his office
7. while talking on the telephone
8. the boat sank
9. after the party was over
10. according to the elaborately printed instructions in the guidebook

1q-r Two other kinds of phrases you should be familiar with are the **appositive** and the **absolute**.

1q Appositives

An **appositive** is a word or group of words that renames or restates, in other terms, the meaning of a neighbouring word. For example, if you start with two simple sentences,

> Marvin is our gardener. He looks after the flowers.

you can reduce the first and combine it with the second:

> Marvin, *our gardener*, looks after the flowers.

Most appositives are nouns or noun phrases that redefine, usually in more specific terms, the nouns they follow. But occasionally an appositive precedes the other noun:

> *A fine gardener*, Marvin deserves our gratitude.

And occasionally another part of speech can function as an appositive, for example a participial (adjectival) phrase:

> Studying assiduously, *reviewing every page of the text*, they prepared for the exam.

or a verb:

> Parse (*analyze grammatically*) some of these sentences.

An appositive can also be a single word, often a name:

> Our gardener, *Marvin*, looks after the flowers.

And, rarely, even a subordinate clause can function as an appositive:

> How I got here—*whether I paid my own way or not*—is none of their business.

Note that an appositive is grammatically equivalent to the term it defines, and could replace it in the sentence:

> Our gardener looks after the flowers.
> A fine gardener deserves our gratitude.
> Reviewing every page of the text, they prepared for the exam.
> Analyze some of these sentences grammatically.
> Marvin looks after the flowers.
> Whether I paid my own way or not is none of their business.

(For the punctuation of appositives, see #37b and #44g.)

Exercise 1q(1) Writing appositives

By reducing one of each pair to an appositive, combine each of the following pairs of sentences into a single sentence. Construct one or two so that the appositive comes first.

1. Joe is a night owl. He sleeps most of the day.
2. The manager is a stickler for accuracy. She insists that we triple-check every set of figures.
3. I must thank my uncle for putting me through school. He is a wealthy man.
4. The mayor believes in ghosts. He attends séances at least once a month.
5. You can save time by preparing carefully. That is, you can take careful notes and draw up a preliminary outline.

Exercise 1q(2) Using appositives

Combine each of the following pairs of sentences into a single sentence by reducing all or part of one of them to an appositive. You may drop some words and change and rearrange others, but don't change the basic meaning. For practice, do some sentences in more than one way.

Example: Hong Kong is one of Asia's busiest ports. It is a major Pacific commercial centre.
  (a) Hong Kong, one of Asia's busiest ports, is a major Pacific commercial centre.
  (b) One of Asia's busiest ports, Hong Kong, is a major Pacific commercial centre.
  (c) One of Asia's busiest ports, Hong Kong is a major Pacific commercial centre.

1. The book I read last weekend is *Fifth Business*. It is the first volume of Robertson Davies's *The Deptford Trilogy*.
2. To become a good doctor is not easy. It takes many years of study and hard work.
3. I always look forward to September. It is the month when the new academic year begins.
4. My hobbies more than occupy my spare time. I collect stamps, play chess, listen to classical music, and eat.
5. Tabloid newspapers seem to go in for sensationalism. They are the smaller, easier-to-hold newspapers.
6. Canada has a larger land mass than any other country except Russia. It is a country with a relatively small population.
7. She was relaxed and confident when she began the race. She was sure she could win.
8. The word *hamburger* is one of the common words we take for granted. It comes from the name of a German city.
9. Dr. Snyder is our family physician. She is a dedicated person who works long hours.
10. Running marathons is not something everyone should try. It is a potentially dangerous sport.

1r

1r   Absolute Phrases

An **absolute phrase** has no direct grammatical link with what it modifies; it depends simply on juxtaposition, in effect modifying the rest of the sentence by hovering over it like an umbrella. Most absolute phrases amount to a sentence with the verb changed to a participle (see #10d). Instead of using two sentences,

> The sky had cleared. The game could finally begin.

you can reduce the first to an absolute phrase modifying the second:

> *The sky having cleared*, the game could finally begin.

If the original verb is a form of *be*, the participle can often be omitted:

> *Her last exam (being) over*, Elana could finally relax.
> In the heavy seas the ship pitched wildly, *its bows (being) sometimes entirely awash*.

Sometimes, especially with certain common expressions, the participle isn't preceded by a noun:

> There were a few rough spots, but *generally speaking* the rehearsal was a success.
> *Judging by the results*, it was not a good campaign.

And sometimes infinitive phrases (see #10a) function as absolutes:

> *To say the least*, the campaign was not a success.

You can also think of many absolutes as *with*-phrases from which the preposition has been dropped:

> *(With) Her last exam finished*, Elana could relax.
> The ship pitched wildly, *(with) its bows sometimes awash*.

And you can think of most absolutes as functioning much like an adverb modifying the rest of the sentence (see #9a and #9d.4):

> *absolute: All things considered*, it was a fair exam.
> *adverb: Unfortunately*, I hadn't studied hard enough.

See also #10i and Exercise 10(5).

Exercise 1r   Writing absolute phrases

Compose five sentences using absolute phrases. You may want to start with pairs of sentences or with sentences containing a *with*-phrase.

1s   Order of Elements in Declarative Sentences

Even if you didn't know the names of some of the bits and pieces, chances are that the samples illustrating the basic sentence patterns felt natural to you; they're the familiar kinds you use every day without even thinking about their structure. Note that the natural order of the elements in almost all the patterns is the same:

> subject—verb
> subject—transitive verb—object(s)—(objective complement)
> subject—linking verb—subjective complement

The only exception is Pattern 6, the expletive, in which the subject follows the verb (see #1k).

This conventional order of *subject—verb—object or complement* has proved itself the most direct and forceful pattern of expression:

> A stitch in time saves nine.
> Beggars can't be choosers.
> Humpty Dumpty had a great fall.
> We are such stuff as dreams are made on.
> We shall defend every village, every town, and every city.
> This was their finest hour.

But this conventional order can be altered to create special stylistic effects or special emphasis, and to introduce occasional pleasing variations:

direct object		*subject*	*transitive verb*	
The dessert, however,		we	ate	with gusto.

subjective complement	*linking verb*	*subject*
Evil	was	the day that I first met that man.

Such inversions aren't wrong, for conventions (or rules) are made to be broken as well as followed; but their very unconventionality demands that they be used sparingly. They are most at home in poetry or highly poetic prose:

> Such thoughts to Lucy I will give . . . .
> No motion has she now . . . .
> Thirty days hath September . . . .
> And now abideth faith, hope, and charity, these three; but the greatest of
>   these is charity.
> Never in the field of human conflict was so much owed by so many to so few.

Elsewhere such variations are rare, since any unusual pattern almost automatically calls attention to itself, something seldom appropriate in expository prose. But used occasionally, and appropriately, they can be highly effective.

Exercise 1s **Using alternative word-orders**

Try composing four or five declarative sentences that vary the standard order of elements in one way or another. Then choose one of your sentences and use it in a paragraph that you think justifies the unorthodox order.

1t   **Order of Elements in Interrogative Sentences**

The conventional order in interrogative sentences usually differs from that for declarative sentences. It is of course possible to use the declarative order for a question—for example in speaking, when one can use stress and end with the rising or falling intonation that usually indicates a question:

> The man bit the dog?

thereby conveying a meaning something like

> What?! Do you mean to tell me that the *man* actually bit the *dog*, instead of the other way around? How very bizarre!

But unless you're recording or imitating dialogue, you won't find this technique easy to use in writing.

Usually, an interrogative sentence, besides ending with the conventional question mark, will take one of the following patterns. If the verb is a single-word form of *be*, it precedes the subject:

verb	subject	subjective complement
Was	Macdonald	an effective leader?

With all other single-word verbs, it is necessary to supply a form of the auxiliary verb *do* before the subject; the main part of the verb then follows the subject in the normal way:

auxiliary verb	subject	main verb
Did	Macdonald	lead effectively?

If the verb is already a verb phrase, the first auxiliary comes before the subject:

auxiliary verb	subject	second auxiliary	main verb
Are	you		going?
Will	Max		speak first?
Have	you	been	drinking?

If the question includes a negative, the *not* goes before or after the subject, depending on whether one uses the less formal, contracted form:

Aren't you going?
Are you not going?

With questions using expletives (Pattern 6; see #1k), the expletive and the verb are reversed:

Were there many people at the meeting?
Was it difficult to believe her?

With so-called "tag" questions, a statement is followed by a verb-pronoun question; note also that a *not* appears in one or the other of the two parts:

Mark has been drinking, hasn't he?
Mark hasn't been drinking, has he?

All the above questions invite a *yes* or *no* answer, perhaps extended by a short clause made up of the appropriate pronoun (or expletive) and auxiliary, such as

Yes, he was. Yes I am. No, I haven't. Yes, there were. No, it wasn't. No, he hasn't. No, he has not.

Note that the negative answers include a *not* in the clause.

The only other common form of question begins with a **question-word**, one of the interrogative adverbs or pronouns; these invite answers beyond a mere *yes* or *no*. When a question begins with an interrogative adverb (see #9a), a form of *do* or another already-present auxiliary comes before the subject:

Why did he say that?
Where (When) are you going?

If an interrogative *pronoun* (see #3c) functions as *subject*, the sentence retains standard declarative word order:

Who will speak first?

If the opening pronoun is the *object* of the verb or a preposition, it is followed by the added auxiliary *do* or the first part of a verb phrase, the subject, and the rest of the verb, just as in the *yes or no* pattern:

Whom did you ask?
What will the speaker deal with? (*or* With what will the speaker deal?)

A similar reversal occurs when an interrogative pronoun functions as a possessive or other adjective (see #8a):

Whose (Which, What) explanation did you favour?
To what (which, whose) problems will the speaker address himself?

See also #11b, on the placement of prepositions in questions.

Exercise 1t **Constructing interrogative sentences**

Select a representative variety of ten or twenty sentences from those you've written for earlier exercises in this chapter and rewrite them as questions. Try using two or more different forms of question for some of the sentences.

1u   The Structure of Imperative Sentences

Although it is possible, especially with emphatic commands, to use the full structure of a declarative sentence:

subject	predicate
You	take that back!
You two in the corner	please stop your chattering.

the conventional form of **imperative sentences** uses only the *predicate*, omitting the *subject* (an understood *you*):

Come into the garden, Maud. (*Maud* is not the subject, but a noun of
    address; see #2b.)
Look before you leap.
Close the door.
Take two aspirins and go to bed.
Proofread carefully.
Hush.

Sometimes, especially in dialogue or informal contexts, even the verb can be omitted; a complement alone does the job:

Careful.   Easy, now.   Steady.

You may think you'll have little use for imperative sentences. But if you ever want to write a set of instructions, you'll need to use a great many of them. And they can provide useful variety in other contexts as well, just as questions can. *Declarative* sentences are unquestionably the mainstay of expression, but *interrogative* and *imperative* sentences are also useful. Use them.

1v   What Is a Sentence?

Now for a different kind of look at these groups of words called sentences. First, just what is a **sentence**? Most standard definitions are unsatisfactory and unrealistic. One of them, for example, says that a sentence is a group of words with a subject and a verb. But the first sentence of this section, just above, lacks a subject-verb combination. And here are some more sentences that lack one or the other or both:

> Yes.   No.   When?   Now or never.   Oh my goodness!   Wow!
> Who, me?   Well, I never!   John.   Spaghetti.
> Come here.   Never mind.   Call me Ishmael.   Sink or swim.

Out of context, such sentences don't tell us much, but they are clearly acceptable units. Moreover, some groups of words do contain a subject-verb combination but are still not sentences: an opening capital letter and a closing period don't make a subordinate clause a sentence:

> I decided to make a list. *Before I went shopping.*
> He bought me the bike. *Which I had stared at in the store the week before.*

The second clause in each of these is a **fragment** (see #1y).

Another common definition claims that a sentence is a complete thought. But *Yes* and *No* aren't satisfyingly complete without the questions that prompted them, nor are some of the other examples without their respective contexts. Nor is there anything necessarily "incomplete" about such words as *dog, hand, chair, liberty, love*—yet these words are not normally thought of as sentences.

Remember that language is primarily speech sound. It is more realistic to define a **sentence** as *a satisfyingly complete pattern of intonation or expression*: that is, a complete utterance. Your voice and natural tone should tell you whether a certain group of words is or is not a sentence. Make it a practice to read your written work aloud, or at least to sound it over in your mind's ear. Doing so will help you avoid serious errors.

1w-y   Major Sentences, Minor Sentences, and Fragments

Sentences—that is, acceptable patterns of expression—are of two kinds, which we call **major** and **minor**. Though this and similar books deal almost exclusively with *major* sentences, and though you won't have much use for *minor* sentences in academic writing, you should understand what minor sentences are so that you can use them occasionally for emphasis or other rhetorical effects or in a piece of dialogue. And you need to be able to distinguish between the minor sentence, which is acceptable, and the fragmentary expression, which is not.

1w   Major Sentences

A **major sentence** is a grammatically independent group of words that contains at least two essential structural elements: a subject and a finite verb (see #1a and #6b, Note). Major sentences constitute 99% or more of most writing. They are the sentences whose basic patterns are illustrated above, in sections #1c to #1k.

1x   Minor Sentences

A **minor sentence** is an acceptable pattern of expression that nevertheless lacks either a subject or a finite verb, or both. But it is easy to supply the missing element or elements from context; for whereas *major* sentences can usually stand by themselves, most *minor* sentences need a context of one or more nearby sentences in order to make sense—most obviously, for example, as answers to questions. The minor sentence, however, like the major, is grammatically independent.

Minor sentences are usually one of the following four kinds:

1. *Exclamations:* Oh! Well, I never! Heavens! Wow! Great Scott! Drat! Incredible!

2. *Questions or responses to questions:* When? Tomorrow. How many? Seven. Why? What for? How come? What else? Really? Yes. No. Please. Perhaps. Certainly.

3. *Common proverbial or idiomatic expressions:* Easy come, easy go. Now or never. In a pig's eye! Sink or swim. Better late than never. Down the hatch.

4. *Minor sentences used for rhetorical or stylistic effect by writers who know how to handle them:* These are more common in narrative and descriptive writing, but they can be effective in other contexts as well. Here is how Charles Dickens begins *Bleak House:*

> London. Michaelmas Term lately over, and the Lord Chancellor sitting in Lincoln's Inn Hall. Implacable November weather. As much mud in the streets, as if the waters had but newly retired from the face of the earth, and it would not be wonderful to meet a Megalosaurus, forty feet long or so, waddling like an elephantine lizard up Holborn Hill.

And so on for three long paragraphs: not a major sentence in sight. Here is how William Zinsser begins his 1969 essay "Nobody Here but Us Dead Sheep":

> Nerve gas in Okinawa. Nuclear explosions in Nevada. Chemical Mace in the eyes. Every day it's something else in American life which strikes me as outlandish.

Clearly the beginning of a piece of writing is a good place to try the effects of a minor sentence or two. A student began an essay this way:

> Money, money, money. It makes the world go round.

And here is a paragraph from another student's essay:

> One of my favourite distractions is my junk drawer. You know, that drawer in the kitchen overflowing with miscellaneous tidbits of memorabilia. The treasure chest of hastily tossed-in articles which may include anything from letters, coupons long past their expiry date, junk mail, and old photos, to the odd sock you thought the washing-machine ate.

1y   **Fragments**

frag   Don't mistake an unacceptable **fragment** for an acceptable minor sentence:

> *frag:* I didn't attend the meeting. *Because I felt that it would be a waste of time.*

The *Because*-clause is a fragment. The period after *meeting* should be changed to a comma so that the subordinate clause can take its rightful place in the sentence. (But note that this *Because*-clause, like many other fragments, would be acceptable as an answer to a question just before it.)

> *frag:* It was a terrible scene. One that I'll never forget.

The clause beginning with *One* should be linked to the preceding independent clause with a comma, not separated from it by a period. It can then take its rightful place as a noun clause in apposition to *scene.*

> *frag:* She gave me back the ring. Being of a forgiving nature.

The participial phrase beginning with *being* is not a separate sentence but an adjective modifying *She*; it should be introduced by a comma, or even moved to the beginning of the sentence:

> *revised:* Being of a forgiving nature, she gave me back the ring.

Note that fragments tend to occur after the independent clauses that they should be attached to.

Fragments are not satisfyingly complete patterns of intonation or expression; learn to recognize them so that you won't make the mistake of treating them like acceptable minor sentences.

Indicate whether the second group of words in each of the following is a minor sentence or a fragment.

1. He stayed in the parking place. Until the time on the meter had run out.
2. Just look at the way she's dressed. Good heavens!
3. You say you've never seen this man? Never?
4. He decided to stay in bed until eleven. It being a Sunday, after all.
5. How much wood can a woodchuck chuck? Plenty.

1z Kinds of Major Sentences

Sentences are usually classified as **simple**, **compound**, **complex**, and **compound-complex**.

1. A **simple** sentence has one subject and one finite verb, and therefore contains only one clause, an independent clause:

$$\overset{\text{s}}{\text{Denis}} \ \overset{\text{v}}{\text{works.}}$$

$$\overset{\text{s}}{\text{The boat}} \ \overset{\text{v}}{\text{leaks.}}$$

$$\text{The dilapidated old} \ \overset{\text{s}}{\text{building}} \ \overset{\text{v}}{\text{collapsed}} \ \text{during the night.}$$

The subject or the verb, or both, can be compound—that is, consist of more than one part—but the sentence containing them will still be **simple**:

Jules and Kim left early. (compound subject)
She *watched and waited.* (compound verb)
The *sergeant and his men moved* down the hill *and crossed* the river. (compound subject, compound verb)

2. A **compound** sentence in effect consists of two or more simple sentences—that is, independent clauses—linked by coordinating conjunctions (see #12a), by punctuation, or by both:

$$\text{The starter's} \ \overset{\text{s}}{\text{flag}} \ \overset{\text{v}}{\text{fell}} \ \text{and the} \ \overset{\text{s}}{\text{race}} \ \overset{\text{v}}{\text{began.}}$$

$$\text{The} \ \overset{\text{s}}{\text{clouds}} \ \overset{\text{v}}{\text{massed}} \ \text{thickly against the hills; soon the}$$

$$\overset{\text{s}}{\text{rain}} \ \overset{\text{v}}{\text{fell}} \ \text{in torrents.}$$

$\overset{\text{S}}{\text{He}}\ \overset{\text{V}}{\text{wanted to fly,}}\ \text{but}\ \overset{\text{S}}{\text{she}}\ \overset{\text{V}}{\text{insisted on going by train.}}$

S   S   V S   V
Gabriel's patience and persistence paid off; he not only won the prize but also
   V
earned his competitors' respect.

S V   S   V   S   V
The day was warm, the breeze was mild, and everyone had a good time.

3. A **complex** sentence consists of one independent clause and one or more subordinate clauses; in the following examples, the subordinate clauses are italicized:

He claimed *that he was innocent.* (noun clause as direct object)
She left *before the party was over.* (adverbial clause modifying *left*)
Ivan is the one *who is most likely to win.* (adjectival clause modifying *one*)
Anita, *who is the most intelligent*, scored highest. (adjectival clause modifying *Anita*)
When the time came, he put his belongings in the suitcase *which he had brought with him.* (adverbial clause modifying *put*, adjectival clause modifying *suitcase*)
Although it was late, they decided to start anyway. (adverbial clause of concession, in effect modifying the rest of the sentence)

Note that, when the meaning is clear, the conjunction *that* introducing a noun clause, or the relative pronouns *that* and *which*, can be omitted:

He claimed *he was innocent.*
. . . the suitcase *he had brought with him.*

But see the note near the end of #37a.

4. A **compound-complex** sentence consists of two or more independent clauses and one or more subordinate clauses:

Because he knew that the job was important, he began very carefully, but as time passed he grew impatient and therefore he failed to obtain the results that he had hoped for.

Analyzing this example:

Because he knew (adverbial clause)
that the job was important (noun clause)
he began very carefully (independent clause)
but (coordinating conjunction)
as time passed (adverbial clause)
he grew impatient (independent clause)
and (coordinating conjunction)
therefore (conjunctive adverb)
he failed to obtain the results (independent clause)
that he had hoped for (adjective clause)

Exercise 1z(1) Recognizing kinds of sentences

Label each of the following sentences as simple, compound, complex, or compound-complex.

1. Although Canada has a vast territory, its population is relatively small.
2. Nobody is going to give you something for nothing.
3. The mechanic who fixed my car yesterday is the same one I took it to last year.
4. The rains came and the river rose.
5. Few things are more pleasant than a lovingly prepared and carefully presented elegant meal consisting of several courses, consumed in good company, with soft background music, and accompanied by noble wines.
6. He saw the book he wanted on the top shelf, but he couldn't reach it.
7. Josephine decided against going for a ride in his flying machine.
8. A philosophy major may learn to think clearly and may even acquire a sense of cultural history, but when she graduates she will probably have difficulty finding a job that makes use of her training.
9. Whether violence on television is responsible for violent behaviour in children, or even in adults, is debatable.
10. Northern oil and gas deposits have created a mixture of benefits and problems for Canadians and Americans alike.

Exercise 1z(2) Constructing different kinds of sentences

(a) Compose three simple sentences.
(b) Compose two compound sentences, each with two independent clauses.
(c) Compose a compound sentence with three independent clauses.
(d) Compose two complex sentences, each with one independent and one subordinate clause.
(e) Compose a complex sentence with one independent and two subordinate clauses.
(f) Compose three compound-complex sentences.

Recycle one or more of your original simple sentences as you go on to the more complicated sentences. Use as many other modifiers—words and phrases—as you want.

CHAPTER II

THE PARTS OF SPEECH AND HOW THEY WORK IN SENTENCES

Introduction: Word Order, Inflection, and the Parts of Speech

As you saw in Chapter I, *word order* helps determine whether a sentence is asking a question or making a statement. But word order is important in another and even more basic way. The order of elements in Pattern 2A (see #1d), for example—subject, verb, direct object—determines *meaning*:

Students need teachers.

Clear enough. We know, from standard English word order, that *Students* is the subject, *need* the verb, and *teachers* the direct object. Reversing the order reverses the meaning:

Teachers need students.

Now we know that *Teachers* are doing the *needing* and that *students* are the objects of the need. If you know a language like German or Latin, you know how different—and in some ways more difficult—they can be; for in such languages it is the *form* of the words, rather than their position, that determines meaning. For example the sentence

Teachers students need.

would, in English, not only sound awkward but also be ambiguous. But the same three words in Latin would be clear because the *forms* of the two nouns would show which was subject and which was object.

The change in a word's form is called **inflection**. A language in which inflection is the key to grammatical or syntactical relations is called *synthetic*; a language like English, whose grammar is predominantly expressed by word order rather than inflection, is called *analytic*. But English isn't a purely analytic language, for it retains some features of its synthetic ancestor, Anglo-Saxon: some words in modern English must be inflected in order for sentences to communicate clearly. If for example you want the noun *boy* to denote more than one young male, you change it—*inflect* it—by adding an *s* to make it plural: *boys*. If you want to use the verb *see* to denote the act of seeing in some past time, you change its form so that you can say, for example, *I saw* or *I have seen* or *I was seeing*.

English words fall traditionally into eight categories called **parts of speech**. Five of these can be inflected in one or more ways:

Noun, Pronoun, Verb, Adjective, Adverb

The other three are never inflected:

Preposition, Conjunction, Interjection

For example the preposition *in* is always *in*; the conjunction *but* is always *but*. (The only exceptions occur when words are referred to *as words*, as in "There are too many *and*'s in that sentence," or in informal usages such as "I don't want to hear any *ifs, ands,* or *buts*" and "He knows all the *ins* and *outs* of the process," where such words function as nouns rather than as structure-words, prepositions and conjunctions.)

Note that the term *inflection* applies only to the change of a word's form *within its part of speech*. That is, when the noun *boy* is inflected for the plural, the new form—*boys*—is still a noun; when the pronoun *they* is inflected to *them* or *theirs*, the new forms are still pronouns. (Again there is an exception: when you inflect a noun or pronoun for the possessive case in front of a noun—the *boy's* coat, *their* idea—you turn it into an adjective; some people, however, thinking of *form* rather than *function*, prefer to call these "possessive nouns" and "possessive pronouns.")

Many words can be changed so that they function as different parts of speech. For example the noun *centre* can be made into the adjective *central*, or the noun *meaning* into the adjective *meaningful*, or the verb *vacate* into the noun *vacation*. Such changes, however, are not inflections but **derivations**; a word can be *derived* from a word of a different part of speech, often by the addition of one or more suffixes: *trust, trustful, trustfully, trustfulness*. And many words, even without being changed, can serve as more than one part of speech; for example:

Have you no *trust* in me? (noun)
I *trust* you. (verb)
She works for a *trust* company. (adjective)

The word *word* itself can be a noun ("Use this *word* correctly"), a verb ("How will you *word* your reply?"), or an adjective ("*Word* games are fun"). The word *right* can be a noun (his legal *right*), an adjective (the *right* stuff), an adverb (turn *right*, do it *right*), or a verb (*right* an overturned canoe). Or consider the versatility of the common little word *over*:

At least we have a roof *over* our heads. (preposition)
The game is *over*. (adjective)
Write that page *over*. (adverb)
How long does an *over* in cricket last? (noun)
"Roger. Message received. *Over*." (interjection)

Shakespeare even has a character say "I'll *over* then to England"—a rare use of *over* as a verb. The *form* of a word, then, doesn't always determine its function. What part of speech a word is depends on its *function* in a particular sentence.

The rest of this chapter discusses the eight parts of speech—their inflections (if any) and other grammatical properties; their subcategories; how they work with other words in sentences; and some of their important derivatives (verbals)—and calls attention to some of their potential trouble-spots, such as **agreement** and a verb's **tenses**.

.2 Nouns

A **noun** (from the Latin *nomen*, "name") is a word that names or stands for a person, place, thing, class, concept, quality, or action: *woman, character, city, country, citizen, ship, garden, machine, silence, vegetable, road, liberty, beauty, river, spring, investigation.* **Proper nouns** are names of specific persons, places, or things and begin with a capital letter: *Dorothy, Rumpelstiltskin, Winnipeg, England,* the *Lusitania.* All the others, called **common nouns,** are capitalized only if they begin a sentence:

> *Liberty* is a precious commodity.
> *Spring* is my favourite season.

or form part of a proper noun:

> Spring Garden Road, Statue of Liberty, Ottawa River

or are personified or otherwise emphasized, for example in poetry:

> Let there be light! said Liberty,
> And like sunrise from the sea,
> Athens arose!
> > (Shelley)

> Our noisy years seem moments in the being
> Of the eternal Silence . . . .
> > (Wordsworth)

(See #47, on capitalization.)

One can also classify nouns as either **concrete**, names of tangible objects (*doctor, elephant, utensil, book, barn*), or **abstract**, names of intangible things or ideas (*liberty, honour, happiness, history*). (See #54.)

Collective nouns are names of collections or groups often considered as units: *army, committee, family, herd, flock.* (See #4e and #7f.)

2a

2a   Inflection of Nouns

Nouns can be inflected in only two simple ways: for **number** and for **possessive case.**

1. For **number:** Most common, concrete nouns that stand for *countable* things are either **singular** (naming a single thing) or **plural** (naming more than one thing). And though proper nouns supposedly name specific persons, places, or things, they too can often logically be inflected for the plural; for example, there are many John *Smiths* in the telephone book, there are several *Londons* (e.g. the one in England and the one in Ontario), and since 1948 there have been two *Koreas*. Most singular nouns are inflected to indicate the plural by the addition of *s* or *es*: *boy, boys; box, boxes*. But some are made plural in other ways: *child, children; stimulus, stimuli*. (For more on the formation of plurals, see #51t.)

Some concrete nouns, however, called **mass** nouns, name materials that are measured, weighed, or divided, rather than items that are counted—for example *gold, oxygen, rice, sand, pasta*. As **uncountable** or **noncountable** nouns, these cannot be inflected for the plural.

Also **uncountable** are abstract nouns and nouns that stand for ideas, activities, and states of mind or being; for example, *honour, journalism, skiing, happiness*. Some nouns, however, can be either countable or uncountable, depending on context. For example:

> The butcher sells meat. (uncountable)
> The delicatessen offers several delicious smoked *meats*. (countable, equivalent to *kinds of smoked meat*)
> They insisted on telling the truth as a matter of *honour*. (uncountable)
> Many *honours* were heaped upon the returning hero. (countable, since an *honour* here is not an abstract quality but designates a specific thing like a medal, a citation, the key to the city, or at least one or another sort of verbal recognition or citation)

(See also #4c, #7g and #8c.6.)

2. For **possessive case: Case** is a term designating the syntactical relation of a noun or pronoun to other words in a sentence. In English, whether a noun is a *subject* (**subjective** case) or an *object* (**objective** case) is shown by word order rather than by inflection. But nouns are inflected for **possessive** case. By adding an apostrophe and an *s*, or sometimes only an apostrophe, you inflect a noun so that it shows possession or ownership: *my father's job, the children's toys, the students' grievances*. (For more on inflecting nouns for possessive case, see #51w.)

2b   Grammatical Function of Nouns

Nouns function in sentences in the following ways:

Subject of a verb (see #1a):

> *Students* work hard.

Direct object of a verb (see #1d):

> Our team won the *championship*.

Indirect object of a verb (see #1f):

> We awarded *Beverly* the prize.

Object of a preposition (see #1f and #1l):

> We gave the prize to *Beverly*. It was a book about *mountain-climbing*.

Predicate noun after a linking verb (see #1h):

> Harold is an *accountant*.

Objective complement (see #1j):

> The judges declared Beverly the *winner*.

An appositive to any other noun (see #1q):

> André, the *policeman*, spotted Roger, the *thief*.
> We gave Beverly the prize, a *book* about mountain-climbing.
> My brother *Masoud* graduated last year.

Nouns in the *possessive case* function as adjectives (see #8a):

> *Maria's* coat is expensive. (Which coat? Maria's.)
> I did a *day's* work. (How much work? A day's.)

or as predicate nouns, after a linking verb:

> The expensive-looking coat is *Maria's*.

Even without being inflected for possessive case, many nouns can also function as adjectives: the *school* paper, *police* procedure, the *automobile* industry, the *dessert* course, and so on (see #59g).

A noun (or pronoun) referring to someone being directly addressed, as in dialogue or in a letter, is called a *noun of address*. Such nouns, usually proper names, are not directly related to the syntax of the rest of the sentence and are set off with punctuation:

> *Yuki*, are you all right?

Soon, *Steve*, you'll see what I mean.
Hey *you*—give me a hand here!

Exercise 2b Recognizing nouns

Identify each noun or noun phrase in the following sentences and determine whether it is functioning as a subject, a direct object, an indirect object, an object of a preposition, a subjective complement (predicate noun), an objective complement, an appositive, or a possessive adjective.

1. Canada's youngest province, Newfoundland, joined Confederation in 1949.
2. The Queen was given a twenty-one gun salute.
3. Halifax's mayor gave the visiting dignitary the key to the city.
4. Old people often think back with pleasure, or regret, on their youth.
5. July was a month to remember: Marsha had never had such a rewarding holiday.
6. Shakespeare wrote many plays, but *Hamlet*, a tragedy, is his best-known work.
7. Too much work makes Jack a dull boy.

3 Pronouns

A **pronoun**, as its name indicates, is a word that stands for (*pro*) or in place of a noun, or at least functions like a noun in a sentence. Most pronouns refer to nouns that come earlier, their **antecedents** (from Latin for *coming before*):

Jack offered an interpretation, but *he* didn't feel confident about *it*.

Here, *Jack* is the antecedent of the pronoun *he*, and *interpretation* is the antecedent of the pronoun *it*. Occasionally an "antecedent" can come after the pronoun that refers to it, especially if the pronoun is in a subordinate clause and if the context is clear—that is, if the pronoun couldn't refer to some other noun (see also #5d):

Although *he* offered an interpretation, *Jack* didn't feel confident about it.

There are eight kinds of pronoun: **personal, impersonal, interrogative, relative, demonstrative, indefinite, reflexive** or **intensive,** and **reciprocal.** Generally, pronouns perform the same functions as nouns: they are most often subjects of verbs, direct and indirect objects, and objects of prepositions; some can also function as appositives and predicate nouns. Some pronouns are inflected much more than nouns, and some require particular care in their use.

The following sections discuss the different kinds of pronoun; their inflections; their grammatical functions in phrases, clauses, and sentences; and the special problems of **case** (#3e), **agreement** (#4-4f), and **reference** (#5-5e).

3a Personal Pronouns

Personal pronouns refer to specific persons or things. They are inflected in four ways:

1. For **person**:

First-person pronouns (*I, we,* etc.) refer to the person or persons doing the speaking.

Second-person pronouns (*you, yours*) refer to the person or persons being spoken to.

Third-person pronouns (*he, she, it, they,* etc.) refer to the person(s) or thing(s) being spoken about.

2. For **number**:

Singular: *I* am writing. *She* is writing.

Plural: *We* are writing. *They* are writing.

(The second-person pronoun *you* can be either singular or plural.)

3. For **gender** (2nd- and 3rd-person pronouns):

Masculine pronouns (*he, him, his*) refer to males.

Feminine pronouns (*she, her, hers*) refer to females.

The **neuter** pronoun (*it*) refers to things or to creatures—such as animals and sometimes babies—whose gender is unknown or irrelevant to the context.

(In the plural forms—*we, you, they,* etc.—there is no indication of gender.)

4. For **case** (see also #3e):

Pronouns that function as **subjects** must be in the **subjective** case:

I paint. *She* paints. *They* are painting.

Pronouns that function as **objects** must be in the **objective** case:

The car hit *them*. Give *her* the book. Give it to *me*.

Pronouns that indicate possession or ownership must be in the **possessive** case:

That book is *his*. This book is *mine*. Where is *yours*?

The following chart shows all the inflections of personal pronouns:

		subject	object	possessive pronoun	possessive adjective
singular	1st person	I	me	mine	my
	2nd person	you	you	yours	your
	3rd person	he	him	his	his
		she	her	hers	her
		it	it		its
plural	1st person	we	us	ours	our
	2nd person	you	you	yours	your
	3rd person	they	them	theirs	their

Possessive (or **pronominal**) **adjectives** always precede nouns; **possessive pronouns** may function as subjects, objects, and predicate nouns. Note that *you* and *it* are inflected only for possessive case, that *his* serves as both possessive pronoun and possessive adjective, and that *her* serves as both objective case and possessive adjective.

Caution: Never use an apostrophe to indicate the possessive case of a *personal pronoun*. Write *hers*, not *her's*; *theirs*, not *their's*. The most common such error is *it's* (contraction of *it is*, and sometimes of *it has*) when what is meant is *its* (possessive form of *it*). The word *it's* ALWAYS means *it is* or *it has*.

3b   Impersonal Pronouns

Especially in relatively formal contexts, the **impersonal pronoun** *one*, meaning essentially "a person," serves in place of a first-, second-, or third-person pronoun:

> *One* must be careful when crossing the street.
> *One* must keep *one's* priorities straight.

The pronoun *it* is also used as an impersonal pronoun in such sentences as the following; note that impersonal *it* is usually the subject of some form of *be* (see #6f) and that it usually refers to time, distance, weather, and the like:

> *It* is getting late. *It's* almost four o'clock.
> *It's* cold. *It* feels colder than *it* did yesterday.
> *It* was just one of those things.
> *It* is a mile and a half from here to the station.

3c   Interrogative Pronouns

Interrogative pronouns are *question-words* used usually at or near the beginning of *interrogative sentences* (see #1t). *Who* is inflected for objective and possessive case, *which* for possessive case only:

subjective	objective	possessive
who	whom	whose
which	which	whose
what	what	

Who refers to persons, *which* and *what* to things; *which* sometimes also refers to persons, as in *Which of you is going?* The compound forms *whoever* and *whatever*, and sometimes even *whichever* and *whomever*, can also function as interrogative pronouns. Here are some examples showing interrogative pronouns functioning in different ways.

As subject:

> Who said that? Which of these books is best? What is the baby's name? Whoever told you that?

As direct object of verb:

> Whom do you recommend for the job? What did you give Aunt Jane for her birthday?

As object of a preposition (see also #11):

> To whom did you give the book? To what do I owe this honour?

As objective complement:

> What did you call me? You've named the baby *what*?

In front of a noun, an interrogative word functions as an **interrogative adjective**:

> Whose book is this? Which car shall we take?

For more on *who* and *whom*, see #3e.

3d   Relative Pronouns

A **relative pronoun** usually introduces an *adjective clause*—called a **relative clause**—in which it functions as subject, object, or object of a preposition. The pronoun links, or *relates*, the clause to an antecedent in the same sentence, a noun or pronoun that the whole clause modifies.

The principal relative pronouns are *who*, *which*, and *that*. *Who* and *which* are inflected for case:

subjective	*objective*	*possessive*
who	whom	whose
which	which	whose
that	that	

Who refers to persons (and sometimes to animals thought of as persons), *which* to things, and *that* to either persons or things. Some examples of how relative pronouns function:

> Margaret, who is leaving in the morning, will call us later tonight. (*who* as subject of verb *is*; clause modifies *Margaret*)
> Joel described the woman whom he had met at the party. (*whom* as direct object; clause modifies *woman*)
> At midnight Tanya began to revise her descriptive essay, which was due in the morning. (*which* as subject of verb *was*; clause modifies *essay*)
> She postponed working on the essay that she was having trouble with. (*that* as object of preposition *with*; clause modifies *essay*)

A relative clause is either **restrictive** and unpunctuated, or **nonrestrictive** and set off with punctuation (see #37). If the relative pronoun in a restrictive clause is the object of a verb or a preposition, it can usually be omitted:

> Joel described the woman [*whom* or *that*] he had met.
> She postponed working on the essay [*that* or *which*] she was having trouble with.

But if the preposition is placed before the pronoun (*with which*), the pronoun cannot be omitted.

When *whose* precedes and modifies a noun in a relative clause, it functions as what is called a **relative adjective**:

> His mother was the one whose advice he most valued.

And sometimes a **relative adverb**, often *when* or *where*, introduces a relative clause (see also #9a):

> Here's an aerial photo of the town where I live. (The clause *where I live* modifies the noun *town*.)
> My parents warned me of a time when I'd regret my decision. (The *when*-clause modifies the noun *time*.)

Sometimes *what* and compounds with *ever* (*whatever, whoever, whomever, whichever*) are also considered relative pronouns, even though they introduce noun clauses (e.g., "Remember *what I said*." "Take *whichever one you want*."). *Who, whom,* and *which* may also introduce such noun clauses.

For more on *who* and *whom*, see #3e. For more on adjective clauses, see #8 and #15a.

3e **Case** (See also #3a.4.)

ca Choosing the correct **number** or **person** of a pronoun is not a problem. But choosing the correct **case** of personal, interrogative, and relative pronouns is sometimes difficult. The main problem is limited to deciding between *subjective* and *objective* case, in only a few kinds of sentences, and only in formal writing. In everyday speech and informal writing, things like "*Who* did you lend the book to?" and "It's *me*" and "That's *her*" upset few people. But in formal writing and strictly formal speech, you should use the correct forms.

If you know how a pronoun is functioning grammatically, you will know which form to use. Here are the kinds of sentences that sometimes cause problems:

1. A pronoun functioning as the *subject* should be in the *subjective* case.

Whenever you use a pronoun as part of a *compound subject* (see #1z.1), make sure it's in the *subjective* case. Someone who wouldn't dream of saying "*Me* am going to the store" could slip and say something like "Susan and *me* studied hard for the examination" instead of the correct

Susan and *I* studied hard for the examination.

If you're not sure, remove the other part of the subject; then you'll know which pronoun sounds right:

[Susan and] *I* studied hard for the examination.

But even a one-part subject can lead someone astray:

ca: *Us* students should stand up for our rights.
revised: *We* students should stand up for our rights.

The pronoun *We* is the subject; the word *students* is an appositive (see #1q) further identifying it, as if saying "We, the students, should . . . ."

2. A pronoun functioning as a direct or indirect *object* should be in the *objective* case.

Again, errors most often occur with a two-part structure—here, a *compound object*. Someone who would never say "The club asked *I* for my opinion" could slip and say "They asked Ingrid and *I* to take part in the play." When you use a pronoun as part of a compound object, make sure it's in the *objective* case. Again, test by removing the other part:

They asked [Ingrid and] *me* to take part in the play.

Caution: Don't slip into what is called "hypercorrection." Since many people say things like "Jake and me went camping," others—not understanding the grammar but wishing to seem correct—use the "and I" form even for an object, when it should be "and me."

3. A pronoun functioning as the *object* of a preposition should be in the *objective* case:

> *ca:* The government sometimes forgets about the needs of we taxpayers.
> *revised:* The government sometimes forgets about the needs of us taxpayers.

Again, since *us* sounds suspect (because it is followed by a noun, as if at the beginning of a sentence like "We taxpayers should . . . ."), speakers and writers sometimes overcorrect and use *we*; but the objective *us* is correct, for it is the object of the preposition *of*. Check your pronoun by removing the appositive noun; *us* will then sound right.

4. A pronoun functioning as a *predicate noun* (see #1h and #14d) after a linking verb should be in the *subjective* case:

> It is *they* who must decide, not *we*.
> The swimmer who won the prize is *she*, over there by the pool.
> It is *I* who will carry the greater burden.

If such usages sound stuffy and artificial to you—as they do to many people—find another way to phrase your sentences; for example:

> They, not we, must decide.
> The swimmer over by the pool is the one who won the prize.
> First prize went to that girl, over there by the pool.
> I will be the one carrying the greater burden.
> I myself will be carrying the greater burden. (In writing, when you can't use speech rhythms and stress for a desired emphasis, an extra word, such as an intensive pronoun like *myself*, often works; see #3h.)

Again, watch out for compound structures:

> *ca:* The nominees are Yasmin and me.
> *revised:* The nominees are Yasmin and I.

5. Pronouns following the conjunctions *as* and *than* in comparisons should be in the *subjective* case if they are functioning as subjects, even if their verbs are not expressed but left "understood":

> Roberta is brighter than *they* [are].
> Aaron has learned less than *I* [have].
> He hasn't learned as much as *I* [have].
> Claude is as tall as *I* [am].

If however the pronouns are functioning as objects, they should be in the objective case:

> I trust *her* more than [I trust] *him*.

See also **so . . . as** in the Usage Checklist, #60.

6. Use the appropriate case of the interrogative and relative pronouns *who* and *whom*, *whoever* and *whomever*. Although *who* is often used instead of *whom* in speech and informal writing, you should know how to use the two correctly when you want to write or speak more formally.

a. Use the *subjective* case for the subject of a verb in a question or a relative clause:

> *Who* is going?
> Dickens was a novelist *who* was extremely popular.

Don't let an intervening parenthetical clause like *you think* or *they believe* mislead you. Test such sentences by removing the clauses; *who* is the subject of the verb:

> *Who* [do you think] will win?
> She is the one *who* [most people say] will win.

And don't be fooled by a verb in the passive voice (see #1e and #6 o-p). *Who* is still the subject of the verb:

> He is a public servant *who* will be long remembered.

If you aren't sure, try substituting *him* or *me*: they will more obviously sound wrong than *whom* might.

b. Use the *objective* case for the object of a verb or preposition:

> *Whom* do you prefer in that role?
> He is the candidate *whom* I most admire.
> To *whom* do you intend to award the prize?
> She is the manager for *whom* the employees have the most respect.

If such usages with *whom* seem to you unnatural and stuffy, avoid them by rephrasing your sentences:

> Who is going to get the prize?
> To which student are you going to award the prize?
> The employees have more respect for her than for the other managers.
> She is the manager that the employees respect most.

c. In noun clauses, the case of the pronoun is determined by its function *in its clause*, not by other words:

How can you tell *who won?*
I can't tell *who will win.*
I'll give the prize to *whomever the judges declare the winner.*
The instructor planned to award a book-prize to *whoever wrote the best essay.*

For the possessive case of pronouns with *gerunds*, see #10h.

Exercise 3e(1)   Using correct pronouns

Underline the correct pronoun in each of the pairs in parentheses.

1. (She, her) and (I, me) will work on the project tonight.
2. There stood Eva, (who, whom) we had just said goodbye to.
3. The judge released the two men (who, whom) had been incorrectly charged.
4. Is Genevieve the person (who, whom) you think will do the best job?
5. This gift will please (whoever, whomever) receives it.
6. The coach advised Anwar and (I, me) not to miss any more practice.
7. (Who, Whom) do you wish to see?

Exercise 3e(2)   Problem pronouns

Make up five sentences that use a personal pronoun in the subjective case (*I, he, she, they*) after a form of the verb *be*, and five sentences using the pronoun *whom* or *whomever* in a correct formal way. Then rewrite each sentence, keeping them correctly formal, but avoiding the possible stuffiness of these usages.

3f   Demonstrative Pronouns

Demonstrative pronouns, which can be thought of as accompanied by a demonstrative gesture, namely pointing, are inflected for *number* only:

singular: this   that
plural: these   those

This and *these* usually refer to something nearby or something just said or about to be said; *that* and *those* usually refer to something farther away or more remote in time or longer in duration; but there are no precise rules:

Try some of *this.*
The clerk was surly; *this* was what upset her the most.

These are the main points I will cover in today's lecture.
That looks decidedly unappetizing.
That was the story he told us the next morning.
Those were his exact words.
Those are the cities you should visit on your holiday.

These pronouns also often occur in prepositional phrases with *like* and *such as*:

Would you go out with someone who dresses like *that*?
I don't need any more friends like *those*!
An alibi such as *this* will not stand up in court.
You can't duck the blame with such an excuse as *that*.

When used in the same way as *this* and *that*, the words *such* and *so* can also function as demonstrative pronouns:

Such was the story he told them.
She didn't like their decision and she told them *so*.

Useful as demonstrative pronouns can be, however, use them sparingly in writing, for they are often vague in their reference. Instead, consider this alternative: When followed by nouns, these words function as *demonstrative adjectives*, and then there's no risk of vagueness: *this* belief, *that* statement, *these* buildings, *those* arguments. See #5c, #28, and **ref** in Chapter XI.

3g   Indefinite Pronouns

Indefinite pronouns refer to *indefinite* or unknown persons or things, or to indefinite or unknown quantities of persons or things. The only major problem with these words is whether they are *singular* or *plural*. Think of indefinite pronouns as falling into four groups:

Group 1: compounds with *body*, *one*, and *thing*. These words function like nouns—that is, they need no antecedents—and they are almost always considered *singular*:

anybody	everybody	nobody	somebody
anyone	everyone	no one	someone
anything	everything	nothing	something

Group 2: a few others that are almost always *singular*:

another   each   either   much   neither   one   other

Group 3: a few that are obviously always *plural*:

both   few   many   several

Group 4: a few that can be either *singular* or *plural*, depending on context and intended meaning:

all   any   more   most   none   some

For discussions of the important matter of grammatical **agreement** with indefinite pronouns, and examples of their use in sentences, see #4c and #7d.

Only *one* and *other* can be inflected for number, by adding s to make them plural: *ones, others* (the words *somebodies* and *nobodies* are rarely used nouns, not pronouns). Several indefinite pronouns can be inflected for possessive case; unlike personal pronouns, they take 's, just as nouns do (or, with *others'*, just an apostrophe):

anybody's	anyone's	everybody's	everyone's
nobody's	no one's	somebody's	someone's
one's	other's	another's	others'

The rest must use *of* to show possession; for example:

That was the belief *of many* who were present.

When in the possessive case, these words function as adjectives. Further, all the words in Groups 2, 3, and 4, except *none*, can also function as adjectives (see #8a):

any boat	*some* people	*few* people
more money	*each* day	*either* direction

The adjective expressing the meaning of *none* is *no*:

Send *no* flowers.

Sometimes the cardinal and ordinal numbers (*one, two, three,* etc., and *first, second, third,* etc.) are also classed as indefinite pronouns, for they often function similarly, both as pronouns and as adjectives:

How many ducks are on the pond? I see *several.* I see *seven.* I see *ten.*
Do you like these stories? I like *some,* but not *others.* I like the *first* and the *third.*
He owns *two* boats.
Tune in for the *second* thrilling episode.

3h   Reflexive and Intensive Pronouns

These pronouns are formed by adding *self* or *selves* to the possessive form of the first- and second-person personal pronouns, to the objective form of third-person personal pronouns, and to the impersonal pronoun *one* (see #3a, #3b).

singular	plural
myself	ourselves
yourself	yourselves
himself ⎫	
herself ⎬	themselves
itself ⎭	
oneself	

A **reflexive pronoun** is used as an object when that object is the same person or thing as the subject:

> He treated *himself* to a candy-bar.   (direct object)
> One should pamper *oneself* a little.   (direct object)
> She gave *herself* a treat.   (indirect object)
> We kept the idea to *ourselves*.   (object of preposition)

These pronouns are also used as **intensive pronouns** to emphasize a subject or object. An intensive pronoun comes either right after the noun it emphasizes or at the end of the sentence:

> Although he let the others choose their positions, Angelo *himself* is going to pitch.
> The professor told us to count up our scores *ourselves*.

They are also used in prepositional phrases with *by* to mean *alone* or *without help*:

> I can do this job by *myself*.

Caution: Do not use this form of pronoun as a substitute for a personal pronoun:

> The boss talked Hank and *me* [not *myself*] into doing the job.

Especially don't use such a *myself* simply to avoid having to decide whether *I* or *me* is correct in a compound subject or object (see #3e).

3i   Reciprocal Pronouns

Like a reflexive pronoun, a **reciprocal pronoun** refers to the subject of a sentence—but this time the subject is always plural. The two reciprocal pronouns are singular, and consist of two words each:

> each other (referring to a subject of two)
> one another (referring to a subject of three or more)

They can be inflected for possessive case by adding 's:

> each other's   one another's

These pronouns express some kind of mutual interaction between or among the parts of a plural subject:

> The President and the Prime Minister praised each other's policies.
> The computers in this office in effect speak to one another automatically.

See **each other, one another** in the Usage Checklist, #60.

4 Agreement of Pronouns with Their Antecedents

agr   Any pronoun that refers to or stands for an *antecedent* (see #3) must **agree** with, be the same as, that antecedent in **person** (1st, 2nd, or 3rd), **number** (singular or plural), and **gender** (masculine, feminine, or neuter). For example:

> *Joanne* wants to go to university so that *she* will be trained to take *her* place in the world.

Since the proper noun *Joanne*, the antecedent, is third person, singular, and feminine, any pronouns that refer to it must also be third person, singular, and feminine: *she* and *her* thus "agree" grammatically with their antecedent.

The following sections (#4a-f) point out the most common sources of error in pronoun agreement. Note that these circumstances are similar to those affecting subject-verb agreement (see #7). Note also that these errors all have to do with *number*—whether a pronoun should be *singular* or *plural*. Mistakes in *gender* and *person* are rare (but see #26, on shifts).

4a   Antecedents Joined by *and*

When two or more singular antecedents are joined by *and*, use a *plural* pronoun:

> The manager and the accountant compared *their* figures.
> Both Jennifer and Chinmoy contributed *their* know-how.

If such a compound is preceded by *each* or *every*, however, the pronoun should be *singular*:

> Each book and magazine in the library has *its* own number.

4b   Antecedents Joined by *or* or *nor*

When two or more antecedents are joined by *or* or *nor*, use a *singular* pronoun if the antecedents are singular:

> The dog or the cat is sure to make *itself* heard.
> Either David or Jonathan will bring *his* car.
> Neither Maylin nor her mother gave *her* consent.

If one antecedent is masculine and the other feminine, rephrase the sentence (see #4d).

Use a *plural* pronoun if the antecedents are plural:

> Neither the players nor the coaches did *their* jobs properly.

If the antecedents are mixed singular and plural, a pronoun should agree with the nearest one. But if you move from a plural to a singular antecedent, the sentence will almost inevitably sound awkward; try to construct such sentences so that the last antecedent is plural:

> *awk:* Neither the actors nor *the director* could control *his* temper.
> *revised:* Neither the director nor *the actors* could control *their* tempers.

See also #7c. (Note that the awkwardness here extended to gender: if the actors included both men and women, neither *his* nor *her* would be appropriate; see #4d.)

4c   Indefinite Pronoun as Antecedent

If the antecedent is an *indefinite pronoun* (see #3g), you'll usually use a *singular* pronoun to refer to it. The indefinite pronouns in Group 1 (the compounds with *body, one,* and *thing*) are singular, as are those in Group 2 (*another, each, either, much, neither, one, other*):

> *Each* of the boys worked on *his* own project.
> *Either* of these women is likely to buy that sports car for *herself.*
> *Everything* has *its* proper place.

Occasionally, *everyone* or *everybody* has an obviously plural sense; a pronoun referring to it should then be plural:

> When the hat had been passed to *everyone* in the room, Anton counted up *their* contributions.

Indefinite pronouns from Group 3 (*both, few, many, several*) are always plural:

> Only a *few* sent *their* condolences.

The indefinite pronouns in Group 4 (*all, any, more, most, none, some*), though they can be either singular or plural, seldom cause trouble; the intended meaning is usually clearly either singular or plural:

> *Some* of the food on the menu could be criticized for *its* lack of nutrients.
> *Some* of the ships in the fleet had been restored to *their* original beauty.

Here the mass noun demands the singular sense for *some,* and the countable noun *ships,* in the plural, demands the plural sense (see #3a). But confusion sometimes arises with the indefinite pronoun *none*. (See also #7d.) Although *none* began by meaning *no one* or *not one*, it now commonly has the plural sense:

> None of the men removed *their* hats.

But with a mass noun, or if your intended meaning is *not a single one*, treat *none* as singular:

> None of the food could be praised for *its* quality.
> None of the men removed *his* hat. (perhaps even change *None* to *Not one*)

When any of these words function as *adjectives*, the same principles apply:

> *Each* boy worked on *his* own project.
> *Either* woman may buy the car for *herself*.
> Only a *few* people sent *their* condolences.
> *Some* food can be praised for *its* nutrition.
> *Some* ships had been restored to *their* original beauty.

Note: The word *every* used as an adjective requires a *singular* pronoun:

> *Every* boy has *his* own project.

4d   **The Problem of the Generic *he*: Avoiding Sexist Language**

Several indefinite pronouns, indefinite nouns like *person*, and many other nouns used in a generalizing way, have raised an additional problem. In the past, if a *singular antecedent* had no grammatical gender, but could refer to either male or female, it was conventional to use the masculine pronoun *he* (*him, his, himself*) in a generic sense, meaning any person, male or female:

> *Everyone* present raised *his* hand.
> *Anyone* who doesn't pay *his* taxes is asking for trouble.
> If a *person* is considerate of others' feelings, *he* will get along better.
> A *writer* should be careful about *his* diction.

Today this practice is regarded as unfair and unrealistic since it implies, for example, that no women were present, that only men pay taxes, that all persons are males, that there are no women writers. Such usages reveal the unconsidered assumption that males are the norm. And merely substituting *she* or *her* in all such instances is no solution, since it is equally sexist. (Some writers alternate between the male and female pronouns for the generic sense, but some readers find that distracting.)

But you can easily avoid sexist language. Colloquially and informally, many people simply use a plural pronoun:

> *agr:* Anyone who doesn't pay *their* taxes is asking for trouble.

But this fosters bad habits; and it is unacceptable to many people who care about language, for it is grammatically incorrect. (Note in the example the clash between the plural pronoun *their* and the singular verb *is*.) Even though a plural pronoun sometimes sounds all right with the antecedent *everyone*:

> Everyone present raised *their* hands.

don't adopt it as a general practice. There are better solutions:

1. If you are referring to a group or class consisting entirely of either men or women, it is only logical to use the appropriate pronoun, whether masculine or feminine (this is less a matter of grammar than of common sense):

> Everyone in the room raised *his* hand.
> Everyone in the room raised *her* hand.

If the group is mixed, try to avoid the problem, for example by using the indefinite article:

> Everyone in the room raised *a* hand.

2. Often the simplest technique is to make the antecedent itself plural: then the plural pronoun referring to it is grammatically appropriate, and no problem of gender arises:

> *All those* in the room raised *their* hands.
> *Those* who don't pay *their* taxes are asking for trouble.
> *Writers* should be careful about *their* diction.

3. If your purpose and the formality of the context permit, you can use the impersonal pronoun *one*:

> If *one* is considerate of others' feelings, *one* will get along better.

But if this sounds stuffy, consider using the less formal second-person pronoun *you* (but see #5e):

> If *you* are considerate of others' feelings, *you* will get along better.

4. Or you can revise a sentence so that no pronoun is necessary:

> Everyone's hand went up.
> In order to get along better, be considerate of others' feelings.

Sometimes the pronoun can simply be omitted:

> A writer should be careful about diction.

5. But if a sentence doesn't lend itself to such changes, or if you want to keep its original structure for some other reason, you can still manage. Don't resort to such awkward and unsightly devices as *he/she, him/her, her/his, him/herself,* or the even worse *s/he.* But an occasional *he or she* or *she or he* and the like is acceptable:

> If anyone complains, *he or she* will be asked to leave.
> A writer should be careful about *her or his* diction.

But do this only occasionally; used often, such terms become tedious and cluttering.

See also **man, woman, lady, etc.** and **person, persons, people** in the Usage Checklist, #60.

4e   Collective Noun as Antecedent

If the antecedent is a *collective noun* (see #2), use either a singular or a plural pronoun to refer to it, depending on context and desired meaning. If the collective noun stands for the group seen as a unit, use a *singular* pronoun:

> The *team* did *its* job well.
> The *committee* announced *its* decision.

If the collective noun stands for the members of the group seen as separate individuals, use a *plural* pronoun:

> The *team* took up *their* starting positions.
> The *committee* had no sooner taken *their* seats than *they* began arguing among *themselves.*

4f   Agreement with Demonstrative Adjectives

Demonstrative pronouns aren't a problem, but demonstrative *adjectives* must agree in number with the nouns they modify (usually *kind* or *kinds* or similar words):

> *agr: These kind* of doctors work especially hard.
> *revised: This kind* of doctor works especially hard.
> *revised: These kinds* of doctors work especially hard.

If *These kinds* or *Those kinds* sounds stuffy or awkward, take a moment to rephrase; for example:

> Doctors such as these work especially hard.

Exercise 4 Correcting agreement errors

Correct any lack of agreement in the following between pronouns and their antecedents. Revise sentences as necessary to avoid possibly sexist use of the generic masculine pronoun.

1. Everybody is free to express their own opinion.
2. Una or Gwendolyn will lend you their textbook.
3. Anyone who doesn't think for themselves can be deceived by advertising.
4. His arguments cannot alter my opinion, for it seems to me illogical.
5. After studying his statements for over an hour, I still couldn't understand it.
6. It is usually a bad sign when a person stops caring about his appearance.
7. Everyone who wants to play the game will be provided with a pencil to write their answers with.
8. All the boys arrived on time, each with their books carried proudly in both hands.
9. In order to make sure each sentence is correct, check them carefully during revision and proofreading.
10. None of the women agreed to those proposals that would limit their rights.

5 Reference of Pronouns

ref A pronoun's **reference** to an antecedent must be clear. If the antecedent is remote, ambiguous, vague, or missing, the meaning of the pronoun, and of the statement it appears in, will not be clear.

5a Remote Antecedent

An antecedent should be close enough to the pronoun to be unmistakable; your reader shouldn't have to pause and search for it. An antecedent should seldom be more than one sentence back. For example:

> People who expect to experience happiness in material things alone may well discover that the life of the mind is more important than the life of the physical senses. Material prosperity may seem fine at a given moment, but in the long run its delights have a way of fading into
> *ref:* inconsequential tedium and emptiness. *They* then realize, too late, where true happiness lies.

The word *People* is too far back to be a clear antecedent for the pronoun *They*. If the second sentence had also begun with *They*, the connection would be clearer. Or the third sentence might begin with a more particularizing phrase, like "Such people . . . ."

5b   Ambiguous Reference

A pronoun should refer clearly to only one antecedent:

> *ref:* When Donna's mother told her that *she* needed an operation, *she* was
> obviously upset.

Each *she* could refer either to Donna (or *her*) or to Donna's mother. When
revising such a sentence, don't just insert explanatory parentheses;
rephrase the sentence:

> *weak:* When Donna's mother told her that she (her mother) needed an opera-
> tion, she (Donna) was obviously upset.
> *clear:* Donna was obviously upset when her mother told her about needing
> an operation.
> *clear:* Donna's mother needed an operation, and she was obviously upset
> when she told Donna about it.
> *clear:* Donna was obviously upset when her mother said, "I must have an
> operation."

Another example:

> *ref:* His second novel was far different from his first. *It* was an adventure story
> set in Australia.

A pronoun like *it* often refers to the subject of the preceding independent
clause, here *second novel*; but *it* is also pulled toward the closest noun or
pronoun, here *first*.
The problem is easily solved by *combining* the two sentences, reducing the
second to a subordinate element:

> *clear:* His second novel, an adventure story set in Australia, was far different
> from his first.
> *clear:* His second novel was far different from his first, which was an adven-
> ture story set in Australia.

5c   Vague Reference

Vague reference is usually caused by the demonstrative pronouns *this* and
that and the relative pronoun *which*:

> *ref:* There were three isolated people leaning against the wall, and it was very
> dark. *This* made Shelagh wary as she approached the bus stop.

(*This* could easily be changed, after a comma, to *which*.) *This* (or *which*)
seems to refer to the entire content of the preceding sentence, but it also
seems to refer specifically to the fact that it was dark. Revision is necessary:

> *clear:* The extreme darkness and the three isolated people leaning against the
> wall made Shelagh wary as she approached the bus stop.

clear: Three isolated people were leaning against the wall, and it was very dark. These circumstances made Shelagh wary as she approached the bus stop.

clear: Three isolated people leaned against the wall, and it was very dark, facts which taken together made Shelagh wary as she approached the bus stop.

A *this* or *which* can be adequate if the phrasing and meaning are appropriate:

clear: Three separate people were leaning against the nearby building, but *this* didn't worry Shelagh, for she was a judo expert. But it was also getting very dark, *which* did make her a little wary as she approached the bus stop.

Another example:

ref: Othello states many times that he loves Iago and that he thinks he is a very honest man; Iago uses *this* to his advantage.

The third *he* is possibly ambiguous, but more serious is the vague reference of *this.* Changing *this* to *this opinion, these feelings, this attitude, these mistakes, this blindness of Othello's,* or even *Othello's blindness,* makes the reference clearer. Even the *his* is slightly ambiguous: "Iago takes advantage of" is better—or just omit *his.*

And don't catch the "this" disease: sufferers from it are driven to begin a large proportion of their sentences and other independent clauses with a *this.* Whenever you catch yourself beginning with a *this,* look carefully to see

1. if the reference to the preceding clause or sentence or paragraph is as clear on paper as it may be in your mind;
2. if the *this* could be replaced by a specific noun or noun phrase, or otherwise avoided, for example by rephrasing or subordinating;
3. whether, if you decide to retain *this,* it is a mere demonstrative pronoun; if so, try to make it a **demonstrative adjective**, giving it a noun to modify—even if no more specific than "This *idea,*" "This *fact,*" or "This *argument*" (see #3f and #28).

And always check to see if an opening *This* looks back to a noun that is in fact singular; it may be that *These* ideas, facts, or arguments would be more appropriate.

5d Missing Antecedent

Sometimes a writer may have an antecedent in mind but fail to write it down:

ref: In the early seventeenth century the Renaissance had concentrated mainly on the arts rather than on developing the scientific part of *their* minds.

The writer was probably thinking of "the people of the Renaissance." Simply changing *their* to *people's* would clear up the difficulty.

ref: After the mayor's speech *he* agreed to answer questions from the audience.

The implied antecedent of *he* is *mayor*, but it isn't there, for the possessive *mayor's* functions as an adjective rather than a noun. Several revisions are possible:

clear: When the mayor finished his speech, he agreed to answer questions from the audience.
clear: After speaking, the mayor agreed to answer questions from the audience.
clear: At the end of his speech the mayor agreed to answer questions from the audience.

Note that in this last version *his* comes before its supposed "antecedent," *mayor*—an unusual pattern, but acceptable if the context is clear (for example, if no other possible antecedent for *his* occurred in the preceding sentence) and if the two are close together.

ref: Whenever a student assembly is called, *they* are required to attend.

Since *student* here functions as an adjective, it is necessary to replace *they* with *students*—and then probably one would want to omit the original *student*. Or one could refer to "an assembly of students" and retain *they*.

ref: Over half the cars were derailed, but *it* did not injure anyone seriously.

Again, no antecedent. Change *it* to *the accident* or *the derailment*, or use passive voice: "but no one was seriously injured." (For passive voice, see #1e, #6p, and #18f.)

5e   Indefinite *you, they,* and *it*

In formal writing, avoid the pronouns *you, they,* and *it* when they are indefinite:

informal: In order to graduate, *you* must have at least sixty units of credit.
formal: In order to graduate, a student must have at least sixty units of credit.

(The impersonal *one* would be all right, but less good because less specific—and stuffier.)

informal: In some cities *they* do not have enough recycling facilities.

formal: Some cities do not have enough recycling facilities.
formal: Some cities' recycling facilities are inadequate.

Although it is correct to use the expletive or impersonal *it* (see #1k and #18f) and say "*It* is raining," "*It* is hard to get up in the morning," "*It* is seven o'clock," and so on, avoid such indefinite uses of *it* as the following:

informal: It says in our textbook that we should be careful how we use the pronoun *it.*
formal: Our textbook says that we should be careful how we use the pronoun *it.*

Exercise 5 Correcting faulty pronoun reference

Correct any faulty pronoun reference in the following:

1. Summer homes make good retreats—for those who can afford it.
2. If it rains on Maui it is soon evaporated into thin air.
3. Huck, the protagonist, is the narrator of the novel. Twain does this to let us see society through the eyes of a boy.
4. Many people believe that success is necessary for happiness, and they work hard to attain it.
5. You cannot suppress truth, for it is morally wrong.
6. Othello swore she was faithful and true and would have bet his life that she wouldn't betray him, but he ends by taking her life for this very reason.
7. The deadline was a month away, but I failed to meet it, for something happened that prevented it.
8. The tone of the poem is such that it creates an atmosphere of romance.
9. In Shakespeare's sonnet 65, it points out the differences between love and time.
10. Television usually shows regular commercial movies but this is more and more supplanted by made-for-TV films.

6 Verbs

Verbs are the most important of the parts of speech. A verb is the focal point of a sentence or a clause. As you saw in Chapter I, standard sentences consist of subjects and predicates: every subject must have a predicate, and the heart of every predicate is its **verb**.

Verbs are often called "action" words; yet many verbs express little or no action. Think of verbs as expressing not only *action* but also *occurrence*, *process*, and *condition* or *state of being*. All verbs *assert* or *ask* something about their subjects, sometimes by *linking* a subject with a complement. Some verbs are single words; others are phrases consisting of two or more words. Here are some sentences with the verbs italicized:

He *throws* curves.
She *flew* in space.
I *thought* for a while.
Gershom *is* a lawyer.
Something *happened* last night.
I *am cooking* spaghetti.
In a week I *will have driven* two thousand kilometres.
Are you *listening*?
The two columns of figures *came out* even.
Will you *be needing* this book later?
The fresh bread *smells* delicious.
They *will set out* for the Amazon in June.

(For a discussion of such two-part verbs as *come out* and *set out*, see #11d-e.)

6a   Kinds of Verbs: Transitive, Intransitive, and Linking

Verbs are classified according to the way they function in sentences.

A verb normally taking a *direct object* is considered a **transitive** verb. *Transitive* means "effecting transition"; a transitive verb makes a transition, conveys a movement, from its subject to its object:

She *has* good taste.
He *introduced* me to his uncle.
Greg never *neglects* his homework.
She *expresses* her ideas eloquently.
He *stuffed* himself with pizza.
Where *did* you *put* that book?

A direct object answers the question consisting of the verb and *what* or *whom*: Introduced whom? Me. Neglects what? Homework. Expresses what? Ideas. Stuffed whom? Himself. Did put what? Book. (See also #1d, #1f, #1i, and #1j.)

A verb that normally occurs without a direct object is considered **intransitive** (see also #1c):

When *will* you *arrive*?
What *has happened* to the beluga whale?
The earthquake *occurred* during the night.
You *should lie* low for a while.
He *lied* to his roommate.
Please *go*.

Many verbs, however, can be either transitive or intransitive, depending on how they function in particular sentences:

I *ran* the business effectively   (transitive)
I *ran* to the store.   (intransitive)
He *paints* pictures.   (transitive)

He *paints* for a living.   (intransitive)
I *can see* the parade better from the balcony.   (transitive)
I *can see* well enough from here.   (intransitive)
He *wished* that he were home in bed.   (transitive)
She *wished* upon a star.   (intransitive)

In fact, few verbs are exclusively either transitive or intransitive, as a good dictionary will show you. Verbs felt to be clearly intransitive can often also be used transitively, and vice versa:

She *slept* the sleep of the just.
He leaned back in the chair and *remembered*.

A third kind of verb is called a **linking** or copulative verb. The main one is *be* in its various forms. Some other common linking verbs are *become, seem, remain, act, get, feel, look, appear, smell, sound,* and *taste*.

Linking verbs don't have objects, but are yet incomplete; they need a **subjective complement**. A linking verb is like an equal sign in an equation: something at the right-hand (predicate) end is needed to balance what is at the left-hand (subject) end. The complement will be either a *predicate noun* or a *predicate adjective* (see also #1g and #1h). Some examples:

Angela *is* a lawyer.   (predicate noun: *lawyer*)
Angela *is* not well.   (predicate adjective: *well*)
Martin *became* a pilot.   (predicate noun: *pilot*)
Martin *became* uneasy.   (predicate adjective: *uneasy*)
The winner *is* Nathan.   (predicate noun: *Nathan*)
The band *sounds* good.   (predicate adjective: *good*)
The surface *felt* sticky.   (predicate adjective: *sticky*)

Occasionally a complement precedes the verb, for example in a question or in a sentence or clause inverted for emphasis:

How *sick* are you?
However *angry* he may have been, he did not let it show.

Like an object, a subjective complement answers the question consisting of the verb and *what* or *whom*, or perhaps *how*: Is what? A lawyer. Became what? Uneasy. Is whom? Nathan. Sounds how? Good. It differs from an object in that it is the equivalent of the subject or says something about it.

Such verbs as *act, sound, taste, smell,* and *feel* can of course also function as transitive verbs: She *acted* the part. He *sounded* his horn. He *smelled* the hydrogen sulphide. I *tasted* the soup. He *felt* the bump on his head.

Similarly, many of these verbs can also function as regular intransitive verbs, sometimes accompanied by *adverbial* modifiers (see #9): The all-clear *sounded*. The garbage *smelled*. We *looked* at the painting. Gerald *is* on the roof. Teresa *is* at home. We *are* here.

But whenever one of these verbs is accompanied by a predicate noun or a predicate adjective, it is functioning as a **linking** verb.

Exercise 6a(1) Using transitive and intransitive verbs

After each transitive verb in the following, supply an object; after each intransitive verb, supply an adverb (or adverbial phrase) or a period. If a particular verb can be either transitive or intransitive, do both.

Examples: Moira *wants* money. (tr.)
Moira *waited* patiently. (intr.)
Moira *waited*. (intr.)
Moira *speaks* loudly. (intr.)
                      with authority. (intr.)
                      her mind. (tr.)

1. Lisa *drinks*	10. Tony *washed*	19. Claudia *relaxes*
2. Murray *talks*	11. Kamala *knelt*	20. Matilda *teaches*
3. Adriana *expects*	12. Yvonne *believed*	21. Su-lin *attempted*
4. They *ordered*	13. Jonathan *flew*	22. Colin *sold*
5. Yukio *learned*	14. Pierre *repaired*	23. Fawad *selected*
6. Council *vetoed*	15. Hilda *drove*	24. Olivier *performed*
7. Brian *responded*	16. Horace *sang*	25. Everyone *breathed*
8. Sonya *planted*	17. Donald *opened*	26. James *bled*
9. Ricardo *bought*	18. We *liberated*	27. Ann *compromised*

Exercise 6a(2) Recognizing subjective complements

In the following, identify the complement of each italicized linking verb as a predicate noun or a predicate adjective.

1. She *was* sorry that he *felt* so ill.
2. Because he *was* a computer expert, he *was* confident that he could write an effective program for the system.
3. The book *became* a best-seller even though it *was* critical of most readers' beliefs.
4. Since the house *was* well insulated, it *stayed* warm throughout the severe winter.
5. Incredible as it *seems*, the casserole *tasted* as good as it *looked* odd.

Exercise 6a(3) Using subjective complements

After each linking verb, supply (a) a predicate noun and (b) a predicate adjective.

Example: Kevin *was*   (a) an engineer.   (b) exhausted.

1. Erika *is*
2. Priscilla *became*
3. Luigi *remained*
4. The government *is*
5. Lorne *had been*

Compose sentences using some common linking verbs other than *be*, *become*, *seem*, and *remain*. Then compose other sentences using the same verbs as either transitive or intransitive verbs, without complements. Can any of them function as all three kinds? Try *smell*, for example, or *act*.

6b   **Inflection of Verbs; Principal Parts**

As well as being the most important, verbs are also the most complex, the most highly inflected of the eight parts of speech. Verbs are inflected

1. for **person** and **number** in order to agree with a subject (#6d);
2. for **tense** in order to show an action's time—present, past, or future—and character (#6g);
3. for **mood** in order to show the kind of sentence a verb is in—indicative, imperative, or subjunctive (#6-l, #6m);
4. for **voice** in order to show whether a subject is active (performing an action) or passive (being acted upon) (#6 o-p).

Every verb (except some auxiliaries; see #6e) has what are called its **principal parts**:

> its **basic** form (the form a dictionary lists)
> its **past-tense** form
> its **past participle**
> its **present participle**

Verbs regularly form both the *past tense* and *past participle* simply by adding *ed* to the basic form:

basic form	past-tense form	past participle
push	pushed	pushed
cook	cooked	cooked

If the basic form already ends in *e*, however, only *d* is added:

move	moved	moved
agree	agreed	agreed

Present participles are regularly formed by adding *ing* to the basic form:

basic form	present participle
push	pushing
cook	cooking
agree	agreeing

But verbs ending in an unpronounced *e* usually drop it before adding *ing*:

| move | moving |
| skate | skating |

And some verbs double a final consonant before adding *ed* or *ing*:

| grin | grinned | grinning |
| stop | stopped | stopping |

For more on these and other irregularities, see #51c-e. Further, good dictionaries list any irregular principal parts, ones not formed by simply adding *ed* or *ing* (and see #6c).

It is from these four parts—the basic form and the three principal inflections of it—that all other inflected forms of a verb are made.

> **Note:** The *basic* form of a verb is sometimes called the **infinitive** form, meaning that it can be preceded by *to* to form an *infinitive*: *to be, to push, to agree*. Infinitives, participles, and gerunds are called **non-finite** verbs, or **verbals**; they *function* not as verbs but as other parts of speech (see #10-10f). **Finite verbs**, unlike non-finite forms, are restricted or limited by person, number, tense, mood, and voice; they function as the main verbs in sentences.

6c   Irregular Verbs

Some of the most common English verbs are **irregular** in the way they make their past-tense forms and their past participles. Whenever you aren't certain about the principal parts of a verb, check your dictionary, or use the following list, which contains most of the common irregular verbs with their past-tense forms and their past participles (where two or more are given, the first is the more common). If you need to, memorize these forms; practise by composing sentences using each form (for example: *Choose* the one you want. I *chose* mine yesterday. Haven't you *chosen* your topic yet?):

basic or present form	past-tense form	past participle
arise	arose	arisen
awake	awoke, awaked	awaked, awoken, awoke
bear	bore	borne (passive *born* for "given birth to")
beat	beat	beaten, beat (occasional)
become	became	become
begin	began	begun
bet	bet, betted	bet, betted
bid (offer)	bid	bid

present form	past-tense form	past participle
bid (order, invite)	bade	bidden
bind	bound	bound
bite	bit	bitten, bit
bleed	bled	bled
blow	blew	blown
break	broke	broken
breed	bred	bred
bring	brought	brought
burst	burst	burst
buy	bought	bought
cast	cast	cast
catch	caught	caught
choose	chose	chosen
cling	clung	clung
come	came	come
cost	cost	cost
creep	crept	crept
cut	cut	cut
deal	dealt	dealt
dig	dug	dug
dive	dived, dove	dived
draw	drew	drawn
dream	dreamed, dreamt	dreamed, dreamt
drink	drank	drunk
drive	drove	driven
eat	ate	eaten
fall	fell	fallen
feed	fed	fed
feel	felt	felt
fight	fought	fought
find	found	found
flee	fled	fled
fly	flew	flown
forbid	forbade, forbad	forbidden
forget	forgot	forgotten, forgot (archaic, poetic)
forsake	forsook	forsaken
freeze	froze	frozen
get	got	got, gotten
give	gave	given
go	went	gone
grind	ground	ground
grow	grew	grown
hang	hung	hung
hang (execute)	hanged	hanged
hear	heard	heard
hide	hid	hidden, hid
hit	hit	hit
hold	held	held
hurt	hurt	hurt

present form	past-tense form	past participle
keep	kept	kept
kneel	knelt, kneeled	knelt, kneeled
knit	knitted, knit	knitted, knit
know	knew	known
lay	laid	laid
lead	led	led
leap	leaped, leapt	leaped, leapt
leave	left	left
lend	lent	lent
let	let	let
lie (recline)	lay	lain
light	lighted, lit	lighted, lit
lose	lost	lost
make	made	made
mean	meant	meant
meet	met	met
mistake	mistook	mistaken
mow	mowed	mown
overcome	overcame	overcome
pay	paid	paid
prove	proved	proved, proven
put	put	put
quit	quit, quitted	quit, quitted
read	read (changes pronunciation)	read (changes pronunciation)
ride	rode	ridden
ring	rang	rung
rise	rose	risen
run	ran	run
say	said	said
see	saw	seen
seek	sought	sought
sell	sold	sold
send	sent	sent
set	set	set
shake	shook	shaken
shed	shed	shed
shine	shone, shined (esp. for "polished")	shone, shined
shoot	shot	shot
shrink	shrank, shrunk	shrunk
shut	shut	shut
sing	sang, sung	sung
sink	sank, sunk	sunk
sit	sat	sat
slay	slew	slain
sleep	slept	slept
slide	slid	slid
sling	slung	slung

present form	past-tense form	past participle
slink	slunk	slunk
speak	spoke	spoken
speed	sped, speeded	sped, speeded
spend	spent	spent
spin	spun	spun
spit	spit, spat	spit, spat
split	split	split
spread	spread	spread
spring	sprang, sprung	sprung
stand	stood	stood
steal	stole	stolen
stick	stuck	stuck
sting	stung	stung
stink	stank, stunk	stunk
strew	strewed	strewn
stride	strode	stridden
strike	struck	struck (or *stricken* for "ill" or "afflicted")
string	strung	strung
strive	strove, strived	striven, strived
swear	swore	sworn
sweep	swept	swept
swell	swelled	swelled, swollen
swim	swam	swum
swing	swung	swung
take	took	taken
teach	taught	taught
tear	tore	torn
tell	told	told
think	thought	thought
thrive	throve, thrived	thrived, thriven
throw	threw	thrown
thrust	thrust	thrust
wake	woke, waked	waked, woken, woke
wear	wore	worn
weep	wept	wept
win	won	won
wind	wound	wound
write	wrote	written

6d   Inflection for Person and Number

In order to agree with a subject (see #7), a verb is inflected for *person* and *number*. To illustrate, here are four verbs inflected for person and number in the *present tense*, using personal pronouns as subjects (see #3a):

	Singular			
1st person	I walk	I move	I push	I fly
2nd person	you walk	you move	you push	you fly
3rd person	he walks	he moves	he pushes	he flies
	she walks	she moves	she pushes	she flies
	it walks	it moves	it pushes	it flies
	Plural			
1st person	we walk	we move	we push	we fly
2nd person	you walk	you move	you push	you fly
3rd person	they walk	they move	they push	they fly

Note that the inflection occurs *only in the third-person singular* and that you simply add *s* or *es* to the basic form (if necessary, first changing final *y* to *i*; see #51d).

6e   **Auxiliary Verbs**

Auxiliary or **helping verbs** go with other verbs to form verb phrases indicating tense, voice, and mood. The auxiliary *do* helps in forming questions (see #1t), forming negative sentences, and expressing emphasis:

> *Did* you arrive in time?
> I *did not* arrive in time.
> She *doesn't* care for asparagus.
> I *did* wash my face!
> I *do* admire that man.

Do works only in the simple present and simple past tenses (see #6g).

But the principal auxiliary verbs are *be, have, will,* and *shall.* They enable us to form tenses beyond the simple present and the simple past, as illustrated in #6g and #6h. *Be* and *have* go with main verbs and with each other to form the perfect tenses and the progressive tenses; *will* and *shall* help form the various future tenses. *Be* also combines with main verbs to form the passive voice (see #6 o-p).

Modal Auxiliaries

There are also what are called **modal auxiliaries**. The principal ones are *can, could, may, might, must, should,* and *would.* They combine with main verbs and other auxiliaries to express such meanings as ability, possibility, obligation, and necessity. For example:

> I *can* understand that.
> There *could* be thunderstorms tomorrow.
> I *would* tell you the answer if I *could.*
> The instructor *may* decide to cancel the quiz.
> I *might* attend, but then again I *might* not.
> You *should* have received the letter by now.
> *Must* we listen to that song again?

The equivalent phrases *able to* (can), *ought to* (should), and *have to* (must) also function as modal auxiliaries, as sometimes do verbs like *let, dare,* and *need* (*Let* me go! *Dare* I ask? *Need* you shout so?).

could, might: *Could* and *might* also serve as the past-tense forms of *can* and *may*, for example if demanded by the sequence of tenses after a verb in the past tense (see # 6i):

> He *was* sure that I *could* handle the project.
> She *said* that I *might* watch the rehearsal if I was quiet.

(For the distinction between *can* and *may*, see **can, may** in the Usage Checklist, #60. For *should* and *would* as past-tense forms, see #6i.2.)

might, may: *Might* and *may* are sometimes interchangeable when expressing possibility:

> She *may* (*might*) challenge the committee's decision.
> He *may* (*might*) have finished the job by now.

But usually there is a difference, with *may* indicating a stronger possibility, *might* a somewhat less likely one:

> Since more rain is forecast, the flood *may* (i.e., *may well*) get worse overnight.
> The weather report says the worst is over, though the river *might* (i.e., *could*, but probably won't) rise still further.

To express a condition contrary to fact (see #6m.2), *might* is the right word:

> If you had studied more systematically, you *might* (not *may*) have passed the course.
> Things soon got better on the farm, though that *might* (not *may*) have happened even without our extreme measures.

That is, you *didn't* study more systematically, and you *didn't* pass the course; and life *did* get better on the farm, but it *didn't* do so without the extreme measures: in both examples, *might* is necessary for a clear expression of a hypothetical as opposed to a factual circumstance. See also **may, might** in #60.

Like forms of *do*, modal auxiliaries can join with the contraction *n't*, and *can* can join with the word *not* itself: *cannot, can't, couldn't, shouldn't, wouldn't, mustn't*. (One isn't likely nowadays to encounter *mayn't*, though *mightn't* still occurs.) Unlike other verbs (see #6d), modal auxiliaries are not inflected for third-person singular:

> I can go. You can go. He or she or it can go.

Nor do these verbs have any participial forms, or an infinitive form (one cannot say *to can*, but must use another verb: *to be able*). But they can work as parts of perfect tenses as well as of simple present and simple past tenses (see #6g). (For more on modal auxiliaries, see #6n.)

6f   *vb*

6f   Inflection of *do*, *be*, and *have*

Do, *be*, and *have* are different from the other auxiliaries in that they have lexical meanings of their own and can therefore also function as main or substantive verbs. (So of course do *can* and *will*—but those are actually different words from the auxiliaries *can* and *will*.) As a substantive verb, *do* most often has the sense of *perform, accomplish*:

> I *do* my job. He *did* what I asked. She *does* her best.

Have as a substantive verb most often means *own, possess, contain*:

> I *have* enough money. July *has* thirty-one days.

And *be* as a substantive can mean *exist* or *live* (a sense seldom used: "I think; therefore I *am*"), but most often means *occur, remain, occupy a place*:

> The exam *is* today. I won't *be* more than an hour. The car *is* in the garage.

(See your dictionary for other meanings of these verbs.)

Even when functioning as auxiliaries, these verbs are fully inflected. Here are the inflections for *do* and *have*, which, as you can see, are irregular:

singular	*1st person*	I do	I have
	2nd person	you do	you have
	3rd person	he does	he has
		she does	she has
		it does	it has
plural	*1st person*	we do	we have
	2nd person	you do	you have
	3rd person	they do	they have
past-tense form		did	had
past participle		done	had
present participle		doing	having

The most common verb of all, *be*, is also the most irregular:

		present tense	*past tense*
singular	*1st person*	I am	I was
	2nd person	you are	you were
	3rd person	he-she-it is	he-she-it was
plural	*1st person*	we are	we were
	2nd person	you are	you were
	3rd person	they are	they were
past participle	been		
present participle	being		

For a fuller discussion of tense, see the next two sections.

6g   Time and the Verb: Inflection for Tense

t

Even though verbs must agree with their subjects in person and number (see #6d, #7-7j), they are still the strongest elements in sentences because they not only indicate action but also control time. The verb by its inflection indicates the *time* of an action, event, or condition. Through its **tense** a verb shows *when* an action occurs:

> *past tense:* Yesterday I *practised.*
> *present tense:* Today I *practise.*
> *future tense:* Tomorrow I *will practise.*

Here the adverbs emphasize the *when* of the action, but the senses of past, present, and future are clear without them:

> I *practised.* I *practise.* I *will practise.*

The chart on page 70 shows all the standard tenses of a verb.

In addition, as the chart on the next page also shows, the verb indicates the *character* or *nature* of an action, sometimes called *aspect*:

The tenses in Group 1, the *simple* tenses, describe *indefinite* actions, actions that occur at or during a given time. They can also describe *habitual* or *repeated* actions.

The tenses in Group 2, the *perfect* tenses (from the Latin *perfectus*, "completed"), describe actions that are *complete* (a) in the present, (b) in the past before some specific time, or (c) in the future, again before some specific time referred to or understood.

The tenses in Groups 3 and 4, the *progressive* tenses, describe *continuing* actions. There is a corresponding progressive tense for each of the other six tenses.

6h   The Functions of the Different Tenses

The tenses of English verbs are generally clear and straightforward. Most people have little or no trouble with them. But there are some peculiarities that you may need to watch. Following are brief descriptions and illustrations of the main functions of each tense. Although these points are sometimes oversimplifications of very complex matters, and although there are other exceptions and variations than those listed, these guidelines should help you to use the tenses properly and to take advantage of the possibilities they offer for clear expression.

Tense	Verb Form

1. Indefinite Aspect: duration of action not specified; may be once only or repeated.

   Simple Present

I-you	paint
he-she-it	paints
we-you-they	paint

   Simple Past

I-you-he-she-it-we-you-they	painted

   Simple Future

I-you-he-she-it-we-you-they	will paint

2. Completed Aspect (add the past participle of the main verb to the indefinite inflection of have).

   Present Perfect

he-she-it	has painted
I-you-we-you-they	have painted

   Past Perfect

I-you-he-she-it-we-you-they	had painted

   Future Perfect

I-you-he-she-it-we-you-they	will have painted

3. Continuing Aspect: Simple (add the present participle of the main verb to the indefinite inflection of *be*).

   Present Progressive

I	am painting
you	are painting
he-she-it	is painting
we-you-they	are painting

   Past Progressive

I	was painting
you	were painting
he-she-it	was painting
we-you-they	were painting

   Future Progressive

I-you-he-she-it-we-you-they	will be painting

4. Continuing Aspect: Perfect (add the present participle of the main verb to the indefinite inflection of *have* and the past participle of *be*).

   Present Perfect Progressive

I-you	have been painting
he-she-it	has been painting
we-you-they	have been painting

   Past Perfect Progressive

I-you-he-she-it-we-you-they	had been painting

   Future Perfect Progressive

I-you-he-she-it-we-you-they	will have been painting

1. *Simple present*

   Generally, use this tense to describe an action or condition that is happening now, at the time of the utterance:

   > The pitcher *throws*. The batter *swings*. It *is* a high fly ball . . . .
   > The day *is* very warm. I *am* uncomfortable. *Are* you all right? I *can manage*.

   But this tense has several other common uses. It can indicate a general truth or belief:

   > Everest *is* Earth's highest mountain.
   > Cheetahs *can outrun* any other animal.
   > The bigger they *are* the harder they *fall*.

   or describe a customary or habitual or repeated action or condition:

   > I *paint* pictures for a living.
   > Anne *spells* her name with an *e*.
   > I always *eat* breakfast before going to school.
   > Hurricane season *arrives* in the fall.

   or describe the characters or events in a literary or other work, or what an author does in such a work (see #6k):

   > Oedipus *searches* for the truth almost like a modern detective.
   > The Seven Dwarfs *whistle* while they work.
   > Chaucer *begins* by introducing his characters.

   or even express future time, especially with the help of an adverbial modifier (see also number 7 below):

   > He *arrives* tomorrow. (adverbial modifier: *tomorrow*)
   > We *leave* for England next Sunday. (adverbial modifier: *next Sunday*)

2. *Simple past*

   Use this tense for a single or repeated action or condition that began and ended in the past (compare number 4 below):

   > I *earned* a lot of money last summer.
   > I *was* out in the field before six every morning.
   > The Battle of Hastings *took place* in 1066.
   > *Did* the Romantic Period *end* when Victoria became queen?
   > I *painted* a picture yesterday.
   > I *painted* pictures last year.
   > I *visited* Greece in 1982, 1988, and 1991.

3. *Simple future*

   Although there are other ways to indicate future time (see for example number 1 above and number 7 below), the most common and straightforward is to use this tense, putting *will* or *shall* before the basic form of the verb:

   > She *will arrive* tomorrow morning.
   > I *will paint* your portrait next week.

I will *paint* pictures next year.
We'll *have* a nice picnic if it doesn't rain.

Shall, once considered correct with a first-person subject (*I*, *we*), is now restricted largely to expressing emphasis or determination, or to unusually formal or polite contexts:

I *shall* never *give in.*
Shall you *be attending* the luncheon?
We *shall expect* you at one, then.

or to first-person questions asking for agreement or permission or advice, where *will* would sound unidiomatic:

Shall we *go?*
Shall I *take* the wheel now?
What *shall* I *do* now?
What *shall* we *give* Bertram for Christmas?

Other questions about the future, in whatever person, asking simply for information, use *will*:

Where *will* you *be* at this time tomorrow?
Will we *arrive* in time?

With the informal contractions *I'll, we'll,* etc., the question of *will* or *shall* doesn't arise. With negatives, the contracted forms of *will not* and *shall not* are *won't* and *shan't*:

Won't we *arrive* on time?
No, I *shan't be able* to attend.

Especially after another verb in the past, *would* and *should* serve as the past-tense forms of *will* and *shall* (see #6i.2).

4. *Present perfect*
Use this tense for an action or condition that began in the past and that continues to the present (compare number 2 above); though considered "completed" as of the moment, some actions or conditions referred to in this tense could continue after the present:

I *have earned* a lot of money this summer.
The Prime Minister *has* just *entered* the room.
The weather *has been* lousy lately.
Her illness *has lasted* for two months.

You can use this tense for something that occurred entirely in the past if you feel that it somehow impinges on the present—that is, if you intend to imply the sense of "before now" or "so far" or "already":

I *have painted* a picture; take a look at it.
She *has told* us how she wants our assignments done.
I *have visited* Greece three times.
We *have beaten* them seven out of ten times.

5. *Past perfect*
   Use this tense for an action completed in the past before a specific past time:

   I *had painted* a picture just before they arrived.
   Though I *had seen* the film twice before, I went again last week.
   They got to the station only a minute late, but the train *had* already *left*.
   I *had hoped* for an A, but I did badly on the exam.

6. *Future perfect*
   Use this tense for an action or condition that will be completed before a specific future time:

   By this time next week I *will have painted* a picture.
   I *will* already *have eaten* when you arrive.

   Sometimes simple future works as well as future perfect:

   Some experts predict that by the year 2000 scientists *will have found* (or *will find*) a cure for cancer.

7. *Present progressive*
   Use this tense for an action or condition that began at some past time and that is continuing now, in the present:

   I *am painting* a picture, so please don't bother me.
   I *am writing* my rough draft.
   The drought on the Prairies *is getting* worse.

   Sometimes the simple and the progressive forms of a verb say much the same thing:

   We *hope* for rain. We *are hoping* for rain.
   I *feel* ill. I *am feeling* ill.

   But usually the progressive form emphasizes an activity, or the singleness or continuing nature of an action, rather than a larger condition or general truth:

   A recession *hurts* many people. The recession *is hurting* many people.
   I *go* to university. I *am going* to university.

Like the simple present, the present progressive tense can also express future time, especially with adverbial help:

> They *are arriving* early tomorrow morning.

You can also express future time with a form of *be* and *going* before an infinitive (see #10a):

> They *are going to appeal* the verdict.

8. *Past progressive*

   Use this tense for an action that was in progress during some past time, especially if you want to emphasize the action or its continuing nature:

   > I remember that I *was painting* a picture that day.
   > He *was driving* very fast.
   > They *were protesting* the council's decision.

   Sometimes the past progressive tense suggests an interrupted action or an action during which something else happens:

   > When the telephone rang I *was shampooing* my hair.
   > Just as he *was stepping* off, the bus started moving.

9. *Future progressive*

   Use this tense for a continuing action in the future or for an action that will be occurring at some specific time in the future:

   > I *will be painting* pictures as long as I can hold a brush.
   > You *will be learning* things for the rest of your life.
   > They *will be arriving* on the midnight plane.

10. *Present perfect progressive*

    Use this tense to emphasize the continuing nature of a single or repeated action that began in the past and that has continued at least up to the present:

    > I *have been working* on this picture for an hour.
    > The dollar *has been declining* in value.
    > Our study-group *has been meeting* once a week since January.

11. *Past perfect progressive*

    Use this tense to emphasize the continuing nature of a single or repeated past action that was completed before or interrupted by some other past action:

I *had been painting* pictures for three years before I finally sold one.

We *had* all *been expecting* something quite different.

I *had been pondering* the problem for an hour when suddenly the solution popped into my head.

12. *Future perfect progressive*

This tense is seldom used. Use it only to emphasize the continuing nature of a future action before a specific time in the future or before a second future action:

If she continues to paint, by the year 2000 she *will have been working* at it for over half her life.

You *will* already *have been driving* for about nine hours before you even get to the border.

Exercise 6h(1) **Using verb tenses**

Choose a few fairly standard verbs—say, three regular verbs and three from the list of irregular verbs (#6c)—and run them through their paces: compose sentences using them in all the tenses illustrated in #6g and #6h.

Exercise 6h(2) **Using auxiliary verbs**

Select ten or so of the sentences you wrote for the preceding exercise and try using *do* and some of the *modal auxiliaries* (see #6e) with them to produce different meanings. For example:

I do paint pictures. I did paint pictures. Didn't you paint pictures? I may have painted pictures. Can you paint? I should be painting the garage. I should have been painting pictures. I shouldn't have tried painting the ceiling. Could I have been painting in my sleep? They must have been painting all night.

6i   Sequence of Tenses

When two or more verbs occur in the same sentence, they will sometimes be of the same tense, but often they will be of different tenses.

1. *Compound Sentences*

In a compound sentence, made up of two or more independent clauses (see #1z), the verbs can be equally independent; use whatever tenses the sense requires:

I *am leaving* (present progressive) now, but she *will leave* (future) in the morning.

The polls *have closed* (present perfect); the clerks *will* soon *be counting* (future progressive) the ballots.

He had made (past perfect) his promise, and the committee *decided* (past) to hold him to it; therefore they *expect* (present) his cooperation.

2. *Past Tense in Independent Clause*

In complex or compound-complex sentences, if the verb in an independent clause is in any of the past tenses, the verbs in any clauses subordinate to it will usually also be in one of the past tenses. For example:

I *told* her that I *was* sorry.
I *had told* him about the man who *would succeed* him.
I *assured* them that I *should be* happy to accept their offer.

Refer to a time *earlier* than that of a past main verb by using the *past perfect* tense:

I *told* him that I *had seen* her the day before.
I *was telling* her about what I *had done*.

But there are exceptions. When the verb in the subordinate clause states a general or timeless truth or belief, or something characteristic or habitual, it stays in the present tense:

Einstein *showed* that space, time, and light *are* linked.
They *found out* the hard way that money *doesn't guarantee* happiness.
She *reminded* him that London Bridge *is* now in Arizona.

And common sense sometimes dictates that other kinds of verbs in subordinate clauses should not be changed to a past tense. If you feel that a tense other than the past would be clearer or more accurate, use it; for example:

I *learned* yesterday that I *will be able* to get into the new program in the fall.

The rule calls for *would*, but *will* is logical and clear.

In an interview yesterday, Smith *said* that he *is* determined to complete the investigation.

To use *was* rather than *is* here would at best be ambiguous, implying that Smith's determination was a thing of the past; if it definitely *was* past, then *had been* would be clearer.

I *had* already *told* him about the man who *will succeed* him next month.

Here the adverb *next month* makes it clear that the succession has not yet occurred; hence the future tense is the logical one. And here is one more example of a sentence in which the "sequence of tenses" rule is best ignored:

> The secretary *told* me this morning that Professor Barnes *is* ill and *will not be holding* class this afternoon.

But unless you firmly believe that another tense is better, use past with past.

6j Verb Phrases in Compound Predicates

When a compound predicate consists of two verb phrases in different tenses, don't omit part of one of them:

> *t:* The party has never and will never practise nepotism.

Rather, include each verb in full or rephrase the sentence:

> *revised:* The party has never practised and will never practise nepotism.
> *revised:* The party has never practised nepotism and will never do so.

6k Tenses in Writing About Literature

When discussing or describing the events in a literary work, it is customary to use what is called the "historical present" tense (see also #6h.1):

> When Hamlet *returns* to Denmark he *meets* Horatio and they *observe* Ophelia's burial.

Other tenses can occur in such a context to indicate times before or after the "now" of the historical present:

> While he *was* away, Hamlet *had arranged* to have Rosencrantz and Guildenstern put to death. Now he *holds* Yorick's skull and *watches* Ophelia being buried. And later he *will meet* his own death in the duel with Laertes. Clearly death *is* one of the principal themes with which Shakespeare *is concerned* in the play.

Note that it is also customary to speak even of a long-dead author in the present tense when one is discussing a particular work; another example:

> In *Moby-Dick* Melville *tells* of mad Ahab's pursuit of the great white whale.

For the tenses of infinitives and participles, see #10b and #10e.

6-1   Mood

English verbs are usually considered to have three moods. The **mood** (or *mode*) of a verb has to do with the nature of the expression it's being used in. The ordinary mood is the **indicative**, used for statements of fact or opinion and for questions:

> The weather forecast for tomorrow *sounds* promising.
> Shall we *proceed* with our plans?

The **imperative** mood is used for most commands and instructions (see #1 and #1u):

> *Put* the picnic hamper in the trunk.
> *Don't forget* the mustard.
> *Be* sure to lock the door.

These offer no difficulty. Only the **subjunctive** mood causes any problems, and those only rarely.

6m   Using the Subjunctive

The subjunctive has almost disappeared from modern English. It survives in some standard expressions or idioms such as "*Be* that as it may"; "*Come* what may"; "Heaven *forbid!*" and "Long *live* the Queen!" Otherwise, you need understand only two kinds of instances where the subjunctive still functions.

1. Use the subjunctive—usually in a *that*-clause—after verbs expressing demands, obligations, requirements, recommendations, suggestions, wishes, and the like:

> It is necessary that we *be* there before noon.
> The judge required that Ralph *attend* the hearing.
> The doctor recommended that she *take* a sea voyage.
> Ruth asked that the door *be* left open.
> I wish [that] I *were* in Paris.

2. Use the subjunctive to express *conditions contrary to fact*, conditions that are hypothetical or impossible or not real—often in *if* clauses or their equivalents:

> He looked as if he *were* going to explode. [But of course he didn't explode.]
> If Lise *were* here she would back me up. [But she *isn't* here.]
> If he *weren't* so stubborn, he'd be easier to get along with. [But he *is* stubborn.]

An *as if* or *as though* clause almost always expresses a condition contrary to fact, but not all *if* clauses do; don't be misled into using a subjunctive where it's not wanted:

wrong: He said that if there *were* another complaint he would resign.

The verb should be *was,* for the condition could turn out to be true: there may be another complaint.

Since only a few subjunctive forms differ from those of the indicative, they are easy to learn and remember. The third-person singular form loses its *s:*

> *indicative:* I like the way she *paints.*
> *subjunctive:* I suggested that she *paint* my portrait.

The subjunctive forms of the verb *be* are *be* and *were:*

> *indicative:* He *is* my friend. (I *am,* you-we-they *are*)
> *subjunctive:* I asked that she *be* my attorney. (that I-you-we-they *be*)

> *indicative:* I know that I *am* in Edmonton.
> *subjunctive:* I wish that I *were* in Florence.

> *indicative:* They *are* not particularly prominent.
> *subjunctive:* They behave as if they *were* royalty.

Note that both *be* and *were* function with either singular or plural subjects. Note also that the past-tense form *were* functions in present-tense expressions of wishes and contrary-to-fact conditions. Other verbs also use their past tense as a subjunctive after a present-tense wish:

> I wish that I *painted* better.

After a past-tense wish, use the standard past-perfect form:

> He wished that he *had been* more attentive.
> She wished that she *had played* better.

Although one often hears and reads informal expressions like "I wish I *was* in Paris" and "If Lise *was* here," the subjunctive is still preferable in formal contexts and is used and expected by many educated people. It isn't dead yet. But if subjunctives worry you, see the next section.

6n Using Modal Auxiliaries and Infinitives Instead of Subjunctives

The *modal auxiliaries* (see #6e) offer common alternatives to many sentences using subjunctives; they express several of the same moods, or modes:

> We *must* be there before noon.
> The doctor told her she *should* (*ought to*) take a sea voyage.
> I wish that I *could be* in Paris.
> He looked as if he *might* explode.

If Lise *could have been* here, she would back me up.
If he *would be* less stubborn, he'd be easier to get along with.
I asked if she *would* paint my portrait.
I asked her if she *would* be my attorney.
I wish that I *could* paint better.

Another alternative uses the *infinitive* (see #10a):

It is necessary for us *to be* there before noon.
The judge ordered Ralph *to attend* the hearing.
Ruth asked us *to leave* the door open.
He seemed about *to explode*.
I told her I wanted her *to paint* my portrait.
I asked her *to be* my attorney.

Exercise 6mn **Using subjunctives**

Compose ten sentences using a variety of subjunctive forms. Then try to revise each so that it uses a modal auxiliary or an infinitive instead of a subjunctive. You should be able to change most if not all of them.

---

60 Voice

There are two voices, *active* and *passive*. The active voice is direct: *I made this boat*. The passive voice is less direct, reversing the normal subject-verb-object pattern: *This boat was made by me* (see #1e). Passive voice is easy to recognize; the verb uses some form of *be* followed by a past participle: *was made*. What in active voice would be a direct object (*boat*), in passive voice becomes the subject of the verb. And passive constructions often leave unmentioned the agent of the action or state they describe: *The investigation was carried out* (*by whom* isn't specified).

6p The Passive Voice

pas   Politicians and civil servants and others are fond of the passive voice: people can promise action without committing themselves to perform it, and they can admit error without accepting responsibility:

passive: Be assured (by whom?) that action will be taken (by whom?).
active: I assure you that I will act.
passive: It is to be regretted (by whom?) that an error has been made (by whom?). The matter will be investigated (by whom?).
active: I am sorry we made an error in your account. I will look into the matter and correct it immediately.

Although the passive voice has its uses, it is seldom preferable to active voice. Passive voice tends to be weak and impersonal. It often leads to fuzziness, wordiness, and even grammatical error. It is also a feature of much jargon (see #59h). Don't get into the habit of using the passive voice; when possible, use the direct and more vigorous active voice. Here are some examples from students' papers:

> *pas:* All of this *is communicated* by Tolkien by means of a poem rather than prose. The poetry *is shown* as a tool which Tolkien employs in order to foreshadow events and establish ideas which otherwise *could* not *be* easily *communicated* to us.

The wordiness and general fuzziness of this passage result largely from the passive voice. A change to active voice shortens it, clarifies the sense, and produces a crisper style. Begin by making the agent the subject; the rest then follows naturally and logically:

> *active:* Tolkien *communicates* all this in poetry rather than prose because with poetry he can foreshadow events and establish ideas that would otherwise be difficult to convey.
> *pas:* And as I stood admiring the small hills, rich grass, and tall poplars, as I had often done before, they *were* now *being compared* with the landscape at home.

The passive voice here serves only to confuse the reader. Clearly the *I* is the only possible agent:

> *active:* And as I stood admiring the small hills, rich grass, and tall poplars, as I had often done before, I *was* now *comparing* them with the landscape at home.
> *pas:* By weeding out the errors in one's writing, good habits *are* also *learned.*

Here the passive is not only awkward and weak but also leads to a *dangling modifier* (see #24). The frequency of such errors is itself a good reason to be sparing with passive voice. Active voice eliminates the grammatical error:

> *active:* By weeding out the errors in one's writing, one also *learns* good habits.

When to use the passive voice (see also #18f)

Use the passive voice only when the active voice is impossible or unnecessarily awkward, or when the passive is for some other reason clearly preferable or demanded by the context. Generally, use passive voice only

1. when the agent, or doer of the act, is indefinite or not known;
2. when the agent is less important than the act itself;
3. when you want to emphasize either the agent or the act by putting it at the beginning or end of the sentence.

For example:

> It *was reported* that there were two survivors.

Here the writer doesn't know who did the reporting. To avoid the passive by saying "Someone reported that there were two survivors" would oddly stress the mysterious "someone." And the fact that someone reported is less important than the content of the report.

> The accident *was witnessed* by more than thirty people.

Here the writer emphasizes the large number of witnesses by putting them at the end of the sentence, the most emphatic place.

No doubt you'll want to use passive voice on other sorts of occasions as well; but don't use it unwittingly or uncritically. Remember: a verb in the passive consists of some form of *be* followed by a past participle (*is shown, was accompanied, to be announced, has been decided, are legalized, will be charged, is being removed*). Whenever you find yourself using such verbs, stop to consider whether an active structure would be more effective.

Caution: Like *mood, voice* operates regardless of tense; don't confuse *passive* with *past.* Passive constructions can occur in any of the tenses.

Exercise 6p | **Revising passive voice**

In the following, change passive voice to active voice wherever you think the revision improves the sentence. Retain the passive wherever you think it preferable.

1. The house was broken into during the night, but only some loose change was taken.
2. After some packing boxes were found, the tedious process of individually wrapping all my valuables began.
3. By planning a trip carefully, time-wasting mistakes can be avoided.
4. The car was driven by Denise, while Yves acted as map-reader.
5. Another factor that makes Whistler's ski resort so popular is the diversity of entertainment that can be found there.
6. Some went swimming, some went on short hikes, some just lay around, and baseball was played by others.
7. Although a daily routine was followed, there was enough variety to keep us from becoming bored.
8. The proposed budget cuts were presented by a committee of economists.
9. According to the Prime Minister, it is hoped that the government's policies will be approved by the electorate at the next election.
10. We were informed by our guide that the cathedral was built in the thirteenth century.

7 Agreement Between Subject and Verb

A verb should agree with its subject in **number** and **person**. We say *I see*, not *I sees*, *he sees*, not *he see*, and *we see*, not *we sees*. Most people automatically use the correct form of the verb to go with the subject's *person*, but sometimes people have trouble making verbs agree with subjects in *number*. Here are the main circumstances to watch out for:

7a Something Intervening Between Subject and Verb

When something plural comes between a singular subject and its verb, the verb must still agree with the subject:

> Far below, a *landscape* of rolling brown hills and small trees *lies* in disharmony with the grim structures of steel and cement.
> *Each* of the poems *has* certain striking qualities.
> *Neither* of the men *was* willing to compromise.
> The whole *experience*—the decision to go, the planning, the ocean voyage, and especially all the places we went and things we saw—*was* consistently exciting.

Similarly, don't let an intervening singular noun affect the agreement between a plural subject and its verb.

7b Compound Subject: Singular Nouns Joined by *and*

A compound subject made up of two or more singular nouns joined by *and* is usually plural:

> Careful thought and attention to detail *are* essential.
> Coffee and tea *were* served on the patio.

Occasionally exceptions occur. If two nouns identify the same person or thing, or if two nouns taken together are thought of as a unit, the verb is singular:

> A husband and father *has* an obligation to share the domestic responsibilities.
> Strawberries and cream *is* a popular dessert.

But if you feel an urge to use a singular verb after a two-part subject joined by *and*, make sure you haven't used two nouns that mean the same thing and that are therefore *redundant* (see #59c):

> *red:* The *strength* and *power* of her argument is undeniable.

Get rid of one or the other, or replace them with some other single word (*force*?).

7c *agr*

> **Caution:** Phrases such as *in addition to, as well as,* and *together with* are prepositions, not conjunctions like *and*. A singular subject followed by one of them still takes a singular verb:
>
> > The cat as well as the dog *comes* when I whistle.
> > Mrs. Hondiak, along with her daughters, *is* attending college this year.
>
> Compound subjects preceded by *each, every,* or *many a* take a singular verb:
>
> > Each dog and cat *has* its own supper-dish.

7c Compound Subject: Parts Joined by *or* or a Correlative

When the parts of a subject are joined by the coordinating conjunction *or* (see #12a) or by the correlative conjunctions *either...or, neither...nor, not...but, not only...but also, whether...or* (see #12b), the part nearest the verb determines whether the verb is singular or plural:

> One or the other of you *has* the key. (both parts singular: verb singular)
> Neither the men nor the women *like* the proposal. (both parts plural: verb plural)
> Neither the mainland nor the islands *are* being treated fairly. (first part singular, second part plural: verb plural)
> Neither my parents nor I *was* to blame. (first part plural, second part singular: verb singular)

Try to avoid the construction in the last example, since it usually sounds awkward (see also #4b). It's easy to rephrase; for example:

> Neither I nor my parents were to blame.
> My parents were not to blame, nor was I.

7d Agreement with Indefinite Pronouns (see also #3g, #4c)

Most indefinite pronouns are singular: *another, anybody, anyone, anything, each, either, everybody, everyone, everything, much, neither, nobody, no one, nothing, one, other, somebody, someone, something.* A few, however, namely *all, any, more, most, none, some,* can be either singular or plural, depending on whether they refer to a single quantity or to a number of individual units within a group:

> *Some* of the money *is* missing. (a single amount; *money* is singular, a mass noun)
> *Some* of the men *are* missing. (a number of men; *men* is plural)
> *All* of this novel *is* good. (a whole novel; *novel* is singular)
> *All* of his novels *are* well written. (a number of novels; *novels* is plural)

Most of the beef *was* overcooked. (a single mass; *beef* is singular)
Most of the cattle *are* grain-fed. (a number of animals; *cattle* is plural)
None of the work *is* finished. (a single unit; *work* is singular)
None of the reports *are* ready. (a number of reports; *reports* is plural)

Although some people still consider *none* always singular, you'll be safe enough if you ask yourself what you mean by it in a particular context. For example:

None of the runners *is* tired yet. (none=*not one*)
None of the runners *are* likely to quit. (none=*not any*)
None but the fainthearted *are* staying behind. (none but=*only they*)

The meaning of the phrase *more than one* is obviously plural, but the force of the word *one* usually dictates a singular verb; if the phrase is broken up, however, a plural verb usually sounds idiomatic:

Of the five answers, more than one *is* probably correct.
More answers than one *are* probably correct.

7e   Subject Following Verb

When the normal subject-verb order is reversed, the verb still must agree with the real subject, not some word that happens to precede it:

There *is* only one *answer* to this question.
There *are* several possible *solutions* to the problem.
Here *comes* the *judge.*
Here *come* the *clowns.*
Thirty days *has September.*
Charging about all over the landscape *were* the *group* of scouts *and* their leader.

When compounded singular nouns follow an opening *there* or *here*, most writers use a plural verb:

There *were* a *computer and* a *copier* in the next room.

But if the compound subject consists of noun phrases or clauses, a singular verb often sounds more idiomatic:

There *was* still an *essay* to be revised *and* a *play* to be studied before he could think about sleep.

If the parts are mixed singular and plural, some writers make the verb agree with the nearest part:

There *was* still the *play* to be read *and* his *lines* to be memorized.

But others find this wrong or awkward. You can easily avoid the issue by rephrasing—and save a few words as well:

> A computer and a copier were in the next room.
> He still had an essay to revise and a play to study before he could think about sleep.
> He still had to read the play and memorize his lines.

An expletive *it* always takes a singular verb—usually a linking verb (see #6a):

> It *is* questions like these that give the most trouble.

For more on the expletives *it* and *there*, see #1k and #59a.

Caution: Don't let a predicate noun determine a verb's number; the verb must agree with the subject of the sentence, not the complement (see #1h and #6a):

> The last *word* in style that year *was* suede shoes and broad lapels.

7f Agreement with Collective Nouns

Collective nouns (see #2) name groups considered as units and therefore usually take singular verbs. But when such a noun denotes the individual members of a group, the verb must be plural:

> The faculty *has* made its decision regarding student representation. (singular)
> The faculty *have* not yet made up their minds about student representation. (plural)
> His family *comes* from Korea. (singular)
> His family *come* from Jamaica, India, and Southern Europe. (plural)
> The audience *was* composed and attentive. (singular)
> The audience *were* sneezing, coughing, blowing their noses, and chatting with one another. (plural)

Such words as *number*, *half*, and *majority* can also be considered collective nouns and either singular or plural:

> A *number* of skiers *are* missing. (*a*: plural)
> The *number* of skiers here *is* quite large. (*the*: singular)
> Half of the women *are* going.
> Half of the team *is* here. OR Half of the team *are* here. (depending on whether the collective *team* is considered singular or plural)

(See also **amount, number** in #60.)

Other terms of quantity, like some of the indefinite pronouns (see #7d), can be either singular or plural:

> Five of those chocolates *is* quite enough for one day.
> Five of us *are* going to the play.

Eggs cost too much.
A *dozen* eggs *costs* too much.
A *dozen* of them *do* not have to take the final exam.
That *quartet plays* very well.
The *quartet pick up their* instruments and the room grows quiet.

7g   Nouns That Are Always Singular or Always Plural

Some nouns, because of their meanings, cannot be inflected for number and will always be either singular or plural. Some examples:

The *gold comes* from the Yukon.   (always singular)
Oxygen is essential to human life.   (always singular)
Mathematics is difficult for some people.   (always singular)
Good *news is* always welcome.   (always singular)
The *scissors are* in the kitchen.   (always plural)
His *trousers are* soaking wet.   (always plural)
Her *clothes are* very stylish.   (always plural)

For more on *mass* and *countable* nouns, see #2a and #8c.6.

7h   Titles of Works; Words Referred to as Words

Titles of literary and other works and words referred to as words should be treated as *singular* even if they are plural in themselves:

The Two Gentlemen of Verona **is** one of Shakespeare's lesser comedies.
The Seasons **is** probably Vivaldi's best-known work.
Heebee-jeebies **is** an out-of-date slang term.

7i   Agreement with Relative Pronouns

Whether a relative pronoun is singular or plural depends on its antecedent (see #4). Therefore when a relative clause has *who, which,* or *that* as its subject, the verb must agree in number with the pronoun's antecedent:

Her success is due to her intelligence and perseverance, which *have overcome* all obstacles. (The antecedent of *which* is *intelligence and perseverance.*)

Errors most often occur with the phrases *one of those...who* and *one of the...who:*

He is one of those people who *have* difficulty reading aloud.
He is one of the few people I know who *have* difficulty reading aloud.

Have is correct, since the antecedent of *who* is the plural *people*, not the singular *one*. The only time this construction takes a singular verb is when *one* is preceded by *the only*; *one* is then the antecedent of *who*:

> He is the only one of those attending who *has* difficulty reading aloud.

Or avoid the problem by simplifying; such constructions are often wordy and cumbersome anyway:

> He has difficulty reading aloud.
> Of those attending, he alone has difficulty reading aloud.

7j Plurals: *criteria, data, media,* etc.

The following words are *plural*; don't use singular verbs with them (see #51t.7):

criteria	data	media	trivia	phenomena	strata

Exercise 7(1) Choosing correct verbs

Underline the correct form of each pair of verbs:

1. Both the house and the cottage are unoccupied, but neither Jason nor Melinda (is, are) interested in moving in.
2. There (is, are) fresh coffee and muffins on the kitchen table.
3. The committee (intends, intend) to table its report today.
4. Susan and her father (is, are) going, but neither Huy nor his mother (plans, plan) to attend.
5. It (was, were) ten years later that war broke out.
6. The library as well as the bookstore (sponsors, sponsor) readings by Canadian authors.
7. Aphra Behn is one of the many early women writers who (is, are) underrated.
8. Unexplained natural phenomena (fascinates, fascinate) the scientific community.
9. Each of the researchers (claims, claim) to have found a vaccine to cure the virus.
10. There (is, are) only two major airlines in that country.
11. Most critics agree that Timothy Findley's *The Wars* (is, are) an important Canadian novel.
12. The number of good movies (has, have) decreased in recent years, but a large number of moviegoers (is, are) still willing to pay the price of admission.
13. Potato chips (ruins, ruin) many a serious diet.
14. All work and no play (makes, make) Jack a dull boy.
15. She is the only one of the journalists who (was, were) present who (thinks, think) the story of the refugees (merits, merit) further investigation.

Exercise 7(2) **Correcting faulty subject-verb agreement**

Revise the following sentences to correct any lack of agreement between subject and verb.

1. Recent studies of the earth's atmosphere indicates that there are more than one hole in the ozone layer.
2. Juliet's love and courage is evident in this scene.
3. Post-modern architecture in North America and Europe have been changing urban skylines.
4. In Canada, the media is largely based in Ottawa and Toronto.
5. This economist writes of the virtue of selfishness, but it seems to me that she, along with those who share her view, are forgetting the importance of cooperation.
6. Everything in this speech, the metre, the repetition of vowels and consonants, and the vibrant imagery, lead us to believe that this is the high point of Othello's love—and, as far as we know from this play, of his life.
7. The migration of whales attract many tourists to this coastal community.
8. A growing number of Tories is questioning her leadership.
9. The rhythm of the lines are quite effective.
10. Indeed, the exercise of careful thought and careful planning seem to be necessary for the successful completion of the project.
11. But scandal, unfair politics, and the "big business" of politics has led to the corruption of the system.
12. But with innovation comes a few risks.
13. There appears to be four different ways of approaching such a problem.
14. My faith and trust in him was complete.
15. The number of jobs available to students under sixteen were very few that year.

---

8 Adjectives

ad   An **adjective** modifies—limits, qualifies, or particularizes —a noun or pronoun. Adjectives generally answer the questions *Which? What kind of? How many? How much?*

> *The black* cat was *hungry*; he ate *five* sardines and drank *some* milk.

8a Kinds of Adjectives

Adjectives fall into two major classes: **non-descriptive** and **descriptive**.

1. The several kinds of **non-descriptive** adjectives include some that are basically *structure-words* (see #1-l):

Articles: *a, an,* and *the* (see #8c).

Demonstrative adjectives (see also #3f): *this* hat, *that* problem, *these* women, *those* books

Interrogative and **relative** adjectives (see also #3c-d): *Which* book is best? *What* time is it? *Whose* opinion do you trust? She is the one *whose* opinion I trust.

Possessive adjectives—the possessive forms of personal and impersonal pronouns (see #3a-b) and of nouns (see #2b); for example: *my* book, *her* car, *its* colour, *their* luck, *one's* beliefs, a *man's* coat, the *river's* mouth, the *car's* engine, *Hamlet's* ego, *Shirley's* job (Note: People who think of *form* rather than *function* prefer to call these "possessive pronouns" and "possessive nouns.")

Indefinite and **numerical** adjectives (see #3g); for example: *some* money, *any* time, *more* fuel, *several* people, *three* ducks, *thirty* ships, the *fourth* episode

2. **Descriptive** adjectives give information about such matters as the size, shape, colour, nature, and quality of whatever a noun or pronoun names:

> a *fast* car; a *delicate* balance; a *large, impressive three-storey gray Victorian* house; a *beautiful* painting; a *brave* man; a *tempting* dessert; a *well-done* steak; a *once-in-a-lifetime* opportunity; *Canadian* literature; a *Shakespearean* play; *composted* leaves; a *fascinating* place *to visit*; *kitchen* towels; a *dictionary* definition; *looking tired and discouraged*, he . . . ; the book *to beat all other books*; the woman *of the hour*; the rabbits *who caused all the trouble*

As these examples illustrate, adjectival modifiers can be single (*fast, delicate, beautiful,* etc.), in groups or series (*large, impressive three-storey gray Victorian*), or in compounds (*three-storey, well-done, once-in-a-lifetime*); they can be proper adjectives, formed from proper nouns (*Victorian, Canadian, Shakespearean*); they can be words that are adjectives only (*delicate, beautiful*) or words that can also function as other parts of speech (*fast, brave, tempting,* etc.), including nouns functioning as adjectives (*kitchen, dictionary*); they can be present participles (*tempting, fascinating*), past participles (*composted*), or infinitives (*to visit*); they can be participial phrases (*looking tired and discouraged*), infinitive phrases (*to beat all other books*), or prepositional phrases (*of the hour*); or they can be relative clauses (*who caused all the trouble*). For more examples see #15a. On the punctuation of nouns in series, see #38; on the overuse of nouns as modifiers, see #59g; on infinitives and participles, see #10a and #10d; on prepositions, see #11; on relative clauses, see #3d, #19c.2, and #37a.

8b Comparison of Descriptive Adjectives

Most descriptive adjectives can be inflected or supplemented for *degree* in order to make *comparisons*. The basic or dictionary form of an adjective is called its **positive** form: *high, difficult, calm*. Use it to compare two things that are equal or similar, or—with qualifiers such as *not* and *almost*—that are dissimilar:

> This assignment is *as difficult as* last week's.
> It is *not nearly so difficult as* I expected.

To make the **comparative** form, add *er* or put *more* (or *less*) in front of it: *higher, calmer, more difficult, less difficult*. Use it to compare two unequal things:

> My grades are *higher* now than they were last year.
> Your part is *more difficult* than mine.

For the **superlative** form, add *est* or put *most* (or *least*) in front of it: *highest, calmest, most difficult, least difficult*. Generally, use it to compare three or more unequal things:

> Which of these mountains is the *highest*?
> He is the *calmest* and *least pretentious* person I know.

It is impossible to set rules for when to add *er* and *est* and when to use *more* and *most*. Some dictionaries tell you when *er* and *est* may be added to an adjective; if you have such a dictionary, and it doesn't give those forms for a particular adjective, use *more* and *most*. Otherwise, you can usually follow these guidelines:

For adjectives of *one* syllable, usually add *er* and *est*:

positive	comparative	superlative
short	shorter	shortest
low	lower	lowest
rough	rougher	roughest
dry	drier	driest
grim	grimmer	grimmest
brave	braver	bravest

You can also use *more* and *most* with many of these. And *less* and *least* are necessary with any of them. (And note the spelling changes in the last three examples; see #51c-e.)

For adjectives of *three or more* syllables, usually use *more* and *most* (or *less* and *least*):

beautiful	more beautiful	most beautiful
troublesome	more troublesome	most troublesome

positive	comparative	superlative
acerbic	more acerbic	most acerbic
ridiculous	more ridiculous	most ridiculous

For most adjectives of *two* syllables ending in *al, ect, ed, ent, ful, ic, id, ing, ish, ive, less,* and *ous* (and any others where an added *er* or *est* would simply sound wrong), generally use *more* and *most* (or *less* and *least*):

formal	more formal	most formal
direct	more direct	most direct
noted	more noted	most noted
potent	more potent	most potent
bashful	more bashful	most bashful
manic	more manic	most manic
candid	more candid	most candid
pleasing	more pleasing	most pleasing
churlish	more churlish	most churlish
restive	more restive	most restive
careless	more careless	most careless
conscious	more conscious	most conscious

For other adjectives of two syllables, you usually have a choice; for example:

gentle	gentler, more gentle	gentlest, most gentle
bitter	bitterer, more bitter	bitterest, most bitter
lively	livelier, more lively	liveliest, most lively
silly	sillier, more silly	silliest, most silly

When there is a choice, the forms with *more* and *most* will usually sound more formal and more emphatic than those with *er* and *est.* In fact, you can use *more* and *most* with almost any descriptive adjective, even one-syllable ones, if you want a little extra emphasis or a different rhythm:

Of all the grim statistics I have seen, these are by far the most grim.

But the converse isn't true: adjectives of three or more syllables, and even shorter ones ending in *ous* and *ful* and so on, almost always require *more* and *most*—unless you want to represent slangy or uneducated dialogue, or to create a humorous effect, as when Alice finds things in Wonderland to be growing "curiouser and curiouser."

Notes:

1. A few common adjectives form their comparative and superlative degrees irregularly:

good	better	best
bad	worse	worst

---

far	farther, further	farthest, furthest
little	littler, less, lesser	littlest, least
much, many	more	most

(And see **farther, further** in the Usage Checklist, #60.)

Good dictionaries list all irregular forms after the basic entry, including those in which a spelling change occurs.

2. Although comparative degree is customarily used when comparing two things and superlative degree for three or more things, superlative degree is also often used for only two things, for example for more emphasis:

> She is the better swimmer (of the two).
> We chose the lesser of the two evils.
> Of the two contestants in the race, she is by far the best.

Caution: Don't double up a comparative or superlative form and write something like *more better* or *most prettiest*. If you want emphasis, use the adverbial intensifiers *much* or *far* or *by far*: much livelier, much more lively, far livelier, far more lively, livelier by far, much the livelier of the two, much the liveliest, by far the liveliest.

Because of their meanings, some adjectives should not be compared: see **unique** in the Usage Checklist, #60. See also #29 and #30, on faulty comparison, and **comp** in Chapter XI.

Exercise 8b Comparing adjectives

Come up with some exceptions: adjectives that don't fit neatly into the guidelines. For example, would you use *er* and *est* with *pat, chic, prone,* and *lost*? Or with *sudden, thorough, malign,* and *sanguine*? Do *er* and *est* work with *slippery*? Do some longer adjectives take *est* comfortably, but not *er*? Think of some descriptive adjectives (other than *unique* etc.) that for some reason don't lend themselves to comparisons at all. (Try some past-participial forms, for example, or words that function primarily as nouns or other parts of speech.)

8c Articles: *a, an,* and *the*

art   Articles—sometimes considered separately from parts of speech—can conveniently be thought of as kinds of adjectives. Like adjectives, they modify nouns. Like demonstrative and possessive adjectives, they are also sometimes called *markers* or *determiners,* because an article always indicates that a noun will soon follow.

The definite article *the* and the indefinite article *a* or *an* are used *idiomatically* (see #58), and often baffle people whose first language isn't English—and no wonder, for it is almost impossible to set down all the rules for their use. Nevertheless, here are a few principles for your guidance.

1. The form *a* of the indefinite article is used before words beginning with a consonant (*a dog, a building, a wagon, a yellow orchid*), including words beginning with a pronounced *h* (*a horse, a historical event, a hotel, a hypothesis*) and words beginning with a *u* or *o* whose initial sound is that of *y* or *w* (*a useful book, a one-sided contest*). The form *an* is used before words beginning with a vowel sound (*an opinion, an underdog, an ugly duckling, an honour*). Similarly, the pronunciation of *the* changes from "thuh" to "thee" before a word beginning with a vowel sound.

2. Generally, the definite article designates one or more particular persons or things whose identity is established by context or a modifier:

> *The* black horse is in *the* barn.
> *The* building is on *the* corner.
> *The* teacher stands in front of *the* class.
> *The* cars are at *the* starting line.

whereas generally a person or thing designated by the indefinite article is not specific:

> He wants to buy *a* horse.
> The library needs *a* new building.
> Each class has *a* teacher.

The indefinite article is like *one*; it can be used only before singular countable nouns. Sometimes it even means *one*:

> I thought I would like the job, but I lasted only *a* week.
> This will take *an* hour or two.

Here are some further illustrations comparing *a* and *the*:

> He gave me *a* gift. (unspecified)
> He gave me *the* gift I had hoped for. (particularized by the modifying clause *I had hoped for*)
> Give me *a* book. (any book that's handy)
> Give me *the* book. (a particular book, one already identified or otherwise clear from the context)
> Look up *schism* in *a* dictionary. (any dictionary)
> Look up *schism* in *the* dictionary. (also meaning *any*, but considering all dictionaries as a class; or implying "the particular dictionary you customarily use.")
> Look up *schism* in *your* dictionary. (the one you own)

3. Articles can also be used generically. *The horse is a beautiful animal*: this emphasizes the *class* "horse" (and is not, here, equivalent to *That*

horse, standing over there by the fence, is a beautiful animal). *A horse is a beautiful animal*: this means the same thing, but using the indefinite article emphasizes an individual member of the class. If no article is used—*Horses are beautiful animals*—the plural *Horses* causes the emphasis to fall on all the individual horses. Compare: *The automobile is a prominent feature of our lives. An automobile is almost a necessity in our society. Automobiles dominate our lives.*

4. Definite articles go with some proper nouns but not with others:

We say	but
Canada	the Dominion of Canada
Great Britain	the United Kingdom
Vancouver Island	the Leeward Islands
Mount Olympus	the Rocky Mountains, the Rockies
Great Slave Lake	the Great Lakes
Hudson Bay	the Bay of Fundy
Dalhousie University	the University of Manitoba

Note that *the* usually goes with plurals, names containing *of*-phrases, and names consisting of a modified common noun (the United *Kingdom*) as opposed to a modified proper noun (Great *Britain*).

5. The definite article can also be used to indicate exclusiveness; *the* is then equivalent to *the only* or *the best* (in both speech and writing, such a *the* is sometimes emphasized):

> He was *the* man for the job.

But if such exclusiveness is not intended, *the* is wrong:

> *art:* She soon becomes *the* good friend of the main character.

Change *good* to the superlative *best* (there can be only one *best*) and the definite article is correct; otherwise, *a* is correct.

6. *Uncountable* nouns, whether *mass* nouns (see #2a) or *abstract* nouns (see #2), take no article if the mass or abstract sense governs:

> *art:* The poem is *a* direct, simple *praise* of God.

Here the *a* must be removed. But notice the difference if a concrete noun is inserted; then the article is correct:

> The poem is *a* direct, simple *hymn* of praise.

If such a noun specifies a particular part of the whole, the definite article is correct:

> *The praise* that she bestowed upon him made him blush.

Look at *the gold* that I panned.

Compare:

He lacks humility.
He lacks *the* humility necessary for that position.

Give me liberty, or give me death.
Give me *the* liberty to know, to utter, and to argue freely according to
   conscience, above all liberties.
The disclosure meant *the* death of his dreams.

Orange juice is good for you.
Drink *the* orange juice I gave you. ("I gave you" or a similar phrase like
   "sitting in front of you" could be omitted as understood.)

It sometimes helps to think of each *the* in such instances as similar to a
demonstrative or possessive adjective:

Her praise was generous.
Look at *my* gold.
Give me *that* liberty above all others.
Drink *your* orange juice.
Drink *that* orange juice sitting in front of you.

If an abstract noun is used in a concrete but not particularized sense, the
indefinite article precedes it; if in a particularized way, the definite article:

That horse is *a* beauty. He is *the* beauty I was telling you about.
This is *an* honour. He did me *the* honour of inviting me.
Hers is *a* very special honesty. She has *the* honesty of a saint.

7. The definite article usually precedes an adjective functioning as a noun
(see #8f):

The young should heed the advice of *the* elderly.
The poor will always be with us.
The French oppose independence for Brittany.
This is *the* most I can do.

But not always:

More is sure to come.
Most will arrive on time.

> **Caution:** Don't put a definite article before *most* when *most* is adverbial:
>
> *art:* What people want *the* most is security.
> *art:* That is what they want *the* most of all.

8. Titles of artistic works are not usually preceded by articles; but usage is inconsistent, and some idiomatically take the definite article. It would never do to say

> *art:* Donne's poetic power is evident in *the* Sonnet X.

Either omit *the* or change it to *his*. And one wouldn't say "the *Alice in Wonderland*" or "the *Paradise Lost*." But it would be natural to refer to "the *Areopagitica*" and "the *Adventures of Huckleberry Finn*." (Of course if *A* or *The* is part of a title, it should be included: *A Midsummer Night's Dream, The Portrait of a Lady*.) If a possessive (or pronominal) adjective or a possessive form of the author's name precedes, no article is needed: "Milton in his *Areopagitica*," "in Milton's *Areopagitica*." One might well speak of Michelangelo's great sculpture as "the *David*" (but "In Florence we saw Michelangelo's *David*"), whereas one would not use the article before the title of Earle Birney's poem, *David*.

9. With names of academic fields and courses, whether proper nouns or abstract common nouns, no article is used:

> She is enrolled in Psychology 301.
> He reads books on psychology.
> He is majoring in English.
> This is a program in English Language and Literature.

But if such terms are particularized common nouns or used adjectivally, the definite article is used:

> She studies *the* psychology of animal behaviour.
> You are learning more about *the* English language.

Yet it would be incorrect to speak of "*the* English literature," unless particularized as *the* English literature of, say, Uganda, India, or the Philippines.

10. The definite article is used before the names of ships and trains:

> the *Golden Hind*, the *Titanic*, the *St. Roch*
> the *Super Chief*, the *Orient Express*

11. Sometimes the indefinite article is used to identify something in a general sense; but once the context has been clearly established, the definite article takes over:

> Tonight I wish to discuss *a* problem that has arisen recently, for I think it is *an* important one. *The* problem to which I refer is that of . . . .

8d *ad*

In each blank, place *a*, *an*, or *the*; or put *O* if no article is needed. If either article could be used, put a slash (/) between them. If an article could be used, but need not, put parentheses around it. Some of the answers will be debatable, and we hope you will debate them.

1. In ____ Canadian society, everyone is considered ____ equal.
2. After five years in ____ business, she decided to enrol in ____ International Relations at ____ University of British Columbia.
3. My sister got ____ award for her work in ____ genetics.
4. ____ news report focussed on ____ earthquake in Japan.
5. I am scheduled to go into ____ hospital just when ____ hospital is expecting ____ nurses' strike.
6. There was ____ controversial documentary on ____ television last night.
7. It was ____ lucky day when I bought ____ ticket in ____ lottery.
8. I think you should put ____ onion in ____ stew.
9. This is ____ picture of ____ amoeba, and notice that ____ picture is magnified ____ thousand times so that we can see ____ amoeba's structure.
10. If you belong to ____ union you must be prepared to honour ____ picket lines.

8d   Placement of Adjectives

Adjectival modifiers usually come just before or just after what they modify. *Articles* always, and other determiners almost always, precede the nouns they modify, usually with either no intervening words or only one or two other adjectives:

> Trying to save *some* money, *the* manager decided to let *his* clerk go.
> *The angry* manager decided to fire *his clumsy* and *forgetful* clerk.

Predicate adjectives (see #1g) almost always follow the subject and linking verb:

> The forest is *cool* and *green* and *full of bird-song*.
> Shortly after his operation he again became *sick*.

Adjectives serving as *objective complements* usually follow the subject-verb-direct object (see #1i):

> I thought the suggestion *preposterous*.

Most other single-word adjectives, and many compound adjectives, precede the nouns they modify:

> The *tall*, *dark*, and *handsome* hero lives on in *romantic* fiction.
> The *weather* map shows a *cold* front moving into the *northern* Prairies.

Phrases like "the map weather" or "a front cold" or "the Prairies northern" are obviously unidiomatic in English. (Note that order can determine meaning; for example, a *cold head* is not the same thing as a *head cold*: here, adjective and noun exchange functions as they exchange positions.)

But deviations are possible. Poetry, for example, often uses inversions for purposes of emphasis and rhyme:

> *Fled* is that music . . . .
> *Red* as a rose is she . . . .
> This Hermit *good* lives in that wood . . . .
> And he called for his fiddlers *three*.

Such inversions also occur outside of poetry—but don't use them often, for when the unusual ceases to be unusual it loses much of its power. But if you want a certain emphasis or rhythm, you can put a predicate adjective before a noun (see also #6a):

> *Frustrated* I may have been, but I hadn't lost my wits.

or a regular adjective after a noun:

> He had faith *extraordinary*.
> She did the only thing *possible*.
> There was food *enough* for everyone.

(And note such standard terms as *Governor General* and *court-martial*.) Compound adjectives and adjectives in phrases are often comfortable after a noun:

> His friend, always *faithful and kind*, came at once.
> Elfrida, *radiant and delighted*, left the room, *secure* in her victory.

Relative clauses and various kinds of phrases customarily follow the nouns they modify:

> He is one inspector *who believes in being thorough*.
> The president *of the company* will retire next month.
> The time *to build* is now!

The only adjectival modifier not generally restricted in its position is the participial phrase (see #10d):

> It was a proposal *welcomed by everyone*.
> *Welcomed by everyone*, the proposal was soon adopted.
> *Having had abundant experience*, Kenneth applied for the job.
> Kenneth, *having had abundant experience*, applied for the job.
> Kenneth applied for the job, *having had abundant experience*.

This movability makes the participial phrase a popular way to introduce variety and to control emphasis (see #18e). But be careful: inexperienced writers sometimes lean too heavily on *ing* phrases to begin sentences; and such phrases can be awkward or ambiguous, especially in the form of a *dangling modifier*:

> *dm:* Having had abundant experience, the job seemed just right for Kenneth.

See #24; see also #23, on misplaced modifiers.

8e   Order of Adjectives

Adjectives usually follow an idiomatic order: an article or possessive or demonstrative comes first; then numbers, if any; then descriptive adjectives, usually in an order moving toward the more specific. Adjectives indicating size, age, and colour usually come in that order. For example:

> the three big old black bears
> my two favourite hiking companions
> that well-known Canadian free-style swimming champion

8f   Adjectives Functioning as Nouns

If preceded by *the* or a possessive, many words normally thought of as adjectives can function as *nouns*, usually referring to people, and usually in a plural sense (see #8c.7); for example:

> the Swedish, the British, the Chinese, the Lebanese
> the free, the brave, the sick and dying, society's poor, the more fortunate, the powerful, the big and the small, the high and the mighty, the wealthy, the starving, the enslaved, the badly injured, their wounded, the uneducated, the unemployed, the underprivileged, her beloved, my dearest, the deceased
> the abstract, the metaphysical, the good, the true

9   Adverbs

ad   Adverbs are often thought of as especially tricky. This part of speech is sometimes called the "catch-all" category, since any word that doesn't seem to fit elsewhere is usually assumed to be an adverb. Yet basically, and for most of our needs, adverbs are similar to adjectives, and only a little more complicated.

9a   Kinds and Functions of Adverbs

Whereas adjectives can modify only nouns and pronouns, adverbs can modify *verbs* (and *verbals*; see #10), *adjectives*, other *adverbs*, and *independent clauses* or whole *sentences*. Adverbial modifiers generally answer such questions as *How? When? Where? Why?* and *To what degree?* That is, they indicate such things as *manner* (How?), *time* (When? How often? How long?), *place* and *direction* (Where? In what direction?), *cause, result,* and *purpose* (Why? To what effect?), and *degree* (To what degree? To what extent?). They also express affirmation and negation, conditions, concessions, and comparisons. Here are some examples:

> *Fully* expecting to fail, he slumped *disconsolately in his seat* and began the examination.

To what degree? *Fully*: the adverb of degree modifies the participial (verbal) phrase *expecting to fail*. How? *Disconsolately*: the adverb of manner modifies the verb *slumped*. Where? *In his seat*: the prepositional phrase functions as an adverb of place modifying the verb *slumped*.

> *For many years* they lived *very happily together in Australia.*

How? *Happily* and *together*: the adverbs of manner modify the verb *lived*. To what degree? *Very*: the intensifying adverb modifies the adverb *happily*. Where? *In Australia*: the adverbial prepositional phrase modifies the verb *lived*. How long? *For many years*: the prepositional phrase functions as an adverb of time or duration modifying the verb—or it can be thought of as modifying the whole clause *they lived happily together.*

> *Fortunately*, the cut was *not* deep.

To what effect? *Fortunately*: a sentence modifier. To what degree? *Not*: the negating adverb modifies the adjective *deep*.

> *Because their budget was tight*, they *eventually* decided *not* to buy a new car.

Why? *Because their budget was tight*: the adverbial clause of cause modifies the verb *decided*—or in a way all the rest of the sentence. When? *Eventually*: the adverb of time modifies the verb *decided*. The negating *not* modifies the infinitive (verbal) *to buy*.

> *Last November* the sun *seldom* shone.

When? *Last November*: the noun phrase functions as an adverb of time modifying the verb *shone*. How often? *Seldom*: the adverb of time or frequency modifies the verb *shone*.

> Driving *fast* is *often* dangerous.

How? *Fast*: the adverb of manner modifies the gerund (verbal) *driving*. When? *Often*: the adverb of time or frequency modifies the adjective *dangerous*.

> *If you're tired*, I'll wash the dishes.

The conditional clause modifies the verb (*'ll wash*).

> *Although she dislikes Los Angeles intensely*, she agreed to go *there in order to keep peace in the family*.

Intensely (degree) modifies the verb *dislikes*. *There* (place) modifies the infinitive *to go*. *Although she dislikes Los Angeles intensely* is an adverbial clause of concession. The prepositional phrase *in order to keep peace in the family* is an adverb of purpose modifying the verb *agreed*. The smaller adverbial prepositional phrase *in the family* modifies the infinitive phrase *to keep peace*, answering the question Where?

> She was *better* prepared *than I was*.

The adverb *better* modifies the adjective *prepared*; it and the clause *than I was* express comparison or contrast.

Adverbs as condensed clauses

Some single-word adverbs and adverbial phrases—especially sentence modifiers—can be thought of as reduced clauses:

> *Fortunately* [It is fortunate that], the cut was not deep.
> *When possible* [When it is possible], let your writing cool off *before proofreading it* [before you proofread it].

Other kinds of adverbs: relative, interrogative, conjunctive

1. The **relative** adverbs *where* and *when* are used to introduce relative (adjective) clauses (see #3d):

> She returned to the town *where she had been born*.
> He did not look forward to the moment *when it would be his turn*.

2. The **interrogative** adverbs (*where, when, why*, and *how*) are used in questions:

> *Where* are you going? *Why? How* soon? *How* will you get there? *When* will you return?

3. **Conjunctive** adverbs usually join whole clauses or sentences to each other and indicate the nature of the connection:

> It was an important question; *therefore* they took their time over it.
> Only fifteen people showed up. *Nevertheless*, the candidate didn't let his discouragement show.
> The tornado almost flattened the town; no one, *however*, was seriously injured.

For more on conjunctive adverbs, see #33h.

9b   Forms of Adverbs; Adjectives and Adverbs

1. *Adverbs ending in* ly

Many adverbs are formed by adding *ly* to descriptive adjectives, for example *roughly, happily, fundamentally, curiously*. Don't use an adjectival form where an adverbial form is needed:

> She is a *careful* driver. (adjective modifying *driver*)
> She drives *carefully*. (adverb modifying *drives*)

2. *Adverbs not ending in* ly

Some adverbs don't end in *ly*, for example *ahead, almost, alone, down, however, long, now, often, quite, since, soon, then, there, therefore, when, where*. Others without the *ly* are identical to adjectives, for example *far, fast, little, low, more, much, well*:

> He owns a *fast* car. (adjective)
> He likes to drive *fast*. (adverb)
> She has a *low* opinion of him. (adjective)
> She flew *low* over the lake. (adverb)

Well as an adjective means *healthy* (I am quite *well*, thank you) or sometimes *satisfactory, right*, or *advisable* (all is *well*; it is *well* you came when you did; it is *well* to prepare carefully). Otherwise *well* is an adverb, and should be used instead of the frequently misused *good*, which is an adjective. Similarly, *bad* is an adjective, *badly* an adverb. Be careful with these often misused forms:

> She did a *good* coaching job. The team played *well*.
> They felt *bad* about the child, who had played *badly* in the game. (*Felt* is a linking verb here.)

See also **good, bad, badly, well** in the Usage Checklist, #60.

3. *Adverbs with short and long forms*

Some common adverbs have two forms, one with *ly* and one without. The form without *ly* is identical to the adjective, but the two do not mean the same thing. Check a dictionary if you aren't sure of the meanings of such pairs as these:

> even—evenly, fair—fairly, hard—hardly, high—highly,
> just— justly, late—lately, near—nearly, right—rightly

With some of the others, the short form is an equivalent of, sometimes even preferable to, the longer form; for example:

> Don't talk so *loud*. Look *deep* into my eyes. They travelled far and *wide*. Come *straight* home.

As for the rest, words such as *cheap, clear, close, direct, loose, quick, quiet, sharp, smooth, strong, tight,* and *wrong* are often used as adverbs, but in formal contexts you should use the *ly* form. Regardless of what the road-signs may say, drive *slowly,* not *slow*.

But if you write instructions, especially a recipe, avoid the opposite error, one found in most cookbooks. It's right to tell readers to "stir the sauce *slowly,*" but wrong to tell them to "slice the onion *thinly.*" You wouldn't tell someone to "sand the wood *smoothly,*" but *smooth*—that is, until it is smooth; so slice the onion [so that it is] *thin,* and chop the nuts [until they are] *fine,* and so on. In such phrases the modifier goes with the noun, not the verb.

4. Real *and* really, sure *and* surely

Don't use the adjectival form where the adverbial is needed:

> Her suggestion was *really* [not *real*] different.
> He *surely* [not *sure*] was right about the weather.

But the second example may sound odd. Most people would stick with *sure* in a colloquial context and use *certainly* in a formal one. And *really* is seldom needed at all: see **very** in the Usage Checklist, #60.

5. *Adjectives ending in* ly

Some common adjectives themselves end in *ly,* among them *burly, curly, early, friendly, holy, homely, leisurely, likely, lively, lovely, lowly, orderly, silly, surly, ugly.* Whatever some dictionaries say, adding another *ly* to these inevitably sounds awkward. And though some dictionaries label such adjectives as adverbs as well (he walked *leisurely* toward the door; she behaved *friendly* toward the strangers), that usage also often sounds awkward. You can avoid the problem by adding a few words or rephrasing:

> He walked toward the door in a leisurely manner.
> She behaved in a friendly way toward the strangers.
> She was friendly toward the strangers.

In a few instances, however, the *ly* adjectives do also serve idiomatically as adverbs; for example:

> He spoke *kindly* of you. She rises *early*. He exercises *daily*. The tour leaves *hourly*. Most magazines are published *weekly* or *monthly*.

And there's no need for *yearly* as an adverb since we have *annually*. (And see **basis** in the Usage Checklist, #60.)

9c   Comparison of Adverbs

Like descriptive adjectives, most adverbs that are similarly descriptive can be inflected or supplemented for degree (see #8b). Some short adverbs without *ly* form their comparative and superlative degrees with *er* and *est*; for example:

positive	*comparative*	*superlative*
fast	faster	fastest
hard	harder	hardest
high	higher	highest
late	later	latest
low	lower	lowest
soon	sooner	soonest

Less and *least* also sometimes go with these; for example:

They ran *least hard* during the second mile.
They still ran fast, but *less fast* than they had the day before.

Adverbs of three or more syllables ending in *ly* use *more* and *most*, *less* and *least*; for example:

happily	more happily	most happily
stridently	less stridently	least stridently
disconsolately	more disconsolately	most disconsolately

Most two-syllable adverbs, whether or not they end in *ly*, also use *more* and *most*, *less* and *least*, though a few can also be inflected with *er* and *est*; for example:

slowly	more slowly	most slowly
grimly	less grimly	least grimly
fully	more fully	most fully
alone	more alone	most alone
kindly	kindlier, more kindly	kindliest, most kindly
often	more often, oftener	most often, oftenest

Some adverbs form their comparative and superlative degrees irregularly:

badly	worse	worst
well	better	best
much	more	most
little	less	least
far	farther, further	farthest, furthest

A few adverbs of place use *farther* and *farthest* (or *further* and *furthest*; see **farther, further** in the Usage Checklist, #60); for example:

down	farther down	farthest down
north	farther north	farthest north

As with adjectives, the adverbs *much*, *far*, and *by far* serve as intensifiers in comparisons:

They live *much* more comfortably than they used to.
She flew *far* lower than she should have.
He practises harder *by far* than anyone else on the team.

9d   Placement of Adverbs

1. *Adverbs modifying adjectives or other adverbs*
An intensifying or qualifying adverb almost always goes just before the adjective or adverb it modifies:

almost always, *very* hot, *only* two, *strongly* confident, *most* surely

2. *Modifiers of verbs*
Whether single words, phrases, or clauses, most modifiers of verbs are more flexible in their position than any other part of speech. Often they can go almost anywhere in a sentence and still function clearly:

Quickly he jumped sideways.
He *quickly* jumped sideways.
He jumped *quickly* sideways.
He jumped sideways *quickly*.

But note that the emphasis—and therefore the overall effect, and meaning—changes slightly. So be sure you know just what you want to say before you decide where to put an adverbial modifier. Don't just stick it in anywhere, assuming that it will do the job you want it to do. Here is another example; note how much you can control the emphasis:

Because she likes drama, Sue *often* goes to the theatre.
Sue, *because she likes drama*, *often* goes to the theatre.
Sue *often* goes to the theatre *because she likes drama*.

And in each version, the adverb *often* could come after *goes* or after *theatre*. Try it.

3. *Adverbs of place*
The preceding example also illustrates the only major restriction on adverbial modifiers of the verb. A phrase like *to the theatre*, like a direct object, almost has to come right after the verb—or with no more than an

often or other such word intervening. But sometimes an adverb of place or direction can come first if a sentence's usual word order is reversed for emphasis or some other reason:

> *Off to market* we shall go.
> *There* she stood, staring out to sea.
> *Where* are you going? (but: Are you going *there*?)
> *Downward* he plummeted, waiting until the last moment to pull the ripcord.

4. Sentence modifiers

Sentence modifiers usually come at the beginning, but they too can be placed elsewhere for purposes of emphasis or rhythm:

> *Fortunately*, the cut was not deep.
> The cut, *fortunately*, was not deep.
> The cut was, *fortunately*, not deep.
> The cut was not deep, *fortunately*.

With longer or more involved sentences, however, a sentence modifier at the end loses much of its force and point, obviously; obviously it works better if placed earlier.

See also #33h, on the placement and punctuation of conjunctive adverbs, and #23, on misplaced modifiers.

Exercise 8-9(1) Recognizing adjectives and adverbs

Underline all the single-word adverbs and circle all the single-word adjectives (including articles) in the following sentences:

1. The recession continued unchecked; it was the third consecutive quarter of slow growth.
2. Although she felt happy in her job, she decided, reluctantly, to express very forcefully her growing concern about office politics.
3. The fireplace screen was too hot to touch.
4. When the hikers were fully rested, they cheerfully resumed the leisurely pace of their climb.
5. Surely the government can find some way to raise the necessary revenues fairly.

Exercise 8-9(2) Correcting misused adjectives and adverbs

Correct any errors in the use of adjectives and adverbs in the following sentences:

1. She concentrated so hardly that she got a headache.
2. The promotion usually goes to the determinedest and skilfullest employee.
3. The temperature had risen considerable by noon.

4. We enjoyed a real good vacation in Fiji.
5. He preferred to wear his corduroy brown old jacket.
6. Nira isn't writing as good as she usually does.
7. Houses are more costlier this year than they were last.
8. The slowlier you drive, the less fuel you use.
9. He treats his closest friends poorest of all.
10. Which member of the opposition party is the more ambitious politician?

Exercise 8-9(3) **Using adjectival and adverbial modifiers**

Enrich and elaborate each of the following basic sentences by adding a variety of adjectival and adverbial modifiers. Use phrases and clauses as well as single words. Try several versions of each, and experiment with placement. (Change tenses of verbs if you wish, and add auxiliaries.)

1. Children play.
2. Politicians lose elections.
3. The camper was bitten by a snake.
4. Hiking gives one an appetite.
5. Travel is broadening.
6. Computers are tools.
7. There are lessons in history.

Exercise 8-9(4) **Using adjectives and adverbs**

Make a list of ten adjectives (other than those listed or discussed above) that can also serve as or be changed into adverbs. Use each adjective in a sentence; then make each an adverb and use those in sentences. Then choose two and compose sentences using them in their comparative and superlative forms as both adjectives and adverbs.

---

10 Verbals: Infinitives, Participles, and Gerunds

Infinitives, participles, and gerunds are called **verbals**, forms that are derived from verbs but that cannot function as main or finite verbs. Verbals are **non-finite** forms—unfinished, not restricted by person and number as finite verbs are (see #6d, and the note at the end of #6b). They function as *other parts of speech*, yet retain some characteristics of verbs: they can have objects, they can be modified by adverbs, and they can express tense and voice. Verbals often introduce *verbal phrases*, groups of words which themselves function as other parts of speech (see #1p). Verbals are well worth cultivating and practising with, for they enable you to inject much of the strength and liveliness of verbs into your writing even though the words are functioning as adjectives, adverbs, and nouns.

10a   Infinitives

People sometimes use a form called the **infinitive** to identify particular verbs. They speak of "the verb *to be*" or "the verb *to live*." (In this book we use the basic or dictionary form, *be, live*; see note in #6b.) An infinitive usually consists of the word *to* (often called "the sign of the infinitive") followed by the basic form: *to be, to live*. Infinitives can function as *nouns, adjectives*, and *adverbs*.

1. *Infinitives as nouns*

> *To save* the horses was his primary intention.

The infinitive phrase *To save the horses* is the subject of the verb *was*. The noun *horses* is the direct object of the infinitive *To save*.

> She wanted *to end* the game quickly.

The infinitive phrase *to end the game quickly* is the direct object of the verb *wanted*. The infinitive *to end* is modified by the adverb *quickly* and has the noun *game* as its own direct object. The subject pronoun *She* is also the subject of the infinitive.

> She wanted me *to stop* the game.

Here the phrase *me to stop the game* is the object of the verb *wanted*; the pronoun *me*, although in the objective case, functions as the subject of the infinitive *to stop*.

2. *Infinitives as adjectives*

> His strong desire *to be* the winner was his undoing.

The infinitive phrase *to be the winner* modifies the noun *desire*. Since *be* is a linking verb, the infinitive is here followed by the predicate noun *winner*.

> The green coupons are the ones *to save*.

The infinitive *to save* modifies the pronoun *ones*.

3. *Infinitives as adverbs*

> She was lucky *to have* such a friend.

The infinitive phrase *to have such a friend* modifies the predicate adjective *lucky*. The noun phrase *such a friend* is the direct object of the infinitive *to have*.

> He went to Calgary *to visit* his sister.

The infinitive phrase *to visit his sister* is an adverb of purpose modifying the verb *went*; *his sister* is the direct object of the infinitive *to visit*.

10b   Tense and Voice of Infinitives (see #6g-h, #6o-p)

Infinitives may be either *present* (to indicate a time the same as or later than that of the main verb):

> She wants me *to go* to South America with her.
> I was pleased *to meet* you.
> I would have liked *to meet* [not *to have met*] you earlier.

or *present perfect* (to indicate a time before that of the main verb); the *to* then goes with the auxiliary *have*, followed by the verb's past participle:

> I was lucky *to have met* the manager before the interview.

Each of these may also take the *progressive* form, using the auxiliaries *be* and *have*:

> I expect *to be travelling* abroad this summer.
> He was said *to have been planning* the coup for months.

Infinitives may also be in the *passive voice*, again putting *to* with the appropriate auxiliaries, then adding a past participle:

> The children wanted *to be taken* to the circus.
> He was thought *to have been motivated* by sheer greed.

Note: After some verbs, an infinitive can occur without the customary *to*; for example: *Let* sleeping dogs *lie*. It *made* me *cry*. We *saw* the man *jump*. He *felt* the house *shake*. I *helped* her (to) *decide*.

10c   Split Infinitives

split   Since an infinitive is a unit, separating its parts can weaken it and often results in awkwardness. The more words that intrude, the more awkward the split:

> *split:* He wanted *to* quickly *conclude* the business of the meeting.
> *split:* She claimed that it was too difficult *to* very accurately or confidently *solve* such a problem in the time allowed.

You can usually avoid or repair such splits by rephrasing or rearranging so the adverbs don't interrupt the infinitive:

> He wanted *to conclude* the business of the meeting quickly.
> She claimed that it was too difficult, in the time allowed, *to solve* such a problem with any degree of accuracy or confidence.

But it is better to split an infinitive than to sound awkward or over-refined:

> The minister promised *to* carefully *study* the circumstances that had led to the decision and the public outcry that followed it.

This is clearly better than the awkward *to study carefully the circumstances* or the stuffy *carefully to study the circumstances*, and *carefully* can't be moved to the end of the sentence. Again:

> It is impossible *to* more than *guess* at her intentions.

The adverbial *more than* can't be moved, though a conscientious writer might insert *do* after *to*, thereby avoiding the problem. If the infinitive includes a form of *be* or *have* as an auxiliary, an adverb before the last part is less likely to sound out of place:

> The demonstration was thought *to have been* carefully *planned.*
> We seem *to have* finally *found* the right road.

Try never to *unnecessarily* or *unintentionally* split an infinitive.

10d   Participles

The **past participle** and **present participle** work with various auxiliaries to form a finite verb's *perfect* and *progressive* tenses (see #6g-h). But without the auxiliaries to indicate *person* and *number*, the participles are nonfinite and cannot function as verbs. Instead they function as *adjectives*, modifying nouns and pronouns:

> *Soaking* himself in the bath, Josef suddenly noticed his *reddened* and *swollen* ankle.

Present participles always end in *ing*, regular past participles in *ed* or *d*. Irregular past participles end variously: *made, mown, broken,* etc. (see #6b-c). A regular past participle is identical to the *past-tense* form of a verb, but you can easily check a given word's function in a sentence. In the example above, the past-tense form *noticed* clearly has *Josef* as it subject; the past participle *reddened*, with no subject, is an adjective modifying *ankle.* More examples:

> *Painted* houses require more care than brick ones.

The past participle *Painted* modifies the noun *houses.*

> *Impressed*, she recounted the film's more *thrilling* episodes.

The past participle *Impressed* modifies the subject, *she*; the present participle *thrilling* modifies the noun *episodes* and is itself modified by the adverb *more.*

> The subject *discussed* most often was the environment.

The past participle *discussed* modifies the noun *subject* and is itself modified by the adverbial *most often.*

Suddenly *finding* himself alone, he became very *frightened*.

The present participle *finding* introduces the participial phrase *finding himself alone*, which modifies the subject, *he*; *finding*, as a verbal, has *himself* as a direct object and is modified by the adverb *suddenly*. The past participle *frightened* functions as a predicate adjective after the linking verb *became*; it modifies *he* and is itself modified by the adverb *very*.

10e **Tense and Voice of Participles** (see #6g-h, #6o-p)

The standard present or past participle indicates a time the same as that of the main verb:

Being the tallest, Luzia played centre.

Strictly speaking, a past participle by itself amounts to passive voice:

Worried by what he'd heard, Joe picked up the phone.

With *ing* attached to an auxiliary, participles can also be in the perfect or perfect-progressive tense, indicating a time earlier than that of the main verb:

Having painted himself into a corner, George climbed out the window.
Having been painting for over two hours, Leah decided to take a break.

Participles in the present-progressive and the perfect tenses can also be in the passive voice:

The subject *being discussed* was the environment.
Having been warned, she knew better than to accept the offer.

> **Caution:** It is particularly important that you know a present participle when you write one. If you use a present participle and think it's functioning as a finite verb, you may well produce a **fragment** (see #1y).

Exercise 10d-e | **Using participles**

Compose sentences using—as single-word adjectives—the present and the past participles of each of these verbs:

care	drive	cut	sleep	trouble
dry	grow	boil	change	rejuvenate

Then add auxiliaries and use them as finite verbs.

Example: stun—stunning—stunned
> She looked *stunning*. It was a *stunning* blow. The *stunned* boxer hit the mat. He lay there, *stunned*.
> He *was stunning* us with his revelations. He *has stunned* others before us. One *can be stunned* by a jolt of electricity.

10f Gerunds

When the *ing* form of a verb functions as a *noun*, it is called a **gerund**:

> Josef gave himself a good *soaking*.
> *Moving* furniture can be hard work.
> Sylvester has a profound fear of *flying*.
> Careful preparation—*brainstorming* and *organizing* and *outlining*—helps produce good essays.

The gerund *soaking* is a direct object, and is itself modified by the adjective *good*. The gerund *Moving* is the subject of the sentence, and has *furniture* as a direct object. The gerund *flying* is the object of the preposition *of*. In the final example, the three gerunds constitute an appositive of the subject noun, *preparation* (see #1q).

10g Tense and Voice of Gerunds (see #6g-h and #6o-p)

As with infinitives and participles, the *perfect* form of a gerund indicates a time earlier than that of the main verb:

> His *having built* the boat himself caused him to boast a little.

Perfect-progressive tense is possible, but unwieldy:

> My *having been feeling* unwell caused me to stay home.
> (Since I had been feeling unwell, I stayed home.)

And a gerund can be in the passive voice, though again a different phrasing will usually be preferable:

> Her *having been told* the rules meant that she had no excuse for doing it wrong.
> His *being praised* by the boss gave him a big lift.

10h Possessives with Gerunds

In formal usage, a noun or a personal pronoun preceding a gerund will usually be in the possessive case:

> *His* driving left much to be desired.
> The trouble was caused by *our* not knowing what to do.
> She approved of *Bob's* cooking the dinner
> I can't understand the *minister's* always refusing to reveal the source of her information.
> Can you explain the *engine's* not starting?

If the gerund is the subject, as in the first example, the possessive is essential. Otherwise, if you are writing informally, and especially if you want to emphasize the noun or pronoun, you needn't use the possessive:

> She approved of *Bob* cooking the dinner rather than Jim.
> Can you imagine the *minister* behaving that way?

Further, in order to avoid awkward-sounding constructions, you usually won't use a possessive form when a noun is (a) abstract, (b) plural, (c) multiple, or (d) separated from the gerund by modifiers (other than adverbs like *not* or *always* when they sound almost like part of the verbal):

> a. He couldn't bear the thought of *disaster striking* again.
> b. The possibility of the *thieves returning* to their hide-out was slim.
> c. There is little likelihood of *Alberto and Maria agreeing* to your proposal.
> d. One might well wonder at a *man* with such a record *claiming* to be honest.

Note: A gerund followed immediately by another noun will sometimes sound awkward or ambiguous unless you interpose *of* or *the* or some similar term to keep the gerund from sounding like a participle: his building (of) boats, your organizing (of the) material, his revealing (of, the, of the) sources, my practising (the) piano.

10i   Verbals in Absolute Phrases

Infinitives and participles (but not gerunds) can function in **absolute phrases** (see #1r):

> *To say the least*, the day was not a success.
> *Strictly speaking*, their actions were not legal.
> She decided to go for a swim, *the day being hot*.
> *All things considered*, the meeting was a success.

Exercise 10(1) Recognizing verbals

Identify each verbal in the following sentences as an infinitive, a past or present participle, or a gerund.

1. Coming as he did from the Prairies, he found the coastal scenery to be stunning.
2. She wanted to fly, and learning was easier than she had expected.
3. My answering service had promised to buzz me if anything startling were to arise.
4. The celebrated performers got top billing for the first showing of the winning film.
5. Trying to study hard with a splitting headache is usually not very rewarding.

6. The party was certain to last until midnight, permitting everyone to eat and drink too much.

7. Turning table legs on a spinning lathe is one way to spend a pleasant and relaxed evening.

8. Sent as he had been from one office to another, Sherman was tired of running back and forth and up and down; he was now resolved to go straight to the top.

9. When doing one's daily exercising, one should be careful not to overstrain already taxed muscles.

10. The contrived plot of the currently running play is enough to make the audience get up and leave the theatre without worrying about the author's supposed talent or his past record of charming tired city-dwellers with rural high jinks.

Exercise 10(2) Using verbals

Here are some exercises to help you get the feel of verbals and to recognize some of the things you can do with them.

a. In short sentences, use three infinitives as nouns, adjectives, and adverbs (if possible; they are less common). Then use each in three longer sentences, again as noun, adjective, and adverb—but expanded into infinitive *phrases*; elaborate the sentences as much as you want. You needn't simply build on the short sentences, but you may.

> *Example: to sit*

> > *noun:* To sit is restful. (subject)
> > I like to sit. (object)
> > One way to relax is to sit. (predicate noun)

> > *adjective:* I need a place to sit. I have an urge to sit.

> > *adverb:* He was determined to sit. She cleared a space in order to sit.

> > *noun phrase:* To sit, feet up, before a quietly crackling fire on a cold winter night, reading a moderately engrossing detective story, is one of the more relaxing pleasures available to modern civilized human beings.

b. Compose ten sentences using some present and past participles to modify different kinds of nouns—subjects, direct objects, indirect objects, objects of prepositions, predicate nouns, objective complements, appositives.

c. Make *ing* forms of five verbs and use them as gerunds—at least one as a subject, one as a direct object, one as a predicate noun, and one as an object of a preposition. Use each first as a single word in a short sentence, then in a longer one as part of a gerund phrase.

If you haven't already done so, try varying the tenses of some of your verbals. Have you put any in passive voice?

Exercise 10(3) Reducing clauses to infinitive phrases

By reducing clauses to phrases, you can often get rid of unnecessary heaviness and wordiness. Practise by reducing each italicized clause in the following sentences to an infinitive phrase that conveys basically the same meaning. Change or rearrange words as necessary.

>   Example: We wondered *what we should do next.*
>   We wondered *what to do next.*

1. He claimed *that he was unbeatable.*
2. He said *that I should help with the chores.*
3. Remember *that you should be at the lab by 2:30.*
4. *If you want a restful weekend,* you must disconnect your telephone.
5. Sherrill thought *that I had given up.*
6. The quarterback's problem was *that he had to decide* what play *he should use next.*
7. She was so confident *that she entered every race.*
8. The police officer said *that we should follow him to the station.*
9. The time *that you should worry about* is the hour before the race.
10. It is said *that break-dancing originated* during street-fights in New York City.

Do any of these strike you as preferable with the clauses left intact? Might one's choice depend on context?

Exercise 10(4) Reducing clauses

This time reduce each italicized clause to the kind of phrase specified in parentheses after each sentence.

>   Example: *As she changed her mind*, she suddenly felt much better. (present participial)
>   *Changing her mind*, she suddenly felt much better.

1. *They did not mince their words*: they made their criticisms forcefully and forthrightly. (present participial)
2. Sometimes the best part of a vacation is *when you plan it.* (gerund)
3. Earning high marks is something *that you can be proud of.* (infinitive)
4. *Because they felt foolish*, they decided to leave early. (present participial)
5. *Because there were only two guests in the hotel*, the manager let most of the staff leave early. (absolute)
6. *The fact that she had won the contest* came as something of a shock to her. (gerund)
7. *Because repeated failures had discouraged them*, they gave up and went home. (past participial)
8. The clown *who had on the funny hat* started turning somersaults. (present participial)
9. *As they dispensed hot soup to the hungry crowd*, they came to understand more about the plight of the homeless. (present participial)
10. *Although bad luck had plagued every step of their preparations*, they managed to produce a highly successful spring festival. (past participial)

Absolute phrases are useful for expressing cause-effect relations or for providing vivid descriptive details. Since they considerably heighten style, don't use them often. But do use them sometimes. For practice, combine each of the following pairs of sentences by reducing one of them (usually the first) to an absolute phrase consisting of a noun and a participle (along with any modifiers). Remember that if the participle is *being*, it can sometimes be omitted (see #1r).

> *Example:* Everyone present agreed. The motion passed unanimously.
> Everyone present agreeing, the motion passed unanimously.
> Dinner was over and the dishes were washed. They sat down to watch a movie on television.
> Dinner (being) over and the dishes (being) washed, they sat down to watch a movie on television.

1. The little girl was very sleepy. Her father carried her upstairs to her bedroom.
2. The car refused to start. They had no choice but to hoof it.
3. His voice was cracking and his eyes were watering. He sat down, hoping he had made his point.
4. The flags waved and the band played. The parade turned the last corner and disappeared.
5. The day was breezy yet warm. They decided to go for a sail on the lake.
6. She smiled and accepted the judgment. Protest, she knew, was futile.
7. Her position was secure. She confidently challenged the members of the board.
8. Extra money was hard to come by. He was forced to curtail his extracurricular activities.
9. The lie in the bushes was unplayable. He dropped the ball in the clear and took a one-stroke penalty.
10. He smiled at the audience and sat down. The effect he wanted had already been sufficiently achieved.

11 Prepositions

Prepositions are structure-words or function-words (see #1-l); they never change their form. A preposition is always part of a *prepositional phrase*, and it usually *precedes* in *position* the rest of the phrase, which always includes a noun or pronoun as the **object** of the preposition:

> This is a book *about* writing.
> She sent the letter *to* her brother.

Make a question of the preposition and *what* or *whom* and the answer will always be the object: *About* what? Writing. *To* whom? Her brother.

11a

11a Functions of Prepositions and Prepositional Phrases

A preposition *links* its object to some other word in the sentence; the prepositional phrase then functions as either an *adjectival* or an *adverbial* modifier:

> He laid the book *on the table*.

Here *on* links *table* to the verb *laid*; the phrase *on the table* therefore functions as an adverb describing *where* the book was laid.

> It was a time *for celebration*.

Here *for* links *celebration* to the noun *time*; the phrase therefore functions as an adjective indicating *what kind of* time.

> **Note:** Occasionally a prepositional phrase can function as a noun, for instance as the subject of a sentence:
>
> > *After class* is a good time to talk to the instructor.

11b Placement of Prepositions

Usually, like articles, prepositions signal that a noun or pronoun soon follows. But prepositions can also come at the ends of clauses or sentences, for example in a question, for emphasis, or to avoid awkwardness or stiffness:

> Which house do you want to look *at*?
> Whom are you buying the book *for*?
> She is the one I want to give the book *to*.
> They had several problems to contend *with*.
> This is the restaurant I was telling you *about*.
> The problem he was dealing *with* seemed insoluble.

Some would prefer "with which he was dealing," especially in a formal context. But it isn't wrong to end a sentence or clause with a preposition, in spite of what many people have been taught; just don't do it when it is unnecessarily awkward, or so often that it calls attention to itself. Remember that Sir Winston Churchill is supposed to have said that it was the sort of usage "up with which I will not put."

11c Common Prepositions

Most prepositions indicate a spatial or temporal relation, or such things as purpose, concession, comparison, manner, and agency. Here is a list of common prepositions; note that several consist of more than one word:

about	beneath	in front of	over
above	beside	in order to	past
according to	besides	in place of	regarding
across	between	in relation to	regardless of
across from	beyond	inside	round
after	but	in spite of	since
against	by	into	such as
ahead of	by way of	like	through
along	concerning	near	throughout
alongside	considering	next to	till
among	contrary to	notwithstanding	to
apart from	despite	of	toward(s)
around	down	off	under
as	during	on	underneath
as for (to)	except	on account of	unlike
at	except for	onto	until
away from	excepting	on top of	up
because of	for	opposite	upon
before	from	out	with
behind	in	out of	within
below	in addition to	outside	without

Exercise 11a-c(1) Recognizing prepositional phrases

Identify each prepositional phrase in the following sentences and note whether each is adjectival or adverbial.

1. He went into town to buy some bacon for his breakfast.
2. There stood a man of about forty, in the hot sunshine, wearing a heavy jacket with the collar turned up.
3. In the morning the president called her secretary on the telephone and told her to come to the office without delay.
4. The bulk of the material was sent ahead in trunks.
5. Louis looked under the table for the ball of yarn that had fallen from his lap.

Exercise 11a-c(2) Using prepositional phrases

Prepositional phrases are essential components of writing, but they can be overdone. These exercises will give you practice both in using them and in avoiding their overuse.

a. *Reducing clauses to prepositional phrases:* You'll use prepositional phrases without even thinking about them; but sometimes you should consciously try to tighten and lighten your style by reducing some clauses to prepositional phrases. Do that with the italicized clauses in the following sentences. Revise in other ways as well if you wish, but don't change the essential meaning.

Example: The cold front *that is over the coast* will move inland overnight.
The cold front *over the coast* will move inland overnight.

1. *If you have enough stamina*, you can take part in all the athletic events.
2. The time *when you could worry* is long past.
3. *Because she was so confident*, she entered every race.
4. Students *who have part-time jobs* must budget their time carefully.
5. We need the advice *that an expert can give us*.

b. Reducing clauses to prepositional phrases using gerunds: Gerunds (see #10f-g) are often used as objects of prepositions. Convert the italicized clauses in the following sentences to prepositional phrases with gerunds.

> *Example: Before she submitted the essay*, she proofread it carefully.
> *Before submitting the essay*, she proofread it carefully.

1. *When I had run* only half a mile, I felt nearly exhausted.
2. *Although he trained rigorously*, he didn't get past the preliminaries.
3. You can't hope to pass *unless you do all the assignments*.
4. *They checked letters carefully*, and caught two spies.
5. He deserves some credit *because he tried so hard*.

c. Getting rid of excessive prepositional phrases: When prepositional phrases come in bunches, they can contribute to wordiness and awkwardness. Practise revising to get rid of unnecessary clutter: cut the number of prepositional phrases in each of the following sentences (shown in parentheses) at least in half.

> *Example:* Some of the players on the football team are in danger of losing their eligibility because of the poor quality of their work for classes and on examinations. (8)
> Because they are doing so poorly academically, some football players may lose their right to play. (reduced to zero)

1. He got to the top of the mountain first by using several trails unknown to his competitors in the race, which was held during the celebration of the centennial of the province's entry into confederation. (9)
2. The feeling of most of the people at the meeting was that the candidate spoke in strident tones for too long about things about which he knew little. (7)
3. The man at the top of the stairs of the old house shouted at me to get away from his door in a hurry. (6)
4. One of the most respected of modern historians has some odd ideas about the beginning of the war between European nations that broke out, with such devastating consequences, in early August of 1914. (8)
5. Economists' predictions about the rise and fall of interest rates seem to be accurate for the most part, but only within the limits of a period of about three or four weeks, at most, and even at that you have to take them with a grain of salt. (10)

11d   Two-part Verbs

English has many two-part and even three-part verbs consisting of a simple verb in combination with another word or words, for example *cool off, act up, blow up, find out, hold up, carry on, get on with, stick up for.* It doesn't matter whether you think of the added words as prepositions, adverbs, or some sort of "particle." Indeed, sometimes it is difficult to say whether a word like *down* in *sit down* is functioning as part of the verb or as an adverb describing how one can sit; but the *down* and *up* in "sit down to a good meal" and "sit up in your chair" seem more like parts of the verbs than, say, the preposition *at* in "He sat at his desk." Usually you can sense a difference in sound: in "He *took over* the operation" both parts are stressed when said aloud, whereas in "He *took* over three hours to get here" only the *took* is stressed; *over* functions separately. Often, too, the parts of a verb can be separated and still mean the same, whereas the verb and preposition or adverb cannot:

> The hecklers were *won over* by his reply.
> He *won* the hecklers *over* with his reply.
> He *won* over his nearest opponent by three strokes.

> They *blew up* the plane.
> They *blew* the plane *up*.
> The wind *blew* up the chimney.

But some two-part verbs cannot be separated, for example *see to, look after, run across, sit up, turn in.*

Some simple verbs can take two or more different words to form new verbs; for example:

> try out, try on; think out, think up; fill up, fill in, fill out; fall out, fall in, fall off

Some can use several different words:

> let alone, let down, let go, let loose, let off, let on, let up
> turn against, turn down, turn in, turn loose, turn off, turn on, turn out, turn over, turn to, turn up
> bring about, bring around, bring down, bring forth, bring forward, bring in, bring off, bring on, bring out, bring over, bring to, bring up

11e   Using Two-part Verbs: Informality and Formality

By consciously using or avoiding these verbs in a piece of writing, you can help control tone. Most of these verbs are standard and idiomatic, but some are informal or colloquial or even slangy, for example *let up, mess up, shake up, trip up* (and see #52). Even the standard ones are often relatively informal—that is, they have more formal equivalents; for example:

> give away _____ bestow; reveal, betray
> give back _____ return

give in	_____	yield, concede
give off	_____	discharge, emit
give out	_____	emit; distribute; become exhausted
give over	_____	relinquish, abandon; cease
give up	_____	despair; stop, renounce; surrender, cede
give way	_____	withdraw, retreat; make room for; collapse

If you choose *buy* as more appropriate to your context than *purchase*, you'll probably also want to use some two-part verbs rather than their more formal, often Latinate, equivalents; for example you'd probably say *put up with* rather than *tolerate*. Or vice versa: if you're writing a strictly formal piece, you may want to avoid the informal terms, or allow in only a couple for contrast or spice. Much writing nowadays, including academic writing, is becoming increasingly informal; any composition that eschewed the kind of vigour these two-part verbs can impart would risk sounding pompous and stiff.

Exercise 11d-e **Using two-part verbs**

---

a. Draw up a list of two-part (and three-part) verbs and their more formal equivalents. Draw on those listed above, but add as many more as you can think of. Take common verbs like *come, go, put, take, get,* and *set,* and try adding on such common prepositions and adverbs as *about, at, away, back, down, in, off, out, over, through, to, up, upon,* and *with.* Consult your dictionary. If you don't find many listed (usually under the entry for the basic verb itself), look in a bigger dictionary, or a learner's dictionary. You shouldn't have to go as far as the *Oxford English Dictionary* to find a substantial number (though you may want to).

b. Compose several sentences—or better yet compose two or three separate paragraphs on different kinds of topics—using as many verbs from your list as you can squeeze in. Read them over, aloud, to see how they sound.

c. Rewrite them, wherever possible substituting more formal verbs for your originals. Now how do they sound?

d. Rewrite again, judiciously mixing the two kinds of verbs. Which version of each piece do you now like the best? Does it depend on the subject? Would it depend at all on your intended audience?

---

12 Conjunctions

Conjunctions are another kind of structure-word or function-word (see #1-1). As their name indicates, conjunctions are words that "join together." There are three kinds of conjunctions: *coordinating, correlative,* and *subordinating.*

12a   Coordinating Conjunctions

1. There are only seven **coordinating** conjunctions. Memorize them:

and   but   or   nor   for   yet   so

When you use a coordinating conjunction, choose the appropriate one (see #28, on faulty coordination). *And* indicates addition, *nor* indicates negative addition (equivalent to *also not*), *but* and *yet* indicate contrast or opposition, *or* indicates choice, *for* indicates cause or reason, and *so* indicates effect or result.

Some can also be other parts of speech: *yet* can be an adverb (It's not *yet* ten o'clock); *so* can be an adverb (It was *so* dark that...), an adjective (That is *so*), a demonstrative pronoun (I liked him, and I told him *so*), and an interjection (*So!*); *for* is also a common preposition (*for* a while, *for* me); even *but* can be a preposition, meaning *except* (all *but* two).

For *punctuation* with coordinating conjunctions, see Chapter IV, especially #33a-c and #44d.

2. *Joining words, phrases, and subordinate clauses*
And, but, or, and *yet* join coordinate elements within sentences. The elements joined should be of equal importance and of similar grammatical structure and function. When joined, they are sometimes called *compounds* of various kinds (see #1z.1). Here are examples of the compounding of various kinds of sentence elements:

> I saw *Jean* and *Ralph*. (two direct objects)
> *Jean* and *Ralph* saw me. (two subjects)
> They *ducked* and *ran*. (two verbs)
> The driver was *short, fat,* and *ugly*. (three predicate adjectives)
> He ate *fast* and *noisily*. (two adverbs)
> The bird flew *in the door* and *out the window*. (two adverbial prepositional phrases)
> *Tired* but *determined*, she plodded on. (two past participles)
> The children *cooked the dinner* and *washed the dishes*. (two verbs with direct objects)
> People *who invest wisely* and *who spend carefully* can weather a recession. (two adjective clauses)
> I travel *when I have the time and money* and *when I can find someone pleasant to accompany me*. (two adverbial clauses)
> The lawyer told him *what he should wear* and *how he should speak*. (two noun clauses)

Obviously the elements being joined won't always have identical structures, but don't risk disappointing readers' natural expectations that compound elements will be fairly parallel. For example it would be weaker to write the last example with one direct object as a clause and the other as an infinitive phrase (see #27, on faulty parallelism):

The lawyer told him *what he should wear* and *how to speak*.

When three or more elements are compounded, the conjunction usually appears only between the last two, though *and* and *or* can appear throughout (called *polysyndeton*), for purposes of rhythm or emphasis:

There was a tug-of-war *and* a sack race *and* an egg race *and* a three-legged race *and* . . . well, there was just about any kind of game anyone could want at a picnic.

And occasionally *and* can be omitted entirely (called *asyndeton*), also for emphasis (see also #38c):

There were flowers galore—fuschias, snap-dragons, jonquils, dahlias, azaleas, tulips, roses, lilacs, camellias—more kinds of flowers than I wanted to see on any one day.

3. *Joining independent clauses*

All seven coordinating conjunctions can join independent clauses to make compound (or compound-complex) sentences (see #1z). The clauses will be grammatically equivalent since they are *independent*; but they needn't be grammatically parallel or even of similar length—though they often are both, for parallelism is a strong stylistic force. Here are some examples:

The players fought, the umpires shouted, *and* the fans booed.
The kestrel flew higher and higher, in ever-wider circles, *and* soon it was but a speck in the sky overhead.
Jean saw me, *but* Ralph didn't.
Will you answer her letter, *or* shall I ask Violet to?
I won't do it, *nor* will she. (With *nor* there must be some sort of negative in the first clause. Note that after *nor* the normal subject-verb order is reversed.)
He began to drive more slowly, *for* it was getting dark.
The economy seemed in good shape, *yet* the market went into a slump.
There was no way to avoid it, *so* I decided to get as much out of the experience as I could.

Note: The conjunction *so* is informal; in formal writing, you can almost always indicate cause-effect relations with a *because-* or *since*-clause instead:

Since there was no way to avoid it, I decided to get as much out of the experience as I could.

And so, however, is acceptable, but don't use it often.

---

4. *Joining sentences*

In spite of what many people have been taught, it isn't wrong to begin a sentence with *And* or *But*, or for that matter any of the other coordinating conjunctions. *For*, however, so similar in meaning to *because*, often sounds awkward at the start of a sentence, as if introducing a fragmentary subordinate clause (see #12c). And *So* often sounds colloquial, even immature. But the rest, especially *And* and *But*, make good openers; it's just that you shouldn't overdo them. An opening *But* or *Yet* can nicely emphasize a contrast or other turn of thought (as in the preceding sentence). An opening *And* can also be emphatic:

> He told the judge he was sorry. And he meant it.

Both *And* and *But* as sentence-openers contribute to paragraph coherence (see #65d). And, especially in a narrative, a succession of opening *And*'s can impart a feeling of rapid pace, even breathless excitement. Used too often, they can become tedious, but used carefully and when they feel natural, they can be effective.

Exercise 12a   Using coordinating conjunctions

Put an appropriate coordinating conjunction in each blank. If more than one is possible, say so.

1. Uta got home late, _____ she had a good excuse.
2. There is only one solution to this problem, _____ I know what it is.
3. You can make an appointment for tomorrow, _____ you can wait until next week.
4. No one likes pollution, _____ some people insist that we have to live with it.
5. Her brother is not cynical, _____ is he insensitive.
6. It was a startling painting, _____ I spent a long time examining it.
7. We were puzzled by the professor's humorous comments, _____ we had expected her to speak seriously on the subject.
8. My mother arrives tomorrow morning, _____ she expects to be met at the airport.
9. The fishing season is postponed two weeks this year, _____ Luis is somehow controlling his impatience.
10. Keep a pressure bandage on that sprain, _____ it will take weeks to heal.

12b   Correlative Conjunctions

Correlative conjunctions come in pairs. They *correlate* ("relate together") two parallel parts of a sentence. The principal ones are *either . . . or, neither . . . nor, whether . . . or, both . . . and, not . . . but,* and *not only . . . but also.* Correlative conjunctions enable you to write sentences containing forcefully balanced elements—but don't overdo them. They are also more at home in formal than in informal writing. Some examples:

> *Either* Rodney *or* Elliott is going to drive.
> Put the suitcase *either* on the bed *or* on the chair.
> She accepted *neither* the first *nor* the second offer.
> *Whether* by accident *or* by design, the number turned out to be exactly right.
> *Both* the administration *and* the student body are pleased with the new plan.
> He was worried *not* about his money *but* about his reputation.
> She *not only* plays well *but also* sings well.
> *Not only* does she play well, *but* she *also* sings well.
> He was worried *not only* about his money *but* about his reputation *as well*.

In the last example, note that *as well* substitutes for *also*. In the next-to-last example, note how *does* alters the strict parallel; and in both the last two examples, note how *also* or its equivalent can be moved away from the *but*. Except for these variations, make what follows one term exactly parallel to what follows the other: *by accident/by design*, *the first/the second*, *plays well/sings well*; that is, write "either *on the bed* or *on the chair*" or "on either *the bed* or *the chair*," but not "either *on the bed* or *the chair*." (See #27, on faulty parallelism.)

Further, with the *not only . . . but also* pair, you should usually make the *also* (or some equivalent) explicit. Its omission results in a feeling of incompleteness:

> *incomplete:* He was *not only* tired, *but* hungry.
> *complete:* He was *not only* tired, *but also* hungry.
> *complete:* He was *not only* tired, *but* hungry *as well*.

If the second part doesn't *add to* or *complete* the first part but merely *intensifies* it, don't include *also*:

> The day was not only hot, but downright stifling.

See #7c for *agreement* of verbs with subjects joined by some of the correlatives.

12c   Subordinating Conjunctions

A **subordinating** conjunction introduces a *subordinate* (or *dependent*) clause and links it to the *independent* (or *main* or *principal*) clause to which it is grammatically related:

> She writes *because* she has something to say.

The subordinating conjunction *because* introduces the adverbial clause *because she has something to say* and links it to the independent clause whose verb it modifies. The *because*-clause is *subordinate* because it cannot stand by itself: by itself it would be a *fragment* (see #1y). Note that a subordinate clause can also come first:

Because she has something to say, she writes articles for magazines.

Even though *Because* does not occur between the two unequal clauses, it still links them grammatically.

That Dilip will win the prize is a foregone conclusion.

Here *That* introduces the *noun* clause *That Dilip will win the prize*, which functions as the subject of the sentence. Note that whereas a coordinating conjunction is like a spot of glue between two things and not a part of either, a subordinating conjunction is an integral part of its clause. In the following sentence, for example, the subordinating conjunction *whenever* is a part of the adverbial clause that modifies the imperative verb *Leave*:

Leave *whenever you feel tired.*

Here is a list of the principal subordinating conjunctions:

after	however	than	when
although	if	that	whenever
as	if only	though	where
as though	in case	till	whereas
because	lest	unless	wherever
before	once	until	whether
even though	rather than	what	while
ever since	since	whatever	why

There are also many terms consisting of two or more words ending in *as*, *if*, and *that* which serve as subordinating conjunctions, including *inasmuch as, insofar as, as long as, as soon as, as far as, as if, even if, only if, but that, except that, now that, in that, provided that, in order that.*

Some subordinating conjunctions can also function as adverbs, prepositions, and relative pronouns. But don't worry about parts of speech. It is easier simply to think of all these terms as *subordinators—* including the relative pronouns and relative adverbs (*who, which, that, when, where*) that introduce adjective clauses. (Strictly speaking, subordinating conjunctions can introduce only adverbial and noun clauses.) If you understand their *subordinating* function, you will understand the syntax of complex and compound-complex sentences (see #1z) and, most important, will be able to avoid *fragments* (see #1y).

Exercise 12c(1) Recognizing subordinate clauses

Identify the subordinate clauses in the following passage and indicate how each is functioning: as adjective, adverb, or noun. (Remember that sometimes relative pronouns are omitted; see #3d and #37a.) What words do the adjectival and adverbial clauses modify? How does each noun clause function? (You might begin by identifying the *independent* clauses; you might also want to mark the subject and verb of each clause, of whichever kind.)

Once upon a time, when he was only seven, Jean-Paul decided that he wanted to be a musician. He especially liked drums, the toy ones his parents had foolishly bought for him to play with. As he grew older, he discovered that there were other kinds of percussion instruments—the piano, for example, and the xylophone. But whenever he asked for a piano, or a xylophone, his parents, who were not well off, had to say no. That he kept on playing with drums, therefore, is not surprising. Eventually he even bought some drums for himself, out of the money he earned delivering papers. When the noise he made became too much, his father set aside a room in the cellar for him to practise in. Then Jean-Paul was happy. And only a few years later (though the time passed rapidly for all of them), Jean-Paul became a regular member of a band that played in local clubs. But his parents, who still thought the noise was awful, never went to hear him. But Jean-Paul was one of those who struck it lucky. And when he suddenly (it was all quite different from what they'd expected) blossomed as a video star—one who had his own band—they didn't know whether they should celebrate or disown him. But since he made lots of money, he felt so generous that he paid off their mortgage and even let them invite him home for holidays. They hope that someday soon he'll even get married, and perhaps settle near them, with his drums and his wife; if he does, then maybe they'll all be able to live more or less happily ever after.

Exercise 12c(2)   Writing subordinate clauses

Combine each of the following pairs of simple sentences into a single complex sentence by subordinating one clause and attaching it to the other with one of the subordinators listed above. You may want to change, delete, or add some words, or reverse the clauses, or otherwise rearrange words. Experiment with different subordinators.

Example: The computer revolution has affected many business and professional people. Its largest impact may prove to have been on the young.
(Though, Although) the computer revolution has affected many business and professional people, its . . . .
The computer revolution has affected many business and professional people, (though, even though) its . . . .

1. The art gallery won't open until next week. The leak in the roof hasn't been repaired yet.
2. I will finish my exams next week. Then I am going to look for a summer job.
3. See that old house on the corner? I used to live there.

4. Canada's gun laws are stricter than those in the United States. We should be thankful for this.
5. Some of the workers have a legitimate grievance. They will probably vote in favour of a strike.
6. Some students may not have paid all their fees. They would not yet be considered officially registered.
7. The Prairies are very dry this year. They haven't been this dry for several years.
8. First you should master the simple sentence. Then you can work on complex sentences.
9. Barking dogs surrounded our mailman. They didn't bite him.
10. The election campaign drew nearer its end. The number of undecided voters decreased.

13 Interjections

An **interjection** is a word or group of words *interjected* or "thrown into" a sentence in order to express emotion. Strictly speaking, interjections have no grammatical function; they are simply thrust into sentences and play no part in their syntax, though sometimes they act like a sentence modifier:

> But—*good heavens!*—what did you expect?
> *Oh*, what fun!
> *Well*, aren't you the sly one!
> *My goodness*, it's been a long day.
> It was, *well*, a bit of a disappointment.

Mild interjections are usually set off with commas. Strong interjections are sometimes set off with dashes and are often accompanied by exclamation points (see #39b and #42c). An interjection may also be a minor sentence by itself (see #1x):

> *Ouch!* That hurt!
> *Well*. So much for the preliminaries. Now comes the hard part.

Review Exercises, Chapter II — Recognizing and using parts of speech

a. Recognizing parts of speech

To test yourself, see if you can identify the part of speech of each word in the following sentences. Can you say how each is functioning grammatically? What kinds of sentences are they?

1. The skyline of modern Toronto provides a striking example of what modern architecture can do.
2. Students with carefully planned programs can begin a new academic year relatively confident that they know what they're doing.
3. Waiter, there's a fly in my soup!
4. Well, to tell the truth, I just did not have the necessary patience.
5. Why should anyone be unhappy about paying a fair tax?
6. Neither the captain nor the crew could be blamed for the terribly costly accident.
7. Forestry is one of the principal industries of British Columbia.
8. The terminally ill are now getting increasingly considerate attention in our hospitals.
9. The elevator business has been said to have its ups and downs.
10. Pamela, please put back the chocolate cake.
11. The minister should pressure the committee to release its data.
12. While abroad I learned to make do with only a backpack.
13. In a few seconds, the computer told us much more than we needed to know.
14. The game was, unfortunately, little more than a brawl, a knock-down-drag-out fight, almost from beginning to end.
15. Help!

b. Using different parts of speech

For fun, write some sentences using the following words as different parts of speech—as many different ones as you can. Each is good for at least two.

shed	plant	still	wrong	round	cross
best	before	train	last	set	near
left	study	cover	fine	rose	down

Writing Effective Sentences:
Basic Elements and Modifiers;
Length, Variety, and Emphasis;
Analyzing Sentences;
Common Errors and Weaknesses

Chapter III deals with the way the various elements work together in sentences. It is designed to enable you to understand how even complicated sentences work, how to control some of that working, and how to avoid common errors. If you have difficulty understanding any of the terms and concepts discussed in this chapter, you may need to review some parts of the first two chapters.

14-15 Basic Sentence Elements and Their Modifiers

14 Subject, Verb, Object, Complement

Consider again the bare bones of a sentence. The two essential elements are a *subject* and a *verb* (see #1a).

14a Subject

The **subject** is what is talked about. More precisely, it is (a) the source of the action indicated by the verb, or (b) the person or thing experiencing or possessing the state of being or the condition indicated by the verb and its complement:

> *Rosa* watched the performance. (*Rosa* is the source of the action of watching.)
> *We* are happy about the outcome. (*We* indicates those experiencing the state of being happy.)
> *Bernice* is a physician. (*Bernice* is the person in the state or condition of being a physician.)
> *Education* is important. (*Education* is what possesses the condition of being important.)

The subject of a sentence will ordinarily be one of the following: a basic noun (see #2), a pronoun (see #3), a gerund or gerund phrase (see #10f), an infinitive or infinitive phrase (see #10a), or a noun clause (see #1o):

> The *cow* chewed slowly. (noun)
> *He* likes to discuss politics. (pronoun)
> *Swimming* is an excellent exercise. (gerund)
> *Throwing frisbees* used to be popular. (gerund phrase)
> It was necessary *to leave*. (infinitive)
> *To study a text closely* is the only way to appreciate it fully. (infinitive phrase)
> *That the firm is solvent* is obvious from these records. (noun clause)

Rarely, a prepositional phrase serves as subject; see #11a.

14b   Finite Verb

The **finite verb** is the focal point of the sentence. It indicates the nature and time of the action (see #6-6p):

> The instructor *will explain* the examination. (action: explaining; time: the future)
> We *rested* halfway up the mountain. (action: resting; time: the past)
> Mr. Wong *has* an M.B.A. (action: having, possessing; time: the present)
> Bernice *is* a neurologist. (action: being something, possessing a condition; time: the present)

14c   Direct Object

If a verb is *transitive* (see #6a), it will have a **direct object** to complete the pattern (see #1d). Like the subject, the direct object may be a noun, a pronoun, a gerund or gerund phrase, an infinitive or infinitive phrase, or a noun clause:

> He will explain the *examination*. (noun)
> The dog accepted *him* as master. (pronoun)
> She enjoys *hiking*. (gerund)
> He enjoys *playing golf*. (gerund phrase)
> They decided *to attend*. (infinitive)
> They want *to learn French*. (infinitive phrase)
> The supervisor knew *that Marie was a good worker*. (noun clause)

Along with a direct object, there may also be an indirect object or an objective complement; see #1f, #1i, and #1j.

14d   Subjective Complement

Similarly, after a *linking verb* (see #6a), a **subjective complement** is necessary to complete the pattern. This complement will usually be either a *predicate noun* or a *predicate adjective* (see #1g and #1h). A predicate noun may be a noun or a pronoun, or (especially after *be*) a gerund or gerund phrase, an infinitive or infinitive phrase, or a noun clause:

> She is a *doctor*. (noun)
> Is this the *one*? (pronoun)
> Her favourite pastime is *skiing*. (gerund)
> The next task is *bathing the dog*. (gerund phrase)
> My first thought was *to run*. (infinitive)
> His ambition was *to drive a fire engine*. (infinitive phrase)
> He remained *what he had always been*: a cad. (noun clause)

A predicate adjective will ordinarily be a descriptive adjective, a participle, or an idiomatic prepositional phrase:

> She became *impatient*. (descriptive adjective)
> The regulations are *annoying*. (present participle)
> She looked *distracted*. (past participle)
> The phone is *out of order*. (prepositional phrase)

The linking verb *be* (and sometimes others) can also be followed by an adverb (I am *here*; he is *in his office*).

These elements—**subject, finite verb**, and **object** or **complement**—are the bare bones of major sentences. They are closely linked in the ways indicated above, with the verb as the focal and uniting element. (For a discussion of the *order* in which these elements occur, see #1s-u.)

15 Modifiers

Other grammatical elements put flesh on the bones. Such elements are called **modifiers**: they limit or describe other elements so as to modify—that is, change—a listener's or reader's idea of them. The two principal kinds of modifiers are *adjectives* (see #8) and *adverbs* (see #9). Also useful, but less frequent, are *appositives* (see #1q) and *absolute phrases* (see #1r and #10i). An adjectival or adverbial modifier, of course, may even be part of the bare bones of a sentence if it completes the predicate after a linking verb (Education is *important*; Peter is *home*). An adverb may also be essential if it modifies an intransitive verb that would otherwise seem incomplete (Peter lives *in an apartment*). But generally modifiers do their work by adding to, enriching, a central core of thought.

15a Adjectival Modifiers (see #8-8b, #8e-f)

Adjectival modifiers modify nouns, pronouns, and phrases or clauses functioning as nouns. They commonly answer the questions *Which? What kind of? How many? How much?* An adjectival modifier may be a single-word adjective, a series, a participle or participial phrase, an infinitive or infinitive phrase, a prepositional phrase, or a relative clause:

Serious athletes keep *their* bodies in *good* condition. (single words modifying nouns immediately following)

They are usually *healthy*. (predicate adjective modifying pronoun *They*)

What you're asking me to do is *ridiculous*. (predicate adjective modifying noun clause *What you're asking me to do*)

Three muscular young men showed up. (series modifying *men*)

Stan jogs around the *football* field. (noun functioning as adjective, modifying *field*)

Sweating, he runs around and around. (present participle modifying *he*)

The team pressed on, *undaunted*. (past participle modifying *team*)

Finally convincing himself, he went on a diet. (present participial phrase modifying *he*)

Geraldine could relax, *having been thoroughly checked by a doctor*. (participial phrase, perfect tense, modifying *Geraldine*)

Tuesday was a day *to remember*. (infinitive modifying *day*)

His ability *to pass up dessert* impressed us. (infinitive phrase modifying *ability*)

The books *on the shelves* are mine. (prepositional phrase modifying *books*)

The salesman, *who by now had his foot in the door*, wouldn't let me interrupt. (relative clause modifying *salesman*)

15b Adverbial Modifiers (see #9-9d)

Adverbial modifiers modify verbs, adjectives, other adverbs, and whole clauses or sentences. They commonly answer the questions *How? When? Where? To what degree?* An adverbial modifier may be a single word, a series, an infinitive or infinitive phrase, a prepositional phrase, or an adverbial clause:

She drove *slowly*. (single word modifying verb *drove*)

The fog was *exceedingly* thick. (modifying adjective *thick*)

She drove *very* slowly. (modifying adverb *slowly*)

She *soon* moved. (modifying verb *moved*)

Obviously, he's not sticking to his diet. (modifying the rest of the sentence)

Slowly, carefully, even tediously, he described his experience. (series modifying verb *described*)

To relax, she listens to music. (infinitive modifying verb *listens*)

He was lucky *to have survived the fall*. (infinitive phrase modifying predicate adjective *lucky*)

They arrived *before noon*. (prepositional phrase modifying verb *arrived*)

He joined *because he believed in their principles*. (clause modifying verb *joined*)

She drove slowly *because the fog was exceedingly thick*. (clause modifying adverb *slowly*, or the whole preceding clause, *She drove slowly*)

Turn out the light *when you're finished*. (clause modifying preceding independent clause)

15c Overlapping Modifiers

The preceding examples are meant to illustrate each kind of adjectival and adverbial modifier separately, in tidy isolation from the other kinds.

And of course such sentences are not uncommon, for relative simplicity of sentence structure can be a stylistic strength. But many sentences are more complicated, largely because modifiers overlap a great deal. Modifiers occur as parts of other modifiers: single-word modifiers occur as parts of phrases and clauses, phrases occur as parts of other phrases and as parts of clauses, and subordinate clauses occur as parts of phrases and as parts of other clauses. Here are examples illustrating some of the possible structural variety (you may want to check sections #1c-k in order to match these sentences and their clauses with the various patterns they include):

> They gazed languidly at the setting sun.

languidly—adverb modifying *gazed*
at the setting sun—adverbial prepositional phrase modifying *gazed*
setting—participial adjective modifying *sun*

> Most of his off-the-cuff remarks fell flat.

of his off-the-cuff remarks—adjectival prepositional phrase modifying *Most*
off-the-cuff—hyphenated prepositional phrase, adjective modifying *remarks*

> Desiring to learn to speak French well, they spent a year in Paris.

Desiring to learn to speak French well—participial phrase modifying *they*
to learn to speak French well—infinitive phrase, object of the participle
    Desiring
to speak French well—infinitive phrase, object of the infinitive *to learn*
well—adverb modifying infinitive *to speak*
in Paris—adverbial prepositional phrase modifying *spent*

> It was daunting to think of the consequences that might ensue.

to think of the consequences that might ensue—infinitive phrase, delayed sub-
    ject of sentence
of the consequences—adverbial prepositional phrase modifying infinitive *to*
    think
that might ensue—relative clause modifying *consequences*
daunting—participle, predicate adjective modifying *subject*

> They cherished the thought, a recurring one for them, that they might
> someday be out of debt.

a recurring one for them—appositive phrase further defining *thought*
recurring—participle modifying *one*
for them—adverbial prepositional phrase modifying *recurring*
that they might someday be out of debt—relative clause modifying *thought*
out of debt—prepositional phrase, predicate adjective after linking verb *might*
    be
someday—adverb modifying *might be*

With the bonus money, he bought what he had dreamed about for years: a computer to play with.

With the bonus money—adverbial prepositional phrase modifying *bought*
bonus—adjective modifying *money*
what he had dreamed about for years—noun clause, direct object of *bought*
about [what]—adverbial prepositional phrase modifying *dreamed*
for years—adverbial prepositional phrase modifying *dreamed*
a computer to play with—appositive phrase modifying the noun clause
to play with—adjectival infinitive phrase modifying *computer*

Because she wanted to become better educated, she enrolled in night school.

Because she wanted to become better educated—adverbial clause modifying the
    independent clause *she enrolled in night school* (or just the verb *enrolled*)
to become better educated—infinitive phrase, direct object of *wanted*
better—adverb modifying *educated*, the predicate adjective after *become*
in night school—adverbial prepositional phrase modifying *enrolled*
night—noun functioning as adjective to modify *school*

He was a man who, being well versed in the finer things of life, knew bad music when he heard it.

who...knew bad music when he heard it—relative clause modifying predicate
    noun *man*
when he heard it—adverbial clause modifying *knew*
being well versed in the finer things of life—participial phrase modifying rela-
    tive pronoun *who*
versed—past participle, predicate adjective after *being*
well—adverb modifying *versed*
in the finer things of life—adverbial prepositional phrase modifying *versed*
of life—adjectival prepositional phrase modifying *things*

The book being one of the kind that puts you to sleep, she laid it aside and dozed off.

The book being one of the kind that puts you to sleep—absolute phrase
of the kind that puts you to sleep—adjectival prepositional phrase modifying
    one
that puts you to sleep—relative clause modifying *kind*
to sleep—adverbial prepositional phrase modifying *puts*

He is the person who knows what must be done when a computer virus strikes.

who knows what must be done when a computer virus strikes—relative clause
    modifying *person*
what must be done when a computer virus strikes—noun clause, direct object
    of *knows*
when a computer virus strikes—adverbial clause modifying verb *must be done*

These examples suggest the kind of richness that is possible, the kind you undoubtedly create at times without even thinking about it. But think about it. Try concocting sentences with these sorts of syntactical complications.

You may be surprised at the kinds of sentences you can turn out when you set your mind to it. You may also discover that working with sentences in this way will help generate material for developing your paragraphs and essays.

15d   Using Modifiers: A Sample Scenario

Suppose you were assigned an essay on the kinds of recreational reading you do. In getting your ideas together and taking notes, you might draft a bare-bones sentence such as this:

> I like novels.

It's a start. But you soon realize that it isn't exactly true to your thoughts. It needs qualification. So you begin modifying its elements:

> I like *modern* novels.

The adjective limits the meaning of *novels*—you're not so fond of older novels. Then you remember that you haven't much liked some recent novels about rich people or heroes and heroines of high romance and adventure, so you add an adjectival prepositional phrase to further limit the word *novels*:

> I like modern novels *about everyday people.*

Then you remember a couple of novels that were both modern and about ordinary people but that were pretty bad; therefore you insert yet another adjective to further qualify, or rather quantify, the noun *novels*:

> I like *most* modern novels about everyday people.

Then you have an attack of logic and realize that *most* implies that you are familiar with *all* such modern novels. But you quickly see a way to revise the sentence so as to convey your thoughts accurately; you take out *most* and put the adverb *usually* in front of the verb:

> I *usually* like modern novels about everyday people.

So far so good. But the sentence somehow doesn't impress you; you suspect that a reader might want a little more information about these "everyday people." Of course you could go on to explain in another sentence or two, but you'd like to get a little more meat into this sentence. Then you have a flash of inspiration: you can help clarify your point and at the same time inject some rhythm and parallelism by adding a participial phrase modifying *people*:

> I usually like modern novels about everyday people *facing everyday problems.*

You rather like it. But working at this one sentence has got your brain going, so before you leave it you think about your reasons for liking such novels. You decide that you like them because they're about people like yourself, and because their problems aren't so much those caused by outside pressures as they are home-grown problems, problems like your own. You feel the words beginning to come, and you consider your options: you can put the explanation in a separate sentence; you can join it to your present sentence with a semicolon or a colon or a coordinating conjunction like *for*, creating a compound sentence; or you can integrate it more closely by making it a subordinate clause, turning the whole into a complex sentence. You decide on the third method, and put the new material in a *because*-clause modifying the verb *like*. And while you're thinking about it, you begin to feel that, given the way your sentence has developed, the word *like* now sounds rather pallid, weak because relatively common; you decide to change it to the more vigorous verb *enjoy*. Now your sentence is finished, at least for the time being:

> I usually enjoy modern novels about everyday people having everyday problems, because I can identify with the characters and share their troubles—and their triumphs.

By adding modifiers, a writer can enlarge the reader's knowledge of the material being presented and impart precision and clarity to a sentence, as well as improve its style. Minimal or bare-bones sentences can themselves be effective and emphatic; use them when they are appropriate. But most of your sentences will be longer. And it is in elaborating and enriching your sentences with modifiers that you as author and stylist exercise much of your control: you take charge of what your readers will learn and how they will learn it.

Exercise 15 Using modifiers

Choose ten of these bare-bones sentences and flesh them out with various kinds of modifiers. Compose several expanded sentences for each. Use some single-word modifiers, but try to work mainly with phrases and clauses, including some noun clauses. Identify each modifier. Keep the sentences simple or complex, not compound or compound-complex (see #1z). (If you don't like our core sentences, make up some of your own.)

The campus was deserted.	Athletes train.
Canadians puzzle Americans.	I enjoy my hobby.
Movies glorify violence.	The meal was superb.
Little things irritate me.	I visited _____.
The child sat still.	I ski.
Save the rain forest.	Money talks.
I read a magazine article.	The roses bloomed.
Advertising insults the audience.	The war ended.

It's not surprising.	The music faltered.
Time is passing.	Manners matter.
Spring is coming.	Stop.

16-18 Length, Variety, and Emphasis

16 Sentence Length

How long should a sentence be? Long enough. A sentence may consist of one word or it may go on for a hundred words or more. There are no arbitrary criteria. If you're curious, do some research to determine the average sentence length in several published works you have handy—for example this book, other texts, a recent novel, a collection of essays, newspapers, magazines. You'll probably find that the average is somewhere between 15 and 25 words per sentence, that longer sentences are more common in formal and specialized writing, and that shorter sentences are more at home in informal and popular writing and in narrative and dialogue. There are, then, some general guidelines, and you'll probably fit your own writing to them automatically. But check your own writing; if you're far off what seems to be the appropriate average, you can do something about it.

16a Short Sentences

If you find that you're writing an excessive number of short sentences, try

1. building them up, elaborating their elements with modifiers, including various kinds of phrases and clauses;
2. combining some of them to form compound subjects, predicates, and objects or complements;
3. combining two or more of them—especially if they are simple sentences—into one or another kind of complex sentence. (Since *compound* sentences are made up of simple sentences joined by punctuation and coordinating conjunctions, they often read like a series of shorter, simple sentences.)

16b Long Sentences

If you find yourself writing too many long sentences, check them for two possible dangers:

1. You may be rambling or trying to pack too much into a single sentence, possibly destroying its unity (see #28) but certainly making it unnecessarily difficult to read. Try breaking it up into more unified or more easily manageable chunks.

17

2. You may simply be using too many words to make your point. Try cutting out any deadwood (see #59).

In either of these kinds of unwieldy sentence, check that you haven't slipped into what is called "excessive subordination"—too many loosely related details obscuring the main idea, or confusing strings of subordinate clauses modifying each other. Try removing some of the clutter, and try reducing clauses to phrases and phrases to single words (see Exercises 10.3, 10.4, and 11a-c.2).

17 Sentence Variety

Both for emphasis (see #18) and for ease of reading—that is, to avoid monotony—vary both the lengths and kinds of your sentences. Examine closely some pieces of prose that you particularly enjoy or that you find unusually clear and easy to read: you will likely discover that they contain both a pleasing mixture of short, medium, and long sentences and a similar variety of kinds and structures.

17a Variety of Lengths

A string of short sentences will sound choppy and fragmented; avoid the staccato effect by interweaving some longer ones. A succession of long sentences may make your ideas hard to follow; give your readers a break—and your prose some sparkle—by inserting a few short, emphatic sentences here and there. Even a string of medium-length sentences can bore readers into inattention. Impart some rhythm, some shape, to your paragraphs by varying sentence length. Especially consider using a short, snappy sentence to open or close a paragraph, and perhaps an unusually long sentence to end a paragraph. They can be effective.

17b Variety of Kinds

A string of simple and compound sentences risks coming across as simple-minded. In a narrative, successive simple and compound sentences may be appropriate for recounting a sequence of events, but when you're writing reasoned prose, let some of the complexity of your ideas be reflected in complex and compound-complex sentences. On the other hand, a string of complex and compound-complex sentences may become oppressive, just as a long string of monumental floats in a parade soon becomes tiresome unless relieved by an occasional clown or tumbler. Give your readers a breather now and then.

17c   Variety of Structures

Try to avoid an unduly long string of sentences that use the same syntactical structure. For example, though the standard order of elements in declarative sentences is subject-verb-object or -complement, consider the possibility of varying that order occasionally for the purpose of emphasis (see #1s and #18). Perhaps use an occasional interrogative sentence (see #1t), whether a rhetorical question (a question that doesn't expect an answer) or a question that you proceed to answer as you develop a paragraph. Even an occasional expletive pattern or passive voice can be refreshing—if you can justify it on other grounds as well (see #1e, #1k, #6p, and #18f); that is, introducing such variety for variety alone can be dangerous.

Especially, don't *begin* a string of sentences with the same kind of word or phrase or clause—unless you are purposely setting up a controlled succession of parallel structures for emphasis or coherence (see #65a). Imagine the effect of several sentences beginning with such words as *Similarly* . . . . *Especially* . . . . *Consequently* . . . . *Nevertheless* . . . . Whatever else the sentences contained, the monotony would be stultifying. Or imagine a series of sentences all starting with a subject-noun, or with a present-participial phrase. To avoid such undesirable sameness, take advantage of the way modifiers of various kinds can be moved around in sentences (see #1q, #1r, #8d, #9d, #11b, and #18e).

18   Emphasis in Sentences

emph   To communicate clearly and effectively, make sure your readers perceive the relative importance of your ideas the same way you do. Learn to control emphasis so that what you want emphasized is what gets emphasized.

You can emphasize whole sentences in several ways:

1. Set a sentence off by itself, as a short paragraph.
2. Put an important sentence at the beginning of a paragraph or, even better, at the end.
3. Put an important point in a short sentence among several long ones, or in a long sentence among several short ones.
4. Shift the style or structure of a sentence to make it stand out from those around it (see #66).

In similar ways you can emphasize appropriate parts of individual sentences. The principal devices for achieving emphasis *within* sentences are position and word order, repetition, stylistic contrast, syntax, and punctuation.

18a   Endings and Beginnings

The most emphatic position in a sentence is its ending; the second most emphatic position is its beginning. Consider these two sentences:

> The flood killed seven people.
> Seven people died in the flood.

Each sentence emphasizes both the *flood* and the *seven people*, but the first emphasizes the *seven people* a little more, whereas the second emphasizes the *flood* a little more. Further, the longer the sentence, the stronger the effect of emphasis by position. Consider the following:

1. The best teacher I've ever had was my high-school history teacher, a lively woman in her early sixties.
2. A lively woman in her early sixties, my high-school history teacher was the best teacher I've ever had.
3. My high-school history teacher, a lively woman in her early sixties, was the best teacher I've ever had.
4. The best teacher I've ever had was a lively woman in her early sixties who taught me history in high school.

Each sentence contains the same three ideas, but each distributes the emphasis differently. In each the last part is the most emphatic, the first part next, and the middle part least. Think of them as topic sentences (see #64a):

> Number 1 could introduce a paragraph focussing on the quality of the teacher but emphasizing her character, her age, and the fact that she was a woman.
> Number 2 could introduce a paragraph focussing more on the quality of her teaching.
> Number 3 could open a paragraph stressing the quality of the teaching and the nature and level of the subject; details of age, gender, and character would be incidental.
> Number 4 may seem the flattest, the least emphatic and least likely of the four, but it could effectively introduce a mainly narrative paragraph focussing on the writer's good experience in the class.

Note that in all four versions the part referring to "the best teacher I've ever had" comes either first or last, since the superlative *best* would sound unnatural in the unemphatic middle position—unless one acknowledged its inherent emphasis in some other way, for example by setting off the appositive with a pair of dashes (see #39b):

> My high-school history teacher—the best teacher I've ever had—was a lively woman in her early sixties.

18b Loose Sentences and Periodic Sentences

Loose is not a pejorative term here. A *loose* or *cumulative* sentence makes its main point in an early independent clause and then adds modifying subordinate elements:

> The day began ominously, with the sun trying in vain to peek between the horizon and the dark clouds that had built up during the night, and the wind leaning heavily on our tent.

Such sentences are common, for they are "loose" and comfortable, easygoing, natural. (Such sentences are also called "right-branching.") At the other extreme is the *periodic* (or "left-branching") sentence, which wholly or partly delays its main point, the independent clause, until the end:

> With the wind leaning heavily on our tent and the sun vainly trying to peek between the horizon and the night's build-up of dark clouds, the day was off to an ominous start.

Full periodic sentences are almost always the result of careful thought and planning; they sound contrived, less natural, and therefore should not be used often. But they can be dramatic and emphatic, creating suspense as the reader waits for the meaning to fall into place. But if you try for such suspense, don't separate subject and predicate too widely, as a student did in this awkward sentence:

> *awk:* The abrupt change from one moment when the air is alive with laughing and shouting, to the next when the atmosphere resembles that of a morgue, is dramatic.

Many sentences, of course, delay completion of the main clause only until somewhere in the middle rather than all the way to the end. To the degree that they do delay it, they are partly periodic, like this one.

18c The Importance of the Final Position

Because the end of a sentence is naturally so emphatic, readers expect something important there; don't disappoint them by letting something incidental or merely qualifying fall at the end, for then the sentence itself will fall: its energy will be dissipated and wasted, its essential meaning distorted. For example:

> *emph:* That was the fastest I've ever driven a car, I think.

The uncertain *I think* should go at the beginning or, even less emphatically, after *That* or *was.*

> *emph:* Cramming for exams can be counterproductive, sometimes.

The qualifying *sometimes* could go at the beginning, but it would be best after *can*, letting the emphasis fall where it belongs, on *cramming* and *counterproductive*.

18d Changing Word Order

Earlier sections point out certain standard patterns: subject-verb-object or -complement (#1c-j); single-word adjectives preceding nouns—or, if predicate adjectives, following them (#8d). But variations are possible, and because these patterns are recognized as standard, any departures from them stand out (see #1s and #8d for examples). But be careful, for if the inverted order calls attention to itself at the expense of meaning, the attempt may backfire. In the following sentence, for example, the writer strained a little too hard for emphasis. Can you achieve it in some less risky way?

> It is from imagination that have come all the world's great literature, music, architecture, and works of art.

18e Movable Modifiers

Many modifiers other than single-word adjectives are movable, enabling you to shift them or other words to where you want them. Appositives can sometimes be transposed (see #1q). You can move participial phrases, if you do so carefully (see #8d). Absolute phrases (see #1r), since they function as sentence modifiers, can usually come at the beginning or the end—or, if syntax permits, in the middle.

But adverbial modifiers are the most movable of all (see #9d). As you compose, and especially as you revise your drafts, consider the possible placements of any adverbial modifiers you've used. Take advantage of their flexibility in order to exercise maximum control over the rhythms of your sentences and, most important, to get the emphases that will best serve your purposes. Some examples:

> We inched our way *slowly and painfully* along the narrow tunnel.

Would the adverbs be more emphatic at the end? Try it:

> We inched our way along the narrow tunnel *slowly and painfully*.

A little better, perhaps. Now try them at the beginning, and instead of *and*, use punctuation to emphasize the slowness:

> *Slowly, painfully,* we inched our way along the narrow tunnel.

Another example, from a student's draft:

> *draft:* When I entered university I naturally expected it to be different from high school, but I wasn't prepared for the impact it would have on the way I lived my day-to-day life.

Clear enough. But the writer decided to try separating the independent clauses and using a conjunctive adverb to get a little more of the emphasis he felt he needed:

> *revised:* When I entered university I naturally expected it to be different from high school. However, I wasn't prepared for the impact it would have on the way I lived my day-to-day life.

But that sounded too stiff (as *However* often does at the beginning of a sentence). After some further fiddling with the adverbs, he came up with this:

> *revised:* When I entered university I expected it to be different from high school—naturally. I was not, however, prepared for the impact it would have on the way I lived my day-to-day life.

Setting *naturally* off with a dash at the end of the first sentence added a touch of self-mockery. And moving *however* a few words into the second sentence not only got rid of the stiffness but also, because of the pause forced by its commas, added a useful emphasis to *not*, now spelled out in full. (For more on *however*, see #33h.)

Caution: When shifting modifiers about, be careful to avoid creating awkwardly misplaced or dangling modifiers. See #23 and #24.

18f   Using the Expletive and the Passive Voice for Emphasis

Two of the basic sentence patterns, the *expletive* (#1k) and the *passive voice* (#1e, #6p), are in themselves often weak and unemphatic; keep them to a minimum and your writing will be clearer and more vigorous. Sometimes, however, they will enable you to achieve a desired emphasis. For example:

> Passive voice can be used to get a certain word or phrase to an emphatic place in a sentence.

Here putting the verb in the passive voice (*can be used*) enables the important phrase *Passive voice* to come at the beginning; otherwise the sentence would have to begin less strongly (for example with *You can use passive voice*). Use expletives and passive voice when you need to in order to delete or delay or otherwise shift the subject of a sentence. Nevertheless, avoid these patterns when possible. Use them only when you have good reason to.

18g emph

18g Emphasis by Repetition

You may wish to repeat an important word or idea in order to emphasize it, to make it stick in your readers' minds. Careless, unintentional repetition can be wordy and tedious (see #59b); but intentional, controlled repetition—used sparingly—can be highly effective, especially in sentences with balanced or parallel structures:

> I especially admired her hands, her long, elegant, piano-playing hands.
> If you want to understand another country you should travel to that country.
> If you have the strength to face the facts, the facts can sometimes give you strength.
> If it's a fight they want, it's a fight they'll get.
> She liked to read sentimental romances, and she tried to turn her own life into a sentimental romance.
> Many North American homes are littered with antiques: antique books, antique silver, antique weapons, antique furniture, and antique junk.

18h Emphasis by Stylistic Contrast

A stylistically heightened sentence—for example a periodic sentence (#18b), a sentence with parallel or balanced structure (#27, #18g), or a richly metaphorical or allusive sentence (#53)—stands out beside plainer sentences. For that reason, such a sentence often appears at the end of a paragraph (see #64c). In the same way, though usually less strikingly, a word or phrase may stand out from its surroundings (and note that such terms often gravitate toward that position of natural emphasis, the end of the sentence):

> She attempted to convince me in the most eloquent terms that I should scram.
> The unprecedented increase in violent crime has rendered everyday existence for many law-abiding citizens a scary process.
> It appears that somewhere in the corridors of power lurks a resident *éminence grise*.

Terms from other languages naturally stand out, but don't make the mistake of using them pretentiously, for many readers are unimpressed by them or even resent them; use one only after due thought, and preferably when there is no satisfactory English equivalent. And be careful not to overshoot: too strong a contrast may jar; the first example above works only because of the intentional humour deriving from the shift to slang.

18i Emphasis by Syntax

Put important points in independent clauses; put lesser matter in subordinate clauses and phrases. Sometimes it can go either way, depending on what you want to emphasize:

> Accepting the booby prize, he grinned fatuously.

Grinning fatuously, he accepted the booby prize.

But more often the choice is determined by the content:

> *emph:* I strolled into the biology laboratory, when my attention was attracted by the pitter-pattering of a little white rat in a cage at the back.
>
> *revised:* When I strolled into the biology laboratory, my attention was attracted by the pitter-pattering of a little white rat in a cage at the back.
>
> *emph:* Choosing my courses carefully, I wanted to get a well-rounded education.
>
> *revised:* Because I wanted to get a well-rounded education, I chose my courses carefully.
>
> *emph:* I had almost reached the top of the ladder when I missed my footing and fell.
>
> *revised:* When I had almost reached the top of the ladder, I missed my footing and fell.

Granted, the original version of the last example could be appropriate in a particular context; but unless you have a good reason, don't distort apparently logical emphasis by subordinating main ideas.

See also #28 and #12c.

18j   Emphasis by Punctuation

Obviously an exclamation point (!) denotes emphasis. But using exclamation points is not the only way, and usually not the best way, to achieve emphasis with punctuation. Try to make your sentences appropriately emphatic without resorting to this sometimes lame and artificial device. Arrange your words so that commas and other marks fall where you want a pause for emphasis (see #18e). Use dashes, colons, and even parentheses judiciously to set off important ideas (see #18a). Occasionally use a semicolon instead of a comma in order to get a more emphatic pause (but only in a series or between independent clauses). Study Chapter IV carefully, especially the following sections: 32c, 32d, 33b, 33h, 33i, 35a, 36, 38c, 38d, 38e, 39b, 39c, 42c, 43g, and 44d.

> **Note:** As much as possible, avoid emphasizing words and sentences with such mechanical devices as underlining and capitalization. See #47r and #49d.

Exercise 16-18   Sentence length, variety, and emphasis

Below are five paragraphs from draft versions of student essays. For practice, revise each one to improve the effectiveness of sentence length, variety, and emphasis. Try not to change the basic sense in any important way, but make whatever changes will make the paragraphs effective.

(a) My father drove up to the campsite and chose an empty spot close to the lake, up against the thickly covered mountainside. We had just unpacked our equipment and set up our tent when an elderly man walked up our path. He introduced himself and told us that he was camped farther up the mountain, about a hundred yards away. He told us that only an hour before, as he walked toward his campsite, he saw a huge black bear running away from it. He said he then drew closer and saw that his tent was knocked down and his food scattered all over the ground. He suggested that we might want to move our camp to a safer place, not so close to this bear's haunts.

(b) The sky promised hot and sunny weather as we quickly finished closing side-pockets and adjusting straps on our packs in preparation for our hike up Black Tusk, which is in Garibaldi Park, a hike which was to be on a trail I had never seen before and which I therefore had been looking forward to with great enthusiasm. And that's what I felt as we set off in the early morning light on the first leg of the journey which would take us to the top in a few hours.

(c) The way time passes can be odd. The mind's sense of time can be changed. I remember an experience which will illustrate this. It happened when I was nine. I rode my bike in front of a car and got hit. I don't remember much about this experience. However, a few details do come to mind. These include the way the car's brakes sounded suddenly from my right. I never even saw the car that hit me. And I remember flying through the air. It was a peculiar feeling. The ground seemed to come up slowly as I floated along. Time seemed almost to have stopped. But then I hit the ground. And then time speeded up. A neighbour ran up and asked if I was all right. My parents pulled our car up. They carefully put me in it. And all of a sudden I was at the hospital, it seemed. It all must have taken twenty or thirty minutes. To me it seemed that only a minute or two had passed since I had hit the ground.

(d) It's not so difficult to repot a houseplant, although many plant-owners procrastinate about doing this because they think it's too messy and time-consuming, when actually repotting takes very little time and effort if you follow a simple set of instructions such as I'm about to give you. And you'll find that when you've done the repotting both you and your plant will benefit from the process because the plant will then be able to receive fresh minerals and oxygen from the new soil which will make it grow into a healthier plant that will give you increased pleasure and enjoyment.

(e) We should all do volunteer work in our communities, I believe. I know that there isn't always a lot of extra time available. But we should make some. Instead of sitting down to watch television, we should do something useful. We could spend two hours with a disabled child. We could take a fatherless young boy or girl to a ball-game. We can help even if we can't find time to leave home, probably. We can volunteer our services from inside our homes. For example we can make telephone calls and type letters. Or we can simply stuff envelopes and put stamps on them. There are hundreds of ways we can volunteer our services to the community. Let's share some happiness with someone else. Let's volunteer our services today.

19 Analyzing Sentences

Practise analyzing your own and others' sentences. The better you understand how sentences work, the better able you will be to write effective and correct sentences.

You should be able to account for each word in a sentence; no essential element should be missing, nothing should be left over, and the grammatical relations among all the parts should be clear. If these conditions aren't met, the sentence in question is likely to be incorrect, misleading, or ambiguous. If words, phrases, and clauses fit the roles they are being asked to play, the sentence should work.

The first step in analyzing a sentence is to establish its basic structure: the *subject*, the *finite verb*, and the *object* or *complement*, if any. (If the sentence is other than a simple sentence, there will be more than one set of these essential parts.) Then proceed to the modifiers of these elements, and then to modifiers of modifiers.

19a   The Chart Method

Here is a convenient arrangement for analyzing the structure of relatively uncomplicated sentences:

The angry coach severely punished the wayward goalie.

Subject	Finite Verb	Object or Complement	Adjectival Modifier	Adverbial Modifier
coach	punished	goalie (direct object of verb *punished*)	The (modifies *coach*) angry (mod. *coach*) the (mod. *goalie*) wayward (mod. *goalie*)	severely (mod. verb *punished*: "how?")

This most beautiful summer is now almost gone.

Subject	Finite Verb	Object or Complement	Adjectival Modifier	Adverbial Modifier
summer	is (linking verb)	gone (pred. adj.)	This (dem. adj. mod. *summer*) beautiful (mod. *summer*)	most (mod. *beautiful*: "to what degree?") now (mod. verb is: "when?") almost (mod. *gone*: "to what degree?")

The very befuddled Roger realized that driving a car was not easy.

Subject	Finite Verb	Object or Complement	Adjectival Modifier	Adverbial Modifier	Other
Roger	realized	that . . . easy (noun clause as dir. obj.)	The, befuddled (mod. *Roger*)	very (mod. *befuddled*)	
driving	was (linking verb)	easy (pred. adj.) car (obj. of gerund *driving*)		not (mod. *easy*)	that (sub. conj.)

In the last example, the items below the dotted line belong to the subordinate clause in this complex sentence.

19b The Vertical Method

For more complicated sentences, you may find a different method more convenient, for example one in which the sentence is written out vertically:

When the canoe trip ended, Philip finally realized that the end of his happy summer was almost upon him.

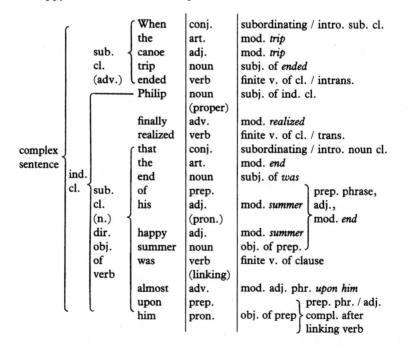

As you can see, this method virtually forces you to account for the grammatical function of every word in the sentence.

19c The Diagramming Method

The old but still serviceable diagramming method has its drawbacks: there is no way to distinguish between adjective and adverb, for example, unless you label each one; and it also requires learning a separate and sometimes complicated system. Nevertheless, it can be useful in revealing the workings of a sentence. Here are sample diagrams of the most common kinds of sentences:

1. Simple Sentences

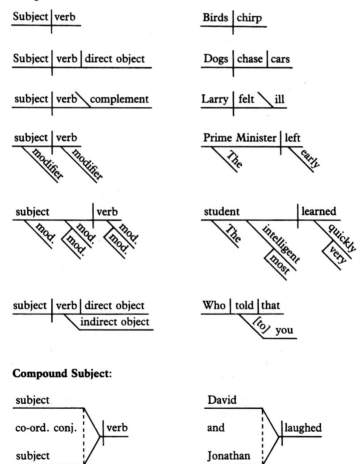

Compound Subject:

Compound Verb:

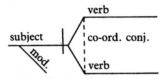

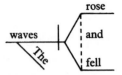

Compound Object:

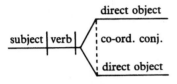

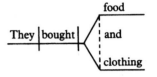

Prepositional Phrases:

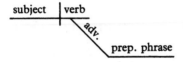

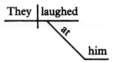

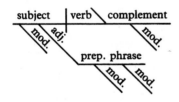

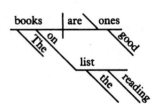

Participial Phrase:

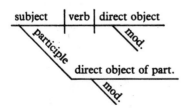

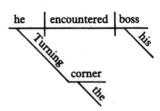

Gerund Phrase as Subject:

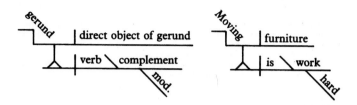

Infinitive Phrase as Noun:

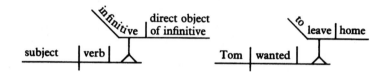

Infinitive Phrase as Adjective:

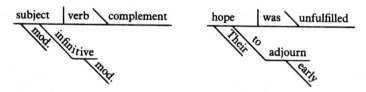

Infinitive Phrase as Adverb:

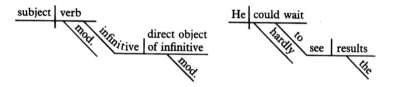

2. Complex Sentences

Noun Clause as Direct Object:

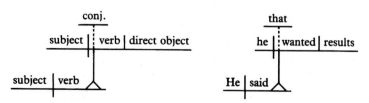

Noun Clause as Object of Preposition:

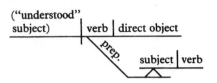

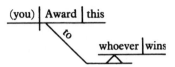

Relative Clause Modifying the Subject:

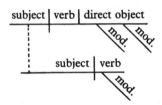

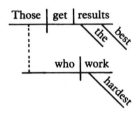

Relative Clause Modifying a Direct Object:

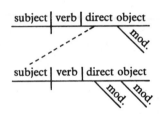

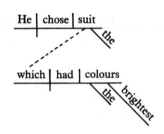

Relative Clause Modifying a Complement:

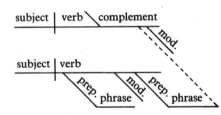

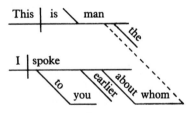

Adverbial Clause:

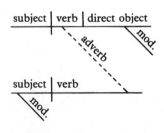

3. Compound Sentences

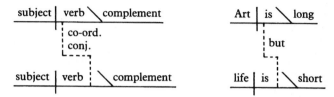

4. Compound-complex sentences are diagrammed following similar patterns.

   Grammatical analysis, by whatever method, is not an end in itself (though some people enjoy it as a kind of game). Its purpose is to give you insight into the accepted structures of the basic unit of communication, the sentence, so that you can construct sound sentences and discover and eliminate errors in your writing. As you become more familiar with such analyses and with the demands of correct sentence structure, you should find the process becoming automatic and the elimination of errors easier.

Exercise 19 **Analyzing sentences**

---

   a. Try analyzing the following sentences by each of the three suggested methods. Doing so should give you a sense of the advantages and disadvantages of each; then you can use or adapt the one you prefer, or use different methods for different kinds of sentences. You may even want to invent your own method.

   1. Police rushed to the scene of the accident.
   2. A chinook is a warm wind blowing eastward off the Rocky Mountains.
   3. Many potentially good films are spoiled by sensationalism.
   4. Both the beaver and the maple leaf are Canadian emblems.
   5. Although she was discouraged, Suki persevered, and after a few more tries she succeeded in clearing the two-metre bar.

   b. Here is a longer, more complicated sentence. For such sentences, the "vertical" method is probably the most convenient. Try it. (You may want to challenge a friend: see which of you can write down the greatest number of grammatical facts about the sentence.)

   Constructed of stone and cedar, the large house that the Smiths built on the brow of Murphy's Bluff—an exposed promontory—was so sturdy that even the icy blasts of the continual north wind in December and January made no impression on it.

20 *frag*

20-31 Common Sentence Errors and Weaknesses

20-22 Fragments, Comma Splices, and Run-on (Fused) Sentences

The three most serious sentence errors are the *fragment*, the *comma splice*, and the *run-on sentence*. Many readers consider the members of this unholy trinity to be signs of illiteracy. Avoid them.

20 Fragments

frag A **fragment** is a group of words that is not an acceptable sentence, either major or minor, but that is punctuated as if it were a sentence (that is, started with a capital letter and ended with a period). The fragment is discussed along with the minor sentence, which it sometimes resembles: see #1x and #1y. See also **frag** in Chapter XI.

21 Comma Splices

cs A **comma splice** is the joining of two independent clauses with only a comma. Although the error stems from a failure to understand sentence structure, we nevertheless discuss it under *punctuation*, since it requires attention to punctuation marks: see #33e-h. See also **cs** in Chapter XI.

22 Run-on (Fused) Sentences

run-on, fs A **run-on** sentence, sometimes called a **fused** sentence, is in fact not a single sentence but *two* sentences run together with neither a period to mark the end of the first nor a capital letter to mark the beginning of the second. So blatant an error that it is usually caused by extreme haste or typographical carelessness, it sometimes, like the comma splice, results from a failure to understand how sentences work. And since a run-on occurs with the same kind of sentence structure as does the comma splice, and like it requires attention to punctuation, we discuss it alongside the other error: see #33j. See also **run-on** in Chapter XI.

23 Misplaced Modifiers

mm

23a Movability and Poor Placement

As we point out in the introduction to Chapter II, part of the meaning in English sentences is conveyed by the position of words in relation to each other. And though there are certain standard or conventional arrangements, a good deal of flexibility is possible (see #1s, #1t, #8d, #11b, and #15). Adverbial modifiers are especially movable (see #9d and #18e). Because of this flexibility, writers sometimes unthinkingly put a modifier where it conveys an unintended or ambiguous meaning, or where it is linked by juxtaposition to a word it can't logically modify. In order to say precisely what you mean, you have to be careful in placing your modifiers—especially adverbs. Note the changes in meaning that result from the different placement of the little word *only* in the following sentences:

> Only his son works in Halifax. (No other member of his family works there.)
> His only son works in Halifax. (He has no other sons.)
> His son only works in Halifax. (He doesn't live in Halifax, but commutes.)
> His son works only in Halifax. (He works in no other place.)

The following sentence demonstrates how misplacement can produce absurdity:

> *mm:* A man soon learns not to scatter his clothes about after he is married in the bathroom.

Obviously the adverbial phrase *in the bathroom* belongs after what it modifies, the infinitive phrase *to scatter his clothes about.* The adverbial clause *after he is married* must be put either at the beginning of the sentence or, set off by commas, after *learns.*

Usually it is best to keep modifiers and the words they modify as close together as possible. Here is an example of an adjective awkwardly out of place:

> *mm:* Love is a *difficult* emotion to express in words.
> *clear:* Love is an emotion (that is) difficult to express.

and an example of a misplaced relative clause:

> *mm:* In 1683, the first St. Cecilia's Day festival was held in London, which is a festival of the performing arts.

London is a festival? Perhaps—especially to those trying to attract tourists. But here the writer meant something else (and we've reduced the clause to an appositive phrase):

> *clear:* In 1683, the first St. Cecilia's Day festival, a festival of the performing arts, was held in London.

23b *mm*

23b *Only, almost, etc.*

Be particularly careful (as illustrated in the preceding section) with such adverbs as *only, almost, just, merely,* and *even.* Colloquially we toss these around like tiddlywinks, but in formal writing we should put them where they clearly mean what we want them to:

> *mm:* Hardy *only* wrote novels as a sideline; his main interest was poetry.
> *clear:* Hardy wrote novels *only* as a sideline; his main interest was poetry.
> *mm:* The students *almost* washed fifty cars last Saturday.
> *clear:* The students washed *almost* fifty cars last Saturday.

23c **Squinting Modifiers**

squint A squinting modifier is a word or phrase put between two elements either of which it could modify. That is, a modifier "squints" so that a reader can't tell which way it is looking; the result is awkward ambiguity:

> *squint:* It was so hot *for a week* we did hardly any work at all.

Which clause does the adverbial phrase modify? It is disturbingly ambiguous, even though the meaning would be about the same either way. A speaking voice could impart clarifying emphasis to such a sentence, but a writer must substitute words or structures for the missing vocal emphasis. Don't try to heal the wound with the mere band-aid of a comma before or after the modifier: it's seldom effective, and can even make the sentence sound more awkward. Revise in some other way. Here, a simple *that* removes the ambiguity:

> *clear:* It was so hot that for a week we did hardly any work at all.
> *clear:* It was so hot for a week that we did hardly any work at all.

Another example:

> *squint:* My father advised me *now and then* to invest in stocks.

This time, rearrangement is necessary:

> *clear:* My father now and then advised me to invest in stocks.
> *clear:* My father advised me to invest now and then in stocks.

Even a modifier at the end of a sentence can in effect squint, be ambiguous. When rearrangement doesn't work, substantial revision will be necessary:

> *ambig:* He was upset when she left for more reasons than one.
> *clear:* He was upset for more reasons than one when she left.
> *clear:* He had more than one reason to be upset when she left.
> *clear:* He was upset because she had more than one reason for leaving.

Note: An awkwardly split infinitive is also caused by a kind of misplaced modifier; see #10c.

Exercise 23 **Correcting misplaced modifiers**

Revise the following sentences to eliminate awkwardness resulting from misplaced modifiers.

1. His outbursts were only viewed as signs of bad temper.
2. I vowed to never discriminate against children when I became an adult.
3. She decided that on this day she would skip dinner entirely in the morning.
4. I could see my grandfather coming through the window.
5. He was naturally upset by her remark.
6. They discussed rebuilding the hotel for three days but decided against it.
7. Another reason why David lives a barren emotional and social life more pertinent to the theme of this essay is his thwarted love for Judith.
8. A piano stands in the centre of the stage with its outline only visible to the audience in the darkness.
9. Farmer Jones only ploughed three acres yesterday.
10. It merely seemed a few days before they were back again.

---

24 Dangling Modifiers

dm   Like a pronoun without an antecedent, a **dangling modifier** has no logical word in the rest of the sentence to hook on to; instead it is left dangling, grammatically unattached, and unfortunately it often tries to attach itself, illogically, to some other word. Most dangling modifiers are *verbal phrases*; be particularly careful with them.

24a Dangling Participial Phrases (see #10d)

> *dm: Striding aggressively into the room*, my eyes fell upon the figure cowering in the corner.

Since the adjectival phrase wants to modify a noun, it tries to hook up with the subject of the adjacent clause, *eyes*. One's eyes may be said, figuratively, to "fall" on something, but they can scarcely be said to "stride." If one were to say, "Striding aggressively into the room, my eyes tripped over the edge of the carpet," the absurdity would be immediately obvious. To avoid the unintentionally humorous dangler, simply change the participial phrase to a subordinate clause:

> *revised: As I strode aggressively into the room*, my eyes fell upon the figure cowering in the corner.

Or, if you want to keep the effect of the opening participial phrase, rework the clause so that its subject is the logical word to be modified:

> *revised:* Striding aggressively into the room, *I* let my gaze fall upon the figure cowering in the corner.

Here is another example, one with no built-in absurdity:

> *dm: Living in a small town*, there wasn't much to do for entertainment.

Provide something for the phrase to modify, or revise the sentence in some other way:

> *revised:* Living in a small town, *we* had little to do for entertainment.
> *revised:* Since we lived in a small town, there wasn't much to do for entertainment.

In the next example, passive voice causes the trouble (see #6p):

> *dm: Looking up to the open sky*, not a cloud could be seen.
> *revised:* Looking up to the open sky, *I* could not see a cloud.
> *revised:* There wasn't a cloud to be seen in the open sky.

24b   Dangling Gerund Phrases (see #10f)

When a gerund phrase is the object of a preposition, it can dangle much like a participial phrase:

> *dm:* After *being informed of the correct procedure*, our attention was directed to the next steps.

Obviously it isn't "our attention" that was "informed." Again the lapse into passive voice is at least partly to blame.

> *revised:* After being informed of the correct procedure, *we* were directed to attend to the next steps.

But this revision is still passive and awkward. Such a sentence can be better revised another way:

> *revised:* After informing us of the correct procedure, the instructor directed our attention to the next steps.

24c   Dangling Infinitive Phrases (see #10a)

> *dm: To follow Freud's procedure*, the speaker's thoughts must be fully known.

Passive voice is again the culprit, depriving the infinitive phrase of a logical word to modify.

revised: To follow Freud's procedure, *one* must know the speaker's thoughts fully.

The next example is more complicated:

dm: *To make the mayor's plan work*, it requires the people's cooperation.

Here the phrase awkwardly seems to be the antecedent of *it*. Dropping the *it* lets the phrase clearly act as a noun; or the sentence can be revised in some other way:

revised: To make the mayor's plan work will require the people's cooperation.
revised: If the mayor's plan is to work, the people will have to cooperate.

24d Dangling Elliptical Clauses

An **elliptical clause** is an adverbial clause that has been abridged so that its subject and verb are only "understood" or implied rather than stated; the subject of the independent clause then automatically serves also as the implied subject of the elliptical clause. If the implied subject is different from the subject of the independent clause, the subordinate element will dangle, sometimes ludicrously:

dm: Once in the army, a person's life is totally regimented.

It isn't "a person's *life*" that is in the army, but the *person*. Either supply a logical subject and verb for the elliptical clause, or retain the elliptical clause and make the other subject logically agree with it:

revised: Once *you are* in the army, *your life* is totally regimented.
revised: Once in the army, *one* finds that one's life is totally regimented.

Another example:

dm: When well marinated, put the pieces of chicken on the barbecue.

Here the understood subject is *the pieces*, but the subject of the independent clause of this imperative sentence is an understood *you*. Give the elliptical clause a subject and verb:

revised: When the pieces of chicken are well marinated, put them on the barbecue.

24e Dangling Prepositional Phrases and Appositives
(see #11 and #1q)

A prepositional phrase can also dangle. In this example, an indefinite *it* (see #5e) is the troublemaker:

> *dm:* *Like a child in a toy-shop*, it is all she can bear not to touch everything.
>
> *revised:* Like a child in a toy-shop, *she* can hardly bear not to touch everything.

And so can an appositive:

> *dm:* *A superb racing car*, a Ferrari's engine is a masterpiece of engineering.

The phrase seems to be in apposition with the noun *engine*, but it is illogical to equate an engine with an entire car (the possessive *Ferrari's* is adjectival). Revise it:

> *revised:* A superb racing car, a *Ferrari* has an engine that is a masterpiece of engineering.

Exercise 24   Correcting dangling modifiers

Revise the following to eliminate dangling modifiers.

1. Feeling carefree and nonchalant, all my problems were forgotten.
2. By using Huck as the narrator we are drawn into his centre of consciousness.
3. In order to ski one must be outdoors, thereby being good for physical and mental health.
4. Looked at in this light, one has to find Hamlet very much like other people.
5. Réamur introduced the idea of testing small sample rods and then studying their structure when fractured.
6. Being the youngest sibling in my family, it is easier for me to understand children.
7. When not going to school or working, my hobbies range from athletics to automobiles.
8. By using this style it added more flair to the story.
9. The colonel began to send groups of reinforcements to the weakened position only to be ambushed along the jungle trails.
10. Whispering in the darkened theatre, our popcorn spilled onto the floor.

25   Mixed Constructions

mix   To begin a sentence with one construction and then absent-mindedly shift to another is at least as awkward as changing horses in midstream:

> *mix:* Physical education can be enjoyable for both the noncompetitive student as well as the competitive one.

The writer set up a *both . . . and* pattern, but then shifted to *as well as* instead of following through with the *and*. Either change *as well as* to *and* or omit the *both*.

> *mix:* Since Spain was a devoutly Catholic country, therefore most of its art was on religious themes.

This writer began with a subordinating *Since,* but then used *therefore* to introduce the second clause, which would be correct only if the first clause had been independent. Drop either the *Since* or the *therefore* (if *Since,* change the comma to a semicolon to avoid a comma splice: see #33e).

Exercise 25 | Correcting mixed constructions

Revise the following to eliminate mixed constructions.

1. Piranesi worked on a colossal scale, putting more emphasis on density rather than on outline.
2. The reason for the drop in production was due to labour troubles.
3. It wasn't until five years later before she returned to the place.
4. I found that the introductory part of the book to be very helpful.
5. The new styles were popular with both men and women alike.
6. Since, for most of us, our earliest recollections are mere fragments of things that made up our childhoods, we therefore must rely on the objects or ideas around us to trigger the past.
7. Just because people like to watch television doesn't mean our society is in a state of decay.

---

26 Shifts in Perspective—Inconsistent Point of View

shift,   Be consistent in your point of view within a sentence—and usually from
pv   one sentence to the next, as well. Avoid awkward or illogical shifts in the *tense, mood,* and *voice* of verbs, and in the *person* and *number* of pronouns.

26a Shifts in Tense (see #6g-h)

> *shift:* The professor *told* us what he expected of us and then he *leans* against the desk and *grins.*

Change *leans* and *grins* to past tense, like *told.*

26b Shifts in Mood (see #6-lm)

> *shift:* If it *were* Sunday and I *was* through with my homework, I would go skiing with you.

Change indicative *was* to subjunctive *were.*

> *shift:* First *put* tab A in slot B; next *you will put* tab C in slot D.

Omit *you will* to correct the shift from imperative to indicative.

26c *shift, pv*

26c   Shifts in Voice (see #60-p)

> *shift:* Readers should not have to read a second time before some sense *can be made* of the passage.
> *shift:* We drove thirty miles to the end of the road, after which five more miles *were covered* on foot.

Such awkward shifts from active to passive could also be marked **pas.** Stick with active voice (and the same subject):

> *revised:* Readers should not have to read a passage a second time before they can make sense of it.
> *revised:* We drove thirty miles to the end of the road and then covered another five miles on foot.

26d   Shifts in Person of Pronoun (see #3a-b)

> *shift:* If *one* wants to learn about trees, *you* should study forestry.

Change second-person *you* to third-person *one* (or perhaps *he or she*).

26e   Shifts in Number of Pronoun (see #3a)

> *shift:* If the committee wants *its* recommendations followed, *they* should have written *their* report more carefully.

The committee changed from a collective unit (*it*) to a collection of individuals (*they, their*); the committee should be either singular or plural throughout. See also #4e and #7f. (The errors in #26d and #26e could also be marked **agr:** see #4.)

27   Faulty Parallelism

fp, //   Parallelism is a strong stylistic technique. Not only does it make for vigorous, balanced, and rhythmical sentences, but it can also help develop and tie together paragraphs (see #65a). Like any other good thing, parallelism can be overdone, but more commonly people underuse it. Of course, if you're writing an especially sober piece, like a letter of condolence, you probably won't want to use lively devices like parallelism and metaphor. But in most writing a good dose of parallel structure is healthful. Build parallel elements into your sentences, and now and then make two or three successive sentences parallel with each other. Here is a sentence from a student's paper on computer crime; note how parallelism (along with alliteration) strengthens the first part, thereby helping to set up the second part:

> Although one can distinguish the malicious from the mischievous or the harmless hacker from the more dangerous computer criminal, security officials take a dim view of anyone who romps through company files.

But be careful, for it is all too easy to slip, to set up a parallel and then muff it. Study the following examples of **faulty parallelism** carefully. (See also #12a-b.)

27a   With Coordinate Elements

Coordinate elements in a sentence should have the same grammatical form. If they don't, the sentence will lack parallelism and therefore be awkward at best.

> *fp:* Mario is wealthy, handsome, and a bachelor.

The first two complements are predicate adjectives, the third a predicate noun. Change *a bachelor* to the adjective *unmarried* so that it will be parallel.

The coordinate parts of compound subjects, verbs, objects, and modifiers should be parallel in form.

> *fp:* Eating huge meals, too many sweets, and snacking between meals can lead to obesity.

This sentence can be corrected either by making all three parts of the subject into gerunds:

> *revised:* Eating large meals, eating too many sweets, and snacking between meals can lead to obesity.

or by using only the first gerund and following it with three parallel objects:

> *revised:* Eating large meals, too many sweets, and between-meal snacks can lead to obesity.

Another example:

> *fp:* He described the computer in terms suggesting a deep affection for it and that also demonstrated a thoroughgoing knowledge of it.

Simply change the participial phrase (*suggesting . . .*) to a relative clause (*that suggested . . .*) so that it will be parallel with the second part.

It is particularly easy for a writer to omit a second *that:*

fp: Marvin was convinced *that* the argument was unsound and he could profitably spend some time analyzing it.

A second *that*, before *he*, corrects the error and clarifies the meaning—for this slip is in effect not only a breakdown of parallelism but also an implied shift in point of view (see #26); it could be marked **shift** or **pv** as well as **fp**; it could also be marked **ambig**. The lack of a second *that* invites or at least allows a reader to take "he could profitably spend some time analyzing it" as an independent clause—expressing the writer's own opinion about what Marvin should do—rather than what the writer intended, a second subordinate clause expressing a part of Marvin's opinion. (See also **pv** in Chapter XI.)

27b With Correlative Conjunctions (see #12b)

Be especially careful when using correlative conjunctions:

fp: Whether for teaching a child the alphabet or in educating an adult about the latest political development, television is the best device we have.

The constructions following the *whether* and the *or* should be parallel; change *in* to *for.*

The correlative pair *not only . . . but also* can be particularly troublesome:

fp: She not only corrected my grammar but also my spelling.

The error can be corrected either by repeating the verb *corrected* (or using some other appropriate verb, such as *criticized* or *repaired*) after *but also:*

revised: She not only corrected my grammar but also corrected my spelling.

or by moving *corrected* so that it occurs before *not only* rather than after it:

revised: She corrected not only my grammar but also my spelling.

Either method makes what follows *not only* parallel in form to what follows *but also.* Obviously the second version is more economical.

27c In a Series

In any series of three or more parallel elements, make sure that little beginning words like prepositions, pronouns, and the *to* of infinitives precede either the first element alone or each of the elements. And don't omit needed articles:

fp: The car was equipped with a CB radio, stereo tape deck, an AM-FM receiver, and a miniature television receiver.

The article *a* is missing before the second item, breaking the parallelism.

> *fp:* He exhorted his followers to obey the rules, to think positively, and ignore criticism.

Since *to* occurs in the first two phrases, it should lead off the third as well—or else be omitted from the second one. If necessary, jot down the items in such a series in a vertical list after the word that introduces it: any slips in parallelism should then be obvious.

Exercise 27 Correcting faulty parallelism

Revise the following in order to repair faulty parallelism.

1. Disagreements were not only apparent between clergy and scientists, but between various elements of the church as well.
2. People adopt roles in life which they are most comfortable with, or will benefit them the most.
3. Not only was our black Snowball like a baby but also very much like a dog.
4. It is necessary that we tighten our belts and to try to control our spending.
5. Part of the scene is not only concerned with the present situation but also prepares the way for the important scene that follows.
6. We are told that we should eat more protein, less fat, and exercise regularly.
7. The elderly are an important part of our society, and our own lives.
8. About 1750, it became clear to the French that the arrival of the few English traders was only the beginning and soon masses of settlers would follow and destroy the French empire in North America.
9. He says that when he grows up he wants to be a teacher, a home-owner, and travel.
10. A pet not only gives an elderly person something to care for, but also a sense of usefulness.
11. Perhaps even the daily newspaper may someday be delivered by co-axial cable rather than a paper-carrier.
12. Soldiers have to cope with obsolete or too few pieces of new equipment.
13. The speaker narrates the poem as if he has walked along the streets at night more than once before and that he is acquainted with what goes on around him during his walks.
14. There are many kinds of smiles. For example there are smiles of pleasure, compassion, humour, contempt, winning, competitive, shared secrets, idiotic grins, leers, gloating, sneers, recognition, friendliness, greeting, social, professional, gratification, spontaneous, contagious, deliberate, suppressed, courtesy, anger, humility, rebellion, embarrassment, and surprise.
15. Everything the fortuneteller told me was happy and exciting: I would marry a rich man, have two children, one who will become a famous hockey player, and the other will be a doctor, travel all over the world, and live until I'm ninety-five, healthy as a young woman.

28 *fc, log, emph, u, sub*

28 Faulty Coordination: Logic, Emphasis, and Unity

fc, log, If unrelated or unequal elements—usually clauses—are presented as co-
emph, ordinate, the result is **faulty coordination**.
u, sub

> *fc:* Watches are usually water-resistant *and* some have the ability to glow in
> the dark.

There is no logical connection between the two clauses—other than that
they both say something about watches. The ideas would be better
expressed in separate sentences. Note also that coordinating two such
clauses produces a sentence lacking in **unity**. Here is another example,
from a student's description of a simple object; the lack of unity is even
more glaring:

> *fc:* One might find this kind of a jar in a small junk shop *and* it can be used
> for anything from cotton balls to rings and things, or just to stand as a
> decoration.

The suggestion about the junk shop should either be in a separate sentence or be subordinated.

Similarly, if two elements are joined by an inappropriate coordinating
conjunction, the result is again faulty coordination—sometimes referred
to as "loose" coordination. Here is an example of this more common
weakness:

> *fc:* Nationalism can affect the relations between nations by creating a distrust-
> ful atmosphere, *and* an ambassador's innocent remark can be turned into
> an insult by a suspicious listener.

The *and* misrepresents the relation between the two clauses; the second is
not an additional fact but rather an example or result of the fact stated in
the first. Simply joining the two clauses with a semicolon or colon would
be better, or changing *and* to *in which*, subordinating the second clause.
The first clause could be made subordinate with an opening *Because*, but
that would distort **emphasis**, since the first clause appears more important (see #18i). Here is another example, from a student's description of
how a particular scene in *Hamlet* should be staged:

> *fc:* In this scene Rosencrantz is the main speaker of the two courtiers; there-
> fore he should stand closer to Hamlet.

This sentence could be marked **sub** or **emph** as well as **fc**. The first clause
would be better subordinated:

> *revised:* Because in this scene Rosencrantz is the main speaker of the two
> courtiers, he should stand closer to Hamlet.

The original *therefore* does express this relation, but the sentence was nonetheless a compound one, tacitly equating the two clauses. Emphasis and clarity are better served by letting the syntax acknowledge the logically subordinate nature of the first clause. The original sentence, then, could also have been marked **log**, though **fc** is more precise. Sometimes, however, **fc** and **log** are about equally applicable:

> *fc, log:* Alliteration is a very effective poetic device when used sparingly but appropriately.

The meaning expressed by *but* here is entirely illogical, since it implies opposition, although it is likely that a poet who uses alliteration sparingly would also use it appropriately. A simple *and* would be a better coordinator.

A particularly weak form of loose coordination overlaps with the "this" disease (see #5c, and Chapter XI under **ref**):

> *fc:* The poem's tone is light and cheery, *and this* is reinforced by the mainly one-syllable words and the regular rhythm and rhyme.

If you ever find such an *and this* in your draft, try to revise it out, for not only is the coordination weak, but the demonstrative *this* is weak as well, since it has no antecedent:

> *revised:* The poem's light and cheery tone is reinforced by the mainly one-syllable words and the regular rhythm and rhyme.

Another kind of faulty coordination links several short independent clauses with coordinating conjunctions, mostly *and*'s; the result is a loose string of seemingly unrelated parts. Such sentences tend to ramble on and on, emphasizing nothing:

> *fc, rambling:* The ferry rates were increased and the bigger commercial vehicles had to pay more to use the ferry service and so the cost of transporting goods rose and the consumers who bought those goods had to pay more for them but they had to pay higher fares on the ferries as well and naturally most people were unhappy about it.

The data needed to make the point are here, but the ineffective syntax leaves the poor reader floundering, trying to decipher the connections and the thought behind the whole thing. The *but* seems to be used less for logic than for variety, and the vague *it* at the end effectively dissipates any emphasis the sentence might have had. A little judicious tinkering sorts out and rearranges the facts, shortens the sentence by almost half, reduces the five coordinating conjunctions to a pair of correlative conjunctions, reduces the six independent clauses to two independent and one subordinate, and achieves at least some emphasis at the end:

revised: Not only did the increased ferry rates cost travellers more, but, since the commercial vehicles also had to pay more, the cost of transported goods rose as well, affecting all consumers.

See also #18i and #16b.

Exercise 28(1) Using subordination

Convert each of the following pairs of sentences into a complex sentence by subordinating one or the other.

1. The book was well written. I did not find it rewarding.
2. The wind was very cold. She wore a heavy sweater.
3. It stopped snowing. He shovelled the driveway.
4. She read a good book. He played solitaire.
5. The meeting was contentious. A consensus was reached.

Exercise 28(2) Correcting faulty coordination

Revise the following sentences to eliminate faulty or loose coordination; keep in mind good subordination, unity, emphasis, and logic. You may also find that you can reduce wordiness.

1. There are no windows in the room, and all lighting is from fluorescent fixtures.
2. At this point Ophelia becomes confused, and this becomes evident when she speaks her next line.
3. Rachel is afraid of God and when Calla takes her to the Tabernacle service she goes crazy.
4. The last appearance of the ghost is in the "closet" scene and the purpose of its appearance is to prevent Hamlet from diverging from his "blunted purpose."
5. We want more than our neighbours and then buy the most ridiculous things.
6. Her experiments with chimpanzees were unusual but they were interesting.
7. Older people have already been through what others are experiencing, and this enables them to help.
8. Experts are not always right, and they are seldom wrong.
9. The city's streets are well paved and some of them badly need repair.
10. He is a genius; some people claim that he is an imposter.
11. The stores are usually the first to remind us that Christmas is coming and set the mood with decorations, music, and advertising.
12. The activity of milking a cow becomes very commonplace to the farmer, but it is fun to do and fascinating to watch.
13. Texans are noted for their chauvinism and they often brag unreasonably about their state's virtues.
14. She prepared diligently for the examination and failed it twice, and then passed it with flying colours the third time.
15. Unemployment is unusually high and one should not expect to be hired at the first place one tries.

29 Faulty Logic

log   Clear and logical thinking is essential to clear and effective writing. For example, don't make sweeping statements unless you support them with specific evidence: over-generalization is one of the most common weaknesses in student writing. Make sure also that the evidence you use is sound and that the authorities you cite are reliable. Such matters are particularly important in argumentative writing—as almost all writing is to some degree. You also want to avoid weak reasoning: such logical missteps as begging the question, reasoning in a circle, jumping to conclusions, and leaning on false analogies can seriously decrease the effectiveness of an essay (see #70e-h).

There are many ways in which logic is important even in something so small as a sentence. The problems discussed in the preceding sections, from *Misplaced Modifiers* on, are in part problems in logic. Following are some examples of other ways in which sentences can be illogical.

Unsound reasoning leads to sentences like this:

log: James's father was proud of him, for he had the boy's picture on his desk.

The conclusion may seem reasonable, but it should at least be qualified with a *probably*, or more evidence should be provided; for there are other possible reasons for the picture's being on the desk. James's mother could have put it there, and the father not bothered to remove it; perhaps he's afraid to. Or he could feel love for a lazy son, but not pride. Or he could be feigning love and pride for appearances' sake, knowing inside that he doesn't feel either. Here's another example:

log: Wordsworth is *perhaps* the first English Romantic poet, *for* his major themes—man, nature, human life—are characteristic of the Romantic style of poetry.

To begin with, the word *perhaps* is pointless: either the writer is making a point of Wordsworth's primacy and there is no "perhaps" about it, or there is no point to be made and the whole clause is superfluous. Even more serious is the way evidence is given to substantiate the statement: if the mere presence in his poetry of themes common to Romanticism makes him first, then all Romantic poets are first. The writer probably meant something like "Wordsworth is the first English Romantic poet to develop the major themes of the Romantic movement." And just how valid is the implication that "human life" is especially characteristic of Romantic writers? No amount of careful writing can overcome muddy thinking.

But even if writers know clearly what they want to say, they have to choose and use words carefully:

log: The town is *surrounded* on one side by the ocean.

If the place were indeed *surrounded*, it would be an island. The correct word here is *bounded*. This error might equally well be designated an error in diction: see #57 and **ww** (wrong word) in Chapter XI.

Writers must also be careful about the way they put sentences together:

> *log:* Having a car with bad spark plugs or points or a dirty carburetor causes it to run poorly and to use too much gas.

Here the sentence structure wins, the writer loses: it could as well be marked **ss** (sentence structure, or sentence sense). The intention is clear, but the verb, *causes*, has as its subject the gerund *having*; consequently the sentence says that the mere possession of the afflicted car is what causes it to run poorly—as if one could borrow a similar car and it would run well. A logical revision:

> *revised:* Bad spark plugs or bad points or a dirty carburetor cause a car to run poorly and to use too much gas.

The parallelism was also weak, for *points* alone wouldn't have caused trouble.

Faulty comparisons are another cause of illogicality:

> *log, comp:* French painting did not follow the wild and exciting forms of Baroque art as closely as most European countries.

Again the meaning is apparent, but the syntax faulty; readers would be annoyed at having to revise the sentence themselves in order to understand it. The sentence says either that "European countries followed the wild and exciting forms of Baroque art" to some degree or that "French painting followed most European countries more closely than it followed the wild and exciting forms of Baroque art," neither of which makes logical sense. Simply completing the comparison straightens out the syntax and permits the intended meaning to come through unambiguously:

> *revised:* French painting did not follow the wild and exciting forms of Baroque art as closely as *did that of* most European countries.

See also **comp** in Chapter XI.

Another kind of ambiguity appears in this sentence:

> *log:* Numerous scientific societies were founded in every developed country.

The intended meaning is probably that every developed country had at least one scientific society—but it could just as well mean that there were *numerous* such societies in each country. See also **ambig** and **cl** (clarity) in Chapter XI.

Here's another kind of illogical sentence:

log: His lack of knowledge of the subject was visible on every page.

The meaning is clear, but it might strike a reader as odd to think of a *lack* being *visible*. Put it more logically:

revised: Every page revealed his ignorance of the subject.

Make sure that nouns are inflected to agree logically with the context:

log: All the students suffered mental stiffness as a result of the unusual exercise involved in using their brain.

Clearly the students possessed *brains*, not just one *brain*.

Sometimes an extra word creeps in and ruins an otherwise logical sentence:

log: Alexander Graham Bell is known as the modern inventor of the telephone.

The writer was probably thinking subconsciously of the telephone as a *modern* invention, and the word just popped into the sentence. Thinking consciously, one sees that the word *modern* implies that there have been one or more earlier, perhaps even ancient, inventors of the telephone.

Finally, make sure your sentences actually say something worth saying. Here's one that doesn't:

log: The mood and theme play a very significant part in this poem.

This could be called an "empty" sentence (the weak intensifier *very* suggests that the writer subconsciously felt the need to prop it up). It would be illogical for the *theme* of a poem to play other than a significant part in it.

Exercise 29 | Improving logic

Revise the following sentences to eliminate errors in logic.

1. As he approached the shore, he felt a challenge between himself and the sea.
2. Milton's influence on other subsequent poets was very great.
3. Some auto accidents are unavoidable, but can be prevented by proper maintenance.
4. Shakespeare fashioned *A Midsummer Night's Dream* around the theme of love and created the characters and situations to illustrate it in the best possible way. Thus he freely used a variety of comic devices in developing the theme.
5. By the use of imagery, diction, symbolism, and sound, we may also see the structure of the plot.
6. It employed the technique of using projected images on a screen and a corresponding taped conversation which visually enforced the lesson.

7. Throughout history man has been discussing and proposing theories about his purpose on earth, and thus far they can be divided into three general camps.
8. Through the use of too much abstract language, jargon, and clichés the clarity and effectiveness of this article have been destroyed.
9. As I think back to the days when we were in our early teens, we had a lot of fun together.
10. After his wife died, his paintings of excited forms changed to quiet ones.

---

30 Faulty Alignment

al Poor **alignment** results when two or more elements in a sentence are illogically or incongruously aligned with each other. Such errors often take the form of a verb saying something illogical about its subject—an error sometimes called faulty *predication*; that is, what is predicated about the subject is an impossibility. For example:

> *al, pred:* Many new inventions and techniques occurred during this period.

An invention could, with some strain, be said to *occur*, but *techniques* do not *occur*. Revision is necessary; one possibility is to use an expletive and the passive voice:

> *revised:* During this period there were many new inventions, and many new techniques were developed.

In the next example the verb repeats the meaning of the subject:

> *al, pred:* The setting of the play takes place in Denmark.
> *revised:* The play takes place in Denmark.
> *better:* The play is set in Denmark.

Errors in predication often occur with a form of *be* and a complement:

> *al, pred:* The amount of gear to take along is the first step to consider when planning a long hike.

But an *amount* cannot be a *step*; drastic revision is needed:

> *revised:* The first step in planning a hike is to decide how much gear to take along.

Note that this also removes the other illogicality: one does not *consider* a *step*; rather the considering, or deciding, is itself the step. Another example:

> *al, pred:* The value of good literature is priceless.

It is not the *value* that is priceless, but the *literature* itself. Here is a similar error, of a common kind:

> *al, pred:* The cost of my used car was relatively inexpensive.
> *revised:* The cost of my used car was relatively low.
> *revised:* My used car was relatively inexpensive.

Other errors in alignment aren't errors in predication, but are similar to them in using words illogically:

> *al:* In narrative, the author describes the occurrences, environment, and thoughts of the characters.

It is logical to speak of characters having thoughts and an environment, but not *occurrences*; substitute *experiences*.

> *al:* Its fine texture was as smooth and hard as a waterworn rock.

This, which illogically equates *texture* and *rock*, is also a form of incomplete comparison. Insert *that of* after *hard as*. (See **comp** in Chapter XI; see also #29.)

> *al:* Beliefs such as being a Christian or a Jew or a Moslem or even an atheist should not cause anyone to be denied a job.

But *being* a Christian, etc., is not a *belief*. One could begin the sentence with *Being*, or one could recast it completely:

> *revised:* People should not be denied jobs because of their religious beliefs, be they Christian, Jewish, Moslem, atheistic, or anything else.

Exercise 30   Improving alignment

Revise the following sentences to remove illogical or incongruous alignment.

1. I decided not to buy it, for the price was too expensive.
2. Even religious principles were being enlightened during this period.
3. It is clear that this general conception of his ability is greatly underestimated.
4. The only source of light in the house came through the windows.
5. Its shape is a rectangle about three times as long as it is wide.
6. The poem expresses the meaningless and useless achievements of war.
7. The character of the speaker in the poem seems weary and tired.
8. The need for such great effort on the part of the reader represents serious weakness in the writing.
9. Life and death was a constant idea in the back of the pioneers' minds.
10. She started university at a very young age.

31 *coh*

31 Sentence Coherence

coh Although the word *coherence* usually refers to the connection between sentences and between paragraphs (see #63-65, #68b), the parts of a sentence must also cohere, stick together. Each sentence fault discussed in the preceding sections is capable of making a sentence incoherent (the dictionary meanings *disjointed, illogical, confused, inconsistent, loose, disorganized* all apply). If a sentence lacks coherence, the fault probably lies in one or more of the following: faulty arrangement (faulty *word order, misplaced modifier*), unclear or missing or illogical connections and relations between parts (faulty *reference*, lack of *agreement, dangling modifier, faulty coordination*, faulty *logic*, incongruous *alignment*), syntactic shift from one part to another (*mixed construction, shift* in point of view, *faulty parallelism*); or the weakness may be due to something that can only be labelled *awkward* or *unclear* (see **awk** and **cl** in Chapter XI). Consult these specific sections as necessary to ensure that your sentences are coherent within themselves.

Review Exercise, Chapters I, II, and III	Sentence errors and weaknesses

The following sentences contain various kinds of errors and weaknesses discussed in the preceding chapters. Decide what is wrong with each sentence, label it with the appropriate correction symbol, and then revise the sentence in order to eliminate the problem. Some of the sentences have more than one thing wrong with them.

1. Our coach is overweight, Hungarian, overpaid, and over forty.
2. One receives this impression when the colour of the picture is considered.
3. Many organic diseases present symptoms that are very similar to autism.
4. Great distances now separate he and his father.
5. The writer's skill was very good.
6. It's true that love and romance come when you least expect it.
7. No player in our school has ever scored as highly as Schmidt did this year.
8. The poem is separated into two parts. The first being his memories and an account of how he reacted to his father's death.
9. Its shape is rounded somewhat resembling a keyhole.
10. I pulled over to the side of the road in a green truck I had borrowed from my roommate, and because the weather was warm I was dressed only in shorts and a bandana, which I had tied around my head.
11. Borelli supposed that there was a tendency for celestial bodies to attract each other but a fluid pressure prevented this.
12. Shakespeare's *Othello* is a brilliant but tragic story of the betrayal of the Moor of Venice by his most trusted friend, Iago.

13. The whole meaning of Housman's poem is that it is better to die young with honour and glory intact than to have someone take it away from you.

14. The forefinger along with the other digits of the hand have enabled us to evolve to the position of being the ruler of the world.

15. He says he would like to have another chance at being premier; but if he couldn't run the government right the first time, how can anyone think he's about to do it right again?

16. Smitty is so eager about Michael's friendship, and this is easy to understand even the first time one reads the story.

17. Those who are actually involved in this Christmas frenzy may find themselves feeling like getting in touch with old friends, making peace with people they haven't been getting along with, giving to their loved ones and even to strangers, decorating, and enjoying each other's company.

18. They preferred to go out with friends to movies and parties than to stay home and watch TV with their families.

19. By creating an atmosphere of concern for the main character we are more open to the message of the story.

20. What a university stands for more than anything else is an institution where one furthers his education.

21. He has an old worn coat which is far too big for him, but alterations are something he has neither money for nor feels the need to get done.

22. At the beginning, she played things very cautious.

23. Her success is credited to her slyness and wit which always prevails over her daughter's weakness.

24. Physical activity of any kind is always beneficial for the individual.

25. At present the fees are already very expensive.

26. Many people think of themselves as a well-educated person when they really are not.

27. The poet suggests that our lives are but a speck in time and there is nothing we can do about it.

28. Good nutrition need not be expensive, for junk food often costs more.

29. The cost of computers are now starting to drop.

30. Ask the average television viewer how many programs he saw more than a few days before he can remember.

31. He had been given instructions on how to repair the engine, but it did not do much good.

32. Old buildings should not be thoughtlessly destroyed and replaced with modern architecture without admiring their quality and detail.

33. Being the youngest of four children, old clothing is something I know a good deal about.

34. The main contrast is between the attitudes of the older children to that of the younger children.

35. Often the cafeteria foods will have sauces and gravies available if people wish, which adds flavour.

36. There are also several phrases in the story that seem to have a dual meaning. One meaning being commonplace and the other having to do with ancient mythology.

37. The poem is about the loss that a child feels when his father dies at a young age.
38. Always look both to the left and the right before you cross a busy street.
39. Unlike many of his contemporaries whose humorous writings quickly faded, Twain's masterpiece has become a classic and will continue to entertain readers for a long time.
40. The man whom they believed was the cause of the trouble left the country.
41. The author uses characterization to develop her characters.
42. Someone who is sensible can judge their own impulses and emotions accurately.
43. Don't give up an aspiring career just to please someone else.
44. Vico's theories omitted many countries because they did not have the highly evolved pattern of civilization as Greece and Rome did.
45. One of the first things that the audience feels towards Hamlet is sympathy for the recent death of his father.
46. Belief in witchcraft and witch-tests declined in later years, but were never completely forgotten.
47. It is not the characters themselves that is important but what they represent.
48. There are several courses that I know I don't want to do.
49. We want to know why Hamlet behaves as he does, and until one is satisfied that one knows, he will always remain a mystery.
50. I rarely throw anything out, because you never know when it might be needed.

CHAPTER IV

Punctuation

p   Two common misconceptions about punctuation:

1. Punctuation is of little consequence; it has little to do with the effectiveness of written English.
2. Good punctuation is a mystery whose secrets are available only to those with a special instinct.

Those who labour under one or both of these errors are almost certain to punctuate poorly, whether through fear or lack of concern or both.

First, good punctuation is essential to clear and effective writing. It helps writers clarify meaning and tone and therefore helps readers understand what writers communicate: try removing the punctuation marks from a piece of prose and then see how difficult it is to read it. Punctuation enables writers to point to meaning that in spoken language would be indicated by pauses, pitch, tone, and stress. In effect, punctuation enables readers to *hear* a sentence the way a writer intends. Commas, semicolons, colons, and dashes also help to clarify the internal structure of sentences; often the very meaning of a sentence depends on how it is punctuated.

Second, the principles of good punctuation are not mysterious or remote; it shouldn't be difficult to master them. Since even poor punctuators depend on punctuation to help them understand what they read, they need only raise their unconscious punctuation-sense to a conscious level in order to control punctuation and help their own readers.

And here yet another misconception needs countering: what are often called the "rules" of punctuation aren't rules but **conventions** (see the Introduction to Part I). For example, English-speakers agree that the word for a small domestic feline animal is *cat*. If you wrote about a *kat*, your readers would probably understand you, but they would wonder why you had strayed from the conventional spelling—and to that extent you would have lost touch with them, disturbed the quality of their understanding of your intended meaning. But if you chose to call the animal a *zyb*, you would have departed completely from the convention—and you would have lost your readers entirely. The "rule" that *cat* is spelled c-a-t is not a moral or legal restraint on behaviour; no one is going to sue you or throw you in jail for spelling it z-y-b. But you would exercise your freedom of choice only by defeating your purpose: clear and effective communication.

Similarly, the conventions of punctuation have come to be agreed upon by writers and readers of English for the purpose of clear and effective communication. Although good writers do sometimes stray from these conventions, they usually do so because they have a sufficient command of them to break a "rule" in order to achieve a desired effect.

A good way to improve your punctuation-sense is to become more aware of others' punctuation. Look not only for good things but also for bad things, weaknesses as well as strengths. If you do this consciously and conscientiously as you read, you will soon acquire a better sense of what punctuation does and how it does it—a sense which you can then apply to your own writing, and which should soon become instinctive.

The following discussions cover the common circumstances and even some relatively uncommon ones. Note that a clear understanding of the principles depends on a clear understanding of the syntax of the sentences in question; if you find it hard to grasp the principles, you may need to review the appropriate sections on grammar and sentence-sense in the preceding chapters. Note further that, far from being straitjackets, many of the principles not only allow but even invite you to exercise a good deal of choice.

Note: *Hyphens* and *apostrophes* are dealt with in Chapter VI, on Spelling. See #51o-s and #51v, respectively.

32-41 Internal Punctuation: Using Commas, Semicolons, Colons, and Dashes

32 The Marks Defined

32a Comma ,

The **comma** is a light or mild separator. It is the most neutral, least obtrusive punctuation mark. It is also the most used mark. Use it to separate words, phrases, and clauses from each other when no heavier or more expressive mark is required or desired. A comma makes a reader *pause* slightly.

Main Functions of Commas

Basically commas are used in only three ways; if you know these rules, you should have little trouble with commas:

1. Generally, use a comma between independent clauses joined by a coordinating conjunction (*and, but, or, nor, for, yet, so*; see #12a; see also #33a and #33e-g):

> We watched the changing of the guard at Buckingham Palace, and then we walked across Hyde Park.

Most of us went back to college in the fall, but Dorothy Wang was tempted
by an opportunity to travel, so she took off for Italy.

2. Generally, use commas to separate items in a series of three or more
(see #38a-b):

It is said that early to bed and early to rise will make one healthy, wealthy,
and wise.
Socrates, Plato, and Aristotle were three early Western philosophers.

See #44c on a common error with such constructions.

3. Generally, use commas to set off parenthetical elements—interruptive
or introductory words, phrases, and clauses and nonrestrictive appositives
or relative clauses (see #34-37 and #39a):

There are, however, some exceptions.
Hearing her flight number called, she began to run.
E. M. Forster's last novel, *A Passage to India*, is both serious and humorous.
Volkswagen Beetles, which were once common on streets and highways, are
a rare sight today.

Other Conventional Uses of the Comma

1. Use a comma between elements of an emphatic contrast:

This is a practical lesson, not a theoretical one.

2. Use a comma to indicate a pause where a word has been acceptably
omitted:

Ron is a conservative; Sally, a socialist.
To err is human; to forgive, divine.

3. Use commas to set off a noun of address (see #2b):

Simon, please write home more often.
Tell me, sir, how you think I should handle this.

4. Generally, use commas with a verb of speaking before or after a quotation (see also #43d-e):

Then Hilda remarked, "I found that movie offensive."
"It doesn't matter to me," said Rominder laughingly.

5. Use commas after the salutation of informal letters (Dear Gail,) and
after the complimentary close of all letters (Yours truly,). In formal letters
a colon is conventional after the salutation (Dear Mr. Hranka:).

6. Use commas correctly with dates. Different forms are possible:

> She left on January 11, 1991, and was gone a month.
> (Note the comma *after* the year.)
> On 11 January 1991 she left for a month's holiday.

With only month and year, you may use a comma or not—but be consistent:

> The book was published in March, 1993, in Canada.
> It was published here in March 1993.

7. Use commas to set off geographical names and addresses:

> He left Fredericton, New Brunswick, and moved to Windsor, Ontario, in hopes of finding a better-paying job. (Note the commas *after* the names of the provinces.)
> Her summer address will be 11 Bishop's Place, Lewes, Sussex, England.

For some common errors with commas, see #44a-h.

32b Semicolon **;**

The **semicolon** is a heavy separator, often almost equivalent to a period or "full stop." It forces a much longer pause than a comma does. And compared with the comma, it is used sparingly. Basically, semicolons have only two functions:

1. Generally, use a semicolon between closely related independent clauses that are *not* joined by one of the coordinating conjunctions (see #12a.1 and #33d):

> Tap water often tastes of chemicals; spring water usually does not.
> There were seventy-five people but room for only fifty; therefore twenty-five had to wait for a second bus.

See #44j on common misuses of the semicolon.

2. Use a semicolon instead of a comma if a comma would not be heavy enough—for example if clauses or the elements in a series have internal commas of their own (see #33b and #38c).

32c Colon **:**

Colons are commonly used to introduce lists, examples, and long or formal quotations, but their possibilities in more everyday sentences are often overlooked. The reason a colon is useful to introduce lists and the like is that it looks forward, anticipates: it gives readers a push toward the next part of the sentence. In the preceding sentence, for example, we intend the colon to give readers a little extra impetus, to set up a sense of expectation about what is coming. It points out, even emphasizes, the relation between the two parts of the sentence (here, a relation in which the second part restates and clarifies what the first part says). A semicolon in that spot would bring readers to an abrupt halt, leaving it up to them to make the necessary connection between the two parts. Here are more examples; in some the anticipatory function of the colon is less obvious, but it is there:

> The garden contained only four kinds of flowers: roses, tulips, geraniums, and chrysanthemums.
> Let me add just this: anyone who expects to achieve excellence must be prepared to work hard.
> It was a lovely time of year: trees were in blossom, garden flowers bloomed all around, the sky was clear and bright, and the temperature was just right.
> It was a warm day: we soon removed our jackets and sweaters.

Nevertheless, don't get carried away and overuse the colon: its stylish effectiveness would wear off if it appeared more than once or twice a page. And see #44k on how to avoid a common misuse of the colon.

MS note: Though some writers will continue to leave two spaces after a colon, one space is enough. And definitely only one space follows colons setting off subtitles or in footnotes or bibliographical entries.

32d Dash ——

The **dash** is a much-abused punctuation mark. Hasty writers often use it as a substitute for a comma, or where a colon would be better—perhaps because they feel insecure about colons. Use a dash only when you have a definite reason for doing so. Like the colon, the dash sets up expectations in a reader's mind. But whereas the colon sets up an expectation that what follows will somehow explain, summarize, define, or otherwise comment on what has gone before, a dash suggests that what follows will be either emphatic or somehow surprising, involving some sort of twist or irony, or at least a complete break in syntax. Consider the following sentence:

> The teacher praised my wit, my intelligence, my organization, and my research—and failed the paper for its poor spelling and punctuation.

Here the dash adds to the punch of what follows it. A comma there would deprive the sentence of much of its force; it would even sound odd, since the resulting matter-of-fact tone would not be in harmony with what the sentence was saying. Only a dash can convey the appropriate *tone* (see the introduction to Part III). Another example:

> What he wanted—and he wanted it very badly indeed—was to be well liked by everyone.

To set off the interrupting clause with commas instead of dashes wouldn't be "incorrect," but it would be weak, for the content of the clause is clearly emphatic. Only dashes have the power to signal that emphasis; commas would implicitly contradict what the clause is saying (as would parentheses; but see the note in #39c).

The dash is also handy in some long and involved sentences, for example after a long series before a summarizing clause:

> The laws of supply and demand, the health of the stock market, the strength of our currency, the world money market, the balance of payments, inflation, unemployment—all these and more go to shape our everyday economic lives, often in ways unseen or little understood.

Note that even here the emphasizing quality of the dash serves the meaning, though its principal function in such a sentence is to mark the abrupt and unusual syntactic break.

But, as with colons, don't overdo it, since dashes are even stronger marks and would lose effectiveness if used often.

Ms note: A typewritten dash is composed of two hyphens with no space before, after, or between them.

33-38 How to Use Commas, Semicolons, Colons, and Dashes

33 Between Independent Clauses

33a Comma and Coordinating Conjunction

Generally, use a **comma** between independent clauses joined by one of the coordinating conjunctions (*and, but, or, nor, for, yet*, and sometimes *so*; see #12a.3):

> The course proved difficult, and she found herself burning the midnight oil.
> It was a serious speech, but he included many jokes along the way, and the audience loved it.
> Jared could go into debt for the sports car, or he could go on driving his old clunker.
> He knew what he should do, yet he couldn't bring himself to take the first step.

If the clauses are short, or if only one of a pair of clauses is short, the comma or commas may be omitted:

The road was smooth and the car was running well and the weather was
   perfect.
The walls were crumbling and the roof was full of holes.

But sometimes even with a short clause the natural pause of a comma
may make the sentence read more smoothly and clearly:

The building was old, and the ivy had climbed nearly to the top of its three
   storeys.

When the clauses are parallel in structure the comma may often be omitted:

Art is long and life is short.
He stood up and she sat down.

When two clauses have the same subject, a comma is less likely to be
needed between them:

It was windy and it was wet. (Note also their shortness and their parallel
   structure—and the alliteration.)
The play was well produced and it impressed everyone who saw it.

> **Caution:** Independent clauses joined by *but* and *yet*, which explicitly mark
> a contrast, will almost always need a comma as well. And when you join
> two clauses with the coordinating conjunction *for*, always put a comma in
> front of it to prevent its being misread as a preposition:
>
> She was eager to leave early, for the restaurant was sure to be crowded.
>
> The conjunction *so* also almost always needs a comma—but remember that
> *so* is considered informal (see #12a.3).

33b   Semicolon and Coordinating Conjunction

You will sometimes want to use a **semicolon** between independent
clauses even though they are joined by a coordinating conjunction. A
semicolon is appropriate when at least one of the clauses contains other
punctuation:

Old as he was, my uncle, Angus, the best farmer in the district, easily won
   the ploughing contest; and no one who knew him—or even had only heard
   of him—was in the least surprised.

or when at least one of the clauses is unusually long:

A politician may make long-winded speeches full of clichés and generalities
   and the sort of things it is obvious everyone wants to hear; but people will
   still vote for him because they like his face.

or when you want the extra emphasis provided by a stronger pause:

> He protested that he was sorry for all his mistakes; but he went right on making them.

33c   Dash and Coordinating Conjunction

Note that in the preceding example a **dash** would have a similar and perhaps even better effect:

> He protested that he was sorry for all his mistakes—but he went right on making them.

For a different rhetorical effect, change *but* to the more neutral *and*; a dash then takes over the contrasting function:

> He protested that he was sorry for all his mistakes—and he went right on making them.

Similarly, consider the slightly different effects of these two versions of the same basic sentence:

> It may not be the best way, but it's the only way we know.
> It may not be the best way—but it's the only way we know.

> **Note:** Of course, even a period could be used between such clauses, since there is nothing inherently wrong with beginning a sentence with *And* or *But*; even as sentence openers, they are still doing their job of coordinating. See #12a.4.

33d   Semicolon Without Coordinating Conjunction

To avoid a *comma splice* (see the next section), generally use a **semicolon** between independent clauses that are not joined with one of the coordinating conjunctions (*and, but, or, nor, for, yet, so*):

> The actual value of the prize is not important; it is the honour connected with it that matters.
> She was exhausted and obviously not going to win; nevertheless she persevered and finished the race.

33e   Comma Splice

cs

Using only a comma between independent clauses not joined with a coordinating conjunction results in a **comma splice**:

> *cs:* The actual value of the prize is not important, it is the honour connected with it that matters.

cs: Being a mere child I didn't fully understand what I had witnessed, I just knew it was wrong.

A semicolon signals that an independent clause comes next. But a comma tells readers that something subordinate comes next; an independent clause coming instead would derail their train of thought. A comma *with a coordinating conjunction* is enough:

The President of the United States is elected, but the members of his cabinet are not.

With few exceptions (see below), a comma *without* a coordinating conjunction is not enough. In most such sentences, then, in order to avoid seriously distracting your readers, use *semicolons*:

Being a mere child I didn't fully understand what I had witnessed; I just knew it was wrong.
Students who work will gain their reward; students who shirk will also gain theirs.
Vancouver, the largest city in British Columbia, is not the capital; Victoria has that distinction.

For a discussion of ways to correct comma splices, see **cs** in Chapter XI.

33f-g Exceptions: Commas Alone Between Independent Clauses

33f Commas with Short and Parallel Clauses

If the clauses are short enough that a reader can take them both in with a single glance, and especially if they are also parallel in structure, a comma rather than a semicolon may be enough:

She cooked, he ate.
Lightning flashed, thunder roared.

33g Commas with Series of Clauses

Relatively short independent clauses in a *series* of three or more, especially if they are grammatically parallel, may be separated by commas rather than semicolons:

I came, I saw, I conquered.
The water was calm, our luck was good, and the fish were biting.
If you want to do well you must pay attention, you must read carefully, you must work diligently, you must write correctly, and you must keep your fingers crossed.

(In the last sentence a dash would work nicely in place of the last comma.)

33h   Caution: Use Semicolons with Conjunctive Adverbs and Transitional Phrases

Be sure to use a **semicolon**—not just a comma—between independent clauses that you join with a conjunctive adverb. Here is a list of most of the common ones:

accordingly	finally	likewise	similarly
afterward	further	meanwhile	still
also	furthermore	moreover	subsequently
anyway	hence	namely	then
besides	however	nevertheless	thereafter
certainly	indeed	next	therefore
consequently	instead	nonetheless	thus
conversely	later	otherwise	undoubtedly

The same caution applies to common transitional phrases such as these:

after this	if not	in the meantime
as a result	in addition	on the contrary
for example	in fact	on the other hand
for this reason	in short	that is

Conjunctive adverbs often have the *feel* of subordinating conjunctions, but they are not conjunctions—although some dictionaries label them as conjunctions for these meanings; rather, think of them as adverbs doing a joining or "conjunctive" job:

> The book's print was very small; therefore she got a headache as she read it.

Here *therefore* works very much like *so*; nevertheless, it is a conjunctive adverb and requires the semicolon.

> He felt well enough to go; however, his doctor ordered him to stay in bed.

Here *however* works very much like *but*; nevertheless, it is a conjunctive adverb and requires the semicolon.

Caution: Note that whereas other conjunctive adverbs will often, but not always, be followed by commas, *however* as a conjunctive adverb (unless it ends a sentence) *must* be followed by a comma to prevent its being misread as a regular adverb meaning "in whatever way" or "to whatever degree," as in "*However* you go, just make sure you get there on time."

Style Note: *However* often sounds stiff and awkward at the beginning of a sentence or clause. Unless you want special emphasis on it—equivalent to underlining it—put it at some other appropriate place in the clause. Often, delaying it just one or two words works best:

> His doctor, however, ordered him to stay in bed.

Since conjunctive adverbs can easily be shifted around within a clause, you may find it helpful to apply that test if you aren't sure whether a particular word is a conjunctive adverb or a conjunction.

33i Dashes and Colons Without Coordinating Conjunctions

Dashes and **colons** may also be used between independent clauses not joined by coordinating conjunctions. Use a dash when you want stronger emphasis on the second clause; use a colon when you want its anticipatory effect—when the second clause explains or enlarges upon the first (see #32c and #32d). In many sentences either a dash or a colon would work; the choice depends on the desired tone or emphasis. For example:

> The novel was dreadful from beginning to end: a plausible plot must have been the last thing on the writer's mind.
> The proposal horrified him—it was unthinkable.
> He took the obvious way out: he turned and ran.
> It was a unique occasion—everyone at the meeting agreed on what should be done.

Note that a comma would not be correct in any of these examples. A semicolon would work, but it would be weak and usually inappropriate (except perhaps in the first example). But note that a *period*, especially in the second and third examples, would achieve a crisp and emphatic effect by turning each into two separate sentences.

33j Run-on (Fused) Sentence

run-on Failure to put any punctuation between independent clauses where there
fs is also no coordinating conjunction results in a **run-on** or **fused** sentence:

> *run-on:* Philosophers' views did not always meet with the approval of the authorities therefore there was constant conflict between writers and the church or state.

A semicolon after *authorities* corrects this serious error. See #22; see also **run-on** in Chapter XI.

Exercise 33(1) **Punctuating between independent clauses**

Insert whatever punctuation mark (other than a period) you think best between the independent clauses in the following sentences. You may decide that some need no punctuation. Could some be punctuated in more than one way?

1. The communications revolution swept North America in the 1980's the personal computer and the fax machine became fixtures in every modern office.

2. Jamil needed some help with his lab report and he thought he knew where he could find it.
3. Puppet shows aren't just for children many adults enjoy them as well.
4. Some people work to live others live to work.
5. It was a fascinating hypothesis but no one seemed eager to support it.
6. They giggled they laughed they collapsed in a heap.
7. The hurricane warning went up and most people began heading inland but as usual some refused to budge.
8. Easy come easy go.
9. The company came closer to bankruptcy than ever before it faced the prospect of losing what a hundred years of hard work and sacrifice had built up.
10. The civil war was over people were jubilant.

Exercise 33(2) | **Correcting comma splices and run-ons**

Correct any comma splices and run-on sentences in the following:

1. I had not been back since my childhood therefore I was very surprised at all the changes that had taken place.
2. The outcome of the game is relatively unimportant it is the intensity of individual performances that matters more.
3. We started to edit the next edition of the newsletter, pretty soon paper was strewn all over the place.
4. Throughout the poem Atwood uses various techniques to get her point across, however, the literal sense is sufficiently clear.
5. But we sat silent, the scene before us on the stage had left us stunned.
6. The Montagues and Capulets can't seem to make peace they can't even pass in the streets of Verona without picking a fight.
7. This advertisement insults female consumers, therefore the product's sales are bound to suffer.
8. Life in those days was a gruelling chore, but that was what made it satisfying.
9. The Berlin Wall stood for almost thirty years, however, it was toppled in just a few weeks.
10. At last we pushed off from the shore, the canoes were buffeted by the rolling waves caused by the tidal flow.

---

34 To Set Off Adverbial Clauses

34a Commas with Introductory Clauses

Generally, use a comma between an introductory adverbial clause and an independent (main) clause:

> After I had selected all the items I wanted, I discovered that I had left my wallet at home.
> Since she was elected by a large majority, she felt that she had a strong mandate for her policies.
> When the party was over, I went straight home.

When the introductory clause is short and when there would be no pause if the sentence were spoken aloud, you may often omit the comma:

> When the party was over I went straight home.
> Once the dam had burst there was no hope for the town.
> Since he felt ill he decided to stay home.

But if omitting the comma could cause misreading, retain it:

> Whenever I wanted, someone would bring me something to eat.
> Long before the sun rose, high above the mountains I could see a jet's contrail streaking the sky.

Whenever you're not sure, use a comma: it will always be acceptable.

34b   Commas with Concluding Clauses

A comma may or may not be needed between an independent clause and a following adverbial clause. If the subordinate clause is essential to the meaning of the sentence, it is in effect *restrictive* and should not be set off with a comma; if it is not essential but contains only additional information or comment, it is *nonrestrictive* and should be set off with a comma (see #37). Consider the following examples:

> I went straight home when the party was over.
> She felt that she had a strong mandate for her policies because she was elected by a large majority.
> He simply could not succeed, however hard he may have tried.
> She did an excellent job on her second essay, although the first one was a disaster.

Most such final clauses will be necessary and won't want a comma. When in doubt, try omitting the clause to see if the sentence still says essentially what you want it to. Consider the following pair; the meanings are different, depending on whether or not there is a comma:

> The conference was a success even though it began in wild confusion.
> The conference was a success, even though it began in wild confusion.

See also #37c.

35 p

Insert commas where you think necessary in the following sentences. Indicate any places where you think a comma would be optional.

1. Although it was almost midnight he knew he had to stay up and finish writing the report.
2. You may begin now if you want to.
3. You may begin whenever you wish.
4. The fruit crop is especially good this year because the spring was unusually warm.
5. Because spring was so warm this year the fruit crop is unusually heavy.
6. Before you move to Peru you should study Spanish.
7. Freedom of speech is certainly a fundamental right though some may not recognize the fact.
8. You can often tell when commas are required if you read sentences aloud and listen for the natural pauses.
9. After she had won the race she seemed oddly less confident than she had before the race began.
10. However you look at the problem you cannot find a simple solution.

35 To Set Off Introductory and Concluding Words and Phrases

35a Adverbs and Adverbial Phrases

Generally, set off a long introductory adverbial phrase with a comma:

After many years as leader of the party, he retired gracefully.
In order to get the best results from your computer, you must follow the instruction manual carefully.
Just like all the other long-time employees, she felt loyal to the company.

Introductory single-word adverbs and short phrases don't need to be set off if the sentence flows smoothly without a comma; try reading these aloud:

Unfortunately the weather didn't cooperate.
Slowly they crept closer to the fire.
With a mighty heave they hoisted the beam into place.
In order to punctuate well you have to feel a sentence's rhythm.
In 1983 they moved to Calgary.

Generally, set off such a word or phrase only if you want a distinct pause, for example for emphasis or qualification or to prevent misreading:

Unfortunately, the weather didn't cooperate.
Generally, follow our advice about punctuation.
Usually, quiet people are easier to work with.

Of the conjunctive adverbs, only *however* must be set off, though the others frequently are as well (see #33h and #44f).

When such words and phrases follow the independent clause, most—but not all—will be restrictive and therefore not set off with commas:

> He retired gracefully after many years as leader of the party.
> You must follow the instruction manual carefully in order to get the best results from your computer.
> They moved to Calgary in 1983.
> She felt loyal to the company, just like all the other long-time employees.
> The weather didn't cooperate, unfortunately.

If you intend the concluding element to complete the sense of the main clause, don't set it off; if it merely provides additional information or comment, set it off. The presence or absence of punctuation tells your readers how you want the sentence to be read.

35b   Participles and Participial Phrases

Always set off an introductory participle or participial phrase with a comma (see #10d):

> Finding the course unexpectedly difficult, she sought extra help.
> Feeling victorious, he left the room.
> Having been in prison so long, he scarcely recognized the world when he emerged.
> Puzzled, she turned back to the beginning of the chapter.

Closing participles and participial phrases almost always need to be set off as well. Read the sentence aloud; if you feel a distinct pause, use a comma:

> She sought extra help, finding the course unexpectedly difficult.
> Higher prices result in increased wage demands, contributing to the inflationary spiral.

Occasionally such a sentence will flow clearly and smoothly without a comma, especially if the modifier is in effect restrictive, essential to the meaning:

> He left the room feeling victorious.
> She sat there looking puzzled.

If the closing participle modifies a predicate noun or a direct object, there usually should not be a comma:

> He was a man lacking in courage.
> I left him feeling bewildered.

But if the participle in such a sentence modifies the subject—that is, if it could also conceivably modify the object—a comma is necessary:

> I left him, feeling bewildered.

Only the presence or absence of the comma tells a reader how to understand such a sentence.

Caution: Don't mistake a *gerund* for a *participle* (see #10d and #10f). A gerund or gerund phrase functioning as the subject should not be followed by a comma (see #44a):

> *participle:* Singing in the rain, we happily walked all the way home.
> *gerund:*   Singing in the rain kept us from feeling gloomy.

Similarly, don't mistake a long infinitive phrase functioning as a subject noun for one functioning as an adverb (see #10a):

> *noun:*   To put together a large jigsaw puzzle in one day without help is a remarkable feat.
> *adverb:*   To put together a large jigsaw puzzle in one day without help, you need to be either gifted or very lucky.

35c Absolute Phrases

Always set off absolute phrases with commas (see #1r and #10i):

> The doors locked and bolted, they went to bed feeling secure.
> Timmy went to his room, head bowed, a tear coursing down his cheek.

Exercise 35 | **Punctuating opening and closing words and phrases**

Insert commas where you think necessary in the following sentences. Indicate any places where you think a comma would be optional.

1. Unnoticed I entered the house by the side door.
2. We walked slowly soaking up the sights and sounds along the waterfront.
3. At the end of the lecture I had no clearer understanding of the subject than I had when I came in.
4. The dishes washed and put away I decided to relax with a good book.
5. The brain regulates and integrates our senses allowing us to experience our environment.
6. Raising prices results in increased wage demands adding to inflation.
7. Following the instructions I poured the second ingredient into the beaker with the first and shook them shutting my eyes in expectation of something unpleasant.
8. Before going to bed I fixed myself a light snack naturally.
9. To make a long story short I found my aunt looking healthier than I'd ever seen her before.
10. Looking strained and furious the coach stared back at the referee without saying a word.

36 To Set Off Concluding Summaries and Appositives

Both **dashes** and **colons** can set off concluding summaries and appositives. Some writers think dashes are best for short concluding elements and colons for longer ones; but what matters isn't their length but their relation to the rest of the sentence. Use colons for straightforward conclusions, dashes for emphatic or unexpected ones. For example, the following sentences express a conventional idea, with the colon straightforwardly, with the dash somewhat emphatically:

> He wanted only one thing from life: happiness.
> He wanted only one thing from life—happiness.

But with a less expected final word the tone changes:

> He wanted only one thing from life—money.

Here a colon would do, since a colon followed by a single word automatically conveys some emphasis; but the vigour of the idea would not be as well served by the quietness of a colon as it is by the dash of a dash. The same principles apply to setting off longer concluding appositives and summaries, though colons are more common; use a dash only when you want to take advantage of its special flavour.

> **Note:** You will sometimes find a comma used to set off a concluding appositive or summary; but a comma is unlikely to be as effective as a colon or a dash, and can even be temporarily misleading.

37 To Set Off Nonrestrictive Elements

Words, phrases, and clauses are **nonrestrictive** when they are not essential to the principal meaning of a sentence; they should be set off from the rest of the sentence, usually with commas, though dashes and parentheses can also be used (see #39). A **restrictive** modifier is essential to the meaning and should not be set off:

> *restrictive:* Anyone wanting a refund should see the manager.
> *nonrestrictive:* Alex, wanting a refund, asked to see the manager.

The participial phrase explains why Alex asked to see the manager, but the sentence is clear without it: "Alex asked to see the manager"; the phrase is therefore not essential and is set off with commas. But without the phrase the first sentence wouldn't make sense: "Anyone should see the manager"; the phrase is essential and is not set off. The question most often arises with *relative clauses* (see #1o and #3d); *appositives*, though usually nonrestrictive, can also be restrictive; and some other elements

37a *p*

can also be in effect either restrictive or nonrestrictive (see #34b and #35a-b).

37a   Restrictive and Nonrestrictive Relative Clauses

Always set off a nonrestrictive relative clause; do not set off restrictive relative clauses:

> She is a woman who likes to travel.

Clearly the relative clause is essential and is not set off.

> Carol, who likes to travel, is going to Greece this summer.

Now the relative clause is merely additional—though explanatory—information: it is not essential to the identification of Carol, who has been explicitly named, nor is it essential to the meaning of the main clause. Being nonrestrictive, then, it must be set off. Consider the following pair of sentences:

> Students, who are lazy, should not expect much from their education.
> Students who are lazy should not expect much from their education.

Set off as nonrestrictive, the relative clause applies to all students, which makes the sentence untrue. Left unpunctuated, the relative clause is restrictive, making the sentence correctly apply only to students who are in fact lazy. Another example:

> The book, which I so badly wanted to read, was not in the library.
> The book which I so badly wanted to read was not in the library.

With the clause set off as nonrestrictive, we must assume that the book has been clearly identified in an earlier sentence. Left unpunctuated, the clause identifies "The book" as the particular one the speaker wanted to read but which the library didn't have.

Note: If you can use the relative pronoun *that*, you know the clause is restrictive; *that* cannot begin a nonrestrictive clause:

> The book that I wanted to read was not in the library.

Further, if the pronoun can be omitted (see #3d), the clause is restrictive, as with *that* in the preceding example and *whom* in the following:

> The person [whom] I most admire is the one who works hard and plays hard.

But don't omit *that* when it is necessary to prevent misreading:

> *cl:* Examples of the quality of art advertisements contain can be found in almost any magazine.

A *that* after *art* prevents misreading the phrase as "art advertisements."

> **Usage note:** *That* is much more common than *which* in restrictive clauses. Indeed, some writers prefer to use *which* only in nonrestrictive clauses. But since *which* has long been commonly used in restrictive clauses, it is absurd to insist upon the distinction. Besides, *which* sometimes simply sounds better.

37b   Restrictive and Nonrestrictive Appositives

Always set off a nonrestrictive appositive:

> Jan, our daughter, keeps the lawn mowed all summer.
> Karl—the man I intend to marry—is tops in all categories.
> Milton's *Paradise Lost* is a noble work of literature, one that will live in human minds for all time.
> Hugh is going to bring his sister, Eileen.

In the last example, the comma indicates that Hugh has only the one sister. Left unpunctuated, the appositive would be restrictive, meaning that Hugh has more than one sister and that the particular one he is going to bring is the one named Eileen.

Some appositives have become parts of names or titles and are not set off; for example:

> William the Conqueror won the Battle of Hastings in 1066.
> The Apostle Paul wrote several books of the New Testament.
> Ivan the Terrible was the first czar of Russia.

Don't mistake a restrictive appositive for a nonrestrictive one:

> *p:* The proceedings were opened by union leader, Peter Smith, with remarks attacking the government.

The commas are wrong, since it is only his name, *Peter Smith*, that clearly identifies him; the appositive is therefore *restrictive*. But alter the sentence slightly:

> The proceedings were opened by the union's leader, Peter Smith, with remarks attacking the government.

Now the phrase *the union's leader*, with its definite article, identifies the man; the name itself, *Peter Smith*, is only incidental information and is therefore *nonrestrictive*.

> *p:* According to spokesman, James Fraser, the economy is improving daily.
> *revised:* According to spokesman James Fraser, the economy is improving daily.
> *revised:* According to the spokesman, James Fraser, the economy is improving daily.

The definite article makes all the difference. But even the presence or absence of the definite article is not always a sure test:

> One of the best-known mysteries of the sea is that of the ship *Mary Celeste*, the disappearance of whose entire crew has never been satisfactorily explained.

The phrase *the ship* is insufficient identification; the proper name is needed and is therefore restrictive. This error most often occurs when a proper name *follows* a defining or characterizing word or phrase. In the reverse order, such a phrase is set off as a nonrestrictive appositive:

> James Fraser, the spokesman, said the economy is improving daily.

See #44g for more on restrictive appositives.

37c   ***Because* Clauses and Phrases**

Adverbial clauses or phrases beginning with *because* (or otherwise conveying that sense) can be a problem when they *follow* an explicit negative. Although they are in effect restrictive, they nevertheless usually need to be set off:

> They don't trust him, because he is a politician.

The comma helps, since without it a reader could ask, "Well, then why *do* they trust him?" That is, the sentence could be read to mean that they do trust him, but for some reason other than that he is a politician. Without the negative, but with the same basic meaning, the comma isn't necessary:

> They distrust him because he is a politician.

When a *because* follows a negative, punctuate the sentence so that it means what you want it to:

> Mary didn't pass the exam, because she had stayed up all night studying for it: she was so groggy she couldn't even read the questions correctly.
> Mary didn't pass the exam because she had stayed up all night studying for it. That may have helped, but her thorough grasp of the material would have enabled her to pass it without the cramming.

Often you can best avoid the possible awkwardness or ambiguity by simply rephrasing a sentence in which *because* follows a negative.

Exercise 37   **Punctuating nonrestrictive elements**

Decide whether the italicized elements in the following sentences are restrictive or nonrestrictive and insert punctuation as required.

1. The student *who takes studying seriously* is the one *who is most likely to succeed.*

2. The novels *I like best* are those *that tell a good story*.
3. This movie *which was produced on a very low budget* was a popular success.
4. Whitehorse *the capital of the Yukon* is a cold place to spend the winter.
5. Cato *the Elder* was one of the principal Stoic philosophers.
6. Sentence interrupters *not essential to the meaning* should be set off with commas.
7. Michel Tremblay *the playwright* is a Quebec writer with a national reputation.
8. The London *which is in Ontario* was named after the London *which is the capital of England*.
9. My twin brother *Greg* is very proud of his wife *Marilyn*.
10. In the view of small-town newspaper editor James Black the storm was nothing to get excited about.

38 Between Items in a Series

38a Commas

Generally, use commas between words, phrases, or clauses in a series of three or more:

> He sells books, magazines, candy, and tobacco.
> She promised the voters to cut taxes, to limit government spending, and to improve transportation.
> Carmen explained that she had visited the art gallery, that she had walked in the park, and that eventually she had gone to a movie.
> He stirred the sauce frequently, carefully, and hungrily.

38b Comma Before Final Item in a Series

The common practice of omitting the final comma, the one before the conjunction, can be misleading. Better always to include it. That final pause will give your sentences a better rhythm, and you will avoid the kind of possible confusion apparent in sentences like these (try adding the final comma and then reading them again):

> For breakfast I like toast, coffee and ham and eggs.
> Your teacher wants your essays to contain not only good ideas, but also good diction, good sentences, good paragraphs, good punctuation and mechanics and good organization.
> They prided themselves on having a large and bright kitchen, a productive vegetable garden, a large recreation room with a huge fireplace and two fifty-foot cedar trees.
> The Speech from the Throne discussed international trade, improvements in transportation, slowing down inflation and the postal service.

38c Semicolons

If the phrases or clauses in a series are unusually long or contain internal punctuation, you will probably want to separate them with semicolons rather than commas:

> How wonderful it is to awaken in the morning when the birds are clamouring in the trees; to see the bright light of a summer morning streaming into the room; to realize, with a sudden flash of joy, that it is Sunday and that this perfect morning is completely yours; and then to loaf in a deck-chair without a thought of tomorrow.
>
> Saint John, New Brunswick; Victoria, British Columbia; and Kingston, Ontario, are all about the same size.

If you want to create emphasis and a slower rhythm, you can separate even short items with semicolons:

> There are certain qualities we expect in our leaders: honesty; integrity; intelligence; understanding.

(The omission of the customary *and* before the final item stylistically heightens the effect, reinforcing the emphasis gained by using semicolons; see #12a.2.)

38d Dashes

You can also emphasize items in a series by putting dashes between them—but don't do it often. The sharpness of the breaks greatly heightens the effect of a series:

> Rising taxes—rising insurance rates—rising transportation costs—skyrocketing food prices: it is becoming more and more difficult to live decently and still keep within a budget.

Here again the omission of *and* adds to the stridency, as do repetition and parallel structure; even the colon adds its touch. But such dashes can also be effective in a quieter context:

> Upon rounding the bend we were confronted with a breathtaking panorama of lush valleys with meandering streams—flower-covered slopes—great rocks and trees—and, overtopping all, the mighty peaks with their hoods of snow.

38e Colons

Colons too can be used in a series—but even more rarely than dashes. Colons add emphasis because they are unusual, but mainly their anticipatory nature produces a cumulative effect suitable when successive items in a series build to a climax:

He held on: he persevered: he fought back: and eventually he won out, regardless of the seemingly overwhelming obstacles.

It blew: it rained: it hailed: it sleeted: it even snowed—it was a most unusual June.

(Note how the dash in the last example prepares for the final clause.)

38f Series of Adjectives

Use commas between two or more adjectives preceding a noun if they are parallel, each modifying the noun itself; do not put commas between adjectives that are not parallel:

He is an intelligent, efficient, ambitious officer.
She is a tall young woman.
She wore a new black felt hat, a long red coat, and a woollen scarf with red, white, and black stripes.

In the first sentence, each adjective modifies *officer*. In the second, *tall* modifies *young woman*; it is a *young woman* who is *tall*, not a *woman* who is *tall* and *young*. In the third, *new* modifies *black felt hat*, *black* modifies *felt hat*, and *long* modifies *red coat*; *red*, *white*, and *black* all separately modify *stripes*.

But it isn't always easy to tell whether or not such adjectives are parallel. One rule of thumb that often helps is to think of each comma as substituting for *and*: try putting *and* between the adjectives. If it sounds logical there, the adjectives are probably parallel and should be separated by a comma; if *and* doesn't seem to work, a comma won't either. For example, you wouldn't say *a black and felt hat* or *a long and red coat*, whereas *red and white and black stripes* is natural. Another aid to remember: usually no comma is needed after a number (*three blind mice*) or after common adjectives for size or age (*tall young woman, long red coat, new brick house*). But sometimes you'll have to rely on instinct or common sense. For example, the following sentences seem fine without commas:

There was an ominous wry tone in her voice.
What caught our eye in the antique shop was a comfortable-looking tattered old upholstered leather chair.

But you might not agree. If you find yourself stuck, you can always rewrite the sentence.

See also #44c.

Exercise 38 Punctuating series

Punctuate the following sentences as necessary.

1. The things I expected from my education were better self-discipline a broader outlook on life and the arts and preparation for a possible career.

2. April May and June are my favourite months.
3. The handsome young man wore gray plaid slacks a yellow turtleneck sweater and a smartly tailored blue blazer with square brass buttons.
4. The nice cute little baby soon began to crawl fall and squall.
5. The recital was over the audience began to cheer and applaud loudly and the pianist who was obviously pleased stood up and bowed.

39 Punctuating "Sentence Interrupters" with Commas, Dashes, and Parentheses: The Punctuation Marks that Come in Pairs

Sentence interrupters are parenthetical elements—words, phrases, or clauses—that interrupt the syntax of a sentence. Although we discuss some of these under other headings, here we stress two points: (1) interrupters must be set off at *both* ends; (2) you can choose among three kinds of punctuation marks to set them off: a pair of commas, a pair of dashes, or a pair of parentheses.

39a Interrupters Set Off with Commas

Set off light, ordinary interrupters with a pair of commas:

Boswell, the biographer of Samuel Johnson, was a keen observer. (nonrestrictive appositive phrase)

This document, the lawyer says, will complete the contract. (explanatory clause)

Thank you, David, for your good advice. (noun of address)

Mr. Hao, feeling elated, left the judge's office. (participial phrase)

At least one science course, such as botany or astronomy, is required of all students. (prepositional phrase of example)

You may, on the other hand, wish to concentrate on the final examination. (transitional prepositional phrase)

Could you be persuaded to consider this money as, well, a loan? (mild interjection)

Grandparents, who are sometimes too indulgent, should not be allowed to spoil their grandchildren. (nonrestrictive relative clause)

But the canned tuna, it now occurs to me, may after all be responsible for our upset stomachs. (clause expressing afterthought)

It was, all things considered, a successful concert. (absolute phrase)

39b Interrupters Set Off with Dashes

Use a pair of dashes to set off abrupt interrupters or other interrupters that you wish to emphasize. An interrupter that sharply breaks the syntax of a sentence will often be emphatic for that very reason, and dashes will be appropriate to set it off:

This document—so says the lawyer, anyway—will complete the contract.
The stockholders who voted for him—quite a sizable group—were obviously
dissatisfied with our recent conduct of the business.
He told me—believe this or not!—that he would never touch liquor again.
Samuel Johnson—the eighteenth century's most eminent man of letters—is
the subject of James Boswell's great biography.

In the last example commas would suffice, but dashes work well because
of both the length and the content of the appositive. Wherever you want
emphasis or a different tone, you can use dashes where commas would
ordinarily serve:

The best student—Denise Dione—was elected class president.
The modern age—as we all know—is a technology-ridden age.

Dashes are also useful to set off an interrupter consisting of a series with
its own internal commas, such as our first sentence in this section; set off
with commas, such a structure can be confusing:

confusing: Sentence interrupters are parenthetical elements, words, phrases,
or clauses, that interrupt the syntax of a sentence.
clear: Sentence interrupters are parenthetical elements—words,
phrases, or clauses—that interrupt the syntax of a sentence.

39c   Interrupters Set Off with Parentheses

Use parentheses to set off abrupt interrupters or other interrupters that
you wish to de-emphasize; often interrupters that could be emphatic can
be played down in order to emphasize the other parts of a sentence:

The stockholders who voted for him (quite a sizable group) were obviously
dissatisfied with our recent conduct of the business.
The best student (her name is Denise Dion) was elected class president.
It is not possible at this time (it is far too early in the growing season) to predict with any confidence just what the crop yield will be.
Speculation (I mean this in its pejorative sense) is not a safe foundation for a
business enterprise.
Some modern sports activities (hang-gliding for example) involve an unusually high element of danger.

Note: By de-emphasizing something striking, parentheses can also
achieve an effect similar to that of dashes, though by an ironic tone rather
than an insistent one.

Caution: Remember, punctuation marks that set off sentence interrupters
come in pairs. If you put down an opening parenthesis you aren't likely to
omit the closing one. But sometimes writers thoughtlessly omit the second
dash or—especially—the second comma. Reading aloud, perhaps with
exaggerated pauses, can help you spot that a mark is missing.

---

40 *p*

Set off the italicized interrupters with commas, dashes, or parentheses. Be prepared to defend your choices.

1. It was seven o'clock in the evening *a mild autumn evening* and the crickets were beginning to chirp.
2. No one *at least no one who was present* wanted to disagree with the speaker's position.
3. One Sunday morning *a morning I will never forget* the phone rang clamorously.
4. Since it was only a mild interjection *no more than a barely audible snort from the back of the room* he went on with scarcely a pause *but with a slightly raised eyebrow* and finished his speech.
5. And then suddenly *out of the blue and into my head* came the only possible answer.

40 Parentheses ( )

Parentheses have three principal functions in nontechnical writing: (1) to set off certain kinds of interrupters (see #39c above), (2) to enclose cross-reference information within a sentence, as we just did and as we do throughout this book, and (3) to enclose numerals or letters setting up a list or series, as we do in this sentence. Note that if a complete sentence is enclosed in parentheses within another sentence (here is an example of such an insertion), it needs neither an opening capital letter nor a closing period. Note also that if a comma or other mark is called for by the sentence (as in the preceding sentence, and in this one), it comes *after* the closing parenthesis, not before the opening one. Exclamation points and question marks go inside the parentheses only if they are a part of what is enclosed. (When an entire sentence or more is enclosed, the terminal mark of course comes inside the parentheses—as does this period.)

41 Brackets [ ]

Brackets (often referred to as "square brackets," since some people use the term *brackets* also to refer to parentheses) are used primarily to enclose something inserted in a direct quotation: see #43j. And if you have to put parentheses inside parentheses—as in a footnote or a bibliographical entry—change the inner ones to brackets.

42 End Punctuation: Period, Question Mark, and Exclamation Point

The end of every sentence must be marked with a period, a question mark, or an exclamation point (but see the note at the end of this section). The **period** is the most common terminal punctuation; it ends the vast majority of sentences. The **question mark** is used to end direct questions or seeming statements that are intended interrogatively. The **exclamation point** is used to end sentences that express strong emotion, emphatic surprise, or even emphatic query. Usually the appropriate choice of mark will be obvious, but sometimes you will want to consider just what effect you want to achieve. Note for example the different effects of the following; in each instance, the end punctuation would dictate the necessary tone of voice and distribution of emphasis and pitch with which the sentence would be said aloud:

> He resigned. (matter-of-fact)
> He resigned! (surprised or emphatic)
> He resigned? (sceptical or surprised)

42a   Period   •

Use a period to mark the end of statements and unemphatic commands:

> It is not as cold this winter as it was last winter.
> Geoffrey Chaucer, the author of *The Canterbury Tales*, died in 1400.
> Don't let yourself be fooled by advertising claims.

A period can also be used after something worded as a question but not meant interrogatively:

> You'll write to us soon, won't you.
> It's a difficult decision to make, isn't it.

Use a period after most abbreviations:

> abbr., Mr., Ms., Ph.D., Dr., Jr., B.A., Mt., Nfld., P.E.I., etc.

Notes: (1) Although *Ms.* is not a true abbreviation, it is usually followed by a period. (2) In England it is conventional to omit the period after abbreviations that include the first and last letter of the abbreviated word: Mr, Mrs, Dr, Bart, ft, Jr, St, etc. (And note in the preceding sentence that a period after an abbreviation at the end of a sentence serves as the sentence's period.)

Periods are not used after metric and other symbols (unless they occur at the end of a sentence):

> km, cm, kg, C, Hz, Au, Zr

Periods are often omitted with initials, especially of groups or organizations, and especially if the initials are acronyms or thought of as a name and written in capital letters:

> UN, UNESCO, RCMP, RAF, NDP, TV, MLA, MP, STOL, CBC

When in doubt, consult a good dictionary. If there is more than one acceptable usage, be consistent: stick with the one you choose.

42b   Question Mark   **?**

Use a question mark at the end of direct questions:

> Who is the greatest philosopher of all time?
> When will the contract expire?

Note that a question mark is necessary after questions that aren't phrased in the usual interrogative way (as might occur if you were writing dialogue):

> You're leaving so early? (i.e., "Are you leaving so early?")
> You want him to accompany you? (i.e., "Do you want him to accompany you?")

A question appearing as a sentence interrupter still needs a question mark at its end:

> I went back to the beginning—what else could I do?—and tried to get it right the second time through.
> The man in the mackintosh (what was his name again?) took a rear seat.

Since such interrupters are necessarily abrupt, dashes or parentheses are the appropriate marks to set them off.

See also #1t.

42c   Exclamation Point   **!**

Use exclamation points after emphatic statements and after expressions of emphatic surprise, emphatic query, and strong emotion—that is, after exclamations:

> He came in first, yet it was only his second time in professional competition!
> What a fine actor!

You don't say so!
Isn't it beautiful today!
Be careful!
Wow!

Caution: Use exclamation points sparingly, if at all, in formal writing. Achieve your desired emphasis by other means: see #18j.

Note: Two other ways to end sentences seldom occur outside narrative fiction. A dash, or more commonly the three dots of ellipsis (see #43i), are sometimes used at the end of a sentence—especially in dialogue or at the end of a paragraph or a chapter—to indicate a pause, a fading away, or an interruption, or to create mild suspense.

---

43 Punctuation with Quotations; Using Quotation Marks " "

Q, q   There are two kinds of quotation: dialogue or direct speech, as in a story, novel, or nonfiction narrative or other essay; and verbatim quotation from a published work or other source, as in a research paper (see Chapter IX). (For the use of quotation marks around titles, see #48a and c.)

43a   Direct Speech

Enclose all direct speech in quotation marks:

> I remember hearing my mother say to my father, "Henry, get your feet off the coffee table."

In dialogue, it is conventional to begin a new paragraph each time the speaker changes:

> "Henry," she said, a note of exasperation in her voice, "please get your feet off the coffee table."
> "Oh, yes," he replied. "Sorry, dear, I keep forgetting."
> She examined it for scratches. "Well, no harm done this time, I guess. But please try to remember."

Even when speeches are incomplete, the part that is verbatim should be enclosed in quotation marks:

> After only two weeks, he said he was "tired of it all" and that he was "going to look for a more interesting job."

43b Q, q

43b Direct Quotation from a Source

Enclose in quotation marks any direct quotation from another source that you run into your own text:

> According to Francis Bacon, "No pleasure is comparable to standing upon the vantage-ground of truth."

1. Prose

Prose quotations that run to no more than four lines are normally run into the text. Quotations of more than four lines should be indented ten spaces and double-spaced (like your text):

```
As Milton puts it, in one of those ringing passages that make his

Areopagitica so memorable:

        I cannot praise a fugitive and cloistered virtue,

        unexercised and unbreathed, that never sallies out and

        seeks her adversary, but slinks out of the race where

        that immortal garland is to be run for, not without dust

        and heat.
```

When a quotation is thus set off, do not add quotation marks around it; but reproduce any quotation marks that appear in the original:

```
        Budgets can be important.  As Dickens has Mr. Micawber say in

David Copperfield,

        "Annual income twenty pounds, annual expenditure nineteen

        nineteen six, result happiness.  Annual income twenty

        pounds, annual expenditure twenty pounds ought and six,

        result misery."
```

> **Note:** If you quote only a single paragraph or part of a paragraph, do not include the paragraph indention; if your quotation takes in more than one paragraph, include the indentions (but not for the first paragraph if you begin your quotation later than its beginning); use three additional spaces for an indention. If you quote multiple paragraphs that are in quotation marks in the original, put such marks at the beginning of each paragraph, but at the end only of the last one.

2. Poetry

Set off quotations of four or more lines of poetry in the same way (though you needn't indent them as much as ten spaces if their line-lengths would make the page look awkward). A quotation of one, two, or three lines of poetry may be set off if you want it to get special emphasis; otherwise run such a quotation into your text. When you run in more than one line, indicate the line-breaks with a spaced slash mark or *virgule*:

> Wordsworth's comment in one of his sonnets almost two hundred
>
> years ago could well be applied to the way we live today: "The
>
> world is too much with us; late and soon, / Getting and spending,
>
> we lay waste our powers: / Little we see in nature that is
>
> ours."

43c Single Quotation Marks: Quotation Within Quotation ' '

Put single quotation marks around a quotation that occurs within another quotation; this is the only standard use for single quotation marks:

> In Joseph Conrad's *Heart of Darkness*, after a leisurely setting
>
> of the scene by the unnamed narrator, the drama begins when the
>
> character who is to be the principal narrator first speaks:
>
> "'And this also,' said Marlow suddenly, 'has been one of the
>
> dark places of the earth.'"

43d With Verbs of Speaking Before Quotations

When verbs of speaking or their equivalent precede a quotation, they are usually followed by commas:

> Helen said, "He will do exactly as I tell him."
> Adriana look up and asked, "What time is it?"

(Note that when a quotation ends a sentence, its own terminal punctuation serves also as that of the sentence.) With short or emphatic quotations, commas often aren't necessary:

> He said "Not yet," so we waited a little longer.
> Someone shouted "Fire!" and we all headed for the exits.

Again, punctuate a sentence the way you want it to be heard; your sense of its rhythm should help you decide. On the other hand, if the quotation is long—especially if it consists of more than one sentence—or if the context is formal, a colon will probably be more appropriate:

> When dinner was over Oscar turned to his hostess and said: "Seldom have I enjoyed a meal more, my dear. The balance of courses was superb, and the wines were the perfect accompaniment."

If the introductory element is itself an independent clause, then a colon or period must be used:

> Oscar turned to her and spoke: "A delicious repast, my dear."

Spoke, unlike *said*, is here an intransitive verb.

If you work a quotation into your own syntax, don't use even a comma to introduce it; for example the word *that* often follows a verb of speaking:

> It is often said that "Sticks and stones may break my bones, but words will never hurt me"—a singularly inaccurate notion.

43e   With Verbs of Speaking After Quotations

If a verb of speaking or a subject-verb combination follows a quotation, it is usually set off by a comma:

> "The Great Lakes are extremely important to the commerce of the area," said the speaker.
> "I think there's a fly in my soup," she muttered.

But if the quotation ends with a question mark or an exclamation point, no other punctuation is added:

> "What time is it?" asked Adriana, looking up.
> "Mr. Chairman! I insist that I be heard!" he shouted.

If the clause containing the verb of speaking interrupts the quotation, it should be preceded by a comma and followed by whatever mark is called for by the syntax and the sense. For example:

> "Since it's such a long drive," he said, "we'd better get an early start."
> "It's a long drive," he argued; "therefore I think we should start early."
> "It's a very long way," he insisted. "We should start as early as possible."

43f   With Quotations Set Off by Indention

Colons are conventionally used to introduce "block" quotations—long quotations set off from your text:

> In one of his *Devotions* John Donne wrote:
>
>> No man is an island, entire of itself; every man is a
>> piece of the continent, a part of the main; if a clod be
>> washed away by the sea, Europe is the less, as well as if
>> a promontory were, as well as if a manor of thy friends
>> or of thine own were; any man's death diminishes me,
>> because I am involved in mankind; and therefore never
>> send to know for whom the bell tolls; it tolls for thee.

But if you work even such a long quotation into your own syntax, as with a *that* after *wrote*, no punctuation is needed.

43g Words Used in a Special Sense

As we do with "block" in #43f above, put quotation marks around words used in a special sense or words for which you wish to indicate some qualification:

> What she calls a "ramble" I would call a twenty-mile hike.
> He had been up in the woods so long he was "bushed," as Canadians put it.

> **Note:** Some writers put quotation marks around words referred to as words, but it is better practice to italicize them (see #49c).

> **Caution:** Don't put quotation marks around slang terms, clichés, and the like. If a word or phrase is so weak or inappropriate that you have to apologize for it, you shouldn't be using it in the first place. And the last thing such a term needs is to have attention called to it. Even if a slang term is appropriate, putting quotation marks around it implicitly insults readers by presuming that they won't recognize a bit of slang when they see it. And do not use quotation marks for emphasis; they don't work that way. (See also the comment on "civilization" on page 10 of the sample research paper, #79.)

43h Other Marks with Quotation Marks

Put *periods* and *commas* inside closing quotation marks; put *semicolons* and *colons* outside them:

> "Knowing how to write well," he said, "can be a source of great pleasure"; and then he added that it had "one other important quality": he identified it simply as "hard work."

We recommend this standard North American practice. (In British usage, periods and commas are also put outside unless they are part of what is being quoted—and single rather than double quotation marks are conventional. Some Canadian writers and publishers follow British practice, putting periods and commas inside closing quotation marks only when they are actually in the material being quoted, as for example with a period at the end of a sentence.) *Question marks* and *exclamation points* go either outside or inside, depending on whether they apply to the quotation or to the whole sentence:

> "What time is it?" she asked.
> Who said, "To be or not to be, that is the question"?
> Did you find out who shouted "God save the Queen!"?

43i Ellipses for Omissions   • • •

If when quoting from a written source you decide to omit one or more words from a sentence, indicate the omission with the three *spaced* periods of an **ellipsis**. For example, if you wanted to quote only part of the passage from Donne quoted at length earlier (#43f), you might do it like this:

```
As John Donne put it, "No man is an island, entire of itself . . .

any man's death diminishes me, because I am involved in

mankind. . . ."
```

When you omit something from the end of a sentence, as here, one period is the sentence period and the other three indicate the omission. Four periods also can indicate the omission of one or more entire sentences, or even whole paragraphs. You need not indicate an ellipsis at the beginning of a quotation unless the quotation could be mistaken for a complete sentence, for example if it began with *I* or some other capital letter:

```
One could say, echoing Donne, ". . . I am involved in mankind. . . ."
```

Don't use an ellipsis at either end if your quotation is a mere word or phrase that could in no way be mistaken for a complete sentence—but make sure such words and phrases fit into your own syntax.

Caution: Don't omit material from a quotation in such a way that you distort what the author is saying or destroy the integrity of the syntax. Similarly, don't quote unfairly "out of context"; for example, if an author qualifies a statement in some way, don't quote it as if it were unqualified.

43j Brackets for Additions, Changes, and Comments [ ]

Keep such changes to a minimum, but enclose in square brackets any editorial addition or change you find it necessary to make within a quotation—for example a clarifying fact or a change in tense to make the quoted material fit the syntax of your sentence:

> The author states that "The following year [1990] marked a turning point in my life."
> One of my friends wrote me that her "feelings about the subject [were] similar to" mine.

Use the word *sic* (Latin for *thus*) in brackets to indicate that an error in the quotation occurs in the original:

> One of my friends wrote me: "My feelings about the subject are similiar [sic] to yours."

See also #77f. For further information on quotations, see the *MLA Handbook for Writers of Research Papers* (3rd edition, 1988).

44 Avoiding Common Errors in Punctuation

44a Generally, do not put a comma between a subject and its verb unless some intervening element calls for punctuation:

> *no p:* His enthusiasm for the project and his desire to be of help, led him to add his name to the list of volunteers.

Don't be misled by the length of a compound subject. The comma after *help* is just as wrong as the comma in this sentence:

> *no p:* Edna, addressed the class.

But if some intervening element, for example an appositive or a participial phrase, requires setting off, use a *pair* of marks (see #39):

> His enthusiasm for the project and his desire to be of help, both strongly felt, led him to add his name to the list of volunteers.
> Edna—the star student—addressed the class.

Occasionally, however, if a subject is unusually long or complicated or heavily punctuated, a comma after it and before the verb can provide a welcome breather:

> Students who come to university looking not for an education but for a good time, to whom classes are a necessary evil and weekend parties the really important occasions, and who feel that teachers and libraries are things to be avoided as much as possible, are not only likely to perform poorly but are also fundamentally wasting their own and everyone else's time and money.

The comma after *possible,* while not essential, does make the sentence easier to read. Sometimes such a comma is required simply to prevent misreading; here the comma after *people* keeps it from being even momentarily mistaken for the subject of the verb *give*:

> The spirit of adventure and the openness to the unexpected sights, sounds, tastes, and people, give independent travellers a familiarity with a place that those on package tours could never have.

44b Do not put a comma between a verb and its object or complement unless some intervening element calls for punctuation. Especially, don't mistakenly assume that a clause opening with *that* always needs a comma before it:

> *no p:* Jeremy realized, that he could no longer keep his eyes open.

The noun clause beginning with *that* is the direct object of the verb *found* and should not be separated from it. Only if an interrupter requires setting off should there be any punctuation:

Jeremy realized, moreover, that he could no longer keep his eyes open.
Jeremy realized, as he tried once again to read the paragraph, that he could no longer keep his eyes open.

Another example:

no p: Ottawa's principal claim to fame is, that it is the national capital.

Here the comma intrudes between the linking verb *is* and its complement, the predicate noun consisting of a *that*-clause.

44c Do not put a comma between the last adjective of a series and the noun it modifies:

p: How could anyone fail to be impressed by such an intelligent, outspoken, resourceful, fellow as Jonathan has proved himself to be?

The comma after *resourceful* is wrong, though it may briefly feel right because a certain rhythm has been established and because there is no *and* before the last of the three adjectives. Don't let yourself be trapped into this error.

44d Generally, don't put a comma between words and phrases joined by a coordinating conjunction; use a comma only when the coordinate elements are clauses (see #33a):

The dog and cat circled each other warily, and then went off in opposite directions.
I was a long way from home, and didn't know how to get there.
She was not only intelligent, but also very industrious.

The commas in these three sentences are all unnecessary. Sometimes a writer uses such a comma for a mild emphasis, but if you want an emphatic pause a dash will probably work better:

The dog and cat circled each other warily—and then went off in opposite directions.

Or the sentence can be slightly revised in order to gain the emphasis:

She was not only intelligent; she was also very industrious.
I was a long way from home, and I had no idea how to get there.

But there are occasions when commas work between coordinate elements other than clauses, times when one wants a slight pause, or a mild emphasis, yet doesn't want to call attention to it with a dash. (We use two such commas in the preceding sentence.) When you do use such a comma, do so with conscious intent; mere instinct or a vague sense of rhythm can all too easily lead you into over-punctuation.

44e   If the two elements joined by a conjunction constitute an emphatic repetition, a comma is sometimes optional:

> I wanted not only to win, but to win overwhelmingly.

This sentence would be equally correct and effective without the comma. But in the following sentence the comma is necessary:

> It was an object of beauty, and of beauty most spectacular.

Again, sounding a sentence over to yourself will help you decide.

44f   Generally, do not set off introductory elements or interrupters that are very short, that are not really parenthetical, or that are so slightly parenthetical that you feel no pause when reading them:

> *no p:* Perhaps, she was trying to tell us something.
> *no p:* But, it was not a case of mistaken identity.
> *no p:* Therefore, he put on his raincoat.
> *no p:* We asked if we could try it out, for a week, to see if we really liked it.

When the pause is strong, however, be sure to set it off:

> It was only then, after dinner, that we were all able to relax.

Often such commas are optional, depending on the pattern of intonation the writer wants:

> In Canada(,) the progress of the seasons is sharply evident.
> In Canada(,) as elsewhere, money talks.
> Last year(,) there was a record wheat crop.
> The committee(,) therefore(,) decided to table the motion.
> After dinner(,) we all went for a walk.
> As she walked(,) she thought of her childhood on the farm.

Sometimes such a comma is necessary to prevent misreading:

> After eating, the dog Irene gave me jumped out the window.
> As she walked, past events in her life crowded before her mind's eye.
> We came to the door of the meeting room and opened it. Inside, a few students were standing about, three or four to a group.

See also #35a.

44g   Don't incorrectly set off titles of literary works and the like as nonrestrictive appositives (see #37b). It's "the ice-breaker *Terry Fox*," not "the ice-breaker, *Terry Fox*." There are, after all, other ice-breakers.

> *p:* In his poem, *Paradise Lost*, Milton tells of the fall, dramatized in the disobedience of Adam and Eve.
> *p:* In the novel, *Great Expectations*, Dickens's theme is that of growing up.

The punctuation makes it sound as though Milton wrote only this one poem and that Dickens's novel is the only novel in existence. The titles are restrictive: if they were removed, the sentences would not be clear. If the context is clear, the explanatory words often aren't needed at all:

> In *Paradise Lost* Milton tells . . . .
> In *Great Expectations* Dickens's theme is . . . .

If an author has in fact written only one novel or poem or play, it would be correct to set off its title. Similarly, it would be correct to set off a title after referring to an author's "*first* novel" or the like—since that would restrict the reference of the word *novel*.

The urge to punctuate before titles of literary works sometimes leads to the even worse error of putting a comma between a possessive and the title; do not do this:

> *no p:* I remember enjoying Coleridge's, *The Rime of the Ancient Mariner.*

44h Do not set off indirect quotations as if they were direct quotations:

> *no p:* In his last chapter the author says, that civilization as we have come to know it is in jeopardy.
> *no p:* If you ask Tomiko she's sure to say, she doesn't want to go.

In an indirect quotation, what was said is being reported, not quoted. If Tomiko is quoted directly, a comma is correct:

> If you ask Tomiko she's sure to say, "I don't want to go."

See also #43a and #43d.

44i Don't put a question mark at the end of indirect questions—questions that are only being reported, not asked directly:

> I asked what we were having for dinner.
> She wanted to find out what had happened the year before.
> What he asked himself then was how he was going to explain it to his boss.

44j Do not put a semicolon in front of a mere phrase or subordinate clause. Use such a semicolon only where you could, if you chose to, put a period instead:

> *p:* They cancelled the meeting; being disappointed at the low turnout.
> *p:* Only about a dozen people showed up; partly because there had not been enough publicity.

Those semicolons should be *commas*. Periods in those spots would turn what follows them into fragments (see #1y); in effect, so do semicolons. Since a semicolon signals that an *independent* clause is coming, readers are distracted when only a phrase or subordinate clause arrives. If you find yourself trying to avoid comma splices and overshooting in this way, devote some further study to the comma splice (#33e) and to learning how to recognize an independent clause (see #1m-n and p).

Similarly, don't put a semicolon between a subordinate clause and an independent clause:

> *p:* In my first few years of school, my formative years, when my hobby was still in its infancy; the sky was alive with wonder.

Change the semicolon to a comma. The presence of earlier commas in the sentence doesn't mean that the later one needs promoting to semicolon; there is no danger of misreading—as there sometimes is when a comma and a coordinating conjunction join two independent clauses (see #33b).

44k   Do not use a colon after a syntactically incomplete construction; a colon is appropriate only after an independent clause:

> *p:* She preferred such foods as: potatoes, corn, and spaghetti.

The prepositional *such as* needs an object to be complete. Had the phrase been extended to "He preferred such foods as these" or "as the following," it would have been complete, an independent clause, and a colon would have been correct. Here is another example of this common error:

> *p:* His favourite pastimes are: fishing, golfing, swimming, and hiking.

Since the linking verb *are* is incomplete without a complement, the colon is incorrect. Remember not to use a colon after a *preposition* or after a form of the verb *be*.

44-l   Never put a comma or a semicolon together with a dash. Such combinations used to be common, but they are now avoided because they contribute little but clutter. Use whichever mark is appropriate.

Review Exercises, Chapter IV   **Punctuation**

---

(1) Correcting punctuation
Correct any errors in punctuation in the following sentences—many from students' papers. You may also want to make other improvements: practise your revising techniques.

    1. It is a question of careful preparation, attentive reading and review.

P

2. I believe, that for a number of reasons, reproductive technology should be carefully regulated.
3. She accepts being an outsider for that is all she has known.
4. Many of his plays are about royalty, as in: *Richard II*, *Richard III*, and *Henry IV*.
5. In Beckett's play, *Waiting for Godot*, there are many tragicomic moments.
6. Claudius now sits on the throne and has married Hamlet's mother Gertrude.
7. With him too, she felt uncomfortable.
8. I didn't like the book on modern astronomy because its contents were incomprehensible to me.
9. The encounter that deepened his feelings more, occurred at age nine.
10. Therefore, Forster praises democracy as well for it allows variety and criticism.
11. This then, was the plan. Return to our campsite for the night, and tackle Black Tusk the next morning.
12. I joined in; haltingly at first and then more confidently.
13. As a person exercises the muscle of the heart becomes stronger, therefore, it can pump more blood while beating less.
14. Three or four horses were easy enough to count but entire herds of cows were beyond my capability.
15. The tip is manufactured from a rubbery substance; especially designed for erasing typographical errors.
16. It was after all, exactly what he had asked for.
17. Crisp memories of laughing eyes, loving smiles and peaceful easy feelings still linger.
18. The same word was used three times in the same paragraph; twice to describe different ideas altogether.
19. The other team had played valiantly, if not desperately till the final whistle.
20. Eighteenth-century mathematicians unlike their counterparts in the seventeenth century, were able to develop both pure and applied mathematics. Leonhard Euler, a notable genius in both these fields contributed invaluably to every branch of mathematics.
21. Another classic film, that explores the effects of war on individual lives, is *Casablanca*.
22. It began to rain, nevertheless, since they were on the sixteenth fairway they went ahead and finished the round.
23. When press secretary, Joanne Tandy, rose to speak a reporter interrupted her.
24. To me this indicates, that although he remembers the details of the events he describes, there is an enormous space of time, between them and the present, that makes them intangible.
25. The sounds of the poem are soft and never harsh which helps create the melancholy tone.
26. The bristles in my hairbrush are no longer uniform—some are missing and others stick out in all directions.
27. It is hard to appreciate freedom, if one has always lived with it.

28. Many books on the reading list interested me but some bored me; one novel in particular.
29. The title and the subtitle indicate the subject, and help us to understand what the essay is discussing.
30. My dictionary is my favourite book not because of its essential function: try to get along without one, but because of some of the extra features I've discovered in it.
31. He moved into residence when he enrolled in first year because he wanted to be part of campus life, and remained there by choice, until he graduated.
32. No one can weigh his deeds but heaven, and we who know of his acts.
33. One moment I was running for my life but in the next, the ground gave way beneath me and I was falling through space. Upon hitting the bottom I thought resignedly; it has got me.
34. Watching the Canada-Russia hockey series was overall a rewarding experience. The one game however, which stands out most in my mind, is the eighth and final game. With the series all tied up, this was a crucial game; for both teams.
35. I don't think I had ever known anybody as a person before, only their exterior characteristics. That is I suppose one of the facts of one's childhood, superficiality reigns supreme. Someone to talk to and listen to, it was a novel experience for me and so it came as rather a shock when he left.

(2) Using punctuation

Punctuate the following sentences as you think best, indicating possible alternatives and places where you think punctuation is optional. Be prepared to defend your choices. Some sentences may not need punctuating. (For all but the last ten, periods are supplied; for those ten, the terminal punctuation is itself part of the exercise.)

1. When the meeting ended he went to a pub for a drink.
2. Fred went home to bed as soon as the meeting was over.
3. There was still much to be done but she decided to call it a night.
4. In 1971 he moved to Halifax Nova Scotia and bought a small business.
5. He felt uneasy about the trip yet he knew he had to go along.
6. I took the book that I didn't like back to the library.
7. Mary Winnie and Cora came to the party together.
8. He had a broad engaging smile.
9. Having heard all she wanted Bridget left the meeting.
10. But once you've taken the first few steps the rest will naturally be easy.
11. The poem was short the novel was long the poem was good the novel better.
12. Perhaps we can still think of some way out of this mess.
13. But Canadians don't think that way they prefer to sit back and wait.
14. Last summer we visited Hastings the site of the battle won by William the Conqueror in 1066.
15. It is not good policy to start writing right away because your work will probably be weak in organization coherence and unity.

p

16. There are only three vegetables I can't tolerate turnips turnips and turnips.
17. The doctor a specialist in family practice made house calls all morning.
18. August 1914 was when the world went to war.
19. He had to finish the novel quickly or he wouldn't be ready for class.
20. We arrived we ate we departed and that's all there was to the evening.
21. You must plan your budget carefully in times of inflation.
22. He is the only man I know who wears a tie every day whatever the season.
23. His several hobbies were philately woodworking chess and fishing.
24. The two opponents settled the question amicably at the meeting and then went home to write nasty letters to each other.
25. I enjoyed both the novel and the poem but the novel which was an adventure story was much easier to read.
26. It was a splendid old stone house surrounded by well-landscaped lush green lawns and approached by a long sweeping gravel driveway.
27. This new machine looking like a caricature of a human being may yet prove beneficial.
28. It was to prove a very important day for Richard the embattled king he having to decide which course to pursue.
29. One August afternoon it was the hottest day of the year she perversely decided to play tennis.
30. He enjoyed the work of Melville Hemingway and Twain even more than that of such a talented successful novelist as Dickens.
31. I found many mistakes in the paper which was a mess from beginning to end.
32. Because of the vast distances the extreme climate rapidly rising costs and far from least important the rights and needs of native peoples the matter of northern development is a difficult problem but some people think that society's increasing demand for energy and other resources dictates that some kind of action be taken that the north be increasingly opened up to technological exploitation.
33. Before I was even half-way through the job my boss told me I could have the rest of the day off.
34. They sat there glowing with pride in their accomplishments.
35. I drove my car which was splashed all over with mud down to the car-wash.
36. She found many mistakes in the paper which were quite serious.
37. It was a simple assignment for the student was asked to write only one page.
38. It was a long hot summer in fact it was so hot I got scarcely any work done.
39. To avoid error he proofread the paper carefully.
40. I kept my distance from Gustav feeling uneasy about his display of temper.
41. If winter is here can spring be far behind
42. As soon as the plane had landed I began to wonder would I be able to fly again without fear

43. Well can you beat that
44. Has anyone ever come up to you on the street and asked Where's the best place in town to eat
45. Later he thought of many things he could have done but at the moment of crisis only one way out occurred to him run like mad
46. Tell me Algernon whether you would write March 16 1962 or put it like this 16 March 1962
47. Wayne's tirade finished Anita said No one will be swayed by such behaviour
48. He said that he would try to calm down
49. I should think she remarked that you could see where your own best interests lie Can't you my dear
50. Then came the reply she'd been hoping for I'll do whatever you think is best

PART
2

MECHANICS

CHAPTER V

MANUSCRIPT CONVENTIONS AND OTHER MECHANICAL CONVENTIONS OF WRITING

45 Manuscript Conventions

ms

45a Format

Unless directed otherwise, follow these conventions when you are preparing a manuscript for submission:

1. Use white paper of good quality, 21 by 28 cm or $8\frac{1}{2}$ by 11 inches. Do not use thin or "onionskin" paper, so-called "erasable" paper, or paper torn from a spiral notebook.

2. If you type, use a good black ribbon, a regular (i.e., not italic) typeface, and keep the type clean. Use unruled paper, and double-space throughout. If you use a word processor, check to make sure its printer output is acceptable to your instructor.

3. If you write by hand, use medium- to wide-ruled paper and write on alternate lines. Use black or blue-black ink. Never submit anything in pencil. Write legibly.

4. Use only one side of each page.

5. Leave margins of about 2.5 cm (1 inch) on all four sides of the page.

6. Number all pages at right margin, about 1.25 cm ($\frac{1}{2}$ inch) from the top. Use Arabic numerals, without periods, dashes, slashes, circles, or other decorations. Your instructor may wish you to include your surname before the number, as a precaution against misplaced pages.

7. Centre the title about 2.5 cm (1 inch) from the top on the first page, and double-space between it and the first line of the text. For a long essay or research paper that cannot easily be folded (see number 14 below), begin about 2.5 cm (1 inch) from the top, at the left margin, and on separate double-spaced lines put your name, your instructor's name, the course number, and the date; then double-space again and put the title, centred. (For an illustration, see Chapter IX, #79. If you wish or are instructed to use a separate title page, for the format of such a page, again see #79.)

8. Capitalize the title correctly (see #47m). Do not put the whole title in capital letters.

9. Do not underline your title or put a period after it. Do not put it in quotation marks (unless it is in fact a quotation); if it includes the title of a poem, story, book, etc., or a ship's name, use italics or quotation marks appropriately (see #48). Do not use the title of a published work by itself as your own title. Some examples:

> The Structure of Keats's "Ode to a Nightingale"
> Thematic Imagery in *A Jest of God*
> "How Are the Mighty Fallen": The Sinking of the *Titanic*

10. Never begin a line with a comma, semicolon, period, question mark, exclamation point, or hyphen. Occasionally a dash or the dots of an ellipsis may have to come at the beginning of a line, but if possible place them at the end of the preceding line.

11. If you type, leave two spaces after any terminal punctuation; use two unspaced hyphens to make a dash, with no space before or after them; and leave spaces before and after each of the three dots of an ellipsis.

12. Indent each paragraph five spaces (about 2.5 cm or an inch in handwritten work). You needn't leave extra space between paragraphs.

13. Be neat. Avoid messy erasures, blots, and strike-overs. If you make more than two or three changes on a page, redo the page. If you are using a word-processor, call up the file, make the appropriate emendations, save the changes, and reprint the page or pages you have revised. To change or delete a word or short phrase by hand, draw a single horizontal line through it and write the new word or phrase, if any, above it. If you wish to insert a word or short phrase, place a caret (∧) *below* the line at the point of insertion and write the addition *above* the line. If you wish to start a new paragraph where you haven't indented, put the

symbol ¶ in the left margin and insert a caret where you want the paragraph to begin. If you wish to cancel a paragraph indention, write "No ¶" in the left margin.

14. If you aren't using a separate title page (see number 7 above), fold the paper vertically, text *inside,* and endorse it on the outside, at the top of the right-hand side (i.e., with the fold to the left) with your name, the course number, the date, the instructor's name, and perhaps also the number of the assignment.

15. If necessary, fasten the pages of an essay together with a paper clip. Never use a staple or a pin. Long essays are sometimes submitted in folders.

45b   Syllabication and Word Division

syl, div

1. Generally, divide only unusually long words: readers don't expect straight right-hand margins with handwritten or typed work, or even with computer-generated material. (*Note:* If your computer will justify the right margin with proportional spacing, fine; if it justifies by leaving irregular spaces between words, check with your instructor, since many people dislike reading such text.)

2. To divide a word, insert a hyphen at the end of a line, after the first part of the word, and begin the next line with the rest of the word. Never begin a new line with a hyphen, and never divide a word at the end of a page.

3. Divide words only between syllables—and don't guess: check your dictionary for a word's syllabication.

4. Never separate a syllable of only one letter, or even of two; especially, don't separate a final *ed*, even if it is a syllable.

5. Try to begin the second part of a divided word with a consonant. For example, *radi-cal*, not *rad-ical*.

6. Try to avoid dividing hyphenated words. If you must divide one, do so only where the hyphen already stands.

Exercise 45b | **Syllabication**

Insert hyphens in the following words where you think their syllables break. Consult your dictionary afterward to see if you were correct. Indicate syllable breaks that should not be used to divide a word at the end of a line.

1. accommodated	11. distinctly
2. apartment	12. Machiavellian
4. befuddled	13. perspicacity
3. appointed	14. philosophical
5. cannibalism	15. prevaricated
6. cognoscenti	16. sentenced
7. commercialization	17. suggestion
8. confused	18. tachometer
9. counterirritant	19. thoroughly
10. differentiating	20. verisimilitude

---

46 Abbreviations

ab   Abbreviations are expected in technical and scientific writing, legal writing, business writing, memos, reports, reference works, bibliographies and footnotes, tables and charts, and sometimes in journalism. In ordinary writing, however, only a few kinds are acceptable. (See also #78b.)

46a   Titles before proper names, with or without initials or given names:

> Mr. Cheung, Mrs. L. W. Smith, Ms. Helene Greco, Dr. David Adams, St. John

46b   In *informal* writing, titles before proper names with initials or given names:

> Prof. Janet Thomson (*but* Professor Thomson)
> Sen. I. C. Power (*but* Senator Power)
> Gen. John S. Hawkins (*but* General Hawkins)
> the Rev. Matthew Markle (*or, more formally,* the Reverend Matthew Markle, the Reverend Mr. Markle)
> the Hon. Jacques Sprat (*more formally*, the Honourable Jacques Sprat, the Honourable Mr. Sprat)

In formal writing, spell out these and similar titles.

46c   Titles and degrees after proper names:

> Timothy Johanson, Jr.
> David Adams, M.D. (*but not* Dr. David Adams, M.D.)
> A. Pullerman, D.D.S.
> Laurel McGregor, Ph.D., F.R.S.C.

Academic degrees not following a name may also be abbreviated:

> Shirley is working toward her B.A.
> Abdul is studying for his M.A. examinations.

46d Standard words used with dates and numerals:

> 720 B.C., A.D. 231, the second century A.D., 7 a.m. (*or* 7 A.M.), 8:30 p.m. (*or* 8:30 P.M.), no. 17 (*or* No. 17)

Note that *A.D.* precedes a date whereas *B.C.* follows one. Note also that some people use *B.C.E.* ("before the common era") and *C.E.* ("common era"), both following the date, instead of *B.C.* and *A.D.*

46e Agencies and organizations commonly known by their initials (see also #42a):

> UNICEF, UAW, CBC, CNN, RCMP, NASA

46f Some scientific, technical, or other terms (usually of considerable length) commonly known by their initials (see also #42a):

> BTU, DDT, DNA, ESP, FM, IPA, MLA, MP, GST, TNT

46g Latin expressions commonly used in English (in formal writing, it is better to spell out the English—or, with *versus*, the Latin—equivalent):

> i.e. (that is), e.g. (for example), cf. (compare), etc. (and so forth), vs. (*versus*), et al. (and others)

Caution:

(a) If you use *e.g.*, use it only to introduce the example or list of examples; following the example or list, write it out:

> Some provinces—e.g. Alberta, Saskatchewan, and New Brunswick—felt
> that they had been poorly represented on the committee.
> Some provinces—Alberta, Saskatchewan, and New Brunswick, for exam-
> ple—felt that they had been poorly represented on the committee.

Note also that if you introduce a list with *e.g.* or *for example* or even *such as*, it is illogical to follow it with *etc.* or *and so forth*.

(b) Generally use a comma after *i.e.*, just as you would if you wrote out *that is*. And usually use one after *e.g.* as well (test for the pause by reading it aloud as *for example*).

(c) The abbreviation *cf.* stands for Latin *confer*, meaning *compare*. Do not use it to mean simply "see"; for that the Latin *vide* (v.) would be correct.

(d) Don't use *etc.* lazily. Use it only when there are at least several more items to follow and when they are reasonably obvious:

> Evergreen trees—cedars, pines, etc.—are common in northern
> latitudes.

> Learning the Greek alphabet—alpha, beta, gamma, delta, etc.—isn't really difficult.
>
> *Wrong:* He considered several possible occupations: accounting, teaching, nursing, etc.
>
> Here a reader can have no idea of what the other possible occupations might be. Further, never write *and etc.*: *and* is redundant, since *etc.* (*et cetera*) means "*and* so forth."

46h   Terms used in official titles being copied exactly:

> Johnson Bros., Ltd.; Ibbetson & Co.; Smith & Sons, Inc.; *Quill & Quire*

> **Caution:** Don't use the ampersand (&) as a substitute for *and*; use it only when copying a title of a company or a publication exactly, as above.

47 Capitalization

cap,
uc   Generally, capitalize proper nouns, abbreviations of proper nouns, and words derived from proper nouns, as follows:

47a   Names and nicknames of real and fictional people and individual animals:

> Lester B. Pearson, Barbara Ward, Magic Johnson, Kenneth Branagh, Clarissa Dalloway, Rumpelstiltskin, Elsa, Rin Tin Tin, Lassie, Washoe, King Kong, Dumbo

47b   Titles when they precede and thus are parts of names:

> Professor Jones (*but* I see that Jones is your professor.)
> Captain John Smith (*but* John Smith was a captain.)
> Rabbi Samuel Small (*but* Mr. Small was our rabbi.)

> **Note:** Normally titles that follow names aren't capitalized unless they have become part of the name: Pat Carney, the senator; Bull Halsey, the admiral; *but* Catherine the Great, Peter the Hermit, Smokey the Bear. Some titles of particular distinction are customarily capitalized even if the person isn't named:
>
> The Prime Minister will tour the Maritimes in May.
> The Queen visited Canada to open the 1976 Olympics.

47c Words designating family relationships when they are used as parts of proper names and also when they are used in place of proper names, except following a possessive:

> Uncle George (*but* I have an uncle named George.)
> There's my uncle, George. (*but* There's my Uncle George.)
> I told Father about it. (*but* My father knows about it.)
> I have always respected Grandmother. (*but* Juanita's grandmother is a splendid old lady.)

47d Place names—including common nouns (*river, street, park*, etc.) when they are parts of proper nouns (see #2):

> Alberta, the Amazon, the Andes, Asia, Banff, Buenos Aires, Mt. Etna, the Gobi Desert, Hudson Bay, Japan, Kejimkujik National Park, Lake Ladoga, the Mississippi River, Moose Jaw, Niagara Falls, Québec, Rivière-du-loup, the Sahara, the Suez Canal, Trafalgar Square, Vancouver Island, Yonge Street

> **Note:** Don't capitalize *north, east, south,* and *west* unless they are part of specific place names (North Dakota, West Vancouver, South America) or designate specific geographical areas (the frozen North, the East Coast, the Deep South, the Northwest, the Wild West, the Far East).

47e The names of the months (January, February, etc.) and the days of the week (Monday, Tuesday, etc.), but not the seasons (spring, summer, autumn, fall, winter). Also capitalize holidays, and holy days and festivals (Christmas, Canada Day, Remembrance Day, Hanukkah).

47f Names of deities and other religious names and terms:

> God, the Holy Ghost, the Virgin Mary, the Bible, the Dead Sea Scrolls, the Torah, the Talmud, Islam, Allah, the Koran, Apollo, Jupiter, Vishnu, Taoism

Note: Some people capitalize pronouns referring to a deity; others prefer not to.

47g Names of nationalities and other groups and organizations and of their members:

> Canadian, Australian, Scandinavian, South American, Irish, San Francisco Giants, Progressive Conservatives, Roman Catholics, Lions, Teamsters, Alcoholics Anonymous

47h Names of institutions, specific buildings, sections of government, historical events, periods, and documents:

> McGill University, The Hospital for Sick Children, the British Museum, the Empire State Building, Westminster Abbey, the Ministry of Labour, the

Renaissance, the French Revolution, the Treaty of Versailles, the Gulf War, the Magna Carta, the Charter of Rights and Freedoms

47i Specific academic courses, but not the subjects themselves, except for languages:

> Philosophy 101, Fine Arts 300, Mathematics 204
> an English course, a major in French
> a history course, an economics major, a degree in psychology

47j Derivatives of proper nouns:

> Shakespearean, French Canadian, Confucianism, Haligonian, Celtic, Québecoise, Christian, Miltonic, Texan, Keynesian, Edwardian, Muscovite

> **Note:** Some words derived from proper nouns—and some proper nouns themselves—are so much a part of everyday usage or refer to such common things that they were never or are no longer capitalized; some examples: bible (in secular contexts), biblical, herculean, raglan, martial, quixotic, hamburger, frankfurter, french fries, champagne, burgundy, roman and italic, vulcanized, macadamized, galvanized, pasteurized, curie, volt, ampere, joule, gerrymander, denim, china, japanned, erotic, bloomers, jeroboam, jeremiad

47k Abbreviations of proper nouns:

> PMO,   TVA,   CUPE,   CUSO,   the BNA Act,   P.E.I.,   B.C.

Note that abbreviations of agencies and organizations commonly known by their initials do not need periods (see #46e), but that abbreviations of geographical entities such as provinces usually do. When in doubt, consult your dictionary. See also #42a.

47-l The pronoun *I* and the vocative interjection *O*:

> O my people, what have I done unto thee? (Micah 6:3)

Do not capitalize the interjection *oh* unless it begins a sentence.

47m In the titles of written and other works, including student essays, use a capital letter to begin the first word, the last word, and all other important words; leave uncapitalized only articles (*a*, *an*, *the*) and any conjunctions and prepositions less than five letters long (unless one of these is the first or last word):

> *A Jest of God*   "The Dead"
> *All About Eve*   *Of Thee I Sing*
> "The Metamorphosis"   "Comin' Thro' the Rye"
> *In Which We Serve*   *As for Me and My House*
> *As the World Wags On*   "Once More to the Lake"
> *Roughing It in the Bush*   *Such Is My Beloved*

But there can be exceptions; for example the conjunctions *Nor* and *So* are usually capitalized, the relative pronoun *that* is sometimes not capitalized (*All's Well that Ends Well*), and in Ralph Ellison's "Tell It Like It Is, Baby" the preposition-cum-conjunction *Like* demands capitalization. (See #48 for more on titles.)

Note: If a title includes a hyphenated word, capitalize the part after the hyphen only if it is a noun or adjective or is otherwise an important word:

> *Self-Portrait*
> *The Scorched-Wood People*
> *Murder Among the Well-to-do*

Capitalize the first word of a subtitle, even if it is an article:

> *The Interior Landscape: The Literary Criticism of Marshall McLuhan*

See #48b for the use of italics in titles.

47n Capitalize the first word of a major or minor sentence—of anything, that is, that concludes with terminal punctuation:

> Modern Art. Now that's a controversial topic. Right?

47o Capitalize the first word of a quotation that is intended as a sentence or that is capitalized in the source, but not fragments from other than the beginning of such a sentence:

> When he said "Let me take the wheel for a while," I shuddered at the memory of what had happened the last time I had let him "take the wheel."

If something interrupts a quoted sentence, do not begin its second part with a capital:

> "It was all I could do," she said, "to keep my head above water."

47p Capitalize the first word of a sentence in parentheses only if it stands by itself, apart from other sentences. If it is incorporated within another sentence, it is neither capitalized nor ended with a period (though it could end with a question mark or exclamation point: see #40 and #42).

> He did as he was told (there was really nothing else for him to do), and the tension was relieved. (But of course he would never admit to himself that he had been bested.)

47q An incorporated sentence following a colon may be capitalized if it seems to stand as a separate statement, for example if it is itself long or requires emphasis; otherwise it is best left uncapitalized:

> There was one thing, she said, which we must never forget: No one has a
> right to happiness that deprives someone else of deserved happiness.
> It was a splendid night: the sky was clear except for a few picturesque clouds,
> the moon was full, and even a few stars shone through. (The first *The*
> could be capitalized if the writer wanted particular emphasis on the
> details.)
> It was no time for petty quarrels: everything depended on unanimity.

47r   Although it is risky and should not be done often, writers who have
good control of tone can occasionally capitalize a personified abstraction or a word or phrase to which they want to impart a special importance of some kind:

> It was no longer a matter of simply getting along adequately; now it was a
> question of Survival.
> Only when it begins to fade does Youth appear so valuable.
> The filching fingers of the monster Inflation reach everywhere.

Sometimes the slight emphasis of capitalization can be used for a
humorous or ironic effect:

> He insisted on driving His Beautiful Car: everyone else preferred to walk the
> two blocks without benefit of jerks and jolts and carbon monoxide fumes.

And occasionally, but rarely, you can capitalize whole words and phrases
or even sentences for a special sort of graphic emphasis:

> When we reached the site, however, we were confronted by a sign warning
> us in no uncertain terms to KEEP OUT—TRESPASSERS WILL BE
> PROSECUTED.
> When she made the suggestion to the group she was answered with a
> resounding NO.

Clearly in such instances there is no need for further indications, such
as quotation marks or underlining, though the last one could end with
an exclamation point.

48 Titles (see also #47m)

title

48a   Put quotation marks around the titles of short works and of parts of
longer works, such as short stories, articles, essays, short poems, chapters of books, songs, and individual episodes of television programs:

> Leonard Cohen's "Suzanne" is both poem and song.
> "Friend of My Youth" is one of Munro's best stories.
> The first chapter of Thoreau's *Walden* is called "Economy."
> "The New Bicycle" is one of the poems in P. K. Page's collection *The Glass Air*.
> I wish they'd repeat "Rumpole and the Old Boy Net."

There can be exceptions, however. For example, the title of each of the four plays in Robertson Davies's book *Four Favourite Plays* deserves italicizing in its own right. And some works, for example Coleridge's *The Rime of the Ancient Mariner* and Conrad's *Heart of Darkness*, although originally parts of larger collections, are fairly long and have attained a reputation and importance as individual works; most writers feel justified in italicizing their titles.

48b Use italics (see #49) for titles of written works published as units, such as books, magazines, journals, newspapers, and plays; for films and television programs; for paintings and sculptures, and for musical compositions (other than single songs), such as operas and ballets:

> *Paradise Lost* is Milton's greatest work.
> Have you read Milan Kundera's *The Unbearable Lightness of Being*?
> *Saturday Night* is a Canadian magazine.
> The scholarly journal *Canadian Literature* is published quarterly.
> I prefer *The Globe and Mail* to the *Winnipeg Free Press*.
> I recommend that you see the Stratford production of *The Tempest*.
> *Rumpole of the Bailey* is repeating again on PBS.
> One tires of hearing Ravel's *Bolero* played so often.
> Michelangelo's *David* is almost worth a trip to Florence.
> Leonardo da Vinci's *The Last Supper* seems to need constant restoration.
> We saw a fine production of Gilbert and Sullivan's *H.M.S. Pinafore*.

Note: Instrumental compositions may be known by name or by technical detail, or both. A name is italicized (Beethoven's *Pastoral Symphony*); technical identification is usually not (Beethoven's Sixth Symphony, or Symphony no. 6, op. 68, in F).

48c If an essay title includes a book title, the book title is italicized:

> "Games and Godgames in *The Magus* and *The French Lieutenant's Woman*"

If a book title includes something requiring quotation marks, retain the quotation marks and italicize the whole thing:

> *From Fiction to Film: D. H. Lawrence's "The Rocking-Horse Winner"*

If a book title includes something that itself would be italicized, such as the name of a ship or the title of another book, either put the secondary item in quotation marks or leave it in roman type (i.e., not italicized):

> *The Cruise of the "Nona"*
> *D. H. Lawrence and* Sons and Lovers: *Sources and Criticism*

49 *ital*

49 Italics

ital   *Italics*—like that—are a special kind of slanting type. In handwritten work or work typed on a standard typewriter, represent italic type by <u>underlining</u>. Some typewriters can produce italics, as can some computers, depending on software and printer. In addition to italics for titles (see #48b), here are their other main uses:

49a   Italicize names of individual ships, planes, and the like:

> the *Golden Hind*, the *Erebus* and the *Terror*, the *St. Bonaventure*, the *Lusitania*, *The Spirit of St. Louis*, *Mariner IX*, the *Columbia*, the *Orient Express*

49b   Italicize non-English words and phrases that are not yet sufficiently common to be entirely at home in English. English contains many terms that have come from other languages but that are no longer thought of as non-English and are therefore not italicized; for example:

> moccasin, wigwam, prairie, genre, tableau, bamboo, arroyo, corral, hara-kiri, chutzpah, spaghetti, goulash, hashish, eureka, litotes, hiatus, vacuum, sic.

There are also words that are sufficiently Anglicized not to require italicizing but that usually retain their original accents and diacritical marks; for example:

> cliché, naïf, cañon, façade, Götterdämmerung, fête.

But English also makes use of many terms still felt by many writers to be sufficiently non-English to need italicizing; for example:

> *ad nauseam, au courant, chez, coup d'état, joie de vivre, outré, raison d'être, savoir faire, Lebensraum, verboten, Weltanschauung, tempus fugit, vade mecum*

Many such expressions are on their way to full acceptance in English. If you are unsure, consult a good up-to-date dictionary; for example, it may label a term such as *ad hoc* "Latin," but for another term, such as *per se*, merely identify Latin as its etymological source.

49c   Italicize words, letters, numerals, and the like when you refer to them as such:

> The word *helicopter* is formed from Greek roots.
> There are two *r*'s in *embarrass*. (Note that only the *r* is italicized; the *s* making it plural stays roman.)
> The number *13* is considered unlucky by many otherwise rational people.
> Don't use *&* as a lazy substitute for *and*.

See also #43g. For the matter of apostrophes for plurals of such elements, see #51v.

49d   Italicize words or phrases—or even whole sentences—that you want to emphasize, for example as they might be stressed if spoken aloud:

> One thing he was now sure of: *that* was no way to go about the task.
> Careful thought should lead one to the conclusion that *character*, not wealth or connections, will be most important in the long run.
> If people try to tell you otherwise, *don't listen to them.*
> Try to remember that *Fredericton*, not Saint John, is the capital of New Brunswick.
> He gave up his ideas of fun and decided instead to finish his education. *And it was the most important decision of his life.*

But like other typographical devices for achieving emphasis (boldface, capitalization, underlining), this method is worth avoiding, or at least minimizing, in ordinary writing, for no merely mechanical means of emphasis is, ultimately, as effective as punctuation, word order, and syntax. Easy methods often produce only a transitory or cheap effect, and repeated use quickly saps what effectiveness they have. Consider the following sentences:

> Well, I felt just *terrible* when he told me that!
> I felt terrible, just terrible, when he told me that.
> I can think of only one way to describe how I felt when he told me that: I felt terrible.

50   Numerals

num   Numerals are appropriate in technical and scientific writing, and newspapers sometimes use them to save space. But in ordinary writing certain conventions limit their use. Use numerals for the following purposes:

50a   For the time of day with *a.m.* or *p.m.*:

> 3 p.m. (*but* three o'clock, three in the afternoon)

50b *num*

50b   For dates:

> November 11, 1918, *or* 11 November 1918

The year is almost always represented by numerals, and centuries written out:

> 1900 was the last year of the nineteenth century, not the first year of the twentieth century. (See #50h.)

> > **Note:** *st, nd, rd,* and *th* go with numerals in dates only if the year is not given; or the number may be written out:
> >
> > May 2, 1951; May 2nd; the second of May; May second

50c   For addresses:

> 2132 Fourth Avenue; 4771 128th Street; P.O. Box 91; Apartment 8

50d   For technical and mathematical numbers, such as percentages and decimals:

> 31 percent; 31%; 37°C; 37 degrees Celsius; 2.54 centimetres; 2.54 cm; 45 rpm

50e   For page numbers and other divisions of a written work, especially in documentation (see #78 and #80):

> page 27, p. 27, (pp. 9-13), pp. 33-38, line 13, lines 3 and 5, (lines 7-9), stanza 2, chapter 4, Chapter 4, Ch. 4, Chapter IV, section 3, section III, Part 2, Book IX, (IX, 120), 2 Samuel 22:3, II Samuel 19:1

(Note that books of the Bible are not italicized.)

50f   For acts, scenes, and line numbers of plays (your instructor may prefer that you use roman numerals for acts and scenes):

> In act 4, scene 2, ...
> See act IV, scene ii, line 77.
> Remember Hamlet's "To be, or not to be" (3.1.56). OR (III.i.56).

50g   Generally, spell out numbers that can be expressed in one or two words; use numerals for numbers that would take more than two words:

> four, thirty, eighty-three, one third, two hundred, seven thousand, 115, 385, 2120, three dollars, $3.48, five hundred dollars, $517

If you are writing about more than one number, say for purposes of comparison or giving statistics, numerals are usually preferable:

Enrollment dropped from 250 two years ago, to 200 last year, to only 90 this year.

Don't mix numerals and words in such a context.

50h Don't begin a sentence with a numeral. Either spell out the number or rewrite the sentence so that the number doesn't come first:

Thirty to forty percent goes for taxes.
Taxes consume from 30 to 40 percent.

num: 750 people showed up to watch the chess tournament.
revised: As many as 750 people came to watch the chess tournament.
revised: The chess tournament drew 750 interested spectators.

Dates are sometimes considered acceptable at the beginning of a sentence, but since some people object to the practice it is worth avoiding. In #50b above we could easily have rewritten the example:

Remember that 1900 was the last year of the nineteenth century, not the first year of the twentieth century.

50i Commas have long been conventional to separate groups of three figures in long numbers: 3,172,450; 17,920. In the metric system, however, along with the rest of SI (Système Internationale, or International System of Units), groups of three digits on either side of a decimal point are separated by spaces; with four-digit numbers a space is optional:

3 172 450   3.1416 or 3.141 6   *but* 3.141 59

This convention does not apply to addresses or amounts of money. For further information about SI consult the *Canadian Metric Practice Guide*, published by the Canadian Standards Association.

> **MS Note:** When typing the Arabic numeral *one*, don't use a capital *I*, since that produces a roman numeral. If your typewriter has no numeral *1*, use lower-case *l*.

CHAPTER VI
Spelling

Some writers have little trouble with spelling; others have a lot. Even confident writers must consult a dictionary occasionally; poor spellers need one open beside them all the time. If you want readers to respect what you write, you must respect it yourself. Misspelled words—among the first things a reader will notice—show a lack of respect.

English spelling isn't as bizarre as some people think, but there are oddities. Sometimes the same sound can be spelled in several ways (fine, offer, phone, cough; so, soap, sow, sew, beau, dough), or a single element can be pronounced in several ways (cough, tough, dough, through, bough, fought; lot, tote, women, lost, tomb, fork, love). When such inconsistencies occur in longer and less familiar words, sometimes only a dictionary can help us. And remember, a dictionary isn't *pre*scribing but *de*scribing: it isn't commanding us to be correct but simply recording the currently accepted *conventions*.

English has changed a great deal over the centuries, and it is still changing. Old words pass out of use, new words are added, conventions of grammar change, pronunciations change—and spelling changes, but not very fast; dictionaries can do a fairly good job of recording what is conventional—"correct"—right now. Words in transition may have more than one acceptable meaning or pronunciation or spelling. The word *pejorative*, for example, has several acceptable pronunciations (lexicographers usually record them in what they consider the order of preference, with the most acceptable or most common first). The past tense of *dream* can be either *dreamed* or *dreamt*. The past tense of *slide* changed from *slided* to *slid* a century or so ago; will the past tense of *glide* someday be *glid*? Just a few years ago *dove* was considered unacceptable—colloquial or dialectal at best—as the past tense of *dive*; now it is at least as acceptable as *dived*. *Clue* is now prevalent, but for centuries it shared acceptability with *clew*. And so on.

In Canada we also have to contend with the influence of British and American spelling on ours. Broadly speaking, Canadian conventions—whether of spelling, punctuation, usage, pronunciation, or whatever—are closer to American than to British, and where they are changing they are changing in the direction of American conventions. Many of us still say "leftenant" instead of "lootenant," but we say and spell *aluminum* rather than *aluminium*. The alphabet still ends in *zed* rather than *zee* for many of us, though the distinction is fading. Most Canadians write *centre* and *theatre* rather than *center* and *theater*; but "skedule" is replacing "shedule" as the pronunciation of *schedule*. Endings in *our* (colour, honour, labour, etc.) exist alongside those in *or*; either spelling is conventional in Canada. The same is true of endings in *ise* or *ize*, though the latter is clearly preferred. We have the useful alternatives *cheque* (bank), *racquet* (tennis), and *storey* (floor); Americans have only *check*, *racket*, and *story* for both meanings. But *draught* is losing ground to *draft*, and *program* and *judgment* are rapidly replacing *programme* and *judgement*. And so on.

Where alternatives exist, either is correct. But be consistent. If you spell *honour*, then write *humour*, *colour*, *labour*; if you choose *analyze*, write *paralyze* and *modernize*; if you choose *centre*, write *lustre* and *fibre*. And if you do choose the *our* endings, watch out for the trap: when you add the suffixes *ous*, *ious*, *ate* or *ation*, and *ize* (or *ise*), you must drop the *u* and write *humorous*, *coloration*, *vaporize*, *laborious*; and there is no *u* in *honorary*.

The point is, there is choice. In this book, for example, we use the *our* ending because we think it is still considered standard outside the popular media. And we use the *ize* ending (where the alternatives exist) because we believe it to be the dominant form. If a particular form is clearly dominant or an acknowledged standard, we think it should be used. (The Spelling List at the end of the chapter includes some words with alternative spellings that might occasionally be troublesome; the one listed first is at least slightly preferable.)

But such dilemmas, if they are dilemmas, are infrequent. The real spelling difficulties, those shared by all writers of English, are of a different sort.

51 Spelling Rules and Common Causes of Error

sp   Many spelling errors result from carelessness or ignorance; self-discipline and a good dictionary are the only cures. Many other spelling errors, however, fall into clear categories. Familiarize yourself with the main rules and the main sources of error.

51a *ie* or *ei*

The old jingle should help: Use *i* before *e* except after *c*, or when sounded like *a* as in *neighbour* and *weigh*.

> *ie:* achieve, believe, chief, field, fiend, shriek, siege, wield
> *ei* after *c*: ceiling, conceive, deceive, perceive, receive
> *ei* when sounded like *a*: eight, neighbour, sleigh, veil, weigh

When the sound is neither long *e* nor long *a*, the spelling *ei* is usually right:

> counterfeit, foreign, forfeit, height, heir, their

But there are several exceptions; memorize them if necessary:

> either, financier, friend, leisure, mischief, neither, seize, sieve, weird

When in doubt, consult your dictionary.

51b cede, ceed, or sede

Memorize if necessary: The *sede* ending occurs only in *supersede*. The *ceed* ending occurs only in *exceed*, *proceed*, and *succeed*. All other words ending in this sound use *cede*: accede, concede, intercede, precede, recede, secede.

51c Final e Before a Suffix

A *suffix* is one or more syllables added to the end of a *root* word to form a new word, usually changing its part of speech. For example:

root	suffix	new word
appear (v.)	ance	appearance (n.)
content (adj.)	ment	contentment (n.)
occasion (n.)	al	occasional (adj.)
occasional (adj.)	ly	occasionally (adv.)

When the root word ends in a silent *e*, certain rules generally apply. If the suffix begins with a *vowel* (*a, e, i, o, u*), the *e* is usually dropped:

desire + able = desirable	forgive + able = forgivable
sphere + ical = spherical	argue + ing = arguing
come + ing = coming	allure + ing = alluring
continue + ous = continuous	desire + ous = desirous
sense + ual = sensual	rogue + ish = roguish

(*Dyeing* retains the *e* to distinguish it from *dying*. If a word ends with two *e*'s, both are pronounced and therefore not dropped: *agreeing, fleeing*.)

If the suffix begins with *a* or *o*, most words ending in *ce* or *ge* retain the *e* in order to preserve the soft sound of the *c* (like *s* rather than *k*) or the *g* (like *j* rather than hard as in *gun*):

notice + able = noticeable	outrage + ous = outrageous

Note that *vengeance* and *gorgeous* have such a silent *e*. (Similarly, words like *picnic* and *frolic* require an added *k* to preserve the hard sound before suffixes beginning with *e* or *i*: *picnicked, picnicking, frolicked, frolicking, politicking*; but *tactical, frolicsome*. Exception: *arced, arcing*.)

If the suffix begins with a *consonant*, the *e* is usually not dropped:

awe + some = awesome	effective + ness = effectiveness
definite + ly = definitely	hoarse + ly = hoarsely

immediate + ly = immediately   mere + ly = merely
immense + ly = immensely   separate + ly = separately
involve + ment = involvement   woe + ful = woeful

(But note a common exception: awe + ful = awful.)

And there is a subgroup of words whose final *e*'s are sometimes wrongly omitted. The *e*, though silent, is essential to keep the sound of the preceding vowel long:

completely	extremely	hopelessness	livelihood
loneliness	remoteness	severely	tasteless

But such an *e* is sometimes dropped when no consonant intervenes between it and the long vowel:

argue + ment = argument   due + ly = duly   true + ly = truly

51d Final *y* After a Consonant and Before a Suffix

When the suffix begins with *i*, keep the *y*:

baby + ish = babyish   carry + ing = carrying
try + ing = trying   worry + ing = worrying

(**Note:** Words ending in *ie* change it to *y* before adding *ing*: die + ing = dying; lie + ing = lying.)

When the suffix begins with something other than *i*, change *y* to *i*:

happy + er = happier   duty + ful = dutiful
fancy + ful = fanciful   duty + able = dutiable
happy + ness = happiness   silly + est = silliest
harmony + ous = harmonious   angry + ly = angrily

Some exceptions: shyly, shyness; slyer or slier, slyly or slily, flier or flyer.

51e Doubling of a Final Consonant Before a Suffix

Double the final consonant of the root if

(a) that consonant is preceded by a single vowel,
(b) the root is a one-syllable word or a word accented on its last syllable, and
(c) the suffix begins with a vowel.

One-syllable words:

bar + ed = barred   bar + ing = barring
fit + ed = fitted   fit + ing = fitting   fit + er = fitter
hot + er = hotter   hot + est = hottest
shop + ed = shopped   shop + ing = shopping   shop + er = shopper

51f *sp*

Words accented on last syllable:

allot + ed = allotted	allot + ing = allotting
commit + ed = committed	commit + ing = committing
occur + ed = occurred	occur + ing = occurring
	occur + ence = occurrence
propel + ed = propelled	propel + ing = propelling
	propel + er = propeller

But when the addition of the suffix shifts the accent of the root word away from the last syllable, do not double the final consonant:

infer + ed = inferred	infer + ing = inferring	BUT *inference*
prefer + ed = preferred	prefer + ing = preferring	BUT *preference*
refer + ed = referred	refer + ing = referring	BUT *reference*

Do not double the final consonant if it is preceded by a single consonant (sharp + er = sharper) or if the final consonant is preceded by two vowels (fail + ed = failed, stoop + ing = stooping) or if the root word is more than one syllable and *not* accented on its last syllable (benefit + ed = benefited, parallel + ing = paralleling) or if the suffix begins with a consonant (commit + ment = commitment).

Note: Unlike *parallel*, other words often double a final *l*, even when they are of two or more syllables and not accented on the final syllable; for example *labelled* or *labeled*, *traveller* or *traveler*. Either form is correct, though the Canadian preference is for the doubled *l*. (Some even double the *l* at the end of *parallel*, in spite of the awkwardly present double *ll* preceding it.) The word *kidnap* is a similar exception, for the obvious reason of pronunciation: either *kidnapped* or *kidnaped* is correct (and *kidnapping* or *kidnaping*). Another is *worship*: either *worshipped* or *worshiped*, *worshipping* or *worshiping*. In both instances, the double final consonant is preferred in Canada.

51f   The Suffix *ly*

When *ly* is added to an adjective already ending in a single *l*, that final *l* is retained, resulting in an adverb ending in *lly*. If you pronounce such words carefully you will be less likely to misspell them:

accidental + ly = accidentally	cool + ly = coolly
incidental + ly = incidentally	mental + ly = mentally
natural + ly + naturally	political + ly = politically

If the root ends in a double *ll*, one *l* is of course dropped: full + ly = fully, chill + ly = chilly, droll + ly = drolly.

> **Note:** Many adjectives ending in *ic* have alternative forms ending in *ical*. But even if they don't, nearly all add *ally*, not just *ly*, to become adverbs—as do nouns like *music* and *stoic*. Again, careful pronunciation will help you avoid error:

alphabetic, alphabetical, alphabetically	drastic, drastically
basic, basically	scientific, scientifically
cyclic, cyclical, cyclically	symbolic, symbolical, symbolically

An exception: *publicly*.

51g   Prefixes

The more you know about how words are put together, the less trouble you will have spelling them. Many spelling errors occur because a writer isn't aware that a particular word consists of a root word with a **prefix** stuck on the front of it. (*Pre* is from a Latin word meaning *before*; *fix* is a root, meaning *fasten* or *place*; the new word is *prefix*.) When a prefix ends with the same letter that the root begins with, the result is a double letter; don't omit one of them:

ad + dress = address	mis + spell = misspell
com + motion = commotion	un + necessary = unnecessary

(Similarly, don't carelessly omit one of the doubled letters in compounds such as *beachhead*, *bookkeeping*, and *roommate*.)

In many words the first letter of a root has "pulled" the last letter of a prefix over, resulting in a double letter. Writers unaware of the prefix sometimes forget to double the consonant. The Latin prefix *ad*, meaning *to, toward, near*, is commonly affected this way; for example it became *af* in front of *facere*, meaning *to do*; hence our word *affect* has two *f*'s. Here are some other examples:

ad	>	ac	in *access, accept, acquire, acquaint*
		al	in *alliance, allusion*
		an	in *annul, annihilate*
		ap	in *apprehend, apparatus, application*
com	>	col	in *collide, colloquial, collusion*
		con	in *connect, connote*
		cor	in *correct, correspond*
ob	>	op	in *oppose, oppress*
sub	>	suc	in *success, succumb*
		sup	in *suppress, supply, support*

Note the structure of the frequently misspelled *accommodate*: both *ac* and *com* are prefixes, so the word must have both a double *cc* and a double *mm*.

Errors also result from mistaking a prefix. A writer who spells *arouse* with a double *rr* doesn't know that the prefix here is simply *a*, not *ad > ar*. A writer who spells *apology* with a double *pp* is unaware that the prefix is *apo*, not *ad > ap* (knowing that the root is from the Greek *logos* would help). Familiarize yourself with prefixes. Here are some words with their prefixes in capital letters; after each is a common misspelling that knowing the prefix would have prevented:

Right	Wrong	Right	Wrong
AFOREmentioned	aformentioned	MILLImetre	milimetre
BY-product	biproduct	MINIature	minature
CONTROversial	conterversial	PENinsula	penninsula
DEscribe	discribe	PERsuade	pursuade
DEstroy	distroy	PERvading	prevading
DIAlogue	diologue	PORtraying	protraying
DISappointed	dissappointed	PROfessor	proffessor

51h   Suffixes

Suffixes too can give trouble. For example, if you add *ness* to a word ending in *n*, the result is a double *nn*: *barrenness, openness, stubbornness*. And remember that the correct suffix is *ful*, not *full*: *spoonful, cupful, shovelful, bucketful, roomful, successful*.

51i   Troublesome Word-endings

Several groups of suffixes—or just think of them as word-endings—consistently plague bad spellers and sometimes trip even good spellers. There are no rules governing them, and pronunciation is seldom any help; one either knows them or does not. Whenever you aren't *certain* of the correct spelling, check your dictionary. The following examples will at least alert you to the potential trouble-spots:

able, ably, ability; ible, ibly, ibility:

Many more words end in *able* than in *ible*, which should help; yet it is the *ible* endings that cause the most trouble:

advisable	inevitable	audible	inexpressible
comparable	laudable	contemptible	irresistible
debatable	noticeable	deductible	negligible
desirable	quotable	eligible	plausible
immeasurable	respectable	flexible	responsible
indispensable	syllable	forcible	tangible
indubitable	veritable	incredible	visible

ent, ently, ence, ency; ant, antly, ance, ancy:

apparent	independent	appearance	flamboyant
confidence	inherent	attendance	hindrance
coherent	permanent	blatant	irrelevant
consistent	persistence	brilliant	maintenance
excellent	resilient	concomitant	resistance
existence	tendency	extravagant	warrant

tial, tian, tiate; cial, cian, ciate:

confidential	influential	beneficial	mathematician
dietitian	martial	crucial	mortician
existential	spatial	emaciated	physician
expatiate	substantial	enunciate	politician

ce; se:

choice	presence	course	expense
evidence	pretence	dense	phrase
fence	voice	dispense	sparse

ative; itive:

affirmative	informative	additive	positive
comparative	negative	competitive	repetitive
imaginative	restorative	genitive	sensitive

51j   Changes in Spelling of Roots

Be careful with words whose roots change spelling—often because of a change in stress—when they are inflected for a different part of speech; for example:

clear, clarity	maintain, maintenance
curious, curiosity	prevail, prevalent
despair, desperate	pronounce, pronunciation
exclaim, exclamatory	repair, reparable
generous, generosity	repeat, repetition

inherit, heritage, BUT heredity, hereditary

51k   Faulty Pronunciation

Incorrect pronunciation often leads to incorrect spelling. Acquire the habit of correct pronunciation; sound words to yourself, exaggeratedly if necessary, even at the expense of temporarily slowing your reading speed. Here is a list of words some of whose common misspellings could be prevented by careful pronunciation:

academic	disgust	hurriedly	predilection
accelerate	disillusioned	immersing	prevalent
accidentally	eerie	insurgence	privilege
analogy	elaborate	interpretation	pronunciation
approximately	emperor	intimacy	quantity
architectural	environment	inviting	repetitive
athlete,	epitomize	irrelevant	reservoir
athletics	escape	itinerary	significant
authoritative	especially	larynx	similar
barbiturate	etcetera	lightning	strength
Britain	evident	limpidly	subsidiary
candidate	excerpt	lustrous	suffocate
celebration	facsimiles	mathematics	surprise
conference	February	negative	temporarily
congratulate	film	nuclear	ultimatum
controversial	foliage	occasional	village
definitely	frailty	optimism	villain
deteriorating	further	original	visible
detrimental	government	particular	vulnerable
dilapidated	governor	peculiar	where
diphthong	gravitation	permanently	whether
disastrous	height	phenomenon	whines
disgruntled	hereditary	philosophical	wondrous

Caution: Don't carelessly omit the *d* or *ed* from such words as *used* and *supposed*, *old-fashioned* and *prejudiced*, which are often carelessly pronounced. And don't write *of* instead of the contracted *'ve* in informal words like *would've*. And don't write or copy so hastily that you omit whole syllables (usually near-duplications in sound). Write carefully—and proofread even more carefully, sounding the words to yourself. Here are some examples of "telescoped" words that occur frequently:

Right	*Wrong*	*Right*	*Wrong*
convenience	convience	institution	instution
criticize	critize	politician	politian
examining	examing	remembrance	rembrance
inappropriate	inappriate	repetition	repition

51-I Confusion with Other Words

Don't let false analogies and similarities of sound lead you astray.

A writer who thinks of a word like	*may spell another word WRONG, like this:*	*instead of RIGHT, like this:*
young	amoung	among
breeze	cheeze	cheese
conform	conformation	confirmation
diet	diety	deity

desolate	desolute	dissolute
exalt	exaltant	exultant
democracy	hypocracy	hypocrisy
ideal	idealic	idyllic
discrete	indiscrete	indiscreet
air, fairy	ordinairy	ordinary
ledge, knowledge	priviledge	privilege
size	rize	rise
religious	sacreligious	sacrilegious
familiar	similiar	similar
stupid	stupifying	stupefying
summer	summerize	summarize
prize	surprize	surprise
tack	tacktics	tactics
rink, sink	zink	zinc

51m Homophones and Other Words Sometimes Confused

Caution: Your word-processing program's "spell-check" will *not* catch mistakes resulting from such confusion of words.

1. Be careful to distinguish between **homophones** (or homonyms), words pronounced alike but spelled differently. Here are some that can be troublesome; look up in the dictionary any whose meanings you aren't sure of; this is a matter of meaning as well as of spelling (and see #57):

aisle, isle	hail, hale
alter, altar	hanger, hangar
assent, ascent	hear, here
bear, bare	heard, herd
birth, berth	hole, whole
board, bored	holy, holey, wholly
border, boarder	idle, idol, idyll
born, borne	its, it's
break, brake	led, lead
by, by-, bi-, buy, bye	lessen, lesson
callous, callus	manner, manor
canvas, canvass	mantel, mantle
capital, capitol	meat, meet, mete
complement, compliment	naval, navel
cord, chord	paid, payed
council, counsel	past, passed
course, coarse	patience, patients
desert (v.), dessert	peddle, pedal
die, dying; dye, dyeing	phase, faze
discreet, discrete	piece, peace
flair, flare	pique, peak, peek
forgo, forego	plain, plane
forth, fourth	populous, populace

pore, pour
pray, prey
precedence, precedents
presence, presents
principle, principal
rain, reign, rein
right, write, rite
ring(er), wring(er)
road, rode, rowed
roll, role
seen, scene
sight, site, cite
soul, sole
sow, sew; sown, sewn
stationary, stationery

straight, strait
surf, serf
there, their, they're
throes, throws
through, threw
to, too, two
vein, vain, vane
vice, vise
waste, waist
wave, waive
way, weigh
weak, week
whose, who's
yoke, yolk
your, you're

2. There are also words that are not pronounced exactly alike but that are similar enough to be confused. Again, look up any whose meanings you aren't sure of:

accept, except
access, excess
adopt, adapt, adept
adverse, averse
advice, advise
affect, effect
afflicted, inflicted
allude, elude
angle, angel
appraise, apprise
anti-, ante-
assume, presume
bisect, dissect
bizarre, bazaar
breath, breathe
careen, career (v.)
censor, censure
choose, chose
climatic, climactic
conscious, conscience
credible, creditable, credulous
custom, costume
decent, descent, dissent
desert (n.), dessert
detract, distract
device, devise
diary, dairy
diffuse, defuse
discomfit, discomfort
elicit, illicit

emigrate, immigrate
eminent, imminent, immanent
ensure, insure, assure
envelop, envelope
exalt, exult
evoke, invoke
finely, finally
flaunt, flout
forbear, forebear
fortunate, fortuitous
founder, flounder
gantlet, gauntlet
Granada, Grenada
hardy, hearty
illusion, allusion
impractical, impracticable
incident, incidence, instance
incredulous, incredible
ingenious, ingenuous
insight, incite
instant, instance
later, latter
lineage, linage
liniment, lineament
loathe, loath
loose, lose
mitigate, militate
moral, morale
persecute, prosecute
practical, practicable

predominate, predominant		subscribe, ascribe	
proceed, precede		tack, tact	
prophecy, prophesy		than, then	
quite, quiet		torturous, tortuous	
rational, rationale		verses, *versus*	
statue, statute		whether, weather	
stringent, astringent		while, wile	

3. Be careful also to distinguish between such terms as the following, for although they sound the same, they function differently depending on whether they are spelled as one word or two:

already	all ready	awhile	a while
altogether	all together		(see also #60)
anybody	any body	everybody	every body
anymore	any more	everyday	every day
	(see also #60)	everyone	every one
anyone	any one	maybe	may be
anytime	any time	someday	some day
anyway	any way	sometime	some time

51n   One Word or Two Words?

Do not spell the following words as two or three separate or hyphenated words; each is one unhyphenated word:

alongside	easygoing	nowadays	straightforward
background	lifetime	outshine	sunrise
buildup (n.)	nevertheless	setback	throughout
countryside	nonetheless	spotlight	wrongdoing

The following, on the other hand, should always be spelled as two unhyphenated words:

a bit	at least	in order (to)
a few	close by	in spite (of)
after all	even though	no longer
all right (NOT alright)	every time	(on the) other hand
a lot	in between	(in) other words
as though	in fact	up to

Terms like *back yard*, *front yard*, *home town*, and *high school* should be written as two words (adjective + noun); when used as adjectival modifiers, they are hyphenated. When in doubt about such terms, consult your dictionary; you may find, as with *insofar*, *in so far*, that either form is acceptable.

> **Note:** The word *cannot* should usually be written as one word; write *can not* only when you want special emphasis on the *not*—equivalent to underlining it.

51o Hyphenation

To hyphenate or not to hyphenate? That is often the question. There are some firm rules; there are some sound guidelines; and there is a large territory where only common sense and a good dictionary can help you find your way. Since the conventions are constantly changing, sometimes rapidly, make a habit of checking your dictionary for current usage. (For hyphens to divide a word at the end of a line, see #45b.) Here are the main points to remember:

1. Use hyphens in compound numbers from twenty-one to ninety-nine: *forty-three, eighty-five.*

2. Use hyphens with fractions used as adjectives:

> A two-thirds majority is required to defeat the amendment.

When a fraction is used as a noun, some writers do not use a hyphen:

> Two thirds of the audience was asleep.

3. Use hyphens with compounds indicating time, when these are written out: *seven-thirty, nine-fifteen.*

4. Use a hyphen between a pair of numbers (including hours and dates) indicating a range: *pages 73-78, June 20-26.* The hyphen is equivalent to the word *to.* If you introduce the range with *from*, write out the word *to*: *from June 20 to June 26.* If you use *between*, write out the word *and*: *between June 20 and June 26.*

5. Use hyphens with prefixes before proper nouns:

all-Canadian	Pan-Slavic	pseudo-Pindaric
anti-Fascist	post-Elizabethan	semi-Gothic
ex-Prime Minister	pre-Christian	Trans-Siberian
non-Communist	pro-Tory	un-English

But there are long-established exceptions; for example:

antichrist	transatlantic	transpacific

6. Use hyphens with compounds beginning with the prefix *self: self-assured, self-confidence, self-deluded, self-esteem, self-made, self-pity,* etc. (The words *selfhood, selfish, selfless,* and *selfsame* are not hyphenated, since *self* is the root, not a prefix.) Hyphens are conventionally used with certain other prefixes: *all-important, ex-premier, quasi-religious.* Hyphens are conventionally used with most, but not all, compounds beginning with *vice* and *by: vice-chancellor, vice-consul, vice-president, vice-regent,*

etc., BUT *viceregal, vicereine, viceroy*; *by-election, by-product*, etc., BUT *bygone, bylaw, byroad, bystander, byword*. Check your dictionary.

7. Use hyphens with the suffixes *elect* and *designate*: *mayor-elect, ambassador-designate*.

8. Use hyphens with *great* and *in-law* in compounds designating family relationships: *mother-in-law, son-in-law, great-grandfather, great-aunt*.

9. Use hyphens to prevent a word's being mistaken for an entirely different word:

> He recounted what had happened after the ballots had been re-counted.
> If you're going to re-strain the juice, I'll restrain myself from drinking it now, seeds and all.
> Once at the resort after the bumpy ride, we sat down to re-sort our jumbled fishing gear.
> If you re-cover that chair before you sell it, you may be able to recover your investment.

10. Use hyphens to prevent awkward or confusing combinations of letters and sounds: *anti-intellectual, doll-like, photo-offset, re-echo, set-to*.

11. Hyphens are sometimes necessary to prevent ambiguity:

> *ambig:* The ad offered six week old kittens for sale.
> *clear:* The ad offered six week-old kittens for sale.
> *clear:* The ad offered six-week-old kittens for sale.

In the following, hyphenating *evening out* removes the possibility of misreading the sentence:

> Some people think we need a social evening-out of benefits and responsibilities.

51p   Compound Nouns

Some nouns composed of two or more words are conventionally hyphenated, for example *free-for-all, half-and-half, half-breed, man-eater, merry-go-round, old-timer, runner-up, safe-conduct, shut-in, tam-o'-shanter, trade-in, well-being*. But many that one might think should be hyphenated are not, and others that may once have been hyphenated, or even two separate words, have become so familiar that they are now one unhyphenated word. Usage is constantly and rapidly changing, and even dictionaries don't always agree on what is standard at a given time. Some dictionaries still record such old-fashioned forms as *to-night* and *to-morrow* as alternatives; use *tonight* and *tomorrow*. Clearly one should consult a dictionary that is both good and up-to-date and use the form it lists first.

51q Compound Modifiers

When two or more words occur together in such a way that they act as a single adjective before a noun, they are usually hyphenated in order to prevent a momentary misreading of the first part: a *well-dressed* man, *greenish-gray* eyes, *middle-class* values, *computer-printed* forms, a *once-in-a-lifetime* chance, a *three-day-old* strike. When they occur after a noun, misreading is unlikely and no hyphen is needed: *The man was well dressed*. But many compound modifiers are already listed as hyphenated words; for example one dictionary lists these, among others: *first-class, fly-by-night, good-looking, habit-forming, open-minded, right-hand, short-lived, tongue-tied, warm-blooded, wide-eyed*. Such modifiers retain their hyphens even when they follow the nouns they modify: *The tone of the speech was quite matter-of-fact*.

> **Caution:** Since one cannot mistake the first part of a compound modifier when it is an adverb ending in *ly*, even in front of a noun, do not use a hyphen:
>
> He is a happily married man.
> The superbly wrought sculpture was the centre of attention.

Exercise 51pq Checking hyphenation

What does your dictionary say about the following? Should they be two separate words, hyphenated, or one unhyphenated word? (As an experiment, look some of them up in more than one dictionary; you'll likely find differences.)

1. dumb waiter	8. nail set	15. south bound
2. duty free	9. pocket book	16. stock pile
3. fish hook	10. power boat	17. time out
4. foot candle	11. pre empt	18. waste paper
5. half life	12. run around	19. wine skin
6. half moon	13. sheep dog	20. world weary
7. home stretch	14. slip stream	21. world wide

51r Suspension Hyphens

If you use two prefixes with one root, use what is called a "suspension" hyphen—even if the prefixes would not normally be hyphenated:

The audience was about equally divided between pro- and anti-Liberals.
You may either pre- or post-date the cheque.
You may choose between the three- and the five-day excursions.

51s   Hyphenated Verbs

Verbs too are sometimes hyphenated. A dictionary will list most of the ones you might want to use; for example: *baby-sit, pan-broil, pistol-whip, pole-vault, re-educate, second-guess, sight-read, soft-pedal, straight-arm, two-time.*

Note that some expressions can be spelled either as two separate words or as compounds, depending on what part of speech they are functioning as; for example:

He works *full time*. He has a *full-time* job.
If you get too dizzy you may *black out*. You will then suffer a *blackout*.
Call up the next group of trainees. The commander ordered a general *call-up*.

Exercise 51o-s   Using hyphens

Insert hyphens wherever they are needed in the following sentences. Consult your dictionary if necessary.

1. The ferry is thirty two and one quarter metres long.
2. The all Canadian team proved too much for even the exchampions.
3. My half sister showed me an old fashioned tintype picture of her greatgrandmother.
4. The fully developed outline will be on your desk by midmorning.
5. The three youths, though well built, looked to me a run of the mill sort.
6. I watched an interesting two hour documentary about an alien smuggling operation.
7. Enjoy our beautiful dining room or take it with you service in one minute or less.
8. In the small town where I grew up there was a once a month barn dance; I miss that small town culture.
9. Much contemporary art is designed to fit readily into the middle class living room or the corporate board room.
10. The average high school graduate today doesn't have much hope of getting a well paying career job.

51t   Plurals (See also #51v.1.)

1. For most nouns, add *s* or *es* to the singular form to indicate plural number:

one building, two buildings	one box, two boxes
one cat, two cats	one church, two churches
one girl, two girls	one wish, two wishes

Add *es* rather than *s* if forming the plural makes an extra syllable, as in the three examples on the right. Sometimes the added *s* alone produces an extra syllable: *fireplaces, adages, cases, blazes, houses.*

2. Some nouns ending in *o* preceded by a consonant form their plurals with *s*, some use *es*, and for some either form is correct; but use the one listed first in your dictionary. Here are a few examples:

altos	echoes	cargoes OR cargos
pianos	heroes	mottoes OR mottos
solos	potatoes	zeros OR zeroes

If the final *o* is preceded by a vowel, usually only an *s* is added: *arpeggios, cameos, ratios, cuckoos, embryos.*

3. For some nouns ending in a single *f* or an *fe*, change the ending to *ve* before adding *s*; for example:

knife, knives	life, lives	shelf, shelves
leaf, leaves	loaf, loaves	thief, thieves

But some simply add *s*:

beliefs	gulfs	safes	griefs	proofs	still lifes

Some words ending in *f* have alternative plurals:

dwarfs OR dwarves	scarfs OR scarves
hoofs OR hooves	wharves OR wharfs

> **Note:** The well-known athletic group called the *Maple Leafs* is obviously a special case, a proper noun that doesn't follow the rules governing common nouns.

4. For nouns ending in *y* preceded by a vowel, add *s*:

bays	buoys	guys	keys	toys	valleys

For nouns ending in *y* preceded by a consonant, change the *y* to *i* and add *es*:

city, cities	cry, cries	kitty, kitties
country, countries	family, families	trophy, trophies

Exception: Most proper nouns ending in *y* simply add *s*:

The group includes two *Marys* and three *Henrys*.
From 1949 to 1990 there were two *Germanys*.

But note that we refer to the *Rockies*, and the Canary Islands are called the *Canaries*.

5. *Plurals of Compounds:* Generally, form the plurals of compounds simply by adding *s*:

backbenchers	forget-me-nots	great-grandmothers
man-eaters	major generals	lieutenant-governors
shut-ins	second cousins	merry-go-rounds

But if the first part is a noun and the rest is not, or if the first part is the more important of two nouns, that one is made plural:

daughters-in-law	jacks-of-all-trades	passers-by
governors general	mayors-elect	poets laureate

But there are exceptions, and—as usual—usage is changing. Note for example *spoonfuls* (this is the form for all nouns ending in *ful*). And a few compounds conventionally pluralize both nouns; for example: *menservants, ups and downs.* And a few are the same in both singular and plural; for example: *crossroads, daddy-long-legs, fancy pants.*

6. *Irregular Plurals:* Some nouns are irregular in the way they form their plurals, but these are common and generally well known; for example:

child, children	foot, feet	mouse, mice	woman, women

Some plural forms are the same as the singular; for example:

one deer, two deer	one series, two series
one moose, two moose	one sheep, two sheep

7. *Plurals of Borrowed Words:* The plurals of words borrowed from other languages (mostly Latin and Greek) can pose a problem. Words used formally or technically tend to retain their original plurals; words used more commonly tend to form their plurals according to English rules. Since many such words are in transition, you will probably encounter both plural forms. When in doubt, use the preferred form listed in your dictionary. Here are some examples of words that have tended to retain their original plurals:

alumna, alumnae	larva, larvae
alumnus, alumni	madame, mesdames
analysis, analyses	nucleus, nuclei
basis, bases	parenthesis, parentheses
crisis, crises	phenomenon, phenomena
criterion, criteria	stimulus, stimuli
hypothesis, hypotheses	synthesis, syntheses
kibbutz, kibbutzim	thesis, theses

Here are some with both forms, the choice often depending on the formality or technicality of the context:

antenna, antennae (insects), antennas (radios, etc.)
apparatus, apparatus, apparatuses

appendix, appendices, appendixes
beau, beaux, beaus
cactus, cacti, cactuses
chateau, chateaux, chateaus
curriculum, curricula, curriculums
focus, foci, focuses
formula, formulae, formulas
index, indices, indexes
lacuna, lacunae, lacunas
matrix, matrices, matrixes
memorandum, memoranda, memorandums
referendum, referenda, referendums
stratum, strata, stratums
syllabus, syllabi, syllabuses
symposium, symposia, symposiums
terminus, termini, terminuses
ultimatum, ultimata, ultimatums
vertebra, vertebrae, vertebras

And here are a few that now tend to follow regular English patterns:

bureau, bureaus   sanctum, sanctums
campus, campuses   stadium, stadiums
genius, geniuses (*genii* for mythological creatures)

Caution: If you want to be considered a careful writer and speaker of English, you should adhere to the following usages:

Data is plural; the singular is *datum*.
Strata is plural; the singular is *stratum*.
Kudos is singular; don't use it as if it were plural.
Trivia is plural; don't use it as if it were singular.
Bacteria is plural; don't use it as if it were singular.
Media is the plural of *medium*; don't use it as if it were singular. (*Mediums* is the correct plural for spiritualists who claim to communicate with the dead.)

Opinion, as well as usage, is divided on the spelling of the plurals of these and similar words. Most writers, for example, find *criterions* and *phenomenons* abhorrent, preferring the original *criteria* and *phenomena*. On the other hand, some don't object to *data* as a singular noun. And *agenda*, originally the plural of *agendum*, is now simply a singular noun with its own plural, *agendas*. Your dictionary should indicate any irregular plurals; if you aren't sure of a word, look it up.

Note: If you use or quote words from other languages that have such diacritical marks as the cedilla, the circumflex, the tilde, the umlaut, or acute or grave accents, write them accurately. For example: *façade, fête, cañon, Götterdämmerung, passé, à la mode.* See also #49b.

Exercise 51t Forming plurals

Write out what you think is the correct plural form of each of the following nouns. Then check your dictionary to see if you were right.

1. aide-de-camp	8. fish	15. museum	22. solo
2. alley	9. fly-by	16. octopus	23. speech
3. bonus	10. glass	17. ox	24. staff
4. bus	11. goose	18. plateau	25. territory
5. cloverleaf	12. handful	19. radius	26. town
6. embargo	13. mongoose	20. serf	27. wife
7. fifth	14. mosquito	21. society	28. yokefellow

51u Third-Person-Singular Verbs in the Present Tense

The third-person-singular, present-tense inflection of verbs is usually formed by following the same rules that govern the formation of plurals of nouns. For example:

I brief him. She briefs me.
I buy. He buys.
I carry. She carries.
I hate. She hates.
I lift. The fog lifts.

I lurch. It lurches.
I portray. He portrays.
I run. He runs.
I try. She tries.
I wish. He wishes.

But be careful, for there are exceptions; for example:

He loafs on weekends and wolfs his food.
She hoofs it to work every day.

Exercise 51u Inflecting verbs

Supply the present-tense, third-person-singular form of each of the following verbs:

1. atrophy	6. condone	11. leaf	16. revoke
2. buy	7. convey	12. mouth	17. search
3. chafe	8. echo	13. rally	18. ski
4. choose	9. go	14. reach	19. swing
5. comb	10. grasp	15. relieve	20. tunnel

51v Apostrophes

apos 1. *For Plurals:* An apostrophe and an s may be used to form the plural only of numerals, symbols, letters, and of words referred to as words:

She knew her ABC's at the age of four.
Study the three R's.
It happened in the 1870's.
Indent all ¶'s five spaces.

Accommodate is spelled with two *c*'s and two *m*'s.
There are four 7's in my telephone number.
There are too many *and*'s in that sentence.

Note that when a word, letter, or figure is italicized, the apostrophe and the *s* are not.

Some people prefer to form such plurals without the apostrophe: Rs, 7s, 1870s, *and*s. But this practice can be confusing, especially with letters and words, which may be misread:

How many *is* are there in *Mississippi*?
Too many *this*s can spoil a good paragraph.

It is clearer and easier always to use the apostrophe, though potentially awkward instances could be rephrased.

Caution: Never use an apostrophe and an *s* to form any other kind of plural—that is, of regular common and proper nouns.

---

2. *To Indicate Omissions:* Use apostrophes to indicate omitted letters in contractions and omitted (though obvious) numerals:

aren't (are not)	they're (they are)
can't (cannot)	won't (will not)
doesn't (does not)	wouldn't (would not)
don't (do not)	goin' home (going home)
isn't (is not)	back in '63
it's (it is)	the crash of '29
she's (she is)	the summer of '42

If an apostrophe is already present to indicate a plural, you may omit the apostrophe that indicates omission: *the 20's, the 90's.*

51w Possessives

apos 1. To form the possessive case of a singular or a plural noun that does not end in *s*, add an apostrophe and *s*:

Alberta's capital	a day's work	the girl's teacher
the car's colour	deer's hides	tomorrow's news
children's books	Emil's briefcase	the women's jobs

2. To form the possessive of compound nouns, use '*s* after the last noun:

The Solicitor General's report is due tomorrow.
Sally and Mike's dinner party was a huge success.

But be careful: if the nouns don't actually form a compound, each will need the '*s*:

Sally's and Mike's translations were markedly different.

3. You may safely and correctly add an apostrophe and *s* to form the possessive of singular nouns ending in *s* or an *s*-sound:

the class's achievement	an index's usefulness
the cross's meaning	Keats's poems
the congress's debates	a platypus's bill

—though some writers prefer to add only an apostrophe if the pronunciation of an extra syllable would sound awkward:

Achilles' heel	Moses' miracles
for convenience' sake	Demosthenes' speeches

But the *'s* is never wrong: Achilles's heel; for convenience's sake; Moses's miracles; Demosthenes's speeches. In any event, one can usually avoid possible awkwardness by showing possession with an *of*-phrase instead of *'s* (see number 5, below):

> for the sake of convenience; the poems of Keats; the miracles of Moses; the bill of a platypus

4. To indicate the possessive case of plural nouns ending in *s*, add only an apostrophe:

> the cannons' roar
> the girls' sweaters
> the Joneses' garden
> the Smiths' cottage

Caution: Do not use apostrophes in possessive personal pronouns: *hers,* NOT *her's; its,* NOT *it's; ours,* NOT *our's; theirs,* NOT *their's; yours,* NOT *your's.* (See also #3a.)

---

5. *Possessive with 's or with of:* Especially in formal writing, the *'s* form is more common with the names of living creatures, the *of* form with the names of inanimate things:

> the cat's tail, the girl's coat, Sherman's home town, the arm of the chair, the contents of the refrigerator, the surface of the desk

But both are acceptable with either category. The *'s* form, for example, is common with nouns that refer to things thought of as made up of people or animals or as extensions of them:

> the team's strategy, the committee's decision, the company's representative, the government's policy, the city's bylaws, Canada's climate, the factory's output, the heart's affections, the law's delay

or things that are "animate" in the sense that they are part of nature:

the dawn's early light, the wind's velocity, the comet's tail, the sea's surface, the plant's roots, the sky's colour

or periods of time:

today's paper, a day's work, a month's wages, winter's storms

Even beyond such uses the *'s* is not uncommon; sometimes there is a sense of personification, but not always:

beauty's ensign, at death's door, freedom's light, *Love's Labour's Lost*, time's fool, the razor's edge, the ship's helm

If it seems natural and appropriate to you, go ahead and speak or write of a *car's engine*, a *book's contents*, a *rocket's trajectory*, a *poem's imagery*, and the like (but don't be surprised if a few people object to the practice).

Conversely, for the sake of emphasis or rhythm you will occasionally want to use an *of*-phrase where *'s* would be normal; for example *the jury's verdict* lacks the punch of *the verdict of the jury*. You can also use an *of*-phrase to avoid awkward pronunciations (see above: those who don't like the sound of *Dickens's novels* can refer to *the novels of Dickens*) and unwieldy constructions (*the opinion of the Minister of Finance* is preferable to *the Minister of Finance's opinion*). Further, whether you use *'s* or just *s* to form the plural of letters, figures, and the like (see #51v.1), it is probably best, in order to avoid ambiguity, to form possessives of abbreviations with *of* rather than with apostrophes: *the opinion of the MLA*, *the opinion of the MLA's*, *the opinion of the MLAs*.

6. *Double Possessives:* Although some people object to them, there is nothing wrong with double possessives—showing possession with both an *of*-phrase and a possessive inflection. They are standard with possessive pronouns and can be used similarly with common and proper nouns:

a favourite *of mine*, a friend *of hers*, a friend *of the family* or *of the family's*, a contemporary *of Shakespeare* or *of Shakespeare's*

And a sentence like "The story was based on an idea of Shakespeare" is at least potentially ambiguous, whereas "The story was based on an idea of Shakespeare's" is clear. But if you feel that this sort of construction is unlovely, you can usually manage to revise it to something like "on one of Shakespeare's ideas." And certainly avoid such double possessives with a *that-* construction: "His hat was just like that of Arthur's"; all would agree that *that* is unlovely.

Exercise 51vw(1)   Using apostrophes

Insert apostrophes where necessary in the following:

1. I dont know whether this book is his or hers, but theres no doubt its a handsome one, and its value on todays market, what its worth now, must surely be greater than its value as a new book, way back in the 1930s.
2. Clearly he doesnt know whats going on: itll take him a weeks study to catch up.
3. Our reports so far ahead of theirs that shell have to work nights to make ends meet.
4. It isnt whom you know but what you know that in the end seals the deal.
5. Dianas guess is closer than Seans, but the jars full and accurate count of beans wont be verified till Mondays announcement.
6. The teachers comments about Guys paper pointed out its errors.
7. Its sometimes a full days work to write a good paragraph.
8. It doesnt matter who wins the game; its rather its quality that counts.
9. When the childrens shouting got too loud, the Joneses neighbours had to shut their windows, but Alice left hers open.
10. Their approach was by ones and twos, whereas ours was a matter of charging in all at once.

Exercise 51vw(2)   Using apostrophes

In the following sentences, supply any missing apostrophes and correct any instances of their misuse, and any associated errors.

1. Now we see wives who, by working and pooling their wages with their husbands, can purchase extra luxury items for the home and family.
2. Able people are often held back by societies structure.
3. The two main characters are each others foils.
4. He acted without a moments hesitation.
5. We will meet again in two days time.
6. Have you read H. G. Well's *The Time Machine*?
7. If it is to perform it's duties properly, the committees frame of reference needs to be made clearer.
8. You can buy boys and girls jeans in any good department store.
9. The Smith's came to dinner.
10. When someone misuses apostrophes, it show's ignorance.

51x   Spelling List

In addition to the words listed and discussed in the preceding pages, many other words often cause spelling problems. Following is a list of frequently misspelled words. If you are at all weak in spelling, you should test yourself on these words, as well as those discussed earlier.

But you should also keep your own spelling list: whenever you misspell a word, add it to your list—and try to decide which rule the error violates or which category of error it falls into. Practise spelling the words on your list until you have mastered them.

absence
absorption
accessible
acclaim
accumulate
acknowledgment or
  acknowledgement
acquaintance
acquire
additional
advertise
adviser or advisor
aesthetic or esthetic
affection
affidavit
aging
allege
alternately
always
amateur
amour
analyze or analyse
analogy
anonymous
anticipated
apartment
appal or appall
approach
architect
arctic
arithmetic
article
atmosphere
audience
automatically
auxiliary
axe or ax
background
beggar
beneficent
benefit
botany
bullet
buoyant
bureau

burglar
buried
cafeteria
calendar
Calvinist
camaraderie
candidate
cannibal
captain
careful
carnival
cartilage
catalogue, catalog
category
cemetery
chagrin
challenge
champion
changeable
chocolate
cinnamon
clamour or clamor
clothed
coincide
colossal
committee
complexion
comprise
comrade
concomitant
conqueror
conscious
consensus
conservative
consider
consumer
control
controlled
convenient
court
courteous
create
criticism
criticize or criticise
crucifixion

curiosity
cylinder
decorative
decrepit
defence or defense
defensive
delusion
desperate
develop
devastation
diameter
dilemma
diminution
dining
diphtheria
dispatch or despatch
dissatisfied
dissipate
divide
doctor
drunkenness
eclectic
ecstasy
efficient
electorate
elegiac
eligible
embarrassment
emancipation
emphasize or
  emphasise
employee
emulate
encompass
encyclopedia
endeavour or endeavor
enforced
engraver
enterprise
epilogue
equip
equipment
equipped
erupt
euphonious

exalt
exaggerate
excel
exercise
exhausted
exhilarating
exorbitant
exuberant
facilities
fallacy
fascinating
feasible
fervour or fervor
filter
flippant
flourish
flyer or flier
focusses or focuses
foreign
foresee
forty
fulfill
fundamentally
furor
gaiety
gauge
genealogy
gleam
goddess
grammar
gray or grey
grievous
guarantee
guard
harass
harmonious
height
heinous
hence
heroine
hesitancy
hindrance
homogeneous
horseshoe
household
humorous
hygienist
hypocrisy
hypocrite
illegal

illegitimate
illiterate
imagery
imagination
imitate
immediate
impious
implementation
importance
imposter
improvise
inadequacy
incidentally
incompatible
indefinite
industrialization
inevitable
influence
injuries
innocent
inoculate
inquire or enquire
integrated
interrupt
intimate
intriguing
jealousy
jeweller or jeweler
jewellery or jewelry
judgment or
   judgement
knowledge
knowledgeable
laboratory
leeches
library
licence or license (n.)
license or licence (v.)
lieutenant
likelihood
lineage
liquefy
liqueur
liquor
luxury
magnificent
mammoth
manoeuvre or
   maneuver
manual

manufactured
marriage
marshal
mattress
meant
medieval
melancholy
menace
metaphor
mineralogy
minuscule
mischievous
molester
monologue
monotonous
monstrous
mould or mold
museum
mustache or
   moustache
naive
necessary
ninety
nosey or nosy
nostrils
numerous
obstacle
occurred
occurrence
offence or offense
omniscient
oneself
operator
opulent
ostracize or ostracise
paralleled or
   parallelled
paralyze or paralyse
paraphernalia
parliament
partner
peculiar
peddler
perfectible
perseverance
personality
personify
personnel
persuade
pharaoh

phony or phoney
plagiarism
playwright
plough or plow
poem
pollution
porous
positioning
possession
practicality
practice (n.)
practise or practice (v.)
predecessors
prejudice
prestige
pretence or pretense
primitive
procedure
proletariat
prominent
proscenium
psychiatry
psychology
pursue
putrefy
puzzled
quandary
quantity
quatrain
quizzically
rarefied
reality
recognize
recommend
reflection
religious
reminisce
repel
repetition

resemblance
rhythm
ridiculous
sacrifice
safety
scandal
sceptic or skeptic
sentence
separate
sheik
shepherd
sheriff
shining
shiny
signifies
simile
sincerity
siphon
simultaneous
skiing
skilful or skillful
smoulder or smolder
solely
soliloquy
species
spectators
speech
sponsor
storey or story (floor)
straddle
strategy
stretched
styrofoam
subconsciously
subsequent
subtly
succinct
succumb
sulphur or sulfur

superintendent
susceptible
suspense
symbolic
symbolize or symbolise
symmetry
synonymous
syrup
tariff
temperament
temperature
territory
theory
therein
threshold
tragedy
trailed
tranquillity or
 tranquility
transferred
troubadour
tyranny
unavailing
undoubtedly
unmistakable
until
usefulness
vehicle
vilify
weary
whisky or whiskey
willful or wilful
wintry
wistfulness
withdrawal
woollen or woolen
woolly
writing
written

PART

3

STYLE AND THE LARGER ELEMENTS OF COMPOSITION

Jonathan Swift's definition of style may be the best, at least for simplicity and directness: "Proper words in proper places make the true definition of a style." In its broadest sense, **style** consists of everything that is not the *content* of what is being expressed. It is the *manner* as opposed to the *matter*: everything that is a part of the *way* something is said constitutes its style.

But though we customarily distinguish between *style* and *content* in order to facilitate discussion and analysis, the distinction is in some ways false, for the two are inseparable. Since the *way* in which something is expressed inevitably influences the effect, it is necessarily part of *what* is being expressed. "I have a hangover" may say essentially the same thing as "I'm feeling a bit fragile this morning," but the different *styles* of the statements create different effects, different meanings. The medium, then, if it is not the entire message, is at least part of it.

An important attribute of style is **tone**, usually defined as a writer's attitude toward both subject matter and audience. Tone in writing is analogous to tone in speech. We hear or describe someone as speaking in a sarcastic tone of voice, or as sounding angry, or jocular, or matter-of-fact. Writing, like speech, can "sound" ironic, conversational, intimate, morbid, tragic, frivolous, cold, impassioned, comic, coy, energetic, phlegmatic, detached, sneering, contemptuous, laudatory, condescending, and so forth. The tone of a piece of writing—whether an essay or only a sentence—largely determines the feeling or impression the writing creates.

The style of a piece of writing, including its tone, arises from such features as syntax, point of view, and even punctuation. But it is largely determined by diction: by choice of words, figurative language, and even sounds.

CHAPTER VII

Diction

d   Diction—a writer's choice of words—is obviously near the heart of effective writing and style. No amount of correct grammar and rhetorical skill can compensate for poor diction. This chapter isolates the principal difficulties writers encounter in choosing and using words, and offers some suggestions for overcoming them.

The first suggestion is the simplest and most basic one: when you think "diction" think "dictionary." **USE YOUR DICTIONARY.** Become familiar with it; find out how it works and discover the variety of information it offers. Good "college" or "desk" dictionaries don't merely give you the spelling, syllabication, pronunciation, and meaning of words; they also offer advice on usage, idioms, and synonyms to help you decide on the best word for a particular context; they list irregularities in the principal parts of verbs, in the inflection of adjectives and adverbs, and in the formation of plurals; they supply etymologies (knowing a word's original form and meaning can sometimes help you decide on its appropriateness for your purpose); they tell you if a word or phrase is considered slang, colloquial, informal, or archaic. And they usually have interesting and useful introductory essays and appendices. Take advantage of the many resources of your dictionary.

52   Level

lev   In any piece of writing, use words that are appropriate to you, to your topic, and to the circumstances in which you are writing. That is, consider the *occasion*, your *purpose*, and your *audience*. Avoid words and phrases that call attention to themselves rather than to the meaning you want to convey. Generally, avoid slang and colloquial or informal terms at one extreme, and pretentious, overly formal, highfalutin language at the other. Of course there will be times when one or the other, or both, will be useful—for example to make a point in a particularly telling way, to achieve a humorous effect, or to make dialogue sound realistic. But it is usually preferable to adopt a straightforward, moderate style, a medium level of diction that neither crawls on its belly in the dirt nor struts about on stilts. (See also #11d.)

52a   Slang

Since **slang** is diction at the opposite extreme from **formal**, it is seldom appropriate in a formal context. There is nothing inherently wrong with slang; it is undeniably a colourful part of the language. But its very liveliness and vigour make it faddish: some slang terms remain in vogue only a few weeks, some linger on for a few years, and new ones are constantly popping up to replace those going out of fashion. Although many slang terms eventually become part of the standard language, much slang is so ephemeral that dictionaries cannot keep up with it.

It is principally slang's transitoriness that makes it risky to use in writing. A word or phrase that is *hot* (or *cool*) when you write it may sound stale and dated soon after. Much slang is also limited to particular social groups, classes, or professions, and it is often regional as well. Hence terms that may be vivid to you and your friends may be unintelligible to an outsider, such as someone older or from a different place (or, given the nature of some slang, a reader who finds them intelligible may also find them offensive).

A writer does well, therefore, to be careful—and conservative. The temptation to enliven one's writing with some pungent slang is often great. It can trap the unwary writer, and tempt even the wary, into sounding not only dated but also artificially chic and clever. Too much spice can ruin the taste of something, especially something delicate—which in a way formal style is.

Yet sometimes a slang term will seem the most effective way to say something. So don't avoid slang entirely; rather, use it only when it is the most appropriate means to a desired end—but use it infrequently and with care. And note that you can't always depend even on dictionaries to help you, for they often disagree about what is and isn't slang. The adjective *strapped*, for example, meaning broke, out of money, has been around at least since the beginning of this century; one current dictionary doesn't even list it, a second labels it *slang*, another calls it *informal*, and yet another assigns it no label, implying that it has entered the general vocabulary and become "respectable."

If tempted to write something slangy, then, think twice, or thrice— and consult not only one or more good dictionaries but also your ear, your common sense, and your good taste.

> **Note:** Remember, if you do use a slang term, do not put quotation marks around it (see #43g).

Exercise 52a   **Thinking about slang**

List as many slang terms as you can think of for each of the following. Which are current in your vocabulary? Which if any would you consider using in an essay? In a letter to a friend? In a letter to a parent or uncle or aunt? In conversation with someone of your own gender? In conversation with someone of the opposite gender?

1. criminal (n.)	6. court (v.)	11. sweetheart
2. mad (adj.)	7. bore (n.)	12. boy
3. intoxicated	8. very good	13. girl
4. cheat (v.)	9. talk (v.)	14. beautiful
5. cheat (n.)	10. stupid person	15. ugly

52b   Informal, Colloquial

inf,
colloq   Even dictionaries can't agree on distinguishing between *slang* and informal or colloquial usage. (Note: Because many people confuse it with *dialectal*, some dictionaries no longer use the label *colloquial*, but use *informal* instead.) Slang terms are in one sense simply extreme examples of the colloquial or informal. Nevertheless, there are many words and phrases that can be labelled *inf* or *colloq*, and although not slang, they do not ordinarily belong in formal writing. For example, unless you are aiming for a somewhat informal level, you should avoid such abbreviations as *prof*, *gent*, and *rev*; and you should also avoid contractions (*can't*, *don't*, etc.), though they are common in speech.

Here are more examples of informal or colloquial usages that most writers think would be out of place in strictly formal writing:

Informal or Colloquial	Acceptable equivalents
absolutely	very; yes
a lot of, lots of, lots	much, many, a great deal of
and such	and so on, and the like
anyplace, everyplace noplace, someplace	anywhere, everywhere, nowhere, somewhere
around	about, approximately
awful	bad, ill, ugly, unpleasant, etc.
be sure and	be sure to
back of, in back of	behind
chance of + gerund (e.g. chance of getting)	chance + infinitive (chance to get)
expect (as in "I expect you want me to go")	suppose, suspect, imagine
figure	think, believe, etc.
fix (verb)	repair, prepare, etc.
fix (noun)	predicament, etc.
funny	odd, peculiar, strange, unusual
guess (as in "I guess that...")	believe, suppose, think
mean	bad, cruel, evil, etc.
most (as in "most everyone")	almost
nice	agreeable, attractive, pleasant, etc.
nowhere near	not nearly, not at all, not anywhere near

out loud	aloud
over with	ended, finished, done
phone	telephone
photo	photograph
plan on + gerund (e.g. plan on going)	plan + infinitive (plan to go)
quite, quite a bit, quite a few, quite a lot, etc.	somewhat, rather, many, a large amount, much, etc.
real, really (as intensive adverb)	very, greatly, surely, etc.
right away, right now	immediately, at once
shape (good, bad, etc.)	condition
show up	appear, arrive; prove better than, best
size up	judge, estimate the strength of, etc.
sure and (as in "Be sure and call")	sure to
terrible, terribly (also as vague intensifiers)	unpleasant, uncomfortable, very, extremely, etc.
try and	try to
wait on	await, wait for
where (as in "I see where we're in for a storm")	that

In addition, many words have been so abused in advertising, used for gushy and exaggerated effect, that they can now seldom be used with precision in formal writing. For example:

awesome, fantastic, marvellous, stupendous, terrific, tremendous

Exercise 52b   **Using formal diction**

Provide formal substitutes for each of the slang or informal terms below. Use your dictionary as necessary. Then compose sentences for at least ten of the listed terms, using them in ways that you think would be acceptable in relatively formal writing.

1. bawl out	11. cuss (v. & n.)	21. jerk
2. beef (v. & n.)	12. cute	22. miss out
3. booze	13. ditch	23. monkey business
4. cheapskate	14. down the tube	24. on the spot
5. chump	15. egged on	25. scrounge
6. con (v.)	16. face the music	26. slapdash
7. conniption	17. fall guy	27. slouch
8. cook up	18. highbrow	28. southpaw
9. crackdown	19. hoofed it	29. square
10. crummy	20. hunch	30. stunner

52c   "Fine Writing"

Unnecessarily formal or pretentious diction is called "fine writing"—here, an ironic term of disapproval. Efforts to impress readers with such writing

fig **53**

almost always backfire. For example, imagine yourself trying to take seriously someone who wrote "It was felicitous that the canine in question was demonstrably more exuberant in emitting threatening sounds than in attempting to implement said threats by engaging in actual physical assault" instead of simply saying "Luckily, the dog's bark was worse than his bite." This is an exaggerated example, of course; but it illustrates how important it is to be natural (within reason) and straightforward. Writers who over-reach themselves often use supposedly elegant terms incorrectly. The student who wrote "Riding majestically down the street on a magnificent float was the Festival Queen surrounded by all her courtesans" was striving for sophistication, but succeeded only in getting an undesired laugh from the reader who knew the correct meaning of *courtesans*.

Exercise 52c **Thinking about "big" words**

For each of the following words, provide one or more equivalents that are less formal, more common or natural. Use your dictionary as necessary. Which of these words are in your own *recognition* vocabulary? Which do you consider to be in your *working* vocabulary? Mark any that you think should *not* necessarily be avoided as pretentious or overly formal in a normal context.

1. ablutions	21. eleemosynary	41. penurious
2. assiduity	22. equitation	42. peregrinations
3. aviate	23. erstwhile	43. propinquity
4. bellicose	24. frangible	44. *raison d'être*
5. cachinnation	25. gustatory	45. rebarbative
6. cinereous	26. habiliments	46. refection
7. circumambient	27. hebdomadal	47. regurgitate
8. collation	28. impudicity	48. repast
9. colloquy	29. ineluctable	49. rubicund
10. comminatory	30. jejune	50. salubrious
11. compotation	31. lubricity	51. sartorial
12. concatenation	32. lucubrations	52. serendipitous
13. confabulate	33. matutinal	53. sesquipedalian
14. conflagration	34. mentation	54. superincumbent
15. contumelious	35. objurgation	55. tenebrous
16. crepuscular	36. obloquy	56. transpontine
17. defenestration	37. oppugnant	57. vilipend
18. divagation	38. orthography	58. visage
19. doff	39. otiose	59. veridical
20. egress	40. pellucid	60. *Weltanschauung*

---

53 Figurative Language

fig

Strictly, **figurative language** includes many "figures of speech," such as personification, synecdoche, metonymy, hyperbole, litotes, and even paradox, irony, and symbolism. Generally, however, the term *figurative language* refers to *metaphoric* language, whose most common devices are the **metaphor** and the **simile**. A **simile** is an explicit comparison which is usually introduced by *like* or *as*:

> The river is *like* a snake winding across the plain.
> She was as carefree *as* a wild canary.

A **metaphor**, on the other hand, is an implicit comparison; the things being compared are assumed to be identical:

> The river *is* a snake winding across the plain.

Often a metaphor is condensed into a *verb*:

> The river *snakes* its way across the plain.

an *adjective*:

> The *serpentine* river meanders across the plain.

or an *adverb*:

> The river winds *snakily* across the plain.

Figurative language is an important element of good style. Writing that lacks it will be relatively dry, flat, and dull. But remember that a good metaphor doesn't merely enhance style; it also sharpens meaning. Use metaphors not simply for their own sake, but rather to convey meaning more effectively. For example, to say that "the hillside was covered with a profusion of colourful flowers" is clear enough; but if one writes instead that "the hillside was a tapestry of spring blossoms," the metaphor not only enriches the style but also provides readers with something *concrete* (see #54a), an *image* (that of the tapestry) that helps them visualize the scene.

53a   Inappropriate Metaphors

If you force a metaphor upon a given expression just to embellish style, it will likely be inappropriate and call attention to itself rather than enhance the desired meaning. It will, to use a rather tired but still expressive simile, stick out like a sore thumb. For example, "the tide of emotion suddenly stopped" doesn't work, since tides don't start and stop; they ebb and flow. And a phrase like "bomb craters blossoming all over the landscape" works only if one intends the inherent discord. And a simile such as "he ran like an ostrich in heat" may confuse the reader with inappropriate associations.

53b   Overextended Metaphors

Extended metaphors can be effective, but don't let yourself become so enamoured with a metaphor that you extend it too far, to the point where it takes control of what is being said:

> When she came out of the surf her hair looked like limp spaghetti. A sauce of seaweed and sand, looking like spinach and grated cheese, had been carelessly

applied, the red flower fastened in her tresses looked like a wayward piece of tomato, and globs of mud clung like meatballs to the pasty pasta of her face. The fork of my attention hovered hesitatingly over this odd dish. Clearly I would need more than one glass of the red wine of remembered beauty and affection to wash it all down.

This may all be very clever, but after the first sentence—the spaghetti image itself being somewhat questionable—one quickly loses sight of the original descriptive intention and becomes mired in all the associated metaphors and similes; in short, a reader is likely to feel fed up and turn to something less fattening and overseasoned. Don't extend a metaphor beyond its usefulness.

53c   Dead Metaphors

One must also guard against dead metaphors and clichés (see #59e). The language contains many dead metaphors like the *leg* of a table, *branching out*, and *flew* to the rescue, which are acceptable since we no longer think of them as metaphors. But many other metaphors, whether altogether dead or only moribund but with little metaphoric force left, can be dangerous. Such hackneyed phrases as *the ladder to success, making mountains out of molehills, nipped in the bud, flog a dead horse,* and *between the devil and the deep blue sea* are usually muddying and soporific instead of enlivening and clarifying.

Occasionally, however, a dead or trite metaphor can be revivified, consciously used in a fresh way. For example, the hackneyed phrase *bit off more than he could chew* was given new life by the person who, discussing Henry James's writing, said that James "chewed more than he bit off." *Sound as a dollar* would these days be more appropriately rendered as "unsound as a dollar." Even a slangy phrase like *chew the fat* might be transformed and updated in a description of people sitting down to "chew the cholesterol." But be careful, for such attempts can misfire; like an overextended metaphor, they sometimes call attention to their own cleverness at the expense of the intended meaning.

53d   Mixed Metaphors

Finally, avoid incongruously mixed metaphors. The person who wrote, of the Great Depression, that "what began as a zephyr soon blossomed into a giant," had lost control of metaphor. The following paragraph about Shakespeare's *Othello* was written by a student who obviously began with the good intention of using metaphors to help describe the almost unbelievable evil of Iago, but who soon became lost in a self-created maze of contradictions and incongruities:

> Iago has spun his web and like a spider he waits. His beautiful web of silk is so fragile and yet it captures the souls of its victims by gently luring them

into his womb. Unsuspecting are those unfortunate creatures who sense the poisonous venom oozing through their veins. It has a tranquil effect, for it numbs the mind with its magical potion. The victims are transformed into pawns as they satisfy the queen's appetite and so they serve their purpose.

Here is a paragraph, also by a student, that not only successfully uses metaphor throughout to create its effect but that is also, in its entirety (note the title and the final clause), a single metaphor:

> At the Movies
>
> I remember once, as a kid, lying on my back watching clouds. Row upon row of factory-perfect models drifted along the assembly line. There went a nifty schooner, flag flying—and look, a snapping toy poodle with the most absurd cut! Next came chilly Greenland, with Labrador much too close for comfort. But the banana split was the best of all. It reminded me how hungry I was, and how close to home. With a jump, I promised myself I'd catch the second feature on the next sunny day.

Certainly, then, use figurative language. It can lend grace and charm and liveliness and clarity to your writing. But beware of its potential pitfalls: inappropriate, overextended, and mixed metaphors.

54 Concrete and Abstract; Weak Generalizations

54a Concreteness and Specificity

conc   Concrete words denote tangible things, capable of being apprehended by our physical senses (*cars, orchestra, flowers, broccoli, fire, walking*). **Abstract** words denote intangible things, like ideas or qualities (*transportation, entertainment, nature, health, destruction, progress*). The more *concrete* your writing, the more readily your readers will grasp it, for the concreteness will provide images for their imaginations to respond to. If you write

> Transportation is becoming a major problem in our city.

and leave it at that, readers might understand you, but you'd be taking a chance on their conjuring up the right kinds of images. But if you write, or add,

> In the downtown core of our city, far too many cars and far too few buses travel the streets.

you know that your readers will understand exactly what you mean: in their minds they will see the traffic jams and the overloaded buses.

Similarly, the less **general** and the more **specific** your writing is, the clearer and more effective it will be. *General* and *specific* are relative terms: a general word designates a *class* (e.g., *modes of transportation*); a less general or more specific word designates members of that class (*vehicles, ships, airplanes*); a still more specific word designates members of a still smaller class (*cars, trucks, trains, buses*); and so on, getting narrower and narrower, the classes and sub-classes getting smaller and smaller, until—if one wants or needs to go that far—one arrives at a single, unique item, a class of one, such as the particular car sitting in your own garage.

Of course it is appropriate to write about "plant life," but try then to narrow it, say, to "flowers"; and if you can write about "pansies," "roses," "daffodils," and so on, you'll be even more effective. Even the generalization "fire" is unquestionably vivid, but "forest fires" makes it sharper, and mentioning the specific example of "the huge fires of 1985" will likely enable you to make your point even more forcibly. Don't vaguely write "We experienced a hot day" when you could write more clearly, "We sweltered all afternoon in the 35-degree heat," or "We enjoyed basking in the hot sun all afternoon." Don't write "I found the city interesting" when you could write "I liked the city's architecture and night life," or, better still, "I was fascinated by the architecture in the city's French quarter, and I took delight in the many fine cafés, restaurants, and jazz clubs that I found there."

The following passage makes sense, but its abstractness and generality prevent it from being very memorable or effective:

> If one makes a purchase that a short time later proves to have been ill-advised due to the rapid deterioration of quality, then it is the opinion of this writer that one has every right to seek redress either by expressing one's displeasure to the individual who conducted the original transaction or, if it should prove necessary, by resorting to litigation.

Inexperienced writers often assume that this kind of language is good because it sounds formal and sophisticated. But notice how much more vivid a revised version is:

> If you buy a car on Thursday and the engine falls out of it on Saturday, I think you should shout "Hey!" to the dealer who sold it to you, and haul him into court if necessary to get back the good money you paid for what turned out to be a pile of junk.

Of course abstract and general terms are perfectly legitimate and often necessary, for one can scarcely present all ideas concretely. Nevertheless, try to be as concrete and specific as your subject will allow.

54b   Weak Generalizations

gen   The most common weakness of student writing is an overdependence on generalizations. Consider: "Women today are no longer content with their traditional roles in life." A reader who accepted such a general assertion would scarcely be a reader worth having, for the statement cries out for illustration, evidence, qualification; it evokes all kinds of questions: All women? In all countries? What "roles" in particular?

What is the force of "traditional" here? Is such discontent really something new? Merely stating a generalization or assumption is not enough; to be clear and effective it must be illustrated and supported by specifics. The amount of support needed will vary, but two props are more than twice as effective as one, and three props—often an optimum number to aim for—are probably twice as effective as two.

Here are two in-class essays on the same topic. Read the first one through:

> Travel can be a very broadening experience for people who go with the intention of having their eyes opened, which may often occur by unpleasant means. Culture shock can be a very unpleasant and hurtful experience to people who keep their eyes and minds closed to different attitudes or opinions. This problem of culture shock is an example of why people should prepare for the unexpected and try to learn from difficult experiences, rather than keeping a closed mind which will cause them to come away with a grudge or hurt feelings.
>
> Besides causing negative attitudes, travel can also confirm the prejudices of people with narrow minds. For example, I once met an Englishman who had travelled around the world visiting the last vestiges of the British empire. He had even travelled to South Africa, and still come away with his colonialist attitudes.
>
> Even if one goes to a country with an open mind, one may still come away with a superficial perception of that country. It takes time to get to know a country and understand its people. The time one spends in a country will thus greatly affect one's perception of that country.
>
> Time is also needed before travelling begins, for people to read and learn about the area they will be going to. This background will enable them to look for things they might otherwise never see, and they will appreciate more the things they do discover. For example, if one knows something about the architecture of a country before one visits it, one can plan one's trip to include visits to buildings of special interest.
>
> Thus an open, well-prepared mind will benefit from the experiences of travel, but otherwise travel is likely to have a very negative, narrowing effect on people's minds.

Now, without looking back at the essay, ask yourself what it said. You will probably have a vague sense of its thesis, and chances are you will remember something about a well-travelled but still narrow-minded Englishman, and perhaps something about the advisability of knowing something in advance about foreign architecture—for those are the only concrete items in the essay. (Think how much more vivid and therefore meaningful and memorable the point about architecture would have been had it included a reference to a specific landmark, such as the Leaning Tower of Pisa or the Taj Mahal or the Parthenon or St. Paul's Cathedral.)

Now read the second essay, noting as you read how much clearer its points are than the relatively unsupported generalizations of the first essay:

Travel can be broadening. The knowledge gained in the areas of historical background, cultural diversity, and the range of personalities encountered in foreign lands gives us a more objective outlook on ourselves, on
Canada and Canadian issues, and on our position as a cog in the great
machine of civilization.

The impact of history upon visitors to foreign lands is immense indeed.
One cannot help but feel somewhat small when looking across valley upon
valley of white crosses in France, coming face to face with the magnitude of
death taking place in World Wars. Before long, one realizes that many of the
events that took place years ago have an effect upon the way in which we live
today. In some areas, scars of the recent past remain. The bits of rubble left
from the once formidable Berlin Wall, for example, remind visitors that the
way they live is not the same way others live, that, indeed, for decades mil-
lions lived grim and limited lives, never dreaming that in their lifetimes revolutionary changes would bring freedom, if not immediate comfort and
prosperity.

This is not to say that there are not pleasant aspects of history as well.
Sixteenth-century cobblestone lanes, usually less than ten feet wide, still
remain in many old English villages, surrounded by Tudor cottages, complete
with thatched roofs, oil lamps, and sculpted wrought-iron fences. Standing in
such an environment and thinking about the writings of masters like
Shakespeare brings out a much deeper and richer taste than merely reading
about them in a cold classroom at home. And places like this remind us of
how our ancestors lived, making it easier to understand the customs and
ideas of the past.

In going through different foreign lands, one cannot ignore the great cultural diversity. This is best illustrated by contrasting Fiestas in Spain and
Oktoberfest in Munich with our own celebrations. Many countries, besides
having different languages (and dialects of those languages), also have their
own dress, holidays, and religious beliefs. This variety is often startling to the
tourist, used to the general homogeneity of such things back here and often
taking it for granted that what is standard for him or her is also the norm
throughout much of the rest of the world.

There is also a wide range of social habits within a country. This is especially true of Britain, which still rigidly clings to its class system. A visitor
from Canada may find it hard to understand such a system, not realizing that
it is a centuries-old tradition; a son always does the same job as the father,
whether knight or knave, and lives in the same place, and often dies there.

Above all, the differences among people from other countries are what
leave a visitor with the most lasting impression. From the beggar in the
slums of Casablanca, to the well-dressed German walking briskly in the
streets of Hanover, to the British executive sipping beer in "the local" on
Hyde Street, there are myriad personalities as one travels through foreign
lands. When we look at the world from this perspective, realizing that we are
not all the same, we are better equipped to understand many of the problems
throughout the world.

Even the next-to-last paragraph, with its feeble topic sentence, is at least
partly saved by the examples that follow—although they aren't very specific. The first essay is not devoid of meaning, for generalizations do have

content, do say something; but the similar meaning in the second is clearer, more forceful; readers will better understand and remember what it said simply because their minds have something concrete and specific to hang on to. (You may wish to compare these two essays in other ways, as well; for example, is the way the second concludes superior to the way the first does?)

Exercise 54(1) Using specific diction

For each of the following words, supply several increasingly specific terms; take at least a few all the way to a single specific item.

1. furniture	6. drink (v.)	11. creature
2. art	7. drink (n.)	12. structure
3. answered	8. winged thing	13. see
4. said	9. seat	14. moved
5. food	10. entertainment	15. literature

Next, compose a paragraph in which you use one of the general terms in the first sentence and which you develop by using increasingly specific terms.

Exercise 54(2) Being concrete and specific

Rewrite this vague and abstract autobiographical paragraph. Try to make it sharp and vivid by supplying concrete and specific details wherever suitable. Or, if you prefer, compose an autobiographical paragraph about yourself.

> When I was still fairly young it became necessary for our large family to move from a small prairie town to a large city. At first we were all a little sad, but after a while we settled into our new environment. When I had finished primary and secondary school, I enrolled in an institution of higher learning, and after pursuing my chosen course of studies for the required number of years I received my degree. With it in my possession, I began the search for suitable employment; however, for some time I met with no success, and I had to accept the help of others in order to get along. But finally I found the sort of thing I was looking for, and the people here seem to feel that I am the right person for the position, and even hint at rapid advancement. Consequently I look forward to a pleasant and rewarding career.

55 Connotation and Denotation

You have to keep **connotation** in mind both to avoid conveying a meaning you don't intend and to enable yourself to convey particular shades of meaning you do intend. A word may **denote** (literally mean) what you want it to, yet **connote** (suggest) something you don't intend. For example, if you describe someone as "skinny" your reader will understand the denotative meaning of "thin" but will also understand you to feel at least somewhat negative; if you in fact approve of the condition (and the person), you'll use a word like "slim" or "slender," for their connotation is favourable rather than unfavourable.

Caution: Never use a thesaurus or a dictionary of synonyms without using a standard dictionary in conjunction with it. Words listed together in such books are not necessarily identical in meaning; they can be subtly different not only in denotation but, especially, in connotation as well. A thesaurus is a good vocabulary-building tool, but it should be used with extreme care, for it can all too easily trap the unwary into saying things they don't mean. As an example, consider the fact that many of the words in each group in the following exercise were listed in a thesaurus simply as synonyms.

Exercise 55 | Recognizing connotation

Label each of the following words as having a favourable (f), neutral (n), or unfavourable (u) connotation; perhaps try to place the words in each group on a spectrum running from *f* to *u*. If you think some could be labelled more than one way, depending on context, be prepared to explain. Use your dictionary if necessary.

1. bawdy blue broad coarse crass crude dirty earthy gross improper indelicate nasty obscene off-colour racy ribald risqué salacious scabrous spicy suggestive tasteless vulgar
2. artless crass dense dull dumb feeble-minded foolish green ignorant inept ingenuous innocent naive obtuse shallow simple slow stupid thick unsophisticated unthinking
3. bony gaunt lank lanky lean rawboned scrawny skinny slender slight slim spare spindly svelte thin trim twiggy underweight weedy
4. flaccid floppy limber limp lissome lithe loose pliant rubbery sapless supple willowy
5. angelic canting cherubic demure devout narrow goody-goody pietistic pious prim puritanical religious saintly sanctimonious strait-laced strict
6. artful clever crafty cunning devious diplomatic foxy greasy guileful insinuating oily scheming slimy slippery sly smooth suave tricky unctuous wily
7. addled baffled befuddled bewildered confounded confused flustered fuzzy irresolute mixed-up mystified perplexed puzzled scatter-brained uncertain undecided wavering
8. bare bold candid clear direct downright flagrant forthright frank gross naked plainspoken stark straightforward unambiguous undisguised
9. arrogance assurance audacity boldness brass brazenness cheek chutzpah effrontery gall highhandedness impertinence impudence insolence nerve pride presumption temerity
10. bookworm brain brainworker egghead genius highbrow intellectual mind pedant pundit sage savant scholar smarty thinker

56 *euph*

56 Euphemism

euph   **Euphemisms** are substitutes for words whose meanings are felt to be unpleasant and therefore in certain circumstances socially or psychologically undesirable. In social settings we tend to ask for the location not of the toilet, which is what we want, but of the restroom, the bathroom, the washroom, the powder room, or even, cutesily, the little boys' or little girls' room. Interestingly, the word *toilet* was itself once a euphemism; as time passes, words tend to go downhill, to acquire a pejorative quality. Hearty words describing various bodily functions, words which once were generally acceptable, have now been replaced with euphemisms—at least in many social settings.

But the process is often abused. Euphemisms are used to gloss over some supposed unpleasantness, or even to deceive. Someone who sweeps floors and cleans washrooms may be called a "sanitary engineer" instead of a "custodian" or "janitor," and garbage collectors are also often called "sanitation engineers." Those who used to be known as "salespeople" or "clerks" are now often called "sales representatives" or "sales associates," or even "sales engineers." Some bank tellers are now "customer service representatives." What was once faced squarely as a depression is now, in an attempt to mitigate its negative implications, termed at worst a "recession," or an "economic downturn," or even a mere "growth cycle slowdown." Government officials who have patently lied admit only that they "misspoke" themselves.

Such euphemisms commonly imply a degree of dignity and virtue not justified by the facts. Calling pornography "mature entertainment" seriously distorts the meanings of both "mature" and "entertainment." Some cloud or attempt to hide the facts in other ways. Workers are "laid off" or "declared redundant" or even "released" rather than "fired." A man who has died in hospital is said to have "failed to fulfill his wellness potential" or undergone a "negative patient-care outcome." A spy is directed to "terminate with extreme prejudice" rather than "assassinate" or "murder." George Orwell, as long ago as 1946 in his essay "Politics and the English Language," referred to such linguistic dishonesty, noting that when "People are imprisoned for years without trial," or executed, or exiled to labour camps, the process "is called *elimination of undesirable elements.*" "Defenseless villages," he remarks, "are bombarded from the air, the inhabitants driven out into the countryside, the cattle machine-gunned, the huts set on fire with incendiary bullets: this is called *pacification.*" Referring to the death of civilians during a war as "collateral damage" or "collateral casualties" doesn't make the victims any less dead. And, in a much less serious context, how many sponsors or television announcers are honest enough to refer to their ads as commercial *interruptions* instead of "breaks" (as if they were something to look forward to, like a coffee break)? And how often are they honestly called "commercials," rather than "messages"?

Other euphemisms help people avoid the unpleasant reality of death, which is often called "passing away" or "loss"; the lifeless body, the cadaver or corpse, is deemed less unpleasant as "remains." Such usages may be acceptable, even desirable, in certain circumstances, since they may enable one to avoid aggravating the pain and grief of the bereaved. But in other circumstances, direct, more precise diction is preferable.

Euphemisms that deceive are obviously undesirable. Others may be acceptable if circumstances seem to justify them; one must exercise taste and judgment. But generally speaking, call a spade a spade.

Exercise 56   Avoiding euphemisms

Supply more straightforward equivalents for the following terms.

1. job action, work stoppage
2. revenue enhancement
3. young offender
4. correctional facility
5. underprivileged, deprived, disadvantaged
6. developing countries
7. senior citizens
8. memorial chapel; memorial park
9. untruth
10. inner cities

57   Wrong Word

ww

Any error in diction is a "wrong word," but a particular kind of incorrect word choice is customarily marked **wrong word**. Don't use *infer* where the correct word is *imply*. Don't write *effect* when you mean *affect*. Don't write *ex-patriot* when you mean *expatriate*. (Such errors are also sometimes marked *spelling* or *usage*: see the lists of often-confused words, #51-l and #51m; and see the Usage Checklist, #60.) But other kinds of wrong word choices occur as well; a few examples from students' papers:

> *ww:* Late in the summer I met my best friend, *which* I hadn't seen since graduation.
> *ww:* Most men would have remembered spending several days in an open *ship* with little water and under the tropic sun as a terrible hardship, but Marlow recalls only that he felt he could "last forever, outlast the sea, the earth, and all men."
> *ww:* Many miles of beach on the west coast of Vancouver Island are *absent of* rocks.

Whom, not *which*, is the correct pronoun for a person (see #3d). The word *ship* won't do for a small vessel like a rowboat; *boat* is the appropriate word here (*boat* can be used for any size vessel, but *ship* is appropriate only for large ones). The wrong phrase came to the third writer's mind; *devoid of* was the one wanted (and see #58, on idiom). See also **nsw** (no such word) in Chapter XI.

Exercise 57 | **Avoiding wrong words**

Correct the wrong words in the following sentences.

1. The conference is intended to focus attention on the problems facing our effluent society.
2. The local orchestra, not renowned as a jazz supporter, was spirited and bombastic.
3. The company's representatives claimed to be authoritarians on the subject.
4. Politicians try to maintain an impressionable image in the eyes of the public.
5. We tried to convince her that her fear was entirely imaginative.
6. Some shoppers stopped buying coffee because they found the price so absorbent, if not gastronomical.
7. The premier of Alberta led his party to the best of his possibilities.
8. He was deciduously on the wrong track with that theory.
9. It was an incredulous display of manual dexterity.
10. The cat was very expansive, weighing over twenty pounds.

---

58 Idiom

id   A particular kind of wrong word choice has to do with **idiom**. An idiom is an expression peculiar to a given language, one that may not make logical or grammatical sense but that is nevertheless customary, "the way it is said." The English expression "to sow one's wild oats," for example, if translated into another language would not have its idiomatic meaning; but French has an equivalent expression, *jeter sa gourme*, which would make little sense if translated into English. Here are some other peculiarly English turns of phrase: to have a go at, to be down in the dumps, to be at loose ends, to feel one's oats. You will notice that these idioms have a colloquial flavour about them, or even sound like clichés; but other similar idioms are a part of our everyday language and occur in formal writing as well; for example: to "do oneself proud," to "take after" someone, to "get along with" someone.

But most errors in idiom result from using a wrong preposition in combination with certain other words. For example, we get *in* or *into* a car, but *on* or *onto* a bus; one is usually angry *with* a person, but *at* a thing; one is *fond of* something or someone, but one has *a fondness for* something or someone. Here, from students' papers, are some examples of errors in idiom:

France was at that time a close ally *to* Sweden. (should be *of*)
She took the liberty *to introduce* herself to the group. (*of introducing*)
He was screaming *of* how dangerous it was for me to walk so near the edge of
the cliff. (*about*)
It is pleasant to live in the dorms and be in close proximity *of* everything on
campus. (*to*)

One must also sometimes be careful about choosing between an infinitive and a prepositional gerund phrase. After some expressions either is acceptable; for example:

He is afraid *to lose.* He is afraid *of losing.*
They are hesitant *to attend.* They are hesitant *about attending.*
They plan *to appeal.* They plan *on appealing.* (informal)

But some terms demand one or the other:

They propose *to go.* They are prepared *to go.*
They insist *on going.* They are insistent *on going.*

Yet sometimes when a word changes to a different part of speech, the kind of phrase that follows must also change:

It was *advisable to forget* what they had seen. He reminded them of the
advisability of forgetting what they had seen.
They *desired to go.* They were *desirous of going.*
It is *important to remember.* She spoke of the *importance of remembering.*

But it isn't always even that simple:

He *intended to go.* He spoke of his *intention to go.* He had every *intention of
going.*

And sometimes a *that*-clause is the only idiomatic possibility:

I asked them *to attend.* I recommended *that they attend.*

See also **different from, different than; let, make; on; recommend**; and **very** in #60.

Idiom is a matter of usage and is not something which logic or grammar can much help with. But a good dictionary can often help. For example, if one looks up *adhere*, one finds that it is to be used with *to*, so one would know not to write "adhere on" or "adhere with." And the writer of the first example in the above list could probably have inferred from the dictionary that whereas one allies oneself, or is allied *to* or *with* another, one is simply an ally *of* the other. Or, should you be worried about using the word *oblivious*, your dictionary will probably inform you that it can be followed by either *of* or *to*. (And see **agree** and **differ** in the Usage Checklist, #60; see also **id** in Chapter XI for more examples.)

59 *w, jarg, etc.*

Other references that help with idiom (and with other matters) are H. W. Fowler's *A Dictionary of Modern English Usage* (revised by Sir Ernest Gowers), Theodore M. Bernstein's *The Careful Writer*, and of course *The Oxford English Dictionary*.

Students for whom English is an additional language will benefit from using specialized learners' dictionaries. *The Oxford Advanced Learner's Dictionary of Current English, The Collins Cobuild English Language Dictionary*, and *The Collins Cobuild Essential English Dictionary* offer a wealth of information about idiomatic uses of articles and prepositions. Detailed entries include examples of idioms used in complete sentences. *A Dictionary of American Idioms* (published by Barron's Educational Series) offers similar help, most of which is as useful to Canadians as to Americans.

And when you don't have any of these references at hand, of course you can always ask a friend whose ear you can trust.

Exercise 58   **Correcting idioms**

Correct the unidiomatic usages in the following sentences.

1. She has an unusual philosophy towards modern technology.
2. He suggested me to use this new product.
3. Last summer I was bestowed with a scrawny, mangy mutt.
4. Desdemona had unquestioning faith of Iago's character.
5. Tanya made us to laugh with stories of her adventures in the Yukon.
6. The analysis is weak because it lacks in specific details.
7. I am amazed with the report's suggestions.
8. Lovers and poets create dream worlds in which only they can inhabit.
9. Ironically, although Huck fails, Tom succeeds to free Jim.
10. The generation gap is evident by their uneasiness of each other's boredom.

---

59   Wordiness, Jargon, and Associated Plagues

w, jarg, etc.

Any diction that decreases precision, clarity, and effectiveness is worth trying to avoid. Using too many words or tired words or fuzzy words can only be harmful. We discuss and illustrate these weaknesses all in one section because they are related, sometimes even overlapping. For example, phrases like "on the order of" and "on the part of 302
" could be labelled *w, trite*, or *jarg*. Jargonauts are fond of wordy and pretentious phrases like "make a determination" (instead of simply *determine*), or "put in place" (for *do* or *done*), or "be of assistance to" (instead of *help*). Why settle for the verb *support* when they can say people "are supportive of" someone or something? "Characterize" is increasingly used instead of simply *call* or *name*. What used to be *comment* or perhaps *commentary* on a

sports program is now being referred to as "commentation." And can you imagine yourself using a word like "progressivity"?

Even without such overlapping, there is an inevitable family relationship among the several groupings—if only because one error or weakness frequently leads to, or is accompanied by, others. Considering them all together rather than separately should give you a better sense of the kinds of weakness they cause. No lists such as those that follow can be exhaustive, for new words and phrases are every day shoving their way into these categories. But try to understand the principles, to get a feeling in your bones for the *kinds* of violations of good writing such terms represent. (If the reason for a given term's inclusion is not immediately apparent to you, the illustrations in the exercises may help to clarify the matter.)

59a Wordiness

w

Generally, the fewer words you use to make a point, the better. Useless words—often called *deadwood*—clutter up a sentence; they dissipate its force, cloud its meaning, blunt its effectiveness. The student who wrote the following sentence, for example, used many words where few would have done a better job:

> *w:* What a person should try to do when communicating by writing is to make sure the meaning of what he is trying to say is clear.

Notice the gain in clarity and force when the sentence is revised:

> *revised:* A writer should strive to be clear.

Expletives

Expletive constructions are a common source of weakness and wordiness (see #1k and #18f). There is nothing inherently wrong with them (there are many in this book—two already in this sentence), and they are natural and invaluable in enabling us all to form certain kinds of sentences the way we want to. Nevertheless they are so easy to use that writers sometimes use them when a tighter and more direct form of expression would be preferable. If you can get rid of an expletive without creating awkwardness or losing desired emphasis, do it. Don't write

> *w:* There are several reasons why it is important to revise carefully.

when you can so easily get rid of the flab caused by the *there are* and *it is* structure:

> *revised:* Careful revision is important for several reasons.
> *revised:* For several reasons, careful revision is important.

> *w:* It is one of the rules in this dorm that you make your own bed.
> *revised:* One rule in this dorm requires you to make your own bed.
> *revised:* In this dorm you have to make your own bed.

> *w:* In this town there are over a hundred people on welfare.
> *revised:* Over a hundred people in this town are on welfare.

The saving in words may not always be great, but such changes can help strengthen your style.

See also Exercise 11a-c(2c), on getting rid of the clutter of an excess of prepositional phrases, and #6p and #18f, on the passive voice.

59b Repetition

rep Repetition can be useful for coherence and emphasis (see #65b, #68b, #18g, #66). But unnecessary repetition usually produces wordiness, and often awkwardness as well. Look at this sentence, by a student:

> *rep:* Looking at the general appearance of the buildings, you can see that special consideration was given to the choice of colours for these buildings.

The sentence is wordy in general, but one could begin pruning by cutting out the needless repetition of *buildings*. Another example:

> *rep:* She is able to make the decision to leave Manawaka and to abide by her decision.

It might be argued that the repetition of *decision* aids emphasis, but "make the decision" could be shortened to "decide," or the final "her decision" could be simply "it."

59c Redundancy

red Redundancy, another cause of wordiness, is repetition of an idea rather than a word. (The term "redundancy" can mean "excess" in general, but it is also used to designate the particular error known technically as "tautology.") Something is redundant if it has already been expressed earlier in a sentence. In the preceding sentence, for example, the word *earlier* is redundant, since the idea of *earlier* is present in the word *already*: repeating it is illogical and, of course, wordy. (Double negatives are a kind of redundancy, and plainly illogical: *can't never, don't hardly*.) To begin a sentence with "In my opinion, I think . . ." is already being redundant. If you say that "Tamiko is a personal friend of mine," you are being redundant, for a *friend* can scarcely be other than *personal*. To speak of a "new innovation" is to be redundant. The television writer describing a movie in which "John Wayne heads a stellar all-star cast" evidently didn't know what "stellar" means. And the person who wrote, in a letter to a prospective employer, that "an interview would be mutually helpful to both of us," probably did not get the job. Here are some other frequently encountered phrases that are redundant because the idea of one word is present in the other as well:

advance planning	general consensus
but nevertheless	low ebb
character trait	mental attitude
climb up	more preferable
close scrutiny	necessary prerequisite
completely eliminate	new record
consensus of opinion	past history
continue on	reduce down
enter into	refer back
erode away	revert back

One common kind of redundancy is called "doubling"—adding an unnecessary second word (usually an adjective) as if to make sure the meaning of the first is clear:

red: The report was brief and concise.

Either *brief* or *concise* alone would convey the meaning. Sometimes an insecure writer goes to even greater lengths:

red: The report was brief, concise, and to the point.

Exercise 59c   **Cutting redundancy**

Revise the following sentences to remove redundancy.

1. If enough food cannot be supplied for all the people in the world, humankind will have to deal with hunger, starvation, and widespread famine.
2. He is adventurous in that he likes a challenge and is willing to try new experiences, but he is not adventurous to the point of insanity, though.
3. Looking ahead into the future, the economist sees even worse conditions.
4. She approached the door with feelings of fear and dread.
5. Golding's *Lord of the Flies* concerns a group of young children, all boys, who revert back to savagery.
6. If one doesn't thoroughly examine every part of the subject fully, one is almost sure to miss something that could be important.
7. Most people would rather flee away from danger than face it squarely.
8. Carol soon realized that she had to make a careful outline first, before she could expect an essay to be well organized.
9. She told him in exact and precise terms just what she thought of him.
10. The hangman in the story does not fit the stereotyped image of an executioner.

Exercise 59abc(1) **Removing wordiness**

Revise the following sentences to eliminate wordiness.

1. Time is a very strong, powerful image in this poem.
2. The courses being offered today require much more research and thought rather than the age old memory work that used to plague the education system not too long a time ago.
3. These were the very things that caused him his misery and his grief.
4. Advances in developments of modern technology greatly contribute to making the equipment necessary for computerization of machinery more and more feasible for potential users.
5. Since he has both positive and negative qualities of human nature, Othello is far from perfect and has many faults.
6. Her refusal to express her feelings caused her to store her problems within herself, which added to her visible instability.
7. Pope and Dryden shared that idea in common.
8. Another device used by the poet was one of repetition.
9. There were two hundred people outside the theatre, pressing against the ropes.
10. In the past six months I have been subjected to moving from two locations to other surroundings.

Exercise 59abc(2) **Reducing wordiness by combining sentences**

Often one can save many words by combining two or more drafted sentences into one. Try doing that with each of the following groups, from students' drafts; cut all the wordiness you can while you're at it.

1. Also, parents who wish to see a game live, but do not want to be disturbed by their children, have no choice except to leave them attended at home. In this case, the parents would have to hire a babysitter. As a result, the parents end up paying the babysitter as well as for the game.
2. In P.E. class she would punish the students who had the least athletic ability. An example of this would be the relays in P.E. class. The team that came in last in the relays would be punished by having to run after class.
3. There are a surprising number of lawyers and stockbrokers playing the game. This may be because these people must thrive on strategic planning to be in those professions in the first place. [And see **gr** in Chapter XI.]

59d   Ready-made Phrases

"Prefabricated" or formulaic phrases that leap to our minds whole are almost always wordy. They are a kind of cliché (see #59e), and often also sound jargony (see #59h). You can often eliminate them altogether, or at least use shorter equivalents:

a person who, one of those who
as of the moment
at the present time, at this time, at this point in time (now), at that time,
    at that point in time (then)
at the same time (while)
by and large
by means of (by)
due to the fact that, because of the fact that, on account of the fact that, in view
    of the fact that, owing to the fact that (because); except for the fact
    that (except that)
during the course of, in the course of (during)
for the purpose of (for, to)
for the reason that, for the simple reason that (because)
in all likelihood, in all probability (probably)
in a very real sense
in character, of a . . . character
in colour
in fact, in point of fact
in height (high)
in length (long)
in nature
in number
in reality
in shape
in size
in spite of the fact that (although)
in the case of
in the event that (if)
in the form of
in the light of, in light of (considering)
in the midst of (amid)
in the near future, in the not too distant future (soon)
in the neighbourhood of, in the vicinity of (about, near)
in this day and age (now, today)
manner, in manner, in a . . . manner
period of time (period, time)
personal, personally
previous to, prior to (before)
the fact that
up until, up till (until, till)
use of, the use of, by the use of, through the use of
with the exception of (except for)
with the result that

And the solidity of such ready-made phrases as *point of view* caused a student unthinkingly to tack *of view* onto *point* in the following sentence: "My dentist made the point of view that candy is bad for our teeth." Two-part verbs (see #11d) sometimes trip up writers in the same way: *fill in* is correct for "*Fill in* this form," but not for "The pharmacist *filled in* the prescription." Don't let your guard down.

59e Triteness, Clichés

trite, Trite or hackneyed expressions, clichés, are another form of wordiness:
cliché they are tired, worn out, all too familiar, and therefore generally contribute little to a sentence. Since they are by definition prefabricated phrases, they are another kind of deadwood that should be pruned. Many trite phrases are metaphors, once clever and fresh, but now so old and weary that the metaphorical sense is weak at best (see #53c); for some people the metaphor is completely dead, which explains errors such as "tow the line" (for "toe the line") and "the dye is cast" (for "the die is cast"), "dead as a doorknob," and "tarnish everyone with the same brush." "To all intents and purposes" now sometimes comes out "to all intensive purposes"; "taken for granted" becomes "taken for granite"; "by a hair's breadth" turns up as "by a hare's breath"; and so on. A student aiming for "time immemorial" instead wrote "time in memoriam." Another referred to the joys of "flying off into the wide blue yonder." And another asserted that a particular poet's message was that "we should make hay while the tide's in." A reviewer of a novel imagined angry characters "tearing the author from limb to limb." Even the once-familiar proverb "The proof of the pudding is in the eating" is now often heard as the relatively meaningless "The proof is in the pudding."

Some clichés are redundant as well: *first and foremost, few and far between, over and above, each and every, one and only, to all intents and purposes, ways and means, various and sundry, all and sundry, part and parcel, in this day and age* (now, today), *in our world today* (now, today), *in our modern world today* (now, today), and so on.

Of course clichés can be useful, especially in speech; they can help one fill in pauses and gaps in thinking and get on to the next point. Even in writing they can sometimes—simply because they are so familiar—be an effective way of saying something. And they can be used for a humorous effect. But in writing, in all such instances, they should only be used consciously. It isn't so much that clichés are bad in themselves as that the thoughtless use of clichés is weak. Generally, then, avoid them. No list can be complete, but here are a few more examples to suggest the kinds of expressions to watch out for:

a bolt from the blue	all things being equal
a heart as big as all outdoors	as a last resort
a matter of course	as a matter of fact

as the crow flies
beat a hasty retreat
brown as a berry
busy as a bee
by leaps and bounds
by no manner of means
by no means
clear as crystal (or mud)
conspicuous by its absence
cool as a cucumber
corridors of power
doomed to disappointment
easier said than done
fast as greased lightning
from dawn till dusk
gentle as a lamb
good as gold
if and when
in a manner of speaking
in one ear and out the other
in the long run
it goes without saying
it stands to reason
lock, stock, and barrel

last but not least
love at first sight
many and diverse
moment of truth
needless to say
nipped in the bud
no way, shape, or form
off the beaten track
on the right track
one and the same
par for the course
pride and joy
raining cats and dogs
rears its ugly head
rude awakening
sadder but wiser
seeing is believing
sharp as a tack
slowly but surely
smart as a whip
strike while the iron is hot
strong as an ox
the wrong side of the tracks
when all is said and done

Watch out also for the almost automatic couplings that occur between some adjectives and nouns. One seldom hears of a circle that isn't a *vicious* circle, or a fog that isn't a *pea-soup* fog, or a tenement that isn't a *run-down* tenement. Mere insight is seldom enough: it must be labelled *penetrating* insight. A few more examples:

acid test
ardent admirers
budding genius
bulging biceps
blushing bride
consummate artistry

devastating effect
drastic action
festive occasion
hearty breakfast
heated opposition
knee-jerk reaction

natty dresser
proud possessor
sacred duty
severe stress
tangible proof
vital role

Several of this kind are redundant as well:

advance notice
advance warning
blazing inferno
cozy (little) nook
end result
final outcome
final result

foreseeable future
just deserts
perfectly clear
serious concern
serious crisis
terrible tragedy
total (complete) surprise

59f Overuse of Nouns

The "noun disease" is another source of deadwood; it is also a form of jargon. The focus of a sentence or clause is its main verb; the verb activates it, moves it, makes it go. Too many nouns piled on one verb can slow a sentence down, especially if the verb is only *be* or some other verb with little or no action in it. Consider the following:

> The opinion of the judge in this case is of great significance to the outcome of the investigation and its effects upon the behaviour of all the members of our society in the future.

The verb in this sentence must struggle to move the great load of nouns and prepositional phrases along to some kind of finish. One could easily improve the sentence by reducing the proportion of nouns to verbs and making the verbs more vigorous:

> The judge's decision will inevitably influence how people act.

A particularly virulent form of the noun disease appears in the piling up of *tion* nouns:

> The depredations of the conflagration resulted in the destruction of many habitations and also of the sanitation organization of the location; hence the necessity of the introduction of activation procedures in relation to the implementation of emergency preparations for the amelioration of the situation.

This example is not so exaggerated as you might think. In any event, here is a simpler version of it:

> Since the fire destroyed not only many houses but also the water-treatment plant for the town, emergency procedures had to be set up quickly.

The verbs now have only a third as much noun-baggage to carry as the original verb *resulted* had. There is nothing inherently wrong with nouns ending in *tion*; the damage is done when they come in clusters.

Note: Avoid other unpleasant patterns of sound and rhythm as well, such as excessive alliteration or too regular a metrical pattern:

> At the top of the tree sat a bird on a branch.

or jarring repetitions of sound:

> They put strict restrictions on lending, which constricted the flow of funds.

or accidental rhyme:

> At that time he was in his prime; the way he later let himself go was a crime.

59g Nouns Used as Adjectives

Another insidious form of the noun disease is the awkward and unnecessary use of nouns as if they were adjectives. Many nouns have long functioned adjectivally, some even becoming so idiomatic as to form parts of compounds:

school board	schoolbook	schoolteacher
bathing suit	bath towel	bathtub
lunch hour	lunch box	lunchroom
fire alarm	fire engine	firewood
space heater	space travel	spacesuit
business school	business card	businessperson

Such nouns-cum-adjectives are normal and acceptable; but the practice can be carried too far. "Lounge chair" is clearly preferable to "chair for lounging," but just as clearly "medicine training" does not conform to the usages of English as well as "medical training" or "training in medicine," nor "poetry skills" as well as "poetic skills" or "skill in poetry." In these last two examples, since there is a standard adjectival form available, the simple nouns need not and should not be so used.

But increasingly in recent years, speakers and writers—especially those in government and business and the social sciences and the like—have settled for or even actively chosen such noun-noun combinations that contribute heavily to the jargon cluttering the language, cumbersome phrases such as *learning situation, resource person, cash position, opinion sampling, communication skills, leadership role.* Newspapers report that "a hostage release is expected tomorrow"; "the release of a hostage" would be better. Even worse is the piling up of several nouns, as in such phrases as "the labour force participation rate," "the Resource Management Personnel Training and Development Program," and "a city park recreation facility area."

Resist this tendency. Do not write, as a student did in a discussion of extracurricular activities, of their taking place "either in a school situation or a community-type situation"; don't talk of "emergency situations" or "crisis situations," but of *emergencies* and *crises.* And, obviously, try to avoid the word *situation* altogether.

Exercise 59g Evaluating nouns used as adjectives

Evaluate the following phrases in which nouns are used as adjectives. Are some unacceptable? Are any acceptable? Would some be acceptable in specific contexts? Comment on them in other ways if you wish.

1. task fragmentation
2. worker injuries
3. product impact
4. computer system
5. efficiency problems
6. job description
7. resource planning
8. customer satisfaction
9. customer billing
10. customer complaints

11. staff organization	16. cost factors
12. labour force	17. work schedule
13. staff training	18. profit outlook
14. safety aspects	19. overkill situation
15. department manager	20. clean-up crew

Note: Many nouns also quite normally function as verbs. But some recent usages have provoked criticism. For example, though some people still object to it, *chair*, as in "chair a meeting," seems now to be commonly accepted, especially in informal writing (see **man** in #60); and *contact*, meaning "get in touch with," is also fairly widely accepted, though some would exclude it from formal writing. Some writers accept *critique* as a verb, but many do not; many also continue to object to *parent* as a verb, and to its gerund *parenting*. Many wince when they hear *dialogue* used as a verb, or of something *transitioning*. And most people who care about the language still deplore referring to someone as having *gifted* another with a present, or *suicided*, or *scapegoated* someone, or *curated* an exhibition, or *debuted* (whether transitively or intransitively), or *authored* a piece of writing. (And note how bad can quickly lead to worse: a recent publisher's brochure for an anthology listed among its attractions the fact that "Two-thirds of the articles are authorized by Canadians.") And unless you're writing specifically about using computers, it's probably wise not to refer to *accessing* and *networking*. And see **-ize** in the Usage Checklist, #60.

59h   Jargon

jarg   The word **jargon** in a narrow sense refers to terms peculiar to a specific discipline, such as psychology or chemistry or literary criticism or computer science, terms unlikely to be fully understood by an outsider. Here we use it in a broader sense, to refer to all the gibberish, the incoherent, unintelligible phraseology that clutters contemporary expression. The private languages of particular disciplines or special groups are less dangerous to the general writer (and reader) than is the gobbledygook and bafflegab that so easily finds its way into the ears and minds and mouths and pens of most of us. As potential jargonauts, we must all be on guard against creeping sociologese and bureaucratese and the like, terms from other disciplines and from business and government that infiltrate everyday language. The unsophisticated, bombarded by such locutions, uncritically and even automatically use them in their own speech and writing, often even assuming that a certain prestige attaches to such language; and so the disease spreads. If you write to communicate rather than merely to impress or obfuscate, you will avoid the pitfalls discussed and illustrated here and in the rest of section #59; you will then impress your readers in the best way.

The following list is a sampling of words and phrases that are virtually guaranteed to decrease the quality of your expression, whether spoken or written. Some of the terms sound pretentious and technical, imported from specialized fields (economics, computers); others are fuzzy, imprecise, unnecessarily abstract; and still others are objectionable mainly because they are overused, whether as true clichés or merely popular jargon, or "buzz words" (which is itself a buzz word). Several of the terms are discussed further in #60, the Usage Checklist that follows; and you will find more examples in the review exercises at the end of the chapter.

access (as a verb)
affirmative, negative
along the lines of, along that line, in the line of
angle
area (see Checklist)
aspect
at that point in time (then)
at this point in time (now)
background (as a verb)
basis, on the basis of, on a . . . basis (see Checklist)
bottom line
case
concept, conception
concerning, concerned
connection, in connection with, in this (that) connection
considering, consideration, in consideration of
contact (especially as verb)
cope
definitely
dialogue (especially as a verb)
escalate
eventuate
evidenced by
expertise
facet
factor
feedback
field (as in "the field of medicine," etc.)
formulate
function
guidelines
hopefully (see Checklist)
identify with
image
impact (especially as verb)
implemented, implementation
importantly
indicated to (for "told")
infrastructure
input, output
in regard to, with regard to, regarding, as regards
in relation to

in respect to, with respect to, respecting
interface
in terms of (see Checklist)
in the final analysis
involved
-ize (-ise) verbs (see Checklist)
level
lifestyle
marginal
meaningful, meaningful dialogue
mega-
motivation
ongoing
on stream
parameters
personage
phase
picture, in the picture
position
posture
profile, low profile
realm
relate to
relevant
replicate
scenario, worst-case scenario
sector
self-image
situated
situation
standpoint, vantage point, viewpoint
structure
time frame
type, -type (see Checklist)
viable
-wise (see Checklist)
worthwhile (see Checklist)

Of course, many of these words are perfectly legitimate and can be used in quite normal and acceptable ways. But even such acceptable words can be used as jargon, and those in this list are among the most likely offenders. For example, why say "He replied in the affirmative" when "He said yes" would do? *Angle* is a good and useful word, but in such expressions as "looking at the problem from a different angle" it begins to become jargon. *Aspect* has precise meanings, but they are seldom honoured; the writer of the following sentence didn't know them, but just grabbed at an all too familiar word: "Due to money aspects, many high-school graduates would rather work than enter university." Here *aspects* has no real meaning at all (and see **due to** in the Checklist, #60).

A phrase like "For financial reasons" or "Because of a need for money" would be far better. A student analyzing a poem fell into the jargon trap: "The third quatrain develops the aspect of time." In trying to revise, the writer fell right back into the trap: "The third quatrain brings in the factor of time"—*factor* being nearly as bad here as *aspect*. Unless you use *case* to mean a box or container, a medical case, a legal case, or a grammatical case, or in phrases like "in case of fire," you are likely to create wordy jargon with it: "In most cases, students who worked hard got good grades." Why not "Most students who worked hard got good grades"? *Interface*, as a noun, has a precise technical meaning; but after social scientists adopted it for their purposes, it began surfacing as jargon, used—even as a verb—by many who are evidently unaware of its meaning. *Realm* means a kingdom, and it can—or once could—be useful metaphorically in phrases like "the realm of poetry" or "the realm of ideas"; but it has long been so loosely and widely applied that most careful writers will avoid it except in its meaning of kingdom. Only as jargon does the verb *relate to* mean "understand" or "empathize" or "interact meaningfully with." And so on. If you read and listen carefully you will often find the listed terms, and others like them, being used in ways that are offenses against clear and concise and precise expression.

> **Caution:** People addicted to wordiness and jargon will prefer long words to short ones, and pretentious-sounding words to relatively simple ones. Generally, choose the shorter and simpler. For example, the shorter of each of the following pairs is preferable:
>
> | | |
> |---|---|
> | analysis, analyzation | existential, existentialistic |
> | connote, connotate | (re)orient, (re)orientate |
> | consultative, consultitative | preventive, preventative |
> | courage, courageousness | remedy (v), remediate |
> | disoriented, disorientated | symbolic, symbolical |

60   Usage: A Checklist of Troublesome Words and Phrases

us   This section features words and phrases that have a history of being especially confusing or otherwise troublesome. Study the whole list carefully, perhaps marking for frequent review any entries you recognize as personal problem spots. Like any such list, this one is selective rather than exhaustive; we have tried to keep it short enough to be reasonably manageable. (Even whole books on usage invariably leave out matters someone else would think important.) As with the list of frequently misspelled words, then, you should keep a list of your own errors of this kind for special study. You can often supplement the information and advice provided here by consulting a good dictionary—especially one that includes notes on usage. See also the index and the following lists and discussions: *Words Sometimes Confused* (#51-l-m), *Slang* (#52a), *Informal, Colloquial* (#52b), *Wordiness* (#59a), *Triteness, Clichés* (#59e), *Overuse of Nouns* (#59f), *Nouns Used as Adjectives* (#59g), and *Jargon* (#59h).

about   (See **on.**)

above, below
Avoid stiff references to something preceding or following in an essay. Rather than "for the *above* reasons," write "for *these* (or *those*, or *the foregoing*, or *the preceding*) reasons"; instead of "for the reasons given *below*," write "for the *following* reasons." If you find yourself writing "as I said above" or "as I will explain below" and the like, organization may be poor; try revising your outline.

absolute   (See **unique**, etc.)

actually   (See **very.**)

affect, effect
Avoid the common confusion of these two words. *Affect* is a transitive verb meaning "to act upon" or "to influence"; *effect* is a noun meaning "result, consequence":

> He tried to *affect* the outcome, but all his efforts had no *effect*.

Proofread carefully, since the error as often as not results from carelessness. (Note: *Effect* can also be a verb, meaning "to bring about, to cause"; see your dictionary for two other meanings of *affect*, one a verb and one a noun.)

afterward, afterwards   (See **toward, towards.**)

aggravate
Often colloquially or informally used to mean "annoy, irritate, anger, vex." But properly speaking, only a condition, not a person, can be *aggravated*, and only if it is already bad; *aggravate* means "make worse":

> Standing in the hot sun will *aggravate* your headache.
> The unexpectedly high tax bill *aggravated* the company's already serious financial condition.

agree to, agree with, agree on
Use the correct preposition with *agree*. One agrees *to* a proposal or request, or agrees *to* do something; one agrees *with* someone about a question or opinion, and certain climates or foods agree *with* a person; one agrees *on* (or *about*) the terms or details of something settled after negotiation, or agrees *on* a course of action.

ain't
A nonstandard contraction, primarily equivalent to *aren't* and *isn't*. Avoid it in all writing unless for deliberate colloquial or humorous effect, as in "If it ain't broke, don't fix it."

all, all of   (See **of.**)

along the lines of   (See **in terms of.**)

alternate, alternative; alternately, alternatively
Alternate (adjective) means by turns, one following another, or every other one. *Alternative* (adjective or noun) refers to one of a number of possible choices (usually two). Don't use *alternate* or *alternately* when the sense has something to do with choice:

> In summer they could water their lawns only on *alternate* days.
> The squares on the board are *alternately* red and black.
> The judge had no *alternative*: he had to dismiss the charges.
> There is an *alternative* method, much simpler than the one you are using.
> She could meekly resign or, *alternatively*, she could take her case to the grievance committee.

Alternate is used legitimately to refer to a substitute or standby: "Each delegate to the convention had a designated *alternate*. She served as an *alternate* delegate."

although, though
These conjunctions introduce adverbial phrases or clauses of concession. They mean the same, but *although* with its two syllables usually sounds smoother, less abrupt, at the beginning of a sentence; *though* is more commonly used to begin a subordinate clause following an independent clause, though it can be slightly emphatic at the start of a sentence. But the two words are not always interchangeable: in *even though* and *as though* one cannot substitute *although*, and *although* cannot serve as an adverb at the end of a sentence or clause.
See also **despite that** and **while.**

among   (See **between, among.**)

amount, number
Use *number* only with countable things (i.e., with plural nouns), *amount* only for something considered as a total or mass (i.e., with singular nouns): a *number* of dollars, an *amount* of money; a large *number* of cars, a large *amount* of traffic. *Number* is usually singular after the definite article, plural after the indefinite article (see #7f).
See also **less, fewer.**

and   (See **while.**)

and / or

Worth avoiding, unless you're writing legal phraseology. Write "We'll get there on foot or horseback, or both," rather than "We'll get there on foot and/or horseback." And with more than two items, *and/or* muddies meaning: "This bread can be made with wheat, barley, *and/or* rye."

angry   (See **mad.**)

anxious

Does not mean simply "eager"; use it only when there is at least some degree of real anxiety, angst.

any more, anymore

For the adverb meaning "now" or "nowadays," both spellings are common (though some dictionaries still don't recognize one or the other). But use it only in negative statements (or positive statements with a negative implication) and in questions ("I don't get around much any more"; "I seldom attend sports events any more"; "Do you lie in the sun anymore?"); in other positive contexts the usage is considered dialectal ("The climate seems to be heating up anymore!").

anyplace, someplace

Colloquial for *anywhere, somewhere.*

anyways, anywheres, everywheres, nowheres, somewheres

Dialectal errors for *anyway, anywhere*, etc.

approach   (See **in terms of.**)

apt   (See **likely, liable, apt.**)

area

The word *area* strictly refers to a physical division of space on a surface. Avoid using it as an unnecessesarily vague term to refer to some abstract division, such as a field of study, a problem, or an activity (the *area* of the social sciences, the *area* of finance, the *area* of biblical interpretation). Weather forecasters and others are also fond of *area* as a substitute for *region, district, neighbourhood* (the eastern Alberta *area*, the Ottawa *area*, the South Bronx *area*). And journalists use it awkwardly as an adjective, e.g. in headlines ("Area man bit by rabid dog"; "Area teenagers march in protest"). These usages too are worth avoiding.

as

To avoid ambiguity, don't use *as* in such a way that it can mean either "while" or "because":

> *ambig:* As I was walking after dark I tripped over a sleeping dog.
> *ambig:* As I turned the flame up too high the grease caught fire.
> *ambig:* The car gathered speed quickly *as* I pressed harder on the accelerator.

Because of such potential ambiguity, some writers have banished *as* in the sense of *because* from their vocabularies. Another awkward use of *as*: In a sentence like

> The book was considered *as* a threat to the church.

as is unnecessary—or else needs something like "as a possible threat" to be fully clear.

See also **like, as, as if, as though,** and **so . . . as.**

as . . . as   (See **equally as** and **so . . . as.**)

as being

Don't follow with *being* when *as* alone is enough:

> He always thinks of himself *as* (not *as being*) the life of the party.
> She sees the deputy minister *as* (not *as being*) an incompetent fool.

as far as . . . is (are) concerned, as far as . . . goes

This construction has a wordy, jargon-like air about it, but if you feel that you need to use it anyway, don't leave it unfinished, as in this example:

> *As far as* financing my education, I'm going to have to get a summer job.

The error may stem from a confusion of *as far as* with *as for.*

as regards   (See **in terms of.**)

as such

Don't use this phrase as if it were equivalent to *thus* or *therefore*:

> *us:* My uncle wants to be well-liked. *As such*, he always gives expensive gifts.

In this phrase *as* is a preposition and *such* is a pronoun that requires a clear antecedent:

> My uncle is a generous *man. As such*, he always give me expensive gifts.

as though   (See **like, as, as if, as though.**)

as to

A stiff, jargony phrase worth avoiding; substitution or rephrasing will almost always improve matters:

> *poor:* He made several recommendations *as to* the best method of
> proceeding.
> *better:* He made several recommendations with respect to the best
> method of proceeding.
> *still better:* He recommended several methods of proceeding.
> *poor:* I was in doubt *as to* which road to take.

better: I was in doubt about which road to take.
still better: I was not sure which road to take.
I did not know which road to take.

As to at the beginning of a sentence may seem more tolerable, but even there it usually sounds awkward; try changing it to *As for.*
See also **in terms of.**

awaiting for

Awaiting is not followed by the preposition *for; waiting* is:

I was *awaiting* the train's arrival.
I was *waiting for* the light to change.

awful, awfully

Colloquialisms when used as intensifiers ("They were *awfully* nice to us"). See **very** and #52b.

a while, awhile

Most authorities object to the adverb *awhile* instead of the noun phrase *a while* in some positions, for example after a preposition such as *for:* sleep *awhile;* sleep for *a while.* Others contend that either form is acceptable.

backward, backwards   (See **toward, towards.**)

bad, badly   (See **good, bad, badly, well.**)

barely   (See **can't hardly, etc.**)

basis, on the basis of, on a . . . basis

Basis is a perfectly good word, but these prepositional phrases using it are worth avoiding when possible, for outside of technical contexts they usually amount to wordy jargon.

She made her decision *on the basis of* the committee's report.

This can easily be improved:

She based her decision on the committee's report.

Again:

He selected the furniture *on the basis of* its shape and colour. (by? for? according to? because of?)

The other phrase is even worse; although it is sometimes useful, more often than not it can profitably be revised out: *on a daily basis* is usually jargon for *daily; on a yearly basis* or *on an annualized basis,* for *annually; on a temporary basis,* for *temporarily; on a regular basis,* for *regularly; on a voluntary basis,* for *voluntarily; on a political basis,* for *politically* or *for political reasons; We'll do this for a week on a trial basis* is jargon for *We'll try this for a week;* and so on *ad nauseam.*
See also **in terms of.**

because   (See **reason . . . is because**; see also #37c.)

because of   (See **due to.**)

being that, being as, being as how

Colloquial or dialectal substitutes for *because* or *since* to introduce a subordinate clause, as is *seeing as (how)*, though *seeing that* is acceptable.

belabour, labour

To *labour* something, as in *labour a point*, is to work too hard at it—to overelaborate or overexplain or overdevelop it—and thus spoil it, detract from its effectiveness. To *belabour* something or someone is to strike or beat, as with a whip or a club, or with strong or abusive language—although *belabour* is sometimes used in the other sense as well.

believe   (See **feel(s).**)

below   (See **above, below.**)

beside, besides

Beside, a preposition, means "next to, in comparison with"; *besides* as an adverb means "in addition, also, too, as well"; as a preposition, *besides* means "in addition to, except for, other than":

> She stood *beside* her car.
> His contributions were minuscule *beside* those of his brother.
> She knew she would have to pay the cost of repairs and the towing charges *besides*.
> *Besides* the cost of repairs, she knew she would have to pay towing charges.
> There was no one on the beach *besides* the three of us.
> *Besides* this, what am I expected to do?

between, among

Generally, use *between* when there are two persons or things, and *among* when there are more than two:

> There is ill feeling *between* the two protagonists.
> There were predictable differences *between* the Liberals and Conservatives during the debate.
> They divided the cost equally *among* the three of them.

On occasion *between* is appropriate for groups of three or more, for example if the emphasis is on the individual persons or groups as overlapping pairs, or on the relation of one particular person to each of several others:

> At the end there remained little bitterness *between* the four men.
> It seems impossible to keep the peace *between* the nations of the world.
> One expects there to be good relations *between* a president and the members of his cabinet.

Between is also commonly used informally or colloquially to refer to more than two, as in the idiom "between you and me and the lamppost."

bi-

Bimonthly and *biweekly*, for example, strictly mean "every two months" and "every two weeks." But since the prefix *bi-* is also coming to mean "twice," *bimonthly* and *biweekly* could mean the same as *semimonthly* and *semiweekly*, i.e. "twice a month" and "twice a week." In order to be clear, therefore, you may want to avoid *bi-* and spell out "every two months," "twice a month," etc. *Semiannually* clearly means "twice a year," and *biannual* ("twice a year") is distinguished from *biennial* ("every two years," "lasting two years")—but again you may want to use *semiannually* or the equivalent phrases, just to be sure.

but   (See **can't hardly, etc.**, and **while.**)

can, may (could, might)

Opinion and usage are divided, but in formal contexts it is still advisable to use *can* to denote ability, *may* to denote permission:

> *May* I have your attention, please?
> He *can* walk and chew gum at the same time.
> He knew that he *might* leave if he wished, but he *could* not make himself rise from his chair.

But both *may* and *can* are commonly used to denote possibility: "Things *may* (*can*) turn out worse than you expect. Anything *can* (*may*) happen." And *can* is often used in the sense of permission, especially in informal contexts and with questions and negatives ("*Can* I go?" "No, you *cannot!*") or where the distinction between ability (or possibility) and permission is blurred ("Anyone with an invitation *can* get in")—a blurring which, inherent in the concepts, is making the two increasingly interchangeable.

See also **may, might.**

can't hardly, etc.

Barely, hardly, never, only, and *scarcely* are regarded as negatives or as having a negative force. Therefore don't use words like *can't, don't, couldn't,* and *without* with them, for the result is an ungrammatical **double negative.** Use instead the positive forms: "I *can* hardly believe it. He *could* scarcely finish on time. He emerged from the ordeal *with* hardly a scratch." (Some writers also consider *but* a word not to be preceded by negatives, especially *can't* or *cannot*; others object only to *cannot but* or *can't help but* as redundant; but many consider both usages acceptable.)

centre around or **about**

An illogical phrase. The meaning of the word *centre* (or *focus*) demands a different preposition:

The discussion centred on the proposed amendment.

Or something can centre *upon, in,* or *at.* One can of course say *revolved around, circled around,* and be quite logical.

compare to, compare with

In formal contexts, use *compare to* to liken one thing to another, to express similarity:

> Shall I compare thee *to* a summer's day?
> He compared his work *to* walking a tightrope.

and *compare with* when you mean "to examine for differences or similarities, or both":

> She compared the sports car *with* the compact to see which would be best for her.
> He compared favourably *with* the assistant she had had the previous year.
> Compared *with* a desk job, farm work is more healthful by far.

complete   (See **unique**, etc.)

comprise, compose

Distinguish carefully between these words. Strictly, *comprise* means "consist of, contain, take in, include":

> The city *comprises* several separate communities.
> His duties *comprise* opening and shutting the shop, keeping the shelves stocked at all times, and running errands.

Compose means "constitute, form, make up":

> The seven small communities *compose* the city.

And never use *comprise* in the passive voice—saying for example that some whole "is *comprised* of" several parts; use *composed.*

continual, continuous

These words are sometimes considered interchangeable, but *continual* more often refers to something that happens frequently or even regularly but with interruptions, and *continuous* to something that occurs constantly, without interruptions:

> The speaker's voice went on in a *continuous* drone, in spite of the heckler's *continual* attempts to interrupt.

For something that continues in space rather than time, *continuous* is the correct adjective: "The bookshelf was *continuous* for the entire length of the hallway."

convince, persuade

These words are often used interchangeably; both mean to cause someone to believe or do something. But for many writers there is still a useful distinction between them: with *convince* the emphasis is more likely to be on the belief, with *persuade* on the action. You either *convince* or *persuade* someone *of* something or *that* something is so, but you *persuade* someone *to do* something. Further, *convince* implies appeal to reason, logic, hard facts; *persuade* implies appeal both to reason and to emotion, feelings. *Convince* also connotes an overcoming of objections, a change of mind. (The distinction is perhaps blurred by the fact that changing one's mind is itself a sort of action.)

could   (See **can, may.**)

culminate

Many writers find this verb awkward when used with a direct object or in the passive voice:

> *us:* He *culminated* his remarks with a strong blast at the opposition.
> *us:* The building was *culminated* by a revolving restaurant and a television tower.

It is safer to use it only intransitively, usually with the preposition *in*:

> Our search *culminates* here.
> His speech *culminated* in a strong blast at the opposition.
> The building *culminated* in a revolving restaurant and a television tower.

despite that

Similar in meaning to *but, nevertheless, however*:

> The weather was poor. *Despite that*, we enjoyed our outing.

Don't use the phrase as if it were equivalent to *though* or *although*:

> *us: Despite that* the weather was poor, we enjoyed our outing.

Despite alone works well: *Despite the poor weather* or *Despite the weather's being poor.* Otherwise, to be used this way it would have to be expanded to the wordy *Despite the fact that* (or *In spite of the fact that*); use *Although* or *Though* or *Even though*.

different from, different than

From is the idiomatic preposition after *different*:

> Your car is noticeably *different from* mine.

Than, however, is becoming increasingly common, especially when followed by a clause and when it results in fewer words:

> The finished picture looks far *different than* I intended it to.

But to avoid the label "colloquial," use the construction with *from*:

> The finished picture looks far *different from* what I intended.

differ from, differ with

To *differ from* something or someone is to be unlike in some way; to *differ with* someone is to disagree, to quarrel:

> She *differed from* her colleague in that she was less prone than he to *differ with* everyone on every issue.

disinterested

A much abused word, the adjective *disinterested* means "impartial, objective, free from personal bias." Although it is often used as a synonym for *uninterested, not interested* (no doubt partly because of increasing use of the noun *disinterest* to mean "lack of interest" as well as "impartiality"), in formal contexts retain the distinction between the two:

> It is necessary to find a judge who is *disinterested* in the case, for he will then try it fairly; we assume that he will not also be *uninterested* in it, for then he would be bored by it, and not pay careful attention.

due to

Rather than risk censure, use *due to* only as a predicate adjective + preposition after a form of the verb *be*:

> The accident was *due to* bad weather.

Many writers object to it as a preposition to introduce an adverbial phrase, especially at the beginning of a sentence; use *Because of* or *On account of* instead:

> *Because of* the bad weather, we had an accident.

As a substitute, *Owing to* is little if any better.

each other, one another

These are interchangeable, though *each other* more often refers to two, *one another* to more than two (see also **between, among**):

> The bride and groom kissed *each other*.
> The five boys traded hockey cards with *one another*.

effect, affect   (See **affect, effect.**)

either, neither

As indefinite pronouns or adjectives, these usually refer to one or the other of two things, not more than two; for three or more, use *any* or *any one*:

> *Either* of these two women can answer your questions.
> *Neither* of the two answers is correct.
> *Any* (*one*) of the four proposals is acceptable.

If *either* or *neither* is part of a correlative conjunction (see #12b), it can refer to more than two:

> Either Howard, Zhang, or Peter will act as referee.

empty   (See **unique,** etc.)

emulate
Does not mean simply "imitate," but rather "vie with, try to outdo."

enormity
Does not mean "immensity, great size, enormousness," but rather "outrageousness, heinousness, atrocity," or at least "immoderateness, immorality":

> In pronouncing sentence, the judge emphasized the *enormity* of the arsonist's crime.

enthuse, enthused
Enthuse and *enthused* are colloquial gush for "show (showed) enthusiasm" or "express (expressed) enthusiasm," as is *enthused* for the adjectival "showing enthusiasm, enthusiastic."

equal   (See **unique,** etc.)

equally as
Avoid this awkward redundancy by dropping one word or the other or by substituting *just as.* In expressions like the following, *as* is unnecessary:

> Her first novel was highly praised, and her second is *equally* good.
> He may be a good jumper, but she can jump *equally* high, if not higher.

In expressions like the following, *equally* is unnecessary:

> In a storm, one port is *as* good as another.
> His meat pies were *as* tasty as hers.

especially, specially
Especially means "particularly, unusually"; *specially* means "specifically, for a certain or special purpose":

> We *especially* want Juan to come; we planned the party *specially* for him.
> It's *especially* cold today; I'm going to wear my *specially* made jacket.

-ess   (See **man, woman, lady,** etc.)

essential   (See **unique,** etc.)

ever

Not needed after *seldom* and *rarely*. Instead of *rarely ever*, you may say *hardly ever*.

everywheres   (See **anyways,** etc.)

farther, further

Although the distinction between these is often overlooked, use *farther* and *farthest* to refer to actual physical distance, and *further* and *furthest* everywhere else, such as when referring to time and degree, and to mean something like "more" or "in addition":

> To go any *farther* down the road is the *furthest* thing from my mind.
> Rather than delay any *further*, he chose the card *farthest* from him.
> Without *further* delay, she opened the meeting.

Further, only *Further* can function as a sentence adverb, as in this sentence.

fatal   (See **unique,** etc.)

fatal, fatalistic   (See **simple, simplistic.**)

feel(s)

Don't loosely use the word *feel* when what you really mean is *think* or *believe. Feel* is more appropriate to emotional or physical attitudes and responses, *think* and *believe* to those dependent on reasoning:

> She *felt* cheated by the decision; she *believed* that she had not been given the benefit of the doubt.
> I *feel* the need of sustenance; I *think* I had better have something to eat.
> I *feel* uneasy about starting tonight; given the state of the weather, I *think* the road may be dangerous.

fewer   (See **less, fewer.**)

figuratively   (See **literally, virtually, figuratively.**)

firstly, secondly, etc.

Since some people find the *ly* ending old-fashioned and unnecessary in enumerations, just say *first, second, third*, etc. Many object only to the word *firstly*, so even if you decide to use *secondly, thirdly*, etc., begin with *first*, not *firstly*.

focus   (See **centre around.**)

following

If you avoid using *following* as a preposition meaning simply "after," you'll avoid both the criticism of those who object to it as pretentious and the possibility of its being momentarily misread as a participle or a gerund:

> *ambig: Following* the game, he kept his eye on the team's captain.

former, latter

Use these only when referring to the first or second of two things, not three or more (when *first* or *last* would be appropriate), and only when the reference is clear and unambiguous—i.e., when it is to something immediately preceding. But, like *above* and *below*, they are worth avoiding if possible.

forward, forwards   (See **toward, towards.**)

from the standpoint (viewpoint) of   (See **in terms of.**)

frontward, frontwards   (See **toward, towards.**)

full   (See **unique,** etc.)

fulsome

Although frequently used as if it meant "full, copious, abundant," especially in the phrase "fulsome praise," the word actually means "overfull, excessive," because insincere, and therefore "disgusting, offensive to good taste," even "nauseating."

further   (See **farther, further.**)

good, bad, badly, well

To avoid confusion and error with these words, simply remember that *good* and *bad* are adjectives, *badly* and *well* adverbs (except when *well* is an adjective meaning "healthy"). See also #9b.2.

> She looks *good*. (She is attractive.)
> That suit looks *bad* on you because it fits *badly*.
> Nathan acted *bad*. (He was naughty.)
> Nathan acted *badly*. (His performance as Hamlet was terrible.)
> I feel *good*. (I am happy, in good spirits.)
> I feel *bad*. (I have a splitting headache.)
> Herman feels *badly*. (He has a poor sense of touch?)
> Sophia looks *well*. (She looks healthy, not sick.)
> This wine travels *well*. (It wasn't harmed by the long train journey.)
> The infielders played especially *well* today; they are all *good* players.
> The steak smells *good*. (My mouth is watering.)
> Your dog doesn't smell *well*. (He's too old to hunt.)

half a(n), a half

Both are correct; use whichever sounds smoother or more logical. (Is *half a loaf* better than *a half loaf*? Is *a half hour* more formal than *half an hour*?) But don't use *a half a(n)*; one article is enough.

hanged, hung

In formal writing, use the past-tense form *hanged* only when referring to a death by hanging. For all other uses of the verb *hang*, the correct past form is *hung*.

happen, occur

These verbs sometimes pose a problem for students with English as an additional language. Both verbs are intransitive and cannot take the passive voice form in any tense.

> *wrong:* The revolution *was happened* in 1917.
> *right:* The revolution *happened* in 1917.

hardly   (See **can't hardly, etc.**)

have, of   (See **of.**)

healthy, healthful

Although *healthy* is common in both senses, in formal writing you will likely want to preserve the distinction, using *healthy* to mean "in good health" and *healthful* to mean "contributing to good health":

> To stay *healthy*, one should participate in a *healthful* sport like swimming.

he or she, his or her, he/she, s/he   (See #4d.)

herself, himself, myself, etc.   (See #3h.)

hopefully

In formal writing, use this adverb, meaning "full of hope," only to modify a verb or a verbal adjective:

> "Will you lend me ten dollars?" I asked *hopefully*.
> Smiling *hopefully*, she began to untie the package.

To avoid the censure of the many people who object to it, and to avoid its potential ambiguity, don't use it as a sentence adverb (in spite of its seeming similarity to such acceptable sentence adverbs as *Happily* and *Fortunately*):

> *us:* Hopefully, the sun will shine tomorrow.
> *ambig:* Hopefully, many people will come to the prize drawing.

Instead use *I hope* or *We hope* or *One hopes* or *It is hoped that* or *It is to be hoped that*.

hung   (See **hanged, hung.**)

imply   (See **infer, imply.**)

impossible   (See **unique,** etc.)

in connection with   (See **in terms of.**)

individual

Not simply a synonym for *person*. Reserve the word *individual* for times when the meaning "distinct from others" is present, or when certain people are being distinguished from a different kind of body or institution:

The *person* (not *individual*) you are referring to is my aunt.
Ramona is very much an *individual* in her behaviour. (I.e., she behaves like
no one else.)
The legal restrictions apply to the company itself, but not to the *individuals*
within it.

It is often safer to use *individual* as an adjective rather than as a noun. But
see also **person, persons, people.**

infer, imply

To avoid possible ambiguity and probable censure, use *imply* to mean
"suggest, hint at, indicate indirectly," and *infer* to mean "conclude by reasoning, deduce." A listener or reader can *infer* from a statement something that its speaker or writer *implies* in it:

Her speech strongly *implied* that we could trust her.
I *inferred* from her speech that she was trustworthy.

The word *inference*, then, means "something inferred, a conclusion"; it
does not mean *implication* or *innuendo*.

infinite   (See **unique,** etc.)

in, into

These are often interchangeable, but usually you will want to use *in* to
indicate location inside of, or a state or condition, and *into* to indicate
movement toward the inside of, or a change of state or condition; i.e.,
generally use *into* with verbs of motion and the like:

He went *into* the kitchen, but she was *in* the library.
We moved *into* our new home *in* the suburbs.
After getting *into* trouble, he was understandably *in* a bad temper.
I assured her I would look *into* the matter.

in regard to   (See **in terms of.**)

in relation to   (See **in terms of.**)

in respect to   (See **in terms of.**)

inside, inside of   (See **of.**)

in terms of

Another example of contemporary clutter. Note that it is similar, sometimes even equivalent, to those other offenders *on the basis of* (see **basis**)
and **-wise.** Although it is common in speech, and though occasionally it is
the precisely appropriate phrase, it is more often vague; worse, it is capable of leading to such inane utterances as this (by a governor of a
drought-stricken state): "We're very scarce in terms of water." If you can
avoid it, especially in writing, do so; don't write sentences like these:

He tried to justify the price increase *in terms of* [on the basis of] the
company's increased operating costs.

In terms of experience [Experience-wise], she was as qualified for the post as
   anyone else applying for it.
In terms of fuel economy, this car is better than any other in its class.
He first considered the problem *in terms of* the length of time it would take
   him to solve it.

when the ideas could so easily be better expressed:

He tried to justify the increase in price by citing the company's increased
   operating costs.
She was as experienced as anyone else applying for the post.
This car has the best fuel economy of any in its class.
First he thought about how long it would take him to solve the problem.

And note the further family resemblance of this phrase to others like
*along the lines of, in connection with, in relation to, in [with] regard to, as
regards, regarding, in [with] respect to,* and *from the standpoint [viewpoint]
of. Perspective* and *approach* are two more words often used in a similar
way. See also #59d and #59h.

in (with) regards to
Drop the *s: in (with) regard to.* *As regards* is acceptable. But see #59h and
in terms of.

into   (See **in, into.**)

irregardless
Nonstandard, as your dictionary should tell you. The prefix *ir* (not) is
redundant with *less*, forming a double negative (see **can't hardly**). The
correct word is *regardless.* (The error probably stems from confusion with
irrespective.)

is because   (See **reason . . . is because.**)

is when, is where
Although often standard ("Early morning *is when* the cocks crow,"
"Home *is where* the heart is"), avoid these phrases in statements of definition, where adverbial clauses following linking verbs are considered
ungrammatical:

   us: A double play *is when* two base runners are put out during one play.
   rev: In a double play, two base runners are put out during one play.
   rev: A double play occurs when two base runners are put out during one play.

Since *occurs* is not a linking verb, the adverbial clause beginning with
when is acceptable. Compare **reason . . . is because.**

its, it's
Don't join the multitudes who can't keep these simple words straight. *Its* is
the possessive form of *it; it's* is the contracted form of *it is,* or occasionally

of *it has* (as in "It's been a long day"). It's easy to slip when writing at speed, so proofread carefully.

-ize

The suffix *-ize* (or *-ise*) has long been used to turn nouns and adjectives into verbs (e.g. *democratize, galvanize, satirize, generalize, harmonize, idolize, modernize, theorize*). But like *-wise*, it is now faddishly overused, especially in business and other jargon (*finalize, concretize, prioritize*), leading even to such absurdities as this: "Let us not forget that the minister voluntarily resigned; had he not, he would surely have been *pressurized* to go." The *-ize* ending remains acceptable in established words, but avoid using it to make new ones. (See **-wise**, and see also the Note in #59g.)

kind of, sort of

Used adverbially, as in "*kind of* tired," "*sort of* strange," these terms are colloquial—as they are also when followed by an article: "I had a bad *kind of an* afternoon"; "She was a rather peculiar *sort of a* guide." More formally and less flabbily, say "I had a bad afternoon" and "She was a rather peculiar guide."

See also **type**, and #4f.

labour   (See **belabour, labour.**)

lack, lack of, lacking, lacking in

Lack in its various forms and parts of speech can sometimes pose problems for students with English as an additional language. Note the following usages:

> This paper *lacks* a clear thesis. (*lack* as a transitive verb)
> A major weakness of his argument was its *lack of* evidence. (*lack* as a noun followed by the preposition *of*)
> *Lacking* confidence, she gave up on her research. (*lacking* as a present participle followed by a direct object)
> *Lacking in* experience, they had difficulty in job interviews. (*lacking* as a present participle in combination with the preposition *in*)

lady   (See **man, woman, lady,** etc.)

latter   (See **former, latter.**)

lay   (See **lie, lay.**)

lend   (See **loan.**)

less, fewer

Fewer refers to things that are countable (i.e., with plural nouns); *less* is sometimes used the same way (e.g. on the signs at the express checkout lanes in supermarkets—"9 items or less"), but usually it is preferable to use it for things that are measured rather than counted or considered as units (i.e., with singular uncountable nouns):

> *fewer* dollars, *less* money
> *fewer* hours, *less* time
> *fewer* shouts, *less* noise
> *fewer* cars, *less* traffic
> *fewer* bottles of wine, *less* wine

See also **amount, number**.

less, least; more, most   (See #8b and #9c.)

let, make

The verbs *let* and *make* are parts of an idiom that causes problems, especially for those with English as an additional language. When *let* or *make* is followed by a direct object and an infinitive, the infinitive does not include the customary *to*:

> *id:* They let me *to borrow* their new car.
> *rev:* They let me *borrow* their new car.

See also the note in #10b.

liable   (See **likely, liable, apt.**)

lie, lay

Since *lay* is both the past tense of *lie* and the present tense of *lay*, some people habitually confuse these two verbs. If necessary memorize their principal parts: *lie, lay, lain; lay, laid, laid. Lie* means "recline" or "be situated"; *lay* means "put" or "place"; *lie* is intransitive; *lay* is transitive:

> I *lie* down now; I *lay* down yesterday; I *have lain* down several times today.
> I *lay* the book on the desk now; I *laid* the book on the desk yesterday; I *have laid* the book on the desk every morning for a week.
> The book *lies* on the desk now; the book *lay* on the desk yesterday; the book *has lain* on the desk for an hour.

However common it may be colloquially, don't use *lay* for *lie*, or *laying* for *lying*; if you do, many people will likely consider you illiterate.

> See also **set, sit**.

like, as, as if, as though

Like is a preposition:

> Roger is dressed exactly *like* Ray.

But if Ray is given a verb, then he becomes the subject of a clause, forcing *like* to serve incorrectly as a conjunction; use the conjunction *as* when a clause follows:

> *us:* Roger is dressed exactly *like* Ray is.
> *rev:* Roger is dressed exactly *as* Ray is.

In slightly different constructions, use *as if* or *as though* to introduce clauses:

> It looks *like* rain.
> It looks *as if* (or *as though*) it will rain.
> He stood there *like* a bronze Apollo.
> He stood there *as though* (or *as if*) he were a bronze Apollo.
> She spent money *as if* (or *as though*) there were no tomorrow.

But don't fall victim to hypercorrection; don't shun *like* for *as* when what follows it is not a clause:

> *us:* Rover stood stiffly alert, pointing, head and tail down, *as* any well-trained dog. (*like*)
> *us:* Nicklaus, just *as* last year's winner, sank a stunning birdie putt on the final hole. (*like*)

likely, liable, apt

Although often used interchangeably, especially in informal contexts, in formal writing use *likely* to mean "probable, probably, showing a tendency, suitable"; *liable* to mean "legally obligated, responsible, susceptible to (usually something undesirable)"; and *apt* to refer to probability based on habitual tendency or inclination:

> A storm seems *likely*. He is *likely* to succeed. This is a *likely* spot.
> She is *liable* for damages. Trevor is *liable* to headaches. He is *liable* to hurt himself.
> Dwight is *apt* to trip over his own feet.

Apt can also mean "exactly suitable" (It was an *apt* remark) and "quick to learn" (Kiki is an *apt* pupil).

literally, virtually, figuratively

Literally means "actually, really." *Virtually* means "in effect, practically." *Figuratively* means "metaphorically, not literally." All too often the first two are used to mean their opposites, or as weak intensifiers:

> *us:* She was *literally* swept off her feet. (i.e., *figuratively*)
> *us:* They were caught in a *virtual* downpour. (It *was* a downpour; drop *virtual*.)

loan, lend

Although some people restrict *loan* to being a noun, it is generally acceptable as a verb equivalent to *lend*—except in such figurative uses as "Metaphors *lend* colour to one's style" and "*lend* a hand."

mad

Common in informal contexts to mean "angry," but in formal contexts usually restricted to the meaning "insane, crazy."

make   (See **let, make.**)

man, woman, lady, -ess, Ms., etc.

Like the generic pronoun *he* (see #4d), the general or generic sense of the word *man* causes difficulties. In order to avoid sexist language, many writers now try to avoid the term *man* where it could include the meaning *woman* or *women*. If you're referring to a single individual, often simply substituting the word *person* will do, or in some contexts *human being*. If you're referring to the race, instead of *man* or *mankind*, use *human beings*, *humanity, people, humankind,* or *the human race*. Instead of *manmade*, use *synthetic* or *artificial* or *manufactured*. Similarly, in compounds designating various occupations and positions, try to avoid the suffix *-man* by using gender-neutral terms such as *firefighter, police officer, letter carrier, worker* or *labourer* (instead of *workman*), *supervisor* or *manager* (instead of *foreman*); and though some people object to it, the suffix *-person* is becoming more and more common: *spokesperson, chairperson* (or just *chair*), *anchorperson* (or just *anchor*), *businessperson, salesperson* (but see #56). See also **person, persons, people.**

Another concern is the suffix *-ess*. Usefully gender-specific (and power-designating) terms like *princess, empress, duchess,* and *goddess* are firmly established, but there is seldom if ever any need to refer to an *authoress* or *poetess* when simply *author* or *poet* will serve; some also object to *actress,* claiming *actor* as better for both sexes, though others argue that gender there is often relevant; *stewardess* has given way to *flight attendant* (perhaps partly as a euphemism); and *waitress* and *waiter* are increasingly being replaced by *server*. The suffix *-ette*, as in *usherette*, is similarly demeaning; use *usher*. And don't use *lady* as a substitute for *woman*.

Further, don't thoughtlessly gender-stereotype occupations and other activities that are increasingly engaged in by both men and women; think about doctors, lawyers, business executives, secretaries, nurses, construction workers, cabdrivers, truckdrivers, family cooks, food-shoppers, fishing enthusiasts, and so on. And don't refer, for example, to a "woman doctor" unless gender is somehow relevant to the context, in which case you'll probably also refer to another doctor as a man, or "male." And if you're writing about English novelists and refer to Charles Dickens, refer also to Jane Austen, not "Miss Austen"; if you subsequently refer to him as simply *Dickens*, refer to her as *Austen*.

Use the title *Ms.* for a woman unless you know that a specific woman prefers *Miss* or *Mrs.*

material, materialistic

Don't use *materialistic* when all you need is the adjective *material*. *Material* means "physical, composed of matter," or "concerned with physical rather than spiritual or intellectual things"; it is often the sufficient word:

Her life is founded almost entirely on *material* values.

Materialistic is the adjectival form of the noun *materialist*, which in turn denotes one who believes in *materialism*, a philosophical doctrine holding that everything can be explained in terms of matter and physical laws. A *materialist* can also be one who is notably or questionably concerned with material as opposed to spiritual or intellectual things and values:

> She is very *materialistic* in her outlook on life.

Unless you intend the philosophical overtones, use the simpler *material*. There is an analogous tendency to use *relativistic* rather than *relative* and *moralistic* rather than *moral*. Consult your dictionary. See also **simple, simplistic**, and **real, realism, realist, realistic**.

may (See **can, may**.)

may, might

Don't confuse your reader by using *may* where *might* is necessary for clarity:

(a) after another verb in the past tense:

> *us:* She thought she may get a raise. (Use *might*.)

In the present tense, either *may* or *might* would be possible:

> She thinks she may get a raise. (It's quite likely that she will.)
> She thinks she might get a raise. (It's less likely, but possible.)

(b) for something hypothetical rather than factual:

> *us:* This imaginative software program *may* have helped Beethoven, but it wouldn't have changed the way Mozart composed.

The word *may* makes it sound as if it is *possible* that the program *did* help Beethoven, which is of course absurd. Use *might*.
For other examples, see #6e.

media (See #7j and #51t.7.)

might (See **may, might** and **can, may**.)

momentarily

Though often used to mean "in a moment, soon" ("We'll be eating *momentarily*"), many prefer to restrict it to meaning "for a moment" ("Her attention wandered *momentarily*"). Since the word is therefore sometimes capable of being misunderstood, some writers avoid it altogether.
See also **presently**.

moral, moralistic (See **material, materialistic**.)

more, most; less, least   (See #8b and #9c.)

more important, more importantly
Although *more importantly* is widely used as a kind of sentence adverb, many writers object to it on grammatical grounds, preferring *more important* (as if it were a shorter version of "what is more important").

Ms.   (See **man, woman, lady,** etc., and #42a.)

muchly
An unnecessary non-word, acceptable only colloquially and facetiously, like *muchness*. See also **thusly**.

myself, herself, himself, etc.   (See #3h.)

necessary   (See **unique,** etc.)

neither   (See **either, neither.**)

never   (See **can't hardly, etc.**)

nowheres   (See **anyways,** etc.)

number   (See **amount, number.**)

occur   (See **happen, occur.**)

of
Usually unnecessary, though not considered incorrect, after the prepositions *off, inside, outside,* and often unnecessary after the pronoun *all,* especially when countable items are not involved:

> She fell *off* the fence.
> He awoke to find himself *inside* a large crate.
> As requested, she remained in the hall *outside* the room for five minutes.
> We had *all* the time in the world.
> *All* (or *All of*) the members were present.

Of is needed with *all* before some pronouns, and usually helps before proper nouns:

> Bring *all of* them. We travelled across *all of* Canada.

And because of the way we speak, such phrases as "would have," "could have," and "might have" often come out as contractions ("would've," "could've," "might've"); and because of the way they *hear* such words, some people mistakenly think the 've is *of* and proceed to write "would of," "could of," "might of," and so on. Unless you're writing dialogue spoken by an uneducated person, avoid this error.
See also **on.**

off, off of   (See **of.**)

on

This preposition is sometimes awkwardly unidiomatic when used as a substitute for *about* or *of*:

> *id:* She had no doubts *on* what to do next. (*about*)
> *id:* I am calling my essay "A Study *on* the Effects of Automation." (*of*)

on account of   (See **due to.**)

one another   (See **each other, one another.**)

only   (See **can't hardly, etc.**)

oral, verbal   (See **verbal, oral.**)

outside, outside of   (See **of.**)

owing to   (See **due to.**)

people   (See **person, persons, people.**)

per

Although useful and at home in technical and business writing, the Latin *per* is usually out of its element in other writing, except when part of a Latin phrase (*per capita, per cent*); especially do not use it to mean simply "by, by means of, through" (as in business contexts: "per bearer") or "according to" ("per your instructions").

perfect   (See **unique, etc.**)

person, persons, people

Partly to avoid sexist language (*man, woman,* the generic *he*), some people overuse the word *person* in what often sounds a limp, wordy, jargony, or even awkward way. Try to avoid it, or instead use *one,* or even *you* (see #4d). In the plural, use *persons* only when the number in question is small, say one or two or three ("Two persons refused to sign the petition") or when you want to emphasize the presence of *individuals* in a group ("Those persons wishing to attend the party should sign up now")—but even then the demonstrative pronoun *those* alone will often serve better ("Those wishing to attend . . ."). Otherwise, use *people,* which is normal even for referring to small numbers: "One or two people may object."

See also **man, woman, lady, etc.** and **individual.**

perspective   (See **in terms of.**)

persuade   (See **convince, persuade.**)

plus   (See **d** in Chapter XI.)

possible   (See **unique, etc.**)

presently

Since some people think that *presently* should mean only "in a short while, soon," and others think that it instead, or also, means "at present, currently, now," resulting in at least occasional ambiguity, many writers try to avoid the word altogether. Use the alternative terms and your meaning will be clear. Besides, *presently* now often sounds pretentious.

See also **momentarily**.

put forth   (See **set forth.**)

quote

In contexts that are at all formal, use this only as a verb; don't use it as a noun, equivalent to "quotation" or "quotation marks."

raise, rise

The verb *raise* is transitive, requiring an object: "I *raised* my hand; he *raises* wheat." *Rise* is intransitive: "The temperature *rose* sharply; I *rise* each morning at dawn." If necessary memorize their principal parts: *raise, raised, raised; rise, rose, risen.*

real, realism, realist, realistic

If necessary, use your dictionary to help you keep these words straight. The student who wrote that "Huxley's novel is not about realistic people" was at best being ambiguous: does *realistic* here mean "lifelike," or "facing facts"? The one who wrote "He based his conclusions not on theory but on realistic observation" probably meant "observation of reality."

See also **material, materialistic**.

real, really   (See **very** and #9b.4.)

reason . . . is because

Although this construction has long been common, especially in speech, many people object to it as (a) redundant, since *because* often means simply "for the reason that," and as (b) ungrammatical, since adverbial *because* should not introduce noun clauses after a linking verb (and for the same reason object to *it is because, this is because,* and the like). However common such phrases may be, we suggest that you avoid them, especially in formal writing, since they are bound to draw criticism— especially *the reason is because*; instead write "the reason is that."

reason why

The *why* is often redundant, as in "The reason why I'm taking Spanish is that I want to travel in Latin America." Always check to see if you need the *why*.

recommend

When this transitive verb appears in a clause with an indirect object, that object must be expressed as a prepositional phrase with *to* or *for*, and it must follow the direct object:

> *id:* She recommended *me* this restaurant.
> *id:* She recommended *to me* this restaurant.
> *rev:* She recommended this restaurant *to me*.

A number of other verbs fit the same idiomatic pattern as *recommend*. Among the most common are *admit, contribute, dedicate, demonstrate, describe, distribute, explain, introduce, mention, propose, reveal, speak, state,* and *suggest*. (Note: With several of these verbs, if the direct object is itself a noun clause, it usually follows the prepositional phrase:

> He admitted to me *that he had been lying.*
> She explained to me *what she intended to do.*)

regarding   (See **in terms of.**)

relative, relativistic   (See **material, materialistic.**)

rise, raise   (See **raise, rise.**)

round   (See **unique,** etc.)

scarcely   (See **can't hardly, etc.**)

seeing as (how), seeing that   (See **being that, being as how.**)

sensual, sensuous

Although the meanings of these words often overlap each other in a given context, *sensuous* usually means "pertaining to the senses, sensitive to beauty, etc." *Sensual*, on the other hand, usually means "pertaining to the body and to the gratification of physical appetites, especially sexual appetites; lewd, carnal":

> Many Canadian poets, responding to the beauty of their natural environment, write *sensuous* poetry.
> The minister emphasized the spiritual quality of "The Song of Solomon" rather than its *sensual* features.

set, sit

Set (principal parts *set, set, set*) means "put, place, cause to sit"; it is transitive, requiring an object: "He *set* the glass on the counter"—though it is standard to say that a hen *sets* (or *sits*) on her eggs. *Sit* (principal parts *sit, sat, sat*) means "rest, occupy a seat, assume a sitting position"; it is intransitive: "The glass *sits* on the counter. May I *sit* in the easy chair?"—though it can be used transitively in expressions like "I sat myself down to listen," "She sat him down at the desk." See also **lie, lay.**

set forth

As a stiff, unwieldy substitute for *express(ed)* or *present(ed)* or *state(d)*, this phrase is an attempt at sophistication that usually misfires. *Put forth* is similarly weak.

shall, will; should, would   (See #6e, #6h.3, and #6i.2.)

she or he, her or his, she/he, s/he   (See #4d.)

simple, simplistic

Don't use *simplistic* when all you want is *simple*. *Simplistic* means "over-simplified, unrealistically simple." Similarly, *fatalistic* does not mean the same as *fatal*. (See also **material, materialistic**.)

since

Since can refer both to time ("Since April we haven't had any rain") and to cause ("Since she wouldn't tell him, he had to figure it out for himself"). Therefore don't use *since* in a sentence where it could mean either:

> *ambig:* Since you went away, I've been sad and lonely.

sit, set   (See **set, sit**.)

so . . . as, as . . . as

In strictly formal contexts, use *so* or *so . . . as* with negative comparisons; use *as* or *as . . . as* only with positive comparisons:

> Barbara was almost *as* tall *as* he was, but she was not *so* heavy.
> He was not *so* light on his feet *as* he once was, but he was *as* strong *as* ever.

someplace   (See **anyplace, someplace**.)

somewheres   (See **anyways**, etc.)

sort of   (See **kind of, sort of**.)

so, so that, therefore

As a conjunction, *so* is informal but acceptable (see #12a.3); just don't overwork it. To introduce clauses of purpose and to avoid possible ambiguity, you will often want to use *so that* or *therefore* instead:

> He sharpened the saw *so that* it would cut the boards properly.
> She cleverly changed her story several times, *so that* we couldn't be sure what actually happened.
> She changed her story several times; therefore we couldn't be sure what actually happened.

specially   (See **especially, specially**.)

square   (See **unique**, etc.)

state

A stronger verb than *say*; reserve *state* for places where you want the heavier, more forceful meaning of "assert, declare, make a formal statement."

straight   (See **unique**, etc.)

substitute

Don't use *substitute* when you mean *replace*—i.e., don't follow it with *by* or *with*; use it only with *for*:

> *us:* The french fries were *substituted by* a tossed salad. (*replaced*)
> *us:* I *substituted* the term paper *with* three shorter essays. (*replaced*)
> *revised:* The waitress kindly *substituted* a tossed salad *for* the greasy french fries.
> *revised:* I was permitted to *substitute* three short essays *for* the term paper.

Substitute can also be used intransitively:

> Because he is off his game this year, Stanley has only *substituted*.
> Mere cleverness cannot *substitute* for common sense.

sure, surely

Don't use *sure* as an adverb. See #9b.4.

suspicion, suspect, suspicious

Suspicion is a noun. *Suspect* is the verb (though it can, if pronounced *sus´-pect*, be an adjective or noun). Though *suspicious* can mean *arousing suspicion*, it is sometimes safer to reserve it for the person in whom the suspicions are aroused, using the adjectival sense of *suspect* for the object of those suspicions; otherwise ambiguity may result (unless the context makes the meaning clear):

> *ambig:* He was a very suspicious man.
> *clear:* I thought his actions suspect.
> *clear:* He was suspicious of everyone he met.
> *clear:* All of us were suspect in the eyes of the police.

tend, tends

This verb is often no more than a mushy filler. Don't say "My French teacher tends to mark strictly" when what you mean is "My French teacher marks strictly."

therefore   (See **so, so that, therefore.**)

these (those) kinds (sorts), this kind (sort)   (See #4f.)

think   (See **feel(s).**)

though, although   (See **although, though.**)

thusly

A pretentious-sounding error for *thus* (and see **muchly**).

till, until, 'til

Till and *until* are both standard, and have the same meaning. *Until* is probably felt to be somewhat more formal, and (like the two-syllable *Although*) is usually preferable at the beginning of a sentence. The contraction *'til* is little used nowadays, except in markedly informal contexts, such as personal letters.

too

Used as an intensifier, *too* is sometimes illogical; if an intensifier is necessary in such sentences as these, use *very*:

> I don't like my cocoa *too* hot. (Well, of course you don't!)
> I don't like my cocoa *very* hot.
> She didn't care for the brown suit *too* much. (How could she possibly care *too* much?)
> She didn't care for the brown suit *very* much.

But often you can omit the intensifier as unnecessary:

> She didn't much care for the brown suit.

And see **very**.

toward, towards

These are interchangeable, but in North American (as opposed to British) English, the preposition *toward* is usually preferred to *towards*, just as the adverbs *afterward*, *forward* (meaning *frontward*), and *backward* are to their counterparts ending in *s*.

true facts

An attempt to be emphatic that backfires into illogic. If there are such things as "true facts" or "real facts," what are "false facts" or "unreal facts"? Let the word *facts* mean what it is supposed to; trying to prop it up with *true* or *real* only makes a reader or listener suspect it of being weak or insincere.

type, -type

Don't use *type* as an adjective or part of an adjective, as in "He is a very athletic *type* person." In any but a technical context, the word *type* almost always has the ring of jargon, even when followed by the obligatory *of* (but NOT by an additional *a* or *an*); without the *of* it is colloquial at best. In general writing, if you can substitute *kind of* for *type of*, do so—but even then check to make sure you really need it, for often it is unnecessary, mere deadwood: "She is an intelligent [kind of] woman." As a hyphenated suffix, *-type* is similarly often unnecessary, as well as being one of the worst results of the impulse to turn nouns into adjectives: "This is a new-type vegetable slicer," or "He is a patriotic-type person." Avoid it.

See also **kind of, sort of**.

unique, absolute, necessary, essential, complete, perfect, fatal, equal, (im)possible, infinite, empty, full, straight, round, square, etc.

In writing, especially formal writing, treat these and other such adjectives as absolutes that cannot logically be compared or modified by such adverbs as *very* and *rather*. Since by definition something *unique* is the *only one of its kind* or *without equal*, clearly one thing cannot be "more unique" than another, or even "very unique"; in other words, *unique* is not a synonym for *unusual* or *rare*. Similarly with the others: one thing cannot be "more necessary" than another. Since *perfect* means "without flaw," there cannot be degrees of perfection. Colloquially, expressions of degree or comparison with these terms are fairly common, especially those like *round, square, full, empty,* and *straight*. But strictly speaking, a thing is either *round* or not; one tennis ball cannot be "rounder" than another. And so on. And note that you can easily get around this semantic limitation by calling one thing, for example, "more nearly perfect," "more nearly round," or "closer to round" than another, or by referring to something as "almost unique" or "nearly unique" (but you could simply call it "very rare" or "highly unusual").

until   (See **till, until, 'til.**)

usage, use, utilize, utilization

The noun *usage* is appropriate when you mean customary or habitual use, whether verbal or otherwise ("British usage," "the usages of the early Christians"), or a particular verbal expression being characterized in a particular way ("an ironic usage," "an elegant usage"). Otherwise the shorter noun *use* is preferable. As a verb, *use* should nearly always suffice; *utilize*, often pretentiously employed instead, should carry the specific meaning "put to use, make use of, turn to practical or profitable account." Similarly, the noun *use* will usually be more appropriate than *utilization*. Phrases like *use of, the use of, by the use of,* and *through the use of* tend toward jargon and are almost always wordy.

verbal, oral

Although these words are commonly used interchangeably, you may want to preserve the still useful distinction between them. *Verbal* regularly means "pertaining to words," which could be either written or spoken. If you mean "spoken aloud," then *oral* is preferable. (In some special contexts *verbal* is often used to mean *oral* as opposed to written: "verbal contract, verbal agreement"—but even these usages can be ambiguous; *oral* and *written* would make the circumstances precisely clear.)

very

When revising, you may find that where you have used *very* you could just as well omit it. Often it is a lazy, vague, or euphemistic substitute for a more precise adverb or adjective:

It was *very* sunny today. (magnificently sunny? torturously sunny?)
I was *very* tired. (exhausted?)
He was *very* intoxicated. (falling-down drunk?)

Her embarrassment was *very* obvious. (It was either obvious or it wasn't; drop *very*, or change it to something like *painfully*.)

The same goes for *really* and *actually*. Such lame intensifiers sometimes even detract from the force of the words they modify.

Note: Before some past participles, it is idiomatic to use another word along with *very*:

You are *very much* mistaken if you think I'll agree without an argument.
Sharon is *very well* rehearsed for the role.

virtually (See **literally, virtually, figuratively.**)

way, ways

In formal usage, especially in writing, don't use *ways* to refer to distance; *way* is correct:

We were a long *way* from home.
They had only a little *way* to go.

well (See **good, bad, badly, well.**)

when, where (See **is when, is where.**)

whereas (See **while.**)

while

As a subordinating conjunction, *while* is best restricted to meanings having to do with time:

While Vijay mowed the lawn Honorée raked up the grass clippings.
She played the piano *while* I prepared the dinner.

When it means *although* (*though*) or *whereas*, it can be imprecise, even ambiguous:

While I agree with some of his reasons, I still think my proposal is better. (*Although* would be clearer.)
While he does the lawn-mowing, she cooks the meals. (Fuzzy or ambiguous; *whereas* would make the meaning clear.)

And it is weakest of all when used as a substitute for *and* or *but*:

The winning team guzzled champagne, *while* the losers sat and sulked.

See also **although, though.**

will, shall (See #6h.3.)

-wise

Just as *-ize* (or *-ise*) has long been used to turn nouns and adjectives into verbs, *-wise* has been used to turn them into adverbs, e.g. of manner or position: *clockwise, crabwise, lengthwise, edgewise, sidewise,* *likewise, otherwise.* But this suffix, in its sense of "with reference to" (and equivalent phrases), is so overused in modern jargon (*moneywise, sales-wise, personnel-wise,* etc.) that it is now respectable mainly as a source of humour ("And how are you otherwise-wise?"). Therefore do not tack it onto nouns, for it produces such inanities as what a politician recently announced: "We've just had our best month ever, fund-raisingwise." It is acceptable in established words, of course, but not, or seldom, in new coinages. You can easily find a way to say what you mean without resorting to it (see **in terms of**):

> *not: Grammarwise,* Stephen is not doing well.
> *but:* Stephen is not doing well with grammar.
> *not: Insurance-wise,* I believe I am well enough protected.
> *but:* I believe I have enough insurance.
> *not:* This is the best car I've ever owned, *powerwise.*
> *but:* This car has more power than any other I've owned.

with regard to   (See **in terms of.**)

with respect to   (See **in terms of.**)

woman   (See **man, woman, lady,** etc.)

worthwhile

Try to find a more precise and concrete way to express the desired meaning. "It was a very worthwhile experience" tells one very little (nor does the *very* succeed in propping up the weak *worthwhile*). Skip the vague statement; instead, describe or explain just what was so worthwhile about the experience. See also #54.

would, should   (See #6e and #6i.2.)

Review Exercise, Chapter VII   **Diction**

Revise the following sentences to strengthen the diction and normalize the usage; correct any other errors you find, as well. (Note: Almost all of the sentences in this and the next exercise are from students' essays or published or broadcast sources, with only minor changes.)

1. They discussed the role of the psychiatrist in athlete motivation.
2. The team comprises a close-knit unit that functions on a collective basis.
3. Strategy-wise, we want to position Scouting in an advantageous situation.
4. Because this particular word occurs frequently throughout the course of the play, it achieves a certain importance.
5. In the winter even less tourist dollars are spent.
6. Her striving to be a perfectionist was evident in her business.
7. Hopefully, this weekend's events will turn out to be successful.
8. He was ignorant as to the proper use of the tools.

9. As is so often the case, one type of error leads to another.
10. This passage is a very essential one in the play.
11. His metaphors really bring out a sinister feeling which one feels while reading it.
12. Eliot sees his poetry as occupying a kind of niche in a long conveyer belt of accumulated knowledge and poetry.
13. She has him literally at her beckon call.
14. He found himself in a powerless situation.
15. I resolved to do my best in terms of making friends and working hard.
16. The hulls of the tankers were ripped open in a majority of cases, dumping countless barrels of oil into the sea.
17. Hamlet spends the whole play trying to reach a situation where he can revenge his father's death.
18. This poem is concerned with the fact that one should grasp an opportunity quickly.
19. He is only in town on a once-in-a-while basis.
20. The Prime Minister is waiting for the premiers to show their bottom lines.
21. As she gave me so much money I thanked her profusely.
22. The deal may not have gone ahead if Anderson hadn't been so patient and persistent.
23. People in watching these shows or movies may develop a love for violence as a result of watching this type of program.
24. This man thought it was incumbent upon him to extract revenge.
25. In Olympic sports nationalism is increasingly becoming a more important factor.
26. She saw that this was the last remaining remnant of a very, very important species.
27. On the government side, the Liberals will stand as a traditional agent attempting to breach the gap between English and French Canada.
28. For more than a million Canadians, back pain is an incapacitating experience which slows ordinary movements and turns routine tasks into tortuous events.
29. The author cites that in one of Macaulay's speeches on the First Reform Bill he said, "Reform, that you may preserve."
30. The form of tenure common in British universities is not an essential, or even a necessary, safeguard.
31. We are all intensely involved in profiting on the expenses of other people.
32. The contribution of the coalition to the passage of the legislation was capitalized on by the opposition.
33. He is as equally at ease hobnobbing with celebrities as he is relaxing in his own home.
34. These instructions are contingent to your acceptance.
35. In Surrey there is a local bylaw prohibiting a man to wear a bathing suit which does not cover his navel.
36. The Prime Minister's reply, he complained, was "warm and gratuitous but not very specific."
37. The series is based on Durrell's childhood recollections of his sojourn to Corfu in the 1930s.

d

38. Iago is regarded by all as an honest, truthful man.
39. The character of Nicholas is recognizable to people who really exist in the world.
40. His heroic deeds were awarded with medals.
41. Thanks to your financial commitment, an alternate to on-air fundraising is possible.
42. This book about a politician will have a negative effect in terms of the interests of his opponents.
43. Clinton has tried to pressurize Congress to go along with his proposals.
44. After going only a hundred miles the ship was forced to return to its point of origination.
45. You'll also be amazed, too, at our low prices on basic apparel.
46. The new program will cost in the realm of five million dollars.
47. You can expect similar-type amounts of precipitation over the long weekend.
48. The minister said that he would not want to be categorized with respect to a reply to that statement.
49. Prospective teachers are required to take a Written Expression Competency Examination.
50. There was a general consensus in the neighbourhood that ambulance service in the area was frequently inadequate regarding response time.
51. Today, environmentalists are trying to substitute the word "buy" with the word "recycle."
52. With the new system in place at the ferry dock, a car on the end of the ramp may not go over.
53. We have to reconsider the proposal in terms of the legal aspects of that situation.
54. I was playing my typical type of game.
55. He was advised to keep his feelings on a spiritual plain for a while yet.
56. It seems like he is rather mad at her for daring to try and deceive him.
57. Frodo continuously fretted about the Ring.
58. The firm will be satisfied if the advertising campaign peaks public interest in their products.
59. I denote a real sense of pride here.
60. One must judge the various proposals on an equal basis.

Omnibus Review Exercise, Chapters I–VII	**Sentence errors and weaknesses**

Each of the following sentences contains at least one error or weakness of a kind discussed in this book; many contain more than one. Practise your proofreading and revising. Label the sentences with the appropriate correction symbols.

1. The nature of his errors were not serious.
2. There was a clear increase in strength of Protestant power, especially in England and Prussia who had benefitted from the treaty of Utrecht.

3. In today's world it is becoming increasingly more difficult to find relatively inexpensive ways to use your liesure time.
4. As far as league standings, this string of successive losses has put the team in an insurmountable hole.
5. We at TSN want to feature a few more Canadian athletes at a young age.
6. There were artists which continued to study and produce classical works and there were artists which developed new ideas in their fields.
7. As for ancient man, being civilized was of no concern to one who was battling the many forces of nature such as hunting wild animals for food and shelter from the weather.
8. Argentina, more than any country in Latin America, was a place of massive immigration over relatively few decades.
9. The reason why their cars don't live as long is because most people have no idea of how to properly look after their cars.
10. There's no golfer who wouldn't give his life to don the coveted green jacket, symbolizing a Masters victory and an automatic life-long membership into the Augusta National Golf Club.
11. This book provides what I think is indisputedly the best account of those troubled years.
12. Friends say the feisty newspaperwoman would have liked to have become an artist.
13. He was charged of embezzling over ten thousand dollars.
14. As a single parent with two high schoolers, it took two jobs to stay afloat.
15. During that period of time we talked to him on a nightly basis.
16. The poem's strange theme states that one is better off dying at a young age rather than growing old.
17. An old Victorian mansion has a mysterious basement room which, by entering allows members of the household to travel through time.
18. I had truly scarred her while she had only embarrassed me.
19. At that point the immigration department closed the door tightly.
20. There's no question it was a tragedy, and there's also no question that it may have been prevented.
21. A hobby such as playing music in a band gives more than just enjoyment, it gives relaxation, self satisfaction, it is educational, and it is competitive.
22. During the long California drought, many water areas, such as lakes and reservoirs, were drying up.
23. This evening's show features a family of nine who is competing in the National Karate Championships.
24. I felt a sudden needle like pain.
25. Based on her findings, she concluded that comedy was more healthful than tragedy.
26. The Board of Directors of *Design for Today* wishes to express their appreciation for assistance from many local individuals and businesses.
27. There are many arguments with respect to the importance of a university education in today's society.

28. In this modern day and age it is not unusual to find people who are ignorantly unaware of the technology of how things in our society work.
29. She had so many assignments over the holiday that she felt bogged under.
30. The police act against violators of this minor law only on a complaint basis.
31. They substituted butter with margarine in the belief that it was healthier.
32. As a soccer fan, recent events have been depressing.
33. The silver mentioned in the beginning and the end of the story not only symbolize freedom but they foreshadow a better future.
34. My grandfather was a very introspective-type individual.
35. He is one of those people, (and there are many of them) who does not understand economics.
36. When there never seems to be enough hours in a day, it's time to get yourself a cellular phone.
37. Tonight's specialty is a dish that is a feast not only for the eyes but a treat for the palate as well.
38. Failure to produce efficiently together with failure to reduce imports have had serious economic consequences.
39. The show employs flashbacks to fill in the protagonist's background as a former Vietnam veteran and ex-New Orleans cop.
40. Our opponent merely sights her party's ideology and says things are all right—but ask yourself, can you afford anymore?
41. The government permits the sale of surplus material abroad on an intermittent basis.
42. I hope you will forgive me pointing out certain weaknesses in your argument.
43. The poor woman had become addicted to the pain killing drug she was taking.
44. The laws were made by the parlament and enforced by a police force, which is a similar system to the present.
45. The room was furnished with the new chrome and plastic furniture but it wasn't very attractive.
46. We shouldn't act in terms of a knee-jerk reaction to the present situation.
47. She concluded from her investigation that under the new policy women employees may in fact receive a smaller increase than they may have otherwise received.
48. The English aristocracy, which was mainly comprised of wealthy landowners, did not however, in spite of their comfortable lifestyle, know the manners and etiquette that seemed to elevate the French aristocracy.
49. He promised he would take me to the movies, in spite of how much work that he hasn't finished yet, but has to do.
50. As a valued Acme Bank customer we are pleased to extend to you the opportunity to apply for a personal loan at exceptional fixed interest rates.
51. Our new call-in sports program is kind of unique.

52. It is the story of one man's answer for the problem of dealing with modern violence.
53. It is a tale of two elderly rascals who each believe he is the grandfather of an orphaned ten-year-old heiress.
54. The feeling of excitement comes across by the imagery.
55. If you look directly at the eclipse of the sun you may risk eye damage.
56. Hamlet is still unsure of whether the ghost was real or not and if so, if it spoke the truth.
57. In ancient times the sun was worshipped as a diety and has always had a leading role in mythology.
58. Computer break-ins have become far too easy to do and the law is ineffective in dealing with this type of problem.
59. The reports are drawn up on an annualized basis.
60. I can only say that my worst fears have been brought to fruition.
61. We were driving on a bumpy, dirt road.
62. Both Irish economies have more in common with each other than either have in common with Britain.
63. The real meaning of Christmas is to celebrate the birth of He who taught the golden rule.
64. Its very difficult for man to perceive his own shortcomings, its all too easy for them to see the weaknesses of others.
65. A major reason as to why religion played such an important role in Elizabethan England was because it was a main pastime that the extremely large working class could afford.
66. At the end of the poem the nightingale flies away and leaves Keats disallusioned.
67. Health experts add that because people are obese for different reasons, and that there are different types of obesity, no one solution will work for everyone.
68. The report claims that the dining room is unacceptable to standards to which convention guests should be presented.
69. Former Anglican minister and *Toronto Star* religious editor Tom Harpur, who covered the Pope's activities as a journalist for several years, spoke to an interviewer about his experience.
70. The dinosaur craze began about ten years ago, and it still hasn't topped out yet.
71. The employees should be able to make their points and they should be given careful consideration.
72. This important matter cannot be taken too lightly.
73. The first step in shopping around for a computer to assist you with your particular business needs is to decide what kind of equipment you will need to meet the needs and size of your company.
74. So many people are obsessed with their weight that the diet industry, whether it be in the form of pills, meal substitutes or a new fad diet, has boomed.
75. He was too mannerly to talk about a subject that did not interest whomever was with him.
76. The resident pastor will officiate the service.
77. Trust is a very important aspect in media effectiveness.

78. The passing of summer into autumn had always been experienced with pleasure while at the same time realizing that winter, the season I dislike the most, would soon be a fact of life.
79. Some people neglect not only their own work, but behave in such a way as to cause everyone else in the office to neglect his.
80. These people are sitting on the cutting edge of computer technology.
81. Looking through the newspapers, the cost of food products are seen to be expensive.
82. The minister said he was "very concerned that our health is not affected by chemicals in the environment."
83. Drugs are a problem nation-wide, society-wise; they are impacting negatively on families.
84. Whale blubber which tastes badly to you and I is a rare delicacy to the northern native.
85. In reply to Mr. Mason's letter, I would suggest that he considers certain facts about democratic institutions.
86. The United Kingdom imposed a ban on South African iron, steel, and gold coins.
87. This team is so good they are almost bound to ultimately win in the end.
88. "Well, Chester, what do you think?" asked the salesman—which struck me as being just too chummy, our not having been formally introduced.
89. The golf tee, simplistic as it may be, is well designed to effectively achieve its specific function.
90. The general secretary of the National Viewers Association said that the film was a "travesty of the Gospel" and local authorities should be pressurised into preventing its showing.
91. He had barely settled into the posh ambassadorial residence than he began stirring up controversy.
92. Unfortunately, the director prefers to evoke his own vanished childhood than to explore the protagonist's moral and psychological dilemna.
93. Paranoia is a mental illness where the person believes that he is being persecuted by others.
94. Maintenance of both the home and the garden, household duties, and small children require enormous amounts of energy from an individual.
95. Secrecy in Parliament, in caucus and especially in budget preparations no longer fit with our hunger to know what is happening to our economy.
96. The author's intention is to prevent us catching no more than a succession of sharp glimpses of himself.
97. Inventor of the geodesic dome and other innovations, Fuller's books and lectures tried to foster optimal use of the resources of what he called "spaceship Earth."
98. Both have the same fate awaiting for them; namely death.
99. Fugitive slaves travelled on the underground railroad alone or in groups of up to thirty in one case.
100. When the police came they didn't arrive with lights flashing and sirens blaring; rather they stole into the grounds stealthily.

Here are ten more sentences, most slightly longer or more complicated than the others, that invite more drastic or thoroughgoing revision.

1. The fact that there are many people who I can relate to, adds to a sense of security for me because I feel that I am liked and I have a position with them in society, which enhances my self-identity.
2. Further implications for disaster in postponing the driving experience to an older age could be encountered in those people wishing to use the car as their primary means of transportation to work or a post-secondary institution.
3. The poem mentions statues, pictures, and stairways, all of these seem to enable the reader to picture Prufrock better and the people he associates with.
4. An older person has already made a lot of mistakes in their life and sharing their mistakes with new generations will keep from every generation having to start from a beginning.
5. I am still not sure whether or not I did the right thing about coming here but everyone thought it was, so here I am.
6. Some people may view Hamlet as a feeble, gutless young man who can't make up his mind about anything and this is what I believed at first. But by reading the play carefully and by observing Hamlet's actions this can't be true.
7. A hobby is often a nice way to relax or to just sit down and read a favourite novel or listen to some music, anything, just as long as it is relaxing.
8. I'm lucky to live in a great country, have a family who I love and am loved in return, have caring relations, acquaintances, and the opportunity to meet strangers who may someday be friends.
9. With no increase in salaries, increased teaching loads, and cutbacks in research facilities, faculty is starting to slip away. The university has already lost at least seven faculty members since January, and there are strong indications of many more to come.
10. By portraying the Queen as being blind to the situation of hate between Hamlet and the King, and the fact that she does not seem to even consider the fact that the King killed her previous husband, the audience's attitude toward the King is made even stronger.

CHAPTER VIII

Elements and Principles of Composition:
Paragraphs, Essays, the Writing Process, Argument, and In-class Writing

Earlier chapters discuss the primary units of communication—sentences—and the fundamental elements of expression that make up sentences, namely words, phrases, and clauses. The principles of unity, coherence, and emphasis that apply to sentences (see #18, #28, and #31) apply also to the larger units, the **paragraph** and the **essay** as a whole. These larger units are the subjects of this chapter, which also provides a step-by-step guide to the **process** of planning and writing an essay, discusses the writing of an **argument**, and offers suggestions for writing in-class essays and examinations.

61 Kinds of Paragraphs

A paragraph can be classified in two ways:

    (a) according to its function in its larger context;

    (b) according to the kind of material it contains and the way that material is developed.

61a   Functions of Paragraphs: Substantive and Nonsubstantive Paragraphs

Introductory, concluding, and **transitional** paragraphs are especially designed to begin or end an essay or to provide links between major sections of an essay. When they do no more, such paragraphs are called **nonsubstantive**; they perform important functions, but they don't contribute significantly to the *ideas* that make up the substance of an essay. All other paragraphs in an essay—those that carry the freight, so to speak—are **substantive** paragraphs.

    Nonsubstantive paragraphs can also contribute to the development of a topic; when they do they are of course partly substantive. For example, an effective beginning or ending is often not a separate paragraph but only a sentence or two, or even just part of a sentence, at the beginning or end of an otherwise substantive paragraph.

61b Kinds of Substantive Paragraphs: Methods of Development in Expository Writing

Only substantive paragraphs can be classified according to the way their material is developed. There are several **methods of development** to choose from. The one or more you elect to use for any given paragraph or essay will depend on the nature of your topic and on your audience and purpose. The principal methods are *description, narration, definition, classification, analysis into parts, process analysis, comparison and contrast, cause and effect,* and *examples and illustrations.*

Description can exist by itself, but it is usually at the service of some other method, most often **narration**, which also can exist by itself. But as a student you will usually be writing **exposition**, "exposing" ideas and meanings for one purpose or another. All of the methods of development listed above can be used in *exposition.*

Further, these methods of development are seldom mutually exclusive. Two or more are often combined in a single paragraph, and a whole essay may use several. Even narration can be used in an expository essay: a sequence of events may serve as an example or illustration, or an anecdote might be used as an analogy in a comparison, or a full-length narrative of personal experience might lead to an expository point.

Some methods are combined in other ways. For example, when you are comparing or contrasting you are also necessarily classifying and defining. And almost any method can be thought of as the supplying of **details** to support or clarify an assertion made early in a paragraph or essay. As long as you maintain the fundamental requirements of *unity* and *coherence*, you can mix and combine these methods in any way that will be effective.

62-66 Unity, Coherence, and Emphasis in Paragraphs

All paragraphs, but especially substantive paragraphs, in order to be effective, must have **unity**, **coherence**, and properly controlled **emphasis**.

62 Paragraph Unity

u An effective substantive paragraph deals with one theme; its singleness of purpose engages readers' minds, focussing their attention on that theme.

63 ¶, *para, coh*

If you allow a paragraph to be disrupted by irrelevant digressions or unnecessary shifts in point of view or focus, readers will lose the thread of your discourse. You will confuse them—and lose them. A paragraph has unity because every sentence in it contributes to its purpose and because nothing in it is irrelevant to that purpose. It is like a tidy, well-wrapped package that will reach its destination without coming apart.

63 Paragraph Coherence

coh   Though a paragraph-package has a homogeneous substance—is unified because every sentence contributes to the development of its single theme or idea—it could still come apart if it didn't have another essential quality: **coherence.** Coherence is sticking-togetherness. It is achieved by packing the contents of a paragraph carefully and by using strong enough paper and tape or string to hold everything together. You can ensure coherence in your writing in two ways:

    (a) by carefully organizing your material, and

    (b) by using the mechanical devices that create structural coherence.

64 Coherence Through Organization: Beginning, Middle, and Ending

A substantive paragraph must have a *beginning*, a *middle*, and an *ending*. Good organization means rational order. Make sure that the beginning adequately introduces the theme, that the middle clearly and logically follows from and develops that statement of theme, and that the ending is a natural conclusion that unobtrusively closes the discussion—and perhaps also, in a larger context, provides a hook for the next paragraph to link onto. (For example, the phrase "without coming apart" at the end of the section on unity, above, is picked up in the next paragraph. But see the **Caution** under #64a.1 below.)

64a The Beginning: Topic Sentences

Most substantive paragraphs open with an explicit statement of theme, called a **topic sentence.** (Purely nonsubstantive paragraphs do not have topic sentences.)

1. *Functions of Topic Sentences*

A good opening topic sentence announces what the paragraph will be about. It is in effect a promise that the rest of the paragraph must make good. If the paragraph is part of a larger context, such as an essay, the topic sentence will usually also perform two other functions:

(a) It will refer to the overall subject of the essay and at least suggest the relation of the paragraph to that subject.
(b) It will provide a transition so that the new paragraph flows smoothly from the preceding paragraph.

> **Caution:** It is sometimes possible, but almost always difficult and risky, to provide forward-looking material at the end of a paragraph. If such material occurs naturally, well and good; but don't struggle to get something transitional into the last sentence of a paragraph. The work of transition should be done by the first sentence of the next paragraph. Tampering with a paragraph's final sentence merely for transitional purposes can easily destroy that paragraph's integrity and effectiveness. See #64c.

2. *Efficiency of Topic Sentences*

Since it has so much to do, a good opening topic sentence, even more than other sentences, should be efficient. Here is one that is not:

> The poet uses a great deal of imagery throughout the poem.

The sentence announces the topic—the poem's imagery—but promises nothing more than to show that the poem contains a lot of it. But offering a long list of images wouldn't develop an idea; it would merely illustrate what should be self-evident. Trying to revise this weak topic sentence, the student inserted the adjective *good* before *imagery*; now the paragraph must at least try to show that the abundant images are good ones (not so easy a task as the writer may have thought). But the focus is still largely on the quantity of imagery, which is not where the focus should be. What is most important is the imagery's function: What does the poet do with the imagery? A little thought might lead to a revision like this—a topic sentence that is *efficient*, that not only has more substance in itself but also suggests the approach the paragraph will take:

> The poem's imagery, most of it drawn from nature, helps to create not only the poem's mood but its themes as well.

The same essay also contained the following inefficient topic sentence:

> In the second stanza the poet continues to use images.

The revision didn't help much:

> In the second stanza the poet continues to use excellent images to express his ideas.

Again, what is needed is something sharper, more specific—an assertion that provides a significant idea that can usefully be talked about, developed. For example:

> The imagery in the second stanza contrasts vividly with that of the first.

or

> In the second stanza images of death begin the process that leads to the poem's ironic conclusion.

A good opening topic sentence should be more than just a label on a box; it should itself be a significant part of the contents of the box. It pays to give close attention to the formulation of your topic sentences, for they can help you achieve both *unity* and *coherence* not only in individual paragraphs but also in an essay as a whole (see #68a-b).

3. Notes on the Placement of Topic Sentences

In the great majority of paragraphs, the development fulfills the promise made in an opening topic sentence. But occasionally, by conscious design, a topic sentence may be placed at the end or even elsewhere in a paragraph. Sometimes delaying a topic sentence can increase readers' interest by creating a little mystery or suspense to get them to read on. And stating a topic at the end of a paragraph takes advantage of that most emphatic position (see #66). Note for example our paragraph below labelled *Coherence Through Orderly Development* (#64b.1). The label identifies the topic, which has two elements; but the paragraph itself refers only to "development" until the end, where the short final sentence explicitly ties it all to the idea of coherence. That *part* of the topic, in other words, we delayed until the end, or climax.

A paragraph's topic, then, though single, may consist of more than one part. Similarly, it may not get stated all in one sentence. In this paragraph and the one preceding, for example, note that not until the end of the *second* sentence is the topic fully clear. It is not uncommon for a paragraph to have a second topic sentence, one that partly restates the topic and partly leads into the body of the paragraph.

And—rarely—a paragraph's topic may not be stated at all, but only implied. Occasionally the focal idea of a paragraph is so clearly and strongly implied that it would insult the reader's intelligence to state it baldly. Another kind of paragraph without a topic sentence often occurs in narratives, or in essays where a strong narrative element is present: sometimes a strong topic sentence can effectively govern two or three paragraphs, though the succeeding paragraphs must begin in such a way that their continuing relation to the preceding paragraph is sufficiently clear—perhaps indicated by no more than an opening *Then* or *When*.

But don't strain for these unusual kinds of paragraph. If they occur in your writing naturally, they will probably be all right; but always check them carefully to make sure they're clear and effective. The topic-sentence-first paragraph is the most common because it is the most natural, clear, and effective. Rest satisfied with that kind unless you have good reason to depart from it.

See also *Notes on Beginnings*, #69-1.

64b The Middle

1. *Coherence Through Orderly Development*

A well-developed substantive paragraph fulfills the promise of its beginning. If for example you were writing a paragraph that began with the last example of a topic sentence above ("In the second stanza images of death begin the process that leads to the poem's ironic conclusion"), you would have to explain "the process" and the irony of the poem's conclusion, and you would have to *show* (not merely assert) how images of death from the second stanza set that process in motion. To fulfill your promise effectively, then, you would have to decide how to organize your material. For example you might first describe the irony of the conclusion and then analyze the images to show how they lead to that conclusion. Or you might start by analyzing the death imagery and then proceed to answer some questions that you could ask yourself: What effect do the images create? How does that effect contribute to the way the poem proceeds? How does that process lead to the conclusion? In other words, after considering the different possibilities, you would *choose* a way of presenting your material; and the order you choose to follow should be one that makes sense: one idea should lead logically to another until you reach your goal. Then your paragraph will be coherent.

2. *Patterns of Development*

Orderly development often occurs automatically as one works through one's ideas in composing paragraphs and essays. But often, too—especially for relatively inexperienced writers—it pays to give some conscious thought to just how a particular paragraph (or essay) can best be shaped. The most common *patterns of development* writers use to make sure their paragraphs are orderly and coherent are the following:

> chronological
> spatial
> moving from general to specific or abstract to concrete, or vice versa (see #54 and Exercise 54[1])
> moving from simple to complex, small to large, minor to major
> rising to a climax
> moving from negative to positive (or vice versa)
> moving from question to answer
> logical progression

Further, some of the *methods of development* discussed above (#61b) themselves impose patterns on the arrangement of ideas in a paragraph. In addition to using narration, with its chronological order (perhaps including a flashback or two), or description, with its spatial order, one can move from cause to effect or from effect to cause, or from a statement about a whole to a division of it into parts (analysis), or from a statement about one thing to a comparison of it with another.

Similarly, as with the methods of development, these patterns are not mutually exclusive. For example if you are moving from small to large or minor to major, you are likely also using the order of climax. Even if you are narrating, and therefore following a generally chronological order, you are probably also telling your story in such a way that the reader's interest will mount as you move through a sequence of events until you finally provide the climax.

64c   The Ending

As you compose and revise your drafts, the endings of your paragraphs will often come naturally, without your having to think about them—but they are likely to do so only if you know, when you begin a paragraph, just where it is going; that is, your paragraphs will be unified and coherent, and their endings will be implicit or even explicit in their beginnings. The concluding sentence of a paragraph, like all the others, should be an organic part of the whole (and see the **Caution** under #64a.1).

The final sentence of a paragraph will most often be a statement—not a mere summary—growing out of the substance of the paragraph, a sentence that brings the topic to a clear and natural finish in an unobtrusive way. A final sentence should round off its paragraph in such a way that readers get the feeling of a satisfying close.

Some Advice for Ending Paragraphs

If a paragraph doesn't seem to be ending naturally, you may have to stop and think consciously about it. Here are a few pointers to help you do that:

1. A good ending may point back to the beginning, but it will not merely repeat it; if it repeats something, it will do so in order to put it in the new light made possible by the development of the paragraph.

2. Usually, don't write a separate final sentence solely for the sake of concluding a paragraph. Above all, don't begin such a sentence with a stiff "In conclusion" or "Thus we see that." Sometimes, indeed, the best way to end a paragraph is simply to let it stop, once its point is made. A too-explicit conclusion will often seem tacked-on, anticlimactic, destroying

the effectiveness of an otherwise good paragraph that has a natural feeling of closure at its end. To maintain coherence, the ending of a paragraph should be as much a functional and organic part of the whole as is the tail of a whale.

3. Sometimes a slight stylistic shift is all that's necessary to mark a paragraph's ending, perhaps no more than an unusually short or long sentence. Or an ending might be marked by an allusion or brief quotation—so long as it is to the point and not there simply for its own sake.

4. As a rule, don't end a paragraph with an indented, set-off ("block") quotation, or even a full sentence of quotation that isn't set off. Even though you carefully introduce such a quotation, if you leave it dangling at the end it will almost inevitably leave a "so what?" feeling in the reader's mind, or a feeling that you have abandoned your paragraph to someone else. Always complete such a paragraph with at least a brief comment that explains the quotation, justifies it, or re-emphasizes its main thrust.

65 Structural Coherence

Careful organization and development go a long way toward achieving coherence. But you will sometimes need to use other techniques as well, providing mechanical links that ensure a smooth flow of thought from one sentence to another.

Composing a paragraph is like fashioning a wooden box or a cupboard. You cut pieces to size, making sure they're square-cornered and that the joints fit together. You can then assemble the pieces and reveal the final product as a well-designed and functional unit. But its *coherence* isn't assured until you nail, screw, or glue the pieces together. This section discusses ways of attaching the pieces to each other so that the assembled parts make a solid whole. Or, to return to our earlier analogy, we're putting the wrapping paper and string or tape on our parcel to ensure that the postal service can deliver it intact.

The main devices for structural coherence are *parallelism, repetition, pronouns and demonstrative adjectives,* and *transitional words and phrases.* Like the methods and patterns of development, these devices are not mutually exclusive: two or more may work together in the same paragraph, sometimes even in the same words and phrases.

65a **Parallelism** (See #17c and #27.)

Parallel sentence structure is a simple and effective way to bind successive sentences together. Similar structural patterns in clauses and phrases work like a call and its echo, or echoes.

But don't try to maintain a series of parallel elements for too long. If the echoes remain obvious they will be too noticeable, and therefore tedious; if you vary the echoes to avoid too monotonous a repetition, they will diminish in power as they get farther from the original. Parallelism, like any other device, should not be overdone.

65b   Repetition

Like parallelism, repetition of words and phrases effectively links successive sentences. But the caution against overdoing is most applicable here. Repetition properly controlled for rhetorical effect can be powerful (Winston Churchill's "We will fight them" speech, Martin Luther King's "I have a dream" speech), but repetition, especially on paper, can also become boring evidence of a writer's limited vocabulary or lack of verbal ingenuity. Structure your repetitions carefully; don't put too many too close together. And generally use the device sparingly.

65c   Pronouns and Demonstrative Adjectives

By referring to something mentioned earlier, a pronoun or a demonstrative adjective clearly constructs a bridge within the paragraph between itself and its antecedent or referent.

> **Cautionary Notes:** It is also possible, of course, to create similar links *between* paragraphs, but be careful
>
> (a) that there is an unambiguous antecedent or referent, and
> (b) that you are not too far away from it.
>
> If you are far beyond the antecedent, or if more than one is possible, you risk confusing your readers rather than building coherence for them. Either way, straight repetition is preferable.
> And make it a point to use demonstrative *adjectives* rather than demonstrative *pronouns*. As adjectives they are clear and they can add emphasis. As pronouns they are not emphatic; rather they can be weak and ambiguous (see #3f, #5c, #8a, #28, and **ref** in Ch. XI).

65d   Transitional Terms

Transitional words and phrases create a logical flow from one part or idea to another by indicating their relation. Obviously one must choose the right transitional signal for a particular spot in order to create successful coherence. Here are some of the more common and useful transitional terms:

Terms showing addition of one point to another:

and,   also,   another,   besides,   further,   in addition,   moreover

Terms showing similarity between ideas:

>again, equally, in other words, in the same way, likewise, similarly

Terms showing difference between ideas:

>although, but, conversely, despite, even though, however, in contrast, in spite of, nevertheless, on the contrary, on the other hand, otherwise, still, though, whereas, yet

Terms showing cause and effect or other logical relations:

>as a result, because, consequently, for, hence, of course, since, then, therefore, thus

Terms introducing examples or details:

>for example, for instance, in particular, namely, specifically, that is, to illustrate

Terms expressing emphasis:

>chiefly, especially, indeed, mainly, more important, primarily

Terms showing relations in time and space:

>after, afterward, at the same time, before, earlier, in the meantime, later, meanwhile, simultaneously, subsequently, then, while, behind, beyond, farther away, here, in the distance, nearby, next, there, to the left

These and other such words and phrases, occurring usually at or near the beginnings of sentences, are the glue that helps hold paragraphs together. But if the paragraph isn't unified to begin with, and if its parts haven't been arranged to fit with one another, then even these explicit transitional terms can't do much good.

Caution: Further, don't overdo such terms. If some other kind of coherence is already present, it won't need propping up with one of these. If a writer feels so insecure about coherence as to add a transitional word or phrase slavishly to nearly every sentence, whether it needs one or not, the writing will be stiff and awkward: the box will look ugly because globs of excess glue show at the joints.

Exercise 63-65   Recognizing coherence

Point out the various means by which coherence is established in the following paragraph, and comment on their effectiveness.

>Unlike those many countries which rose to nationhood out of tragic bloodbaths, Canada was built by men and women expressing the best

qualities of human nature. It was built by the courage and stamina of explorers and the stalwart crews of *coureurs de bois* who allowed no obstacles to impede them. It was built by the staunch pioneering spirit and energy of those men and women who literally hacked homes out of the wilderness. It was built by the faith and determination of people who willingly gave the best that was in them to make life better for themselves and their children. Although blood was shed in the process of creating this nation, it owes its being, principally, not to lives lost in its cause but to lives lived in its cause.

66 Emphasis in Paragraphs

emph Just as in a sentence, so in a paragraph the most emphatic position is its ending and the second most emphatic position is its beginning (see #18a). That is another reason the opening or topic sentence is so important a part of a paragraph. And an ending, because of its emphatic position, can make or break a paragraph.

But structure and diction are also important. Parallelism and repetition both create emphasis. Independent clauses are more emphatic than subordinate clauses and phrases. Precise, concrete, and specific words are more emphatic than vague, abstract, and general ones. A "big" word will stand out among plainer terms; a slang expression or colloquialism will stand out in the midst of more formal diction. A long sentence will stand out among several shorter ones; a short sentence will stand out among longer ones. Keep these points in mind as you compose and revise your paragraphs; let emphasis contribute to the effectiveness of your writing.

67 Length of Paragraphs

There is no arbitrary optimum length for a paragraph. The length of a paragraph will be determined by the requirements of the particular job it is doing. In narration or dialogue, a single sentence or a single word may constitute a paragraph. In complex exposition or argument, a paragraph may go on for a page or more—though such long paragraphs are rare in modern writing. Most substantive paragraphs, however, consist of at least three or four sentences, and seldom more than nine or ten. Transitional paragraphs are usually short, sometimes only one sentence. Introductory and concluding paragraphs will be of various lengths, depending on the complexity of the material and on the techniques of beginning and ending that the writer is using.

Sometimes, even in exposition, if a particular point deserves special emphasis, it may be put into a one-sentence paragraph.

67a Too Many Long Paragraphs?

If you find that you are writing many longish paragraphs, you may be overdeveloping, piling more into a paragraph than its topic requires. Or you may be rambling, not weeding out irrelevant material. Or you may be damaging unity by making one paragraph deal with two or more topics that should be dealt with in separate paragraphs.

67b The Importance of Adequate Development

But the more common weakness among inexperienced writers is to settle for paragraphs that are too short to develop their topics sufficiently. The body of a paragraph must be long enough to *develop* a topic satisfactorily; merely restating or summarizing the topic is not enough. If you find yourself writing many short paragraphs, you may not be adequately developing your main ideas. Or you may be endangering coherence by splintering your discussion into small parts: when you revise, check to see if two or more related short paragraphs can be integrated to form one substantial paragraph.

67c Variety

Try to ensure that any extended piece of writing you produce contains a variety of paragraph lengths: long, short, medium. A constant similarity of paragraph lengths can be almost as tedious for a reader as a constant similarity of sentence lengths (see #17a). For the same reason, you should also try to provide a variety of patterns (#64b.2) and methods (#61b) in your paragraphs. For example parallelism, however admirable a device, would likely become tiresome if it were the basic pattern in several successive paragraphs.

Normally, then, the paragraphs that make up a more extensive piece of writing will vary in length. Simply ensure that each of your paragraphs is as long or as short as it needs to be. And whatever their length, make sure that your paragraphs actually go somewhere rather than just tread water. See also #68c.

61-67 Review: A Sample Paragraph with an Analysis

The paragraph that follows illustrates principles discussed in the preceding pages of this chapter. The student who wrote the paragraph has gone on to analyze her work. You should consider analyzing several paragraphs of your own writing in the same way in order to assess the strengths and weaknesses of your handling of this important part of writing.

(1) The word "recession" has become for this generation what the word "Depression" must have been for our grandparents' generation. (2) Rarely can a person pick up a newspaper or tune in to a news broadcast these days without encountering standard stories on the debilitating effects of the economic downturn or the dangers of slow and no growth. (3) These dangers are now so familiar to us that we sometimes forget to pay attention to them as we should. (4) We shrug at reports that money markets are quaking and that investors are losing the nerve to invest in any but the most conservative ventures. (5) We yawn at studies of consumers afraid of losing their jobs in the shrinking employment market, and we accept the conventional wisdom that they react by refusing to make big purchases. (6) We accept that manufacturers react in turn by cutting inventories and jobs, thus making their contribution to a vicious spiral of decline. (7) However much we may have learned to live with recession, we don't have to be geniuses or even economists to understand that recession is a complex set of domino effects that is incredibly difficult to reverse once it gets started.

Analysis of the Paragraph:

Function

The paragraph is *substantive* as far as a reader can determine without the context of the whole essay.

It deals with substantial ideas about recession.

Methods of Development

The principal method here is *cause and effect*.

There is also an element of *comparison* in sentence 1.

The writer illustrates the effects of recession with a number of specific *details* (see sentences 4, 5, and 6).

Theme or Unity

The paragraph focusses on this generation's response to the effects of the current recession.

Coherence

The topic sentence of this seven-sentence paragraph is sentence 2.

Sentence 1 establishes a comparison between recession and depression and makes a gesture toward comparison in its introduction of the paragraph.

Sentence 3 follows up on the topic sentence by suggesting that we do not regard recession with as much attention as we should.

Sentences 4, 5, and 6 examine the effects or consequences of recession and continue to emphasize our nonchalant attitudes toward them.

Sentence 7 recognizes that the causes and effects of recession are complex and long-lasting.

Patterns of Development

The paragraph moves from *general to specific* and from *abstract to concrete* as it develops from its opening generalizations about recession and our reactions to it, to more specific illustrations of these effects, to a closing observation that recession is complex and difficult to reverse.

Structural Coherence

Sentence 2 is linked to sentence 1 by "economic downturn" and "slow and no growth"—both synonyms for recession.

Sentence 3 repeats the key word "dangers" from sentence 2 and also begins with the demonstrative adjective (and transition) "these."

Sentence 4 repeats the pronoun "we" from sentence 3.

Sentences 5 and 6 are parallel to sentence 4: each begins with "we" plus a verb.

Sentence 7 repeats "we" and the key word "recession."

Emphasis

Nothing in the paragraph is strikingly emphatic; the tone is intended to be sober. But there is some appropriate emphasis.

Sentence 3 is shorter than the average and is therefore slightly sharper as it sets up the parallel of sentences 4, 5, and 6.

The parallelism of 4, 5, and 6 is itself emphatic.

Sentence 5 itself contains parallel independent clauses and is therefore additionally emphatic.

Sentence 7 is the longest in the paragraph, adding to the emphasis it has by being last.

The verbs "shrug" and "yawn" convey a little extra flavour, and the reference to "domino effects" in sentence 7 offers at least a touch of emphasis through its image.

Length and Development

The paragraph, with its seven sentences, can be said to be of average length, and its development is sufficient for its purposes.

Review Exercises, 61-67 Working with paragraphs

1. Compose topic sentences that will effectively begin paragraphs on *five* of the following:
   a. To explain to a ten-year-old how an internal combustion engine works
   b. To describe to the police a traffic accident you witnessed
   c. To tell a friend about your experience of seeing an accident happen
   d. To introduce an essay on the history of engines from steam to jet
   e. To recount an anecdote about one of your relatives in order to illustrate his or her character
   f. To describe your dream-house
   g. To analyze a particular short poem
   h. To explain why you are attending college or university
   i. To introduce a short essay about something important you learned on your last holiday abroad
   j. To explain what *beauty* means to you

2. Write paragraphs developing *two* of the topic sentences you composed for Exercise 1.

3. a. Identify and illustrate the patterns and methods of development you used in writing each of the paragraphs for Exercise 2.
   b. How did you ensure that your paragraphs are unified?
   c. Identify and illustrate the techniques you used to make your paragraphs coherent.
   d. What did you intend to achieve with your final sentence for each paragraph? How did you do it? Are your endings effective? If not, work on them until they are and then return to answer these questions.

4. Here are a dozen substantive paragraphs from essays written by students. They range in quality from good to poor. Analyze and evaluate each one (you may also wish to assign rankings to them). Consider specifically each of the principles discussed in the preceding pages:

> methods of development
> unity
> coherence (organization; placement and effectiveness of topic
>   sentences; patterns of development; effectiveness of endings;
>   devices of structural coherence)
> emphasis
> length and adequacy of development

and anything else you think relevant. For example, does a particular paragraph make a promise and then fulfill it? When you are through analyzing, evaluating, and criticizing, practise your own writing skills by revising at least the weaker paragraphs to get rid of their worst defects as paragraphs, and to make any other stylistic improvements you think are needed.

a.   Physical activity is good for people. It contributes greatly to a person's physical and mental well-being. The schedules of varsity teams are very demanding. The swim team has eleven practices a week, of which eight are mandatory—two a day, each an hour and a half in length. The workouts consist of approximately four thousand metres each. The program also consists of running, weight training, and flexibility exercises. Not only does this sort of exercise keep a person in good physical shape, but it also increases their mental awareness. Because you are up and active before classes begin, you are more mentally and physically awake than if you had just gotten out of bed.

b.   It was five generations ago when my paternal ancestors travelled from Czechoslovakia to London and then sailed to the New World. My grandfather finds great joy in telling us about these early settlers. It seems they were very happy to establish themselves in this new "land of opportunities." They were able to purchase a large amount of good farming land near a lake in northern Ontario. Soon others came to settle nearby, and my great-great-grandparents were an integral part of this Canadian community. And Grandpa tells us that it was he and his brothers who built the hydroelectric dam to provide the electricity for this growing village. My grandmother taught in the local schoolhouse, and their children sold garden vegetables and worked as housekeepers for the growing number of Americans who were building summer houses by the lake. I think that the feeling of inferiority from having to work for these rich Americans reinforced my forebears' strong sense of Canadianism. These feelings have been passed on to my generation.

c.   Besides having stronger hearts, well-conditioned runners tend to have slender bodies. Running will only help you lose weight if the food consumption is controlled. Losing weight and maintaining your new weight at the appropriate level, however, depends on the proper balance between your intake of calories and your expenditure of energy.

d.   The storyteller makes use of animal metaphors to describe an individual's character by naming him after the animal whose stereotyped personality he possesses. The importance of living creatures in folk tales is twofold. First, the folk tale is used to teach the tribe's children the significance of individual species; and second, the use of animal names suggests a great deal about a character's personality.

e.   A cold, wet, west-coast winter's day. I was weary from cursing all day. I was wet and exasperated. My crew-truck had spent most of the day on a precarious tilt with two wheels down a bank (someone had tried to turn it around for me); I had it coaxed back onto the road just by quitting time. Now, at day's end, I wallowed in the warmth of its heater while waiting for the crew.

f.   In order to have control over language, writers must understand the denotation and connotation of words. This understanding becomes particularly important when two words are similar in meaning but are not truly synonymous. If such similar but not synonymous words are carelessly handled, writers may grossly misuse them. This will have an adverse effect on the clarity of their work, and will probably mislead and confuse the reader. Misleading the reader is a pitfall to be avoided. This pitfall can only be avoided by a writer's understanding such words and using them carefully so as not to produce ambiguity.

g.   Although the words *ignorance* and *stupidity* are often used interchangeably, there is a difference between them. *Ignorance* is defined as lack of knowledge and *stupidity* is defined as lack of intelligence. To call a person ignorant implies that the person does not know all that is known or can be learned. To call a person stupid implies that the person lacks the ability to learn and know. The words are similar in that they both indicate a deficiency in knowledge or learning, but they differ in that one signifies a permanent condition and the other a condition that may be only temporary. Ignorant people can educate and inform themselves. Stupid people have a dullness of mind which it is difficult or impossible to change.

h.   I believe that Jean Piaget's research has clearly shown that games and rule-making contribute to child development. Children learn much about autonomy and democracy while testing the rules of games. In his early research he chose 1100 children along with the game of marbles to reach his conclusion. The choice of the game of marbles was a good one since it requires no referee and no adult supervision. It is played from early childhood to pre-teens. One six-year-old when asked who he thought had made the rules replied, "God, my father and the town council." At about eleven years children agree that they can change the rules themselves. Piaget has shown that the game of marbles provides a way for children to test the quality of rules and the necessity of rules.

i.   If you intend to go gold panning there are a certain number of items that should be included in your equipment. The most obvious is the gold pan. There are two types of gold pans. They are metal and plastic. Plastic pans are molded from tough space-age plastic. They are said to be better than metal pans because they don't rust and they are lighter. They also have small riffles formed in the plastic that effectively trap the gold. Metal pans are constructed from heavy gauge' steel and vary in size from six to sixteen inches in diameter.

j.   Everything looks beautiful from the saddle of my horse, especially on a crisp fall day. Even the autumn sun as it glints through the fretwork of golden poplar trees that border the road. The track ahead is muddy and well-trampled by many horses' feet. I can hear the clatter of hooves on the concrete, then the soft sucking sound of the mud as we gain momentum and move out to begin our ride. After we gain considerable speed, it happens. That wondrous sensation when horse and rider become one glorious moving body. I feel it now as my horse takes full rein while the blood surges and pounds in my ears and the wind frees my hair as it stings my face. Time ceases to exist here in a world of exhilarating revelation as I become giddy with pleasure. Tired, my horse slows down. The spell is broken. The sun has disappeared completely, and the wind is beginning to rise in bone-chilling forecast of the dreary winter days to come. I will be back again, soon.

k.   Many people are under the impression that the Driver Training Programs offered to sixteen- and seventeen-year-old students prepare them to be capable drivers. I found the program very useful, but then I was nearly eighteen when I received my licence. Some authorities on the subject believe that the programs give students a false sense of security—a very dangerous thing.

l.   Structurally, there are in the subject paragraph fourteen sentences of varying lengths; the shortest sentence, #12, has nine words, while the longest, #6, has fifty-two. The opening sentence contains twelve words, and from there on the sentences alternate from short to long through to the end of the paragraph. The paragraph ends, surprisingly, with another twelve-word sentence. The alternation or variance of sentence lengths helps to keep the paragraph interesting by keeping the rhythm varied and not letting tedious repetition set in.

---

68   Essays: Unity, Coherence, and Emphasis

The principles of composition apply with equal validity to the essay as a whole and to each of its parts: what holds true for the sentence and the paragraph also holds true for the essay as a whole.

68a   Unity

u   Like a sentence or a paragraph, an essay should be unified. That is, it should be about one subject, and everything in it should contribute to the elucidation of that subject. If your paragraphs are themselves unified, and if you make sure that the first sentence of each paragraph refers explicitly (or implicitly but unmistakably) to your overall subject (see #64a.1), then your essay itself will be unified.

68b Coherence

coh There should be coherence not only between words and between sentences, but also between paragraphs. If the beginning of each paragraph provides some kind of transition from the preceding paragraph, the essay will almost surely be coherent. The transitional words and phrases listed above (#65d) and others like them are often useful for establishing the necessary connections between paragraphs—but don't overdo it by slavishly using them to begin every paragraph. Often you can create the link by repeating a significant word or two from the preceding paragraph, usually from somewhere near its end, and sometimes you can make or strengthen the link with a demonstrative adjective, or even a pronoun (but see the **Cautionary Notes** in #65c). Of course there must be an inherent connection between one paragraph and the next—a function of the *unity* of an essay—or not even explicit transitions will be effective. (See also #64a, on topic sentences.)

68c Emphasis

emph Just as in a sentence or a paragraph (see #18a and #66), the most emphatic position in an essay is its ending, and the second most emphatic position is its beginning. That is why it is important to be clear and to the point at the beginning of an essay, usually stating the thesis explicitly (see #69-l.3), and why the ending of an essay should be forceful. Don't, for example, conclude with mere repetition of points you've just made. And since the last thing readers see is usually what sticks most vividly in their minds, essays often use climactic order, beginning with simple or less important points and ending with more important or complex ones (see #64b.2).

Further, the length of a paragraph automatically suggests something about the importance of its contents. Although a short, sharp paragraph can be emphatic in its own way, generally a long paragraph will deal with a relatively important part of the subject. As you look over your work, check to make sure you haven't skimped on an important point, and also that you haven't gone on for too long about a relatively minor point (see #67).

69 The Steps of Planning, Writing, and Revising an Essay

No effective essay can be a mere random assemblage of sentences and paragraphs. It must have a shape, a design, even if only a simple one.

How does one get from the zero of a blank mind to the desired finished product? By taking certain steps—because a piece of writing, like any other end product, is the result of a *process*. The nine steps that any writer must take, whether consciously or not, fall into three major stages:

Stage I: Planning
   Step 1. Finding a subject
   Step 2. Limiting the subject
   Step 3. Determining audience and purpose
   Step 4. Gathering data
   Step 5. Classifying and organizing the data
Stage II: Writing
   Step 6. Writing the first draft
Stage III: Revising
   Step 7. Revising
   Step 8. Preparing the final draft
   Step 9. Proofreading

Sometimes one or more steps may be obviated; for example if you are assigned a specific topic, steps 1 and 2, perhaps even 3, will already be taken care of. And often several parts of the process will be going on at the same time; for example there is often a good deal of interaction among the first five steps. Sometimes the order will be different; for example you may not be clear about your purpose until you have finished steps 4 and 5. And sometimes as late as step 7, revising, you may have to go back and rethink your purpose, or dig up more material, or even limit your topic further, or expand it. But all the steps have to happen somehow, somewhere, somewhen, for a finished piece of writing to be produced.

And even though some of these steps often occur automatically, relatively inexperienced writers should follow them rigorously and self-consciously, particularly if the projected essay is long or complicated, like a term paper or a research paper.

69a   Step 1: Finding a Subject

If a subject has not been assigned, you must find one for yourself. Some people think this is among the most difficult parts of writing an essay, but it needn't be, for subjects are all around us and within us. A few minutes free-associating with a pencil and a sheet of paper, jotting down and playing around with any ideas that pop into your head, will usually lead you at least to a subject area if not to a specific subject. Or look around you and let your mind wander over whatever comes into your field of vision. Or look out the window: What do you see? What does it mean? Or scan the pages of a magazine or newspaper to stimulate a train of thought; editorial and letters pages are usually full of interesting subjects to write about, perhaps to argue about. Or think about people: your immediate family and other relatives, your friends, or people you particularly dislike, or acquaintances with interesting cultures different from your own. Or think about your hobbies or favourite sports, or about your academic pursuits, or about your travels, or simply about some of the little things you do every day and why you do them. The possibilities are almost endless.

Obviously, try to find a subject that interests you, one that you will enjoy working with. Do not, in desperation, pick a subject that bores you, for then you may well handle it poorly, and probably bore your readers as well. If, on the other hand, you are assigned a topic that doesn't particularly interest you, try to make it a learning experience: immerse yourself in it; you may be surprised at how interesting it can become.

69b   Step 2: Limiting the Subject

Once you have a subject, limit it: narrow it to a topic that you can develop adequately within the length of essay you want or have been asked to write. More often than not, people start with subjects that are too big to handle except with broad generalizations. Seldom do they come up, right off the bat, with a topic like what people's toothbrushing habits reveal about their characters, or the dominant image cluster in a particular short story, or the inefficiency of the library building; they're more likely to start with some vague notion about personal hygiene, or how enjoyable the story was, or campus architecture. To save both time and energy, to avoid frustration, and to guarantee a better essay, be merciless with yourself at this stage. If anything, overdo the narrowing, for at a later stage it's easier to broaden than it is to cut.

For example you might decide you want to write about "animals"; but that's obviously far too broad. "Domestic animals" or "wild animals" is narrower, but still too broad. "Farm animals," perhaps, or "farm animals I have known"? Better, but still too large, for where would you begin? How thorough could you be in a mere 500 or even 1000 words? When you find yourself narrowing your subject to something like "Homer, the spoiled pig on my uncle's farm" or "my pet dachshund, Rex" or "why I don't own a cat" or "the experience of living next door to a noisy dog" or "the day Dobbin kicked the barn door down"—then you can with some confidence look forward to developing your topic with sufficient thoroughness and specificity. (See also #54.)

Exercise 69ab   Finding and limiting subjects

List ten broad subject areas that you have some interest in. Then, for each, specify two narrowed topics, (a) one that would be suitable for an essay of about 1500 words (six double-spaced typed pages) and (b) one for an essay of about 500 words. (Feel free to list more than two topics if you wish.)

Examples: Clothing. (a) Campus fashions.   (b) My closet.
How to dress for   Ten uses for a pair
winter hiking.   of old socks.

69c

Nature.	(a)	Why we need	(b)	My pet cactus.
		more parks.		How to build a
		Water imagery in		simple bird-feeder.
		a sonnet.		

69c   Step 3: Determining Audience and Purpose

1. *Audience*

You write a personal letter to a specific reader. If you write a "Letter to the Editor" of a newspaper, you have only a vague notion of your potential readership—namely anyone who reads that newspaper; but you will know where almost all of them live, and knowing only that much could give you something to aim at in your letter; and of course you'll know what they've been reading. The more of a handle you can get on your audience, the better you can control your writing to make it effective for that audience. Always try to define or characterize your audience for a given piece of writing as precisely and specifically as possible.

Much of the writing you do for school may have only one reader: the teacher. But some assignments may ask you to address—or pretend to address—some specific audience. And sometimes teachers ask students to write "for an audience of your peers." In the absence of any other guideline, that's not a bad rule of thumb: write for your classmates, or perhaps for some imaginary student who will occupy your seat or live in your room next year. Sometimes teachers read out or distribute students' work to other students; even if they don't, when they read and criticize your work they may think of themselves as reading over your shoulder, so to speak, or as playing the role of editor.

2. *Purpose*

All writing has the broad purpose of communicating ideas. And in school you write for the special purpose of demonstrating your ability and your knowledge to your teacher. But you'll be able to write more effectively if you think of each essay as having one of three primary rhetorical purposes:

- (a) to inform
- (b) to convince or persuade
- (c) to entertain

Few essays, however, are so single-minded as to have only one of these purposes. For example a set of instructions will have the primary purpose of informing readers how to do something, but it may also be trying to convince them that this is the right or best way to do it. And in order to interest them more, it may also be written entertainingly. An analysis of a poem may seem to be pure exposition, explaining how the poem works and what it means, but at least implicitly it will also be trying to persuade readers that this interpretation is the correct one. An argument will necessarily include exposition. An entertaining or even whimsical piece may well have a satiric thrust or some kind of implicit "lesson." And so on. Usually one of the three purposes will dominate, but one or both of the others will often be present as well. (And see #70 below, on writing arguments.)

The clearer your idea of just what you want to do in an essay, and why, and for whom, the better you will be able to make effective rhetorical choices. You may even want to begin by writing down, as a memo to yourself, a detailed description or "profile" of your audience and as clear a statement of your purpose as you can formulate, and tape it to the wall over your desk. If your ideas become clearer as the work proceeds, you can refine these statements. In any event, as you go through the process of writing, never take your mental eyes off your *audience* and your *purpose*.

Exercise 69c **Thinking about audience and purpose**

Choose some fairly simple and personal subject (for example your typical day at school, the state of your finances, your best or worst class, how different university is from high school, why you need a computer, your athletic ambitions). Write two letters on the topic (300-500 words for each) to two distinctly different kinds of people—for example different in age, background, education, philosophy of life, closeness of acquaintance with you. In an accompanying paragraph, briefly account for the differences between your two letters. Did your purpose change when you changed audiences?

69d Step 4: Gathering Data

An essay can't survive on just vague generalizations and unsupported statements and opinions; it must contain specifics—facts, details, particulars. Whatever your subject, you must gather material somewhere, by reading, talking to others, or—especially if the subject draws on your personal experience—simply thinking about it. And don't stop when you think you have enough; collect as much information as you can, even two or three times what you can use, for then you can *select* the best and discard the rest.

1. *Brainstorming*

If you are expected to generate material from your own knowledge and experience (instead of doing formal research), you may at first think of yourself as hard-up for ideas. But you're not. Sit down with a pencil and a sheet of paper, write your topic in the centre or at the top, and begin jotting down ideas. Put down everything that comes into your head about it. Let your mind run fast and free. Don't bother with sentences, don't worry about spelling, don't even pause to wonder whether the words and phrases are going to be of any use. Just keep scribbling. It shouldn't be long before you've filled the sheet with possible ideas, questions, facts, details, names, examples. You may even need to use a second sheet.

It may help if you also brainstorm your larger subject area, not just the narrowed topic, since some of the broader ideas could prove useful.

2. Using Questions

Another way to generate material: ask yourself questions about your subject or topic and write down the answers. Start with the reporter's standard questions—Who? What? Where? When? Why? How?—and go on from there with more of your own: What is it? Who is associated with it? In what way? Where and when is it, or was it, or will it be? How does it work? Why is it? What causes it? What does it cause? What are its parts? What is it a part of? Is it part of a process? What does it look like? What colour is it? What is it like or unlike? What is its opposite? What if it didn't exist? Is it good, or bad? Such questions and the answers you get will make you think of more questions, and so on; soon you'll have more than enough potentially useful material.

You may even find yourself writing consecutive sentences—beginning, that is, to *develop* your points—since some questions prompt certain kinds of responses. For example, asking *What is it?* may lead you to begin defining your subject; *What is it like or unlike?* may lead you to begin comparing and contrasting it, classifying it, thinking of analogies and metaphors; *What causes it?* and *What does it cause?* may lead you to begin exploring cause-and-effect relations; *What are its parts?* or *What is it made of?* could lead you to analyze your subject; *How does it work?* or *Is it part of a process?* may prompt you to analyze and explain a process.

Exercise 69d Generating material

Using two of your narrowed topics from Exercise 69ab, brainstorm them and bombard them with questions to see how much material you can generate. Then try the same techniques with the larger subjects to see if that will yield any additional useful material. You might also want to try getting together with one or two friends or classmates and bouncing ideas and questions off one another.

69e Step 5: Classifying and Organizing the Data

1. Classifying

As you brainstorm a subject and jot down notes and answers, you'll begin to see connections between one idea and another and start putting them in groups or drawing circles around them and lines and arrows between them. When you have finished gathering material, finish this job of classification. You should soon find yourself with several groups of related items, which means that you will have classified your material according to some principle which arose naturally from it. During this part of the process you will probably also have discarded the weaker or less relevant details, keeping only those which best suit the subject as it is now beginning to take shape; that is, you will have selected the best.

For a tightly limited subject and a short essay, you may have only one group of details; but for an essay of even moderate length, say 750 words or more, you will probably have several groups.

> **Caution:** Try to classify your material in such a way that you end up with several groups or parts—but not more than six or seven: an essay with more than seven parts risks being unwieldy for both writer and reader. Similarly, an organization of only two parts risks falling into two large lumps, sometimes referred to as a "broken-backed" essay; if your material calls for organizing into only two parts, take extra care to ensure that the whole is unified and coherent.

2. *Organizing*

Now put the classified groups into some kind of order. Don't accept the first arrangement that comes to mind; consider as many different arrangements as the material will allow, and then select the best one. (For the most common kinds of order, see the *Patterns of Development* in #64b.2.) And don't simply let things line up by chance, for the order should appear necessary rather than accidental or arbitrary. Ideally, the groups and their details should speak to you, as it were, demanding to be arranged in a particular way because it is the most effective way.

Exercise 69e   Classifying and organizing data

Use the material you generated for the two topics in Exercise 69d. Classify each mass into groups of related items and arrange each set of groups into the best kind of order you can think of for them. In a few sentences, explain why you chose each particular order. Try also to justify them in terms of your audience and purpose.

69f-j   Outlining

69f   The Thesis Statement and the Outline

The last part of the planning or "pre-writing" stage is the formulation of a **thesis statement** and the construction of an **outline**.

During the first four steps you gradually increase your control over your proposed essay: you find and narrow a subject, you think about audience and purpose, you gather data and generate ideas, and you classify and arrange your material. At some point while you are doing all this—certainly by the time you finish it—you should have formulated at least a tentative thesis, a statement that identifies your subject and points the way to what you want to say about it.

This *thesis statement* or *thesis sentence* performs the same function for an outline that a *topic sentence* does for a paragraph. It leads off the outline, the ordered groups become *main headings* with roman numerals, and the details that make up each group, if they aren't simply absorbed by the main heading, become subdivisions of it in various levels of *subheadings*. And though tentative sketches of a possible beginning and ending aren't essential to an outline, it's usually worth trying to think of something of the sort at this stage; you can easily change them later if you think of something better. Here is an example, a student's outline for a short essay:

Thesis Statement: I see three main reasons for the increasing popularity of ceramics as a hobby.

Beginning: With more time available, many people are taking up creative arts and crafts. Ceramics is becoming one of the more popular such hobbies. Why?

   I. Relatively easy to learn
      A. No natural "artistic" ability needed
      B. Patience and determination needed
      C. Not expensive
  II. Practicality
      A. Useful household items
      B. Decorative items
      C. Useful as gifts
 III. Psychological benefits
      A. Outlet for creativity
      B. Self-satisfaction, accomplishment
      C. Escape from frustrations of daily grind

Ending: Have you got a few new-found leisure hours each week? Maybe you too would enjoy pottering about with ceramics.

Note the layout of an outline: numerals and letters are followed by periods and a space or two; subheadings are indented at least two spaces past the beginning of the first word of a main heading. Few outlines will need to go beyond one or two levels of subheading (see #69j.5), but if further subdivision is necessary, here is the the correct way to indicate successive levels:

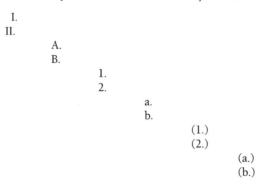

69g The Importance of Outlining

Don't make the mistake of thinking that outlining is mere busy-work, a waste of time and effort. If you draw up a required outline *after* you've written an essay, then indeed you waste time and effort, for such an outline will help you only if it reveals some structural malformation in your essay and forces you to go back and rewrite it—which means you've wasted time and effort.

A conscientious outline drawn up *before* you write an essay will usually save you both time and effort. Writing the draft will be easier and smoother because it follows a plan: you know where you're going. You can avoid such pitfalls as unnecessary repetition, digression, and awkward, illogical, or otherwise incoherent organization. You should no more start writing an essay without an outline than you would take a trip into unfamiliar territory without a good map. An outline keeps the traveller from taking wrong turns, wandering in circles, or getting lost altogether.

Keep in mind too that an outline is not a straitjacket. If as you write and revise you think of a better way to organize a part of your essay, or if some part of the outline proves clumsy when you try to set it down in paragraphs, or if you suddenly think of some new material that should be included, by all means do what you think best and revise your outline accordingly. You may even need to refine your thesis statement in order to reflect changes in your ideas. The virtue of an outline in any such instance is that rather than drifting about rudderless, you are in complete control of any changes you make because you make them consciously and carefully—and you will also have a record of them if you want to recheck them later.

69h Kinds of Outlines

Except perhaps for instinctive geniuses and people with exceptionally good luck, outlining of some kind is necessary for a good essay. The more complicated the essay, the more important the outline. A short, relatively simple essay can sometimes be outlined in your head or with a few informal jottings; but even a short essay is usually easier to write if you've made a formal outline first.

The method of outlining you use may be your own choice or it may be dictated by your instructor or by the nature of a project. Some people like the *topic outline* with its brief headings and subheadings, as in the example above (#69f). Sometimes a *paragraph outline* will work well, one that simply lists the proposed topic or opening sentences of the successive paragraphs that will eventually form the essay. But the one kind of outline that consistently recommends itself is the *sentence outline*, for it is virtually foolproof.

69i   Sentence Outlines

Since every entry in a sentence outline is a complete sentence, it is impossible to fool yourself into thinking you have something to say when in fact you don't. For example, imagine you are planning an essay on various cuisines and, in a topic outline, you put down the heading "Chinese food." But if you lack experience of Chinese food, you might find when you sit down to write your draft that you have little or nothing to say about it. In a sentence outline, you will be forced to make a statement about it, perhaps something like "Although Chinese food sometimes seems strange to Western tastes, it never fails to be interesting." With even such a vague sentence before you, you can more easily begin supplying details to develop your idea; the act of formulating the sentence guarantees that you have at least some ideas about whatever you put down.

Another virtue of a sentence outline is that, when properly handled, it is self-constructing. In a topic or other relatively informal outline, the thesis statement should set up or contain the main headings—either implicitly, as in the example in #69f, or explicitly, as in the example below. In a sentence outline the headings and subheadings work the same way. For example, "Although Chinese food sometimes seems strange to Western tastes, it never fails to be interesting" automatically leads into two subheadings: "A. Chinese food sometimes seems strange to Western tastes," and "B. Chinese food never fails to be interesting." (Such partial repetition is natural to a good sentence outline; it may seem stiff and clumsy, but it is a strength, since it fosters coherence and unity within each part of an essay and in an essay as a whole.)

As an illustration, here is a student's sentence outline:

Thesis Statement: Three major causes of the Russian Revolution were the Great War, poor working conditions, and the influence of political groups.

Beginning: No doubt many contributing factors helped bring about one of the twentieth century's major historical events, the Russian Revolution of 1917. In retrospect, however, three important ones seem to stand out.

I. The Russian Revolution was partly caused by the First World War's great destruction of life and by its hampering of industrial modernization.
   A. The war caused widespread death and disillusionment.
   B. The war impeded any steps by industry toward modernization.

II. Poor working conditions, both past and present, contributed to the Russian Revolution.
   A. The poor working conditions that led to Bloody Sunday and the 1905 Revolution caused a resentment that was still smouldering in 1917.
   B. Lack of reasonable concessions in working conditions, such as an eight-hour day, caused resentment among the working class.

III. The Russian Revolution was precipitated by the two-fold actions of influential political groups.

    A. Political groups stirred up the working class, playing on their disaffection and resentment.

    B. Political groups provided the leadership to coordinate the actions of the enraged masses.

Ending: (Perhaps summarize main events and point to some of the historic repercussions of it all. Has the rest of the world learned anything from its understanding of these events?)

See also the outline for the sample research essay, #79.

69j   Constructing Sentence Outlines

To put together a good sentence outline, follow these rules:

1. Make every item from the thesis statement down to the last sub-subheading a single complete major sentence.

2. Use only simple or complex sentences; do not use compound sentences. Since the independent clauses of a compound sentence could themselves be written as separate sentences, it may mean that two or more headings are masquerading as one. If you find yourself writing a compound sentence, try to rephrase it; if you can't comfortably convert it to simple or complex, rethink the point: some reorganization or other revision is probably necessary.

> **Note:** Although questions can be rhetorically effective in an essay, avoid interrogative sentences in an outline; they seldom lend themselves to the requirements of a tightly structured outline.

3. In any kind of outline you must supply at least two subheadings if you supply any at all; a heading cannot be subdivided into only one part. If under *I* you have an *A* then you must also have at least a *B*; if you have a *1* you must also have at least a *2*, and so on. If you find yourself unable to go beyond one subheading, it probably isn't a subdivision at all but an integral part of the main heading, and should be incorporated into it.

4. The headings or subheadings at each level should be reasonably parallel with each other; that is, I, II, III, etc. should have about the same level of importance, as should subheadings A, B, C, etc. under a given main heading, and 1, 2, 3, etc. under each of these. One way to help achieve this balance is to make the sentences at any given level as much as possible syntactically parallel—that is, the same kinds of sentences and sentence patterns. (A and B under I should be parallel, but an A and B under II or III need not be parallel with those under I—though they may well be.)

> **Note:** As with the major parts of an essay, having more than six or seven subheadings under any one heading risks being unwieldy.

5. Few outlines need to go beyond one level of subheading. If an essay is unusually long or complicated, you may find it helpful or necessary to break things down to a second or even third level of subheading. But remember that headings and subheadings should mostly state ideas, propositions, generalizations; the supporting facts can be supplied at the writing stage. If you find yourself including several levels of subheading, you may already be at the level of facts and details; although this is not necessarily wrong, it can be wasteful (you may find yourself thinking of different details when you actually begin writing), and it can lure a writer into producing a mechanical-sounding essay.

> **Caution:** Whatever kind of outline you use, don't label the first main heading (roman numeral I) "Introduction" or the last one "Conclusion." By definition, introductions and conclusions are not substantive parts of an essay. If you include them as numbered parts of an outline, you may be misled about what constitutes the actual body of your material.
>
> In fact, try not to think of "Introductions" and "Conclusions" as parts of an essay. If you acquire the habit of calling them "Beginnings" and "Endings" instead, you will more easily avoid writing a stiff paragraph of "introduction" simply because you think it's called for, or starting a final paragraph with the almost always unnecessarily stiff phrase "In conclusion."

Exercise 69f-j(1)   Writing thesis statements and outlines

Return to the two topics you've been working with from Exercise 69ab through 69e. If you haven't already done so, formulate a thesis statement for each topic. Make each a single simple or complex sentence. Try to compose the sentences in such a way that each foreshadows the major divisions of the outline to come. Then construct the two outlines. Make at least one of them a sentence outline. Include a statement of audience and purpose with each outline.

Exercise 69f-j(2)   Revising weak outlines

One of the most important functions of an outline is to let you see a graphic representation of a projected essay so that before you begin drafting the essay you can catch and correct structural and other flaws (repetition, overlap, illogical organization, introductory material masquerading as part of the body, inadequate thesis statements, subheadings that aren't really subdivisions, and so on). Here are some outlines drafted by students for possible essays. Analyze them critically; pretend that they are your own and that you'll have to try to write essays based on them. Detect their flaws, both major and minor, and then try to revise each so that it could guide you through the first draft of an essay. Do any of them seem simply unworkable, unsalvageable? If so, why?

(1) *Thesis Statement:* Natural greenery is necessary for recreation, to relieve monotony, to provide aesthetic value, and it is also an important life-sustainer.

   I. Natural greenery for recreation is necessary in that it is essential to enable us to have fields, playgrounds, and parks.

   II. To relieve monotony natural surroundings are important in that they take you away from the tensions of the city, away from all the cement-gray colour, and offer you an isolated island away from people.

   III. In all its beauty natural greenery may be looked upon as having aesthetic value in such things as parks, gardens, and scenery.

   IV. As a life-sustainer greenery is important in providing oxygen, vegetation, and materials for food and shelter.

(2) *Thesis Statement:* Reading is a creative exercise for the imagination.

   I. Reading forces people to visualize settings of stories.

   II. Reading forces people to visualize the appearance of characters.

   III. Some plots force people to imagine the endings of stories or to fill in missing parts of stories.

   IV. Science-fiction stories provide people with inspiration that allows their imaginations to wander.

(3) *Thesis Statement:* Why disadvantaged children have low achievement in school.

   I. Poverty's effects on physical growth.

   II. Little opportunity to learn appropriate roles right from infancy.

   III. Lack of linguistic stimulation.

   IV. Not enough help from society.

(4) *Thesis Statement:* Getting involved, meeting people, and travelling are a few benefits of playing high-school basketball.

   I. Playing basketball helps you to get more involved in your school.

   II. It is quite easy to meet people while on the basketball team.

   III. One of the main benefits is the chance to travel and see other schools.

(5) *Thesis Statement:* The effects of television on our lives.

   I. There are too many shows pertaining to sex and violence on television.

       A. Many shows on TV lead people to accept violence as a way of life.

       B. Children are left to formulate their own opinions on sex.

   II. Many people centre their entire lives on TV.

   III. Advertising on TV disillusions people.

       A. Most ads deceive people into buying things they don't need.

   IV. There are some good educational shows on TV.

(6) *Thesis Statement:* Stress is a problem in university that must be dealt with.

   I. Different types of stress and what causes them.

       A. Unhealthy: stress overload, too much work, not enough rest, bad nutrition.

    B. Healthy stress levels: small amounts of pressure, beneficial to some extent, help one learn and grow.

    C. Emotional: family problems, love problems, depression, loneliness, unable to concentrate.

    D. Physical: work too hard, overdoing it, too much pressure, health problems.

  II. Problems that arise with stress.

    A. Sustained stress: heart attacks, health problems.

    B. Common symptoms: ulcers, insomnia, irritability, sweaty or clammy hands, fidgetiness, higher pulse rate.

 III. Treatments: How to cope.

    A. Physical: relax, read, take up a hobby, watch TV, do something relaxing.

    B. Emotional: relax mind, meditation, exercise.

    C. Serious stress: psychotherapy, counselling, get mind away from problems.

(7) *Thesis Statement:* Cross-country is a sport which requires a lot of endurance, will-power, and speed.

   I. Cross-country is a sport which requires a lot of practice.

  II. One needs a lot of will-power and concentration in order to run a very long distance.

 III. The weather can influence the pace of the runner.

(8) *Thesis Statement:* Traditional religious beliefs play a major role in African life.

   I. The religions are based on animism, the belief that everything has a spirit.

    A. The spirits can have an effect on human life.

      1. The effect can be good.

      2. The effect can be bad.

    B. The spirits of dead ancestors are believed to have great influence on the living.

  II. Many tribes keep a witch doctor and a sorcerer in the village.

    A. The witch doctors and sorcerers protect the people from evil spirits.

    B. The witch doctors protect the land from evil spirits.

 III. Colourful religious ceremonies are performed.

    A. Dancing and feasting are performed to please the spirits.

    B. Dancing and feasting are performed to promote the welfare of the tribe.

(9) *Thesis Statement:* Raising a litter of six cairn terriers is a learning experience!

   I. The pre-whelp period is a time of preparation for both the bitch and her owner.

  II. The actual birth never fails to awaken a sense of wonder at the miracle of life.

 III. As the puppies grow, the work-load of their care increases.

 IV. Happy, healthy puppies are fun to have: in caring for them, one learns many things.

(10)   I. Introduction: running has been around since the time of the caveman.
      II. Benefits
         A. Cardiovascular system
            1. Builds up the heart, reduces heart attacks
            2. Nausea, dizziness
            3. Increases stamina: muscles, breathing
            4. Pulse rate
         B. Psychological effects
            1. Reduce bad habits
               a. Decreases urge to smoke and drink
            2. Relieve tension; clears the head; expands consciousness
            3. Enjoying fresh air
            4. Sense of accomplishment
         C. Weight control
     III. Before and after a run: to avoid injuries, preparation is important, as is slow return to normal
         A. Warming up
         B. Cooling down (slow jogging, walking, mild calisthenics) to avoid dizziness, nausea, cramps
         C. Stretching exercises
     IV. Conclusion: running will continue, and grow in popularity.

When you have finished working on these outlines, go back and examine your own two outlines from the preceding exercise. Do you see any possible weak spots in them? If necessary, revise them.

Can you think of some possible titles for these potential essays—both these others and your own? Try.

Exercise 69f-j(3)   **Constructing and using outlines**

Construct outlines for proposed essays on three of the following:

1. The pros and cons of keeping dogs, cats, birds, fish, or other animals as pets.
2. The methods used by politicians to influence voters.
3. The state of freedom of speech in Canada.
4. How to cook your favourite dish.
5. Your favourite winter sport.
6. The importance of good manners.
7. The pros and cons of minority government.
8. "Why I plan to be a _____."
9. Last year's popular music.
10. How to be lazy.

Check your outlines carefully for any weaknesses, and revise them as necessary.

69k   Step 6: Writing the First Draft

With a good outline to follow, the work of drafting may seem little more than supplying transitions between paragraphs and parts. But the point is that with the shape of the whole laid out, one can concentrate on the real job of writing: finding the right words, generating the right kinds of sentences, and constructing good paragraphs.

Notes:
(1) Sometimes a main heading and its subheading from the outline will become a single paragraph in the essay; sometimes each subheading will become a paragraph; and so on. The nature and density of your material will determine its treatment.
(2) It may be possible to transfer the thesis statement to the essay unchanged, but more likely you will want to change it to fit the style of the essay. The requirements of the outline may well have demanded a stiffish statement that would be inappropriate in the essay itself.

69-1 Notes On Beginnings

1. *Postponing the Beginning*

Starting the actual writing can be a problem: most writers have had the experience of staring at a blank sheet of paper or computer screen for an uncomfortable length of time, trying to think of a good way to begin. If you have no beginning in mind at this point, don't waste time trying to think of one. Plunge right into the body of the essay and write it as rapidly as you can. When the first draft is finished, you'll know exactly what you have written—and therefore what it is that needs to be introduced; you can then go back and do the beginning with relative ease. In fact, writers who write a beginning first often discard the original version and write a new one, either because the essay that finally took shape demands a different kind of beginning, or simply because while in the heat of composition they thought of a better one.

2. *Beginning Directly*

Just as it isn't a good idea to begin a final paragraph with "In conclusion," so it's generally not good practice to open with something like "In this essay I will discuss" or "This essay is concerned with." Don't talk about yourself and your essay; talk about your topic. Rather than begin by informing readers of what you are going to say (and then at the end reminding them of what you have said), start with something substantial and if possible attention-getting (and end with something similarly sharp and definitive). Occasionally, however, when an essay is unusually long or complicated, it can be helpful to explain in advance, to provide readers with what amounts to a brief outline (just as it is then often necessary to provide some summary by way of conclusion).

3. *Subject and Thesis*

However you begin, it is always necessary to identify your subject, and usually also to state your thesis, somewhere at or near the beginning—almost never later than the first paragraph. For example, even if your title is something like "Imagery in Donne's 'The Flea,' " you must still, preferably in your first sentence, mention both the author and the title of the poem. The title of your essay is not a part of its content; the essay must be able to stand on its own.

Special circumstances may on occasion dictate delaying the full statement of a thesis to near the end, for example as part of a strategy of building to a climax—though you will probably provide at least some indication of your thesis near the beginning, perhaps in general terms. Or sometimes a thesis can be broken into several parts to be stated at intervals in the course of an essay. Or you may want to be mysterious or otherwise suspenseful. But be careful: such intentions may easily backfire. Readers generally don't like being kept in the dark. (See also #70d.2.)

4. *Direct, Smooth, Economical: Some Examples*

Begin as directly, smoothly, and economically as you can. Here for example are three ways an essay with the title "Imagery in Donne's 'The Flea' " might begin; note how differences in order, punctuation, and wording make each succeeding one better than the one before:

1. In the poem "The Flea," by John Donne, there is a great deal of imagery.
2. John Donne, in his poem "The Flea," uses imagery to . . . .
3. The imagery in John Donne's "The Flea" . . . .

Here is the beginning of an essay on one of Shakespeare's sonnets. The writer can't seem to get the engine warmed up:

> William Shakespeare, famous English poet and writer of plays, has always been known for the way he uses imagery to convey the point he is making in a particular piece of work. Shakespeare's Sonnet 65 is no exception to this, and this is one of the better examples of his work that I have studied, for illustrating his use of imagery.
>
> The best example in the sonnet comes in lines four and six, where Shakespeare compares a "summer's honey breath" and a "wrackful siege of battering days."

Compare this with another student's beginning on the same topic:

> Shakespeare's Sonnet 65 expresses its meaning through imagery. The poet appeals to a person's knowledge of visible properties in nature in an attempt to explain invisible properties of love and time.

Rather than vacillating as the first writer has done, this writer has taken control of the material immediately. Even though no particular image has yet been mentioned, the second writer, in two crisp sentences, is far beyond where the first writer still is, though well into a second paragraph.

Here is another example of a weak beginning. That the writer was in difficulty is shown by the jargon, awkwardness, and poor usage in the first sentence, the cliché and the illogicality in the second sentence, and the vague reference and wordy emptiness of the third:

> With all aspects considered, a person's graduating year from high school is a very unique experience. It is filled with a seemingly endless variety of memories, dreams, and emotions. I would imagine this is experienced by almost everyone and I most certainly am not an exception.

The writer's own revision proves that the difficulties were merely the result of floundering, trying too hard to make a beginning; had the beginning been written after the essay was otherwise complete, it might have taken this form in the first place:

> There are few things in life that can match the significance of one's high-school graduation year. At least that is the way it seems soon after one completes it.

Exercise 69-1 Evaluating beginnings

Here are five beginnings from student essays; the last two are on the same topic and were written in class. Which ones are good and which ones are weak? Point out the contrasting characteristics that enable you to evaluate them relative to each other.

(1)   Five months of backpacking left me tired, dirty, and eager for a nice fresh bed. But my backpack and I would take just one more night train, to see and experience just one more city. One of Europe's best, they told me. And this thought was far more thrilling than taking a hot shower.
West Berlin. A city on its own. . . .

(2)   Problems relating to a society affect all its inhabitants; hence, all its inhabitants must take part in curing society's ills. I find that society is plagued by problems such as degenerating slums, growing unemployment, and increasing racism. Cultural conflicts have been the root of most of our problems; thus, if the situation is to improve, some changes must occur.

(3)   For many people, their first thought after the ring of the alarm clock is of a steaming cup of coffee. Their stumble to the kitchen for this pick-me-up blends with their dreams. The sleepy eyes that measure out the fragrant brown granules flick open after their owners have savoured that first morning cup of coffee. After a strong cup of coffee, most people perform physical and mental tasks at the peak of their ability.
The reason is caffeine.

(4)   The poem, "To an Athlete Dying Young," written by A. E. Housman, structurally contains different periods of time in its stanzas. The different stanzas refer to different times. The rhythm of the poem is

not uniform in beat. However, it has a consistent rhyme scheme. This poem is also an example of a dramatic monologue.

(5)   "Quit while you're ahead" may be an old and worn-out saying, but it aptly applies to A. E. Housman's poem "To an Athlete Dying Young." In this dramatic monologue the speaker seizes upon this idea as a means of consoling the athlete, or those who mourn him. Beauty and victory are fleeting. Not only does the eternal passing of time always bring change, but once our "peak" has been reached, there is no place to go but down. Rather than growing old and watching new athletes break his records, the young athlete in the poem dies at an early age. His victory garland is preserved, "unwithered," by death.

69m-o The Final Steps

The product of rapid composition is a first draft. Although some first drafts may come very close to being acceptable finished products, don't gamble on it. There are three more steps to be taken before you should consider an essay finished: *Revising*, *Preparing the Final Draft*, and *Proofreading*.

69m Step 7: Revising

Revision (re-vision, literally "scrutinizing again") is an extremely important stage of writing, far too often neglected by inexperienced or weak writers. And don't assume that giving your draft a quick once-over is enough. Writers who care at all about the quality of their work revise a piece of writing at least two or three times. Many writers revise five or even ten or more times before they consider it finished. In fact, the process of revision could be said to be never-ending, for one can almost always find something that can be changed for the better.

Revise carefully, slowly, looking for any way to improve what you've written. Don't aim just to correct errors made in haste, but also to improve diction, sentence structure, punctuation, coherence, paragraphing, and so on. Some writers find that going through a draft for one thing at a time is effective—for example, going through it looking only at paragraphing, then going through it again looking only at sentences, then at punctuation, then at diction, and so on. Weaker writers should discipline themselves to revise in this careful way, concentrating on one thing at a time. And of course be particularly careful with matters you know to be potential weak spots in your writing.

Pretend that you are a hypercritical reader looking for weaknesses and errors. In order to do this effectively, try to allow yourself a cooling-off period; wait as long as possible between the drafting and the revising—at least two or three days—so that you can look at your own work with more objectivity.

You should find the *Omnibus Checklist* (Chapter XII) helpful during your revisions.

69n   Step 8: Preparing the Final Draft

When you are through revising a piece of writing, carefully prepare the final draft, the one that will be presented to your reader or readers. Once the work is out of your hands it's too late to change anything; make sure it's in good shape when it leaves your hands. It should be neat, and it should be in the appropriate format for the kind of writing it is. For most of your academic writing, follow carefully the *Manuscript Conventions* listed and discussed in #45.

69o   Step 9: Proofreading

Proofreading will have been taking place during revision, of course, and perhaps even during drafting; but when what you consider to be the final copy of your essay is ready, go over it yet again. Rarely will this final proofreading not prove worthwhile, for despite earlier careful scrutiny, you will probably discover not only typographical errors but also hitherto unnoticed errors in spelling, punctuation, or grammar.

Do your proofreading with exaggerated care. Read each sentence, as a sentence, SLOWLY; but also read each word as a word; check each punctuation mark, and consider the possibility of adding some or removing some or changing some. Particularly when you proofread for spelling errors, do so as a separate process, and do it by starting at the end and reading, one word at a time, backward, so that you won't get caught up in the flow of a sentence and overlook an error.

And do NOT put full trust in any of the spelling, grammar, and style checks that are part of or designed to be used with word-processing programs. They can't possibly cover all the matters that need attending to; even the spelling checks can't spot a carelessly misspelled word that happens to be the same as some other correctly spelled word—for example, leave the *r* out of *through* and you have *though*; nor can they tell you that you've mistaken, say, *discrete* for *discreet*.

70   Argument: Writing to Convince or Persuade

Most of the principles of composition are even more important in argument than in other kinds of writing—though as we imply earlier (#69c.2), other kinds of writing, especially exposition, often include an element of argumentation. But when your principal purpose is to convince or persuade—when you are writing what can be called an *argument*—there are several additional points and principles to keep in mind. Here are some brief suggestions and some practical advice to help you write effective arguments. (See also **convince, persuade** in #60.)

70a Subject

When you are focussing on your subject for an argumentative essay, keep in mind that there is no point in arguing about easily verifiable facts or generally accepted assumptions (2+2=4; the sky looks blue; good nutrition promotes good health; oil is a nonrenewable energy source). One cannot argue about facts, only about what the facts mean. Various political parties might well differ in the way they interpret election results, but not about the results themselves. But since an argument depends on logical reasoning, when you argue about opinions based on facts you will necessarily use factual data to support your contentions. A collection of unsupported opinions is not an argument but merely a series of assertions.

Similarly, one cannot logically argue about matters of taste. You can't argue that blue is a prettier colour than green; you can only assert that *you* find it prettier, perhaps because of some childhood association.

The subject of an argument must be something that is supposedly capable of verification, though the fact that it is being argued about at all indicates that its verification is not easy or to be taken for granted.

70b Audience

When your *purpose* is to convince or persuade, your knowledge of your *audience* and your constant awareness of that audience are crucial. Consider for example how differently you would have to handle your material and your tone depending on whether you were writing to an audience of (a) people who are basically sympathetic to your position, (b) people who are entirely neutral, or (c) people who are likely to be hostile to your position. Since the effectiveness of an argument depends partly on your gaining and holding the confidence of your readers, or at least getting them to listen to you willingly and with a reasonably open mind, it is vital that you avoid anything that might put them off.

Know your audience. Are your readers largely men? women? elderly? young? well-educated? middle-class? business people? students? politically conservative? "green"? wealthy? poor? artistic? part of an ethnic minority? sports lovers? car owners? family oriented? animal lovers? And so on. The more you know about your potential readers, the better you will know both what kinds of things to avoid in order not to alienate them and what kinds of things to use in order to appeal to them, to attract them toward your position.

70c Evidence

When you are gathering material for an argument, look especially for concrete, specific, precise, factual data that you can use to support your generalizations (see #54b). The effectiveness of your argument will in part depend on the quality and the quantity of the *evidence* you provide both to support your position and to counter your opposition. For example try to find some statistics you can cite, or some expert you can quote (the appeal to authority), or some common experience or assumption about life that you can remind your readers of (the appeal to common sense). You may be able to make good use of your own experience or that of someone you know well.

But be sure that the evidence you gather and use is both *reliable* and *relevant*. Don't cite a film star as an authority on a medical question; don't cite the results of an experiment that has been superseded by later experiments; don't discuss the styling and upholstery of a car if you're arguing about which car provides the most efficient transportation.

70d   Organization

Take extra pains when you are laying out your material. And be sure to construct—carefully—a detailed formal outline. Here are some specific points to keep in mind:

1. *Emphasis*

Usually you will want to save your strongest point or points for last, the most emphatic position. But since the beginning is also emphatic, don't open with a weak or minor point. It is usually best to begin with strength and then deal with minor points and proceed to the end in the order of *climax*. (See also #18, #66, #68c.)

2. *Thesis*

In an argument, your thesis statement is in effect a *proposition* that you intend to support or attack; you want to prove or disprove it, at least to the satisfaction of your readers. For that reason, it usually appears at the beginning, just as a formal debate begins with a reading of the proposition to be debated. Occasionally, however, you can delay your statement of the thesis until at or near the end, letting a logical progression of reasoning lead up to it. But don't try for this dramatic effect unless you're sure it will work better than stating your proposition up front; for example, consider whether your readers might be put off, rather than drawn in, by being kept in the dark about just what your proposition is. (See also #69-l.3.)

3. *Methods of Development*

Arguments can make use of any of the methods of development: narration (an illustrative anecdote), description (a detailed description of something it is important for readers to understand clearly), comparison and contrast, analysis, and so on (see #61b). But be careful with *analogy* (see #70h.9): never use an analogy as the central pillar of an argumentative structure, for opponents can too easily break it down; use analogy, if at all, only as an extra illustration or as one of several minor props. And do give strong consideration to *cause-and-effect* analysis (What caused it? What does it cause? What will it cause?), often a mainstay of argument: you argue for or against something because of what has happened or is happening or will happen as a result of it.

4. Patterns of Development

Similarly, an argument can use any one or more of the common patterns of development (see #64b.2). It is likely, for example, to follow a logical progression, to move from general to specific or from specific to general, and to rise to a climax. But there is one further pattern that often occurs in argument: like a formal debate, many arguments move back and forth between *pro* and *con*, between statements supporting your *pro*position and statements *con*futing your opponent's position (see #70f, and sample essay number 6 in Chapter X).

70e-h How to Argue: Reasoning Logically

70e Being Reasonable

Appeal to common sense; appeal to authority; above all, appeal to *reason*. Demonstrate your respect for your readers' intelligence by appealing to it; they are then more likely to respect you and your arguments. If you appeal to prejudices and baser instincts you may get through to a few, but thoughtful readers won't respond favourably to such tactics. Appeals to people's emotions (sympathy for the poor or sick, love of children, feelings of patriotism, fear of injury) can be effective *additions* to an appeal to reason, but they are not a valid substitute for it. Similarly, if you're conducting a reasoned argument you will usually want to adopt a *moderate tone*. Stridency and sarcasm may win points with readers who are already thoroughly in agreement with your position—but then you wouldn't be arguing so much as preaching to the converted and just showing off.

70f Including the Opposition

Be fair: bring in any major opposing points. If you try to sway your readers by mentioning only what favours your side, they will lose faith in you because they'll likely themselves be thinking of counter-arguments and conclude that you are unfairly suppressing unfavourable evidence. By raising opposing points and doing your best to refute them convincingly, or at least to play them down, you will not only strengthen the logic of your argument but also present yourself as a reasonable person, willing to concede that there is another side to the issue. Moreover, by in effect taking on the role of both sides in a debate, you can often impart a useful back-and-forth movement to your argument, and you can see to it that after demolishing the final opposition point you end on one—or better, two or three—of your own strongest points.

70g   Using Induction and Deduction

The two principal methods of reasoning, *induction* and *deduction*, occur both separately and in combination in argument. You should know how each works, and it sometimes helps to be aware of which one you are using at any given point so that you can use it effectively and avoid its potential pitfalls.

1. *Induction*

Inductive reasoning argues from the particular to the general. It uses specific examples to support a general proposition. A team of chemists will argue that their new theory is correct by describing the results of several experiments which point to it. If you want people to vote for mayoral candidate A rather than B, you could point to several instances of A's actions on behalf of the city while on city council—and also perhaps point to several instances of B's harmful decisions. If you wanted to argue against a proposal to cut back on the athletic program at your school, you could cite the major ways in which the program benefits the school and its students; you could also interview other students to show that the majority agree with you.

Inductive reasoning cannot *prove* anything; it can only establish degrees of probability. Obviously the number of examples affects the force of such arguments. If the chemists can point to only two successful experiments, their claim for their theory would remain weak; if they can cite a hundred consecutive successes, their argument would be convincing: there would be a strong likelihood that the experiment would work again if tried for the 101st time.

But don't overdo it: if in a speech or a written argument you detailed fifty noble acts of candidate A and fifty ignoble acts of candidate B, you would probably bore or anger your audience and turn them against you and your proposition. You would do better to describe a few actions on each side and try to establish that those actions were *representative* or *typical* of the two candidates' official behaviour.

Similarly, if you interviewed students about the athletic program, you would need to talk to enough of them for your sampling to be considered representative; if you polled only PE majors, you could hardly claim that their opinions were typical. And though the sampling would have to be large for the results to be convincing, it would be the total number that would carry weight—as on a petition—not the detailed opinions of each individual student.

In addition, you must be able to explain away any notable exceptions among your examples—possible opposition arguments. For example if one of their experiments failed miserably, the chemists would need to show perhaps that at that time their equipment was faulty, or that one of their ingredients had accidentally become adulterated. If candidate A had once voted to close a useful facility, you could try to show that financial exigency at that time left no choice, or that the facility, though generally perceived as beneficial, was in fact little used and therefore an unnecessary drain on the city's resources. If you explicitly acknowledge such exceptions and show that they are unimportant or atypical, they can't easily be used against you by a hostile reader.

2. Deduction

Deductive reasoning argues from the general to the particular. It begins with facts or generally accepted assumptions or principles and applies them to specific instances. For example we all know that oil and other fossil fuels are nonrenewable energy sources that will presumably someday be depleted; and we also know that the world's energy needs are increasing at an accelerating rate. Basing their argument on those two facts, people conclude that it is increasingly important for us to discover or develop alternative sources of energy.

The standard way of representing this process of thinking is the *syllogism*:

> *Major premise:* All mammals are warm-blooded animals.
> *Minor premise:* Whales are mammals.
> *Conclusion:* Therefore whales are warm-blooded animals.

Syllogistic reasoning is a basic mode of thought, though commonly in everyday thinking and writing one of the premises is omitted as "understood"; for example if a student says "This term paper is due tomorrow, so I'll have to finish it tonight," the assumed second premise ("I don't want to hand the paper in late") goes without saying.

Deductive reasoning, unlike inductive reasoning, can establish proof, but only if the premises are correct and you follow the rules. For example, if one of the premises is negative, the conclusion must be negative—and *two* negative premises cannot lead to a conclusion at all. The term common to both premises—called the "middle" term (in the example, *mammals*)—cannot appear in the conclusion. Most important, if the conclusion is to be an absolute certainty, this "middle" term must in at least one of the premises be all-inclusive, universal, what is called "distributed"; that is, it must refer to all members of its class, usually with an absolute word like *all, every, no, none, always, never*. If instead it is qualified by a word like *some, most,* or *seldom,* the conclusion can only be a probability, not a certainty (and if *both* premises include such a qualifier, they cannot lead to a conclusion):

> Most mammals are viviparous.
> Whales are mammals.
> Therefore whales are probably viviparous.

Here of course one could reason further that since whales are not among the oviparous exceptions (platypus, echidna), they are indeed viviparous.

Obviously, for a conclusion to amount to certainty both premises must be true, or accepted as true:

> No mammals can fly.
> Whales are mammals.
> Therefore whales cannot fly.

Here the conclusion is *valid* (the reasoning process follows the rules), but it is not *sound*, since the first premise with its categorical *no* excludes the bat, a flying mammal. Such a conclusion, even if true (as this one is), will be suspect because it is based on a false premise.

If one argues that

> All mammals are four-legged animals.
> Whales are mammals.
> Therefore whales are four-legged animals.

the conclusion, however valid, is not only unsound but untrue as well. To be accurate, the first premise would have to refer to *some* or *many*; the conclusion would then have to be something like "whales may be four-legged animals." Here the absurdity is obvious. But it is not uncommon to hear something like "X must be anti-business; after all, he is in favour of preserving the rain-forests." Here the absurdity may not appear so obvious, but in the syllogism underlying this reasoning the first premise would read something like "Anyone who argues for preserving the environment is against business"; again, changing *Anyone who argues* to the correctly qualified *Some people who argue* renders the conclusion unsound.

Be careful whenever you find yourself using—or thinking—absolute terms like *all* and *everyone* and *no one* and *must* ("Everyone benefits from exercise"; "All exams are unfair"; "[All] Scots are stingy"; "Lawyers are overpaid"; "No one cares about the elderly"; "Vitamin E must be good for you"): you may be constructing an implicit syllogism that won't stand up, one that your opponents can turn against you. Use such qualifiers as *most* and *some* and *sometimes* when necessary; you won't be able to establish absolute proof or certainty, but you may still have a persuasive argument.

3. *Combining Induction and Deduction*

Induction and deduction often work together. For example, when you cite instances from A's record, you use induction to establish the general proposition of your candidate's worthiness. But then you implicitly turn to deduction, using that generalization as the basis for a further conclusion: "Candidate A has done all these good things for our city in the past; therefore when elected mayor he or she will do similar good things." (Would the unstated second premise—"A person who behaved in a certain way in the past will continue to behave that way in the future"— require some qualification?)

70h   Detecting and Avoiding Fallacies

If you are mounting a counter-argument, it often pays to look for flaws in your opponent's reasoning, such as hidden assumptions and invalid syllogisms. There are several other kinds of recognized—and recognizable— logical fallacies to look for, and of course to guard against in your own writing. Most of them amount to either avoiding evidence or distorting evidence, or both, and some are related to or overlap with others. Here are the main ones to watch for:

1. *argumentum ad hominem*

"Argument directed at the person"—trying to evade the issue by diverting attention to the person: "Byron lived an immoral life; therefore his poetry is bound to be bad." Byron's morality is irrelevant to a discussion of the aesthetic quality of his poetry. "My opponent is obviously not fit to be mayor; he never goes to church, and his daughter was arrested last year for shoplifting." Neither the candidate's non-attendance at church nor his daughter's arrest—whether or not she was guilty—necessarily has any bearing on the candidate's fitness for office. Such tactics, according to their degree of directness or nastiness, are referred to as *innuendo* or *name-calling* or *mud-slinging*. A similar tactic uses *guilt* (or *virtue*) *by association* in an attempt to get one person's or thing's qualities to rub off on another, even though the connection may not be real or relevant: a brand of coffee is not necessarily better because a famous actress is paid to say it is, nor a politician necessarily evil because he once had his picture taken with someone later convicted of a crime.

2. *argumentum ad populum*

"Argument directed at the people"—evading the issue by appealing to mass emotion. Like *argumentum ad hominem*, this technique uses appeals to prejudices, fears, and other feelings not—or not clearly—relevant to the issue. Often by using what are called "glittering generalities," it calls upon large and usually vague, unexamined popular feelings about religion, patriotism, home and family, tradition, and the like. One version of it, called the "bandwagon" approach, associates mass appeal with virtue: if so many people are doing this or thinking that or drinking this or wearing that, it must be right or good. Most people don't want to be thought of as not in the swim.

3. red herring

A false or misleading issue dragged across the trail to throw the dogs off the scent. The new matter may be interesting, but if it is fundamentally irrelevant to the question being argued it is a red herring. *Ad hominem* points are red herrings, diverting a reader's or listener's attention from the main question by injecting the issue of personality.

4. hasty generalization

Jumping to a conclusion; arriving at a generalization for which there is insufficient evidence—such as the chemists with only two successful experiments to point to (see #70g.1). Another example: just because you and a friend didn't like the food you were served at a particular restaurant, you aren't justified in asserting that the restaurant is a bad one; maybe other people would have liked the food, or maybe the regular chef was ill that day. But if you've had several such experiences, and can find other people who've had similar ones, you'll be closer to establishing that those experiences were typical and therefore sufficient to generalize upon.

5. begging the question

Assuming as true something that needs to be proved: "The government should be voted out of office because the new tax they've just imposed is unfair to consumers." The unfairness of the tax needs to be established before it can be used as a premise. Similar to question-begging is **circular reasoning**, in which a reason given to support a proposition is little or no more than a disguised restatement of the proposition: "Her consistently good cooking is easy to explain: she's an expert at all things culinary." Or the circle of logic may have a larger circumference: "I'm convinced that my new computer is the best one I could have bought for my needs. The man who sold it to me assured me it was, and if anyone in town knows all about computers, surely he does. He wouldn't feature this brand if he didn't know it was the best."

6. *post hoc ergo propter hoc*

"After this, therefore because of this"—oversimplifying the evidence by assuming that merely because B follows A in time, B must be caused by A. It's true that thunder is caused by lightning, but the subsequent power failure may have been caused not by the lightning but by a tree blown down across the power line. Think about common superstitions: if you always wear your green socks during an exam because you think they bring you good luck, you are a victim of the *post hoc* fallacy. "As soon as the new government took office, the price of gasoline went up"—but there could be a complex set or chain of causes, perhaps including oil companies' fear of possible new policies; or the price hike might have nothing to do with the new government, the timing being coincidental. Be careful not to oversimplify cause-and-effect relations.

7. either-or

Also called "false dilemma"—oversimplifying an issue by presenting it as consisting of only two choices when in reality it is more complex than that. Some questions do present two clear choices: one either gets up or stays in bed; either one has had German measles or one has not; either one votes in an election or one doesn't. But most arguable issues are not matters simply of black and white; there is often a large area of gray between the extremes. One doesn't have to vote for either A or B; one can perhaps find a third candidate, or one can stay home and not vote for anyone. "If you aren't for us, then you must be against us!" Nonsense; one could be neutral, impartial, uninterested, or committed to a third option. "If I don't pass this course, my life will be ruined." An obvious exaggeration. "The administration at this school is either indifferent to students' needs or against students in general." Neither unpleasant alternative is likely to be true. This insidious pattern of thinking underlies a good deal of what we think of as prejudice, bigotry, and narrow-mindedness: "If you're not a good Christian, then you're not really religious." "If you're not religious, you're unpatriotic." "The choice is between democracy and dictatorship." Don't oversimplify; acknowledge the rich complexity of most issues.

8. exaggerating the trivial

Distorting the evidence by treating a minor point as if it were a major one. If the point is your own, discerning readers will infer that you lack substantial evidence and have had to fall back on weak arguments. If the point is an opposing one, they will infer that you can't refute major points and are trying to make yourself look good by demolishing an easy target. "We should all give more to charity because being generous can give us a warm feeling inside"—worth mentioning perhaps, but not worth dwelling on. "Those who are against raising tuition point out that students are happier if they have a little pocket-money. Now let's examine this argument carefully . . . ." No—better leave it alone; it could scarcely be taken seriously as an argument.

On the other hand, don't distort the evidence by trivializing opposition points that *are* important.

9. false or weak analogy

Oversimplifying the evidence by arguing that because two things are alike in some features, they are necessarily alike in one or more others as well. You can say that learning to ride a bicycle is like learning to play the piano: once you learn, you seldom forget; but you would scarcely go on to argue that one should have a bicycle tuned periodically or that one should mount a tail-light on the piano for safety while playing at night. Analogies can provide interesting and concrete illustrations; by suggesting similarities they can help define or clarify or explain or emphasize something—see for example our analogies between constructing paragraphs and cabinet-making (#65 and #65d) and between an outline and a road map (#69g). Analogies cannot produce proof; they can seldom produce even strong probability; but they can assist in the job of persuasion. We would not expect our analogy to convince you of the importance of an outline, but we hope that, by adding its concrete touch, we help you to understand and perhaps to accept our assertions.

One fairly common argument claims that because city or provincial or other governments are in some ways similar to large business organizations, they need experienced business people to run them. The more similarities you can point to, the stronger the argument. The trouble with this and other arguments from analogy, however, is that no matter how many specific similarities you can come up with, your opponents can usually keep ahead of you by citing an even greater number of specific and significant differences. Try it.

10. equivocation

Using a term in more than one sense; being ambiguous, whether accidentally or intentionally: "It is only natural for intelligent people to reject this idea. And as science tells us, natural law is the law of the universe; it is the law of truth, and must be obeyed." Aside from the cheap appeal to snobbery and self-esteem (we all like to think we are "intelligent," but just what is "intelligence"?) and the appeal to the prestige of "science" in the modern world (but just how infallible is science?) and the imposing but vague term *universe* and the glittering abstraction *truth*, do the two occurrences of the word *natural* jibe with each other? And is a natural *law* comparable to legislation passed by a government and enforced by police and the courts? Don't be attracted by nebulous nonsense, and don't let the meanings of words shift as you move from one phrase or sentence to the next. Choose and use your words carefully.

11. *non sequitur*

"It does not follow"—any flaw in reasoning. When for whatever reason a general proposition does not follow logically from the particular examples cited to support it, or a conclusion does not logically follow from its premises, it is a *non sequitur*. The term would apply to any of the fallacies discussed above and also to such leaps of emotional logic as "She's an attractive woman; she'd make a good prime minister," and "I've put a great deal of time and effort into this project; the grade it gets should reflect that fact."

Exercise 70(1) Detecting faulty reasoning

Point out the weak reasoning in each of the following. Identify any particular fallacies committed.

1. She's a liberal, so she's sure to use the taxpayer's money for all sorts of give-away programs, for that's what "liberal" means: generous.
2. Your advertisement says that you want someone with experience as a computer programmer. I've had a year's experience as a computer programmer, so I'm clearly the person you want for the job.
3. Since aspirin can be harmful to some people—or to anyone, if it is overused—it should either be taken off the market or made available by prescription only.
4. He's bound to have an inferiority complex. Look how short he is!
5. Novels written by women often have women as protagonists. Since this novel has a woman as protagonist, it was probably written by a woman.
6. In the past my garage has kept my car running well, but this year they've hired a new mechanic and my car is always acting up. Obviously the new mechanic is incompetent.
7. Dogs make better pets than cats because when they wag their tails they're happy; cats flick their tails when they're angry.
8. This critic says Jane Austen's novels are second-rate, but since he's known to be a Marxist his judgment won't stand up.
9. If I am not elected, the world will come to an end.
10. Student opinion is overwhelmingly in favour of dropping the second-year English requirement. I took a poll among my fellow science-majors, and over 80% of them agreed.
11. The police are supposed to protect society from criminals. When they give me parking tickets they're not doing their job, for I'm not harming society and I'm certainly not a criminal.
12. We've had an unusually cold winter, no doubt as a result of the eruption of that Philippine volcano last year.
13. Movie stars live glamorous lives. They must be much happier than most other people.
14. This party is for higher tariffs and lower taxes, and so am I. That's why I am loyal to the party and always vote for its candidate.
15. People who live and work together constitute a social community, and in a democracy social communities should have a measure of self-government. Since the university is such a community, and since the vast majority of those participating in its life are students, it follows that students should have a major say in the running of the university.
16. Politicians are all a bunch of crooks. Look for example at _____ and _____. And don't forget _____.
17. Advertising is like fishing. Advertisers use something attractive for bait and reel out their lines to dangle the bait in front of us. They think of consumers as poor dumb fish, suckers who will swallow their stuff hook, line, and sinker. And there's a lesson for us in that: if you bite you'll get hurt, for there's always a nasty hook under the

bait. The only way to protect yourself is to make sure you don't fall for any advertiser's pitch.

Exercise 70(2) Analyzing arguments and recognizing persuasive techniques

(a) In an essay, analyze three or four current magazine advertisements for different kinds of products. Point out all the techniques of persuasion you can find in them. Do they appeal more to emotion than to reason? Are they guilty of any particular fallacies?

(b) Look over a week's worth of the editorial and letters pages of a local city or campus newspaper. Select and analyze three or four editorials or letters in order to discover their argumentative techniques.

(c) Find a more extended piece of argumentative writing in a magazine with national circulation. Try to find one arguing about some issue of national importance. Analyze it as an argument. Consider its subject, its audience, its structure, its methods of reasoning, its possible weaknesses, and so on. Assign it a grade.

Exercise 70(3) Including the opposition

In the following sentence outline for an argumentative essay, the student took little account of points the opposition might raise. Read through it carefully, listing as many opposition arguments as you can think of; then recast the outline so as to include those arguments. You can improve the outline in other ways as well. If you find the counter-arguments compelling, you may want to recast the thesis so that you are arguing for the other side. Include in the revised outline one or more sentences each for both a possible beginning and a possible ending of the essay. Think up a good title.

Thesis statement: In my opinion, it is better to watch sports events at home rather than in a stadium.

I. By staying home, sports fans save money on tickets, transportation, and babysitters.
    A. The cost of watching a game at home is a mere fraction of the cost of a ticket to get into a stadium.
    B. Any kind of transportation is an additional cost to a sports fan who goes to a stadium.
        1. Cars require fuel and parking.
        2. Taxis are expensive.
        3. Public transit is too slow.
    C. Parents who wish to see a game live must hire a babysitter.
II. Television viewers have the comforts and conveniences of staying at home.
    A. They have easy access to relatively inexpensive refreshments and to washroom facilities.

      B. They can sit in an open and relaxed manner.
         1. Stadium seats are too compact and uncomfortable.
         2. Bad weather causes outdoor fans even more discomfort.
      C. When one is in a large crowd it is often difficult to concentrate on a game.
   III. Television offers its viewers the best coverage of any kind of game.
      A. Instant replays and close-ups clarify important events in a game.
      B. Sportscasters provide play-by-play coverage with informative commentary.
      C. Television keeps its viewers entertained during intermission periods.

Exercise 70(4) **Writing an argument**

Carefully plan and write an argument of between 1000 and 1250 words (4-5 double-spaced typed pages) on some local issue—perhaps something you found while working on part (b) of Exercise 70(2). Take a position you sincerely believe in. Don't pick a topic that you can't deal with fairly thoroughly. Be sure to take into account any major opposition arguments.

---

71 Writing In-Class Essays and Essay Examinations

Writing an essay in class or during an examination is just like writing an essay in your own room, in the library, or anywhere else—except that you have to do it faster: you don't have time to think at leisure and at length. Therefore you need to make the best use of the time you have. All the principles discussed earlier in this chapter still hold, but here is some additional advice to help you work quickly and efficiently:

1. On an examination, *read the whole paper through* right away. If it has more than one part, budget your time: before you start thinking and writing, decide just how much time you will need or can afford to spend on each part.

2. *Read* the topics or questions *carefully*. Don't, in haste, misread or misinterpret. Don't read wishfully, finding in a question what you want to find instead of what is actually there.

3. *Follow instructions*. If you're asked for an argument, *argue*. If a question asks you to *analyze* a poem, don't simply give your opinion or evaluation of it. If it asks you to *justify* or *defend* your opinions or conclusions, don't simply assert them. If it asks for *comparison and contrast*, don't spend overlong on just one side of the matter. If it asks you to *define* a term or concept, don't simply describe it or give an example of it, and don't

ramble on about your feelings about it or your impressions of it. And so on.

4. *Take time to plan.* Don't panic and begin writing immediately. Think for a few minutes. The more time you spend planning, the easier and surer the writing itself will be. Do a little quick brainstorming. Take the time to make at least a sketch outline, with a *thesis* or proposition and a list of main points and supporting details; you will then be less likely to wander off the topic or change your thesis as you proceed. It's often a good idea to limit yourself to three or four main points, or parts (in addition, that is, to a beginning and an ending).

5. *Get started.* Once you've drawn up your plan, start writing. If necessary, leave several lines or a page blank at the beginning and plunge right into your first point. Don't waste time trying to think of a beginning if one doesn't occur to you quickly; you can come back and fill it in later. Quite possibly you won't need to supply a separate "beginning" at all. In any event, don't waffle. Get to the point quickly and stay with it. Make your thesis clear early on—that may be all you need by way of a beginning. Often you can pick up some key words or phrases from the question or topic and use them to help frame a thesis and get yourself going.

6. *Write carefully.* Whereas on a home essay you may well write your draft hurriedly and spend most of your time revising, here you have to do most of your revising as you go along (another reason it's important to have a *plan*; without one, you could, as you pause to tinker with a sentence, forget your thread of continuity, your line of argument). And you won't have time to do much revising; your first efforts at sentences will often have to do. Furthermore, unless you make an utterly illegible mess, *don't* waste time recopying.

7. Aim for *quality*, not *quantity*. *More* is not necessarily *better*. Of course your essay must be of reasonable length, and sometimes a required minimum length will be specified. What is most important is that you adequately *develop* your subject by developing each of your main points. But don't try to impress by going on and on, for then you will likely ramble, lose control of your thesis and your organization, and commit writing errors because of haste.

8. *Be specific.* Provide examples, illustrations, evidence. By all means generalize, but *support* your generalizations with specific and concrete details.

9. *Conclude effectively*. Don't tack on a stiff conclusion, especially one that is nothing more than lame repetition. Try somehow to refer to or restate your thesis, and if necessary refer again to your three or four main points, but do so in a way that adds something new. Sometimes a single concluding sentence can make a good clincher, especially if it suggests or underscores some result or effect growing out of what your discussion has said.

10. *Proofread carefully*. Leave yourself enough time to look for the kinds of careless mistakes we all make when writing fast. Don't just run your eyes over your sentences, assuming that any errors will leap out at you, even though that may give you the illusion that you've checked your work. Read carefully. If you know that you're prone to certain kinds of errors, look specifically for them.

If you consult only one or two outside sources in order to write an essay—for example some critical comment on a literary work—it will be easy enough to keep track of your sources and the notes you take from them so that you can provide the necessary documentation (see **ack** and **doc** in Chapter XI). But when you are writing a full-fledged research paper, one depending predominantly on outside sources, the task of keeping things straight can be formidable. The following chapter outlines the process of writing such a paper and points out the precautions one must take to work accurately and efficiently.

But first, just what is a "research" paper? At one extreme, it is simply the culmination of a fact-finding process: the writer locates information about a subject and presents it in a coherent report. At the other extreme, a writer consults outside sources, interprets and evaluates them, and then produces an essay which is a piece of original thinking; though based upon the information gathered by research, it is nevertheless an expression of a new attitude toward the subject. Most research papers fall somewhere between these extremes. A particular assignment or occasion will usually call for a particular kind of result. But though only graduate students writing dissertations are really expected to produce substantial and original contributions to knowledge, you should make a research essay represent your independent thought as much as possible, however much it may be based on facts and ideas gathered from outside sources; always try to draw your own conclusions. A research paper that presents data in a mechanical way is no more than a pastiche, a cut-and-paste job, involving the writer's own intelligence only in deciding what data to present and in what order.

A student who is assigned or chooses an unfamiliar research topic, and who explores that topic conscientiously, may eventually produce an unoriginal report, but that student will learn a good deal in the process. And in the process of exploring an unfamiliar subject and writing about it, a student will also learn a good deal about how to do research and present the results. For the undergraduate, or for any inexperienced writer, learning about *method* is important. Chapter IX is intended to make that learning easier than it might otherwise be. Following the conventions established by the Modern Language Association of America in the *MLA Handbook for Writers of Research Papers* (3rd edition, 1988), it provides examples of the name-page method of parenthetical documentation, followed by a sample research essay, with accompanying comments, illustrating the matters discussed in the body of the chapter. The chapter concludes with brief discussion and examples of other methods of documentation.

CHAPTER IX

THE PROCESS OF WRITING A RESEARCH PAPER

An essay based on library research is still an essay: it should conform to the principles governing any good essay. But research essays also require writers to follow procedures which are not a part of writing other kinds of essays. This chapter discusses and illustrates the steps of writing a research essay and the details that you must keep in mind in order to do a good job. All the matters discussed are important. They are not intended merely to show you things you *may* do, but rather to show you the kinds of things you *must* do in order to produce a good essay without wasting time and energy and without risking serious error. Some of the steps and details may seem absurdly mechanical, and some may look like unnecessary fiddling, but all of them are important, and all of them have proved useful to many writers.

> **Note:** The techniques outlined here are of course not the only possible ones, but they are tested ones. An instructor may wish you to follow a different method, for example to make out note or bibliography cards in a different way or to cross-reference material in a special way. Indeed, after some experience you may yourself devise or discover different or additional ways of safeguarding accuracy and increasing efficiency. No one method is sacrosanct: the important thing is to *have* a method. The alternative is likely to be confusion, error, and wasted effort.

72 The Library and Its Resources

Learn your way around your library: whether on a conducted tour or on your own, explore its layout, its reference facilities, its other holdings, its catalogues, its whole system—in a word, its resources. And don't be afraid to ask librarians for help. Once you feel reasonably at home in what may be a vast and complex building or group of buildings, you can begin to use the library as it is intended to be used.

72a The Catalogues

You will find different kinds of cataloguing systems in different libraries, or even in a single library. Most libraries have converted or are in the process of converting to computer catalogues. Many libraries also store information about their holdings in a **microcatalogue** using some kind of microform (microprint, microcard, microfilm, microfiche) which you can read in the catalogue area. If your library has not converted to such a system, or uses one only for material acquired after a certain date, you will be using a **card catalogue**, in which a library's holdings are listed on cards, one item to a card (an "item" may consist of several volumes), and kept in drawers or trays.

In any one of these systems, listings are usually cross-referenced (found under more than one heading) in order to make it easier to find what you need. If you know only the author of a book, look in the Author Catalogue; if you know the title, look in the Title Catalogue. These two are often combined in one Author-Title Catalogue. If you aren't seeking a specific book but are interested in a particular subject, look in the Subject Catalogue. In a small library, all three catalogues may be combined. Some libraries also have a Shelf Catalogue, with items arranged by **call numbers** and therefore in the same order as the books on the shelves. Such a catalogue may also double as a location file, if the library has branches. There may also be a Serial List of periodicals (magazines, newspapers, journals).

72b   Reference Books

A library's reference section contains many sources of information. Here is a sampling to suggest the kinds of reference books usually available and some of the standard or more useful items in each category. (Note that some items could also appear in other categories than where they are listed.) Find out for yourself what reference aids are in your library; make your own search through the reference section: you may be astonished at the quantity and variety of information available.

Find out also what computerized resources your library provides. In addition to on-line computer catalogues, many libraries are now offering users access to vast amounts of reference material on compact discs commonly referred to as CD-ROMs. For example, the latest edition of *The Oxford English Dictionary* is available in this form, as are the *MLA International Bibliography* and *ERIC* (the Educational Resources Information Center's database of education-related literature). *Linguistics and Language Behavior Abstracts, Environment Abstracts,* and *Sport Bibliography* are available on CD-ROM, as are such indexes of indexes as *Literary Criticism Index* and *Biography and Genealogy Master Index.* You may also want to look into the possibilities for gathering and exchanging information through the world-wide computer network known as *Internet.*

Before you begin work on any particular project, browse through some of the relevant reference sources in order to get an idea of what kind of information is available. In addition, as you explore you will often find that an article in an encyclopedia or a book on a given subject will itself include bibliographical information; by following such leads you can save much of the time you might otherwise spend searching for sources.

Note: Since many reference books—especially dictionaries, encyclopedias, and the like—are frequently updated in revised editions or with supplements, we omit dates of publication; we also omit names of authors, editors, and compilers, since often they too change or are added to in successive editions. Simply find and use the latest edition available—or select an earlier edition if it is more relevant to your topic; for example, the 11th edition of *The Encyclopædia Britannica* (1910–1911) may be more helpful than a recent edition, especially for some subjects in the humanities. For many indexes and the like, we give the year when coverage began; that is, "1900–" means "from 1900 to the present." With these, even if you're working on a current topic, you should go back at least a few years in search of relevant material.

Catalogues, Bibliographical Aids, and Reference Guides (General)

Basic Reference Sources: An Introduction to Materials and Methods
Bibliographic Index: A Cumulative Bibliography of Bibliographies (1938-)
A Bibliography of Canadian Bibliographies
Books in Print; Paperbound Books in Print
Canadian Books in Print
Cumulative Book Index
Current Bibliographic Directory of the Arts and Sciences
Gale Directory of Publications and Broadcast Media (1869-)
Guide to Basic Reference Materials for Canadian Libraries
Guide to Reference Books
Guide to the Use of Books and Libraries
Microform Research Collections: A Guide
National Union Catalogue
The New York Public Library Book of How and Where to Look It Up
The New York Times Guide to Reference Materials
Topical Reference Books
Union List of Scientific Serials in Canadian Libraries
Union List of Serials Held by Libraries of the United States and Canada; New Serial Titles
Union List of Serials in the Social Sciences and Humanities in Canadian Libraries
Walford's Guide to Reference Material
A World Bibliography of Bibliographies

Dictionaries and Other Word-Books

Abbreviations Dictionary
Acronyms, Initialisms, & Abbreviations Dictionary
Allusions—Cultural, Literary, Biblical, and Historical: A Thematic Dictionary
The American Heritage Dictionary of the English Language
Brewer's Dictionary of Phrase and Fable
A Concise Dictionary of Canadianisms
A Dictionary of American English on Historical Principles
A Dictionary of American Idioms
A Dictionary of Canadianisms on Historical Principles
A Dictionary of Contemporary American Usage
Dictionary of Foreign Phrases and Classical Quotations

Dictionary of Foreign Terms
Dictionary of Foreign Words and Phrases
A Dictionary of Modern English Usage
Dictionary of Newfoundland English
A Dictionary of Slang and Unconventional English
Dictionary of Word and Phrase Origins
Etymological Dictionary of the English Language
Funk & Wagnalls New Standard Dictionary of the English Language
Funk & Wagnalls Standard Handbook of Synonyms, Antonyms, and Prepositions
Gage Canadian Dictionary
Harper Dictionary of Contemporary Usage
The Harper Dictionary of Foreign Terms
The Houghton Mifflin Canadian Dictionary of the English Language
Idioms and Phrases Index
Illustrated Dictionary of Place Names: United States and Canada
Modern American Usage: A Guide
New Dictionary of American Slang
Nouveau Petit Larousse Illustré
Origins: A Short Etymological Dictionary of Modern English
The Oxford Advanced Learner's Dictionary of Current English
The Oxford Dictionary of English Etymology
The Oxford English Dictionary on Historical Principles; The New Shorter Oxford
    English Dictionary on Historical Principles; The Concise Oxford Dictionary of
    Current English
The Penguin Canadian Dictionary
Practical English Usage
The Random House Dictionary of the English Language
Roget's International Thesaurus
Roget's II: The New Thesaurus
The Scottish National Dictionary
Webster's Dictionary of English Usage
Webster's Third New International Dictionary of the English Language

Quotations, Proverbs

Bartlett's Familiar Quotations
Chambers Book of Quotations
Colombo's Canadian Quotations
The Dictionary of Canadian Quotations and Phrases
Dictionary of Quotations
The Harper Book of Quotations
The Home Book of Humorous Quotations
The International Thesaurus of Quotations
The Macmillan Book of Proverbs, Maxims, and Famous Phrases
The Macmillan Treasury of Relevant Quotations
A New Dictionary of Quotations on Historical Principles from Ancient
    and Modern Sources
The New Quotable Woman
The Oxford Dictionary of English Proverbs
The Oxford Dictionary of Quotations
Proverbs, Maxims, and Phrases of All Ages

Periodical and Other Indexes (General)

Alternative Press Index (1973-)
Arts and Humanities Citation Index (1976-)
British Humanities Index (1962-)
Canadian News Index (1979-) [continues *Canadian Newspaper Index, Canadian Magazine Index, Canadian Business Index, Canadian Index*]
Canadian Newspaper Index (1977-1979)
Canadian Periodical Index 1920-1937; 1938-1947 (1964-)
    Canadian Index to Periodicals and Documentary Films (1948-1963)
Comprehensive Index to English-Language Little Magazines
Current Events
Dissertation Abstracts; Dissertation Abstracts International
Essay and General Literature Index (1900-)
French Periodical Index (1973-)
Guide to Indian Periodical Literature (1964-)
Index to Commonwealth Little Magazines (1925-)
Index to the Times/The Times Index (1785-)
Indian Press Index (1968-)
International Index to Periodicals (1907-1960)
    International Index (1960-1965)
    Social Sciences and Humanities Index (1965-1974)
    Social Sciences Index (1974-)
    Humanities Index (1974-)
Le Monde: Index Analytique (1967-) (covers from 1944)
The New York Times Index (1851-)
Poole's Index to Periodical Literature (1802-1906)
Popular Periodicals Index (1973-)
Readers' Guide to Periodical Literature (1900-)
Répertoire analytique d'articles de revues du Québec (1972-)
Ulrich's International Periodicals Directory
The Wall Street Journal Index (1958-)

Book Reviews (General)

American Reference Books Annual (1970-)
Book Review Digest (1905-)
Book Review Index (1965-)
Canadian Book Review Annual (1975-)
Children's Book Review Index
Combined Retrospective Index to Book Reviews in Humanities Journals 1802-1974
Combined Retrospective Index to Book Reviews in Scholarly Journals 1886-1974
Current Book Review Citations (1977-)
An Index to Book Reviews in the Humanities
The New York Times Book Review Index (1896-)

Encyclopedias (General)

Academic American Encyclopedia
The Canadian Encyclopedia
Chambers's Encyclopædia
Collier's Encyclopedia

Colombo's Canadian References
The Encyclopædia Britannica
Encyclopedia Americana
Encyclopedia Canadiana
Encyclopedia International
The New Columbia Encyclopedia
The Random House Encyclopedia

Collections of Facts and Opinions; Yearbooks; Chronologies; Atlases and Gazetteers

The Americana Annual (1923-)
The Annual Register: A Record of World Events (1758-)
Atlas of World Issues (1989-)
The Book of Key Facts: Politics, Wars, Science, Literature, The Arts
Britannica Book of the Year (1938-)
Canada Gazetteer Atlas
Canada Year Book
Canadian Almanac & Directory (1847-)
Canadian News Facts (1967-)
Columbia-Lippincott Gazetteer of the World
Cultural Atlas of Africa
Demographic Yearbook; Annuaire démocratique (1948-)
Editorials on File (1970-)
The Europa World Year Book (1926-)
Facts on File: A Weekly World News Digest (1940-)
Facts on File Yearbook (1940-)
Gallup Opinion Index (1965-)
Geographical Abstracts (1966-)
Historical Atlas of Canada
Information Please Almanac (1947-)
National Geographic Atlas of the World
New Cosmopolitan World Atlas
New International Year Book (1907-)
The New York Public Library Book of Chronologies
The New York Public Library Desk Reference
The New York Times Encyclopedic Almanac
Official Associated Press Almanac (1969-)
The People's Chronology
Statesman's Year Book (1864-)
The Times Atlas of the World
The Timetables of History
Webster's New Geographical Dictionary
Who Was When?: A Dictionary of Contemporaries
The World Almanac and Book of Facts (1868-)
The Year Book of World Affairs

History, Politics

African Encyclopedia
The Almanac of American Politics

The Almanac of British Politics
America: History and Life (1964-)
The American Historical Association's Guide to Historical Literature
American Political Dictionary
Arctic Bibliography (1953-)
Australian Public Affairs Information Service: Subject Index to Current Literature
    (1945-)
Bibliography of British History
The Cambridge Ancient History
The Cambridge Medieval History
The Canadian Annual Review of Public Affairs (1902-1938)
    Canadian Annual Review (1960-1970)
    Canadian Annual Review of Politics and Public Affairs (1971-)
China: An Annotated Bibliography of Bibliographies
China Facts and Figures Annual (1978-)
Combined Retrospective Index to Journals in History 1838-1974
Combined Retrospective Index to Journals in Political Science 1886-1974
The Concise Maori Handbook
A Current Bibliography on African Affairs (1962-)
Current Geographical Publications (1938-)
Cyclopaedia of India
Cyclopedia of American Government
Dictionary of American History
A Dictionary of British History
Dictionary of Human Geography
Dictionary of Political Analysis
Dictionary of Political Science and Law
Dictionary of Politics
Encyclopedia of Asian Civilizations
Encyclopedia of Newfoundland and Labrador
Encyclopedia of the Third World
An Encyclopedia of World History
Everyman's Dictionary of Dates
Foreign Affairs Bibliography
Government of Canada Publications
Guide to Historical Literature
A Guide to Reference Materials on India
The Harper Dictionary of Modern Thought
Harper Encyclopedia of the Modern World
Harvard Guide to American History
Historical Abstracts (1955-)
Historic Documents (1972-)
The History of Canada: An Annotated Bibliography
Index to Book Reviews in Historical Periodicals (1973-)
International Bibliography of Historical Sciences (1926-)
International Political Science Abstracts (1951-)
Lemprière's Classical Dictionary of Proper Names Mentioned in Ancient Authors
Monthly Catalogue of United States Government Publications
The New Cambridge Modern History
The Oxford Classical Dictionary

The *Oxford Companion to American History*
The *Oxford Companion to Canadian History and Literature*
Peace Research Abstracts Journal (1964-)
Political Science: A Bibliographical Guide to the Literature
The *Political Science Reviewer: An Annual Review of Scholarship*
Public Affairs Information Service Bulletin: Annual Cumulated Bulletins, Cumulative Subject Index (1915-)
A *Reader's Guide to Canadian History*
The *Statesman's Year-Book* (1864-)
The *Times Atlas of World History*
Yearbook of the United Nations (1946-)

Biography (General)

Biography and Genealogy Master Index
Biography Index: A Cumulative Index to Biographical Material in Books and Magazines (1946-)
Cambridge Biographical Dictionary (UK: *Chambers Biographical Dictionary*)
Canadian Who's Who (1910-)
Chambers Biographical Dictionary
Current Biography (1940-)
Dictionary of American Biography
Dictionary of Canadian Biography
Dictionary of National Biography (British)
Encyclopedia of American Biography
The *International Who's Who* (1935-)
The *Macmillan Dictionary of Canadian Biography*
The *McGraw-Hill Encyclopedia of World Biography*
Notable American Women: A Biographical Dictionary
Webster's Biographical Dictionary
Who's Who (British) (1849-)
Who's Who in America (1899-)
Who's Who of American Women (1958-)
Who Was Who
Who Was Who in America

Science and Technology

Abstracts of North American Geology (1966-)
ACM Guide to Computing Literature
Agricultural Index (1916-1964); *Biological and Agricultural Index* (1964-)
American Men and Women of Science
Applied Ecology Abstracts (1975-1979); *Ecology Abstracts* (1980-)
Astronomy and Astrophysics Abstracts (1969-)
Bibliography and Index of Geology
Bibliography of Current Computing Literature (1967-)
Bibliography of North American Geology
Biological Abstracts (1926-)
British Technology Index (1962-)
The *Cambridge Encyclopædia of Astronomy*
The *Cambridge Encyclopedia of Earth Sciences*

Chemical Abstracts (1907-)
Computer and Control Abstracts (1969-)
Computer Dictionary and Handbook
Computer Literature Index (1980-)
Computer Yearbook (1972-)
Concise Encyclopedia of the Sciences
Dictionary of Biology
Dictionary of Computers, Data Processing, and Telecommunications
A Dictionary of Genetics
A Dictionary of Geology
A Dictionary of Physics
A Dictionary of Science Terms
Dictionary of Scientific Biography
Encyclopedia of Bioethics
The Encyclopedia of Chemistry
Encyclopedia of Computer Science and Engineering
The Encyclopedia of Oceanography
The Encyclopedia of Physics
The Encyclopedia of the Biological Sciences
Encyclopedic Dictionary of Mathematics
The Engineering Index (1884-)
Environment Abstracts
The Environment Index (1971-)
General Science Index (1978-)
Geophysical Abstracts
A Guide to the History of Science
The Harper Encyclopedia of Science
Henderson's Dictionary of Biological Terms
Index Medicus (1899-)
Industrial Arts Index (1913-1957)
    Applied Science and Technology Index (1958-)
    Business Periodicals Index (1958-)
International Dictionary of Medicine and Biology
International Encyclopedia of Chemical Science
Larousse Encyclopedia of Astronomy
McGraw-Hill Basic Bibliography of Science and Technology
McGraw-Hill Encyclopedia of Environmental Science
McGraw-Hill Encyclopedia of Science and Technology
Oxford Dictionary of Computing
The Penguin Dictionary of Science
Physics Abstracts
Pollution Abstracts
Prentice-Hall Encyclopedia of Mathematics
Reference Sources in Science and Technology
Science Abstracts
Science Citation Index (1961-)
Science Reference Sources
Smith's Guide to the Literature of the Life Sciences
Sourcebook on the Environment: A Guide to the Literature
Stein and Day International Medical Encyclopedia

The Timetables of Science
Universal Encyclopedia of Mathematics
Van Nostrand's Scientific Encyclopedia
Who's Who in Ecology (1973-)
World Survey of Climatology
The Zoological Record (1864-)

Social Sciences; Education

Abstracts in Anthropology (1970-)
Biographical Dictionary of Psychology
Canadian Education Index (1965-)
Combined Retrospective Index to Journals in Sociology 1895-1974
Contemporary Psychology (1956-)
Criminal Justice Abstracts
Criminal Justice Periodicals: A Selected Bibliography
Criminology and Penology Abstracts
Current Anthropology (1960-)
Current Index to Journals in Education (1969-)
A Dictionary of Anthropology
Dictionary of Education
A Dictionary of Psychology
A Dictionary of Sociology
A Dictionary of the Social Sciences
Education Index (1929-)
Encyclopedia of Crime and Justice
The Encyclopedia of Education
Encyclopedia of Educational Research
Encyclopedia of Human Behavior: Psychology, Psychiatry, and Mental Health
Encyclopedia of Psychology
Encyclopedia of Social Work
Encyclopedia of Sociology
Encyclopedia of the Social Sciences
Guide to the Literature of Education
The Harvard List of Books in Psychology
International Bibliography of Social and Cultural Anthropology (1955-)
International Bibliography of Sociology (1951-)
International Bibliography of the Social Sciences
International Encyclopedia of the Social Sciences
A London Bibliography of the Social Sciences (1931-)
Physical Education Index (1978-)
Police Science Abstracts
Psychological Abstracts (1927-)
A Reader's Guide to the Social Sciences
RIE: Resources in Education (ERIC)
Royal Anthropological Institute Index to Current Periodicals (1963-)
Social Sciences Citation Index (1956-)
Social Sciences Index (1974-)
Sociological Abstracts (1953-)
Studies on Women Abstracts (1983-)
Women's Studies: A Checklist of Bibliographies

Women's Studies Index
Women Studies Abstracts (1972-)
The World of Learning

Economics and Business

The Arthur Andersen European Community Sourcebook
Business Periodicals Index (1958-)
The Cambridge Economic History of Europe
Canadian Index [continues *Canadian Business Periodicals Index* and *Canadian Business Index*] (1975-)
Cumulative Bibliography of Economic Books (1954-)
A Dictionary of Economics
Economic Abstracts (1953-)
Encyclopedia of Advertising
Encyclopedia of Economics
The Encyclopedia of Management
Everyman's Dictionary of Economics
Handbook of Modern Marketing
Index of Economic Articles (1886-)
Industrial Development Abstracts (1971-)
International Bibliography of Economics (1952-)
Journal of Economic Literature (1963-)
The McGraw-Hill Dictionary of Modern Economics
Survey of Economic and Social History in Canada (1976-)
World Agricultural Economics and Rural Sociology Abstracts (1959-)

Philosophy, Religion, Mythology, Folklore

Analytical Concordance to the Bible
The Anchor Bible
The Anchor Bible Dictionary
A Baptist Bibliography
A Bibliography of Canadian Folklore in English
Bibliography of English-Language Works on the Bábí and Bahá'í Faiths 1844-1985
Black African Traditional Religions and Philosophy: A select bibliographic survey of the sources from the earliest times to 1974
Bulfinch's Mythology
The Cambridge History of Islam
Catholic Almanac (1904-)
The Concise Encyclopedia of Western Philosophy and Philosophers
A Concordance of the Qur'an
Cruden's Complete Concordance to the Old and New Testaments
Cyclopædia of Biblical, Theological, and Ecclesiastical Literature
The Dartmouth Bible
A Dictionary of Chinese Mythology
A Dictionary of Christian Biography
A Dictionary of Hinduism
A Dictionary of Non-Christian Religions
Dictionary of Philosophy
Dictionary of the Bible

Dictionary of the History of Ideas
Encyclopedia Judaica
Encyclopedia of Bioethics
The Encyclopedia of Eastern Philosophy and Religion: Buddhism, Hinduism, Taoism, Zen
The Encyclopedia of Islam
An Encyclopedia of Occultism
The Encyclopedia of Philosophy
An Encyclopedia of Religion
Encyclopedia of Religion and Ethics
Encyclopedia of the American Religious Experience
Encyclopedia of the Hindu World
The Encyclopedia of Unbelief
Encyclopedic Dictionary of Religion
Everyman's Dictionary of Non-Classical Mythology
Funk & Wagnalls Standard Dictionary of Folklore, Mythology, and Legend
The Golden Bough: A Study in Magic and Religion
A Handbook of Greek Mythology
Harper Bible Dictionary
Index to Fairy Tales, Myths, and Legends (1926-)
Index Islamicus
Index to Book Reviews in Religion
Index to Jewish Periodicals (1963-)
International Bibliography of the History of Religions (1954-1979); Science of
    Religion (1980-)
International Standard Bible Encyclopedia
The Interpreter's Bible
The Interpreter's Dictionary of the Bible
The Interpreter's One-Volume Commentary on the Bible
Larousse World Mythology
The Macmillan Bible Atlas
The Mennonite Encyclopedia
Motif-Index of Folk-Literature: A Classification of Narrative Elements in Folktales,
    Ballads, Myths, Fables, Mediaeval Romances, Exempla, Fabliaux, Jest-Books and
    Local Legends
The Mythology of All Races
Nelson's Complete Concordance of the Revised Standard Version Bible
The New Bible Dictionary
New Catholic Encyclopedia
A New Dictionary of Christian Theology
The New Schaff-Herzog Encyclopedia of Religious Knowledge
The New Standard Jewish Encyclopedia
The Oxford Dictionary of Saints
The Oxford Dictionary of the Christian Church
The Penguin Dictionary of Religions
The Philosopher's Index (1967-)
A Popular Dictionary of Sikhism
A Rationalist Encyclopædia
A Reader's Guide to the Great Religions
Religion Index (1949-)
Religions, Mythologies, Folklores: An Annotated Bibliography
Religious Books 1876-1982

Religious Books and Serials in Print 1982-1983
Religious Periodicals Directory
Shinso Hanayama Bibliography on Buddhism
Who's Who in Egyptian Mythology

The Arts

Art Index (1929-)
Arts and Humanities Citation Index (1978-)
Baker's Biographical Dictionary of Musicians
Bryan's Dictionary of Painters and Engravers
The Concise Oxford Dictionary of Ballet
The Concise Oxford Dictionary of Music
Crowell's Handbook of World Opera
The Dance Encyclopedia
A Dictionary of Canadian Artists
Dictionary of Contemporary Music
Dictionary of Contemporary Photography
A Dictionary of Musical Terms
A Dictionary of Symbolism
A Dictionary of Symbols
The Encyclopedia of Dance and Ballet
The Encyclopedia of Jazz
Encyclopedia of Music in Canada
Encyclopedia of Painting
Encyclopedia of Pop, Rock, and Soul
Encyclopedia of Popular Music
Encyclopedia of the Arts
Encyclopedia of the Great Composers and Their Music
Encyclopedia of the Opera
Encyclopedia of World Architecture
Encyclopedia of World Art
Focal Encyclopedia of Photography
A History of Western Music
An Illustrated Encyclopedia of Traditional Symbols
The International Cyclopedia of Music and Musicians
The Larousse Encyclopedia of Music
The Lives of the Painters
McGraw-Hill Dictionary of Art
The Music Index (1949-)
Music Lovers' Encyclopedia
New Dictionary of Modern Sculpture
The New Grove Dictionary of Music and Musicians
The New Harvard Dictionary of Music
The New Oxford Companion to Music
The New Oxford History of Music
The Oxford Companion to Art
The Oxford Companion to the Decorative Arts
The Praeger Encyclopedia of Art
Symbols and Legends in Western Art
A Treasury of Opera Biography

Drama, Film, Television

Annual Index to Motion Picture Credits
Bibliographic Guide to Theatre Arts (1975-)
The Brock Bibliography of Published Canadian Plays in English 1776-1978
Canada on Stage: Canadian Theatre Review Yearbook
The Complete Encyclopedia of Television Programs
Contemporary Dramatists (1973-)
Contemporary Theatre, Film, and Television (1984-)
Dictionary of Films
Dramatic Criticism Index
The Encyclopedia of World Theater
Film Canadiana (1969-)
The Film Encyclopedia
The Filmgoer's Companion
Film Literature Index (1973-)
Film Review Index (1986-)
Halliwell's Filmgoer's Companion
A History of English Drama
International Bibliography of Theatre (1982-)
The International Encyclopedia of Film
International Index to Film Periodicals (1972-)
International Motion Picture Almanac
International Television Almanac (1956-)
The Macmillan Film Bibliography
Magill's Survey of Cinema
McGraw-Hill Encyclopedia of World Drama
Modern World Drama: An Encyclopedia
The Motion Picture Guide
The New York Times Film Reviews (1913-)
The New York Times Theater Reviews (1920-)
The Oxford Companion to Film
The Oxford Companion to the Theatre
Play Index (1949-1987)
Radio and Television: A Selected, Annotated Bibliography
Television Drama Series Programming: A Comprehensive Chronicle (1959-)
TV Facts
Variety International Showbusiness Reference
The World Encyclopedia of Film

Literature and Language

Abstracts of English Studies (1958-)
Annual Bibliography of Commonwealth Literature (1964-)
Annual Bibliography of English Language and Literature (1920-)
A Bibliography of the English Language from the Invention of Printing
    to the Year 1800
A Biographical Dictionary of English Women Writers 1580-1720
The Bloomsbury Guide to English Literature
The Bloomsbury Guide to Women's Literature
Calendar of Literary Facts
The Cambridge Guide to World Literature

Canadian Literature Index: A Guide to Periodicals and Newspapers (1985-)
The Cambridge History of English Literature
Cassell's Encyclopedia of World Literature
Children's Book Review Index (1975-)
Children's Literature Abstracts (1973-)
Children's Literature: An Annotated Bibliography of the History and Criticism
Children's Literature Review
Columbia Dictionary of Modern European Literature
A Complete and Systematic Concordance to the Works of Shakespeare
A Concise Chronology of English Literature
The Concise Oxford Dictionary of Literary Terms
Contemporary Authors (1962-)
Contemporary Literary Criticism (1973-)
Contemporary Novelists (1972-)
Contemporary Poets (1970-)
Critical Writings on Commonwealth Literature: A Selective Bibliography to 1970, with a List of Theses and Dissertations
A Dictionary of British and American Women Writers 1660-1800
Dictionary of Literary Biography
A Dictionary of Literary Terms and Literary Theory
An Encyclopedia of British Women Writers
Encyclopedia of World Literature in the 20th Century
The Feminist Companion to Literature in English
Fiction Catalog (1908-)
A Handbook to Literature
A History of the English Language
Index to Children's Poetry
Letters in Canada (1935-)
Linguistic Bibliography (1939-)
Linguistics and Language Behavior Abstracts (1967-)
Literary Criticism Index
Literary History of Canada
A Literary History of England
Literary History of the United States
Macmillan History of Literature Series
Magill's Bibliography of Literary Criticism
MLA International Bibliography of Books and Articles on the Modern Languages and Literatures (1922-)
The New Cambridge Bibliography of English Literature
Nineteenth-Century Literary Criticism
The Oxford Companion to American Literature
The Oxford Companion to Australian Literature
The Oxford Companion to Canadian Literature
The Oxford Companion to Canadian Theatre
The Oxford Companion to Children's Literature
The Oxford Companion to Classical Literature
The Oxford Companion to English Literature
The Oxford Companion to French Literature
The Oxford Companion to German Literature
The Oxford Companion to Spanish Literature
The Oxford Companion to the English Language

The Oxford History of English Literature
The Penguin Companion to American Literature
The Penguin Companion to Classical, Oriental, and African Literature
The Penguin Companion to English Literature
The Penguin Companion to European Literature
Poetry by Women to 1900: A Bibliography of American and British Writers
Poetry Index Annual (1982-)
Princeton Encyclopedia of Poetry and Poetics
The Reader's Encyclopedia
A Reference Guide to English, American, and Canadian Literature
A Reference Guide to English Studies
A Research Guide to Science Fiction Studies
Selective Bibliography for the Study of English and American Literature
Short Story Index (1953-)
Short Story Index: Collections Indexed, 1900-1978
Something about the Author: Facts and Pictures about Contemporary Authors
        and Illustrators of Books for Young People (1971-)
Survey of Modern Fantasy Literature
Survey of Science Fiction Literature
Twentieth-Century Literary Criticism
The Who's Who of Children's Literature
Women's Magazines 1693-1968
World Authors: A Biographical Dictionary
The World Encyclopedia of Comics
The Year's Work in English Studies (1919-)
The Year's Work in Modern Language Studies (1929-)

Sports and Games

Encyclopedia of Physical Education, Fitness, and Sports
The Oxford Companion to Sports and Games
Sport and Leisure: A Journal of Social Science Abstracts (1989-)
Sport Bibliography
SportSearch

73 Collecting Data: Sources

73a The Preliminary Bibliography

Once you have decided on or been assigned a subject, the first step in gathering information is to compile a **preliminary bibliography**. By consulting various sources (for example periodical indexes, essay indexes, general and particular bibliographies, encyclopedias, and dictionaries, and of course your library's own catalogues, starting probably with the subject catalogue), make a list of possibly useful sources of information about your topic. Next, look in the appropriate catalogues to find out which items on your list are available in your library, and record the call number of each one (you will already have done this for items you first found in the catalogues).

73b   Bibliography Cards

When you begin looking at the actual books and articles on your list, you should do two things:

1. First, as soon as you locate a book or article, make out a **bibliography card** for it. (Use the small 8 × 12 cm or 3 × 5 inch index cards.) With cards you can keep track of material easily: you can keep them in handy alphabetical order, insert new cards as you find new sources, and put aside cards for sources you think are of no use to you.

> **Caution:** Do not throw away any of these cards, even if you think they will be useless, for at a later stage you may decide to use some of them after all. In fact, don't throw away anything: keep all your notes, jottings, scribblings, lists, and drafts, for they may prove useful later when you want to check back on something or, in the light of new discoveries, restore something you earlier discarded.

You will save time if you record the bibliographical information exactly as it will appear later in your bibliography (see #78a, #79, #80a, #80b; see also Chapter X, essay 17). Make sure you record this information accurately and completely: double-check spellings, dates, page numbers, and so on.

> **Cautionary Note:** Some writers prefer not to make a list but instead to enter each item on a card as soon as they come across it in a bibliography or other source. This does save one step, but if you choose to follow such a method, be careful: as soon as you come upon the actual book or article, check your card against it for accuracy, because bibliographies and other lists sometimes contain errors, for example in spelling or punctuation or even dates. One could argue, then, that copying the information from the actual item onto a card also saves a step.

2. Second, peruse the book or article to see how useful it looks, and jot down, on the card, a quick note to yourself about its likely worth as a source. For example, note whether it is promising or appears to be of little or no use, or whether it looks good for a particular part of your project, or whether one part of it looks useful and the rest not. Be as specific as you can, for a glance at such a note may later save you the trouble of a return trip to the library. You may also want to write a label, called a **slug** (see #74c), on each card, indicating what part of your subject it pertains to (e.g. keyed to your preliminary outline—see #74); this information too could save you extra trips. For the same reason, you might note on a card just how thorough your examination of the source was; that is, if you just glanced at it, you may want to return to it, but if you found it so interesting that you read it carefully and even took notes, then you will know that you need not return to it later. And, in case you do want to return to a source, save yourself time by recording the call number of each item.

Here are two sample bibliography cards that go with the sample research paper later in this chapter. Note the arrangement and completeness of the bibliographical information, the slugs in the upper right corners, the writer's notes to herself in the lower right, and the library call numbers in the lower left.

I. The Maker

Kiely, Robert. "Frankenstein." Mary Shelley.
Ed. Harold Bloom. Modern Critical Views.
New York: Chelsea, 1985. 65–80.

PR5398   — critical examination of VF's behaviour
M25   — useful source
1985

III. The Myth

Forry, Steven Earl. Hideous Progenies:
Dramatizations of "Frankenstein" from
Mary Shelley to the Present. Philadelphia:
U of Pennsylvania P, 1990.

PR5397   — a central source on variations in the
F73   Frankenstein story
F67   — useful bibliography
1990   — interesting illustrations!

---

74 Taking Notes

When you have compiled your preliminary bibliography and begun consulting the items it lists, you will also be taking some notes—a process that will accelerate as you go along, until your collection of bibliography cards is complete, at least for the moment, at which time you will only be taking notes in preparation for your outline and first draft. Your preliminary research should be relatively casual, for you will still be exploring your subject, investigating and weighing its possibilities, and attempting to limit it (see #69b) as much as necessary.

At some point during this early stage you should be able to construct a **preliminary outline** (see #69f-j), which of course will be subject to change as you go along. It may be only sketchy at first, but even such an outline will help you decide what kinds of notes to take.

At first you may be uncertain about the usefulness or relevance of some of the material you come across. Be generous with yourself: take many notes. If you toss aside a book that doesn't look useful now, you may discover later that you need it after all; it is better to spend a few minutes taking some careful notes than to spend an hour or two on a return trip to the library only to find that the book has been borrowed by someone else. Use it while you have your hands on it.

For your notes you will need a separate stack of index cards. If you use the same size cards as you used for your bibliography, use a different colour. Or use the larger 10 × 15 cm or 4 × 6 inch cards, especially if your writing is large. On each **note card** you will include at least three things: (1) the note itself, (2) the exact source, and (3) a label or slug indicating just what part of your subject the note pertains to.

74a   The Note Itself

1. Include only one point on each card. The reason for using cards is that it is easy to shuffle them around, to arrange them as you see fit at various stages. If you try to cram too much information onto one card, you won't be able to move it so easily; you may even have to recopy part of the material onto another card so that you can shift it to where you want it. Don't include two or three closely related points on one card unless you are certain that they will occur together in your essay.

2. Be as brief as possible. If for some reason your note must extend beyond one side of a card—if for example it is an unusually long summary or quotation—it can be continued on the back of the card. But be sure to write a large OVER in the bottom right-hand corner so that you won't forget that there is more to the note than appears on the front side. Or continue the note on another card. If you ever do use more than one card for a single note, be sure to repeat the listing of the source at the top of each card, and number the cards. For example, if a note extended to three cards, number them *1 of 3, 2 of 3,* and *3 of 3.*

3. Distinguish carefully between direct quotation and paraphrase or summary (see #77). Generally, use little direct quotation; quote only when you feel strongly that the author's own way of putting something will be especially effective in your essay. When you do quote directly, be extremely careful: your quotation must accurately reproduce the original, including its punctuation, spelling, and even any peculiarities that you think might be incorrect (see item 10 below); do not "improve" or in any way alter what you are copying. In fact, it is a good idea to double-check your copying for absolute accuracy immediately after doing it, and then to mark it as checked (a check mark, or double check mark, perhaps in red, at the right-hand edge will do). And when you do quote directly, put exaggeratedly large quotation marks around the quotation so that you cannot possibly later mistake it for summary or paraphrase. This safeguard is particularly important when a note is part quotation and part summary or paraphrase: the oversize quotation marks will help keep your work clear.

4. If a note consists of a combination of (a) summary or paraphrase or quotation and (b) your own interjected thoughts or explanations or opinions, *enclose your own ideas in square brackets*—or, to be even safer, in double square brackets [[ ]]; you might even want to initial them. This will prevent you from later assuming that the ideas and opinions came from your source rather than from you.

5. As much as possible, *express the material in your own words when taking notes*. The more you can digest and summarize information at the note-taking stage, the less interpreting you will need to do later—and it will never be fresher in your mind than at the time when you are taking the note. If you fail to assimilate it then, you may well have to return to the source to find out just why you quoted it in the first place. It is all too easy to forget, over a period of days, weeks, or even months, just what the point was.

6. When you quote, or even paraphrase or summarize, *do so from the original source if possible*. Second-hand quotations may be not only inaccurate but misleading as well. Seek out the most authoritative source—the original—whenever possible, rather than accept someone else's reading of it. Similarly, if more than one edition of a source-book exists, use the most authoritative or definitive one—usually the most recent.

7. *Distinguish between facts and opinions*. If you are quoting or paraphrasing a supposed authority on a subject, be careful not to let yourself be unduly swayed. Rather than note that "aspirin is good for you," say that "Dr. Jones claims that aspirin is good for you." Rather than write that "the province is running out of natural resources," say that "the Premier believes, after reading the report given him by his investigating committee, that the province is running out of natural resources." The credibility of your own presentation may well depend on such matters.

8. When you are quoting, or even just summarizing or paraphrasing, *be careful with page numbers*. If a quotation runs over from one page to another in your source, be sure to indicate just where the change occurs, for you may later decide to use only a part of the material, and you must know just which page that part came from in order to provide accurate documentation. A simple method is to indicate the end of a page with one or two slashes (/ or //).

9. Whenever you insert explanatory material in a quotation, use square brackets (see #43j).

10. When there is something in a quotation that is obviously wrong, whether a supposed fact or in the writing, such as a spelling error, insert [sic] after it (see #43j).

11. Whenever you omit a word or words from a quotation, use three spaced periods to indicate the ellipsis (see #43i).

74b The Source

In the upper left-hand corner of each note card, identify the source. Usually the last name of the author and a page number will suffice. But if you are using more than one work by the same author, you must include at least a shortened title of the particular work from which the note comes. Indeed, it is a good idea always to include the title, for later in your note-gathering you may come across a second work by an author you are already using; with a title on each card, no confusion can possibly arise. If the note comes from more than one page, indicate the inclusive page numbers; the note itself will show where the page changes (see #74a.8). (When the bibliography is complete, number the bibliography cards, if only to make it easier to put them back in order if you drop them or otherwise mix them up. But it is unwise to use this number alone to identify the source of a particular note. Be cautious: use the author's name and at least a short title.)

74c The Slug

In the upper right-hand corner of each note card, write a *slug*, a word or brief phrase identifying the topic of the note, and if possible indicating just what part of your essay the note belongs in—and be as specific as possible: this slug will be helpful when it comes to organizing the cards before writing the essay. If you've prepared a good outline, a key word or two from its main headings and subheadings, along with their numerals, will be the logical choice to use as a slug on a card.

74d

> **Caution:** *Use ink or type* everything on your note and bibliography cards. Pencil writing can easily become smudged and illegible. Further, guard against the impulse to invent private symbols and abbreviations; they may make the writing of notes easier at first, but over even a short time you can all too easily forget what your own code means. Except for standard abbreviations (but not even these in material you are quoting), write everything out in full. Similarly, if you don't type or use a word processor for your note-taking, be sure to write legibly.

74d   Cross-Referencing: Numbering the Cards

If your project is unusually complex, you may want to devise some system for cross-referencing closely related note cards, or even ones you think might later prove to be closely related. One way to do this is to number the cards, say at top-centre, when you are through taking notes, and to make your cross-references to these numbers. Indeed, it is important, when the cards are all arranged, to number them consecutively; imagine how long it would take, should you drop a stack of a hundred or so cards, to put them back into the correct order without the aid of such numbers. Be sure that your cards are organized according to your outline, or that your outline has been changed to conform to the organization of your cards.

74e   Recording Your Own Ideas

In addition to taking notes from other sources, preserve your own ideas, insights, and flashes of inspiration as you go along. However fragmentary or tentative they may seem at the time, they may well turn out to be valuable at a later stage. Even if you suddenly have so strong an idea about something that you feel sure you will remember it forever, *write it down*; otherwise there is a good chance you will forget it, for another strong idea may dislodge it just a few minutes later. As with regular notes, restrict these to one idea per card. Even though there won't be an outside source listed in the upper left-hand corner, take the extra precaution of putting your initials there, or of putting double square brackets around the note, or both, so that you can't possibly later wonder where it came from. And of course put an appropriate slug in the upper right-hand corner.

For sample note cards illustrating these points, see #79.

75   Writing the Essay

When your research is complete and all the note cards you intend to use are in the desired order, you are ready to begin writing the essay. If your note-taking has been efficient—that is, if you have kept quotation to a minimum, assimilating and interpreting and evaluating as much as possible as you went along, and if you have included among the cards a sufficient number containing only your own ideas—then the essay will almost write itself; you will need do little more than supply any necessary transitions as you move from card to card and follow your outline. (Of course the usual steps of revising and proofreading must follow the writing of the first draft, as described in the preceding chapter; see #69m-o.)

75a Keeping Track of Notes in Your Drafts

As you write your first draft, proceeding from card to card, include in your text the information that will eventually become part of your documentation. That is, at the end of each quotation, paraphrase, summary, or direct reference, enclose in parentheses the last name of the author and the relevant page number or numbers—and also at least a short title, if you are using more than one work by the same author. Similarly, if two or more authors have the same surname, you will also include the appropriate first name, or just an initial.

If you are using a system of parenthetical documentation, such as that of the MLA, which is the principal system illustrated in this text (see #78a), or that of the APA (see #80a), the final form of your notes will be the same as or similar to these parenthetical notes in your drafts.

If you are using the "number" method (see #80b), do the same until you prepare the final draft, when you will change each parenthetical reference to the appropriate number in the list of references. This number will appear in either parentheses or brackets, sometimes accompanied by a page number or date or author's name; and in some versions the number will be a superscript, like a footnote number.

If you are using the system of *The Chicago Manual of Style*, which calls for footnotes (or endnotes) and an alphabetized bibliographical list at the end (see #80c), do the same, converting to numbered footnotes or endnotes only when you are preparing the final draft.

Note: If you have access to a computer and know how to use a good word-processing program, you may want to compile your bibliography and write your outline and notes by that method, though some writers with computers still prefer to use cards, to have the actual physical objects in their hands. Nevertheless, with a computer you can arrange and rearrange material at will, which is especially helpful in drafting and revising your essay. But you must still be careful, since a computer will not correct any errors you make. Further, many writers who use computers don't trust themselves to proofread on the screen, but will print out hard copy to go over carefully. Remember to "save" files on the hard disk at frequent intervals, and when you rework material always leave a back-up file on the hard disk. For example, when you revise a first draft, make sure to retain a copy of the original draft, just in case you aren't happy with the way the revision turns out; then you can retrieve the original and try again. (But keep a copy of that first attempt, for you may decide after all to return to *it* again.) And you will probably want to make back-up copies of everything on a separate disk as well, in case of power failure or other disaster.

---

76 *ack*

76 Acknowledgment of Sources

ack The purpose of documentation is three-fold:

1. It acknowledges a writer's indebtedness to particular sources;
2. It lends weight to a writer's statements and arguments by citing authorities to support them, and also demonstrates the extent of a writer's investigation of a topic;
3. It enables an interested reader to pursue the subject further by consulting cited sources, or possibly to evaluate a particular source or to check the accuracy of a reference or quotation, should it appear questionable.

76a "Common Knowledge"

It is not necessary to provide documentation for facts or ideas or quotations that are well known, or "common knowledge"—such as the fact that Shakespeare wrote *Hamlet*, or that Hamlet said "To be or not to be," or that Sir Isaac Newton formulated the law of gravity, or that the story of Adam and Eve appears in the book of Genesis in the Bible, or that the moon is not made of green cheese. But if you are at all uncertain whether or not something is "common knowledge," play safe: it is far better to over-document and appear a little naive than to under-document and commit **plagiarism**.

One rule of thumb is that if a piece of information appears in three or more different sources, it qualifies as "common knowledge" and need not be documented. For example, such facts as the elevation of Mt. Logan, or the population of Peterborough in a given year, or the date of the execution of Louis Riel, can be found in dozens of reference books. But it can be dangerous for a student, or any non-professional, to trust to such a guideline when dealing with other kinds of material. For example, there may be dozens of articles and books referring to or attempting to explain something like a quark, or the red shift, or black holes, or discoveries at the Olduvai Gorge, or Freudian readings of "The Turn of the Screw," or the importance of mitochondria, or deep structure in linguistic theory, or the warnings about a nuclear winter, or neo-Platonic ideas in Renaissance poetry, or the nature and consequences of the great potato famine, or the origin of the name *Canada*; nevertheless, it is unlikely that a relatively unsophisticated writer will be sufficiently conversant with such material to recognize and accept it as "common knowledge." If something is new to *you*, and if you have not thoroughly explored the available literature on the subject, it is far better to acknowledge a source than to try to brazen it out and slide something past the reader.

When the question of "common knowledge" arises, ask yourself: *common to whom?* Your readers will probably welcome the explicit documentation of something that they themselves do not realize is, to a few experts, "common knowledge." Besides, if at any point in your presentation you give your readers even the slightest cause to question your data, you will have lost their confidence. Be cautious: document anything about which you have the least doubt.

77 Quotation, Paraphrase, Summary, and Plagiarism

Quotation must always be exact, verbatim. **Paraphrase**, on the other hand, reproduces the content of the original, but in different words. Paraphrase is a useful technique because it enables writers to make use of source material while still using their own words and thus to avoid too much direct quotation. But a paraphrase, to be legitimate, may not use significant words and phrases from an original without enclosing them in quotation marks. A paraphrase will usually be a little shorter than the original, but it need not be. A **summary**, however, is by definition a condensation, a boiled-down version that expresses only the principal points of an original passage.

Direct quotation, obviously, must be documented: a reader of a passage in quotation marks will expect to be told who and what is being quoted. But some writers make the serious error of thinking that only direct quotations need to be documented; on the contrary, it is important to know and remember that *paraphrase and summary must also be fully documented.* Failure to document them is **plagiarism**, a form of theft.

To illustrate, here is a paragraph, a direct quotation, from Rupert Brooke's *Letters from America,* followed by (a) legitimate paraphrase, (b) illegitimate paraphrase, (c) combination paraphrase and quotation, (d) summary, and (e) a comment on plagiarism.

```
Such is Toronto.  A brisk city of getting on for half a million

inhabitants, the largest British city in Canada (in spite of the

cheery Italian faces that pop up at you out of excavations in the

street), liberally endowed with millionaires, not lacking its due

share of destitution, misery, and slums.  It is no mushroom city

of the West, it has its history; but at the same time it has

grown immensely of recent years.  It is situated on the shores of

a lovely lake; but you never see that, because the railways have

occupied the entire lake front.  So if, at evening, you try to

find your way to the edge of the water, you are checked by a
```

region of smoke, sheds, trucks, wharves, storehouses, "depôts,"
railway-lines, signals, and locomotives and trains that wander on
the tracks up and down and across streets, pushing their way
through the pedestrians, and tolling, as they go, in the American
fashion, an immense melancholy bell, intent, apparently, on some
private and incommunicable grief. Higher up are the business
quarters, a few sky-scrapers in the American style without the
modern American beauty, but one of which advertises itself as the
highest in the British Empire; streets that seem less narrow than
Montreal [sic], but not unrespectably wide; "the buildings are
generally substantial and often handsome" (the too kindly Herr
Baedeker). Beyond that the residential part, with quiet streets,
gardens open to the road, shady verandahs, and homes, generally
of wood, that are a deal more pleasant to see than the houses in
a modern English town. (Brooke 80-81)

The parenthetical reference for this block quotation begins two spaces after
the final punctuation mark. It includes the author's surname and the page
numbers on which the original appeared. The complete bibliographical
entry for Brooke's work would appear in the list of "Works Cited" as follows:

Brooke, Rupert. <u>Letters from America</u>. London: Sidgwick
and Jackson, 1916.

(For more information about handling quotations, see #43.)

77a   Paraphrase

During his 1913 tour of the United States and Canada, Rupert
Brooke sent back to England articles about his travels. In one
of them he describes Toronto as a large city, predominantly
British, containing both wealth and poverty. He says that it is
relatively old, compared to the upstart new cities further west,
but that nevertheless it has expanded a great deal in the last
little while. He implies that its beautiful setting is spoiled
for its citizens by the railways, which have taken over all the
land near the lake, filling it with buildings and tracks and
smell and noise. He also writes of the commercial part of the
city, with its buildings which are tall (like American ones) but
not very attractive (unlike American ones); one of them, he says,

```
claims to be the tallest in the British Empire.  (He pokes fun at

Baedeker for being over-generous with his comments about the

city's downtown architecture.)  The streets he finds wider than

those of Montreal, but not too wide.  Finally he compares

Toronto's attractive residential areas favourably with those of

English towns (80-81).
```

This is legitimate paraphrase. Even though it uses several words from the original (*British, railways, tracks, American, British Empire, streets, residential, English town*[s]), they are a small part of the whole; more important, they are common words that it would be difficult to find reasonable substitutes for without distorting the sense. And, even more important, they are used in a way that is natural to the paraphraser's own style and context. For example, had the writer said "in the American style" or "the entire lake shore," the style (and words) would have been too much Brooke's. Paraphrase, however, does not consist in merely substituting one word for another, but rather in assimilating something and restating it in your own words and your own syntax.

The parenthetical reference contains only the page numbers, since the author is named in the text. Similarly, though it comes at the end of a long paragraph, it is clear because the paragraph begins by identifying its overall subject and because the writer has carefully kept Brooke's point of view apparent throughout by including him in each independent clause (a technique which also establishes good coherence): *Rupert Brooke, he describes, He says, He implies, He also writes, he says, He pokes fun, he finds, he compares.*

77b Illegitimate Paraphrase

An illegitimate paraphrase of Brooke's paragraph might begin like this:

```
Brooke describes Toronto as a brisk kind of city with nearly half

a million inhabitants, with some Italian faces popping up among

the British, and with both millionaires and slums.  He deplores

the fact that the lake front on which it is situated has been

entirely occupied by the railways, who have turned it into a

region of smoke and storehouses and the like, and trains that

wander back and forth, ringing their huge bells (80-81).
```

The parenthetical reference does not protect such a treatment from the charge of plagiarism, for too many of the words and phrases and too much of the syntax are Brooke's own. The words and phrases we have italicized are all "illegitimate": a flavourful word like *brisk*; the intact phrases *half a million inhabitants* and *Italian faces*; *popping up*, so little different from *pop up*; and so on. Changing *the railways have occupied the entire lake front* to the passive *the lake front . . . has been entirely occupied by the railways*, or *trains that wander up and down* to *trains that wander back and forth*, or *tolling . . . an immense . . . bell* to *ringing their huge bells*, does not make them the writer's: they still have the diction, syntax, and stylistic flavour of Brooke's original, and therefore constitute plagiarism.

Had the writer put quotation marks around "brisk," "Italian faces . . . pop[ping] up," "millionaires" and "slums," "lake front," "it is situated," "occupied," "a region of smoke," "trains that wander," and "bell[s]," the passage would, to be sure, no longer be plagiarism—but it would still be illegitimate, or at least very poor, paraphrase, for if so substantial a part is to be left in Brooke's own words and syntax, the whole might as well have been quoted directly: the writer would have done little more than lightly "edit" the original.

77c   Paraphrase and Quotation Mixed

A writer who felt that a pure paraphrase was too flat and abstract, who felt that some of Brooke's more striking words and phrases should be retained, might choose to mix some direct quotation into a paraphrase:

```
In Letters from America, Rupert Brooke characterizes Toronto as
"brisk," largely British, and as having the usual urban mixture
of wealth and poverty.  Unlike the "mushroom" cities farther west,
he says, Toronto has a history, but he points out that much of
its growth has nevertheless been recent.  He notes, somewhat
cynically, that the people are cut off from the beauty of the
lake by the railways and all their "smoke, sheds, trucks, wharves,
storehouses, 'depôts,' railway lines, signals, and locomotives
and trains" going ding-ding all over the place (80-81).
```

This time the context is very much the writer's own, but some of the flavour of Brooke's original has been retained through the direct quotation of a couple of judiciously chosen words and the cumulatively oppressive catalogue. The writer is clearly in control of the material, as the writer of the preceding example was not. (See also #77f below.)

77d   Summary

A summary, whose purpose is to substantially reduce the original, conveying its essential meaning in a sentence or two, might go something like this:

```
Brooke describes Toronto as large and mainly wealthy,

aesthetically marred by the railway yards along the lake,

with wide-enough streets and tall but (in spite of Baedeker's

half-hearted approval) generally unprepossessing buildings,

and a residential area more attractive than comparable English

ones (80-81).
```

It is appropriate to refer to an author by name in your text—and the first time by full name, as in versions (a) and (c). If for some reason you do not want to bring the author's name into your text (for example if you were surveying a variety of opinions about Toronto and did not want to clutter your text with all their authors' names), then your text might read in part like this, with the author's surname tucked away in the parenthetical reference:

```
Toronto was once described as "brisk," large, and encumbered with

railways and tall but ugly buildings (Brooke 80-81).
```

77e   Plagiarism

Had one of the foregoing versions of the passage not mentioned Brooke, nor included quotation marks, nor ended with documentation, it would have been guilty of outright *plagiarism*, passing off Brooke's words or ideas, or both, as the writer's own, whether intentionally or not. Do not, either by design or by accident, commit plagiarism. If you have any doubts whatever about what does or does not constitute plagiarism, or about whether you are treading on dangerous ground in something you are writing, ask your instructor about it: it is too serious a matter to remain uncertain about. Plagiarism that is clearly unintentional may provoke only a warning, though it could be punished more severely; plagiarism that is clearly or even just possibly intentional may draw punishment ranging from a zero for the essay to dismissal from the course or even from the institution.

See **ack** and **doc** in Chapter XI.

77f   Altering Quotations to Fit Context

When you include quoted material within one of your own sentences, you may have to alter it in one way or another in order to incorporate it smoothly. That is, you may have to change the grammar, syntax, or punctuation of a quotation to make it conform to that of your own sentence.

Note how the writers have altered the quoted material in the following examples. (See also #43j.)

The original quotation (from Mary Shelley's *Frankenstein; or, The Modern Prometheus*):

> I am by birth a Genevese; and my family is one of the most distinguished of that republic. My ancestors had been for many years counsellors and syndics; and my father had filled several public situations with honour and reputation. He was respected by all who knew him for his integrity and indefatigable attention to public business. He passed his younger days perpetually occupied by the affairs of his country; a variety of circumstances had prevented his marrying early, nor was it until the decline of life that he became a husband and the father of a family.

(a) altered for pronoun reference:

```
Victor Frankenstein begins his story by stating that "[he is]
by birth a Genevese; and [his] family is one of the most
distinguished of that republic" (Shelley 31).
```

The first-person pronouns have been changed to third person in order to fit the third-person point of view in the sentence as a whole. The changed pronouns and the accompanying verb (*is* for *am*) appear in square brackets. (The opening *he is* could have been left outside the quotation, but the writer preferred to incorporate the parallelism within the quotation.)

(b) altered for consistent verb tense:

```
As we first encounter him in the description at the beginning of
Victor's narrative, Victor's father is a man "respected by all
who [know] him for his integrity and indefatigable attention to
public business" (Shelley 31).
```

The verb in square brackets has been changed from past to present tense to conform with the tense established by the *is* of the student's sentence.

(c) altered for punctuation:

```
The first words of Victor Frankenstein's narrative--"I am by
birth a Genevese" (Shelley 31)--reveal a narrator preoccupied
with himself, his birth, and his nationality.
```

The semicolon of the original has been dropped to avoid its clashing with the enclosing dashes of the student's own sentence.

(d) selective quotation:

```
The first paragraph of Victor's narrative focusses more on
Victor's father than on any other member of the Frankenstein
```

family. Victor takes pains to describe him as a man of "honour
and reputation. . . . respected by all who knew him for his
integrity and indefatigable attention to public business" and
"perpetually occupied by the affairs of his country" (Shelley
31). A first-time reader of the novel might well be forgiven for
assuming that Victor's narrative will be more a tribute to his
father than an account of his own creation of a monster.

Here, the student writer has selected key words and phrases from the
opening paragraph of Victor Frankenstein's narrative in order to make a
point about the novel's focus. The ellipsis indicates that material has been
omitted in the interests of the student's own sentence structure.

Exercise 77　Paraphrasing and summarizing

Here are two more paragraphs from Rupert Brooke's *Letters from America.*
For each, write (a) a paraphrase, (b) a paraphrase with some quotation
mixed in, and (c) a summary. Include a parenthetical reference in the MLA
style for each piece you write.

(1) Ottawa came as a relief after Montreal. There is no such sense of strain
and tightness in the atmosphere. The British, if not greatly in the majority,
are in the ascendancy; also, the city seems conscious of other than financial
standards, and quietly, with dignity, aware of her own purpose. The
Canadians, like the Americans, chose to have for their capital a city which
did not lead in population or wealth. This is particularly fortunate in
Canada, an extremely individualistic country, whose inhabitants are only
just beginning to be faintly conscious of their nationality. Here, at least,
Canada is more than the Canadian. A man desiring to praise Ottawa would
begin to do so without statistics of wealth and growth of population; and
this can be said of no other city in Canada except Quebec. Not that there are
not immense lumber-mills and the rest in Ottawa. But the Government
farm, and the Parliament buildings, are more important. Also, although the
"spoils" system obtains a good deal in this country, the nucleus of the Civil
Service is much the same as in England; so there is an atmosphere of Civil
Servants about Ottawa, an atmosphere of safeness and honour and massive
buildings and well-shaded walks. After all, there is in the qualities of Civility
and Service much beauty, of a kind which would adorn Canada. (54-55)

(2) Winnipeg is the West. It is important and obvious that in Canada there
are two or three (some say five) distinct Canadas. Even if you lump the
French and English together as one community in the East, there remains
the gulf of the Great Lakes. The difference between East and West is possibly
no greater than that between North and South England, or Bavaria and
Prussia; but in this country, yet unconscious of itself, there is so much less to
hold them together. The character of the land and the people differs; their
interests, as it appears to them, are not the same. Winnipeg is a new city. In
the archives at Ottawa is a picture of Winnipeg in 1870—Mainstreet, with a
few shacks, and the prairie either end. Now her population is a hundred

thousand, and she has the biggest this, that, and the other west of Toronto. A new city; a little more American than the other Canadian cities, but not unpleasantly so. The streets are wider, and full of a bustle which keeps clear of hustle. The people have something of the free swing of Americans, without the bumptiousness; a tempered democracy, a mitigated independence of bearing. The manners of Winnipeg, of the West, impress the stranger as better than those of the East, more friendly, more hearty, more certain to achieve graciousness, if not grace. There is, even, in the architecture of Winnipeg, a sort of *gauche* pride visible. It is hideous, of course, even more hideous than Toronto or Montreal; but cheerily and windily so. There is no scheme in the city, and no beauty, but it is at least preferable to Birmingham, less dingy, less directly depressing. It has no real slums, even though there is poverty and destitution.   (102-03)

78 Documentation

doc   In order to be effective, documentation must be complete, accurate, and clear. Completeness and accuracy depend on careful recording of necessary information as you do your research and take notes. Clarity depends on the way you present that information to your reader. You will be clear only if your audience can follow your method of documentation. Therefore it is important that before you begin any research project, you investigate the method of documentation you need to use. There are four main methods:

(a) The *name-page* method, currently recommended by the Modern Language Association (MLA), and in wide use in the humanities (see #78a, and also #79, the sample research paper);

(b) the *name-date* method, recommended by the American Psychological Association (APA), and used in some of the social and other sciences (see #80a);

(c) the *note* method, recommended by the MLA until 1984, and still preferred in some disciplines and by some individual writers and instructors (see #80c);

(d) the *number* method, used mainly in some of the sciences (see #80b).

Which method you choose will depend on what discipline you are writing in and on the wishes of the instructor for whom you are writing. But you should familiarize yourself with all of them, or at least with those you will most often find in your textbooks and in your research for various courses.

    In the examples and advice that follow, we place the greatest emphasis on the name-page method because it is the one you are most likely to encounter in your courses in the humanities. However, in #80a-c we provide brief descriptions and examples of the APA's name-date method, the number method, and the note method, the last of which is also illustrated by the final sample essay (no. 17) in Chapter X.

78a The Name-Page Method

The virtues of this method of citation over the old note method are obvious: simplicity and efficiency. No footnotes or endnotes are needed. Using this method, you provide a short, usually parenthetical, reference to each source in the body of your paper. Then, at the end of the essay, in a list titled "Works Cited," alphabetized by surname of authors or editors (or title, when no author is named), you provide complete bibliographical information about all the sources you have used.

Here are examples of the basic patterns of in-text parenthetical references, followed by a list of works cited. (See also the examples in #77-77d, and the sample research paper, #79.) Note that parenthetical references are usually placed at the end of the sentence in which the citation occurs; but if a sentence is necessarily long and complicated, a reference may be placed earlier, immediately after the citation itself.

A work by one author

Those who examine the issue argue that "most present-day democracies have a goal of promoting the health and happiness of children" (Gottlieb 239).

Note that the parenthetical reference includes the author's surname and a page reference, with no intervening punctuation, and that the page number is not preceded by the abbreviation "p." The closing period follows the parentheses. If you can include the author's name in your text, the reference will be shorter and simpler:

Beatrice Gottlieb has argued that "most present-day democracies have a goal of promoting the health and happiness of children" (239).

If you cite an entire work rather than a specific part of a work, try to include the author's name in your text; then no parenthetical reference will be necessary:

In "Might may be right?" S. F. Whitaker discusses the seeming change taking place in the usage of <u>may</u> and <u>might</u>.

A work by two authors

Close study of a number of texts has led to the conclusion that "European and American narrative literature has concentrated its attention on male characters who occupy powerful public roles from which women have almost always been excluded" (Gilbert and Gubar 67-68).

A work by three authors

Vancouver has long been a city obscured by the beauty of its natural setting; that is, "Vancouver looks so good that it is easy to overlook its buildings" (Kalman, Phillips, and Ward 9).

A work by more than three authors

In the parenthetical reference, supply the name of the first-listed author, followed by the Latin abbreviation *et al.* (for Latin *et alii,* "and others"):

Tone has been defined as "the expression of the writer's feelings and opinions about the subject and toward the audience" (Donald et al. 412).

Two or more works by the same author

Cite the author's last name and the first word in the title of the work that distinguishes it from the titles of other works by the same author:

Her novels begin quietly. One opens with "The river flowed both ways" (Laurence, <u>Diviners</u> 3); another opens with "Above the town, on the hill brow, the stone angel used to stand" (Laurence, <u>Stone</u> 3).

As noted elsewhere, if you identify the author by name in a sentence in your text, you need not repeat the name in the parenthetical reference to that sentence or to a subsequent one, assuming that the identification remains clear:

Margaret Laurence's novels are notable for their quiet, understated beginnings. One for example opens with "The river flowed both ways" (<u>Diviners</u> 3); another begins, "Above the town, on the hill brow, the stone angel used to stand" (<u>Stone</u> 3).

A work by a government agency or a corporate author

Revenue Canada's <u>Special Income Tax Guide</u> for 1993 begins with the announcement that it uses "plain language to explain the most common income tax situations" (2).

You could include the name of such a source within a full parenthetical reference, but it is usually better to identify it in your text.

A work by an anonymous author

When a magician dies, his or her friends and colleagues gather
for a service known as "the broken-wand ceremony" ("Mere" 43).

This anonymous essay, entitled "Mere Stick," appeared in *The New Yorker*
magazine in August 1993. A short version of the title replaces the author's
surname in the parenthetical reference. In the list of works cited, such
items are alphabetized by title.

An anonymous article in a reference book

Mary Leapor's poem "'An Essay on Woman' is strongly feminist"
("Leapor")--and its title is likely intended to echo that of
Pope's An Essay on Man.

Such items are usually short, often appearing on a single page, and therefore don't require a page number in the reference; they are easily located,
since articles in such reference books are arranged alphabetically. Note
that the reference is inserted after the first clause; the second clause
expresses the opinion of the writer, not the source.

A multivolume work

When you cite one volume from a work of two or more volumes, include
the volume number in the parenthetical reference, followed by a colon
and a space, and then the page number:

The preface to Literature in Canada emphasizes that the oral
tradition has a part to play in the literary history of this
country (Daymond and Monkman 2: xii).

Quotation at second hand

Always try to quote from primary sources. If you quote from a secondary
source, be careful to identify it, since if it contains any error you will then
not be blamed for it. Sometimes, of course, as when someone quotes from
another's conversation, the indirect source may be the only one available.
For example:

On being told that it was impossible to refute Berkeley's
assertion that matter doesn't exist, Samuel Johnson energetically
kicked a large stone so that his foot bounced back off it,
saying, "I refute it thus" (qtd. in Boswell 333).

Similarly, if the source of a desirable quotation is not supplied, you may well have to rely on the secondary source (and in this example there is the further complication of translation):

```
And there is Cézanne's remarkably perceptive statement about
Monet: "Monet is nothing but an eye--but what an eye!" (qtd. in
Haftmann 35).
```

By specifying "Vol. 1" in the list of works cited and adding at the end that the work consists of two volumes (see the list of "Works Cited" below), one need include only the page number here in the parenthetical reference.

A work of literature

Many major works of pre-contemporary literature—fictional and non-fictional prose, plays, poems—have been published in several different editions. To enable readers to locate quotations in any edition they may have access to, parenthetical references to such works should include or consist of clear indications of text divisions other than the page numbers of the particular edition you happen to be using. If you begin with a page number, follow it with a semicolon and then add the other information, using clear abbreviations. Some examples:

(a) prose works

```
Jane Austen presents readers of Pride and Prejudice with the
heroine's father, the likable Mr. Bennet, an "odd . . . mixture
of quick parts, sarcastic humour, reserve, and caprice" (3; vol.
1, ch. 1); only much later do we learn that these in part
contribute to his serious shortcomings as a father.
```

```
In her 1792 A Vindication of the Rights of Woman, Mary
Wollstonecraft claimed that the inadequate education women then
received made them like "savages," with their "immoderate
fondness for dress, for pleasure, and for sway" (187; ch. 13,
sect. 3).
```

```
William of Orange's "powerful" memory enabled him to learn and
use several languages besides his native Dutch (Macaulay 2: 162;
ch. 7).
```

(b) a play in prose

In Chekhov's <u>The Cherry Orchard</u>, Trofimov says to Anya, "The whole of Russia is our orchard" (59; act 2).

(c) a play in verse (see also #50f)

Before he leads his soldiers into battle, Henry dons a disguise and circulates among them, eliciting their opinions about his performance as king with comments such as "I think the King is but a man, as I am" (<u>Henry V</u> 4.1.101-02).

With verse plays, you need not include page numbers at all, since act, scene, and line numbers clearly locate the citation.

(d) a poem

In "The Wind through St. John's," Earle Birney writes of a wind so powerful that "it shakes the seaward shacks of the poor" (line 116).

The line number tells a reader precisely where in the work the quotation comes from; no page number is needed. Since the abbreviations *l.* and *ll.* could be confused with numerals, spell out *line* and *lines*. Subsequent references to the same poem need not include the words *line* or *lines*; the number will be enough.

(e) a long poem with divisions

Those who find Satan heroic are overlooking Milton's flat statements, for example that the Father of Lies is "in pain, / Vaunting aloud, but racked with deep despair," and that his "words . . . bore / Semblance of worth, not substance" (1.125-26, 528-29).

The second set of line numbers is separated from the first by a comma. Again, no page numbers are needed.

(f) the Bible

In the biblical account of the Flood, Noah is presented as a dutiful servant of God, "a just man and perfect in his generations" (Gen. 6.9).

A standard abbreviation of the book is followed by a space, the chapter number, a period, and the number of the verse or verses being cited.

Citing more than one source

If you wish to cite more than one source in a single parenthetical reference, simply write each in the usual way and separate them with a semicolon:

```
Basically, a symbol is "a thing that stands for something else"
or anything that "seems to represent or stand for some reality
other than itself" (Lemon 72; Bevan 275).
```

Using notes as well as parenthetical references

If occasion demands, you may also use an occasional note along with the name-page method. For example, if you think that a reference must consist of or include some comment or explanation, make it a footnote or endnote rather than an obtrusive parenthetical reference. But keep such notes to a minimum; if you cannot comfortably include such discursive comments in your text, it may be that they aren't truly relevant after all. Try to limit such notes to (a) those commenting in some useful way on specific sources, such as a "See," "See for example," or "See also" note, and (b) those listing three or more sources, which might be unwieldy as a parenthetical reference.

In the text, insert a superscript numeral where you want to signal the note (usually at the end of a sentence). Begin the note by indenting five spaces, followed by a superscript numeral corresponding with the one in the text, then another space, and then the note. If you use a footnote, put it at the bottom of the page, four lines below your text; single-space the note, but double-space between notes. If a note carries over to a second page, type a line across the page two spaces below the text and continue the note two spaces below the line. If you use endnotes, put them on a separate page, headed *Notes*, following the text and before the list of works cited, and double-space them.

Here is the way the sources referred to in the preceding examples would be listed at the end of an essay, beginning on a separate page:

Works Cited

```
Austen, Jane.  Pride and Prejudice.  Ed. Mark Schorer.  Boston:
     Houghton, 1956.
Bevan, Edwyn.  Symbolism and Belief.  1938.  Boston: Beacon,
     1957.
Birney, Earle.  Last Makings: Poems.  Toronto: McClelland, 1991.
```

Boswell, James. <u>Life of Johnson</u>. Ed. C. B. Tinker and R. W.
    Chapman. Oxford Standard Authors. London: Oxford UP, 1953.

Chekhov, Anton. <u>Three Plays: The Cherry Orchard, Three Sisters,</u>
    <u>Ivanov</u>. Trans. Elisaveta Fen. London: Penguin, 1951.

Daymond, Douglas, and L. Monkman. <u>Literature in Canada</u>. 2 vols.
    Toronto: Gage, 1978.

Donald, Robert B., et al. <u>Models for Clear Writing</u>. 3rd ed.
    Englewood Cliffs: Prentice, 1994.

Gilbert, Sandra M., and Susan Gubar. <u>The Madwoman in the Attic:</u>
    <u>The Woman Writer and the Nineteenth-Century Literary</u>
    <u>Imagination</u>. New Haven: Yale UP, 1979.

Gottlieb, Beatrice. <u>The Family in the Western World from the</u>
    <u>Black Death to the Industrial Age</u>. New York: Oxford UP,
    1993.

Haftmann, Werner. <u>Painting in the Twentieth Century</u>. Trans.
    Ralph Manheim. Vol. 1. London: Lund Humphries, 1960. 2
    vols.

Kalman, Harold, Ron Phillips, and Robin Ward. <u>Exploring</u>
    <u>Vancouver: The Essential Architectural Guide</u>. Vancouver:
    UBC Press, 1993.

Laurence, Margaret. <u>The Diviners</u>. Toronto: McClelland, 1974.

---. <u>The Stone Angel</u>. New Canadian Library 59. Toronto:
    McClelland, 1968.

"Leapor, Mary." <u>The Feminist Companion to Literature in English</u>.
    Ed. Virginia Blaine, Isobel Grundy, and Patricia Clements.
    New Haven: Yale UP, 1990.

Lemon, Lee T. <u>A Glossary for the Study of English</u>. New York:
    Oxford UP, 1971.

Macaulay, Thomas Babington. <u>The History of England from the</u>
    <u>Accession of James the Second</u>. 5th ed. 2 vols. London:
    Longman, 1849.

"Mere Stick." <u>The New Yorker</u> 23-30 Aug. 1993: 43-44.

Milton, John. <u>Paradise Lost</u>. <u>The Complete Poetical Works of John Milton</u>. Ed. Douglas Bush. Boston: Houghton, 1965.

Revenue Canada. <u>Special Income Tax Guide</u>. Ottawa: Supply and Services Canada, 1993.

Shakespeare, William. <u>King Henry V</u>. Ed. John H. Walter. The Arden Shakespeare. London: Methuen, 1954.

Whitaker, S. F. "Might may be right?" <u>English Today</u> July 1987: 35-36.

Wollstonecraft, Mary. <u>A Vindication of the Rights of Woman</u>. Ed. Carol H. Poston. New York: Norton, 1975.

Some of the above listings also illustrate how to handle certain other details and kinds of sources: an editor's name (Austen, Milton, Shakespeare, Wollstonecraft); the inclusion of subtitles (Chekov, Gilbert and Gubar, Kalman et al.); the original publication date for a republished book (Bevan); a translator (Chekhov, Haftmann); three hyphens and a period indicating another work by the preceding author (Laurence); the name of a series (Boswell, Laurence's <u>The Stone Angel</u>, Shakespeare); identifying an edition (Boswell, Donald, Macaulay); an article from a weekly or bi-weekly magazine ("Mere"—in this instance a double issue); a monthly or bi-monthly magazine (Whitaker). Note that a work by four or more authors may be listed by the first author only (Donald, Robert B., et al.); but if you choose, for whatever reason, you may list all of the authors, in the order in which they appear on the title page: Donald, Robert B., Betty Richmond Morrow, Lillian Griffith Wargetz, and Kathleen Werner. Note also the short form of publishers' names, such as Houghton (Houghton Mifflin Company), Yale UP (Yale University Press), McClelland (McClelland and Stewart), Prentice (Prentice Hall).

Here are some examples of parenthetical references and corresponding biblio-graphical listings for other kinds of sources:

An essay in an edited anthology

As W. J. Harvey has pointed out, "<u>Bleak House</u> is for Dickens a unique and elaborate experiment in narration and plot composition" (146).

Harvey, W. J. "Chance and Design in <u>Bleak House</u>." <u>Dickens and the Twentieth Century</u>. Ed. John Gross and Gabriel Pearson. Toronto: U of Toronto P, 1962. 145-57.

An article in a journal with continuous pagination throughout a volume

That Canadians have increasingly sought out post-secondary education is supported by statistics such as these:

> University enrollments increased gradually, doubling from 1920 to 1945, and then experienced explosive growth from 1960 to 1980 such that more than twenty times as many Canadians would receive a degree in 1990 as their grandparents had in 1920. (Harrigan 811)

Note that if a quotation is set off by indention, the parenthetical reference follows two spaces after the closing punctuation.

Harrigan, Patrick. "The Schooling of Boys and Girls in Canada."
    Journal of Social History 23 (1990): 803-16.

Note that in the bibliographical entry the title of the journal is followed by a single space, then the volume number, another space, the year of publication in parentheses, a colon, another space, and the inclusive page numbers for the article. End the entry with a period. Do not include the issue number, the month, or the season of the issue.

An article in a journal with separate pagination for each issue

The formal study of Canadian literature at Canadian colleges and universities began ever so slowly at the beginning of the twentieth century: "Canadian literature was first taught at a post-secondary institution in Canada in 1907: it was the subject of a summer course at the Macdonald Institute, an affiliate of the Ontario Agricultural College" (Fee 22).

Fee, Margery. "Canadian Literature and English Studies in the
    Canadian University." Essays on Canadian Writing 48 (1992):
    20-40.

This particular journal uses only issue numbers. Were there a volume number as well, the issue number would follow it in the entry. For example, 19.2 would mean that the article appeared in the second issue of volume 19.

An editorial

One perhaps not surprising result of the recession and the lack of jobs "is that young people have started to stay in school longer" (Lewis).

```
Lewis, Robert. "A Lost Generation?" Editorial. Maclean's 14
     Mar. 1994: 2.
```

A review

```
In all of New York City, there is only one high school for the
deaf. This school--its students and its philosophy--is the
subject of some controversy, according to a recent book (Rymer
1).
```

```
Rymer, Russ. "The Sounds of Silence." Rev. of Train Go Sorry,
     by Leah Hager Cohen. New York Times Book Review 13 Mar.
     1994: 1+.
```

In this and in the next example, listing the page numbers as 1+ indicates that the review begins on page 1 of this part of the newspaper and continues not on page 2 but rather on one or more later pages.

A newspaper article

```
A recent report in The Globe and Mail suggests that Canada's
"national-unity debate" "is starting to look like a grudge match
between Quebec and the West" (Delacourt A1).
```

```
Delacourt, Susan. "Western Canada comes out swinging." Globe
     and Mail 9 June 1994: A1+.
```

The item begins on page 1 of section A; the plus sign means that it is continued on some later page other than page 2.

Interviews

This category includes interviews published in newspapers, magazines, books; interviews broadcast on radio or television; and interviews conducted by researchers themselves. In your text, include a parenthetical reference for a published interview; for a broadcast or research interview include the necessary information about the review, but without page numbers. In the Works Cited entry, include the identification "Interview" for a published or broadcast interview, and "Personal interview" or "Telephone interview" for one you conducted yourself.

(a) published interview

```
Thomas King describes his novel Medicine River as a book about "a
very human side of Native life" (King 111).
```

```
King, Thomas. Interview. Contemporary Challenges: Conversations
     with Canadian Native Authors. Ed. Harmut Lutz. Saskatoon:
     Fifth House, 1991. 107-16.
```

(b) broadcast interview

In a recent interview on <u>Morningside</u>, Maureen Matthews and Roger Roulette spoke of one paradox in the lives of Ojibway people in northern Ontario. That is, they reported that although many young people are fluent in the Ojibway language, few of them are familiar at all with traditional ways represented by the drum ceremony.

Matthews, Maureen, and Roger Roulette. Interview. <u>Morningside</u>.
    CBC Radio. Toronto. 14 Mar. 1994.

(c) research interview

Jean Davis, an economic forecaster with a special interest in Pacific Rim trade, reported in a recent interview that the current economic recovery depends in part on a quick recovery in the Japanese economy.

Davis, Jean. Personal interview. 13 Feb. 1994.

Here are examples of "Works Cited" entries for a few other kinds of sources:

A lecture

Piper, Peter. Lecture. Philosophy 303. Capricorn U. 18 Mar.
    1994.

A television program

"Rumpole's Last Case." Writ. John Mortimer. With Leo McKern.
    <u>Rumpole of the Bailey</u>. Mystery. PBS. KCTS, Seattle. 17
    Mar. 1994.

A recording

Eliot, T. S. "The Love Song of J. Alfred Prufrock." <u>T. S. Eliot
    Reading Poems and Choruses</u>. Caedmon, TC 1045, 1955.

Kennedy, Nigel, violin. Violin concertos. By William Walton.
    Cond. André Previn. Royal Philharmonic Orchestra. EMI,
    CDC 7 49628 2, 1987.

If you are emphasizing the work of the composer or conductor of a musical work, put the appropriate name first.

A film

Begin with the underlined title (unless you are emphasizing a particular contributor, such as the writer or director, or a performer), followed by the director, the distributor, and the date:

<u>Schindler's List</u>. Dir. Steven Spielberg. Universal, 1994.

You may wish to include other information as well—whatever you think relevant to your use of the item; for example:

<u>Schindler's List</u>. Dir. Steven Spielberg. Screenwriter, Steven
    Zaillian. Music by John Williams. With Liam Neeson, Ben
    Kingsley, Ralph Fiennes, and Caroline Goodall. Based on
    Thomas Keneally's novel. Universal, 1994.

A videocassette

<u>Waiting for Godot</u>. Videocassette. Dir. Alan Schneider. Films
    for the Humanities, 1976.

Like the preceding entry, this one begins with the underlined title (unless you are emphasizing a particular contributor, such as the writer or director, or a performer), followed by the director, the distributor, and the date.

A painting

David, Jacques Louis. <u>The Death of Socrates</u>. Metropolitan
    Museum of Art, New York.

If you are working from a published photograph, include the necessary data; for example, the above entry could be continued this way:

    . . . . B & w illus. 9 in <u>The Romantic Rebellion: Romantic
    versus Classic Art</u>. By Kenneth Clark. New York: Harper,
    1973.

The "B & w" abbreviation is necessary because this book also contains a numbered series of colour plates.

A personal letter

Day, A. F. Letter to the author. 1 Apr. 1993.

Material from an information service

Cull, Philip. <u>Resource-Based Learning: A Strategy for
    Rejuvenating Canadian History at the Intermediate School
    Level</u>. 1991. ERIC ED 343 829.

This item is listed in the RIE (*Resources in Education*) volumes for 1993, put out by ERIC (Educational Resources Information Center). Vol 27 of RIE includes a resumé of the item.

If an item has been separately published, include that information as well:

Laforge, Lorne. <u>Second Language Teaching in the Canadian</u>

   <u>University</u>. Alberta Teachers Association, Edmonton. Modern

   Language Council. <u>Alberta Modern Language Journal</u> 16, 1977–

   78. ERIC ED149617.

78b Some Abbreviations Commonly Used in Documentation and Notes (see also #46g)

adapt.	adapted by, adaptation
anon.	anonymous
bk.; bks.	book; books
c., ca.	(Latin *circa*) about, approximately (with dates: c. 1737)
cf.	(Latin *confer*) compare (NOT "see")
ch.; chs.	chapter; chapters (also chap.; chaps.)
col.; cols.	column; columns
comp.; comps.	compiler, compiled by; compilers
cond.	conductor, conducted by
dir.	director, directed by
diss.	dissertation
ed.; eds.	editor, edited by, edition; editors, editions
e.g.	(Latin *exempli gratia*) for example
et al.	(Latin *et alii*) and others
etc.	(Latin *et cetera*) and so forth
ex.	example
f.; ff.	and the following page(s) or line(s)—e.g., pp. 21ff.
fig.; figs.	figure; figures
fwd.	foreword, foreword by
i.e.	(Latin *id est*) that is
illus.	illustrator, illustrated by, illustration(s)
introd.	introduction, introduced by
l.; ll.	line; lines (but see ex. on p. 429)
ms.; mss.	manuscript; manuscripts
n.; nn.	note; notes (usually with page numbers: 37n.; p. 73, nn.2–4; or without periods: 37n, 73nn2–4)
natl.	national
N.B., n.b.	(Latin *nota bene*) note well, take notice
n.d.	no date of publication given
no.; nos.	number; numbers
n.p.	no place of publication given, no publisher
n. pag.	no pagination
n.s.	new series
OED	*Oxford English Dictionary*

op.	opus, work
P	Press (see UP)
p.; pp.	page; pages
par.	paragraph
perf.	performed by, performer
pl.	plate; plural
pref.	preface, preface by
prod.	producer, produced by
pub., publ.	publisher, published by
qtd.	quoted
q.v.	(Latin *quod vide*) which see
rev.	revision, revised, revised by, review, reviewed by
rpt.	reprint, reprinted by
sec., sect.	section
ser.	series
sic	(Latin) thus (see #43j)
st.; sts.	stanza; stanzas
supp.; supps.	supplement; supplements
trans.	translated by, translator
U, Univ.	University
UP, U...P	University Press
v.	(Latin *vide*) see
vol.; vols.	volume; volumes
writ.	written by, writer.

79 Sample Research Paper with Comments

This sample research paper conveniently illustrates many of the details discussed in the preceding pages. The combined essay and commentary will repay your close attention.

Title Page

Although the *MLA Handbook for Writers of Research Papers* does not call for a separate title page, many instructors will prefer that you use one, as did the instructor of the class for which the following paper was written. Here is what the sample research paper's title page looked like:

Perspectives on Frankenstein:

The Maker, the Monster, the Myth

by

Jessica Lee

English 207

Professor Peters

17 March 1994

Other arrangements are possible, of course, but this is a fairly standard one: the title and subtitle are centred about a third or a fourth of the way down; the author's name, also centred, follows several lines lower; and the course, instructor, and date (each centred) come nearer the bottom of the page. Note the double-spacing between the lines in each part.

If no title page is included, the information is grouped at the upper left of the first page, about 2.5 cm from the top (the surname plus page number, at upper right, should be about 1.25 cm from the top):

```
                                                              Lee 1

Jessica Lee

Professor Peters

English 207

17 March 1994
                        Perspectives on Frankenstein:

                    The Maker, the Monster, the Myth

         [And the text would begin here, double-spaced like the other

lines.]
```

A title page is not counted as a page for numbering purposes, and pages containing preliminary material such as outlines and prefaces are not considered part of the regular pagination but are instead numbered with small roman numerals.

Commentary on the outline:

This instructor also required that an outline be submitted with the research paper, but urged that it be kept relatively simple. A working outline will almost surely be much more complicated, but for the purposes of an outline to aid the reader, as opposed to one designed to aid the writer, a simple outline, going only to one level of subheading, will usually be sufficient. The writer here managed to keep hers to one page.

Usually, further subheadings can easily be supplied, even by the reader. Under I-B, for example, there could be these subheadings, probably along with other specific points drawn from paragraphs 7 through 12; indeed, Lee's working outline probably included something like them:

1. Frankenstein abandons his creature and fails to take responsibility for the life he has produced.

2. Frankenstein is not there to save his brother, nor does he come forward to save Justine Moritz from conviction for his brother's murder.

3. Frankenstein's failure to understand the creature's threats leads to the deaths of those he loves most: his best friend, his bride, and his father.

Outline

Thesis Statement: <u>Frankenstein</u> challenges readers to consider
three difficult issues: the role of the creator, the role of
his creature, and the nature of the story-cum-myth.

Beginning: <u>Frankenstein</u>, born of a competition among friends, has
become an enduring story and a lasting cultural symbol. It
poses a challenge to readers who like simple plots and
characters, for it presents a number of puzzles, especially
in its narrative structure and its central characters.

I. The Maker: In Victor Frankenstein, Mary Shelley created a
complex character.

    A. Victor is full of contradictions.

    B. Victor's admirable qualities are overshadowed by his
Promethean mistakes.

II. The Monster: In the monster, Mary Shelley created a second
protagonist who is both sympathetic and appalling.

    A. Though the creature is rejected by his creator, his
early character is human-seeming and sympathetic.

    B. The creature's ultimate character is that of a monster
reacting against human mistreatment.

III. The Myth: Over time, Shelley's characters have been
appropriated and even distorted by popular culture.

    A. The mythmakers have made Victor into a mad scientist.

    B. The mythmakers have given the monster the name of his
creator and have robbed him of his voice.

Ending: The Frankenstein story is as relevant today as when it
was written. Despite its flaws, it is a minor classic.

Commentary on the text:

Note that the writer's surname and the page number appear 1.25 cm from the top and at the right margin, with no accompanying punctuation or other marks. Since a title page is included, the title is not repeated at the beginning of the essay. The text begins 2.5 cm from the top. Left, right, and bottom margins are also 2.5 cm. The essay is double-spaced throughout, including the list of Works Cited at the end—but not the three discursive notes, which are single-spaced. For other matters of format **and** manuscript conventions see Chapter V and the commentary on the list of Works Cited at the end of the essay.

Epigraph: The epigraph which begins the essay is drawn from Mary Shelley's own introduction to the 1831 edition of *Frankenstein*. It emphasizes the importance of Shelley's own view of her work—an idea that Lee will return to several times in her paper.

Note: The paragraphs of the actual essay should not be numbered; they are numbered here, however, so that we can refer to them clearly in this commentary.

Paragraph 1: The opening paragraph, with its references to biographical details, provides background on an important theme of this paper—the process of the writing of *Frankenstein*. And it includes a short quotation—the phrase "hideous progeny"—woven into one of Lee's sentences; this phrase, like the epigraph, is drawn from Shelley's 1831 introduction.

Mary Shelley's "three companions" were the poet Percy Bysshe Shelley (soon to become Mary's husband), the poet Lord Byron, and their friend Dr. Polidori. Lee preferred not to identify them here, since she felt they would distract from her focus on Mary. And she also omits the fact, as stated by Mary Shelley in her introduction, that it was Byron's suggestion that they each write a ghost story. Do you think she made the right decision, or do you feel that she should have mentioned these details?

Paragraph 2: Whereas paragraph 1 focusses on Mary Shelley as the writer of *Frankenstein* and provides a short narrative explaining how she came to write the work, paragraph 2 moves the focus from the writer to the reader and provides a contrast between nineteenth- and twentieth-century readers of the novel.

(Continued on next left-hand page.)

> I busied myself <u>to think of a story</u>,--a story to rival
> those which had excited us to this task. One which
> would speak to the mysterious fears of our nature, and
> awaken thrilling horror--one to make the reader dread
> to look round, to curdle the blood, and quicken the
> beatings of the heart. (Shelley 8)

(1) It all began innocently enough. An eighteen year old spending a rainy summer holiday with a circle of her friends found herself in the middle of a contest--a story-writing contest. Her three companions--two of them poets and the other a doctor--challenged her and one another to write ghost stories to pass the time and to entertain one another. She could not have known that she would win the competition hands down, that her story would survive even through the end of the twentieth century, and that the novel she once described as her "hideous progeny" (10) would become a mystery as well as a ghost story, a number of films as well as a book, and a cultural symbol featured in everything from Hallowe'en parties to billboards to television advertising. If Mary Shelley could have foreseen what was to become of her <u>Frankenstein; or, the Modern Prometheus</u>, she would have been amazed, amused, and perhaps even appalled.

(2) Mary Shelley's story, born after months of writer's block, poses a set of challenges for today's readers--challenges different from those that might have faced readers who picked it up when it was first published. To the readers of the early nineteenth century, it might have seemed just an unusual story from an interesting young bohemian, but those who read the book

Paragraph 2 also briefly analyzes the challenges today's readers face when first encountering a novel very different from the film, television, and other cultural images that have sprung from it. These remarks explain why Lee makes the paradoxical comment that today's readers "know too much and too little" about the plot and characters of the original Frankenstein story.

Paragraph 2 ends (except for a closing comment) with a lengthy but apt quotation supporting the claims Lee has made in the paragraph. She thus uses her research findings in an important way, namely citing an authoritative source to support and flesh out a conclusion she has herself reached independently. Note that she chooses to quote rather than paraphrase Lavalley, because he makes his argument in clear and lively language that fits the tone she is attempting to establish in her own prose. In short, she has concluded that Lavalley's comment will strengthen the substance and the readability of her paper.

Unlike the parenthetical reference following the epigraph on page 1, the reference following Lavalley's words includes only the page number, since Lee has already mentioned the author in her sentence introducing the quotation.

Paragraph 3: The third paragraph begins to round out the introduction.

(Continued)

today know too much and too little about the plot and the
characters before they read the first paragraph. In short, they
come to the novel with a large number of cultural assumptions and
with great expectations, some of which are bound to be
disappointed. Critic Albert J. Lavalley sums up the contemporary
reader's dilemma in this way:

> Most of us first became acquainted with Frankenstein
> and his terrifying creation not through the pages of
> Mary Shelley's 1818 novel but through our childhood
> Saturday afternoons at the movies or leisurely sessions
> before the family television set. By the time we read
> the novel the images from various films are so firmly
> imprinted on our minds that it is almost impossible not
> to filter the events and images of the book through the
> more familiar ones of the films. We are apt to distort
> the novel to fit a familiar mold, miss what is fresh or
> unfamiliar in it, and react with discomfort and
> disappointment. (243)

Indeed, modern readers of Frankenstein have their work cut out
for them.

3   Today's marketing wizards might say that Frankenstein
suffers from all the symptoms of a product that has been
over-exposed to the consumer. Lavalley's comments lead one to
see that readers of the Film and Television Age who like their
novelists to provide pat styles, plots, and characters rather
than to lay down challenges and to provoke difficult questions
may well find Frankenstein to be beyond them. In fact, the story

The assertion that Shelley's novel deserves careful and thoughtful reading provides a transition from Lavalley to brief quotations from Levine.

Rather than using another block quotation so soon after that from Lavalley, Lee has excerpted the quotation from George Levine's essay to suit her style and purpose. Compare the original quotation with the way she uses it in her paper:

> But while *Frankenstein* is a phenomenon of popular culture, it is so because it has tapped into the center of Western feeling and imagination: we can hear echoes of it, not only in Gothic fiction, science fiction, and fantasies of all sorts, but in far more "respectable" works, written before the glut of popular cinematic distortions. *Frankenstein* has become a metaphor for our own cultural crises, and survives even yet in high literary culture whose professors may have seen Boris Karloff stumbling through the fog, hands outstretched, at least once too often.

Excerpting it as she did also allowed her to do a little editing; for example she omitted the "not only," which lacked the balancing "also" or "as well" after the following "but" (see #12b); she then supplied an "as well" of her own, since she felt it made for a clearer construction.

With Levine's help, Lee argues that *Frankenstein* is a work of considerable importance to those who wish to understand some of the central themes of Western culture as they are expressed in fiction, thus pointing ahead to part III of the paper.

Paragraph 4: Paragraph 3 leads to paragraph 4, in effect the paper's thesis, a sentence suggesting that the essay will focus on two characters—the creator, Victor Frankenstein, and his nameless creation—and on their relationship with each other, and on the reasons Mary Shelley's story has survived to become a myth. The thesis thus elaborates on the title, showing that the argument will concentrate on Frankenstein the Maker, Frankenstein the Monster, and Frankenstein the Myth. And though paragraph 4 presents the thesis rather baldly, it doesn't break the continuity of the introduction, since it also acts partly as a transition between paragraphs 3 and 5.

Paragraph 5: This paragraph concludes the introductory section, returning to ideas mentioned in paragraphs 2 and 3 about the difficulties readers may have with the novel. It begins by offering two critical perspectives on the novel as a whole. The first is a paraphrase of Barbara Johnson's characterization of *Frankenstein* as a set of three fictional autobiographies. The second comes in the form of a direct quotation from an essay by Peter Brooks. Lee chose to quote Brooks directly because his comments serve as a useful introduction to her own perspective on *Frankenstein* as a complicated narrative structure which reminds her of a Chinese puzzle. Paragraph 5 thus functions as a good preparation for the discussion of Victor Frankenstein's narrative that follows.

is one that pays and repays close reading, careful consideration, and spirited debate, for it "is a phenomenon of popular culture," as George Levine has observed, precisely "because it has tapped into the center of Western feeling and imagination. . . ." Its echoes are discernible, he says, "in Gothic fiction, science fiction, and fantasies of all sorts," as well as "in far more 'respectable'" pre-cinematic works; he calls it "a metaphor for our own cultural crises" (3).

④ The novel itself challenges readers to consider the most profound and difficult questions about the relationship between the creator and the creature, while the transformation and the staying power of the story--its survival in various forms over decades and even centuries--lead us to wonder about how and why a work of fiction becomes a lasting myth rather than a dusty volume sitting unread on a library shelf.

⑤ Whatever else it has become, Frankenstein began as a book, and a complicated book at that. It has been described by one critic as a novel of three interlocking autobiographies (Johnson 57) and by another as a "story-within-a-story (which is a story-within-a-story-within-a-story)" (Brooks 591). Mary Shelley tells her story to the reader; Robert Walton tells his story to his sister; Victor Frankenstein tells his story to Robert; and the creature tells his story to his maker, Victor Frankenstein. With its narratives within narratives, the novel is a little bit like a Chinese puzzle, and readers must sometimes have the feeling that they will never quite reach a full understanding of it all.

⑥ One of the most fascinating and troubling of Shelley's

Paragraphs 6, 7, and 8: These paragraphs present Lee's analysis of Victor Frankenstein. She supports her perspective with several brief quotations from the text—thus also indicating that she has read the novel closely and carefully. The quotations come from note cards she prepared during her research; for example:

Shelley 27   Walton's Relationship with VF   I

[Walton's fourth letter ends with an outpouring of emotion for VF:]

"*I begin to love him as a brother; and his constant and deep grief fills me with sympathy and compassion.*"

(AND)

"*I have found a man who, before his spirit had been broken by misery, I should have been happy to have possessed as the brother of my heart.*"

[NOTE *Walton's use of the adjectives* "gentle," "wise," *and* "cultivated" *to describe* VF.]

Shelley 54-55   VF's Description of His Own   I
                                            Scientific Methods

[VF *mentions* <u>*only in passing*</u> *what he must do in creating his* "human being."]

① "*Who shall conceive the horrors of my secret toil, as I dabbled among the unhallowed damps of the grave, or* <u>*tortured the living animal*</u> *to animate the lifeless clay?*" (54)

② "*I collected bones from charnel-houses; and disturbed, with profane fingers, the tremendous secrets of / the human frame.*"

                    page break   (54-55)

[Note *how quickly he passes over these details.*]

Paragraph 7: This lengthy paragraph focusses on the theme of Victor Frankenstein's "Promethean" mistakes. The allusion to Prometheus is the first of several in the paper. Lee assumes that her reader has a good understanding of the myth of Prometheus and needs no explanation of it. Do you think her assumption about her audience is correct? Could those who don't know just look it up?

(Continued)

Lee 4

puzzles is Victor's account of his own life. As Walton listens
to the man whom he calls "a brother" (27), and as he retells that
man's story in his letters to his sister, he comments on the
"wildness" and "madness" in Victor's eyes and describes him as
"melancholy and despairing" (25). Yet Walton also praises
Frankenstein in the most glowing terms as "noble," "gentle,"
"wise," and "cultivated" (27). The man at the centre of the
novel is thus a contradiction. And therefore it seems to me
difficult for a reader to share Walton's enthusiasm for Victor
Frankenstein. In his passion for knowledge and power, he makes
too many mistakes and hurts too many people to earn the reader's
devotion, and the structure of Mary Shelley's narrative helps
keep the reader at just enough of an emotional distance to ensure
that kind of response.

  For all of his diligence as a university student and all of
his talent as a scientist, Victor Frankenstein makes Promethean
mistakes in his creation of the monster that he originally
envisions as "a human being" (53). He errs in isolating himself
from his family, his friends, and the real world when he decides
to immerse himself for six years in the life of Ingolstadt.
During that time, he does become the "Modern Prometheus" of the
novel's subtitle, for he aspires to the power of the gods: he may
not steal fire, but he does try to steal the power to give life.
The problem for him is that he must traffic in pain and death in
order to create life. Naively, he assumes that he can create
beauty from the torture of living animals and the "bones from
charnel-houses" (Shelley 54). Looking back on the early days of

The first parenthetical reference needs only a page number, since it is clear that the "he" who thinks of himself as creating "a human being" is Victor Frankenstein himself; the reference is to the novel. But the second reference is not so clear; a reader might think "bones from charnel houses" was from some other source than Victor; to be safe, Lee includes the author's name.

At the end of paragraph 7 Lee has chosen to quote at length rather than to paraphrase Victor's justifications of his experiments because she has decided that it is essential to emphasize *exactly* what he thought and felt as he set about creating life. (Note: Near the end of the quotation, the word *devoted* is used in its now obsolete sense of "doomed" or "cursed.")

Paragraph 8: The principal method of development in this paragraph is that of causation. The first sentence presents the topic—Victor's lack of wisdom as a creator—and the sentences following present the causes of or reasons for that lack of wisdom. In building this part of her argument, Lee draws on the arguments of three critics: Barbara Johnson, Mary K. Patterson Thornburg, and Chris Baldick. She quotes briefly from Johnson, paraphrases Thornburg, and quotes at length from Baldick. (Note: She encloses the quoted phrase "spark of life" in single quotation marks, as it is in Baldick's text; this form is standard in British publications.) The paragraph also illustrates various ways in which sources can be referred to and credited: Johnson's name appears in the main part of the sentence, and so the parenthetical reference includes the page number only. Thornburg's surname is included in the parenthetical reference because she is not named in the main part of the sentence. Baldick's name and the title of his book appear in the main part of the sentence (Lee omits the book's subtitle, knowing that she will include it in the list of Works Cited); only the page number appears in the parenthetical reference.

(Continued)

his experiment, he tells Walton how he then felt:

> A new species would bless me as its creator and source;
> many happy and excellent natures would owe their being
> to me. No father could claim the gratitude of his
> child so completely as I should deserve theirs.
> Pursuing these reflections, I thought, that if I could
> bestow animation upon lifeless matter, I might in
> process of time (although I now found it impossible)
> renew life where death had apparently devoted the body
> to corruption. (54)

Clearly, Victor believed without question that his work would
produce happy results for himself, his creature, and the entire
human race.

(8)   Tragically, however, Victor's skills as a scientific
technician do not translate into wisdom as a creator. He wants
to play at being God and then absolve himself of all
responsibility for his creature's life; or as Barbara Johnson
puts it, he "usurps the female role by physically giving birth to
a child" (63) and then abandons his son to a world completely
unprepared to welcome or accept him. Another critic suggests
that Frankenstein is a victim of his successes as a scientist
(Thornburg 71), but a careful consideration of Victor's own
testimony suggests that Chris Baldick is closer to the truth--
that Victor is a Promethean failure as a scientist--when he
observes in his book In Frankenstein's Shadow that

> The parts, in a living being, can only be as beautiful
> as the animating principle which organizes them, and if

Note: Ending a paragraph with a block quotation—especially a long one—is generally not a good stylistic practice (see #64c.4). Do you think it works well enough here, or should Lee have provided at least a brief comment, perhaps a summary or partial restatement, to end the paragraph more effectively? (See e.g. how she concluded paragraphs 2 and 7 above.) If questioned or criticized, could Lee adequately defend her practice here?

Paragraphs 9, 10, 11, and 12: The aim of these four paragraphs is to explain and prove the student's argument that Frankenstein is a complex and controversial character. Paragraph 9 moves the essay from its focus on Frankenstein's comments on his thoughts and feelings before the monster's birth to his story of his actions and inactions in the period following the birth. Paragraph 10 suggests a parallel between the story-within-a-story structure of the narrative (see paragraph 5) and the patterns of repetition in that part of the plot dealing with Frankenstein's behaviour after the creature's birth. Paragraphs 11 and 12 provide the evidence from the text needed to support the claims made in paragraph 10. In her presentation of incidents from the text that show Frankenstein abandoning his responsibility for his experiment, Lee again demonstrates how carefully she has read the novel. She is equally careful to avoid plot summary (a mere rehashing of the events of the story) and refers to incidents at various points in the text only for the purpose of supporting her argument and proving her point.

Paragraph 10: Note that in the last sentence of this paragraph Lee has added an *s* in square brackets to Kiely's word *crime*, thus making it fit with *sins* in the next phrase. She assured herself that in doing so she did not violate the sense of Kiely's original, which reads in part as follows:

> Frankenstein's crime against nature is a crime against womanhood. . . . Frankenstein later beholds the monster . . . "eliminate" his younger brother, his dearest friend, and his beloved Elizabeth.
>
> All the crimes are sins against life in the bloom of youth and beauty, but the murder of the woman is the most effectively presented and, in a way, the most carefully prepared.

Was she correct?

this 'spark of life' proceeds, as it does in Victor's
creation, from tormented isolation and guilty secrecy,
the resulting assembly will only animate and body forth
that condition and display its moral ugliness. (35)

9   The critical disagreements over Victor Frankenstein indicate
that he is a controversial character. He is, furthermore, a
puzzling character because he defies definition. Before his
creature comes to life, readers can see him as a naive human
being trying too hard to be a god, or as a man trying too hard to
be a woman, or even as a child trying too hard to be a parent.
Then, on that "dreary night of November" (57) on which he crosses
the threshold from thinking about his experiment to performing
it, he shows just how woefully unprepared he is to fill any of
the roles he has chosen for himself. Once the creature opens his
dull yellow eyes, takes his first breath, and moves his stiff
limbs, the intellectual game that Frankenstein has been playing
becomes serious business, and his naiveté is replaced by what can
only be called cowardice.

10   Once Mary Shelley expands her narrative focus to include the
creature as well as his creator, she establishes a pattern of
repetition in her plot that is at least as significant as the
story-within-a-story pattern in her narrative. Time and again,
Victor turns away from his creature and abdicates his fundamental
responsibilities as a god and as a parent. Once his mistakes
affect someone other than himself, they become "crime[s] against
nature. . . . sins against life" (Kiely 74).

11   The crimes of the Prometheus of ancient times resulted in

Paragraph 11: This paragraph opens with an allusion to the ancient myth of Prometheus and explains how Shelley has presented her "modern" version of the myth. In supporting her views, Lee paraphrases the views of critic Robert Kiely (already quoted in paragraph 10), whose essay "*Frankenstein*" is reprinted in *Mary Shelley*, a volume in the *Modern Critical Views* series, edited and with an introduction by Harold Bloom. (See #73b.2 for a copy of her bibliography card for this source.)

Paragraph 11 also includes a discursive footnote indicated by the superscript numeral *1* after the period ending the fourth sentence. This note includes information about the various ways in which Frankenstein's unnamed creature is referred to in the text. Lee could have included this information in the body of her essay, but she decided that it would unduly inflate an already long paragraph, and therefore put it in a discursive footnote at the bottom of the page. Note that she rejected the alternative of placing her note on a separate page preceding the Works Cited page at the end of her essay. She wanted her reader to refer to this additional material immediately, and decided that she could best ensure that by putting the note at the foot of the page. (Had the note been put on a separate page at the end, it would have been double-spaced. As a footnote, it begins four lines below the text, and is single-spaced.) Lee didn't feel that she needed to supply page numbers for the quoted terms, since "wretch," for example, occurs over a dozen times, "monster" and "fiend" at least half-a-dozen, and so forth. Note that she also took the opportunity to get in a further relevant point about the similarity between Victor and his creature, a point developed a couple of paragraphs further on.

Note, in the fifth sentence, that Lee has editorially added an *s* in square brackets to the word *fever*, quoted from the novel, in order to give it the plural sense necessary for her sentence.

his own suffering; with each new day, he found himself chained to a rock, condemned to experience the pain of having his liver consumed by a hungry eagle. Shelley's modern Prometheus, in his retreats from the creature and his repeated failures to speak the truth, makes others suffer and virtually ensures the deaths of those whom he admires and loves. The evidence of Frankenstein's negligence is sufficiently strong to support Robert Kiely's view that Shelley deliberately sets out to undercut her hero (73). Frankenstein is callous when he abandons his newborn creature just moments after he has brought him to life; he is neither maternal nor paternal when he fails to give the creature a name.[1] Time and again he falls ill with "nervous fever[s]" (62) that one critic has diagnosed as "hypochondria, or male hysteria" (London 262), and at one point in his confession to Walton, he admits that he takes laudanum to get himself through the difficult days after his illnesses (184). Thus, the creator is conveniently indisposed at the very time when he should be intervening to prevent tragedy.

12   Once he abandons his child on the world's doorstep, Victor Frankenstein, for all his expressions of guilt, fails to take responsibility for the consequences of his dreams and actions. He is not there to prevent the creature from murdering his little

[1] While many have come to refer to the creature himself as "Frankenstein," Shelley gave the creature no name. But in the novel he is variously referred to as, among other things, "the wretch," "the monster," "the daemon," "the devil," and "the fiend," often with accompanying adjectives. Interestingly, Victor several times also applies the most common of these terms, "wretch," to himself.

Paragraph 13: This paragraph acts as a transition to the second major point of the thesis. It points back to Victor, the subject of the previous paragraphs, and points forward to the creature. Here, Lee argues that the creature and the creator—the maker and the monster of the essay's title— are more similar than Frankenstein ever recognizes. The last sentence of the paragraph signals that the student is about to discuss in detail what the monster's narrative reveals about him and about his resemblance to his maker.

Paragraph 14: This paragraph makes an important point that will be further developed in the last part of the essay. It emphasizes the significant differences between and among the various versions of the Frankenstein story. Here Lee argues that the reader's response to the story is sensitive to the sound of the narrative, while the audience that sees the story enacted in a film or on the stage will come away with a lasting visual impression of the monster. This idea of disparity between the text and the performance was first raised in paragraph 2.

(Continued)

brother William; he will not speak to stop the conviction and
execution of the innocent Justine Moritz for the murder. He
cannot bring himself to keep his promise of a mate for his lonely
creature, and he thus ensures the murder of his best friend,
Clerval. He cannot seem even to arrive at a common-sense reading
of the creature's threat to strike on his wedding night, and so
he creates the circumstances in which his bride, Elizabeth, is
strangled. And everything Victor does and fails to do adds to
the blows his father has to bear, so contributing quite directly
to his death as well.

(13)   Gifted and idealistic, a young university student full of
promise, Victor Frankenstein is nevertheless a force for
destruction. And ironically, the creature he sees as so
different from him with his "watery eyes . . . shrivelled
complexion and straight black lips" (57) is in fact a being made
in Frankenstein's own image. The resemblances between
Frankenstein and his monster are, in fact, more numerous than
Frankenstein is capable of seeing. The monster's eloquent
narrative, located at the heart of the novel, reveals these
resemblances.

(14)   One of the most important decisions Mary Shelley made in <u>her</u>
act of creation was to give the monster a mind, a heart, and a
voice. The viewers of various stage and film versions of
<u>Frankenstein</u> may remember the visual image of the creature more
than anything else about him, but careful readers of the text
remember that voice in all its anger and eloquence. For them, it
is at least as powerful as the anguished voice of Victor

Lee ends paragraph 14 with comments from two critics who have argued for the humanness and goodness of Victor Frankenstein's creature. She has drawn her information from two note cards written during her research:

Ketterer 33	Distortions of the Monster II

"*If Mary was influenced by these automata, it is only appropriate that many commentators have distortedly viewed Frankenstein's organic monster as the major precursor of science fiction's robots, androids, and other intelligent machines.*"

Cude 220	Sympathetic Views of II the Monster

"*In fact, by comparison with the human beings of the novel, the monster must be acknowledged a potentially superior being.*"

[*Note that Cude's argument is a very strong defence of the creature.*]

Paragraphs 15 and 16: These paragraphs focus on Lee's own analysis of the creature's narrative. Like previous sections of the paper, they are based on a close reading of the text. Note that Lee supports her own interpretation with an allusion to the idea of the narratives as autobiographies—a theory offered by the critic Barbara Johnson (see paragraph 5). She adds further support through direct quotation of the primary source—the novel itself.

Frankenstein. The creature may be horrifying to the eye, and his appearance may prompt all who encounter him to doubt his humanity, but the tone of his voice and the power of his story and his argument make him sound unmistakably human. One critic has refuted the idea that the creature is something less than human by observing that "many commentators have distortedly viewed Frankenstein's organic monster as the major precursor of science fiction's robots, androids, and other intelligent machines" (Ketterer 33), and another has gone so far as to suggest that he is "a potentially superior being" (Cude 220).

15 Victor Frankenstein may loathe the sight of his creature, but he is the one who brings his voice alive for Walton and for us as readers, and he reports the creature's narrative in a way that seems authentic. He editorializes very little, but when he does, most notably in Chapter XVII when he stops to comment on the creature's plea for a mate, he shows that his monster has much more than brute strength: he also has a formidable power of persuasion.

16 The first part of the creature's autobiography is amazing because it provides such a vivid and moving account of the first days of life. We are so accustomed to newborns and infants who lack the ability to tell us where it hurts and how it all feels: we know that they can explain nothing to us of the first sensations of being alive, and we know that we have lost all memory of these sensations as adults. The monster, if monster he is, puts those first sensations into words for all of us when he describes the experience of being overwhelmed by his untried

Paragraph 17: This paragraph focusses on a transition point in the creature's narrative: it examines what Lee describes as his childhood and adolescence. At the end of the paragraph, she refers to an essay by Marcia Tillotson which she goes on to discuss and to cite in paragraphs 18-20. The amount of space that the student devotes to Tillotson's interpretation of the text indicates that she is one of the more important sources informing this paper.

Note the student's use of quotation marks around the word *civilization* in the second sentence. She has chosen this as a quick way of suggesting her ironic use of the word. Often such a technique achieves a cheap effect at best. Do you find it effective here? (See #43g for comments on similar uses of quotation marks.)

Paragraph 18: Lee uses this paragraph to cite an important part of Marcia Tillotson's argument: her discussion of Percy Shelley's reaction to his wife's work, and in particular his reaction to the monster. The passage Lee cites is an unusual one, for it contains a comment of Shelley's within Tillotson's comment. Thus, Lee is quoting a quotation within a quotation, and to distinguish Shelley's words from Tillotson's she must be careful with quotation marks and indention. The entire passage, quoted from Tillotson, is enclosed in double quotation marks, while Percy's words are first enclosed in single quotation marks, then indented in a block quotation. Clearly, careful use of punctuation here is essential to a reader's understanding.

The block quotation also requires a discursive footnote, for Tillotson had drawn Percy Shelley's words from another source, and like Lee, she must give full credit to that source in a citation which appears at the end of her essay. Note that the information in the footnote includes the title of Percy Shelley's review (enclosed in quotation marks), the title of the book in which Tillotson found the review (underlined), the editor of the book, and (enclosed in parentheses) the place of publication, the name of the publisher, and the year of publication. The page reference for the quotation follows the parenthesis, and in turn is followed by a period.

senses: "I saw, felt, heard, and smelt, at the same time . . ."
(102). The creature's account of his first discoveries--of light
and darkness, of food and pain, of birdsong and fire--conveys his
first thoughts about the world in simple yet eloquent language.
His confusion is a response that most readers can identify
strongly with, for each of us has experienced the bewildering
pain and pleasure of life. In this part of his narrative, the
creature seems almost like one of us.

(17)   When the creature moves out of the world of nature and into
the world of human "civilization," he begins to use his intellect
as well as his senses. In effect, he moves from his infancy
through his childhood and adolescence, still without any help or
support from his parent and maker. The part of the creature's
autobiography recounting this part of his life is memorable and
moving. It presents the reader with a character who slowly
realizes that he is doomed to an isolation and loneliness that
will never be relieved. In her essay "'A Forced Solitude': Mary
Shelley and the Creation of Frankenstein's Monster," Marcia
Tillotson claims that this part of the creature's story elevates
him, making him the novel's second protagonist (168).

(18)   To help make her point, Tillotson turns to Percy Bysshe
Shelley, noting that "Although Mary Shelley based the character
of Frankenstein on Percy, the poet identified not with the
scientist but with the monster." She then goes on to point out
that, "Applying the moral he had found, 'Treat a person ill and
he will become wicked,' Percy came to this conclusion:

      It is thus that too often in society those who are best

Paragraph 19: The opening question constitutes a change of pace and adds to the variety of Lee's sentences, and also leads to tight paragraph coherence when followed by an answer. And quoting the phrase "neglect and solitude of heart" from the preceding paragraph makes clear the close connection between these two paragraphs. Like paragraph 18, this paragraph focusses on an individual's response to the monster, but here Lee concentrates on Mary Shelley's response rather than on that of Percy Shelley.

Here is how the note card for her main point looked; she encloses her own thought in double brackets in order to clearly separate it from Tillotson's:

Tillotson 167-75	Mary Shelley's View of the Monster	II

Throughout her essay, Tillotson refers to autobiographical explanations for the choices Shelley makes— ⟦*particularly in her decisions about characterization.*⟧ *She suggests that the isolation MS felt in her own life allowed her to make the monster's complaints about his loneliness and isolation utterly believable.*

Paragraph 20: This paragraph again begins with Tillotson, then presents Lee's own evidence for her belief that the creature is generous by nature. She is preparing to argue that the creature was made violent and brutal, not born that way. The note contains Lee's own thoughts and the textual evidence to support them; again, brackets clearly mark her own ideas:

Mine	⟦My View of the Monster⟧	II

⟦*The world is prejudiced against the creature. He reaches out time and again, but each time that he does, he is rejected— violently.*

Examples?
1. *VF's desertion of the monster after his birth*
2. *The man in his shack—runs away*
3. *child saved from drowning—monster shot at!*
4. *Mr. DeLacey—Felix runs him off*
5. *William Frankenstein—pushes him away*⟧

(Continued)

qualified to be its benefactors and its ornaments are
branded by some accident with scorn, and changed by
neglect and solitude of heart into a scourge and a
curse." (174)[2]

The outpouring of sympathy for the creature, then, is not
accidental and not just a product of late twentieth-century
thought.

  How was Mary Shelley so well able to portray this "neglect
and solitude of heart" in a creature who is ultimately a violent
and dangerous criminal? Readers and critics over the years have
looked to the author's own life for answers to this question.
Throughout her essay, Tillotson argues that Mary Shelley herself
suffered from "neglect and solitude of heart" both in her
childhood and in her life with Percy Shelley. The writer in her
might have identified with the creator, Victor Frankenstein, but
the child who had grown up without a mother and with a father
distracted by his second marriage, his other children, and his
struggle to make ends meet as a writer and philosopher must have
identified very much with the creature abandoned and forced to
make his way through life on his own.

20 Tillotson explains Shelley's close identification with her
"hideous progeny" in a memorable sentence: "The world has no more
use for a loving monster than it has for a thinking woman" (172).

---

[2] Tillotson quotes from a review of Frankenstein written by
Shelley, but not published before his death. Her source for this
material is "Review of Mary Shelley's Frankenstein," in Shelley's
Prose, or The Trumpet of a Prophecy, ed. David Lee Clark
(Albuquerque: U of New Mexico P, 1954) 307-08.

Evidently Lee has struggled a bit with the structure of the last sentence of paragraph 20. Do you think her decision to include a substantial parenthetical comment in the middle of her sentence has worked? Can you see any way that she might have revised for greater clarity and emphasis in this sentence?

Paragraphs 21, 22, and 23: These three paragraphs focus on the climax of the creature's narrative: his confrontation with Frankenstein and his demand that his maker give him a mate. Chapter XVII of the novel presents this climactic meeting, and in examining it Lee focusses on the ways in which it moves the creature into his adulthood, shows him at the critical moment when he will choose a peaceful or a violent life, and demonstrates his growing power of persuasion.

Paragraph 21: This paragraph is long chiefly because it contains another long quotation from the novel. In the context of what Lee has to say about the creature's voice in the last sentence of paragraph 23, can you explain why she has chosen to use the creature's words rather than paraphrase them? Do you think she made a good choice here?

The narrative itself reveals an eloquent, sensitive individual
who tries time and again to fit himself into a world utterly
prejudiced against him before he turns to a life of revenge and
all the violence that accompanies it. The creature tries to
approach individuals--whether they be his creator, the isolated
man in his shack, the child in danger of drowning, the blind Mr.
De Lacey, or the little William Frankenstein--in a spirit of
generosity. He tries to watch and to learn from others, and
indeed he does (that is, he learns about family, and he acquires
language and literacy), but every approach he makes ends in
disaster.

21   There is nothing monstrous in the creature's behaviour at
first; in fact, the most monstrous behaviour comes from those who
reject him so violently. In this part of the narrative, with its
careful repetition of similar incidents, Mary Shelley makes an
unmistakable and effective case for the view that the creature
was not born a monster; he was made one by his experiences. He
was never innately evil. Whatever flaws of plot, style, and
characterization may weaken Shelley's novel, this image of the
creature turned from helpless child to wounded adolescent to
bitter and violent adult is powerful. The reader well
understands the creature's transformation when, after numerous
rejections, Shelley gives him these lines:

> I am malicious because I am miserable. Am I not
> shunned and hated by all mankind? You, my creator,
> would tear me to pieces, and triumph; remember that,
> and tell me why I should pity man more than he pities

Paragraph 22: This paragraph concentrates on the monster's reasons for demanding companionship.

Do you think it was necessary to include Shelley's name in the parenthetical reference?

Paragraph 23: This paragraph concentrates on Victor's reasons for accepting the creature's arguments.

(Continued)

> me. . . . Shall I respect man, when he contemns me?
> Let him live with me in the interchange of kindness;
> and, instead of injury, I would bestow every benefit
> upon him with tears of gratitude at his acceptance.
> But that cannot be; the human senses are insurmountable
> barriers to our union. (145)

The creature's acute awareness of just how antagonistic others are toward him and his certainty that he can do nothing to change this antagonism make him sympathetic and make this passage one of the most powerful of the entire novel.

(22) Very few human creatures can live without some form of companionship. The monster, whether he is human or not, has this same need for a companion. That the need is an urgent one becomes clear when he demands what seems to him "reasonable and moderate" (Shelley 145): a mate. He has seen family and romantic love during the time spent observing the De Laceys, and he wants the comfort of such love too. He has also seen with horror his own capacity for violence, and in his own mind he sees living apart with someone like himself to be a way to immunize himself against his tendency to react to the cruel world with equal cruelty.

(23) When the monster makes his impassioned plea for a bride, he reaches a high point--at least in terms of his ability to use his persuasive powers and his emotional appeals to elicit sympathy and consent from the man who has made him and then abandoned him in the world. When Victor Frankenstein agrees to his creature's request, he is not just stalling for time; he seems genuinely

The last sentence of paragraph 23 also conveys in its diction Lee's strong sympathies for the creature. What she does here demonstrates an important point that writers of research papers sometimes overlook: that one can and often must adopt an argumentative stance when the weight of the evidence collected entitles one to draw conclusions and express views.

Note that in quoting from Macdonald and Scherf, Lee retains the comma before the first ellipsis, making the quoted phrase easier to read. The comma was in the original sentence: "Shelley's most revolutionary idea, however—giving the monster an articulate voice—is too revolutionary for Scott, who feels that it destroys the monster's 'mysterious sublimity.' " No ellipsis is needed at the end, since the two-part phrase is obviously fragmentary and could not be mistaken for a sentence.

Paragraph 24: This paragraph launches the last of the three major sections in the body of the paper: the myth of Frankenstein. The first sentence refers to two important ideas raised earlier: the power of the voices telling the story and the puzzles created by the complicated characters Shelley has created. The second sentence, a short, emphatic one, takes up another important idea when it concentrates on the endurance of the story. In launching into a discussion of myth—a word with many denotations and connotations—Lee is careful to define it in her terms when she draws on the discussion that Chris Baldick presents at the beginning of *In Frankenstein's Shadow.*

When Lee quoted the phrase "unsettling characterization" in the first sentence, she didn't have to include an ellipsis either before or after it, since it is obvious, as with the quoted phrase in paragraph 23, that something has been left out.

Paragraph 25: This paragraph introduces and seeks to describe Forry's book, which was as important to Lee's research on myth as Tillotson's essay was to her discussion of readers' responses to the novel (see paragraphs 17-20). Because she wants to give her reader an overview of the entire work, she chooses not to quote it. Has Lee given you as a reader a clear sense of what the book is about? (See #73b.2 for a copy of her bibliography card for this source.)

Note that Forry's book provides an example of a title within a title. Lee has indicated Shelley's title within Forry's by enclosing it in quotation marks. Her other option would have been to leave Shelley's title in roman type (i.e., not underlined; see #48c).

moved and genuinely persuaded. He breaks his promise only when
he is out of range of the creature's anguished voice. Thus,
Shelley's "most revolutionary idea, . . . giving the monster an
articulate voice" (Macdonald and Scherf 35), indicates just how
far she went to make Victor's creature a powerful, eloquent
spokesman for the rights of those who are not beautiful or
graceful or particularly lovable.

(24) The sounds of Shelley's novel and the puzzles created in its
"unsettling characterization" (Macdonald and Scherf 35) linger
long after the final chapter draws to a close. First novel or
not, flawed effort or not, <u>Frankenstein</u> endures. It is not
unique in standing the test of time, but it is unusual in the way
that it has become what Baldick labels "a modern myth," which he
defines as a "timeless" story of "lasting significance" (1-2).
Successive generations of readers and creative artists have added
to or subtracted from Shelley's vision to such an extent that she
might hardly recognize her characters and her original plot in
the versions of <u>Frankenstein</u> we see around us today.

(25) The myth-making surrounding <u>Frankenstein</u> has produced
countless variations on the original text--many of them discussed
in lively detail in Steven Earl Forry's 1990 book, <u>Hideous
Progenies: Dramatizations of "Frankenstein" from Mary Shelley to
the Present</u>. Forry discusses the powerful attraction that
Shelley's novel had for producers of melodrama and burlesque on
the London stage in the 1820s. He shows how film-makers began to
commit the story to celluloid as early as 1910, and he recounts
the details of Hollywood's appropriation of the tale in the

Paragraph 26: This paragraph begins with two brief quotations from Robert Jameson's *The Essential Frankenstein.* These quotations introduce the topic of the popularization of the Frankenstein story and prepare the reader for a discussion of the ways in which Victor and the Monster have been changed over the years. Lee maintains that these changes, while revealing popular beliefs and prejudices, have diminished the power of both characters as Mary Shelley created them.

classic 1931 <u>Frankenstein</u> starring Boris Karloff as the monster. Forry concludes that, in the shadow of Karloff's performance, actors and film-makers have turned the <u>Frankenstein</u> story into everything from comedy to science fiction thriller to cult classic.

26 Over time, then, what Robert Jameson calls this "tale of darkness" has become a myth that has "infiltrated every conceivable medium, from novel, play, and poem, to film, video, and rock song" (7). Many creative and not-so-creative individuals have seized their opportunities to make their versions of what Shelley referred to in her introduction to the 1831 edition of <u>Frankenstein</u> as "so very hideous an idea" (5), but the most significant changes to the original tale have involved Shelley's two puzzling protagonists. Victor Frankenstein, the gifted young university student who set out to challenge death and God and human biology in his Promethean experiments, the protagonist who maintains that he is "not recording the vision of a madman" (52) in his narrative, has been made into the mad scientist, living in his gothic mansion and implanting the brain of a criminal into his creature--all with the assistance of his faithful, grotesque, and comic servant Fritz. This madness makes all that Frankenstein does explicable, but it also makes his behaviour less interesting, less complex, less of a puzzle. The mythmakers have diminished him in the process of explaining him, and in so doing have revealed how suspicious many of us in this culture are of the scientist and how anxious we are about the power of science to redefine life.

Paragraph 27: This paragraph deals with the curious way in which the names of characters in Shelley's story have been confused over time. Lee cites Forry's book in offering an explanation for the circumstances leading to the misnaming of the monster as Frankenstein.

Paragraph 28: This paragraph presents Lee's own conclusions about the consequences of popular culture's coming to view Frankenstein the Monster as a being incapable of speech. Lee sketched out the ideas for this paragraph on a note card:

Mine	The Distortion of the Creature by Popular Culture—III, para. 28
⟦TOPIC: *The decision to take away the creature's voice*	
EFFECT? *– still possible to move the audience with a silent creature*	
BUT	
– The sympathy we feel cannot be as great when the creature is rendered as less than human *– are we "humancentric"* *– does inability to speak = less than human??* ⟧	

(Continued)

27   While many of the mythmakers have rendered Victor insane,
they have transformed his creature beyond recognition. He has
acquired a name, for one thing. Forry suggests that the
unofficial christening of the creature as Frankenstein occurred
in 1826 when actor T. P. Cooke, who played the role of the
creature, referred to him by his maker's name in reference to a
poetic dramatization entitled <u>The Devil Among the Players</u> (28-
29). Along with a name, the creature has over time also acquired
a sharper physical image. The figure that Victor Frankenstein
had difficulty describing to Walton in the novel has been
replaced by the awkward giant in the ill-fitting suit--his head
squared, his eyebrows meeting over the bridge of his nose, his
neck pierced on the right and the left side by those trademark
metal bolts.

28   Popular culture has robbed the monster of the power of his
voice--the source of his eloquence and persuasiveness. Of all
the changes made to the creature, this is the most important.
His isolation and anger can still be conveyed in a silent
performance or even in one punctuated by grunts and groans, but
without that voice, the creature has a harder and harder time
moving any audience to feel that he is worthy of the kind of
sympathy that human beings give to one of their own who is
suffering unjustly. The emphasis on the appearance of the
creature at the expense of the sound of his voice thus diminishes
him just as surely as the mythmaking surrounding Victor
Frankenstein diminishes him. The more monstrous the monster
becomes to us, the less troublesome is his fate. And if the

Note the word *humancentric* in the last sentence of paragraph 28. Why has Lee put it in quotation marks? Has she made a good decision in this instance?

Paragraphs 29-31: These three paragraphs bring the paper to a close. In ending her essay, Lee has tried to do something other than simply restate the points she has already offered and supported in detail in the body of her paper. Instead, she has aimed for a more memorable and distinctive conclusion, one which considers the ways in which some current scientific and ethical debates are similar to those raised by *Frankenstein*.

Paragraph 29: This paragraph begins with a quotation from a poem, two lines that refer to the connection between myth and reality; the quotation supports Lee's view that the original story and the subsequent variations on it are all part of what *Frankenstein* means. Then come three sentences that effectively close the discussion of the "myth," and a final sentence that provides a transition from that discussion to the final two paragraphs, which constitute the paper's ending.

The quotation from Birney is of lines 31 and 32 of a 35-line poem; would identifying the line numbers have helped, or is a parenthetical reference unnecessary for so short a poem?

Paragraph 30: This paragraph occasions the third and last of the paper's discursive footnotes. In citing a comment from *Time*, certainly a publication reflecting our popular culture, Lee shows how references to *Frankenstein* arise naturally in a discussion of current scientific experiments having to do with the creation of life in the laboratory.

changes to Victor reflect some of our fears of science and
scientists, the changes to the creature show our "humancentric"
biases and our tendency to assume that awkwardness, ugliness, and
cruelty are somehow less than human.

(29)   In his poem "The Bear on the Delhi Road," Earle Birney
wrote, "It is not easy to free / myth from reality." These lines
certainly apply to Mary Shelley's story. The novel is the
reality; the myth consists of the many variations on Shelley's
original theme. The novel has kept alive vital questions; the
myth has trivialized the maker and the monster until they have
sometimes lost the power to horrify and to mystify. While the
myth and the reality have become inseparable, together they have
kept alive the idea that human attempts to manufacture life take
human creators and the creatures whose lives they shape down an
uncertain and frightening path.

(30)   In this age of recombinant DNA experiments and test-tube
babies, the questions raised by the Frankenstein story are as
provocative as ever.[3] We still struggle with our fears about
scientific advances and wonder whether the day will come when
they threaten our humanness. We still ask (as the creature does)

---

[3] In its cover story of October 11, 1993, Time Magazine
showed the continuing relevance of the Frankenstein story when it
reported,

> The notion that life arose quickly and easily has
> spurred scientists to attempt a truly presumptuous
> feat: they want to create life--real life--in the lab.
> What they have in mind is not some monster like
> Frankenstein's, pieced together from body parts and
> jolted into consciousness by lightning bolts, but
> something more like the molecule in that thimble-size
> test tube at the Scripps Research Institute. (Nash 44)

Paragraph 31: This final paragraph brings the essay full circle when it refers to George Levine's comments about *Frankenstein*, since he was first cited in the third paragraph. Here at the end of the paper, Lee uses Levine's comments on the flaws in Shelley's novel and on its importance as a minor classic to re-emphasize a point she has made several times—that *Frankenstein* is a significant novel, weaknesses and all.

The penultimate sentence in this paragraph uses the three key words that appear in the title of the essay: maker, monster, myth. And the final sentence takes the reader back to the first four sentences of paragraph 1, sentences focussing on the unusual origins of Shelley's novel, thus ending the essay with a strong sense of closure.

about our place in the world; we still wonder (as Victor
Frankenstein does) about our responsibility toward those whom we
bring into the world. We still ask how far is too far in the
quest for knowledge and progress.

(31)   George Levine is right to describe <u>Frankenstein</u> as a minor
novel, "radically flawed by its sensationalism, by the inflexibly
public and oratorical nature of even its most intimate passages"
(3). But he is also right to suggest that <u>Frankenstein</u> is
"arguably, the most important minor novel in English. . . .
larger and richer than any of its progeny and too complex to
serve as mere background" (3). Taken together, the maker, the
monster, and the myth show that Mary Shelley made the right
decision when she decided to pay attention to her nightmare and
commit it to print. Without doubt, she deserved to win that
ghost-story contest.

Pages 19 and 20 constitute the Works Cited section. Here Lee lists all the works she has quoted, paraphrased, or otherwise referred to in her essay.

Format:

1. Begin on a new page; number pages continuing from the essay.
2. Center the heading 2.5 cm from the top. Double space between heading and first entry, and within and between entries.
3. Begin each entry at the left margin. When an entry exceeds one line, indent each subsequent line five spaces.
4. Note carefully the punctuation and spacing within the entries. Follow a colon with one space and a period with two spaces.
5. List entries alphabetically (usually according to surname of author or editor). Do not number the entries, and do not group them according to kinds of sources (books, articles, etc.).

Lee's *Works Cited* includes a variety of books and articles. Here are some comments on specific points in the entries (see #78a for further examples):

Jameson: A typical entry for a book. It includes the author's surname and his full first name, separated by a comma and followed by a period and two spaces. The title of the book is appropriately capitalized and underlined (or italicized), and is also followed by a period and two spaces. The publication information begins with the city of publication, which is followed by a colon, a space, the name of the publisher, a comma, another space, and the year of publication.

Brooks: An entry for a journal with continuous pagination. It is organized as follows: author's last name; comma; space; first name; period; two spaces; title of article, enclosed in quotation marks, with a period inside the closing quotation mark; two spaces; name of scholarly journal, underlined (or italicized); one space; volume number of the journal; one space; year of publication, enclosed in parentheses; colon; one space; inclusive page numbers of the article; period. Note that the title of the novel, *Frankenstein*, included within the title of the article, is underlined (or italicized)—as also in the titles of the articles by Lavalley, Levine, and London.

Birney and **Lavalley:** Citations for works in anthologies, the first an anthology of poetry, the second an anthology of essays. The title of each anthology is italicized and followed by the names of the editors. See also the entries for Johnson, Kiely, Levine, Tillotson. The page numbers are separated from the rest by a period and two spaces, rather than by a colon and one space, as in entries for periodicals (Brooks, Cude, London, Nash).

Ketterer and **Thornburg:** Books in a series. The information about each series—its name and the number of the item within it—appears between the book's title and the publication data. The Johnson and Kiely entries are also for works in series, but there is no number for the books, only the names of the series.

Works Cited

Baldick, Chris. <u>In Frankenstein's Shadow: Myth, Monstrosity, and Nineteenth-century Writing</u>. Oxford: Clarendon, 1987.

Birney, Earle. "The Bear on the Delhi Road." <u>15 Canadian Poets</u>. Eds. Gary Geddes and Phyllis Bruce. Toronto: Oxford UP, 1970. 5-6.

Brooks, Peter. "Godlike Science/Unhallowed Arts: Language and Monstrosity in <u>Frankenstein</u>." <u>New Literary History</u> 9 (1978): 591-605.

Cude, Wilfred. "Mary Shelley's Modern Prometheus: A Study in the Ethics of Scientific Creativity." <u>Dalhousie Review</u> 52 (1972): 212-25.

Forry, Steven Earl. <u>Hideous Progenies: Dramatizations of "Frankenstein" from Mary Shelley to the Present</u>. Philadelphia: U of Pennsylvania P, 1990.

Jameson, Robert. <u>The Essential Frankenstein</u>. London: Bison, 1992.

Johnson, Barbara. "My Monster/My Self." <u>Mary Shelley's "Frankenstein."</u> Ed. Harold Bloom. Modern Critical Interpretations. New York: Chelsea, 1987. 55-66.

Ketterer, David. <u>Frankenstein's Creation: The Book, The Monster, and Human Reality</u>. English Literary Studies Monograph Series 16. Victoria, BC: U of Victoria, 1979.

Kiely, Robert. "<u>Frankenstein</u>." <u>Mary Shelley</u>. Ed. Harold Bloom. Modern Critical Views. New York: Chelsea, 1985. 65-80.

Lavalley, Albert J. "The Stage and Film Children of <u>Frankenstein</u>: A Survey." <u>The Endurance of</u> Frankenstein:

Nash: An entry for an article appearing in a popular magazine.

Macdonald and Scherf: An entry for the introduction to a particular scholarly edition of *Frankenstein*. It cites the editors in the usual author-position, and then specifies the Introduction, followed by the title of the work, and the edition reproduced in the book, namely that of 1818; then—after "By"—the name of the author herself, Mary Wollstonecraft Shelley; and finally the publication information followed by a period and the inclusive page numbers for the introduction and another period.

In the entries for Forry, Johnson, and Thornburg, book titles include the title of the novel itself, which is then enclosed in quotation marks, and the whole book title underlined. To illustrate an alternative method, in the Lavalley and Levine entries, where the novel's title also occurs within the book title, we have left the novel's title without underlining (i.e., in roman type). (In the entry for Kiely, the title of the novel is itself also the title of Kiely's article; hence the word *Frankenstein* is underlined, but the quotation marks are not.)

Note that the entries for Lavalley and Levine refer to essays from the same collection, that edited by Levine and Knoepflmacher. Lee chose to cite each essay as if it had come from a separate book. To avoid the repetition, she could have chosen to use cross-referencing, listing the collection itself as a separate entry, under the editors' names, and the individual essays under their authors' names, like this:

```
Lavalley, Albert J.  "The Stage and Film Children of

    Frankenstein: A Survey."  Levine and Knoepflmacher 243-89.

Levine, George.  "The Ambiguous Heritage of Frankenstein."

    Levine and Knoepflmacher 3-30.

Levine, George, and U. C. Knoepflmacher, eds.  The Endurance of

    Frankenstein: Essays on Mary Shelley's Novel.  Berkeley: U

    of California P, 1979.
```

Since this method results in an additional entry, we think Lee chose correctly. But if there were three or more essays from the same collection the duplication would be greater, and such cross-referencing might be preferable, since it would likely result in overall simplification.

<u>Essays on Mary Shelley's Novel</u>. Eds. George Levine and U. C. Knoepflmacher. Berkeley: U of California P, 1979. 243-89.

Levine, George. "The Ambiguous Heritage of <u>Frankenstein</u>." <u>The Endurance of</u> Frankenstein: <u>Essays on Mary Shelley's Novel</u>. Eds. George Levine and U. C. Knoepflmacher. Berkeley: U of California P, 1979. 3-30.

London, Bette. "Mary Shelley, <u>Frankenstein</u>, and the Spectacle of Masculinity." <u>PMLA</u> 108 (1993): 253-67.

Macdonald, Lorne, and Kathleen Scherf, eds. Introduction. <u>Frankenstein; or, The Modern Prometheus</u>. 1818. By Mary Wollstonecraft Shelley. Peterborough, ON: Broadview, 1994. 11-43.

Nash, J. Madeleine. "How Did Life Begin?" <u>Time</u> 11 Oct. 1993: 43-48.

Shelley, Mary. <u>Frankenstein, or, The Modern Prometheus</u>. Ed. M. K. Joseph. The World's Classics. Oxford: Oxford UP, 1969.

Thornburg, Mary K. Patterson. <u>The Monster in the Mirror: Gender and the Sentimental/Gothic Myth in "Frankenstein."</u> Studies in Speculative Fiction 14. Diss. Ball State U, 1984. Ann Arbor: UMI, 1987.

Tillotson, Marcia. "'A Forced Solitude': Mary Shelley and the Creation of Frankenstein's Monster." <u>The Female Gothic</u>. Ed. Juliann E. Fleenor. Montreal: Eden, 1983. 167-75.

80a   The Name-Date Method

This system is common in the social sciences; the standard guide is the *Publication Manual of the American Psychological Association*, 3rd ed. (1983). Like the name-page method, it uses parenthetical references in the text, but instead of listing the author and the page in the source where the cited material occurs, it lists the author and the date of publication of the source. Since in the sciences reference is often made to the argument or evidence presented by an entire work, page numbers are seldom necessary:

> There are many remarkable parallels between the way artists and scientists look at the world around us (Shlain, 1991).

But if you refer to a particular part of the source, or if you quote from it, supply the relevant page number or numbers:

> As Leonard Shlain (1991) reminds us, "Space, time, and light are of profound interest to both the physicist and the artist" (p. 28).

Note that, as in the name-page method, if you name the author in the text, you don't include the name in the parenthetical reference.

Here are some further examples of name-date parenthetical references, followed by some examples of bibliographical entries:

A work with one author

> Trevor-Roper (1947) presents a detailed account of the defeat and death of Adolf Hitler.

A work with two or more authors

> Although it is true that "the religious and secular customs of the community sometimes helped women who had been assaulted or harassed, nothing could lessen the impact of war on the countryside and its inhabitants" (Anderson & Zinsser, 1988, 1: pp. 115-116).

The fact that the citation comes from volume 1 of a two-volume work could also be noted in the bibliographical list of references. Note that in APA style an ampersand rather than *and* separates two authors in a reference, that the abbreviations "p." and "pp." are used for "page" and "pages," and that all three digits of the closing page number are included.

If a work has two authors, list both names each time it is referred to. If it has three, four, or five authors, list all of them the first time, but only the first and *et al.* (not italicized or underlined) thereafter. If it has six or more authors, list only the first and *et al.* each time, including the first.

As with the name-page system, the bibliography, here labelled "References," consists of a list of all works cited, alphabetized by authors' surnames, beginning on a new page after the essay. Here are a few sample entries:

References

Anderson, B. S., & Zinsser, J. P. (1988). <u>A history of their own: Women in Europe from prehistory to the present</u>. 2 vols. London: Penguin, 1989.

Dawson, V. P. (1988). The scientist in shirt-sleeves: Charles Bonnet's letters on parthenogenesis. In D. C. Mell, Jr., T. E. D. Braun, & L. M. Palmer (Eds.), <u>Man, God, and nature in the Enlightenment</u> (pp. 193-203). East Lansing: Colleagues Press.

Dunbar, M. J. (1977). <u>Environment and good sense: An introduction to environmental damage and control in Canada</u>. Montreal: McGill-Queen's University Press.

Gould, S. J. (1980). <u>The panda's thumb: More reflections in natural history</u>. New York: W. W. Norton.

Gould, S. J. (1991). <u>Bully for brontosaurus: Reflections in natural history</u>. New York: W. W. Norton.

Jung, C. G. (1916). <u>Psychology of the unconscious</u>. (B. M. Hinkle, Trans.). New York: Moffat, Yard.

Mills, C. W. (1956a). <u>The power elite</u>. New York: Oxford University Press.

Mills, C. W. (1956b). <u>White collar: The American middle classes</u>. New York: Oxford University Press.

Sharma, M. C., Kivlin, J. E., & Fliegel, F. C. (1975). Environmental pollution: Is there enough public concern to lead to action? <u>Environment and Behavior</u>, <u>7</u>, 455-471.

Shlain, L. (1991). <u>Art & physics: Parallel visions in space,</u>
<u>time, and light</u>. New York: William Morrow.

Trevor-Roper, H. R. (1947). <u>The last days of Hitler</u>. New York:
Macmillan.

Note the following features in the above entries, including differences
from the format used in the name-page system:

(a) The list is double-spaced throughout.

(b) Second and subsequent lines are indented only three spaces.

(c) Only initials are used, not first and middle names—hence it is not
evident from this list that, e.g., in the first and second items,
Anderson (Bonnie), Zinsser (Judith), Dawson (Virginia) and Palmer
(Lucia) are women.

(d) For a work by more than one author, all authors' names are in reverse
order, not just the first.

(e) The year of publication goes after the name(s) of the author(s)—
though in some versions of this method it goes at the end (for a
book) or after the volume number (for a journal).

(f) Only the first word of a title and subtitle, and any proper nouns, are
capitalized.

(g) There are no quotation marks around the title of an essay or article.

(h) Publishers' names are given in full, omitting only terms like "&
Company," "Co.," "Inc."

(i) The volume number of a journal is underlined.

(j) Two or more works by the same author are listed in chronological
order. Two or more works by the same author, but published in the
same year, are listed alphabetically (by first major word in title), with
a, b, c, etc. after the year.

As with other systems, there will likely be variations among different disciplines. For more information and examples, consult an appropriate style
manual. And check with your instructor if necessary.

80b   The Number Method

Methods of documentation in the natural, physical, life, and applied sciences vary more than those in the social sciences and the humanities—
though you may find that a course in one or another of these sciences
asks you to use the name-page, name-date, or even note method, just as a
course in one of the social sciences, or even one in the arts, may require
you to use the number method.

Most of the sciences, and their scientific journals, use a form of the number method. Numbers in the text refer to specific items in a numbered list of "References" at the end. The numbers in the text may appear in parentheses or as superscript numbers; for example:

```
Hawking (3) discusses black holes at some length.
```

```
Hawking discusses black holes at some length.[3]
```

The reference may be to more than one source, listing the items in numerical order:

```
Several recent articles have discussed this continuing

investigation (4, 7, 18, 21).
```

Some versions call for the number(s) to be underlined, which helps by distinguishing the item number from a page number if a specific passage is being referred to:

```
Hawking says that the term "black holes" was coined in 1969, but

that the idea goes back over two hundred years (3, 81).
```

The sources in the numbered list of references may appear simply in the order in which they are referred to; sometimes, however, the list is ordered and numbered alphabetically. In either instance, a second or further citation of a particular source would simply repeat the relevant number. An entry might look like this:

```
3. Hawking, S.  A brief history of time: From the big bang to

   black holes.  Toronto: Bantam, 1988.
```

And sometimes the numbers in the text will be in brackets rather than parentheses; sometimes the parenthetical reference will include not only a page number but a volume number, a date, or even an author's surname. In the bibliography, the place of publication sometimes follows the name of the publisher. Some systems use no quotation marks or underlining at all; others use quotation marks around book titles, or put authors' names in capital letters, or put volume numbers in bold type; dates sometimes come early, sometimes late. Sometimes endnotes stand in place of a list of references. And so on. The variations in method and format between one discipline and another, or even within one discipline, are so many that you should always find out what your instructor prefers, and if necessary consult an appropriate style manual, such as one of the following: *CBE Style Manual* (Council of Biology Editors), *Handbook for Authors of Papers in American Chemical Society Publications*, *A Manual for Authors of Mathematical Papers*, *Style Manual for Guidance in the Preparation of Papers* (American Institute of Physics).

80c   The Note Method

This method also appears in different versions, for example that discussed in the *MLA Handbook for Writers of Research Papers* and that in the more comprehensive *Chicago Manual of Style*. Again, if your instructor wishes you to use this method, find out just which version is wanted. For example, with a complete set of endnotes or footnotes, a bibliography may be considered unnecessary duplication. Sample essay number 17 in the next chapter illustrates most of the basic forms for notes and for bibliographical entries.

PART 5

SAMPLE ESSAYS, CORRECTION SYMBOLS, AND OMNIBUS CHECKLIST

CHAPTER X

SAMPLE STUDENT ESSAYS WITH COMMENTS AND GRADES

The sample essays which follow are actual essays written by students. Some were written in response to specific assignments; others developed under such general instructions as "Write an extended definition" or "Write an argument." The essays vary in length, kind, and quality. The marginal and final comments focus on matters of content, structure, and style. They will differ from those that other instructors would make, but we believe that they are accurate and fair and that they focus on criteria that all instructors will use in measuring the quality of a student's writing. The grades we have assigned may not be exactly what others would have given, but we believe that they are reasonably accurate and that most instructors would agree with them. Since grading methods vary from institution to institution, here is how our letter grades would translate into other systems:

A	I	80-100%	Very Good to Excellent
B	II	68-79%	Fairly Good to Good
C-D	Pass	50-67%	Passably Weak to Fair
F	Fail	0-49%	Very Poor to Poor

Some comments on the individual essays that follow

The first three essays are brief expositions on the same topic and represent a range of quality from excellent to very poor. Essay 4 could be called a brief informal or expressive argument. Essay 5 is a brief argument. Essay 6 is a more elaborate argument. Number 7 is also an argument, but of a special kind: it was written in reponse to a request for an essay using irony in the manner of Jonathan Swift's "A Modest Proposal"; since the student chose to commit a few deliberate errors as a part of the characterization of the speaker, he labelled them in the margin so that he wouldn't be blamed for them. Essay 8, an argument, contains such serious problems in organization, development, and expression that it was assigned a failing grade. Essay 9 is a brief definition. Essay 10 is a more ambitious exercise in definition and classification. Essays 11 through 17, unmarked and ungraded, are included for the purposes of practice and discussion. The final essay, number 17, basically an exercise in classification and definition, is a research report using a relatively traditional version of the note method of documentation.

(Note: Essays 10, 11, 13, 15, and 17 were written by second- and third-year university students; the rest were written by first-year students.)

Sample Essay No. 1

1

The Days of the Pioneers

The first Canadian was a hardy man from France. He
worked all day for bread. Today's Canadian works half the
day for cake. The pioneers worked to lay the foundations.
We work to add the playroom and the bar.

good opening ¶

The *fermier* paid very little for his estate. He built
his home without blueprints. His prime tools were the axe,
the saw, and the hammer. When the house was ready, he did
not sit in his den and read his newspaper. He had to clear
the land so he could eat and feed his children.

that?

oops! rephrase to avoid ambig

He got up at four in the morning, when it was pitch
black outside. No streetlights lit his pathway to the
outbuildings where his animals were. He worked for three
hours until breakfast. His breakfast was not habit, but
necessity. He ate oatmeal, pancakes, and bacon, and drank
coffee with thick cream. His daily routine varied with the
season, not the time of the fiscal year. In spring, he
cleared the land, then plowed and planted. He helped his
animals have their young. In summer he cleared more land,
and cultivated his crops. In autumn he harvested. Winter
brought some resting time, but the *fermier* still had many
chores to do.

good details

p necessary?

ploughed?

a well-crafted ¶

The man and his wife worked as a team on the farm.
Togetherness came naturally. They did not have to strive
for it. The children came, for family planning was unheard
of. They were made a part of the working unit. They
cleaned the chicken coop, hoed the garden, and watched the

coord with ; ?

in what sense? watched over?

490   *Sample Essays*

2

[margin: agr/shift]

inevitable baby. The family <u>was</u> united, for <u>they</u> needed

[margin: preferred sp?]

each other. The nearest neighbor was often miles away. *[caret with "u" below "neighbor"]*

Family loyalty was only one of the <u>fermier</u>'s loyalties.

[margin: ✓ good // ss]

He was a lover of his land, working with it until he died.
He remembered his <u>mother</u> country, holding dear <u>her</u> language *[margin: try gender-neutral language here?]*
and customs. He was loyal to his Church, loving the priest
and attending the masses.

[margin: ✓ good emphatic rep]

This man, this pioneer, experienced days of

discouragement, days when his crops failed, days when his

children died. He experienced days of hardship, when the

elements raged. But he had a goal, a purpose, which was

immediate and urgent. He earned his bread. The Canadian of

today does not have this immediate goal, and his cake is

tasteless.

Well done. Good simple and clear expression, with some
pleasing crispness. Think about that suggested semicolon;
its use would have added just that extra bit of
finesse. Some paragraphs look a bit short, but each
has unity and is adequately developed. Effective
opening and closing image. You perhaps over-rely on
loose sentences in the s-v-obj pattern; try for
more variety in future assignments.

Sample Essay No. 2

1

The Days of the Pioneers

[handwritten margin annotations throughout]

wo
to avoid split (see 10c)

If the North American people of today were (to suddenly)

p not needed

go back in time, to the days of the pioneers, they would

w?

find life very hard to endure. The pioneers did not have

red

log (only some ?)

all the modern conveniences of today. They travelled in

covered wagons, had to hunt for their food, and slept

outdoors with only a canvas roof over their heads.

unlikely!

They were constantly travelling. Because of this they

led very insecure and uncertain lives. Education was

vague

limited because there were no schools, and the children, at

awk — no p

¶ lacks unity

an early age were expected to assist in the daily chores.

id

Survival depended on each person in the family doing his

or her?

utmost in whatever job he was expected to do.

or she?

ref—see 5a

They led very simple lives. There were no motion

topic sent. not linked to thesis?

pictures they could go to for entertainment, no laundromats

fp

to take the clothes to when there were too many clothes to

rep, w

be washed at home, no restaurants to go to when mother was

too tired to cook dinner. Because they had no electricity,

log shaky at best

pas

everything was done by manual labour. Since they worked so

hard and because there were no beauty parlours, make-up, or

face cream, the women grew haggard at an early age. The men

also aged quickly because of the worries and hardships of

vague

coh— tr needed

life. The family worked together as a closely knit unit.

close-knit?

The children had no outside activities outside of the

awk rep

ref?

family, which kept them from seeing each other for days at a

log?

time. Because of this closeness, there was no juvenile

X

deliquency or teen-age crime which is so rampant today.

ref? p?

oversimplification

contradicts "worries" a few sentences back

The pioneer's sole <u>worry</u> was survival. He did not have
Sentences lack climactic order
to even <u>think</u> of such things as the atomic bomb, politics *split necessary?*
and frustrations at the office. His time was occupied by
protecting himself and his family from Indians and wild
animals, and providing enough food to eat, <u>and enough fuel</u> *p? awk //*
to keep them warm.

(If) a person of today were to go back in time to the
days of the pioneers, (one) (wonders) (if) in spite of the *awk log, ss*
hardships, the simplicity of pioneer life would make him
basically happier person than he is in the modern world. *Ends on rather vague note*

X

(D) You're fairly careful with mechanics, though your proofreading
was inadequate. Some good contrasts, but lacking in
effective sharpness of detail. (Is "face cream" etc.
really worth bringing in?) Some flavour of cliché ("at
an early age" applied to both women and children
becomes meaningless). Some awkwardness of expression,
and logic and coherence are weak throughout. Watch out
for loose reference of which and that. And your thesis
needs a stronger focus: it should do more than just
list the items you will develop.

Sample Essay No. 3

THE DAYS OF THE PIONEER FARMER —— *ms: not all caps*

lc (passim) The Pioneers in Alberta led an exciting and adventurous
meaning? farming life as compared to the quiet domesticated life the *art. not needed?*
people lead now. ∧ Inconveniences of farmers in Pioneer days — *art. needed*
agr seems unsurmountable to us with all our conveniences. *very awk sentence*
sp d?

Although there are many aspects of this life, the *weak d* *ref*
weak d farming life has the most vivid impression on my *¶ too short*
imagination.

seq. of tenses — see 61
awk dm Starting in the spring when the crops must be sowed,
the farmer did not sit on a tractor an pull a seeder over *X*
his land; he hitched eight or twelve horses to a seeder and
id? walked every stretch of land, as the horses did. As time *d, us*
meaning? was a precious period in seeding, he worked from dawn to *meaning?*
=/passim dusk; unlike the present day farmer. The work went slowly; *awk*
the present day farmer can accomplish five times what the *only that? i.e.,*
Pioneer farmer accomplished. In the mid-day break the *in the same time?*
Pioneer had his dinner, but before he was eating he had to *†*
red first go through the ritual of unhitching, watering and *P*
or 12? feeding his eight horses. After his meal the horses must be *†*
re-hitched, and the slow work continued. Present day
farmers come in with the tractor, give it gas and grease,
shift and in no time at all he is returned back to the field. *cliché red*
wo? Once the Pioneer had his seeding completed he had to wait *true today too?*
d? till summer, while nature provided for his crops. If *cl?*
pl? locusts should strike or choking weed invade his fields he
prep would be helpless in defending them. It was not a matter of *to defend?*
needed, spraying his fields to insure its results. A dry year would *ref*
or "them"
is ambig

Could this long ¶ be divided?

mean a poor yield; there was no irrigation to guarantee a ~~does it, really?~~

successful crop. If his crop survived the trials of nature, ~~d, ambig?~~

he had a harvest in August.

wo for //

nice sentence

August not only meant the harvest of his crop but a *also*

spell of long hot days, if the weather agreed. Now by had *d? X*

he cut his crop, and with his hands he bound the sheaves. A

†

job which would take the Pioneer farmer from August to mid- *not much different*

October, takes the present farmer four to six weeks.

above, was plural

Not only did the Pioneer farmer have to cope with *awk—"with Nature"?*

Nature's trial but also there was a constant menace of the *weak expletive, and awk*

P

Indians; a ridiculous thought of the farmer of today. He *garbled sense*

had to protect his crops from fire set by the Indians or

even protect himself from harm. At nights it was maybe a *X* *weak?*

d?

matter of hustling to the fort for protection within the

P   *X*

high walls; where as todays farmer relaxes in front of a *X — apos*

television set. It could be that todays farmer has the *X*

P

conveniences but he certainly does not have the excitment *X*

and adventure of the Pioneer.

F *This essay is highly unsatisfactory. It lacks a strong thesis and rests on a number of unsupported generalizations — especially in the last two paragraphs. There are some good details, but they're so badly handled that the paper must fail. Work on punctuation, syntax, and idiom. Think carefully about your meaning before you compose sentences. For help with prepositions, try The Oxford Advanced Learner's Dictionary of Current English. And discipline yourself to proofread carefully, so as to avoid all the careless errors.*

Sample Essay No. 4

1

[handwritten: ms — caps]

What am I doing here?

Years ago, two men were helping to build a cathedral.
A passerby stopped and asked: "What are you doing here?" "I
am just laying bricks," the first man grumbled. The second
replied, "I am building a monument to God's glory." *[handwritten: good anecdotal opening ✓]*

[handwritten: drab, jargon-like ←] In the present situation, the student is like the two *[handwritten: whose "present situation"?]*
workers. When he asks himself the question, "What am I
[handwritten: no comma] doing here?", he may reply in one of two ways. His answer *[handwritten: unnecessarily vague]*
depends on the range of his view of life.

[handwritten: perhaps no ¶?] The student may be "just laying bricks." Plodding *[handwritten: This ¶ also vague—lacking concreteness]*
through work without any connective thought or unifying
[handwritten: ww? cl?] goal, he has only a short view of his efforts. He finds as
little satisfaction as the first worker, labouring without
plan or point at an aimless, backbreaking task. On the
other hand, the student may be building a memorial. He sees
a point to his work beyond the confusion of courses,
[handwritten: p—comma needed] experiences and years. The student is laying a foundation
for his life. Looking beyond the immediate job, he is able
to see a goal, to recognize a purpose to his work.

The answer to "What am I doing here?" holds the key to
[handwritten: After the gender-neutral "person," all the he's and his's seem wrong.] satisfying living. If the student, indeed any person,
recognizes his own end, he will not just be laying bricks; *[handwritten: two unfortunate meanings here, besides the one you intend! purpose?]*
he will be building a memorial. He will not merely be
existing; he will find satisfaction in getting nearer his
goal. He will know why he is here.

 [handwritten: An interesting way of discussing the question. Good work overall; clear and well organized. But weakened by that central vagueness. The "two ways" need to be made more sharply evident in the last two paragraphs. And note the slips in diction and punctuation.]

496   *Sample Essays*

Sample Essay No. 5

1

"Don't Shoot! I'm Only A Minor."   *lc*   *good title*

X—2 words   Everyday it seems like youths are becoming more and   *us*

more criminal, developing an unhealthy disrespect for the   ✓

laws that are created to protect them. Many youths think

p: no P.? dash? us   it's just a game to steal, anything from candies to cars.   *good allit.*

This type of attitude is not good for any society.   *rather vague thesis*

One morning, several months ago, as I waited in my

living room for my friend to pick me up for school, I picked   }*rep worth avoiding*

Do we need this detail?   up the copy of the Wednesday edition of the local paper,

which had just been delivered. The words "Youth Stabbed in   ✓*good detail*

Lewis Park" stood out in big bold letters at the top of the

front page. A young male who had recently graduated from my

p: 2 or none   high school and who often hung out there at lunch, had been

hospitalized after receiving a stab wound in the stomach.

Two days later the front page was much the same. The

feature article was about two teenagers in ski masks who had

held up a local grocery store at knife point. These

al   articles are only a few incidents in the increasingly

lawless activities of the youth, which range from stealing   *awk with art; the young? (all of them? Avoid sweeping statements.)*

us   =/   hood ornaments off of exotic cars to cold blooded murder, in

my small home town and across Canada.   ∧

awk rep   Some people would argue that the people who commit

these crimes are just "kids," impressionable youngsters who

don't really know what they're getting themselves into.

ago?   That's ridiculous. Two summers past I worked with my uncle

pron— see 3h   building houses. One day on our lunch break, myself and ⓐ   }*cut one article (see us)*

half ⓐ dozen tradesmen were sharing stories and the topic

2

moved to the criminal trend in teenagers' behaviour. I
recall a story told by one of the men about a friend of his.
One night someone broke into the man's house, and he and his
Verb form? wife were <u>woken</u> by the noise of the intruder. The man went
to the closet to get his shotgun and proceeded cautiously
down the stairs. As he entered the kitchen he saw the dark
form of the trespasser. The man raised his gun toward the
intruder and bellowed, "Get your hands up or I'll shoot." *use ⚪ ?*
The intruder replied in a boyish voice, "Don't shoot! I'm
only a minor."

These "kids" know very well what they're doing and they
ref? (5b) know they can get away with <u>it.</u> Teenagers are very *another sweeping statement*
intelligent and cunning. They know how the laws work and
they know that unless they're of legal age they don't really
have to pay for the crimes they commit. Young offenders are
usually only put on probation and given <u>a number of</u> *w rep — delete at least one "a number of"*
<u>community hours, a number of hours</u> they must spend doing
volunteer work in the community. The maximum sentence they
would have to serve is much <u>smaller</u> than the sentence an *ww? shorter?*
adult would receive, and the young offender's identity is
protected.

I think it is time <u>that</u> the lawmakers of our country *for...to?*
needs mention in preceding ¶ as well? sit down and seriously rethink our <u>Young Offenders Act</u>. It
just doesn't do the job anymore. Changes in social
conditions, like increased unemployment rates, <u>higher taxes,</u>
Do these really affect young people, or mainly adults? <u>and cutthroat competition in the workplace</u> and in the school
system, all brought about by recent recessions and increased

98   *Sample Essays*

competition in the global marketplace have caused many
Canadians to change their moral views. I think the Young
Offenders Act should be revamped to reflect these changes in
the way many youths think and act.

P

You need to make the connection clearer—especially here at the end of your argument.

(B) *You've tackled a serious subject and generally handled it well. The best feature of your argument is its attention to evidence showing how the problems you cite disturb you and affect your everyday life; you've made good use of specific examples. The weakest element of your argument is your tendency to generalize about today's youth as if all of them think and act the same; beware of sweeping, all-inclusive statements, for they undermine rather than enhance an argument's effectiveness. You need to qualify arguments in order to make them effective. Your control of diction is basically good, but note some errors in style — e.g. the awkward and unnecessary repetition; and think about those slips in punctuation so that you won't repeat them.*

Sample Essay No. 6

1

lc ?

Handle With Care

consider reversing order

Patent medicines and vitamins are bought in increasing quantities by people every day. They are placed on open *which people?* shelves in stores to be bought without prescription by individuals who have little knowledge of what the chemical

awk wo

effects will be on their bodies. Many of the drugs are potentially harmful; they should be removed from the shelves, and their sales more strictly controlled. To be sure, many of the drugs that are so readily available to

Consider dividing this long opening ¶ to produce a stronger focus.

consumers are helpful in relieving irritating conditions, and are not harmful if administered properly. But people *?* have come to believe that many drugs on the shelves are not harmful at all. Certain medicines have become so commonly used that they are taken as panaceas and administered for any discomfort. The drug universally known under one brand name, "aspirin," is an obvious example. People take one, or *?*

Does aspirin soothe stomach pain, or aggravate it?

two, or several aspirin tablets for headaches, stomach pains, insomnia, nervous and emotional upsets--the whole range of disturbances--and many parents use aspirin to dose *some ? Avoid broad generalizations* their children at the first sign of hyperactivity! These common cures are not safe when used in excess or when taken

W, awk — use

without being needed. Medicines are drugs, and when used incorrectly, drugs can be poison.

unnecessarily ?

Of course one might say that the government cannot be *Is this true? How about helmets for cyclists? and seat belts?* expected to pass regulations protecting people from

comb? ; that

themselves. Individuals are expected to exercise their own intelligence when using drugs. However, this reasoning

wo — better delayed ?

assumes that the public is given information that will help it to act wisely. Unfortunately, that is not so. Most of the information received by society today is transmitted *Vague d* through popular media. What the public hears about patent medicines is conveyed via radio and television in the form of advertising. Drug companies have launched extensive campaigns designed to tell people how accessible drugs are *?* and how little they cost. The advertisements are little *⌐* more than popularity contests between brands. To the *awk wo ~* consumer, what is the value of a film clip showing a famous actor loading a shopping cart with fancy packages picked off a shelf in a drug store? It is all very well to be told *p* that in a conveniently located store, the prices are always "right," but that says nothing about the drugs. The message is to buy.

Of course, some may say that instructions about dosage *will argue?* are on the package of every medicine. Moreover, individual *every package of ?* drug companies often warn the public about misuse of their products. But in an advertisement, the warning against the detrimental effects of the drug is cleverly disguised. For example, there are several medicines on sale that are too *Do you mean for sale?* strong for children's use. When one company says (boasts) that its product is "not even recommended for children," the message somehow gets mixed up. Adults are made to feel that they are part of an exclusive class of people who can, and *interesting interpreta-tion* therefore should, rush out and buy the product. No one would rationally accept this line of reasoning, but this kind of advertising appeals to the emotions, and <u>people</u>

a rather sweeping statement

think what they are made to feel.

✓ an effective concession

Still, one must admit that many of these products are helpful in controlling ailments or in maintaining proper health, and that more stringent control of sales would cause

ambig ref

prices to rise. <u>This</u> may be so, but after all, medicines are used by many people who do not need them. If these drugs--including vitamins--were less available or cost more, people would find alternative, more natural ways of maintaining good health. For instance, exercise can cure

✓ good p, for emph

many ailments as quickly as aspirin; and regular exercise is a better preventive medicine than regular doses of patented, bottled cure-alls. Moreover, many people would soon discover that the body functions very well on a proper diet without daily vitamin supplements. Indeed, the body is designed to assimilate what it needs from good food. In this age of technology, people are beginning to forget that the human race survived for generations before nourishment

no p?

was compressed into little capsules, and the entire daily requirement swallowed with a drink of water in one gulp.

I will concede that there are <u>individuals</u> who do need to use these drugs or vitamins regularly, and other <u>people</u>

both rather vague

who need to use them occasionally. Nevertheless, there is no good reason for the excessive use of medicine <u>found</u> in

pas

which?

today's society. <u>People</u> have mistakenly concluded that if a drug can make them "better" when they are sick, then by the

4

p not needed?

same principle, that drug will improve their condition when
they are not sick. ∧ What could possibly be "better" than
good health? Overdosing oneself with medicine is not the
way to find out. In fact, (excessive) drug use will surely
cause (more harm than good). Drug companies have had ample
time to warn the public about the need to take care when
using their products. More stringent methods are obviously
required.

But, for coh & emph use of drugs?

Is this a tautology?

ww? Do you mean controls?

Ⓐ—

A thoughtful and thought-provoking argument, for the most part
presented clearly and sharply. The introduction could use some
polishing (the length and the introduction of specific
evidence tend to blur the focus); but your thesis is
solid. Your final point could perhaps be stronger and the
concluding recommendation more specific, but the ending
is effective. The argumentative structure is good
throughout, with alternating pros and cons, though here and
there it seems a little stiff; the machinery clanks a
bit. When you revise this for resubmission, see if you can
smooth the bumps a little. You do a particularly good
job of refuting arguments counter to your position, but
you could strengthen your argument by replacing or
qualifying frequent sweeping references to "people" and
their habits of abusing over-the-counter remedies. And consider
naming the products being advertised, and the "famous
actor" plugging them. Note also the several stylistic and
mechanical errors.

Sample Essay No. 7

Guaranteed Satisfaction

In the past two years, violence in hockey has become a major concern of thousands of sports fans in North America.

pron ✓ Myself being a sports fan, I too have witnessed the disgusting changes which have taken place in the professional and junior hockey ranks. I have spent hours deliberating over this problem and am happy to announce a sure-fire solution.

This solution will benefit all parties involved. It will definitely pick up the attendance at every game. We all know how quickly it has been falling lately, and surprisingly in a few cities which, until two years ago, always had sell out crowds. This increase in attendance *sp* $(=/)$ will certainly put more money into the owners' bank accounts and consequently more money into the players' wallets.

frag ✓ Especially in our favourite players' wallets, the "goons," who are grossly underpaid while providing the fans with most of the entertainment. Sales in the concessions and the souvenir booths at the rink are bound to go up. The possibilities are endless. I cannot see any loopholes in my

p & awk ref proposal which could, if properly carried out, turn hockey
ww ✓ into the blooming business it once was, but this time on a scale at least three times as large.

awk wo—try "the wallets of our favourite players" (because of the following appositive)

try "my proposal, a proposal which"

First off, we must rid ourselves of some unnamed politicians across the nation, who have spoiled the game by *sp (passim), p* charging some of the league's best players with such

sp attrocities as creating a public disturbance, brutality,

assault with a lethal weapon (hockey sticks), and even
manslaughter. After being pressed with such charges, these
players, and the teams they play for, have to think twice
before they touch, let alone slug, punch, kick and beat up a   *p*
player on the opposite side. Thus the quality of the game
is destroyed. Who wants to watch a team which is afraid to   *that ?*
fight? I'm sure that with a bit of pushing and kicking in
the right places we could easily rid ourselves of these
cruel polititians who are out to destroy our fun.

    Secondly, after the polititians are out of the way, we
must solve the problem of the players who will not fight.
Many players, whom I cannot blame, are still leary of
fighting after two years of government suppression. It is
hard to get back in the swing of things (arms, sticks, legs,
log? etc.) after two years of idleness. But I'm sure the owners
id ✔ will not put up much of a fight to the second part of my
proposal.

    The players would surely start fighting again if there
was a little cash up for grabs. If a cash bonus was awarded   *mood (subjunctive)*
sp to players who were profficient in acts of violence or even
inf ✔ for the guys who tried hard to be, we would see plenty of
action at every game. The owners need not worry about
p? losing money since the increased attendance would make up
for it three times over. We could easily urge the Hockey
Night in Canada crew to include a weekly series of fights
=/ for between period entertainment. It would be something
like "hockey showdown" but with the toughest guys in the   *Q, and caps?*
        comma?

3

league. A trophy could be included in the year end hockey
awards, for toughest player in the league. We could call it
the Goon Trophy or the Entertainer Award. They both amount
to the same thing.

p? mm? [margin, left of "awards"]
=/ [margin, right of "hockey"]

I am sure that everyone will agree that this proposal
can do nothing but improve our present day hockey. Our own
little hockey players will finally have idols which deserve
respect. It will also open up many new jobs. There will be
a need for many new doctors and dentists (and they will do
good business), since there will always be a few players on
any team who are not quite tough enough. Our labourers will
get their chance by building many new hospitals. We could
call them Hockey Hospitals. Bookies could make a killing,
taking thousands of bets on some bloody good fights. Of
course sponsors for the televised games could get a big
chunk of extra business. Like I said before, the list goes
on and on.

ww ✓ [margin]
=/ [margin, right]
slang ✓ [margin]
gr (us) [margin]
id ✓ [margin]

I do not wish any credit endowed upon me for this
modest proposal. A few of my friends forced me to write it.
I am in the toothpaste business anyway and I don't stand to
make any money from this. My friends guarantee your
satisfaction, though.

This sentence seems odd. . . .

These friends are other sports fans who are only
satisfied by brutality.

and this one seems
downright anticlimactic.
Why not omit both?

B− Good details, good "errors." But
unfortunately your unintentional errors seriously mar this
otherwise effective and enjoyable "modest proposal." Too bad you can't
blame your appalling misspellings on your persona. Both the opening
and — especially — the closing could be much improved. Work on
spelling! And learn about hyphens.

Sample Essay No. 8

Living with Animals

awk shift of person

Human beings have always depended on animals to meet our needs. Animals have been used as food, labour, drug *for? (al)* testing and even entertainment. All these uses for animals *awk rep* are useful, even vital for human needs, but management of animal uses must be responsible. *explain how?*

al? *P*

Order? Above, you list food first.
Animals can be seen as the first slaves of man. Many pictures can be formed of oxen plowing fields of horses *pas XP* pulling carts. I refered to animals as slaves but no one *SP, P* opposed it as no one should. Animals were the only way to *↑ shift, al* get things done faster and more economically. There weren't *what things?* any harmful effects as the animals were well kept for *cared for?* they were more important as labourers than broken down *as? awk ss* Chags. But as labour techniques developed, animal labour became obsolete and is now very insignificant. *weak us* *log?*

ref, P
P, P, us, us
useful?
double or nothing
true? where?
jumps to 4th point!

Animal entertainment is ever present in todays society *apos* as it was over a thousand years ago. Even as far back as *X (prep)* Roman times, event such as chariot racing and bear-baiting, *X (pl)* animals have been a source of entertainment. Horse racing and the circus have substituted for entertainment of the *now substitute?* past but the same enjoyment is there. Animal rights *P* activists have spoken out against poor treatment of animals in circuses. This is absurd. Why would the circus harm the *Don't be too sure.* things which make the circus thrive? It is, however, a *Vague d, ref* reminder that we should not take advantage of the rights of *log of d?* animals as they are living beings as well. *what "rights"?* *P, us*

After labour, animals are seen as food. Animals have *more faulty order; sense also weak (cl)*

provided mankind with food ever since we learned how to
catch them. Some animals were hunted to extinction, which *and still are being?*
e.g.?
us, P is sad as they will be lost forever but with better food *log (are)*
management animals can be a food source forever. It's
sometimes sad to think that some animals live their whole *log?*
pl life producing food or becoming food, but then again what *confuses issue*
P(?) did I eat today: eggs, milk, beef, so I can't really *P (dash?)*
complain. *"but...." — weak afterthought, non sequitur — weak d*

coh-tr needed Killing animals may save human lives. Using test *ss - sp - (al)*
animals gives researchers better understanding of diseases
and can also be used to test potentially life saving drugs, *=/*
all in search of a cure. It is true that hundreds of *awk-dm?*
//? may animals may die so that a few humans live, but then the *human beings*
X future will safer against disease and may result in a better *al, awk*
world. The ends justify the means. *Rather a sweeping generalization!*

beings Humans use animals to meet human needs. I do not
oppose this, but we must understand that animals are a
al(again)! limited resource, and careful management of animal uses must *perfunctory, though well expressed*
pas be practised so that the world will not feel the loss of *d?*
another species. *Unrealistic, since many species have become extinct, and many are becoming so, at an increasing rate*

F There's just too much wrong with this: arrangement, development, examples, clarity, logic, sentence structure, tense, number, reference, diction, punctuation.... There's enough error here to sink the ship two or three times over. The makings are here for an interesting and effective exposition-cum-argument; the essay is packed with ideas and opinions—you clearly have a good deal to say on the topic. But this reads like a very rough draft or even just hastily scribbled notes. You'll have to concentrate on organization and on careful editing and proofreading when you correct and revise this.

Sample Essay No. 9

Beginning ¶ has focus and thesis, but it doesn't
give a reader much incentive to read on.   1

Responsible Government

p unnecessary   Here, in Canada, we enjoy the benefits of responsible

government. In responsible government the cabinet, or

governing body, is directly responsible to the elected

ambig (*x-in?* representatives of the legislature, who, in turn, are   *p necessary?*

pl ?   responsible to their elector, the people. Through this

inc comp   transfer of responsibility, a greater control can be exerted   ) *wo?*
(than   ) *ambig*
what?)   on the machinery of government by the populace.

In this country, we become more aware of the workings

of responsible government when a minority governement is in   X *sp*

no P   power. The term "minority government," means that the

combined votes of the opposition parties exceed the number

of votes of the party in power. Then, if the legislature

does not agree with the cabinet and it is defeated, the   *ambig ref*

caps   prime minister is required to submit the question in dispute

dash? or   to the people; that is, call a general election. This   *vague ref*
supply
he must   clearly shows how the prime minister and his cabinet are   *caps*
(// ss)   directly responsible to the legislature. *—or her?*   *weak ¶ conclusion*

There are many benefits of this system of government. *Vague & bland*
                                                        topic sentence
We, as citizens of Canada, are assured of our control over

the affairs of our country. No leader can become

Are the
meanings) authoritarian or radical because he is (always) answerable for   *p (see 37c)*
of these   ) *or she/her?*
terms as   his actions. Therefore, the governing body, the (cabinet),   *p unnecessary*
clear as
you   (always) has the good interests of the people in mind when
think ?
          planning and executing government business. They,   *agr, shift*

themselves, were elected by the people--not appointed as the) *more p*
cabinet is in the United States where the government is only   ) *needed ?*

> *guaranteed? never self-serving? Your sweeping generalizations,*
with their double-barrelled always, are automatically suspect.

Are you saying that the U.S. cabinet is representative— always, in every administration? Is that true? What does "representative" mean here? [2]

representative, not responsible--and so must be directly
concerned for the welfare of the people.

_no P_

    We have seen, how, in responsible government, the great
mass of people exert power over the chosen ones who govern
them and how these few, in turn are responsible to them.   In
this system democracy is in its most complete form.

p: 2 or none

conclusion seems rather stiff

Have you proved this very strong claim in the body of your essay?   weak

meaning? Perhaps consider Switzerland? ancient Athens?

C-

For the most part you form sentences fairly well—which makes the slips stand out all the more glaringly. You handle the definition fairly competently, though you often express your points rather uncritically —which becomes a serious weakness when you move beyond definition and into what is at least partly argument. Your statements are also sometimes unnecessarily flat, self-evident; you need to work on shaping sharper, more focussed thesis and topic sentences, and on supporting your claims with specific examples and fuller explanations. Be on guard against ambiguity. And you certainly need to work on improving your punctuation.

Sample Essay No. 10

Curiosity

Proverbially?
(still a fine
opening
sentence)

Traditionally considered a killer of cats, curiosity is a human quality of ill-repute. People often view it with suspicion and mistrust, assuming that it is a counter-productive--even destructive--attribute. But such assumptions are not necessarily true. Although it can be both counter-productive and destructive, curiosity is more often productive. It is normal to be curious about one's surroundings. A little curiosity is a necessary thing.

nice sentence
variety in this
opening
paragraph

✓

The earliest recorded usage of the word dates from the late fourteenth century, when Wyclif used it in a sermon: "Bi this answere moun we se how curiouste of science or unskilful coveitise of cunnynge, is to dampne" (The Oxford English Dictionary). In 1380, "curiouste" indicated a "disposition to inquire too minutely into anything." Since then, it has been used to describe human characteristics such as caution, attention to detail, skill, proficiency, "excess [attention] unduly bestowed on matters of inferior moment," nicety and subtlety. But all of these meanings are obsolete. Now curiosity is simply "a desire to know and learn," and it can be divided into two distinct types: one that removes our humanity and another that gives us humanity.

Some readers
might
appreciate a
"translation"
of this.

The first type, dehumanizing curiosity, is an "inquisitiveness in reference to (. . .) matters which do not concern one." And it itself can be subdivided into rabid and morbid forms. Rabid curiosity is plain nosiness, the

a good strong
transition

By omitting
the O.E.D.'s
"trifles
better wo?
or," aren't you unfairly altering the definition
to suit your own purposes?

desire to have knowledge of the activities of others. The
rabidly curious live for gossip--for them, other people are
dehumanized novelties, creatures to be observed and
discussed. This attitude shows in both their mundane
dealings with their associates and their fanatical interest
in celebrities. They love to speculate about their friends
and acquaintances, and even about people they don't know.
The results include office-mates discussing the sleeping
habits of their co-workers, <u>People</u> magazine, and <u>Lifestyles</u>
<u>of the Rich and Famous</u>. This is the stuff that slander and
libel are made of.

interesting examples

good tr

Morbid curiosity is quite similar to rabid curiosity,
except that its fascination is with what other people are
suffering, rather than with what they are doing. It is a
desire to have a spectator's (or second-hand) knowledge of
pain and misfortune. The morbidly curious follow ambulances
and fire engines. They stop and stare at the scenes of <u>car</u>
accidents, and they listen to the police band radio. Films
such as <u>Faces of Death</u> (a movie that <u>is made up of</u> explicit
footage of various forms of death, including death in a
slaughterhouse, death by hanging, and death in the electric
chair) are created for the morbidly curious. For these
worshippers of grim spectacle, the sacrifice is their own
humanity and the humanity of those who suffer.

traffic, better?
pas not necessary

The second type of curiosity--"a feeling of interest
leading one to inquire about [things]"--ennobles those who
experience it. It too can be subdivided: into innate and

still using the OED, one presumes — but why bother changing its "anything" to "[things]"?

intellectual forms. Innate curiosity is the motivation to
learn about one's environment, to determine the limits of
what one can and cannot do; it is a desire for knowledge for
the sake of survival and comfort. The innately curious have
a desire to nose around, a need to learn as much about their
own worlds (whatever size their worlds may be) as they can.
They love to explore, to travel, to experience. This is

∫-p helps

what children, travellers and most people in new situations
have in common--innate curiosity.

strong tr &
a nicely
balanced
topic
sentence

Intellectual curiosity begins where innate curiosity
ends; it is a desire for knowledge for its own sake. There *weak*
is a need to learn, so that one can learn still more, so *expletive*
that one can fill in some of the gaps between what one
perceives and what one knows. The intellectually curious
experience a hunger for the ideas of others, assimilating *ss a bit*

∫? and ?
(smoother)

these then generating ideas of their own. They attempt to *awkward*
define the limits of their own universes, then expand these
limits. After that, they try to determine the new limits
and to expand them again, and again, and still again. *Interesting— but*
might this
Intellectual curiosity is the cause and an ever-expanding *term briefly*
universe is the effect. Without intellectual curiosity, *puzzle*
because of its
there would be no intellectual growth. *standard*
meaning?

Curiosity, in all its forms, is a matter of asking
questions. It is the motivation to question relationships
between oneself and people, between people and people, *I find*
between people and the universe, between the universe and *this a bit*
oneself--a need to fill in some of the blanks. But posing *strained.*

questions can be a dangerous pastime; many have been

ostracized for doing less and many have died. It may be

true, the old saying, that curiosity kills cats, but the

other old saying, that cats have nine lives, may also be

true. According to the folk <u>rhyme</u>, "Curiosity killed the

cat / But satisfaction brought it back." Perhaps

satisfaction gives cats their many lives.

So whereas satisfaction may be a catalyst in the

rebirth of cats, curiosity is a catalyst in the renaissance

of human beings, enabling us to change and grow.

Admittedly, there are <u>things that aren't worth knowing,</u> but

there are many things to question, many things to learn,

many things to know. Without all <u>facets</u> of curiosity, the

questioning, the learning and the satisfaction, people (and

cats too) would be boring creatures, complacent and static

to the end.

[Handwritten margin annotations:]

4

A few specific examples would help.

rhyme? where?

e.g. the "trifles" you omitted earlier?

Here, they undermine the logic of your classification a bit.

d? Think of its physical meaning.

And consider the logic: "all facets," and "the questioning, the learning, and the satisfaction," could as well include the "rabid" and "morbid," could they not? In another way, then, your perhaps too facile conclusion undermines the effectiveness of the piece.

(A) In spite of my quibbles, this is an excellent essay, a fine job of defining and classifying. It is energetic, witty, intelligent, original, graceful; it is interesting to read, and not just because of the surprises and delights to be found in each paragraph. I offer a few suggestions for improvement, but you should nevertheless be proud of this effort.

Sample Essay No. 11

Analysis of Hamlet's Remembrance Soliloquy (I.v.92-112)

> *Hamlet.* O all you host of heaven! O earth! What else?
> And shall I couple hell? O fie! Hold, hold, my heart,
> And you, my sinews, grow not instant old,
> But bear me stiffly up. Remember thee?
> Ay, thou poor ghost, while memory holds a seat
> In this distracted globe. Remember thee?
> Yea, from the table of my memory
> I'll wipe away all trivial fond records,
> All saws of books, all forms, all pressures past
> That youth and observation copied there,
> And thy commandment all alone shall live
> Within the book and volume of my brain,
> Unmixed with baser matter. Yes, by heaven!
> O most pernicious woman!
> O villain, villain, smiling, damnèd villain!
> My tables--meet it is I set it down
> That one may smile, and smile, and be a villain.
> At least I am sure it may be so in Denmark. *[Writes.]*
> So, uncle, there you are. Now to my word:
> It is "Adieu, adieu, remember me."
> I have sworn't.

What is Shakespeare's *Hamlet*? It is a tragedy, a calamity, and a gigantic puzzle, to begin with. The play's central character is a young man with great gifts of intellect, and yet all of his talents cannot save him or the people around him when he decides to follow the commandment of a ghost which haunts the night. In this, his second soliloquy, Hamlet, more alone than ever, expresses his horror at the truth, his rage at those who have betrayed his father, and his determination to remember his oath of vengeance against his father's killer.

This soliloquy in blank verse comes near the end of the first act, immediately following Hamlet's terrifying meeting with a figure whom he accepts as the tormented spirit of his dead father. The soliloquy marks the first turning point in the play, for from this point on, Hamlet is never quite the same. Now, Hamlet has some evidence—or at least testimony —to back up his previous suspicions about the evil nature of the new king, Claudius. Before this speech, Hamlet has been brooding about a marriage he regards as deeply sinful, but he has pledged to hold his tongue about it; now, he is committed to taking action against a murderer and an illegitimate king. From this point on, Hamlet's life of scholarship and romance and friendship is all but dead; he is about to become a man obsessed and an actor playing the role of a madman all too well.

Hamlet's character is complex: he is brilliant, sad, funny, brutal, kind—an incredible mixture of elements. He is a man caught in a struggle between his reason and his passions. In this speech, the passion emerges first. In two exclamations and two questions, he begins his speech with strong emotions of shock and horror. He prays to heaven, shouts at earth, and wonders about hell as he does elsewhere in the play when his passions overcome his reason. He speaks of his own physical weaknesses and describes his mind metaphorically as "a distracted globe." In the first of many pledges, he promises to "wipe away all trivial fond records" and give up everything that has meant anything to him: his books, his sayings, his youthful interests. In a way, Hamlet becomes old and careworn before the audience's eyes as the ghost retreats with the rising of the sun.

The most emotional part of the soliloquy comes when Hamlet expresses his thoughts about his mother and his new stepfather. His mother is a "most pernicious woman," the word "pernicious" suggesting one who is deeply evil. Claudius for his part is "a villain," a "smiling villain," and Hamlet is having a hard time understanding how one so corrupt--so sinful--could appear to be so amiable, such a smiling, polished, perfect king.

Just when Hamlet's passion seems about to boil over into an act of public violence against his "aunt-mother" and "uncle-father," his mind asserts itself and reason prevails in him for the time being. The physical action of Hamlet in this passage matches this physical change. When Hamlet picks up his diary to write about his experience, he shows himself trying to organize the experience with his student's mind. He makes notes about what he has seen; he writes an essay about it. Such an action is but the first example of Hamlet's many attempts to make order out of a disordered, disjointed, and rotten world.

Apart from revealing the complexities of Hamlet's character, this soliloquy presents the audience with several themes. It shows us Hamlet as a Dane deeply disgusted by his own country because it is a place where one may smile and prosper and be a villain. It shows us that the world for Hamlet has become, in just a few minutes on the battlements, a place in which the appearance of a man may not match at all the reality of his soul. In this passage, the word "memory" becomes a refrain, and the reader must wonder how Hamlet could ever forget what he has heard in the chill of the night. The last line, "I have sworn't," echoes other moments in the play in which characters swear oaths: the soldiers' pledge to keep the ghost secret; Ophelia's and Laertes's pledge to follow their father's advice; Gertrude's pledge to abandon Claudius's bed after Hamlet has "cleft [her] heart in twain" in the closet scene. Like the others, Hamlet has a dreadful time--a tragic time--living up to the pledge. In Denmark, it seems, pledges are made to be broken or at least forgotten.

This soliloquy is important to the play, then, as a contributor to the plot, the characterization, and the theme. Without it, the audience would be deprived of a turning point in the plot; it would lose a glimpse at Hamlet's brilliant, embattled mind; it would lose an opportunity to understand the ironic gap between what is and what seems--even in the highest realms of government and power. Without the remembrance soliloquy, in short, *Hamlet* just wouldn't be *Hamlet*.

Sample Essay No. 12

The Museum of Anthropology

I entered through one set of large glass double doors and stepped into a silence that was almost deafening. For some reason, museums seem to cause people to cease their loud chattering and whisper instead, and the Museum of Anthropology is no different. Although there was a number of people browsing inside, the place was silent. Maybe it's because of the impressive artifacts housed throughout the building. Native Indian carvings of all sizes, from small jewelry boxes to objects which dwarf a man, line walls and floors on display for the public to behold. Totem poles sit beside glass cases holding silver jewelry, canoes beside cedar statues, and moccasins beside wooden masks. After investigating the First Nations displays, I wandered into Gallery Five, where on presentation was an exhibit of early Canadian Jews. This section displayed the trials that Jews endured as they set up lives in the Canadian provinces. From here I went to the section of the museum that contains Research Collections. This section is composed of large glass cases holding more than 12 000 items from various regions of the world, such as the South Pacific, India, the Orient, and Latin America. From here I returned to the lobby and exited the museum through one set of large glass double doors and returned home.

Sample Essay No. 13

To the Editor:

Not long ago, I sat down after Sunday dinner and turned on the television to watch Mike Wallace do his weekly hatchet job on 60 Minutes. Instead, what I saw was a report by Ed Bradley on the lives of those countless people who live on the Skid Roads of major American cities. One particular image sticks in my mind; in fact, you could even say that it's been haunting me. At one point in the story, Bradley stopped to talk with an old black man who was living in two big cardboard boxes by the side of what looked like a freeway. It was late at night, and it was cold enough that you could see Bradley's breath as he talked, and there was a black man living inside a cardboard box. It was like a bad dream--like some weird variation on the old nursery rhyme about the old woman who lived in a shoe. If such a scene were enacted on the stage, it would be considered absurd, perhaps even funny. But here, it was real life.

So why am I haunted by this image? It is hardly a surprise that people are down and out, especially at a time when so many governments have decided to become modern-day Scrooges--disciples of Reaganomics. I guess that part of my response is a reaction to the question that Bradley asked in the course of his story. He asked whether societies have a moral responsibility to take care of the people who fall by the wayside as the rest of us are so frantically clawing our way up the ladder of success. Should we take care of those strange men who wander the streets talking to themselves in monologues that never seem to end? Should we provide food and shelter for the bag ladies who wander the streets on hot summer nights dressed in heavy coats, clutching their possessions to their sunken chests? Or should we just keep stepping around them--shaking our heads, mumbling under our breaths about bums, and trying to forget them as quickly as we possibly can?

What shocked me was that the comfortable people who responded to Bradley's questions didn't even hesitate, didn't even make a show of that now defunct emotion known as brotherly love. They were virtually unanimous in answering that they didn't want to see, hear about, or help these human ruins. Spend the tax money on modern armaments, on new china for the White House Dining Room, on state dinners, on cost-benefit analyses, on paper clips--but never on a bit of stew and a mattress for some poor guy who can't make it through the day without a bottle of muscatel.

About this time, I expect that many of my readers have pulled out the handy "bleeding heart liberal" label and are about to affix it angrily to the end of this letter. But don't be too hasty. Behind my emotional heart there lies a mind that wonders about the logic in the argument of those who would turn their backs on the fact of Skid Roads. To abandon these men and women to their cardboard boxes is to say that we have before us a problem that we are incapable of solving. And to say that is to say that this system that we so revere is flawed. Furthermore, what is the logical consequence of leaving the problem to fester?

Sample Essay No. 14

THE GLORY OF IT ALL

We live surrounded by music. What is more, modern technology has placed at our disposal every kind of music, from virtually every period in history and every corner of the globe. Of course, music from different eras serves as a link between people, a common ground. In Peter Shaffer's Amadeus, the audience is transported back in time to view the world of music as it was in the eighteenth century. Although Amadeus mirrors timeless real-to-life struggles, the play's major themes, revenge, fame versus talent, and jealousy are presented through ironies in character, plot, and language.

Throughout the play, Shaffer uses twists in character to present the theme of revenge. A prime example of character irony is presented when Salieri realizes that Mozart will be remembered as the most brilliant composer of his time. In order for Salieri to become "immortal" he must make it known that he murdered the brilliant Mozart, so that, "Whenever men say Mozart with love, they will say Salieri with loathing!" The irony is furthered at the end of the play, when Salieri overhears his claim is "believed in truth by no one but...himself," and realizes he will never be recognized for his efforts.

The theme of fame versus talent is emphasized through various examples of irony in plot. Right from the opening scenes, Salieri makes it clear that, "(he) want(s) fame," and although his talents do not compare to Mozart's, he pursues his goal with fierce determination, taking full advantage of his influential post as court composer. Knowing all along that Mozart is a musical genius, Salieri "get(s) the piece(s) cancelled" to delay Mozart's inevitable fame. Yet even as he does this, Salieri's fame continues to rise steadily "Almost as if (he) were being pushed deliberately from triumph to triumph!" above his talented victim Mozart. Though he dedicates his life to becoming famous, Salieri even admits, "Goodness could not make me a good composer."

The play's major theme, jealousy, is expressed primarily by means of ironies in language. At the beginning of the play, in retrospect, Salieri says ironically, "I wanted to blaze, like a comet, across the firmament of Europe," which is an apt description of his short-lived presence as a well-known eighteenth century composer. In addition, throughout the play, Salieri becomes increasingly envious of Mozart; he even describes a serene Adagio (K.361) as "...pain! Pain as I had never known it." It is at this point in the play that the audience may be certain that Salieri has a mean and jealous passion for Mozart's work. After this point, Shaffer reinforces the theme of jealousy through further ironic speech when Salieri is seducing Mozart's wife: "Take a true look. I've no cunning," he tells her sympathetically. Salieri neatly sums up his feelings towards jealousy, "It's not a passion I understand," an extremely ironic understatement from a man whose world is consumed by it.

In Shaffer's <u>Amadeus</u>, the themes of revenge, fame versus talent, and jealousy are presented most effectively by means of twisted situations involving character, plot, and language.

Shaffer, Peter.   <u>Amadeus</u>.   Harmondsworth: Penguin, 1981.

Sample Essay No. 15

Reflections on a Tourist Poster

Hey, lady! Yes, you--the one smiling up from the smokeless campfire on that poster advertising Canada's great outdoors. Did anyone ever tell you your eyes exactly match the lake water behind you? I guess everybody must, the colour is so remarkable. I never have seen a lake that colour; it's exactly the same aquamarine green that bath salts turn the water in my tub. Still, the fish must like it--I see you have four nice ones lined up in the pan beside your shiny aluminum coffee pot. Who caught those fish, anyway? Certainly not those two immaculate children playing games over on the lake shore; surely not your perfect husband, poised with his foot up on a convenient tree stump. He's too shiny-new! All polished teeth and polished boots, he looks like he just walked out of Eaton's catalogue. I wonder why I always look like I went swimming after the fish I try to catch. Well, it doesn't matter, really. I'll let you get back to your breakfast preparations and your plans for a perfectly marvelous day. I only stopped to ask you: Doesn't it ever rain where you are? Don't the campsites get overcrowded sometimes? Who are you really supposed to be?

Sample Essay No. 16

Help Save Our Environment; Get Involved!

Some people feel that university students do not have significant roles to play in the effort to save our environment. I strongly disagree with this attitude. Students can play significant roles in the effort by learning about major environmental problems, getting involved in environmental groups, and changing their lifestyles so that they don't harm the environment.

In order to play important roles in the effort to save our environment, students must first learn about the major hazards to the environment. It is essential to have knowledge regarding these problems if you wish to get involved. Problems such as the burning of the rain forests in South America, or the Valdez oil spill in Alaska, have grave effects on the environment of Canada. The destruction by fire of the rain forests is producing large amounts of carbon dioxide, and this gas is replacing the oxygen the trees worked so hard to produce through photosynthesis. The Valdez oil spill has killed off many sea animals and birds, and the spill may have affected B.C.'s salmon run as well.

Once you have learned about the environmental problems, it is probable that you will get involved in one, or possibly several, environmental groups. These groups will help you to take an active role in saving our environment. Environmental groups will use many methods to protect our environment. Letter-writing campaigns to government officials, the formation of clean-up crews to fight pollution, the contribution of money to aid in clean-ups, and the boycott of a polluting company's products are some of the tactics used. Greenpeace is probably the most well-known environmental group, as its "Save the Whales" logo is almost universal.

When involved in an environmental group, one becomes more aware of how certain everyday events are harmful to the environment. A basic change in your lifestyle will lessen the damage to our environment. For example, instead of using an aerosol spray deodorant, use a stick deodorant, because aerosol sprays harm the ozone layer. In addition, use biodegradable bags whenever it is possible to do so. If you're really serious about saving our environment, you could even boycott McDonald's, as the containers for their "food" are hazardous to the environment.

To sum up, I feel that university students can play significant roles in the effort to save our environment. Students can do so by gaining knowledge about the environment, getting involved in environmental groups, and making changes in their lifestyles in order to protect the environment.

Sample Essay No. 17

Symbolism in Communication

People communicate with each other in many different ways, but symbolism would seem to be the principal way, for language is itself a symbolic device. Alfred North Whitehead puts it bluntly: "A word is a symbol."[1] But language is so complex. S. I. Hayakawa says that "Of all forms of symbolism, language is the most highly developed, most subtle, and most complicated."[2] Most of us have enough trouble just reading, writing, and speaking our native tongue, let alone trying to figure out its fundamental nature and its complicated workings. But because communication is crucial in any society, understanding how we communicate is very important. In what follows, I have tried to piece together various ideas about language and symbolism that at least begin to make sense to me in order that I may make sense to you and perhaps get you, too, to think about the nature of symbolism. I have discovered, in the process, that although there is still a great deal of disagreement among the experts--philosophers, linguists, communications theorists, literary critics, semioticians (or semiologists), and so on--there has also, during recent decades, come to be a fair amount of consensus about what a symbol is and how it works. And that, in spite of my rather sweeping title, is where I want to focus.

My dictionary defines a symbol as "Something that represents something else by association, resemblance, or convention, especially, a material object used to represent something invisible," and as "A printed or written sign used to represent an operation, element, quantity, quality, or relation, as in mathematics or music." A flag stands for a country and its principles, a rose for beauty; X stands for the operation of multiplying, <u>Au</u> for the element gold. That's a start, but there's more of interest to be said. In <u>Communications: The Transfer of Meaning</u>, for example, Don Fabun distinguishes between audible symbols such as words or exclamations, and visible symbols such as pictures, objects, or written characters. He talks about human communication being symbolic of an experience: the symbol used to relate an experience is not the experience, but a new event. When we use or perceive symbols they are events, not just objects.[3] Fabun goes on to say that common symbols have no meanings of their own; the person doing the communicating has the meaning.[4] To me this says that the interpretation of a symbol depends on the background of the communicator. But according to Philip Wheelwright in <u>The Burning Fountain: A Study in the Language of Symbolism</u>, for a symbol to work there must also be a "fit interpreter," someone who knows how to understand its meaning. For example, "The word 'dog' carries a definite meaning for those who know the English language, and quite possibly no meaning at all for others."[5]

Wheelwright is interested in what he calls "expressive" or "depth language" as opposed to mere "literal language."[6] Both are symbolic, of course, since all words are symbols. But expressive language uses such things as symbolism,

metaphor, and analogy in a "poetic" way to refer to things
that are "real, but of a different order of being from that
of common familiarity."[7] Before he discusses such literary
uses of symbolism, however, he tries to define what a symbol
is. Many basic definitions are similar. For example, a
symbol is "a thing that stands for something else" or
anything that "seems to represent or stand for some reality
other than itself."[8] Wheelwright goes a little further.
"A symbol," he says, "owes its symbolic character to the
fact that it stands for something other than, or at least
more than, what it immediately is."[9] Many authorities point
out that the word symbol comes from the Greek symballein,
"to throw together," or symbolon, "token," referring to one
part of something that has been broken in two;[10] some then
conclude that a symbol doesn't properly stand for "something
else" but for something larger of which it is a part; for
example a particular rose would be a single concrete
instance of the entire abstract concept of beauty. This
definition would exclude such things as plus signs and
chemical "symbols"--and perhaps even words, for the word
rose would then apparently be merely a "sign" standing for
or pointing to a real or imagined rose which could in turn
act as a symbol. I prefer Wheelwright's definition, for it
seems to me more realistic to include both "something other
than" and "or at least more than" as what symbols can stand
for. Indeed, for Susanne K. Langer in her important 1942
book Philosophy in a New Key: A Study in the Symbolism of

Reason, Rite, and Art, mathematical symbols are fundamental
to our understanding of what symbolism is and how it works,
for what such abstractions symbolize is not "data"--facts or
objects--but "concepts," even fictitious ones such as
"imaginary numbers."[11]

Nevertheless, distinguishing between signs and symbols
is key to defining what a symbol is. Wheelwright does this
as he characterizes symbols further.[12] First, he says, a
symbol is not, like a traffic light, a "signal" directing us
to do something. He quotes from Langer, who says that a dog
hearing a familiar name immediately expects the person named
to be present, or that if you say "dinner" the dog expects
to be fed; people, however, often use "signs" that don't
refer to anything in their immediate vicinity.[13] "If I say:
'Napoleon,'" notes Langer, "you do not bow to the conqueror
of Europe as if I had introduced him, but merely think of
him."[14] Even animals, she says, can use signs, for example
in the well-known "conditioned reflex," and "the use of
signs is . . . . the beginning of intelligence."[15] But
"symbolism is the recognized key to that mental life which
is characteristically human and above the level of sheer
animality."[16] "Most of our words," she adds, "are not signs
in the sense of signals. They are used to talk about
things, not to direct our eyes and ears and noses toward
them." And signs used in that way "are not symptoms of
things, but symbols."[17] We use "representative signs"--that
is, symbols--not so much for "practical" or "utilitarian"

purposes as for their own sake, in order to think about things, and in ritual and art.[18]

Symbols, then, are signs; in fact they are a subclass of signs; but signs are not necessarily symbols. For example, Wheelwright's second point is that a symbol is not like a "natural sign," such as dark clouds indicating a coming rainstorm. "A natural sign," he says, "is not used with any purpose or intention of communicating; it works by causal efficacy alone." Smoke, for example, we commonly take to be a "sign" of fire, but it doesn't "symbolize" fire.[19]

According to Wheelwright, a symbol must also have "a certain stability: it endures beyond one or two occasions." Thumbing the nose, for example, he says is an established "symbol of contempt," whereas some other gesture of contempt, a spontaneous one such as perhaps a sudden snort, would not be a symbol. Nor would a landscape that triggered memories of one's childhood be symbolic, he claims; it would merely be "an associative stimulus."[20] But I think others might disagree with him on this point. I don't see why something should be any less symbolic just because it's a one-shot event. To use his own criterion of _intention_,[21] if I wrote a letter and purposely misspelled the recipient's name to show my disrespect, wouldn't that be a symbolic act? If I did it accidentally or out of ignorance it might convey a similar meaning, but I suppose then it would be more a _sign_ or _symptom_ of my attitude rather than a _symbol_. In any event, Wheelwright does say that if such a gesture or scene or other experience were made part of a literary work, it could be developed into a symbol. He mentions, among other examples, Eliot's waste land and Proust's piece of cake dipped in tea.[22] I would think that a particular scene in a painting or a film could be made similarly symbolic.

Consideration of symbolism in literature is (fortunately) beyond the scope of this paper, although William York Tindall in The Literary Symbol suggests many interesting lines of thought. For example he remarks that "symbolism is the necessary condition of literature"[23] and also says that any literary work as a whole is itself a symbol.[24] One point, however, that may (or may not) help us understand symbolism is its relation to metaphor. Tindall quotes the poet Yeats: "All poetic metaphors are symbols";[25] but he himself seems to stop short of equating the two, claiming only that symbols are "founded on analogy" and are therefore "related to metaphor,"[26] and acknowledging that as it becomes more suggestive rather than direct in its comparison, "metaphor approaches symbol."[27] In A Handbook to Literature, however, C. Hugh Holman distinguishes between the two more sharply: a metaphor, he says, "evokes an object in order to illustrate an idea or demonstrate a quality, whereas a symbol embodies the idea or the quality." But then he wipes out this clear separation: "As W. M. Urban said, 'The metaphor becomes a symbol when by means of it we embody an ideal content not otherwise expressible.'"[28] M.

H. Abrams, however, maintains the distinction by pointing to the fact that a metaphor (or simile) requires a "paired subject," as in Robert Burns's "O my love's like a red, red rose," whereas a symbol, as in William Blake's poem "The Sick Rose," lacks a "paired subject";[29] such a symbol, then, could be described as relatively "open-ended" in its signification.[30] I finally find myself preferring the looser way of approaching the matter, such as when Nelson Goodman says that metaphors are an "economical, practical, and creative . . . way of using symbols. In metaphor," he says, "symbols moonlight."[31]

But to get back to signs and symbols. According to John Fiske, Roland Barthes was the first to set up a system for analyzing signs and meaning. The key to his theory is a distinction between two kinds of signs. He says that signs have a denotative, "commonsense," or "obvious" meaning, but that they can also have a connotative meaning. For example, imagine two photos of the same street scene, one in cold and contrastive black and white, the other in warm colour and with a soft focus: the two pictures would <u>denote</u> the same street, seen at the same time and from virtually the same angle, but in their <u>connotation</u> they would be far apart.[32] In addition to connotation and what he calls "myth" ("a culture's way of thinking about something"), Barthes points to a third way that signs work, namely as symbols. "An object becomes a symbol when it acquires through convention and use a meaning that enables it to stand for something

else." For example there are status symbols (a Rolls Royce
is more than just a car) and religious symbols (baptism is
more than just getting dunked in the water).[33] And we're
back to part of my dictionary definition and to
Wheelwright's criterion of "stability."

Fiske goes on to discuss metaphor, which I've looked at
briefly, and metonymy, where a part stands for a whole--
which sounds like one of the basic senses of symbolism.[34]
But I think this forest already has enough trees in it.
Obviously authorities agree or disagree about definitions
and classifications of signs and symbols and so on,
depending, I suppose, on the degree to which they have
developed their own theories. The list of terms and the
questions about them go on and on (Is body-language
symbolic? Is tone of voice symbolic?), and perhaps there
are no firm answers on the horizon; but there are at least
things to think about. For example we can think about
literary symbolism, since poets, naturally, use "expressive"
language as well as everyday, straightforward language.
Poetry is therefore symbolic in a different way or to a
different degree than is a memo or a recipe. But a
scientific formula is also made up of symbols. And a phone
book is full of symbols, for of course names are symbols.[35]

Symbolism, then, is more than just a literary device,
something some of us seem to think poets and other writers
use just to make it difficult for us to understand their
poems and stories and novels. Symbols are the essence of

our lives as human beings. Wheelwright notes that "Langer offers the highly suggestive hypothesis that man's basic need, the one function that most truly distinguishes him from beasts, is the need for <u>symbolization</u>, the need to form conceptions of things."[36] As she emphasizes, symbolization is "an act <u>essential to thought</u>, and prior to it. Symbolization is the essential act of mind."[37] I agree with Langer and Wheelwright. I have to. I look at the world around me and I clearly see that we are unique in our will, if not our need, to think about things, to understand why things are--to make symbols. And language is our principal way of symbolizing. As Langer says, "Words are certainly our most important instruments of expression, our most characteristic, universal, and enviable tools in the conduct of life. Speech," she says, "is the mark of humanity."[37]

I know that communication, person to person, works for me in many ways I will never understand, and it will continue to work for me whether I ever understand it or not. But if understanding symbolism better can help us to communicate with one another more effectively, further work is worth the effort. This ending, then, can for me be only a beginning.

Notes

1 Alfred North Whitehead, _Symbolism: Its Meaning and Effect_ (New York: Macmillan, 1927), 10.

2 S. I. Hayakawa, _Language in Thought and Action_, 4th ed. (New York: Harcourt Brace Jovanovich, 1978), 22.

3 Don Fabun, _Communications: The Transfer of Meaning_, Rev. ed. (Beverly Hills: Glencoe, 1968), 15-16.

4 Fabun, 19.

5 Philip Wheelwright, _The Burning Fountain: A Study in the Language of Symbolism_, Rev. ed. (Bloomington: Indiana Univ. Press, 1968), 8.

6 Wheelwright, 3-4, 73-101.

7 Wheelwright, 5.

8 Lee T. Lemon, _A Glossary for the Study of English_ (New York: Oxford Univ. Press, 1971), 72; Edwyn Bevan, _Symbolism and Belief_ (1938; Boston: Beacon, 1957), 275.

9 Wheelwright, 6.

10 See for example Sylvan Barnet, Morton Berman, and William Burto, _A Dictionary of Literary Terms_ (Boston: Little, Brown, 1960), 84, and J. A Cuddon, _A Dictionary of Literary Terms and Literary Theory_, 3rd ed. (Oxford: Blackwell, 1991), 939.

11 Susanne K. Langer, _Philosophy in a New Key: A Study in the Symbolism of Reason, Rite, and Art_ (1942; New York, Mentor-NAL, 1948), 14.

12 Wheelwright, 9-11.

13 Langer, 24.

[14] Langer, 48.

[15] Langer, 22-23.

[16] Langer, 21.

[17] Langer, 24.

[18] Langer, 29-30.

[19] Wheelwright, 10; and see Langer, 45-46.

[20] Wheelwright, 11.

[21] See Wheelwright, 7.

[22] Wheelwright, 13.

[23] William York Tindall, _The Literary Symbol_ (1955; Bloomington: Indiana Univ. Press, 1958), 68.

[24] Tindall, 4, 10; see also Lemon, 72.

[25] Tindall, 36.

[26] Tindall, 12.

[27] Tindall, 64.

[28] C. Hugh Holman, _A Handbook to Literature_, 4th ed. (Indianapolis: Bobbs-Merrill, 1980), 436.

[29] M. H. Abrams, _A Glossary of Literary Terms_, 4th ed. (New York: Holt, Rinehart and Winston, 1981), 195-96.

[30] M. M. Liberman and Edward E. Foster, _A Modern Lexicon of Literary Terms_ (Glenview, IL: Scott, Foresman, 1968), 115.

[31] Nelson Goodman, "Metaphor as Moonlighting," _On Metaphor_, ed. Sheldon Sacks (Chicago: Univ. of Chicago Press, 1979), 180.

[32] John Fiske, _Introduction to Communication Studies_ (London: Methuen, 1982), 90-91. Langer (51-52) discusses

denotation and connotation somewhat differently: for her

both are symbolic functions, as opposed to mere

"signification," since they involve "conception."

[33] Fiske, 95.

[34] Fiske, 96-100.

[35] See Wheelwright, 16.

[36] Wheelwright, 10; see Langer, 32.

[37] Langer, 33.

[38] Langer, 36.

Works Cited

Abrams, M. H. A Glossary of Literary Terms. 4th ed. New
    York: Holt, Rinehart and Winston, 1981.

Barnet, Sylvan, Morton Berman, and William Burto. A
    Dictionary of Literary Terms. Boston: Little, Brown,
    1960.

Bevan, Edwyn. Symbolism and Belief. 1938. Boston: Beacon,
    1957.

Cuddon, J. A. A Dictionary of Literary Terms and Literary
    Theory. 3rd ed. Oxford: Blackwell, 1991.

Fabun, Don. Communications: The Transfer of Meaning. Rev.
    ed. Beverly Hills: Glencoe, 1968.

Fiske, John. Introduction to Communication Studies.
    London: Methuen, 1982.

Goodman, Nelson. "Metaphor as Moonlighting." On Metaphor.
    Ed. Sheldon Sacks. Chicago: Univ. of Chicago Press,
    1979.

Hayakawa, S. I. Language in Thought and Action. 4th ed.
    New York: Harcourt Brace Jovanovich, 1978.

Holman, C. Hugh. A Handbook to Literature. 4th ed.
    Indianapolis: Bobbs-Merrill, 1980.

Langer, Susanne K. Philosophy in a New Key: A Study in the
    Symbolism of Reason, Rite, and Art. 1942. New York:
    Mentor-NAL, 1948.

Lemon, Lee T. A Glossary for the Study of English. New
    York: Oxford Univ. Press, 1971.

Liberman, M. M., and Edward E. Foster. A Modern Lexicon of

<u>Literary Terms</u>. Glenview, IL: Scott, 1968.

Tindall, William York. <u>The Literary Symbol</u>. 1955.
Bloomington: Indiana Univ. Press, 1958.

Wheelwright, Philip. <u>The Burning Fountain: A Study in the
Language of Symbolism</u>. Rev. ed. Bloomington: Indiana
Univ. Press, 1968.

Whitehead, Alfred North. <u>Symbolism: Its Meaning and Effect</u>.
New York: Macmillan, 1927.

CHAPTER XI

THE CORRECTION SYMBOLS EXPLAINED

This chapter provides an alphabetical list of the abbreviations or "correction symbols" commonly used in marking students' essays, followed by a few other symbols and proofreader's marks often used in such marking. Most listed symbols are followed by brief explanations of their meaning and of the steps necessary to correct or revise the particular errors or weaknesses, including one or more examples of each. Instructors who don't use all the symbols listed or who use some not listed will advise their students accordingly. We have included all the most common symbols and provided cross-references for those that have more than one form; some instructors, for example, will use *fs* (fused sentence) to indicate that egregious error, but since we believe most will refer to it as a *run-on* sentence, we have made that the main entry.

When you approach a marked paper for the purpose of correction and revision, you will probably consult this chapter first. If the brief explanation you find here doesn't enable you to correct a specific error, follow the cross-reference to the fuller discussion elsewhere in the book; only a few of the categories listed below, such as *awk, nsw,* and *ss,* are not discussed specifically elsewhere.

Reminder: These symbols are also listed inside the back cover.

abbr Undesirable or Incorrect Abbreviation

Generally, avoid abbreviations in formal writing. Instead of *e.g., viz., etc.,* use the more formal expressions *for example, namely, and so forth.* Some abbreviations are so common that they are almost a substitute for the full term. For example, we often speak or write of British Columbia as *B.C.* and of Prince Edward Island as *P.E.I.,* but never of Alberta as *Alta.* or of Ontario as *Ont.* Abbreviations like *B.C.* and *P.E.I.* are acceptable in writing (but the name should be spelled in full the first time it appears), whereas *Alta.* and *Ont.* are not. Whenever you aren't sure, avoid the abbreviation; the full word or words will never be inappropriate.

See #46 for more information about abbreviations.

ack Acknowledgment of Sources

Whenever you include in an essay information, ideas, or wording that you obtained from any other written source, you must acknowledge your indebtedness in accordance with the conventions of documentation; this holds true even if you aren't writing a full-fledged research paper. Even specific information from lectures and conversations should usually be acknowledged.

Failure to indicate indebtedness is **plagiarism**, or literary theft. Instructors and institutions usually apply severe penalties for such dishonesty.

See #76-80c, passim. See also **doc** *(Documentation)*.

ad Adjectives and Adverbs Confused or Misused

The most likely kind of error in this category is the use of either an adjective or an adverb where the other should appear. For example:

> *ad:* He doesn't present his arguments very good.

Here the adjective *good* should be replaced by the adverb *well*. (See #9b.2 and **good, bad, badly, well** in #60).

See #8 and #9.

agr Agreement

1. *Agreement between subject and verb:* A finite verb must agree with its subject in person and number.

> *agr:* The falseness of the paper daffodils were to her like a mild insult.

The singular *falseness,* not the plural *daffodils,* is the subject; to agree in number, therefore, the verb should be *was,* not *were.*

See #7.

2. *Agreement of pronouns with their antecedents:* A pronoun must agree in person and number with its antecedent, the word—usually preceding it— to which it refers.

> *agr:* When the teacher asked for volunteers, nobody in the class raised their hand.

The indefinite pronoun *nobody* is singular; to agree with it in number, the pronoun referring to it should also be singular. But to avoid sexist language, you would not use the formerly common *his,* but rather *his or her*—or avoid the problem by rephrasing the sentence: "When the teacher asked for volunteers, not a single hand went up" (see #4d).

See #4. For shifts in the person and number of pronouns, see **shift, pv** *(Point of View)* and #26d-e.

al Illogical or Incongruous Alignment of Elements

Revise to remove the illogicality. For example it may be a matter of faulty predication:

> *al, pred:* His job as a schoolteacher was one way he could earn the
> community's respect.

But a *job* is not a *way*. The sentence needs revising:

> *revised:* His job as a schoolteacher helped earn him the community's respect.
> *revised:* One way he could earn the community's respect was by being a
> schoolteacher.

Other alignment errors also result from trying to make words behave in ways that their meanings don't permit:

> *al:* The general believed that acts such as cowardice and insubordination
> should be severely punished.

But cowardice and insubordination are not *acts*.

> *revised:* The general believed that acts of cowardice and insubordination
> should be severely punished.

See #30; see also **log** *(Logic)* and **comp** *(Incomplete Comparison)*.

ambig Ambiguous

Ambiguity is a kind of lack of clarity that lets a reader understand something in two different ways. Although ambiguity is sometimes intentional, for example in poetry, where it can enrich the meaning, it has no place in expository prose, where it only confuses the reader and thus obscures the meaning.

> *ambig:* The Prime Minister was in favour of elimination of price controls and
> tax reductions.

Here coordination appears to link *price controls* and *tax reductions*—a possible, but unlikely, political stance. The ambiguity can be removed by rearrangement or by changing the syntax:

> *clear:* The Prime Minister was in favour of tax reductions and the elimination
> of price controls.
> *clear:* The Prime Minister was in favour of reducing taxes and eliminating
> price controls.

In this second version, the parallel gerunds *reducing* and *eliminating* help enforce the intended meaning.

See also **cl** *(Clarity)*, **dm** *(Dangling Modifier)* and #24, **mm** *(Misplaced Modifier)* and #23, **fp** *(Faulty Parallelism)* and #27, **p** *(Punctuation)* and Chapter IV, and **ref** *(Faulty Reference)* and #5b.

apos **Apostrophe Missing or Misused**

1. An apostrophe indicates the possessive inflection of nouns. Here the necessary apostrophe is omitted:

> *apos:* She mended the girls dresses.

Without an apostrophe, one can't tell whether the possessive *girls* is singular *(girl's)* or plural *(girls')*.

2. An apostrophe is NOT used for the possessive case of personal pronouns:

> *wrong:* her's, your's, their's

3. An apostrophe indicates the omission of letters in contractions; to omit such an apostrophe is to misspell the word; some examples:

he'll (he will)	shouldn't (should not)
hasn't (has not)	we're (we are)
it's (it is)	you're (you are)

4. Don't confuse a contraction with a possessive form:

> *wrong:* Who's book is this? *(Whose)*
> *wrong:* Is this where *your* going to sleep? *(you're)*

Note: Contractions are out of place in formal writing. If you want a relatively informal tone, however, they are not only permissible but desirable. See #52b.

See #51v-w for complete information on the apostrophe.

art **Article Missing or Misused**

> *art:* At end of the story everyone is happy again.

Supply the missing *the* before *end.*

> *art:* It was an humiliating experience.

Change *an* to *a.*

> *art:* It was at this point in the life that he decided to reform.

Remove *the* or change it to *his.*

See #8c; see also **id** *(Idiom)* and #58.

awk **Awkwardness**

k *Awk* (or *k*) is the symbol many teachers use when they know something is wrong with a sentence but can't put a finger on any particular error, or when the combination of several faults is unusually complicated. *Awk* could be translated as something like "Take this sentence into the shop for diagnosis and repair." Awkwardness can stem from several causes, among them the following:

> It can result from laziness or haste, from indiscriminately writing down the first thing that pops into one's head.
>
> It can occur when an unsophisticated writer overelaborates diction and sentence structure, mistakenly thinking that such a style will impress a reader; simple expression is often the most effective and even the most elegant. See **w** (*Wordiness*) and #59.
>
> It often results from clumsy use of the passive voice (see **pas** and #6p),
>
> or from poor punctuation (see Chapter IV),
>
> or from confused thinking, imprecise diction, and insufficient explanation.

Here are some examples of awkward sentences from students' essays, each followed by an attempt to straighten it out:

> *awk:* Caught up in this new way of life, I felt a closer existence to every thoughts of today.
> *revised:* Caught up in this new way of life, I felt more intimately involved in contemporary thought.
> *awk:* Now, as I began to get some feeling of confidence restored in me, I thought how silly my previous experience had been.
> *revised:* Now, as I regained confidence, I realized how foolish my response to the earlier experience had been.
> *awk:* I looked for a familiar face among that great sea of faces, but this was done in vain.

Here faulty idiom (*among* instead of *in*), the passive voice (*was done*), and unnecessary coordination (along with wordiness) combined to produce a slovenly sentence.

> *revised:* I looked in vain for a friend in that great sea of faces.
> *awk:* The essay is written in a way that he relates his beliefs to the reader, but does not force the reader to digest his beliefs.
> *revised:* The writer explains his beliefs although he does not expect the reader to share them.
> *awk:* The poem also gives a sense of lightness in the way it rhymes and in its metre.
> *revised:* The poem's rhymes and metre contribute to its light tone.
> *awk:* During the eighteenth century, chemistry became a real science instead of the previous alchemy.

revised: In the eighteenth century chemistry became a true science, evolving out of and replacing the pseudoscience of alchemy.

awk: In the poem, "To an Athlete Dying Young," by A. E. Housman, the author poses an argument of why the athlete benefited from dying young.

revised: In A. E. Housman's poem "To an Athlete Dying Young," the speaker argues that it was fortunate for the athlete to die so young.

ca Case of Pronoun Wrong

The case of a pronoun depends on its function in its own clause or phrase. A pronoun that is a subject or a complement must be in the subjective case:

ca: Hans and *me* dug the ditch ourselves. (*I*)
ca: He's the one *whom* I predicted would win the race. (*who*)
ca: That is *her*. (*she*)

A pronoun that is an object of a verb or a preposition must be in the objective case:

ca: They told Albert and *I* to leave. (*me*)
ca: It was up to Peggy and *I* to finish the job. (*me*)
ca: It doesn't matter *who* you take with you. (*whom*)

See #3e. For information about the possessive case of nouns and pronouns, see #2a.2, #2b, #3a-d, #8a, #10h, and #51w.

cap Capitalization Needed or Faulty

cap: Near Hudson bay in the Northwest Territories is the region known as the barrens.

corrected: Near Hudson Bay in the Northwest Territories is the region known as the Barrens.

See #47; see also **lc** (*Lower Case*).

cl Lack of Clarity

Like awkwardness, a lack of clarity can result from many causes. The parts of a sentence may fail to go together in a meaningful way, or the words chosen to express an idea may not do so adequately, or the writer may have had only a vague idea in the first place.

cl: There is also a general sense of irony in the plot or story behind the play.

What is a *general sense* as opposed to a *sense*? What is a *sense of irony* as opposed to *irony*? Why the choice of *plot or story*? And how is it that the plot (or story) is *behind* the play? It is impossible to be sure what the writer meant, but here is a clear sentence that uses the major features of the original: "There are ironic elements in the plot of the play."

> *cl:* This blessing is intended to restore faith in God when things happen such as death which you don't understand and want to blame God for letting them happen.

This sentence could also have been marked *awk*, but the muddiness of the thought and its expression seems to be its principal fault. Sorting it out and adding some logic as well as some careful syntax produce a clearer and more succinct version:

> *revised:* This blessing is intended to restore faith in God, which may be lost when incomprehensible events like death make one question God's justice.

But here is an example of an unclear sentence that remains impenetrable; not even the context offered any help to understanding it:

> *cl:* Absurdist plays work on the situation in much greater detail than the dramatic level.

Here is another sentence that goes astray; one can only wonder what the intended meaning was:

> *cl:* He compares the athlete's achievements and victories to that of death.

Sometimes even punctuation is part of the trouble:

> *cl, p:* Before I really had time to think they wanted me to report for work in the morning.

A comma after *think* makes it likely that a reader will understand the sentence on the first reading rather than the second or third.

See also **ambig** *(Ambiguous)*, **awk** *(Awkward)*, #5, and #23-31.

cliché **Cliché**

See **trite** *(Trite, Worn-out, Hackneyed Expression)*.

coh **Not Coherent; Continuity Weak**

Coherence is weak or faulty when there is insufficient transition between two sentences or two paragraphs. The first sentence of a paragraph, whether it is the topic sentence or not, should in some way provide a connection with the preceding paragraph. Similarly, sentences within paragraphs should flow smoothly from one to another. Here for example are two sentences which are not smoothly connected:

> *coh:* Rachel is invited both to dine at Willard's and to go out with Calla. Despite her desire to accept one of the invitations she declines both of them because it is her mother's card night.

Granted that the idea of the invitations is present in both, and granted that a reader can more or less work out the connection, a *But* to begin the second sentence or a *however* (between commas) after the word *invitations* would provide the necessary coherence and make the reader's task much easier.

See #63-65d and #68b; see also **tr** (*Transition Weak or Lacking*) and *Sentence Coherence*, #31.

colloq Colloquialism

See **inf** (*Informal, Colloquial*).

comb Combine Sentences

An instructor may write *coord* (Coordinate) or *sub* (Subordinate), or even *coord or sub* together, to indicate that some kind of improvement (e.g. economy, coherence, logic, or just a decrease in choppiness) could be gained by putting two (or more) sentences together. Sometimes, however, rather than specify *coord* or *sub*, perhaps because neither seems particularly desirable, an instructor may write *comb*, meaning simply "Combine these sentences into one in the way you think best." In the following, for example, which could as well have been marked *w* (*Wordiness*), the improvement is obvious:

> *w, comb:* The whiteness of the snow piled on their outstretched branches gave their green colour an extra richness. This added attractiveness seemed to enhance their beauty.
> *revised:* The whiteness of the snow piled on their outstretched branches gave their green colour an extra richness, enhancing their beauty.

See **coord** (*Coordination Needed*), **sub** (*Subordination Needed*), #28, and Exercises 1q, 10(4,5), 12c(2) and 59abc(2).

comp Incomplete Comparison

inc Revise to correct incomplete or illogical comparisons.

> *comp:* She is a better skater than any girl on the team.
> *revised:* She is a better skater than any other girl on the team.
> *revised:* She is the best skater on the team.
> *comp:* Life in a small town is better than a big city.
> *revised:* Life in a small town is better than (life) in a big city.

    comp: I think tomato juice is as good, if not better, than orange juice.
    revised: I think tomato juice is as good as, if not better than, orange juice.
    revised: I think tomato juice is as good as orange juice, if not better.
    comp: Fresh vegetables have more vitamins.
    revised: Fresh vegetables have more vitamins than canned or frozen ones.
    comp: I like skiing more than David.
    revised: I like skiing more than David does.
    revised: I like skiing more than I like David.

Note that **ambig** (*Ambiguous*), **cl** (*Lack of Clarity*), or **log** (*Logic*) would be an appropriate mark for some of these sentences.

See #29 and #30.

conc Insufficient Concreteness

Revise by increasing the concreteness of your diction. Replace abstract words and phrases with concrete ones, or expand upon general and abstract statements with specific and concrete details.

    conc: Seymour was a very deep young man.

The word *deep* here is suggestive, but too abstract to be very meaningful. *Deep* could mean any one of several different things here (consult your dictionary); more information, especially in the form of concrete examples, would enable a reader to understand precisely what the writer meant to convey. Here are two sentences whose vague abstractness and illogical circularity (see #70h, under *begging the question*) render them almost meaningless:

    conc, log: The author makes the setting so good that it is very convincing.
    conc, log: The characters are presented as fully described people.

Don't write empty sentences like those. Inject some specific, concrete content.

See #54.

coord Coordination Needed; Combine Sentences

When two sentences are closely related, for example in expressing a contrast, it is usually preferable to combine them, using either punctuation or a coordinating conjunction (see #12a-b) or both.

    coord: Life in the North can be very challenging. Life in a large city offers
        more variety.
    revised: Life in the North can be very challenging, but life in a large city
        offers more variety.

Depending on context and desired emphasis, such sentences could also be joined with a semicolon, or one or the other could be subordinated with a beginning *though* or *whereas*.

See also **sub** *(Subordination)*, **comb** *(Combine Sentences)*, **cs** *(Comma Splice)*, **coh** *(Coherence)*, and **fc** *(Faulty Coordination)* and #28.

cs Comma Splice

A comma splice results from putting a comma between two independent clauses that are not joined with a coordinating conjunction; "splicing" the clauses together with only a comma is not enough.

> *cs:* The flight from Vancouver to Toronto takes only about four hours, it seems to last forever.

The comma is not enough. A semicolon (or period) would be "correct," but a poor solution because the two clauses obviously are closely related. Here the desired contrast would best be emphasized either by using an appropriate coordinating conjunction along with the comma:

> The flight from Vancouver to Toronto takes about four hours, but it seems to last forever.

or by using a subordinating conjunction to change one of the clauses to a subordinate clause:

> Although the flight from Vancouver to Toronto takes only about four hours, it seems to last forever.

Another example:

> *cs:* Contemporary Canadian poetry is, if nothing else, at least plentiful, it pours daily from a number of influential presses.

Here, since the second clause illustrates the idea expressed in the first, a coordinating conjunction would not be the most appropriate connector. Using *for* would work, but it would be better to emphasize the syntactic integrity of the second clause by simply changing the comma to a semicolon. Even a colon would work well (see #32c and #33i). Here is an instance where a colon would be the preferred mark to replace the comma:

> *cs:* Slavery took hold in the South for purely economic reasons, large numbers of workers were needed to attend to the large plantations.

Comma splices, then, can be corrected by replacing the offending comma with an appropriate mark—usually a semicolon, sometimes a colon, or even a period if you decide to turn the clauses into two separate sentences—or by showing the relation between the two clauses with a precise coordinating or subordinating conjunction. Or sometimes you can reduce one of the clauses to a modifying phrase:

cs: The poem gives us several clues to the poet's attitude toward death, one of these is the imagery.

revised: The poem gives us several clues to the poet's attitude toward death, one of these being the imagery.

See #33e and h; for exceptions, see #33f-g. See also **comb** *(Combine Sentences)*, **coord** *(Coordination)*, **fc** *(Faulty Coordination)*, **sub** *(Subordination)*, and Exercises 10(3), 10(4), and 11a-c(2).

d Faulty Diction

Errors in diction are often marked with one or another specific symbol, such as *ww* (wrong word), *nsw* (no such word), *inf* (informal or colloquial), or *id* (idiom). But sometimes a teacher will simply use *d*, implying either that the error does not fall into one of the particular categories or that the student is expected to find out just what the specific error is. In either event, the first thing the writer should do is consult a dictionary; *d* could be said to stand for *dictionary*.

> If we regard the poem in this way, the recurring images of the "unwatered," aimless, barren mind of modern man would be one of the
> *d:* musical themes, and the imagery of water *plus* its symbolism of replenishment would be another.

In this otherwise well-wrought sentence, the word *plus* creates a stylistic disturbance. *Plus* is normally a mathematical term; it is not a conjunction, nor appropriate to this context. In an expository context the meaning of *plus* is usually conveyed by the conjunction *and*; the preposition *with* would also serve the meaning here.

Diction can also be poor by being weak or imprecise. In the following sentence, for example, the word *outlined* is inadequate for the job it is being asked to do:

> *d:* The program should be *outlined* in such a way that learning can take place in the field as well as in the classroom.

A word like *designed*, *planned*, or *organized* would be better.

See Chapter VII. See also **inf** *(Informal, Colloquial)*, **conc** *(Concreteness)*, **id** *(Idiom)*, **jarg** *(Jargon)*, **nsw** *(No Such Word)*, and **ww** *(Wrong Word)*.

dev Development Needed

This mark indicates that an idea, point, or subject needs to be further developed, expanded upon. The weakness occurs most often in the form of an inadequately developed paragraph. Revise by supplying details, examples, or illustrations, by defining or explaining, or by some other method appropriate to the particular instance.

See #54, #61b, #64b, and #67b.

div **Word Division**

See **syl** *(Syllabication)*.

dm **Dangling Modifier**

> *dm:* Running around the corner of the building, a newsstand suddenly loomed in front of me.

Correct a dangling modifier either by changing it so that it no longer dangles:

> *corrected:* As I ran around the corner of the building, a newsstand suddenly loomed in front of me.

or by providing a logical noun or pronoun for it to modify:

> *corrected:* Running around the corner of the building, I was suddenly confronted by a newsstand looming before me.

See #24.

doc **Documentation**

Use the correct forms for your notes (whether parenthetical, at the foot of the page, or collected at the end) and your bibliography. In Chapter IX, on the Research Paper, you will find model notes and bibliographical entries. See #78 and 80. See also #79 and Chapter X, essay 17.

See **ack** *(Acknowledgment of Sources)*.

emph **Emphasis Weak or Unclear**

Make the marked sentence or paragraph properly emphatic by rearranging or by otherwise clarifying the relationship among its parts.

> *emph:* The older generation of our society, like the younger, is also continually confronted with both beneficial and harmful advertisements which are effective on our society in some way or other.

A flabby sentence in general—and what little strength it has is mostly dissipated by the limp final prepositional phrase; simply removing it would sharpen the end of the sentence, which is its most emphatic part. But further improvement can be gained by sorting out and rearranging its content and cutting the repetition and deadwood:

> *revised:* All of society—not just the young but the older generation as well—is bombarded by advertising which can be beneficial as well as harmful.

This may not be the best possible version, but at least its emphasis is clear.

See #18, #66, and #68c; see also **fc** *(Faulty Coordination)* and #28.

euph Euphemism

Avoid unnecessary *euphemism* ("good sounding," though not necessarily good in fact). Often directness and precision are preferable to even well-intentioned delicacy and vagueness. Is someone lacking money to buy enough food really made to feel better by being described as "disadvantaged" rather than "poor"?

When you are tempted to use a euphemism to avoid an unpleasant reality (for example describing a person as "inebriated" or "in a state of intoxication" rather than "drunk"), consider the possible virtues of being direct and succinct instead.

See #56.

fc Faulty Coordination

Faulty coordination occurs when unrelated clauses are presented as coordinate, or when related clauses are linked by punctuation or coordinating conjunctions which fail to indicate the relation correctly.

> *fc:* Chaucer was born in 1340 and he was the greatest poet of medieval England.

The coordinating conjunction *and* is misleading: Chaucer's birth-date and the extent of his reputation are not significantly related or equal in value. The significant comment is contained in the second clause; the opening clause contains a minor fact which should be subordinated to the main statement:

> *revised:* Chaucer, who was born in 1340, was the greatest poet of medieval England.
> *revised:* Chaucer (1340-1400) was medieval England's greatest poet.

Here is another example in which the second of two clauses is more important; the first clause should be subordinated or even changed to a participial phrase:

> *fc:* He had worked all summer at handsome wages and he had earned enough to see him through the next year at university.
> *revised:* Since he had worked all summer at handsome wages, he had earned enough to see him through the next year at university.
> *revised:* Having worked all summer at handsome wages, he had earned enough to see him through the next year at university.

See #28; see also **comb** (*Combine Sentences*), **coord** (*Coordination*), and **sub** (*Subordination*).

fig Inappropriate or Confusing Figurative Language

Revise to change or remove figurative language (similes, metaphors) that is inappropriate or mixed.

> *fig:* Physical Education provides a stepping stone on which students can learn what to do with their leisure time.

The image of a stepping stone adds nothing but oddity to this sentence. Some more appropriate figure may have been in the writer's mind, but the statement is probably better without the metaphor:

> *revised:* Physical Education offers students an opportunity to learn how to use their spare time.

Here is an example of a mixed metaphor:

> *fig:* Like a bolt from the blue the idea grabbed him, and it soon grew into one of his most prized pieces of mental furniture.

One of the troubles with clichés that are dead metaphors is that we often fail to visualize them; result: absurdity. The *bolt from the blue*, even if allowed, could scarcely *grab* anyone, nor could it grow (like a plant?) into a piece of furniture. The urge to be metaphorical backfired on the writer. Don't thoughtlessly juxtapose incongruous images.

See #53 and #59e.

fp Faulty Parallelism

// Revise by making coordinated elements grammatically parallel.

> *fp:* For me England brings back memories of pleasant walks in Cornwall on some windblown lea, looking out to sea dressed in warm woollen jerseys, and feeling a warmth brought about by being with my family in that place.

The three objects of the preposition *of* here are all nouns, but *looking* and *feeling*, unlike *walks*, are gerunds. Repeating *of* before each gerund would help, but it is better to make the three grammatically parallel (and the phrase "dressed in warm woollen jerseys" seems more appropriate to the windblown lea than to looking out to sea):

> *revised:* For me England brings back pleasant memories of walking on some windblown lea in Cornwall, dressed in warm woollen jerseys, looking out to sea, and feeling a warmth brought about by being with my family in that place.

There is also the kind of awkwardness in which a parallel structure breaks down—or isn't sufficiently built up:

> *fp:* During my visit I had the chance to get involved with the children, help with the shopping and cooking—all of which helped make the experience enjoyable.

The sentence structure implies that we're going to be given more than two things—and the phrase "all of which" makes it sound as though we have been. Perhaps the writer subconsciously thought of "shopping" and "cooking" as separate items; but the parallelism is in the verbs *get involved* and *help*. That is, the implied parallel series after *to* is not fulfilled.

> *revised:* During my visit I had the chance to get involved with the children and to help with the shopping and the cooking; these activities helped make the experience enjoyable.

Alternatively, a third element could be supplied, or *cooking* could be governed by a third verb, such as "participate in."

See #27.

frag Unacceptable Fragment

Word groups punctuated as sentences but which don't fulfill the requirements of sentences are usually unacceptable. Any word group that cannot stand by itself and communicate effectively is suspect.

> *frag:* Corbett was chosen to be the next attorney general. He being clever and remarkably well versed in the law.

The second part here has no verb (*being* is a participle), nor is it an acceptable minor sentence. It should be set off with a comma as part of the preceding sentence.

> *frag:* The convention was held at the Cornish Hotel. Because it has a large banquet room which would accommodate us all.

The second part is a subordinate clause dependent on the predicate of the preceding sentence, and should be set off with a comma.

> **Note:** Fragmentary patterns can sometimes be used effectively as a stylistic device by skilled writers. If you deliberately use a fragmentary pattern in an essay, perhaps indicate the fact in a marginal note so that, without penalizing you for it, your instructor can tell you if it works.

See #1x, #1y, and #20.

fs Fused Sentence

See run-on.

gen Inadequately Supported Generalization

See #54b and conc (*Insufficient Concreteness*).

gr Error in Grammar

Although errors such as *agr, dm, ref,* and *t* fall into the category of grammatical error, instructors will sometimes simply mark an error *gr* either because it includes more than one kind of mistake or because they want a student to learn by discovering what the particular error is. Or an instructor may want to emphasize that a usage like "The reason . . . is because" is not just a matter of careless wording but an error in grammar (see **reason . . . is because** in #60).

id Faulty Idiom, Unidiomatic Usage

Idiom refers to the forms of expression and the structures peculiar to a particular language. Idioms are not necessarily logical or explicable in grammatical terms. Errors in idiom most often occur with prepositions, as in the following examples:

> *id:* The extent of Creighton's influence *towards* our view of Canadian history is not fully appreciated. (*on*)
> *id:* Iago has a reputation *of* honesty. (*for*)

See #58; see also **art** (*Articles*) and #8c.

inc Incomplete Comparison

See comp.

inf Inappropriate Informal or Colloquial Diction

Replace the inappropriate word or words with something more formal.

> *inf:* He is the most *stuck-up* boy in the class. (*conceited, vain, egotistical, snobbish*)

See #52b.

ital Italics Needed or Incorrect

Correct by italicizing or by removing unwanted italics. (In typed or handwritten material, italics are represented by <u>underlining</u>.)

> *ital:* "A Night to Remember" is about the sinking of the Titanic.
> *corrected:* A Night to Remember is about the sinking of the *Titanic*.

See #49; see also *Titles*, #48.

jarg Jargon

Revise to avoid unnecessary jargon.

> *jarg:* A truly professional-type player, he seemed able to judge every move from the standpoint of its bottom-line effect.
> *revised:* A true professional, he seemed able to judge the ultimate effect of every move he made.

See #59h.

k Awkward

See awk.

lc Lower Case

Change incorrect capital letter(s) to lower case.

> *lc:* You can now find Champagne made elsewhere than in France. (*champagne*)
> *lc:* I had always planned to get a University education. (*university*)

See #47.

leg Legibility, Illegible

Re-do any messy or poor handwriting or struck-over typing that cannot be read clearly.

lev Inappropriate Level of Diction

See #52.

log Logic: Illogical as Phrased; Logicality of Reasoning Questioned

Illogic underlies many different kinds of error and much weak writing and thinking. Nevertheless, **log** is frequently the mark used to indicate an error of logic arising out of the way something has been phrased. For example:

> *log:* Insecurity is a characteristic basic to Davies's nature and it becomes a consistent weakness of his throughout the play.

If insecurity *is* a basic characteristic, it can scarcely *become* consistent in the course of the play; and it can scarcely *become* consistent *throughout* the play, since *throughout* logically contradicts the meaning of *become*. Here is another example:

> *log:* In giving a precise definition of what this mental science is, Asimov is very vague.

The illogicality is obvious. At least three meanings are possible:

clear: Asimov fails to provide a precise definition of this mental science.
clear: Asimov's definition of this mental science is very vague.
clear: Asimov deals only vaguely with this mental science and makes no attempt to define it.

See also #28, #29, **al** *(Alignment)* and #30, and #70e-h.

mix Mixed Construction

A shift from one syntactical pattern to another within a single sentence:

mix: The choice was between junk food that would be filling or a smaller but nourishing meal.

To revise, decide on one pattern or the other:

revised: The choice was *between* junk food that would be filling *and* a smaller but nourishing meal.
revised: We could choose *either* junk food that would be filling *or* a smaller but nourishing meal.

In the last version, the word *either* could be omitted.

See #25.

mm Misplaced Modifier

Revise by moving the modifying word or phrase to the logical place in the sentence.

mm: Sauron wished to be the Dark Lord of Middle-earth, and *almost* had enough power to succeed *twice.*
revised: Sauron wished to be Dark Lord of Middle-earth, and twice had almost enough power to succeed.

See #23; see also **wo** *(Word Order).*

ms Improper Manuscript Form or Conventions

Conscientious writers are careful to follow certain conventions pertaining to the form and presentation of a manuscript. These include such things as indenting paragraphs clearly, leaving two spaces after periods, not underlining one's own title, being consistent with punctuation marks, and leaving spaces between the dots of an ellipsis.

See Chapter V.

nsw No Such Word

Don't make up words (unless perhaps for humorous purposes). If you can't think of a particular word you want, try consulting a thesaurus. If you use a word that looks or sounds unusual, that doesn't quite ring true, consult a good dictionary to see if it's there. A little extra care will enable you to avoid using such concoctions as these, all of which occurred in students' essays:

ableness (ability)	fruitition (fruition)
afraidness (fear)	infidelous (unfaithful)
artistism (artistry)	irregardless (regardless,
condensated (condensed)	irrespective)
cowardism, cowardness	nonchalantness (nonchalance)
(cowardice)	prejudism (prejudice)
deteriorized (deteriorated)	prophesize (prophesy)
disgustion (disgust)	scepticalism (scepticism)
enrichen (enrich)	superfluosity (superfluity,
freedomship (freedom)	superfluousness)

And don't make the kind of mistake a popular magazine did in a recipe, listing "2 cups frozen corn" among the ingredients, and beginning the instructions with "Unthaw corn."

num Incorrect Use of Numerals

See #50 for the conventions governing the use of numerals.

org Organization Weak or Faulty

Repetition, choppiness, lack of proportion or emphasis, haphazard order—all these and more can be signs of poor organization. It may be necessary to rethink your outline.

See #64, #69e-j, and #70d.

p Error in Punctuation

Punctuation marks are symbols that should be just as meaningful to readers as are the symbols of speech (words) with which they are associated in writing. In speech, "punctuation" takes the form of inflections of voice, pauses, and changes in pitch or intensity. In order to communicate clearly and effectively on paper, one must be as careful with punctuation as one is with words and syntax. When you find *p* in the margin, refer to Chapter IV to find out not only *what* is wrong or weak, but also *why* it is so.

para **Paragraphing**

¶ See #61-67.

pas **Weak Passive Voice**

This mark means that in the reader's opinion the sentence in question would be better served by a verb in the active voice than by one in the passive voice—some form of *be* followed by a past participle, making the subject of a clause the receiver of the action: Jo brought the ice (active); The ice was brought by Jo (passive).

> *pas:* Davies always finds his fears *being played upon* by Mick.
> *active:* Davies always finds that Mick *plays upon* his fears.
> *active:* Mick always *plays upon* Davies's fears.
> *pas:* In these lines the comparison of himself and his lover to flies *is made*.
> *active:* In these lines the speaker *compares* himself and his lover to flies.

See #6p. See also #18f.

passim Latin for *throughout*; used to indicate that an error, such as the misspelling of a name, needs to be corrected throughout an essay.

pred **Faulty Predication**

See **al** *(Alignment)* and #30.

pron **Error in Use of Pronoun**

This abbreviation usually marks such errors and weaknesses as the use of an intensive pronoun as a casual substitute for a personal pronoun, or the overuse of vague demonstrative pronouns, or perhaps *which* to refer to a person.

See also **agr** *(Agreement)*, **ca** *(Case of Pronoun Wrong)*, **ref** *(Weak or Faulty Pronoun Reference)*, and **shift** *(Shift in Perspective)*.

pv **Point of View Inconsistent**

See **shift** *(Shift in Perspective)*

Q **Error in Handling of Quoted Material or Quotation Marks**

Sometimes this correction symbol will refer to nothing more than the careless omission of quotation marks (usually at the end of a quotation). But it could also refer to incorrect punctuation with quoted material, awkwardly introduced quoted material, and the like. If the error so marked is not an obvious one, you may have to consult the section on quotation, #43, to find out what is wrong. See also #77, on handling quotations in research writing.

red **Redundancy**

Redundancy can mean simply wordiness, but it is often used to refer specifically to the awkward and unnecessary repetition of the meaning of one word in another word. In the sentence "But he was not unfriendly though," the *But* and the *though* do the same job; one of them must go (obviously the *though*, since it is informal and also weakens the end of the sentence: see **although, though** in #60, and #18c). Here are two more examples:

> *red:* Throughout the entire story the tone is one of unrelieved gloom.

Since *throughout* means *all through, from beginning to end*, the word *entire* merely repeats what has already been said.

> *revised:* Throughout the story the tone is one of unrelieved gloom.

But this is still redundant, for if the tone is *unrelieved*, it must be constant throughout the story. Hence further tightening is possible:

> *re-revised:* The story's tone is one of unrelieved gloom.

Again:

> *red:* Puck's playful pranks include tricks on housewives and village maids.

Here the writer's choice of the word *pranks* is accurate and effective, but since *pranks* are *frolicsome tricks*, the addition of the adjective *playful* is redundant and decreases the effectiveness. One might even want to get rid of the word *tricks*:

> *revised:* Puck plays pranks on housewives and village maids.

See #59c; see also **w** (*Wordiness*).

ref **Weak or Faulty Pronoun Reference**

Pronouns must refer to their antecedents in a clear way. The following sentence, for example, is muddled because it isn't clear whom the pronouns refer to:

> *ref:* Because of all the attention which Seymour and Buddy gave to Franny and Zooey when *they* were young children, *they* never allowed *them* to develop *their* own ideas of life.

One can, by careful reading, extract the sense of this sentence, but it is the writer's job to make the meaning clear, not the reader's to puzzle it out.

> *revised:* When Franny and Zooey were young, Seymour and Buddy gave *them* so much attention that the children were never able to develop their own ideas of life.

One clear pronoun instead of four confusing ones (and the redundant *young children* has been broken up as well). Here is another example:

> Merlin's power, quite naturally, is partially a result of his "Sight" and what
> *ref:* are thought to be his magical powers. An example of *this* is given during the battle between King Ambrosius and the Saxons.

Clearly one must also be careful with demonstrative pronouns: here the reference of *this* is obscure. Probably in the writer's mind *this* somehow referred to the entire idea expressed in the first sentence. In other words, *this* has no precise antecedent, and the reference is therefore loose at best. A clearer and more precise version (clearing up the awkward parallelism and the passive voice as well) is possible:

> *revised:* Merlin's power derives from a combination of his Sight and his reputed magic. The battle between King Ambrosius and the Saxons provides an illustration of this fact.

Changing the demonstrative pronoun to a demonstrative adjective usually makes things clearer. But the passage is still clumsy and wordy. Try again, combining the sentences:

> *revised:* As the battle between King Ambrosius and the Saxons illustrates, Merlin's power derives from a combination of his Sight and his reputed magic.

See #5; see also #4.

rep Weak, Awkward, or Unnecessary Repetition

Another kind of wordiness that requires pruning. Although repetition is often useful for achieving emphasis and coherence, unnecessary repetition only encumbers.

> *rep:* The snow was falling heavily, but I didn't mind the snow, for I have always enjoyed the things one can do in the snow.

The repetition of *snow* at the end is all right, but the middle one must go; replace *the snow* with *it*, or—better yet—with nothing at all.

See #59b.

run-on Run-on or Fused Sentence

fs Failure to put any punctuation between two independent clauses not joined by a coordinating conjunction results in a run-on sentence. Since a run-on is often merely a careless slip, caused by writing too fast and not proofreading carefully, it should be easy to prevent.

> *run-on:* Vancouver is the most beautifully situated city in Canada it also has
>   some ugly slums.

Like the comma splice, a run-on can be corrected by inserting a semi-colon, by inserting a comma and a coordinating conjunction, by subordinating one of the clauses and inserting a comma, or even by inserting a period.

See #22 and #33j; see also **cs** *(Comma Splice).*

shift Shift in Perspective; Point of View Inconsistent or
pv Unclear

Revise to remove the awkward or illogical shift in tense, mood, or voice of verbs, or person or number of pronouns.

> *shift:* One should never forget *your* snowshoes. (*one's*)
> *shift:* It was four in the afternoon, beginning to get dark, and we *are* still only
>   half-way down the mountain. (*were*)

See #26.

Perspective can also seem to shift because of a lack of parallelism:

> *shift, fp:* Ralph said that it was raining and he preferred to stay home.

If "he preferred to stay home" is meant as a part of what he said, then a second *that* is required after *and*; otherwise, "he preferred" could be taken as parallel to "Ralph said." That is, without the second *that*, "he preferred" would be from the writer's point of view rather than Ralph's.

See #27a.

sp Spelling

If you misspell a word, don't simply try to guess how it should be corrected, for you may get it wrong again. Check the word in your dictionary, and take the opportunity to find out all the dictionary can tell you about the word—not only for the sake of learning something, but also because studying the word will help fix it and its correct spelling in your mind. Then check Chapter VI to see if your error fits any of the categories discussed there; if it does, study the principles involved. And keep a list of the words you misspell so that you can review it as often as necessary to become thoroughly familiar with their correct spellings.

split Unnecessary Split Infinitive

See #10c.

squint Squinting Modifier

A modifier that is ambiguous because it seems to look both ways, so that a reader can't be sure which of two elements it is supposed to modify. Revise as necessary to make the modifier attach itself where you want it.

See #23c.

ss Sentence Structure or Sentence Sense

Sometimes an instructor will put *ss* (or just *s*) in the margin opposite a sentence to indicate that something is wrong with its sense or its structure, leaving it to the writer to discover what the problem is. It may for example be a grammatical error, or a faulty arrangement, or a lack of clarity. Or the sentence may be faulty in some way not covered by any of the more specific categories. If this mark appears often, you may need to review the first three chapters.

stet Latin for *Let it stand.* This mark indicates that you were right the first time, that when you changed something, such as a punctuation mark or the spelling of a word, you should have left it the way it was. To correct, therefore, merely restore it to its original form. (Note that an instructor will be able to advise you this way only if you cancel a word or phrase with a single neat line through it; if you blot it out entirely, you may never find out that your first instinct was correct.)

sub Subordination Needed; Combine Sentences

> *sub:* Forster has also done a superb job in his use of examples. His examples are clear and precise.
> *revised:* Forster has also done a superb job in his use of examples, which are clear and precise.

As two sentences (or even as one sentence consisting of two independent clauses) this example is wordy. Even the revised version could be tightened:

> *revised:* Forster has also done a superb job of providing clear and precise examples.

See also **coord** (*Coordination*), **comb** (*Combine Sentences*), **fc** (*Faulty Coordination*) and #28, **coh** (*Coherence*), #1n-p, #12c, and #18i.

syl Syllabication

This mark, or sometimes *div*, for *word division*, indicates that you have incorrectly or inappropriately broken a word at the end of a line. Consult your dictionary to see where the syllable breaks occur in the word. If that isn't the problem, check #45b, *Syllabication and Word Division*, to find out what is wrong.

t Error in Tense

> I often think back to the day, five years ago, when I bought my first horse.
> *t:* To many people this wouldn't be very exciting, but I *have wanted* a horse for as long as I *can* remember.

Change the present perfect *have wanted* to the past perfect *had wanted*, and the present *can* to the past *could*.

See #6g-k.

title Manuscript Conventions for Titles

> See #48.

tr Transition Weak or Lacking

Provide some kind of transitional word or phrase, or improve upon an existing one, or otherwise improve the transition at the place indicated—which will be either between two paragraphs or between two sentences.

See **coh** (*Coherence*), #64, #64a.1, #65c-d, and #68b.

trite Trite, Worn-out, Hackneyed Expression
cliché

As the following example illustrates, some clichés will simply be wordy and therefore wholly or partly expendable; others will have to be replaced with something fresher; and often the sentence will require other rewording as well:

> *trite:* It *goes without saying* that *over the years many and diverse* opinions have been held regarding the origin of the universe.
> *revised:* Ever since people began thinking about it, astronomers and others have held many different opinions about the origin of the universe.

Here the passive voice of *have been held* was also contributing to the sluggishness of the sentence.

See #59e.

u Unity of Sentence, Paragraph, or Essay Is Weak

See #28, #62, and #68a.

uc Upper Case

Change to upper case (capital) letter(s). See **cap** and #47.

us Usage

A subcategory of diction, this refers specifically to the kinds of problems discussed in *A Checklist of Troublesome Words and Phrases*, #60.

var Variety

Try to improve the variety of lengths, kinds, and patterns of your sentences (see #17) or your paragraphs (see #67c).

vb Verb Form

This abbreviation will mark an error in the form of a verb, for example an incorrect inflection or an incorrect principal part of an irregular verb.

See #6b-g.

w Wordiness

If you find this mark haunting the margins of your essays, you may have to take drastic measures. Try thinking of words as costing money, say a dollar apiece; perhaps that will make it easier to avoid a spendthrift style. Mere economy, of course, is not a virtue; never sacrifice something necessary or useful just to reduce the number of words. But don't use several words where one will not only do the same job but do it better, and don't use words that do no real work at all. Here are some examples of squandered words:

> *w:* In today's society, Canada has earned herself a name of respect with everyone in the world.
> *revised:* Canada has earned universal respect. ($11 saved)
> *w:* His words have a romantic quality to them.

The phrase *to them* does no work. In fact, its effect is negative because it destroys the emphatic crispness of the meaningful part of the sentence. Cut it and save $2.

> *w:* Hardy regarded poetry as his serious work, and wrote novels only in order to make enough money to live on.
> *revised:* Hardy regarded poetry as his serious work, and wrote novels only to make a living. ($5 saved)

> *w:* Othello's trust in Iago becomes evident during the first encounter that the reader observes between the two characters.
> *revised:* Othello's trust in Iago becomes evident during their first encounter. ($8 saved)
> *w:* The flash of lightning is representative of God's power.
> *revised:* The flash of lightning represents God's power.

Only $2 saved, but the sentence is much more direct and vigorous.

See #59, especially #59a; see also **red** (*Redundant*) and #59c, and **rep** (*Repetition*) and #59b.

wo Word Order

A misplaced modifier is one kind of faulty word order, but there are other kinds not so easily classified.

> *wo:* She was naturally hurt by his indifference.
> *revised:* Naturally she was hurt by his indifference.

The potential ambiguity could also have been removed by putting commas around *naturally*, but that would slow the sentence down (though it would also emphasize the word).

> *wo:* I will never forget the day July 17, 1991, when I began my first job.
> *revised:* I will never forget July 17, 1991, the day I began my first job.
> *wo:* The image created in the advertisement is what really makes us buy the product and not the product itself.
> *revised:* The image created in the advertisement, not the product itself, is what makes us buy it.

This is not the only possible revision, of course, but it is the simplest, and the sentence is now clearer and less awkward.

> *wo:* Only at the end was clearly revealed the broad scope of the poem and the intensity of the emotions involved.

There seems no justification for such awkward distortion of normal sentence order.

> *revised:* Only at the end were the poem's broad scope and the intensity of its emotions revealed.

Note: In a stated comparison using *similar to, superior to,* or *inferior to,* a noun modified by the adjective should precede, not follow it:

> *wo:* The film has a similar plot to that of Shakespeare's *The Tempest.*
> *revised:* The film has a plot similar to that of Shakespeare's *The Tempest.*

See **mm** (*Misplaced Modifier*) and #23, #1s-t, #8d-e, #9d, and #11b.

ww **Wrong Word**

This category of diction error covers those mistakes which result from confusion about meaning or usage. For example:

> *ww:* England is a nation *who* has brought the past and the present together.

The pronoun *who* refers to persons, not things; usage demands *that* or *which* in this context (see #3d, and #37a, Usage note).

> *ww:* He came to the meeting at the special *bequest* of the chairman.

A glance at the dictionary confirms that *bequest* cannot be the right word here; the writer probably confused it with *request* and *behest*.

See #57; see also #51-lm.

Here are a few other symbols often used in marking essays:

ℒ	Delete, omit.
¶ ; *no* ¶	Paragraph; no paragraph; see *para.*
//	Parallelism; see *fp.*
X	Obvious error (e.g., typographical).
∧	Something omitted? Insert.
=/	Insert hyphen.
∽	Transpose.
◡	Close up.
#	Space; more space.
?	Something questionable or unclear: Is this what you mean?
✓	Something especially good.

CHAPTER XII

OMNIBUS CHECKLIST FOR PLANNING AND REVISING

Ask yourself these questions before you consider any piece of writing finished. If you can conscientiously answer all of them in the affirmative, your essay should be not just adequate, but good.

1. **During and after planning the essay, ask yourself these questions:**

Subject	Have I chosen an interesting subject? (**#69a**)
	Have I sufficiently *limited* my subject? (**#69b**)
Audience and Purpose	Have I thought about *audience* and *purpose*?
	Have I written down a statement of purpose and a profile of my audience? (**#69c**)
Data	Have I collected or generated *more than enough material*? (**#69d**)
Organization and Outline (**#69e-j**)	Does my *thesis statement* (T.S.) state a proposition about the subject?
	Is each heading and subheading on my outline, including the T.S., a *single complex or simple sentence*?
	Have I *at least three and no more than seven* main headings?
	Is the content of my T.S. *equal* to that of the main headings combined?
	Is the content of each heading *equal* to that of any subheadings under it?
	Are my main headings reasonably *parallel*?
	Are the items in each set of subheadings reasonably *parallel*?
	Does each set of subheadings consist of *at least two and not more than seven*?
	Have I chosen a good *order* for the main parts?
	Have I chosen a good *order* for each set of subparts?

2. **During and after revising the essay, ask yourself these questions:**

Title	Does the *title* of my essay clearly indicate the subject?
	Does the *title* contain something to catch a reader's interest?

Structure	Does my *beginning* in some way try to engage a reader's curiosity or interest?
	Have I kept the *beginning* reasonably short? (#69-l)
	Have I clearly stated my *subject* (and perhaps my *thesis* as well) somewhere near the beginning? (#69-l.3)
	Does my *ending* convey a sense of completion? (#68c, #71.9)
	Have I kept my *ending* short enough, without unnecessary repetition and summary?
Unity *Development* *Emphasis*	Is my essay *unified?* Do all its parts contribute, and have I avoided digression? (#68a)
	Have I been sufficiently *particular, specific,* and not left any generalizations unsupported? (#54)
	Have I devoted an appropriate amount of space to each part? (#68c)
Paragraphs	Does the first sentence of each paragraph (except perhaps the first and last, and any merely transitional ones) somehow *mention the overall subject* of the essay? (#64a.1, #68a)
	Does the first sentence of each substantive paragraph clearly state the topic, or part of the topic—or, if it isn't the first sentence, is the *topic sentence* effective where it is placed? (#64a)
	Is each substantive paragraph *long* enough to *develop* its topic adequately? (#67b)
	Does each paragraph *conclude* adequately, but not too self-consciously? (#64c)
Coherence	Do the sentences in each paragraph have sufficient *coherence* with each other? (#63-65)
	Does the first sentence of each paragraph provide a clear *transition* from the preceding paragraph? (#64a.1, #68b)
	Is the *coherence* between sentences and between paragraphs *smooth?* Have I inserted any unnecessary transitional devices? (#65c-d)
Sentences	Is each sentence (especially if it is compound, complex, or long) *coherent* within itself? (#31)
	Is each sentence clear and sufficiently *emphatic* in making its point? (#18)
	Have I used a *variety of kinds, lengths, and structures* of sentences? (#17)

Have I avoided the passive voice except where it is clearly necessary or desirable? (#6p, #18f)

Diction (Ch. VII)	Have I used *words* whose meanings I am sure of, or checked the *dictionary* for any whose meanings I am not sure of?

Is my diction sufficiently *concrete* and *specific*? (#54a)

Have I avoided *unidiomatic* usages? (#58)

Have I weeded out any unnecessary repetitions and other *wordiness*? (#59a-c)

Have I excluded *jargon* and unnecessary *clichés* and *euphemisms* from my diction? (#59d-h, #56)

Have I avoided unintentional *slang* and *informal* diction, as well as *overformal* diction? (#52)

Have I avoided inappropriate or confusing *figurative language*? (#53)

Have I avoided *sexist language*? (#4d; **man, woman,** etc. in #60)

Grammar   Are all my sentences *grammatically* sound—free of dangling modifiers, agreement errors, incorrect tenses and cases, and the like? (**Chs. II and III**)

Have I avoided *run-ons* and unacceptable *fragments* and *comma splices*? (#33j, #1y, #33e)

Punctuation (Ch IV)   Is the *punctuation* of each sentence correct and effective?

Have I read them aloud with special attention to the punctuation?

Spelling (Ch. VI)   Have I checked all my words—reading backwards if necessary—for possible *spelling* errors?

Mechanics   Have I carefully *proofread*, and corrected all careless and typographical errors? (#69o)

Is my manuscript neat and legible? Does it conform to all the *manuscript conventions*? (**Ch. V**)

Have I introduced and handled all *quotations* properly? (#43, #77)

Have I checked all *quotations* for accuracy? (#77)

Acknowledgment   Have I *acknowledged* everything that requires acknowledgment? (#76, #77)

Have I double-checked my *documentation* for accuracy and correct form? (#78a, #80, Ch. X.17)

The Last Step   Have I read my essay aloud as a final check on how it sounds?

INDEX

spatial order in, 343
descriptive adjectives, 90-93
    comparison of, 91–93 (Ex, 93)
    as predicate adjectives, 133
-designate, hyphenated, 253
despite that, not for though, etc., 308
details
    development by, 339
    in outlines, 366
determiners, markers, 93, 98
development
    adequate, 349, 552
    generating material for, 137–38, 359–60
        (Ex, 360)
    methods of, 339, 344, 376–77
    patterns of, 343–44, 377
diacritical marks, 236, 258
diagramming sentences, 151–56
dialogue
    indention with, 207
    punctuation of, 207
diction, 269–330, 552 (Ex, 330-32)
    big words, 272–73, 299 (Ex, 273)
    checklist for revising, 572
    checklist of usage, 299–330
    clichés, 275, 292–93, 566
    concrete, abstract, 276–80 (Ex, 280)
    connotation and denotation, 280-81 (Ex, 281)
    contrasting, for emphasis, 146
    "doubling," 289 (Ex, 289)
    euphemisms, 282–83, 554 (Ex, 283)
    expletives, 287–88
    faulty, 552
    figurative language, 273–76, 555
    "fine writing," 272–73 (Ex, 273)
    formal, 121–22, 271–73, 557 (Ex, 122, 272,
        273)
    formal and informal, list, 271–72
    general and specific, 276–80 (Ex, 280)
    idiom, 284–86 (Ex, 286)
    informal, colloquial, 271–72, 557 (Ex, 122, 272,
        273)
    jargon, 286–87, 294–99, 558
    levels of, 269–73 (Ex, 122, 270-71, 272, 273)
    logic of, 171–73
    no such word (nsw), 560
    nouns used as adjectives, 35, 90, 295
        (Ex, 295–96)
    nouns used as verbs, 296
    overuse of nouns, 294–99
    ready-made phrases, 291–92
    redundancy, 288–89, 292, 293, 562 (Ex, 289)
    repetition, 288, 563
    slang, 270 (Ex, 270-71)
    triteness, clichés, 275, 292–93, 566
    wordiness, 286–99 (Ex, 289–90)
    wrong word, 283–84, 569 (Ex, 284)
    See also words.
dictionaries, 269, 281, 286
    for correct diction, 552
    for hyphenation, 252 (Ex, 254)
    for idioms, 286
    list of, 286, 395–96

of quotations, 396
    for spelling, 240, 564
    of synonyms, 281 (Ex, 281)
    usage labels in, 269
Dictionary of American Idioms, A, 286
different from, different than, usage of, 308–09
differ from, differ with, usage of, 309
dilemma, false, fallacy, 383
direct discourse. See direct quotations.
directions, capitalization of, 231
direct objects, 9–11, 12, 58 (Ex, 9, 11, 60)
    as basic elements of sentences, 132
    diagrammed, 151–54
    different elements as, 132
    infinitive phrases as, 17, 132
    interrogative pronouns as, 39
    noun clauses as, 15–16, 132, 150, 153–54
    nouns as, 35, 132
    of transitive verbs, 9–11, 58
direct questions, 206
direct quotations, 208–09
discursive documentary notes, 430
    examples, 455, 463, 475, 538–39
disinterested, uninterested, usage of, 309
dissertations, documentation for, 481
distribute, idiom, with indirect object, 324
distribution, in syllogisms, 379
dividing words, syllabication, 227, 566 (Ex, 228)
do
    as auxiliary verb, 22–24, 66
    inflection of, 68
    in interrogative sentences, 22–24
documentation, 416, 424–37, 482–86, 537–415,
        553
    abbreviations used in, 437–38
    forms of, 424
    name-date method (APA), 424, 482–84
    name-page method (MLA), 424, 425–37
    note method (CMS), 424, 486, 537–41
    number method (CBE, etc.), 424, 484–85
    parenthetical, 425–30, 432–35, 482
    purposes of, 416
    sample bibliography, 478–81, 540–41
    sample endnotes, 537–39
    sample footnotes, 455, 463, 475
    "Works Cited" list, 425, 430-32, 478–81, 540–41
    See also bibliography; and listings of specific
        kinds of sources.
double comparatives, 93
double negatives, 306, 316
double possessives, 262
double superlatives, 93
"doubling," wordiness of, 289 (Ex, 289)
drafts
    final, 374
    first, rough, 369–72, 414–15
    footnotes or endnotes in, 415
    parenthetical references in, 415
drama
    documentation of, 429, 431, 432
    reference books, 406
due to, usage of, 309
due to the fact that, wordy, 291

formal writing, 271–73 (Ex, 272, 273)
  abbreviations in, 228
  contractions in, 271, 545
  Latinate verbs for, 122
  quotations, colons with, 209–10
format
  manuscript, 225–27
  of outlines, 362
former, latter, usage of, 312
forward, forwards, usage of, 327
Fowler, H. W., *A Dictionary of Modern
    English Usage*, 286
fractions, hyphenation of, 252
fragments, 27, 112, 156, 217, 556 (Ex, 28)
from the standpoint (viewpoint) of, as jargon, 298,
    315
frontward, frontwards, usage of, 327
full, unique, etc., usage of, 327–28
fulsome, usage of, 312
function-words. *See* structure-words.
funny, as informal, 271
further
  as conjunctive adverb, 188
  as transitional term, 346
further, farther, usage of, 311
further, furthest, in comparison of adverbs, 106
furthermore, as conjunctive adverb, 188
fused sentences. *See* run-on sentences.
future
  adverbial modifers for, 71, 74
  expressed by present progressive tense, 74
  expressed by present tense, 71
future perfect progressive tense, 70, 75
future perfect tense, 70, 73
future progressive tense, 70, 74
future tense, 70, 71–72

gazetteers, 398
gender
  of personal pronouns, 37–38, 48
  and sexist language, 50-52, 319, 543
general and specific, 276–80 (Ex, 280)
generalizations
  in argument, 375, 378
  "glittering generalities," fallacy, 381
  hasty, fallacy, 382
  weak, 171, 277–80, 550 (Ex, 280)
general-specific order, 343
general truth, present tense for, 71
generating material, 137–38, 359–60 (Ex, 360)
generic *he*, sexist, 50-52, 543
genitive case. *See* possessive case.
geography, reference books, 398–400
gerund phrases, 16, 113–14
  dangling, 160
  diagrammed, 152
  as direct objects, 16, 132
  as predicate nouns, 132–33
  as subjects, 16, 132
gerunds, 113–14, 194
  as direct objects, 132
  no commas with, 194
  as non-finite verbs, 62

possessives with, 113–14
  as predicate nouns, 132–33
  as subjects, 132, 153
  tense and voice of, 113
  as verbals, 108, 113–14
get, as linking verb, 59
give, in two-part verbs, 121–22
"glittering generalities," fallacy, 381
glossary, usage checklist, 299–330
gobbledygook, 296
good, bad, badly, well, usage of, 312
government publications, documentation of, 426,
    432
government sections, capitalized, 231
Governor General
  order of, 99
  plural of, 257
grades, 489
grammar, 2–3
  case, 34, 37–38, 41–44 (Ex, 44)
  defined, 2
  errors in, 557
  mood, 77–80 (Ex, 82)
  sentence structure, 5–176 passim
  tense, 69–77 (Ex, 75)
  voice, 80-82
  See also parts of speech; sentences.
grave accent, 258
great-, hyphen with, 253
groups and members, capitalized, 231
guess, as informal, 271
guilt by association, fallacy, 381

hackneyed expressions, 275, 292–93, 566
half, agreement with, 86
half a, a half, usage of, 312
*Handbook for Authors of Papers in American
    Chemical Society Publications*, 485
handwritten work, 225
hanged, hung, usage of, 312
happen, occur, intransitives, usage of, 313
hardly, in double negatives, 306
hardly ever, for *rarely ever*, 311
hasty generalization, fallacy, 382
have
  as auxiliary verb, 66
  inflection of, 68
have, of, confusion of, 248, 321
he, generic, 50-52, 543
headings, outline, 362–66
healthy, healthful, usage of, 313
helping verbs. *See* auxiliary verbs.
hence
  as conjunctive adverb, 188
  as transitional term, 347
he or she, his or her, he/she, s/he, etc., 52
herself, himself, myself, etc., 47
his or her, he or she, he/she, s/he, etc., 52
historical events, periods, documents, capitalized,
    231–32
historical present tense, 77
history, reference books, 398–400
homophones, homonyms, 249–51

as indirect objects, 35
infinitives as, 109, 132, 135, 136, 153
inflection of, 34, 260-62
kinds of, 33
mass, 34
number of, 34
as objective complements, 12, 35 (Ex, 12)
as objects of prepositions, 35
as objects of verbs, 35
overuse of, 294–99
possessive case, 34, 35, 260-62
predicate, 11, 35, 59, 132–33 (Ex, 12, 60)
prepositional phrases as, 118
proper, 33, 95, 252
reference of pronouns to, 53–57 (Ex, 57)
as subjective complements, 11 (Ex, 11, 12)
as subjects, 35, 132
uncountable, 34
as verbs, 296
nowhere near, informal, 271
nowheres, somewheres, anyways, anywheres,
    dialectal, 302
n.p., 437
n. pag., 437
nsw (no such word), 560
number
    agreement of pronoun and antecedent in,
        48–52, 543 (Ex, 52)
    agreement of subject and verb in, 83–88, 543
        (Ex, 88–89)
    of collective nouns, 52, 86–87
    of demonstrative adjectives, 52
    of demonstrative pronouns, 44–45, 563
    of indefinite pronouns, 45–46
    inflection of nouns for, 34
    inflection of verbs for, 61, 65–66
    of parts of an essay, 361, 366
    of personal pronouns, 37, 48
    of pronouns, 37, 44–48, 48–52 (Ex, 53)
    of reciprocal pronouns, 47–48
    of reflexive and intensive pronouns, 46–47
    of relative pronouns, 87–88
    shifts in, 164
    of verbs, 65–66
    of words referred to as words, 87
    See also agreement; reference.
number, agreement with, 86
number, amount, usage of, 301
numbering
    of footnotes, 430, 455, 463, 475
    of note cards, 414
    of pages, 225
    of sections of outlines, 362
number method of documentation, 484–85
numbers
    at beginning of sentence, 239
    cardinal and ordinal, 46
    compound, 252
    footnote, placement of, 430
    spelled out, 238
numerals, 237–39
    abbreviations with, 229
    for addresses, 238

at beginning of sentence, 239
for dates, 238
in metric system, 239
for pages, chapters, etc., 238
for parts of plays, 238
plurals of, 259–60
roman, 238, 362
for technical numbers, 238
for time of day, 237
for years, 238
numerical adjectives, 90

O, vocative, capitalized, 232
objective case, 34
    of infinitives, 109
    of interrogative pronouns, 39
    of personal pronouns, 37–38
    of pronouns, 41–43
    of relative pronouns, 39–40
objective complements, 12 (Ex, 12)
    interrogative pronouns as, 39
    nouns as, 35
    placement of, 98
objects
    case of pronouns as, 41–43
    compound, 123–24
    direct, 9–11, 12, 17, 35, 39, 58, 132 (Ex, 9, 11, 60)
    examples in analyzed sentences, 149–54
    gerunds as, 16, 132
    indirect, 10, 35 (Ex, 11)
    infinitives as, 17, 109, 132, 135, 136, 153
    noun clauses as, 15, 132, 150, 153, 154
    placement in declarative sentences, 21–22
    placement in questions, 23–24
    of prepositions, 35, 39, 154
    relative pronouns as, 39–40
    of verbals, 109, 112, 113
    of verbs, 9–11, 35, 39, 58–59, 132
oblivious of, . . . to, 285
occur, happen, intransitives, usage of, 313
of
    after *all, off, inside, outside,* 321
    after *could, would, might,* 321
    on no substitute for, 322
    to show possession, 261–62
    wordy, 321
of, have, confusion of, 248, 321
off, of after, 321
old-fashioned, misspelled, 248
omissions
    of *and* in series, 124, 200
    apostrophes for, in contractions, 260
    commas for, 181
    ellipses to indicate, 211–12
    of *that*, 29, 166, 196
on, not for *about* or *of*, 322
on account of, due to, usage of, 309
one
    to avoid sexism, 51
    impersonal pronoun, 38, 56
    indefinite pronoun, singular, 45, 49, 84
one another, each other
    as reciprocal pronouns, 47–48

verbals, 62, 108–14 (Ex, 112, 114–16)
  in absolute phrases, 114 (Ex, 117)
  gerunds, 113–14
  infinitives, 109–11 (Ex, 116)
  participles, 111–12 (Ex, 112)
  See also gerunds; infinitives; participles.
verb phrases, 16, 66–68, 77. *See also* auxiliary verbs.
verbs, 57–88, 567
  agreement with subjects, 83–88 (Ex, 88, 89)
  as appositives, 18
  aspect of, 69–70
  auxiliary, 22–23, 66–68 (Ex, 75)
  basic (infinitive) form of, 61–65
  compound, 28
  defined, 57
  as essential elements, 7, 132
  finite, 62, 132
  functions of, 57
  hyphenated, 255
  inflection of, 61–82
  intransitive, 58–59 (Ex, 60)
  irregular, 62–65
  kinds of, 58–59
  linking, 11, 13, 59, 132–33 (Ex, 60)
  modified by adverbs, 100-02
  mood of, 78–79
  non-finite, 62. *See also* verbals.
  number of, 65–66
  with objective complements, 12, 35, 39, 98
  objects of, 9–12, 35, 37–38, 39–40, 58–59, 132
  past-participial forms, 61–65
  past-tense forms, 61–65
  person of, 65–66
  placement in declarative sentences, 21–22
  placement in interrogative sentences, 22–24
  in predicate, 7
  present-participial forms, 61–62
  principal parts of, 61–65
  of speaking, punctuation with, 181, 209–10
  tenses of, 69–77
  third-person-singular present of, 259 (Ex, 259)
  transitive, 9–12, 58–59 (Ex, 60, 61)
  two-part, 121–22 (Ex, 122)
  voice of, 9–10, 80–82, 145 (Ex, 10, 82)
vertical method, sentence analysis, 150
very, usage of, 328–29
very much, very well, idiom, 329
vice-, hyphenated, 252–53
vide, v., 229, 438
videocassette, documentation of, 436
viewpoint, as jargon, 298, 315
virgule, slash
  in notes, 413, 448
  in quotations of verse, 209
virtually, figuratively, literally, usage of, 318
viz., 542
vogue words, buzz words, 297
voice, 80-82 (Ex, 82)
  active, 9, 80-82
  of gerunds, 113
  of infinitives, 110
  of participles, 112
  passive, 9–10, 80-82, 145 (Ex, 10, 82)

shifts in, 164
vs., versus, 229

wait on, as informal, 272
way, ways, usage of, 329
well, good, bad, badly, usage of, 312
what
  as interrogative pronoun, 39
  in noun clauses, 40
whatever
  as interrogative pronoun, 39
  in noun clauses, 40
when
  as interrogative adverb, 102
  as relative adverb, 40
  as transitional term, 342
when, where, in definitions, 315
where
  as interrogative adverb, 102
  as relative adverb, 40
where, as informal for *that,* 272
whereas, for *while,* 329
whether . . . or, 125–26
  agreement with, 84
  parallelism with, 166
which, 283
  as interrogative pronoun, 39
  as relative pronoun, 40, 87
  in restrictive clauses, 40
  vs. *that,* 40, 197
whichever
  as interrogative pronoun, 39
  in noun clauses, 40
while
  although, though, whereas for, 329
  as for, 302
  possible ambiguity of, 329
  weak for *and* or *but,* 329
who
  as interrogative pronoun, 39
  as relative pronoun, 40
who, whom, whoever, whomever, 43–44 (Ex, 44)
whoever
  as interrogative pronoun, 39
  in noun clauses, 40
whom
  avoiding stuffiness of, 43
  as interrogative pronoun, 39
  not *which,* for a person, 283
  in noun clauses, 40
  in restrictive clauses, 40
whomever
  as interrogative pronoun, 39
  in noun clauses, 40
whose
  as interrogative pronoun, 39
  as relative adjective, 40
  as relative pronoun, 40
why, interrogative adverb, 102
will, auxiliary verb, 66
will, shall, 71–72
-wise, as jargon, 298, 314, 329–30
with regard to, as jargon, 297, 314–15

LIST OF EXERCISES

The Canadian Writer's Handbook

THIRD EDITION